2 0 0 0
CHILDREN'S WRITER'S & ILLUSTRATOR'S MARKET

800 EDITORS & ART DIRECTORS WHO BUY YOUR WRITING & ILLUSTRATIONS

EDITED BY
ALICE POPE

W9-BXM-618

WRITER'S DIGEST BOOKS
CINCINNATI, OHIO

Managing Editor, Annuals Department: Cindy Laufenberg
Supervisory Editor: Barbara Kuroff
Production Editor: Pamala Shields
Writer's Digest Books website: www.writersdigest.com

International Standard Serial Number 0897-9790
International Standard Book Number 0-89879-935-X

Cover designed by Clare Finney
Cover illustration by Jeffrey Pelo

Attention Booksellers: This is an annual directory of F&W Publications. Return deadline for this edition is April 30, 2001.

Contents

Page 131

© Arthur Howard

Markets

Page 167

210 Magazines

The latest information on writing and illustration opportunities in children's periodicals is offered here, from general, large-circulation magazines to small religious take-home papers.

260 Greeting Cards, Puzzles & Games

Companies listed in this section offer an array of freelance opportunities in specialty markets—from wrapping paper, birthday cards and party decorations to stickers and jigsaw puzzles.

270 Play Publishers & Producers

This section contains information on regional, community and summer theater play producers including musical requirements, limits on cast sizes and recently performed works.

280 Young Writer's & Illustrator's Markets

Here are listings of publications looking for material from writers and illustrators age 18 and under.

Resources

Page 50

© Tim Coffey

From the Editor

In *Snowflake Bentley*, the 1999 Caldecott-winning picture book by Jacqueline Briggs Martin, illustrated by Mary Azarian, there's a spread that shows a young Wilson Bentley catching falling snowflakes, while a group of kids nearby builds a snow fort and tosses snowballs. Reading the book, I was immediately struck by that image.

"When his mother gave him an old microscope," Martin's text reads, "he used it to look at flowers, raindrops, and blades of grass. Best of all, he used it to look at snow. While other children built forts and pelted snowballs at roosting crows, Willie was catching single snowflakes. Day after stormy day, he studied the icy crystals."

Bentley had a passion for studying nature, especially snow. "He said snow was as beautiful as butterflies, or apple blossoms." He spent hours perfecting his technique of photographing single snowflakes, collecting samples and working on his photos. Those around him laughed at his idea of capturing the images of snowflakes on film. They didn't understand his passion.

This book also got me thinking—I bet writers and illustrators can really relate to Snowflake Bentley. I bet you can relate to having your passion misunderstood by family or friends. (They don't get why you need to spend hours at your computer or drawing table. They think it's a little funny that you keep a notebook or sketchbook with you all the time. They wonder when you're going to give up this silly idea of getting published and get a "real job.")

And like writing and illustrating, Bentley's work was solitary. He spent hours alone working on his project, just as you spend hours alone crafting a story or creating an image. But you have an advantage Bentley did not—there are others like you. Bentley was the first person to photograph snow crystals. No one else was doing what he did. No one else could empathize with his passion.

As a writer or illustrator of children's books you've got many peers. You can find them by joining the Society of Children's Book Writers and Illustrators. (See page 307 for an interview with SCBWI's Executive Director Lin Oliver.) You can join online listservs, visit chatrooms or post on message boards. You can organize a critique group and get together in person or online. And throughout the pages of *Children's Writer's & Illustrator's Market*, you can read the stories and advice of other writers and illustrators. (See page 140 for an interview with Jacqueline Briggs Martin.)

If there are writers and illustrators you'd like to hear from in future editions of this book, I welcome your ideas. If there are topics you'd like to see covered, I welcome those suggestions as well. (I got the idea to add our new Agents & Art Reps section from writers I talked to during a workshop in Verla Kay's chatroom. See page 180 for an interview with Kay.)

Illustration © Mary Azarian

If you've not yet made a resolution for 2000, I have three suggestions: pledge to stick with your passion; vow to interact with your peers; and promise the next time you see falling snow to think about butterflies and apple blossoms.

Alice Pope, cwim@fwpubs.com

Just Getting Started? Some Quick Tips

If you're new to the world of children's publishing, buying *Children's Writer's & Illustrator's Market* may have been one of the first steps in your journey to publication. What follows is a list of suggestions and resources that can help make that journey a smooth and swift one:

1. Make the most of *Children's Writer's & Illustrator's Market*. Be sure to read How to Use This Book to Sell Your Work on page 4 for tips on reading the listings and using the indexes. Also be sure to take advantage of the articles and interviews in the book. The insights of the authors, illustrators, editors and agents we've interviewed will inform and inspire you.

2. Join the Society of Children's Books Writers and Illustrators. SCBWI, almost 12,000 members strong, is an organization for those interested in writing and illustrating for children from the beginner to the professional level. They offer members a slew of information and support through publications, a website, and a host of regional advisors overseeing chapters in almost every state in the U.S. and in several locations around the globe (including France, Japan and Australia). SCBWI puts on a number of conferences, workshops and events on the regional and national level (many listed in the Conferences & Workshops section of this book). For more information contact SCBWI, 8271 Beverly Blvd., Los Angeles CA 90048, (323)782-1010, or visit their website: www.scbwi.org. Also see the Insider Report with SCBWI Executive Director Lin Oliver in page 307.

3. Read newsletters. Newsletters, such as *Children's Book Insider*, *Children's Writer* and the SCBWI *Bulletin*, offer updates and new information about publishers on a timely basis and are relatively inexpensive. Many local chapters of SCBWI offer regional newsletters as well. (See Helpful Books & Publications on page 348 for contact information on the newsletters listed above and others. For information on regional SCBWI newsletters, visit www.scbwi.org and click on "publications.")

4. Read trade and review publications. Magazines like *Publishers Weekly* (which offers two special issues each year devoted to children's publishing available on newsstands), *The Horn Book*, *Riverbank Review* and *Booklinks* offer news, articles, reviews of newly-published titles and ads featuring upcoming and current releases. Referring to them will help you get a feel for what's happening in children's publishing.

5. Read guidelines. Most publishers and magazines offer writer's and artist's guidelines which provide detailed information on needs and submission requirements, and some magazines offer theme lists for upcoming issues. Many publishers and magazines state the availability of guidelines within their listings. Send a self-addressed, stamped envelope (SASE) to publishers who offer guidelines. You'll often find submission information on publishers' and magazines' websites. And while you're on the Web, visit www.writersdigest.com for a searchable database of about 1,150 guidelines.

6. Look at publishers' catalogs. Perusing publishers' catalogs can give you a feel for their line of books and help you decide where your work might fit in. Send for catalogs with a SASE if they are available (often stated within listings). Visit publishers' websites which often contain their full catalogs. You can also ask librarians to look at catalogs they have on hand. You can even search Amazon.com (www.amazon.com) by publisher and year. (Click on "book search" then "publisher, date" and plug in, for example, "Atheneum" under "publisher" and "1999" under year. You'll get a list of all the Atheneum titles published in 1999 which you can peruse.)

7. Visit bookstores. It's not only informative to spend time in bookstores—it's fun, too! Frequently visit the children's section of your local bookstore (whether a chain or an independent) to see the latest from a variety of publishers and the most current issues of children's magazines. Look for books in the genre you're writing or with illustrations similar in style to yours, and spend some time studying them. It's also wise to get to know your local booksellers—they can tell you what's new in the store and provide insight into what kids and adults are buying.

8. Read, read, read! While your at that bookstore, pick up a few things, or keep a list of which books interest you and check them out of your library. Read and study the latest releases, the award winners and the classics. You'll learn from other writers, get ideas and get a feel for what's being published. Think about what works and doesn't work in a story. Pay attention to how plots are constructed and how characters are developed or the rhythm and pacing of picture book text. It's certainly enjoyable research!

9. Take advantage of Internet resources. There are innumerable sources of information available on the Internet about writing for children (and anything else you could possibly think of). It's also a great resource for getting (and staying) in touch with other writers and illustrators through listservs and e-mail, and can serve as a vehicle for self-promotion. (Visit some authors' and illustators' web pages for ideas. See Useful Online Resources on page 351 for a list of helpful websites.)

10. Consider attending a conference. If time and finances allow, attending a conference is a great way to meet peers and network with professionals in the field of children's publishing. As mentioned above, SCBWI offers conferences in various locations year round (see www.scbwi. org and click on "events" for a full calendar of conferences). General writers' conferences often offer specialized sessions just for those interested in children's writing. Many conferences offer optional manuscript and portfolio critiques as well, giving you a chance for feedback from seasoned professionals.

11. Network, network, network! Don't work in a vacuum. You can meet other writers and illustrators through a number of the things listed above—SCBWI, conferences, online. Attend local meetings for writers and illustrators whenever you can. Befriend other writers in your area (SCBWI offers members a roster broken down by state)—share guidelines, share subscriptions, be conference buddies and roommates, join a critique group or writing group, exchange information and offer support. Get online—sign on to listservs, post on message boards, visit chatrooms. (America Online offers them. Also, visit author Verla Kay's website for information on weekly workshops. See Helpful Internet Resources for more information.) Exchange addresses, phone numbers and e-mail addresses with writers or illustrators you meet at events. And at conferences don't be afraid to talk to people, ask strangers to join you for lunch, approach speakers and introduce yourself, chat in elevators and hallways. Remember, you're not alone.

12. Perfect your craft and don't submit until your work is its best. It's often been said that a writer should try to write every day. Great manuscripts don't happen overnight—there's time, research and revision involved. As you visit bookstores and study what others have written and illustrated, really step back and look at your own work and ask yourself—honestly—*How does my work measure up? Is it ready for editors or art directors to see?* If it's not, keep working. You may want to ask a writer's group for constructive comments, or get a professional manuscript or portfolio critique.

13. Be patient, learn from rejection and don't give up! Thousands of manuscripts land on editors' desks; thousands of illustration samples line art directors' file drawers. There are so many factors that come into play when evaluating submissions. Keep in mind that you might not hear back from publishers promptly. Persistence and patience are important qualities in writers and illustrators working for publication. Keep at it—it will come. It can take a while, but when you get that first book contract or first assignment, you'll know it was worth the wait. (Read First Books on page 45 for proof.)

How to Use This Book to Sell Your Work

As a writer, illustrator or photographer first picking up *Children's Writer's & Illustrator's Market*, you may not know quite how to start using the book. Your impulse may be to flip through the book and quickly make a mailing list, then submit to everyone in hopes that someone will take interest in your work. Well, there's more to it. Finding the right market takes time and research. The more you know about a company that interests you, the better chance you have of getting work accepted.

We've made your job a little easier by putting a wealth of information at your fingertips. Besides providing listings, this directory includes a number of tools to help you determine which markets are the best ones for your work. By using these tools, as well as researching on your own, you raise your odds of being published.

USING THE INDEXES

This book lists hundreds of potential buyers of freelance material. To learn which companies want the type of material you're interested in submitting, start with the indexes.

The Age-Level Index

Age groups are broken down into these categories in the Age-Level Index:
- **Picture books** or **picture-oriented material** are written and illustrated for preschoolers to 8-year-olds.
- **Young readers** are for 5- to 8-year-olds.
- **Middle readers** are for 9- to 11-year-olds.
- **Young adults** are for ages 12 and up.

Age breakdowns may vary slightly from publisher to publisher, but using them as guidelines will help you target appropriate markets. For example, if you've written an article about trends in teen fashion, check the Magazines Age-Level Index under the Young Adult subheading. Using this list, you'll quickly find the listings for young adult magazines.

The Subject Index

But let's narrow the search further. Take your list of young adult magazines, turn to the Subject Index, and find the Fashion subheading. Then highlight the names that appear on both lists (Young Adult and Fashion). Now you have a smaller list of all the magazines that would be interested in your teen fashion article. Read through those listings and decide which ones sound best for your work.

Illustrators and photographers can use the Subject Index as well. If you specialize in painting animals, for instance, consider sending samples to book and magazine publishers listed under Animals and, perhaps, Nature/Environment. Illustrators can simply send general examples of their style (in the form of tearsheets or postcards) to art directors to keep on file. The indexes may be more helpful to artists sending manuscripts/illustration packages. Always read the listings for the potential markets to see the type of work art directors prefer and what type of samples they'll keep on file, and send for art or photo guidelines if they're available.

The Poetry Index

This index lists book publishers and magazines interested in submissions from poets. Always send for writer's guidelines from publishers and magazines that interest you.

The Photography Index

You'll find lists of book and magazine publishers, as well as greeting card, puzzle and game manufacturers, that buy photos from freelancers in the Photography Index. Copy the lists and read the listings for specific needs. Send for photo guidelines if they're offered.

USING THE LISTINGS

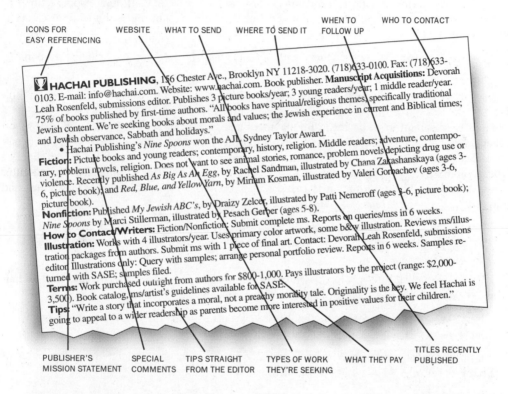

Many listings begin with one or more symbols. (Refer to the inside covers of the book for quick reference.) Here's what each icon stands for:

- **N** indicates a listing is new to this edition.
- ⊞ indicates a listing is a book packager or producer.
- ⊡ indicates a company publishes educational material.
- ✤ indicates a listing is Canadian.
- ✓ indicates a change in contact information from last year's edition.
- **A** indicates a publisher only accepts submissions through agents.
- ♛ indicates a company's publications have received awards recently.

In the Book Publishers section, you'll find contact names after **Manuscript Acquisitions** and **Art Acquisitions**. Contact names in Magazines follow boldface titles such as **Fiction Editor**, **Articles Editor** or **Art Director**. Following contact information in many of these listings are mission statements. Read these to get a general idea of the aim of certain publishers and magazines to help you decide whether to explore them further.

The subheadings under each listing contain more specific information about what a company needs. In Book Publishers and Magazines, for example, you'll find such things as age levels and subjects needed under the **Fiction** and **Nonfiction** subheads. Here's an example from a listing in the Book Publishers section:

Fiction: Picture books: adventure, animal, contemporary, fantasy, humor. Young readers: animal, contemporary, humor, sports, suspense/mystery. Middle readers: adventure, humor, sports. Young adults: humor, problem novels.

Also check the listings for information on how to submit your work and response time. In Book Publishers and Magazines, writers will find this information under the How to Contact/Writers subhead:

How to Contact/Writers: Query with outline/synopsis and 2 sample chapters. Reports on queries in 6 weeks.

For information on submission procedures and formats, turn to Before Your First Sale on page 8.

Also look for information regarding payment and rights purchased. Some markets pay on acceptance, others on publication. Some pay a flat rate for manuscripts and artwork, others pay advances and royalties. Knowing how a market operates will keep you from being shocked when you discover your paycheck won't arrive until your manuscript is published—a year after it was accepted. This information is found under **Terms** in Book Publishers, Magazines and Play Publishers. Here's an example from the Magazines section:

Terms: Pays on acceptance. Buys first North American serial rights or reprint rights. Pays $50-100 for stories/articles. Pays illustrators $75-125 for b&w or color inside; $150-200 for color cover.

Under **Tips** you'll find special advice straight from an editor or art director about what their company wants or doesn't want, or other helpful advice:

Tips: "We are looking for picture books centered on a strong, fully-developed protaganist who grows or changes during the course of the story."

Additional information about specific markets in the form of comments from the editor of this book is set off by bullets (●) within listings:

● This publisher accepts only queries and manuscripts submitted by agents.

Many listings indicate whether submission guidelines are available. If a publisher you're interested in offers guidelines, send for them and read them. The same is true with catalogs. Sending for catalogs and seeing and reading about the books a publisher produces gives you a better idea whether your work would fit in. (You should also look at a few of the books in the catalog at a library or bookstore to get a feel for the publisher's material.) Note that a number of publishers offer guidelines and catalogs on their websites, and a searchable database of more than 1,150 writer's guidelines is available at www.writersdigest.com.

Especially for artists and photographers

Along with information for writers, listings provide information for photographers and illustrators. Illustrators will find numerous markets that maintain files of samples for possible future assignments. If you're both a writer and illustrator, look for markets that accept manuscript/illustration packages. You'll find sample illustrations from various publishers sprinkled throughout the listings. These illustrations serve as examples of the kind of art these particular companies buy. Read the captions for additional information about the artwork and the market.

If you're a photographer, after consulting the Photography Index, read the information under the Photography subhead within listings to see what format buyers prefer. For example, some want 35mm color transparencies, others want b&w prints. Note the type of photos a buyer wants to purchase and the procedures for submitting. It's not uncommon for a market to want a résumé and promotional literature, as well as tearsheets from previous work. Listings also note whether model releases and/or captions are required.

Especially for young writers

If you're a parent, teacher or student, you may be interested in Young Writer's & Illustrator's Markets. The listings in this section encourage submissions from young writers and artists. Some may require a written statement from a teacher or parent noting the work is original. Also watch for age limits.

Young people should also check Contests & Awards for contests that accept work by young writers and artists. Some of the contests listed are especially for students; others accept both student and adult work. These listings contain the phrase **open to students** in bold. Some listings in Clubs & Organizations and Conferences & Workshops may also be of interest to students. Organizations and conferences which are open to or are especially for students also include **open to students.**

COMMON ABBREVIATIONS

Throughout the listings, the following abbreviations are used:
- **ms** or **mss** stands for manuscript or manuscripts.
- **SASE** refers to a self-addressed, stamped envelope.
- **SAE** refers to a self-addressed envelope.
- **IRC** stands for International Reply Coupon. These are required with SAEs sent to markets in countries other than your own.

Before Your First Sale

If you're just beginning to pursue your career as a children's book writer or illustrator, it's important to learn the proper procedures, formats, and protocol for the publishing industry. This article outlines the basics you need to know before you head to the post office with your submissions.

FINDING THE BEST MARKETS FOR YOUR WORK

Researching publishers well is a basic element of submitting your work successfully. Editors and art directors hate to receive inappropriate submissions—handling them wastes a lot of their time, not to mention your time and money, and they are the main reason some publishers have chosen not to accept material over the transom. By randomly sending out material without knowing a company's needs, you're sure to meet with rejection.

If you're interested in submitting to a particular magazine, write to request a sample copy, or see if it's available in your local library or bookstore. For a book publisher, obtain a book catalog and check a library or bookstore for titles produced by that publisher. Many publishers and magazines now have websites that include catalogs or sample articles (websites are given within the listings). Studying such materials carefully will better acquaint you with a publisher's or magazine's writing, illustration and photography styles and formats.

Most of the book publishers and magazines listed in this book (as well as some greeting card and paper product producers) offer some sort of writer's, artist's or photographer's guidelines for a self-addressed, stamped envelope (SASE). Guidelines are also often found on publishers' websites. It's important to read and study guidelines before submitting work. You'll get a better understanding of what a particular publisher wants. You may even decide, after reading the submission guidelines, that your work isn't right for a company you considered. For access to a searchable database of more than 1,150 publishers' guidelines, visit www.writersdigest. com.

SUBMITTING YOUR WORK

Throughout the listings you'll read requests for particular elements to include when contacting markets. Here are explanations of some of these important submission components.

Queries, cover letters and proposals

A query letter is a no-more-than-one-page, well-written piece meant to arouse an editor's interest in your work. Many query letters start with leads similar to those of actual manuscripts. In the rest of the letter, briefly outline the work you're proposing and include facts, anecdotes, interviews or other pertinent information that give the editor a feel for the manuscript's premise—entice her to want to know more. End your letter with a straightforward request to write (or submit) the work, and include information on its approximate length, date it could be completed, and whether accompanying photos or artwork are available.

Arthur Levine, editor-in-chief of Scholastic imprint Arthur Levine Books, recommends writers send queries that present their books as a publisher's catalog would present them. Read through a good catalog and examine how the publishers give enticing summaries of their books in a spare amount of words. It's also important that query letters give editors a taste of your writing style. For more on the topic, and examples of successful queries, see Writing Effective Query Letters on page 20. For good advice and more samples of queries, cover letters and other correspondence, consult *How to Write Attention-Grabbing Query & Cover Letters*, by John

Wood (Writer's Digest Books).
- **Query letters for nonfiction.** Queries are usually required when submitting nonfiction material to a publisher. The goal of a nonfiction query is to convince the editor your idea is perfect for her readership and that you're qualified to do the job. Note any previous writing experience and include published samples to prove your credentials, especially samples related to the subject matter you're querying about.
- **Query letters for fiction.** More and more, queries are being requested for fiction manuscripts. For a fiction query, explain the story's plot, main characters, conflict and resolution. Just as in nonfiction queries, make the editor eager to see more.
- **Cover letters for writers.** Some editors prefer to review complete manuscripts, especially for fiction. In such cases, the cover letter (which should be no longer than one page) serves as your introduction, establishes your credentials as a writer, and gives the editor an overview of the manuscript. If the editor asked for the manuscript because of a query, note this in your cover letter.
- **Cover letters for illustrators and photographers.** For an illustrator or photographer the cover letter serves as an introduction to the art director and establishes professional credentials when submitting samples. Explain what services you can provide as well as what type of follow-up contact you plan to make, if any.
- **Résumés.** Often writers, illustrators and photographers are asked to submit résumés with cover letters and samples. They can be created in a variety of formats, from a single page listing information, to color brochures featuring your work. Keep your resume brief, and focus on your achievements, including your clients and the work you've done for them, as well as your educational background and any awards you've received. Do not use the same résumé you'd use for a typical job application.
- **Book proposals.** Throughout the listings in the Book Publishers section, publishers refer to submitting a synopsis, outline and sample chapters. Depending on an editor's preference, some or all of these components, along with a cover letter, make up a book proposal.

A *synopsis* summarizes the book, covering the basic plot (including the ending). It should be easy to read and flow well.

An *outline* covers your book chapter by chapter and provides highlights of each. If you're developing an outline for fiction, include major characters, plots and subplots, and book length.

Sample chapters give a more comprehensive idea of your writing skill. Some editors may request the first two or three chapters to see how your material is set up. Find out what the editor wants before writing or revising sample chapters.

Manuscript formats

When submitting a complete manuscript, follow some basic guidelines. In the upper-left corner of your title page, type your legal name (not pseudonym), address and phone number. In the upper-right corner, type the approximate word length. All material in the upper corners should be typed single-spaced. Then type the title (centered) almost halfway down that page, the word "by" two spaces under that, and your name or pseudonym two spaces under "by."

The first page should also include the title (centered) one-third of the way down. Two spaces under that type "by" and your name or pseudonym. To begin the body of your manuscript, drop down two double spaces and indent five spaces for each new paragraph. There should be one-inch margins around all sides of a full typewritten page. (Manuscripts with wide margins are more readable and easier to edit.)

Set your computer or typewriter on double-space for the manuscript body. From page two to the end of the manuscript, include your last name followed by a comma and the title (or key words of the title) in the upper-left corner. The page number should go in the top right corner. Drop down two double spaces to begin the body of each page. If you're submitting a novel, type each chapter title one-third of the way down the page. For more information on manuscript formats, read *Writer's Digest Guide to Manuscript Formats*, by Dian Buchman and Seli Groves, or *Manuscript Submissions*, by Scott Edelstein (both Writer's Digest Books).

Picture book formats

The majority of editors prefer to see complete manuscripts for picture books. When typing the text of a picture book, don't include page breaks and don't type each page of text on a new sheet of paper. And unless you are an illustrator, don't worry about supplying art. Editors will find their own illustrators for picture books. Most of the time, a writer and an illustrator who work on the same book never meet. The editor acts as a go-between and works with the writer and illustrator throughout the publishing process. *How to Write and Sell Children's Picture Books*, by Jean E. Karl (Writer's Digest Books), offers advice on preparing text and marketing your work.

If you're an illustrator who has written your own book, create a dummy or storyboard containing both art and text, then submit it along with your complete manuscript and sample pieces of final art (color photocopies or slides—never originals). Publishers interested in picture books specify in their listings what should be submitted. For some tips on creating a dummy, see Nuts & Bolts for Illustrators on page 28. Also refer to *How to Write and Illustrate Children's Books and Get Them Published*, edited by Treld Pelkey Bicknell and Felicity Trotman (North Light Books), or Frieda Gates's book, *How to Write, Illustrate, and Design Children's Books* (Lloyd-Simone Publishing Company).

Writers may also want to learn the art of dummy making to help them through their writing process with things like pacing, rhythm and length. For a great explanation and helpful hints, see *You Can Write Children's Books*, by Tracey E. Dils (Writer's Digest Books). Also see Dils's article Setting Writing Goals That Work! on page 38.

Mailing submissions

Your main concern when packaging material is to be sure it arrives undamaged. If your manuscript is less than six pages, simply fold it in thirds and send it in a #10 (business-size) envelope. For a SASE, either fold another #10 envelope in thirds or insert a #9 (reply) envelope which fits in a #10 neatly without folding.

Another option is folding your manuscript in half in a 6×9 envelope, with a #9 or #10 SASE enclosed. For larger manuscripts use a 9×12 envelope both for mailing the submission and as a SASE (which can be folded in half). Book manuscripts require sturdy packaging for mailing. Include a self-addressed mailing label and return postage.

If asked to send artwork and photographs, remember they require a bit more care in packaging to guarantee they arrive in good condition. Sandwich illustrations and photos between heavy cardboard that is slightly larger than the work. The cardboard can be secured by rubber bands or with tape. If you tape the cardboard together, check that the artwork doesn't stick to the tape. Be sure your name and address appear on the back of each piece of art or each photo in case the material becomes separated. For the packaging use either a manila envelope, foam-padded envelope, brown paper or a mailer lined with plastic air bubbles. Bind non-joined edges with reinforced mailing tape and affix a typed mailing label or clearly write your address.

Mailing material first class ensures quick delivery. Also, first-class mail is forwarded for one year if the addressee has moved, and can be returned if undeliverable. If you're concerned about your original material safely reaching its destination, consider other mailing options, such as UPS or certified mail. If material needs to reach your editor or art director quickly, use overnight delivery services.

Remember, companies outside your own country can't use your country's postage when returning a manuscript to you. When mailing a submission to another country, include a self-addressed envelope and International Reply Coupons or IRCs. (You'll see this term in many

Canadian listings.) Your postmaster can tell you, based on a package's weight, the correct number of IRCs to include to ensure its return.

If it's not necessary for an editor to return your work (such as with photocopies) don't include return postage. You may want to track the status of your submission by enclosing a postage-paid reply postcard with options for the editor to check, such as "Yes, I am interested," "I'll keep the material on file," or "No, the material is not appropriate for my needs at this time."

Some writers, illustrators and photographers simply include a deadline date. If you don't hear from the editor or art director by the specified date, your manuscript, artwork or photos are automatically withdrawn from consideration. Because many publishing houses and companies are overstocked with material, a minimum deadline should be at least three months.

Unless requested, it's never a good idea to use a company's fax number or e-mail address to send manuscript submissions. This can disrupt a company's internal business.

Keeping submission records

It's important to keep track of the material you submit. When recording each submission, include the date it was sent, the business and contact name, and any enclosures (such as samples of writing, artwork or photography). You can create a record-keeping system of your own or look for record-keeping software in your area computer store. The 2000 *Writer's Market: The Electronic Edition* CD-ROM (Writer's Digest Books) features a submission tracker that can be copied to your hard drive.

Keep copies of articles or manuscripts you send together with related correspondence to make follow-up easier. When you sell rights to a manuscript, artwork or photos you can "close" your file on a particular submission by noting the date the material was accepted, what rights were purchased, the publication date and payment.

Often writers, illustrators and photographers fail to follow up on overdue responses. If you don't hear from a publisher within their stated response time, wait another month or so and follow up with a note asking about the status of your submission. Include the title or description, date sent, and a SASE for response. Ask the contact person when she anticipates making a decision. You may refresh the memory of a buyer who temporarily forgot about your submission. At the very least you'll receive a definite "no," and free yourself to send the material to another publisher.

Simultaneous submissions

If you opt for simultaneous (also called "multiple") submissions—sending the same material to several editors at the same time—be sure to inform each editor your work is being considered elsewhere. Many editors are reluctant to receive simultaneous submissions but understand that for hopeful freelancers, waiting several months for a response can be frustrating. In some cases, an editor may actually be more inclined to read your manuscript sooner if she knows it's being considered by another publisher. The Society of Children's Book Writers and Illustrators cautions writers against simultaneous submissions. The official recommendation of SCBWI is to submit to one publisher at a time, but wait only three months (note you'll do so in your cover letter). If no response is received, then send a note withdrawing your manuscript from consideration. SCBWI considers simultaneous submissions acceptable only if you have a manuscript dealing with a timely issue.

It's especially important to keep track of simultaneous submissions, so if you get an offer on a manuscript sent to more than one publisher, you can instruct other publishers to withdraw your work from consideration.

AGENTS AND REPS

Most children's writers, illustrators and photographers, especially those just beginning, are confused about whether to enlist the services of an agent or representative. The decision is strictly one that each writer, illustrator or photographer must make for herself. Some are confident with their own negotiation skills and believe acquiring an agent or rep is not in their best interest. Others feel uncomfortable in the business arena or are not willing to sacrifice valuable creative time for marketing.

About half of children's publishers accept unagented work, so it's possible to break into children's publishing without an agent. Some agents avoid working with children's books because traditionally low advances and trickling royalty payments over long periods of time make children's books less lucrative. Writers targeting magazine markets don't need the services of an agent. In fact, it's practically impossible to find an agent interested in marketing articles and short stories—there simply isn't enough financial incentive.

One benefit of having an agent, though, is it may speed up the process of getting your work reviewed, especially by publishers who don't accept unagented submissions. If an agent has a good reputation and submits your manuscript to an editor, that manuscript may actually bypass the first-read stage (which is done by editorial assistants and junior editors) and end up on the editor's desk sooner.

When agreeing to have a reputable agent represent you, remember that she should be familiar with the needs of the current market and evaluate your manuscript/artwork/photos accordingly. She should also determine the quality of your piece and whether it is saleable. When your manuscript sells, your agent should negotiate a favorable contract and clear up any questions you have about payments.

Keep in mind that however reputable the agent or rep is, she has limitations. Representation does not guarantee sale of your work. It just means an agent or rep sees potential in your writing, art or photos. Though an agent or rep may offer criticism or advice on how to improve your work, she cannot make you a better writer, artist or photographer.

Literary agents typically charge a 15 percent commission from the sale of writing; art and photo representatives usually charge a 25 to 30 percent commission. Such fees are taken from advances and royalty earnings. If your agent sells foreign rights to your work, she will deduct a higher percentage because she will most likely be dealing with an overseas agent with whom she must split the fee.

Be advised that not every agent is open to representing a writer, artist or photographer who lacks an established track record. Just as when approaching a publisher, the manuscript, artwork or photos, and query or cover letter you submit to a potential agent must be attractive and professional looking. Your first impression must be as an organized, articulate person.

For listings of agents and reps, turn to our new Agents & Art Reps section. Also refer to *Guide to Literary Agents* for listings of agents; for listings of art reps, consult *Artist's & Graphic Designer's Market*; and for photo reps, see *Photographer's Market* (all Writer's Digest Books).

The Business of Writing & Illustrating

A career in children's publishing involves more than just writing skills or artistic talent. Successful authors and illustrators must be able to hold their own in negotiations, keep records, understand contract language, grasp copyright law, pay taxes and take care of a number of other business concerns. Although agents and reps, accountants and lawyers, and writers' organizations offer help in sorting out such business issues, it's wise to have a basic understanding of them going in. This article offers just that—basic information. For a more in-depth look at the subjects covered here, check your library or bookstore for books and magazines to help you, some of which are mentioned. We also tell you how to get information on issues like taxes and copyright from the federal government.

CONTRACTS & NEGOTIATION

Before you see your work in print or begin working with an editor or art director on a project, there is negotiation. And whether negotiating a book contract, a magazine article assignment, or an illustration or photo assignment, there are a few things to keep in mind. First, if you find any clauses vague or confusing in a contract, get legal advice. The time and money invested in counseling up front could protect you from problems later. If you have an agent or rep, she will review any contract.

A contract is an agreement between two or more parties that specifies the fees to be paid, services rendered, deadlines, rights purchased and, for artists and photographers, whether original work is returned. Most companies have standard contracts for writers, illustrators and photographers. The specifics (such as royalty rates, advances, delivery dates, etc.) are typed in after negotiations.

Though it's okay to conduct negotiations over the phone, get a written contract once both parties have agreed on terms. Never depend on oral stipulations; written contracts protect both parties from misunderstandings. Watch for clauses that may not be in your best interest, such as "work-for-hire." When you do work-for-hire, you give up all rights to your creations.

Some reputable children's magazines, such as *Highlights for Children*, buy all rights, and many writers and illustrators believe it's worth the concession in order to break into the field. However, once you become more established in the field, it's in your best interest to keep rights to your work. (Note: magazines such as *Highlights* may return rights after a specified time period, so ask about this possibility when negotiating.)

When negotiating a book deal, find out whether your contract contains an option clause. This clause requires the author to give the publisher a first look at her next work before offering it to other publishers. Though it's editorial etiquette to give the publisher the first chance at publishing your next work, be wary of statements in the contract that could trap you. Don't allow the publisher to consider the next project for more than 30 days and be specific about what type of work should actually be considered "next work." (For example, if the book under contract is a young adult novel, specify that the publisher will receive an exclusive look at only your next young adult novel.)

For more tips on contracts, Society of Children's Book Writers and Illustrators members can find information in *The SCBWI Publications Guide to Writing and Illustrating for Children* (chapter 13: Answers to Some Questions About Contracts). Contact SCBWI at 8271 Beverly Blvd., Los Angeles CA 90048, (323)782-1010, or visit their website: www.scbwi.org. Additional contract tips are available on The Authors Guild website, www.authorsguild.org. (Members of the guild can receive a 75-point contract review from the guild's legal staff.) See the website for membership information and application form, or contact The Authors Guild at 390 W. 42nd St., 29th Floor, New York NY 10036, (212)563-5904. Website: www.authorsguild.org.

Book publishers' payment methods

Book publishers pay authors and artists in royalties, a percentage of either the wholesale or retail price of each book sold. From large publishing houses, the author usually receives an advance issued against future royalties before the book is published. Half of the advance amount is issued upon signing the book contract; the other half is issued when the book is finished. For illustrations, one-third of the advance should be collected upon signing the contract; one-third upon delivery of sketches; and one-third upon delivery of finished art.

After your book has sold enough copies to earn back your advance, you'll start to get royalty checks. Some publishers hold a reserve against returns, which means a percentage of royalties is held back in case books are returned from bookstores. If you have a reserve clause in your contract, find out the exact percentage of total sales that will be withheld and the time period the publisher will hold this money. You should be reimbursed this amount after a reasonable time period, such as a year. Royalty percentages vary with each publisher, but there are standard ranges.

Book publishers' rates

According to the latest figures from the Society of Children's Book Writers and Illustrators, picture book writers can expect advances of $3,500-5,000; picture book illustrators' advances range from $7,000-10,000; text and illustration packages can score $8,000-10,000. Royalties for picture books are generally about five percent (split between the author and illustrator) but can go as high as ten percent. Those who both write and illustrate a book, of course, receive the full royalty.

Advances for chapter books and middle-grade novels vary slightly from picture books. Hardcover titles can fetch authors advances of $4,000-6,000 and 10 percent royalties; paperbacks bring in slightly lower advances of $3,000-5,000 and royalties of 6-8 percent. Fees for young adult novels are generally the same, but additional length may increase fees and royalties.

As you might expect, advance and royalty figures vary from house to house and are affected by the time of year, the state of the economy and other factors. Some smaller houses may not even pay royalties, just flat fees. First-time writers and illustrators generally start on the low end of the scale, while established and high-profile writers are paid more.

Pay rates for magazines

For writers, fee structures for magazines are based on a per-word rate or range for a specific article length. Artists and photographers have a few more variables to contend with before contracting their services.

Payment for illustrations and photos can be set by such factors as whether the piece(s) will be black and white or four-color, how many are to be purchased, where the work appears (cover or inside), circulation, and the artist's or photographer's prior experience.

Remaindering

When a book goes out of print, a publisher will sell any existing copies to a wholesaler who, in turn, sells the copies to stores at a discount When the books are "remaindered" to a wholesaler, they are usually sold at a price just above the cost of printing. When negotiating a contract with a publisher you may want to discuss the possibility of purchasing the remaindered copies before they are sold to a wholesaler, then you can market the copies you purchased and still make a profit.

KNOW YOUR RIGHTS

A copyright is a form of protection provided to creators of original works, published or unpublished. In general, copyright protection ensures the writer, illustrator or photographer the power to decide how her work is used and allows her to receive payment for each use.

Essentially, copyright also encourages the creation of new works by guaranteeing the creator power to sell rights to the work in the marketplace. The copyright holder can print, reprint or copy her work; sell or distribute copies of her work; or prepare derivative works such as plays, collages or recordings. The Copyright Law is designed to protect work (created on or after January 1, 1978) for her lifetime plus 50 years.

If you collaborate with someone else on a written or artistic project, the copyright will last for the lifetime of the last survivor plus 50 years. The creators' heirs may hold a copyright for an additional 50 years. After that, the work becomes public domain. Works created anonymously or under a pseudonym are protected for 100 years, or 75 years after publication. Under work-for-hire agreements, you relinquish your copyright to your "employer."

Copyright notice and registration

Some feel a copyright notice should be included on all work, registered or not. Others feel it is not necessary and a copyright notice will only confuse publishers about whether the material is registered (acquiring rights to previously registered material is a more complicated process).

Although it's not necessary to include a copyright notice on unregistered work, if you don't feel your work is safe without the notice, it is your right to include one. Including a copyright notice—© (year of work, your name)—should help safeguard against plagiarism.

Registration is a legal formality intended to make copyright public record, and can help you win more money in a court case. By registering work within three months of publication or before an infringement occurs, you are eligible to collect statutory damages and attorney's fees. If you register later than three months after publication, you will qualify only for actual damages and profits.

Ideas and concepts are not copyrightable, only expressions of those ideas and concepts. A character type or basic plot outline, for example, is not subject to a copyright infringement lawsuit. Also, titles, names, short phrases or slogans, and lists of contents are not subject to copyright protection, though titles and names may be protected through the Trademark Office.

You can register a group of articles, illustrations or photos if it meets these criteria:
* the group is assembled in order, such as in a notebook;
* the works bear a single title, such as "Works by (your name)";
* it is the work of one writer, artist or photographer;
* the material is the subject of a single claim to copyright.

It's a publisher's responsibility to register your book for copyright. If you've previously registered the same material, you must inform your editor and supply the previous copyright information, otherwise, the publisher can't register the book in its published form.

For more information about the proper way to register works, contact the Copyright Office, Public Information Office, (202)707-3000. The forms available are TX for writing (books, articles, etc.); VA for pictures (photographs, illustrations); and PA for plays and music. (To order copyright forms by phone, call (202)707-9100.) For information about how to use the copyright forms, request a copy of Circular I on Copyright Basics. All of the forms and circulars are free. Send the completed registration form along with the stated fee and a copy of the work to the Copyright Office.

For specific answers to questions about copyright (but not legal advice), call the Copyright Public Information Office at (202)707-3000 weekdays between 8:30 a.m. and 5 p.m. EST. Forms can also be downloaded from the Library of Congress website: http://lcweb.loc.gov/copyright. The site also includes a list of frequently asked questions, tips on filling out forms, general copyright information, and links to other sites related to copyright issues. For members of SC-

BWI, information about copyrights and the law is available in *The SCBWI Publications Guide to Writing and Illustrating for Children* (chapter 6: Copyright Facts for Writers).

The rights publishers buy

The copyright law specifies that a writer, illustrator or photographer generally sells one-time rights to her work unless she and the buyer agree otherwise in writing. Many publications will want more exclusive rights to your work than just one-time usage; some will even require you to sell all rights. Be sure you are monetarily compensated for the additional rights you relinquish. If you must give up all rights to a work, carefully consider the price you're being offered to determine whether you'll be compensated for the loss of other potential sales.

Writers who only give up limited rights to their work can then sell reprint rights to other publications, foreign rights to international publications, or even movie rights, should the opportunity arise. Artists and photographers can sell their work to other markets such as paper product companies who may use an image on a calendar, greeting card or mug. Illustrators and photographers may even sell original work after it has been published. And there are now galleries throughout the U.S. that display the work of children's illustrators.

Rights acquired through the sale of a book manuscript are explained in each publisher's contract. Take time to read relevant clauses to be sure you understand what rights each contract is specifying before signing. Be sure your contract contains a clause allowing all rights to revert back to you in the event the publisher goes out of business. (You may even want to have the contract reviewed by an agent or an attorney specializing in publishing law.)

The following are the rights you'll most often sell to publishers, periodicals and producers in the marketplace:

First rights. The buyer purchases the rights to use the work for the first time in any medium. All other rights remain with the creator. When material is excerpted from a soon-to-be-published book for use in a newspaper or periodical, first serial rights are also purchased.

One-time rights. The buyer has no guarantee that she is the first to use a piece. One-time permission to run written work, illustrations or photos is acquired, then the rights revert back to the creator.

First North American serial rights. This is similar to first rights, except that companies who distribute both in the U.S. and Canada will stipulate these rights to ensure that another North American company won't come out with simultaneous usage of the same work.

Second serial (reprint) rights. In this case newspapers and magazines are granted the right to reproduce a work that has already appeared in another publication. These rights are also purchased by a newspaper or magazine editor who wants to publish part of a book after the book has been published. The proceeds from reprint rights for a book are often split evenly between the author and his publishing company.

Simultaneous rights. More than one publication buys one-time rights to the same work at the same time. Use of such rights occurs among magazines with circulations that don't overlap, such as many religious publications.

All rights. Just as it sounds, the writer, illustrator or photographer relinquishes all rights to a piece—she no longer has any say in who acquires rights to use it. All rights are purchased by publishers who pay premium usage fees, have an exclusive format, or have other book or magazine interests from which the purchased work can generate more mileage. If a company insists on acquiring all rights to your work, see if you can negotiate for the rights to revert back to you after a reasonable period of time. If they agree to such a proposal, get it in writing.

Note: Writers, illustrators and photographers should be wary of "work-for-hire" arrangements. If you sign an agreement stipulating that your work will be done as work-for-hire, you will not control the copyrights of the completed work—the company that hired you will be the copyright owner.

Foreign serial rights. Be sure before you market to foreign publications that you have sold only North American—not worldwide—serial rights to previous markets. If so, you are free to market to publications that may be interested in material that's appeared in a North American-based periodical.

Syndication rights. This is a division of serial rights. For example, if a syndicate prints portions of a book in installments in its newspapers, it would be syndicating second serial rights. The syndicate would receive a commission and leave the remainder to be split between the author and publisher.

Subsidiary rights. These include serial rights, dramatic rights, book club rights or translation rights. The contract should specify what percentage of profits from sales of these rights go to the author and publisher.

Dramatic, television and motion picture rights. During a specified time the interested party tries to sell a story to a producer or director. Many times options are renewed because the selling process can be lengthy.

Display rights or electronic publishing rights. They're also known as "Data, Storage and Retrieval." Usually listed under subsidiary rights, the marketing of electronic rights in this era of rapidly expanding capabilities and markets for electronic material can be tricky. Display rights can cover text or images to be used in a CD-ROM or online, or may cover use of material in formats not even fully developed yet. If a display rights clause is listed in your contract, try to negotiate its elimination. Otherwise, be sure to pin down which electronic rights are being purchased. Demand the clause be restricted to things designed to be read only. By doing this, you maintain your rights to use your work for things such as games and interactive software.

RUNNING YOUR BUSINESS

An important part of being a freelance writer, illustrator or photographer is running your freelance business. It's imperative to maintain accurate business records to determine if you're making a profit as a freelancer. Keeping correct, organized records will also make your life easier as you approach tax time.

When setting up your system, begin by keeping a bank account and ledger for your business finances apart from your personal finances. Also, if writing, illustration or photography is secondary to another freelance career, keep separate business records for each.

You will likely accumulate some business expenses before showing any profit when you start out as a freelancer. To substantiate your income and expenses to the IRS, keep all invoices, cash receipts, sales slips, bank statements, canceled checks and receipts related to travel expenses and entertaining clients. For entertainment expenditures, record the date, place and purpose of the business meeting as well as gas mileage. Keep records for all purchases, big and small—don't take the small purchases for granted; they can add up to a substantial amount. File all receipts in chronological order. Maintaining a separate file for each month simplifies retrieving records at the end of the year.

Record keeping

When setting up a single-entry bookkeeping system, record income and expenses separately. Use some of the subheads that appear on Schedule C (the form used for recording income from a business) of the 1040 tax form so you can easily transfer information onto the tax form when filing your return. In your ledger include a description of each transaction—the date, source of income (or debts from business purchases), description of what was purchased or sold, the amount of the transaction, and whether payment was by cash, check or credit card.

Don't wait until January 1 to start keeping records. The moment you first make a business-related purchase or sell an article, book manuscript, illustration or photo, begin tracking your profits and losses. If you keep records from January 1 to December 31, you're using a calendar-year accounting period. Any other accounting period is called a fiscal year.

There are two types of accounting methods you can choose from—the cash method and the accrual method. The cash method is used more often: you record income when it is received and expenses when they're disbursed.

Using the accrual method, you report income at the time you earn it rather than when it's actually received. Similarly, expenses are recorded at the time they're incurred rather than when you actually pay them. If you choose this method, keep separate records for "accounts receivable" and "accounts payable."

Satisfying the IRS

To successfully—and legally—work as a freelancer, you must know what income you should report and what deductions you can claim. But before you can do that, you must prove to the IRS you're in business to make a profit, that your writing, illustration or photography is not merely a hobby.

The Tax Reform Act of 1986 says you should show a profit for three years out of a five-year period to attain professional status. The IRS considers these factors as proof of your professionalism:

- accurate financial records;
- a business bank account separate from your personal account;
- proven time devoted to your profession;
- whether it's your main or secondary source of income;
- your history of profits and losses;
- the amount of training you have invested in your field;
- your expertise.

If your business is unincorporated, you'll fill out tax information on Schedule C of Form 1040. If you're unsure of what deductions you can take, request the IRS publication containing this information. Under the Tax Reform Act, only 30 percent of business meals, entertainment and related tips, and parking charges are deductible. Other deductible expenses allowed on Schedule C include: car expenses for business-related trips; professional courses and seminars; depreciation of office equipment, such as a computer; dues and publications; and miscellaneous expenses, such as postage used for business needs.

If you're working out of a home office, a portion of your mortgage interest (or rent), related utilities, property taxes, repair costs and depreciation may he deducted as business expenses—under special circumstances. To learn more about the possibility of home office deductions, consult IRS Publication 587, Business Use of Your Home

The method of paying taxes on income not subject to withholding is called "estimated tax" for individuals. If you expect to owe more than $500 at year's end and if the total amount of income tax that will be withheld during the year will be less than 90% of the tax shown on the current year's return, you'll generally make estimated tax payments. Estimated tax payments are made in four equal installments due on April 15, June 15, September 15 and January 15 (assuming you're a calendar-year taxpayer). For more information, request Publication 533, Self-Employment Tax.

The Internal Revenue Service's website (www.irs.ustreas.gov/) offers tips and instant access to IRS forms and publications.

Social Security tax

Depending on your net income as a freelancer, you may be liable for a Social Security tax. This is a tax designed for those who don't have Social Security withheld from their paychecks. You're liable if your net income is $400 or more per year. Net income is the difference between your income and allowable business deductions. Request Schedule SE, Computation of Social Security Self-Employment Tax, if you qualify.

If completing your income tax return proves to be too complex, consider hiring an accountant (the fee is a deductible business expense) or contact the IRS for assistance (look in the White

Pages under U.S. Government—Internal Revenue Service or check their website, www.irs.ustrea s.gov.). In addition to numerous publications to instruct you in various facets of preparing a tax return, the IRS also has walk-in centers in some cities.

Insurance

As a self-employed professional be aware of what health and business insurance coverage is available to you. Unless you're a Canadian who is covered by national health insurance or a full-time freelancer covered by your spouse's policy, health insurance will no doubt be one of your biggest expenses. Under the terms of a 1985 government act (COBRA), if you leave a job with health benefits, you're entitled to continue that coverage for up to 18 months—you pay 100 percent of the premium and sometimes a small administration fee. Eventually, you must search for your own health plan. You may also need disability and life insurance. Disability insurance is offered through many private insurance companies and state governments. This insurance pays a monthly fee that covers living and business expenses during periods of long-term recuperation from a health problem. The amount of money paid is based on the recipient's annual earnings.

Before contacting any insurance representative, talk to other writers, illustrators or photographers to learn which insurance companies they recommend. If you belong to a writers' or artists' organization, ask the organization if it offers insurance coverage for professionals. (SCBWI has a plan available. Look through the Clubs & Organizations section for other groups that may offer coverage.) Group coverage may be more affordable and provide more comprehensive coverage than an individual policy.

Writing Effective Query Letters

BY KARMA WILSON

What can evoke the interest of the world's toughest editor? What can break down the dreaded "no unsolicited manuscripts" barrier? What can leap over staggering slushpiles in a single page? A query letter. But not just any query letter, only . . . The Super Query! Don't feel too intimidated. Writing a super query isn't as hard as you might imagine.

Read on for a step-by-step walk through writing query letters that includes advice from three of today's leading editors: Emma Dryden, senior editor of Margaret K. McElderry Books; Melanie Cecka, editor at Viking Children's Books; and Barbara Stretchberry, managing editor of *American Girl* magazine.

No matter what genre you write—fiction, nonfiction, magazine articles, or novels, chances are you'll have to write query letters. And if you want your manuscripts requested by editors, you *must* write them well. If you're ready to correspond with an editor, you've already struggled to learn the basic components of a good story. Query letters have many parallels with good stories. They must say much with few words. They must grab your audience (editors!). And they must have a beginning, middle and end. Let's start at the beginning.

THE NAME GAME

The first thing you'll write on your query letter—the editor's name—can make or break it. If you get that wrong, chances are the letter you labored over will be filed under "R," for rejection. The first rule is to never address a query to a vague entity, such as "Dear Editing Department." Always address your letter to a specific editor or the acquisitions editor.

The second rule is to make certain you have the editor's name correct! Cecka, editor at Viking Children's Books, warns, "Never, under any circumstances, put another editor's name on a manuscript mailed to me. It may be an innocent mistake, but it also qualifies for instant rejection."

No problem, right? You have the current edition of *Children's Writer's & Illustrator's Market* in your hot little hands! You'll just look up the editor's name there. Think again. Though *Children's Writer's & Illustrator's Market* works hard to provide readers with the most up-to-date publisher guidelines and information, editors tend to move from house to house faster than you can say "form rejection." A quick call to the publishing house (numbers are listed in *Children's Writer's & Illustrator's Market*) is well worth the small long distance charge. Just ask the receptionist if the editor in question is still on staff, in the same position. While you're on the phone, inquire if the publisher is accepting queries, as policies tend to change as often as editors do— no sense in wasting good postage. A little research goes a long way. Once you've addressed your letter, you can start your first paragraph.

THE HOOK

The first paragraph is generally the most difficult to write. You must sum up your manuscript in one or two sentences—and make it sound not only interesting, but irresistible. This is your "hook" or your "sound-bite."

KARMA WILSON *is a freelance writer and children's author. Her first picture book* Bear Snores On, *illustrated by Jane Chapman, will be a fall, 2001 release from Margaret K. McElderry Books. Wilson lives in Bonners Ferry, Idaho with her husband and three young children.*

The best examples of sound-bites are in publishers' catalogs. Publishers try to "hook" book buyers in the same way writers try to hook editors. Studying publishers' catalogs is one way to learn what editors look for in a query. If you're querying a magazine, read current issues. Most have a page devoted to what's coming up in future editions which contains excellent examples of hooks for magazine articles and stories.

If you are connected to the Internet, you have an invaluable resource for studying good "hooks." Go to book sellers websites like Amazon.com (www.amazon.com) or Barnes and Noble Online (www.barnesandnoble.com), and look up children's books. (You can search for specific titles or search by publisher name and year.) For each book there is a synopsis provided by the publisher. They are usually no more than a small paragraph and describe the book's theme and story line succinctly. Study these carefully, then consider your own manuscript. Imagine your manuscript has been accepted (this should be second nature to you). What sound-bite would the publishers use to sell your book?

Remember, no matter what publishing house or magazine you are querying, editors appreciate a synopsis that is short and to the point. Dryden, senior editor of McElderry Books, explains, "A query letter should sell me the book in a very brief amount of time and space."

Stretchberry, managing editor of *American Girl* magazine says, "The most important factor in receiving a query is that I want to know quickly what the idea is. Writers who do not present their ideas in a clear, brief way make it harder for me to understand just what I should be getting excited about." So don't meander. Jump into your query with both feet—and be quick about it.

WHYS AND HOWS

Now that you've reeled the editor in with your zingy first paragraph, use your second paragraph to explain why you are qualified to write this story or article. If it is a nonfiction article you're pitching, list your research sources and any interviews you have conducted. If it's a novel or picture book, give some insight into why you think your story needs to be read by today's readers.

Dryden says, "If at all possible, I like a writer to do some market research and explain to me what niche their manuscript can fill." Cecka expresses similar thoughts, "I think it's always important for an author to keep up on market trends, to know what's selling and what's not, and to recognize potentially untapped areas in children's literature and why their writing may work well there."

So ask yourself some tough questions. What niche *does* your book fill? Why should a publisher invest money in you and in your story? How does your book or article stand apart from others already on the market? You'll need firm answers to these questions before writing a query. Study the market to make sure your manuscript is unique and is suited to the publisher or magazine you are targeting.

Stretchberry explains the importance of good market research. "By not reading and understanding the content of *American Girl*, a writer cannot possibly sell me an idea. We have a very specific style, and by reading and studying several back issues, a writer should be able to see why we choose the stories we do. Our writer's guidelines are easily obtainable. By not researching our preferred word length or subject matter, the query will be hard to place in *American Girl*." Do your homework. It's time consuming and can be tedious, but the payoff is worth it.

WRITING CREDITS

In the next paragraph, list any previous writing experience or credits you may have, as well as memberships to children's writing organizations such as the Society of Children's Book Writers and Illustrators (SCBWI).

Many new writers panic at the thought of having no previous experience. Remember, the story idea, and not a long list of credits, is the deciding factor to most editors.

At *American Girl* magazine, credits will not make or break a sale. Stretchberry explains, "I try to evaluate each idea on its own merit. Previous sales and contest placements will not overcome a weak query letter.''

Dryden adds, ''Credits are helpful, but I look more at the subject matter and tone of the story that is being described.'' If you don't have credits, skip this section. But whatever you do, *do not* draw attention to your lack of experience with sentences such as, ''Though I've never been published, I have a deep love of children's literature.'' This will only label you as an amateur.

If you have credits, list two or three that apply to the type of manuscript for which you are querying. Do not list credits for different genres altogether. For instance, don't query a children's book publisher with multiple credits from adult travel magazines. You may write interesting travel articles, but that really has no bearing on your ability to write for children.

Credits, while not essential, can be helpful. Cecka likes to see relevant credits in query letters. ''I think it's always worthwhile to know that a writer has prior publishing experience—it suggests that the writer may have familiarity with some of the more artful aspects of the publishing process, such as working with an editor on revisions. Some very good writers just happen to write lousy cover letters!'' So, use any credits you have to your best advantage. If you have none, take comfort in the fact that a good idea can outweigh lack of experience.

THE ENDING

The last paragraph is a no-brainer. You'll want to mention that you've included a self-addressed, stamped envelope (SASE) for the editor's reply. If you are sending sample chapters, according to guidelines, tell the editor if you want them back (be sure your SASE has adequate postage). Also, use this opportunity to display your good manners by thanking the busy editor for taking time to read your query. Make sure your query letter is no longer than one page, and go through it carefully to check grammar and spelling (this will be read by an editor, after all). Now relax. Your query letter is done!

See, writing a Super Query isn't so hard. Of course, editors are individuals and have their own specific needs and tastes, so you won't be able to please them all. But with a little insight into the minds of editors, and these basic guidelines, you can avoid the common mistakes that are Kryptonite to queries. (Be sure to look at the example letters that follow for comments from editors on letters that resulted in sales and an example of what *not* to do.) Now, all that's left is to print out your Super Query and mail it off. Up . . . up . . . and away!

Submitting to an Agent? Cover Letter Tips

When submitting manuscripts to an agent for consideration, it's necessary to include a cover letter. You can follow many of the same rules you'd use when writing query letters to publishers (discussed in the above article.) "There are certainly obvious things—legible, typed, well-written, no spelling errors, no grammatical errors and inclusion of a SASE," says Agent Steven Malk of Writers House. "A good cover letter should tell a little bit about the author and the book. I always think it's helpful if an author can pitch her book, because I'm going to turn around and pitch it to publishers."

It's a good exercise, Malk says, for a writer to tell what's great about her book, why it should be published, and who it might appeal to. "It's going to catch my eye if someone comes up with a hook for her story or if she says, 'This is going to appeal to people who like Peggy Rathmann' or 'This should be very popular with 2- to 4-year-olds.' "

However, just as with querying publishers, the bottom line is the quality of the work. Says Malk, "I really like a good cover letter—it makes an impression on me. But your work's going to speak for itself no matter what." (Turn to page 26 for Malk's comments on a successful query letter and page 297 for an Insider Report with the agent.)

Successful Query

Overall: short, professional, courteous, not effusive, gushing or cute; not pushy or trying too hard; businesslike format. The letter is all it needs to be; it's the manuscript that should be a work of art.

990 Hatch Street
Acceptanceville NY 14555
(716)555-2192

July 7, 1997

Dinah Stevenson, Executive Editor
CLARION BOOKS
215 Park Avenue South
New York NY 10003

The polite reminder that we corresponded before is welcome; I might not have remembered her name or the previous contact, and the fact that I found an earlier letter interesting predisposes me to read this one.

Dear Ms. Stevenson:

You were kind enough to respond positively to my previous query regarding three Korean folk tales. Enclosed for your consideration are the first three chapters of a novel for young readers.

The chapters were so good I would have wanted to see the balance of the manuscript in any case. But I would have requested the manuscript on the basis of this letter even without seeing a sample.

Title: Seesaw Girl (approx. 8,000 words)
Setting: Seoul, Korea, mid-17th century
Main character: Jade Blossom, a 12-year-old girl from a noble family
Synopsis: A Korean seesaw looks like an American seesaw, except that it is used by standing and jumping. No one knows who invented it, but perhaps it was a young girl like Jade Blossom. Forbidden by her family and tradition to leave the Inner Court of her house, she invents the seesaw to see beyond the walls.

Description is concise and can be taken at a glance; contains several elements I found compelling.

Please let me know at your earliest convenience if you would be interested in seeing the entire manuscript. The query/synopsis is being submitted to multiple publishers.

I'm glad to know that the whole manuscript is available and that author doesn't expect to sell the project on the basis of the sample material. Also glad to be informed that it's being offered multiply.

I am a first-generation Korean-American, born and raised in the U.S. When I was born, my parents made the unusual decision to speak no Korean at home, so my native language is English. Despite the fact that we did not speak Korean, our home retained much of traditional Korean culture, including a Korean seesaw.

Author's interest in, and exposure to, Korean culture makes me more confident about the accuracy and sensitive handling of material unfamiliar to me. Author's personal connection to subject matter often makes for a better book.

I have worked as a journalist and editor, and am currently teaching English as a Second Language. This is my first attempt at a novel for young people.

Thank you for your consideration.

Sincerely,

Work background isn't entirely relevant, but it establishes her as a professional interested in writing, language and education.

Fine with me that this promising writer is unpublished—I like working with first timers and building a relationship from the start of the writer's career.

Linda Sue Park
Encs: ms/SASE

Linda Sue Park queried Clarion about *Seesaw Girl* after getting a personal rejection from Executive Editor Dinah Stevenson on a previous query. Clarion published *Seesaw Girl* in 1999. Coments on Park's successful letter provided by Stevenson.

Successful Query

Overall: the tone is positive and for me, inviting—if a query catches my interest, the article most likely will also.

9034 Foxhunter Lane
Published, PA 18555
January 5, 1996

Rosalie Baker,
Editor
Calliope
Cobblestone Publishing, Inc.
7 School Street
Peterborough, NH 03458

shows research which is important for Calliope.

Dear Ms. Baker:

The compactness of phrases and the fact that each is accurate and to-the-point caught my attention immediately.

Color of kings, symbol of highest office, and the hue indelibly linked with their great city, *Tyrian purple* is one of the more fascinating notes in the Phoenicians' extensive history. The little murex sea-snail—source of the purple dye—provided Phoenicia with a source of wealth and acclaim. In my 800-word article, *Calliope* readers can learn just how Tyrian purple was produced, and discover the dyes' importance to the people of Phoenicia.

Clearly tells me that the author has given thought to article and what she will write.

shows author is aware of and will keep age of our audience in mind.

To accompany this article, I'll also provide you with directions on how your readers can safely and easily make their own purple dye, using just a few ingredients from the supermarket. This activity, based on information from a dyeing workshop instructor, will run about 300 words.

This tells me activity is accessible to wide audience and that it is practical.

Reinforces my feeling that author strives for accuracy.

I last wrote for you in December 1990, when "Spoken Music" appeared in *Cobblestone*. Since then I've also written for *Highlights* and *Spider* magazines and am the author of *Accessible Gardening for People with Physical Disabilities* (Woodbine House, 1994).

Important—this information clearly tells me Janeen enjoys writing and is willing to spend time researching and preparing material.

I appreciate your consideration and look forward to hearing from you.

Sincerely,

Janeen R. Adil

Enc.

Janeen R. Adil's query to *Calliope* resulted in a sale. Since her piece appeared in the September/October 1996 issue, Adil's work has appeared in at least a dozen subsequent issues of *Calliope*. Comments on her successful letter provided by Editor Rosalie Baker.

Successful Query

Grace Maccarone, *Executive Editor* (*Nice to include title*).
Cartwheel Books
555 Broadway
New York, NY 10012

July 20, 1998

Pertinent to us given our Hello Reader! line. Nice beginning.

Holiday titles are a big part of our list. Good point to make in opening paragraph.

Dear Ms. Maccarone:

I am writing to query if you would be interested in seeing my easy reader, entitled *The Scare Dare: Three Stories To Test If You Are A Scaredy Cat.*

This 1125 word manuscript includes three individual scary stories:

   In the first story, *The Cemetary*, Kate chases her cat, Luna, into a dark cemetary during a rain storm and is startled when her white cat appears to have turned black.

   In *Home Sweet Home*, Ben becomes frightened while he is out trick-or-treating. When he rushes back home, however, the loud boos inside his own house are even more scary . . . until he overcomes his fear and solves the mystery.

   In the final story, *Bones in the Bed*, Dave takes his dog trick-or-treating, but the trick is on Dave when his dog fills up Dave's bed with what seems to be arm and leg bones.

Important detail for easy reader— determines level.

All three stories are intriguingly spooky but not overly frightening for the target age group of kindergarten through third grade children. Each story is resolved with a logical twist that is humorously surprising, not supernatural. In a unique feature suggested by the title, a narrator's challenge to the reader to keep reading if (s)he dares is included in italics between each story. As this is a difficult technique to describe, I am including the first story and its corresponding narrator tags as a sample of the text to help you better evaluate your potential interest.

These are important distinctions for this age group.

Good idea—pique interest. Without sample, we might not pursue.

I hope you will share my enthusiasm for this manuscript. As a children's librarian with the San Francisco Public Library, I know first hand the perennial popularity of scary stories with 5-8 year olds and believe this reader would be very marketable. I have previously published an article in the *School Library Journal* and am a member of the Society of Children's Book Writers and Illustrators.

Enhances her credibility—she knows her readership. Might have mentioned at top.

Thank you for your consideration. I look forward to hearing from you.

Sincerely Yours,

Both noteworthy!

Kathleen Keeler
2410 Ashland Avenue
Happy Valley, CA 94555
(415)555-9047

Kathleen Keller's book, now called *I Dare You: Stories to Scare You*, is a fall 2000 Cartwheel Books release. Comments on Keeler's successful letter provided by Liza Baker, Cartwheel Books acquisitions editor. (See First Books on page 45 for more about Keeler's book.)

Successful Query

August 6th, 1998

Dear Mr. Malk,

Here is *Stop Pretending*, my poetry collection for young adults. It won the SCBWI Work-in-Progress Grant last fall. We spoke about it at the SCBWI Conference in Los Angeles. It tells the story of what happened to me and my family when my older sister had a nervous breakdown on the eve of my thirteenth birthday.

I had the immense good fortune to study poetry at UCLA with Myra Cohn Livingston for the last two years of her life. It was Myra who encouraged me to write *Stop Pretending*.

Since Myra's death, a group of her Master Class students have continued to meet and critique one another's work. These fine poets, most of whom have been widely published, helped give me the courage to delve into memories which were often dark and disturbing.

I'm delighted to share this story with you now, and I hope one day to be able to share it with teenagers all across the country. I like to think that this book could help them to feel less alone in whatever their struggles might be.

Thank you so much for taking the time to read it. I have included a SASE for your convenience.

Sincerely,

Sonya Sones
662 Hobby Horse Lane
Next Newbery CA 92555

Handwritten annotations:

- Excellent

- This is a good, concise description of the book.

- Lets me know that she studied with one of the best poets in the business—to her credit.

- It's great that she's in a good critique group.

- Very good. This tells me why she's writing the book and that she's sincere.

- It's helpful to remind me that we met before.

- Good. she knows the target audience.

- Professional

Sonya Sones sent this letter along with her manuscript for *Stop Pretending* to Agent Steven Malk who promptly agreed to represent her. Her book was soon snapped up by HarperCollins. See First Books on page 45 for more on Sones. Comments on her successful letter provided by Malk. (See his Insider Report on page 297.)

Very Bad Query

If you don't have credits, it's not necessary to mention it.

Makes an editor cringe.

Don't send them a picture book! Shows she didn't do her homework.

Editorial Department
Only Nonfiction Publications
6574 Hardcover Street
New York NY 10021

Find a name. (Also note that the majority of children's book editors are female.)

Don't say this—it simply won't matter to an editor.

Dear Sir:

Evidence she's not familiar with the genre.

Enclosed is my 5,000-word picture book *Murray the Helper Monkey*. I've read it to my grandson's kindergarten class and some kids in my neighborhood and they all think it should be published. It's a rhyming story that's a lot like Dr. Seuss's books. I also sent it to 45 other publishers.

Although it's go to mention sub mitting multi, this shows she didn't research publishers.

I haven't been published anywhere accept my church bulletin, but I've been writing for a year in my spare time. I've been married for 32 years, and I have 3 children and 7 grandchildren, so I've been reading books to kids for years! I also love to garden. Last year I grew a tomato that look an awful lot like Beverly Cleary. Maybe that would make a good book.

Oops! should be "except." Watc grammar an usage.

Another oops! sure to proofre well.

One idea at time.

Please don't call in the next two weeks because I will be out of town. If I don't hear from you after that, I'll call you.

Bad, bad, bad

I know you'll love *Murray the Helper Monkey!*

Sincerely,

Leave out impertinent personal information.

Follow-up with a postcard in a few months if you haven't gotten a response; don't call in two weeks.

Wilma Wannabe-Published
3982 No Way Lane
Slushville KY 46555

Not a good closing—don't make assumptions. Thank editor for considering your work and mention that you enclosed a SASE.

Don't forget phone number (and fax and email if you have them). Make it as easy as possible for the editor to contact you.

This letter is the cliché bad query—it's what *not* to do when submitting. Avoid these pitfalls that scream "unprofessional."

Nuts & Bolts for Illustrators

BY JOAN HOLUB

As an illustrator interested in working with children's publishers, you can show your artwork to art directors or editors in a variety of ways—by mail, via a website, in a face-to-face meeting, at a conference portfolio review, or by dropping off your portfolio at a publishing house. Which is most effective? It depends on the publisher's preferences and how much research and planning you do prior to your presentation.

Researching the market before submitting is an important step in the marketing process for illustrators. Learning about the styles of art various publishers prefer can help you decide which ones to approach. If your style is cartoony, for example, and you find a publisher only produces lavish, realistically illustrated books, you'll know to leave them off your mailing list.

It's helpful to visit bookstores to see which publishers are publishing what kinds of books. Many publishers will mail their catalogs to you if you request one. You can often get a catalog by sending a self-addressed, stamped envelope (SASE), or calling to ask for one. You can also visit publishers' websites which often offer access to their complete catalogs.

At some publishing houses, art directors review art. At others, editors do. Get submission information, including publisher's names and addresses, from sources like *Children's Writer's & Illustrator's Market* and The Society of Children's Book Writers and Illustrators (SCBWI) annual market survey.

What kinds of samples should you show?

Whether you're mailing promotional pieces or showing a portfolio, art directors are generally looking for artists who can draw the subjects most often shown in children's books—kids and animals. However, only show what you can draw well. If you are great at drawing kids, but don't draw animals well, don't include animal illustrations among your sample pieces. Art directors also like to see how you draw adults—especially moms, dads, grandparents, teachers.

Your samples should include scenes that show action and background. Try to create a scene that suggests a story. That will show an art director or editor that you are capable of illustrating a story, not just isolated subjects. I don't recommend illustrating scenes from a well-known fairy tale unless you have a very unique vision. Art directors see too many Snow Whites and Cinderellas, so this can be a turn-off.

Don't show samples of a style in which you don't want to work. This sounds obvious, but some artists make this mistake and are then offered an assignment they won't enjoy. Avoid showing only portraits or any work that was obviously a school assignment.

Sending samples by mail

The most cost-effective and efficient way to show your illustrations to most art directors and editors is by mailing samples to them. Here are some basic guidelines to follow when putting together mailing packages. For more detailed imformation on putting together effective promo pieces see For Illustrators: Super Self-Promotion Strategies on page 67.

JOAN HOLUB, *formerly associate art director at Scholastic, is the illustrator and author of many books for children, including her upcoming book* Abby Cadabra, Super Speller *(Grosset & Dunlap). Visit Joan's website at www.joanholub.com for more examples of her artwork and information about her books.*

• Send 3-10 photocopies of your best work, unfolded and inside a 9×12 or larger envelope. Include as many good color copies as you can afford (at least 2 or 3). The rest can be black and white. Staple them together on the upper left corner. Put your name, address, and phone number on each piece, preferably in the same location. Getting a rubber stamp made with this information will make labeling your samples easy.

• Avoid sending odd-sized or oversized samples. Slides are inconvenient for some art directors to view and photos can easily get lost. Sending $8\frac{1}{2} \times 11$ photocopies is best since it's an easy size for art directors to file. Never send original art unless it has been requested by the art director and you have arranged for its safe return.

• Include a short business-like cover letter stating your interest in obtaining illustration assignments. Don't sound flippant, needy, whiny or boastful. List publications in which your art has appeared as well as other art-related qualifications, such as memberships in illustration organizations or awards.

• Mail to the name of the art director (rather than just to "Art Director") if possible. Otherwise, your carefully prepared submission may not reach the right person. Assume your submission will not be returned, unless you request it and include a SASE. It's best to let the art director keep your samples on file. They may not have the right book for you to illustrate right away, but something might come along months or years later. This does happen!

• Mail updates of new work at least annually.

Getting your portfolio reviewed

Meeting an art director face-to-face is a great way to show your work, but many art directors and editors are too busy to schedule meetings. If you can't arrange a meeting, don't despair. Most publishers will allow artists to drop off a portfolio for review when the artist is visiting an area where publishers are located. Since things do get lost, include only duplicates of your work that can be insured at a reasonable cost. Only show originals when you can be present for the review. Label your portfolio with your name, address and phone number.

It's a good idea to have at least two portfolios ready to send at all times. It often happens one art director will request to see your portfolio after you've already sent it to another art director. The Children's Book Council has a detailed list of each art director's requirements for portfolio review, which is available to its members or online at www.cbcbooks.org.

Attending conferences that include portfolio reviews can also be a good way to get your illustrations seen by publishers. The Children's Illustrators Conference held annually in May in New York City by the Society of Illustrators is an excellent event. For a fee, you can leave your portfolio in a private viewing room along with many other portfolios. When you pick up your portfolio at the end of the day, you'll receive an envelope containing any comments or requests left for you by editors and art directors who have viewed your portfolio.

The Society of Children's Book Writers and Illustrators offers a Portfolio Display option for illustrators attending their National Conference held every summer in Los Angeles. (Contact SCBWI Illustration Coordinator Priscilla Burris at burrisdraw@aol.com for more information. Burris also maintains a file of illustrators' samples for interested art directors and editors.)

What should be in your portfolio?

Here are some guidelines to follow when putting together your portfolio:

• Include 15-25 pieces of original as well as published work if you have it. Include dummies and published books if you have them. Some art directors like to see a variety of styles. Others like to see the continuity of one style. Take only your best work.

• Display your work in a small portfolio with clear acetate sleeves. It's not necessary to frame, mount or cover your work unless it's something that could be easily damaged by handling.

• Include samples to leave behind. If you're dropping off your portfolio, consider including a comment sheet that the reviewer can fill in and leave in your portfolio. This can provide you with an indication of an art director's interest, and you may get some helpful feedback as a result.

Website promotion

The Internet is gradually becoming an effective method of introducing artwork to publishers. Some art directors and editors like to visit an individual illustrator's website as a method of becoming familiar with his or her artwork when considering the illustrator for a project. If you don't know how to create a website and don't want to learn, consider a website that specializes in designing and hosting pages that show the work of many illustrators. They usually charge a fee. For more information on using a website for promotion, see For Illustrators: Super Self-Promotion Strategies on page 67.

Making a quick and simple book dummy

Illustrators, especially those who also write, may want to create a book dummy for viewing by editors and art directors. A dummy is simply a rough mock-up of a picture book showing how the text and art of a story flows.

It's important to note that picture books are usually 32 pages plus a cover (and perhaps endpapers). The typical layout of a picture book is as follows:
- page 1: half title page
- pages 2-3: double page title spread
- page 4: copyright and dedication page
- pages 5-32: text

This format can vary. For instance, the copyright page can be on page 32, the half title page can be eliminated, or the text can begin on page 3 or 4. Odd numbered pages are always on the right, and even numbered pages are always on the left side of a spread. (Examine some of your favorite picture book for examples.)

It's best to make your dummy a common size such as 8×10 or $8\frac{1}{2} \times 11$. Decide whether to make it square, vertical or horizontal. Your publisher, or you and your publisher together, will determine the actual size of the book after your manuscript is purchased. So the size you choose for your dummy is not especially crucial at the submission stage.

Note: Before you begin final art for a book, be sure to ask for the exact dimensions that have been decided upon. If you are told that the book is to be 8×10, that means the book is vertical—8 inches wide and 10 inches tall. The first number indicates the width. But double-check with the art director whether the book is vertical or horizontal, just to be safe.

Dummies are most often illustrated in pen or pencil, but nearly any medium can be used. Some artists create loose dummy sketches. Others make them more detailed. Do what suits your book's needs. Here are a few basic steps to follow as you as you create a book dummy:

Step 1: Creating a blank book. For a 32-page picture book plus a cover, you will need 9 sheets (1 for covers, 8 for text) of 11×17 paper. I use ledger-size copier paper and lay the

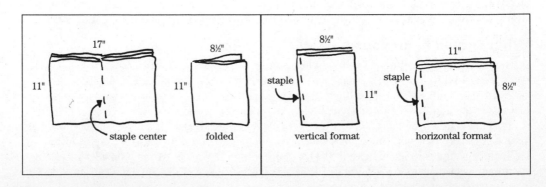

staple center   folded   vertical format   horizontal format stacked pages flat, and staple them 3-4 times along the center line against an undamageable hard surface. (I use my concrete patio. Do this *very* carefully—don't stab yourself or ruin your floors.) Then fold the dummy in half.

An even simpler method is to take 18 sheets (2 for covers, 16 for text) of $8\frac{1}{2} \times 11$ paper and staple sheets together along one edge. No folding needed. You can trim your dummy down to a smaller size if desired.

Step 2: Assembling the text. If possible, type your story on a computer (or typewriter) in the approximate size it will print—probably 14- to 18-point. (Note: Handwritten lettering can be difficult to read or look unprofessional. If your book has few words or if you plan to hand letter the type in your book, a hand-lettered dummy is OK. But be sure it is neat and legible, and submit a typewritten manuscript along with your dummy.)

Cut your story apart, and attach the text of your story in place on pages of your dummy. Do this in a way that will allow you to move your text around later. I've tried various methods such as tape, wax or a nonpermanent adhesive.

This process of distributing your story throughout a given number of pages will help you discover if your story is too long or too short. Now you know how much space is left for your sketches. Is rewriting in order for a better fit?

Step 3: Adding the art. Draw illustrations on tracing paper and place them in the dummy. You can also sketch directly in your dummy, but I don't do this because it can result in a messy look from too many erasures.

If portions of your text are not illustratable—if there's no action to illustrate—you'll find out during this step and more rewriting may be necessary. You will probably move your type around on the pages during this stage, as you decide what works best with your sketches.

Many authors create simple dummies for planning purposes. These are usually not submitted to a publisher, but are used by the author to fine-tune the pacing of the text before they submit a manuscript.

It's not necessary to submit a dummy with your manuscript, particularly if you are not an illustrator. However, if you are unpublished and do hope to illustrate your book, you should at least try to include one to three color photocopies of finished artwork illustrating your story, along with your dummy.

Never mail unrequested original art. Never send your only dummy. Always keep a copy of it.

What if you have several illustration styles?

If you have more than one illustration style, like I do, it can both work for and against you. On the plus side, the fact that you can work in several styles means that you are versatile. So you have the potential to be considered for a wider variety of illustration assignments. One of your styles might be suitable for novel jackets and another suitable for textbook work, while yet another might be suitable for picture book work. Different publishers may be interested in different aspects of your work, so it's easy to stay busy.

On the negative side, having several styles can cause confusion. Suppose someone at a publishing house has seen your colorful, contemporary picture book style and suggests you to the art director as a possible illustrator for a picture book project. Perhaps the art director might then do some research on you. He or she might locate several books that you've illustrated. But what if the art director happens to only come across the somewhat adult style you use for novel jackets or the conservative style you generally reserve for textbook work? The art director may assume that those are your typical styles.

Without contacting you to learn that you have other styles, the art director may decide that your styles (the only ones he's seen) are wrong for the project. He may move on to another illustrator and you'll never know what happened.

If you're a multi-style artist, it's also important to remember to ask which style the art director has in mind when you are given a book to illustrate. Don't assume the style you had in mind is the one they chose you for and the style in which they expect to see their book illustrated. Ask before beginning work and avoid a potential disaster. I find that the pluses far outweigh the negatives with regard to working in a variety of styles. Variety allows me creative freedom, keeps my work fresh and makes my job lots of fun.

Joan Holub has several illustration styles, which she often combines. She alternates painting in watercolor, gouache and acrylic, while drawing with pen, pencils or even paint! Though the mediums might be the same in some of these sample illustrations, the drawing or painting style differs. *The 100th Day of School* (Scholastic) was illustrated in pencil and watercolor; *Pen Pals* (Grosset & Dunlap) was illustrated in pen and watercolor; *Happy Monster Day!* (Scholastic) was illustrated in gouache, acrylic and watercolor; all were painted on Arches watercolor paper.

Making the Most of the Internet

If you haven't discovered it yet, the Internet can be a *SuPER* resource for writers. It offers *Su*pport, *P*romotional opportunities, access to *E*ditors and agents and endless material for *Re*search.

SUPPORT

Before I went online, I felt isolated and lonely. No one else I knew was trying to write for children, and I had no way of getting feedback on my stories. Enter the Internet, which knows no geographic boundaries. Suddenly, I found peers from across the United States who were struggling with the same issues I was. I participated in various critique groups, shared setbacks and joys; I had found a community of writers.

You, too, can find support and encouragement from the online community of writers, through bulletin boards, e-mail critique groups, private mailing lists and other resources.

Bulletin boards. A bulletin board is a public place where you can post messages and others can answer. They are the staple of the early Internet experience and continue in some form on many websites. Check bulletin boards of online service providers, such as America Online, for a group of writers who are already meeting online. Join a public mailing list for writers like www.inkspot.com/tk/network/mailing.html. Visit chat rooms where other children's writers gather such as the Children's Writing Resource Center (www.write4kids.com). Also check listings for Internet Relay Chat (IRC), a text-only worldwide chat area containing thousands of channels for any interest.

E-mail critique groups. One support activity desired by writers is a way to obtain feedback on their manuscripts. A fresh eye will often spot mistakes or have new insights that will help you revise effectively. Drawing from people you meet on bulletin boards, friends from conferences, or other long-distance contacts, you can ask several people if they want to join you in an online critique group. Decide early on procedures and ground rules for sending manuscripts to the entire group and getting feedback. How often can you post, what if one member doesn't participate in critiquing, etc.? For more information, read Sue Bradford Edwards's article, How to Create Your Own E-mail Critique Group (www.utahlinx.com/users/kcummings/cghowto.htm).

Private mailing lists. The easiest way to create your own community is to start a private mailing list. Mailing lists allow you to post to a central address, which forwards your message to everyone on the list. Start by adding writing friends from across the country. As they recommend the list to others, the community will grow and mature. One list I'm a member of passes along information about publishers and editors, discusses issues about the craft of writing, celebrates sales and commiserates over rejections, reports on regional conferences, networks, and sometimes empathizes with personal problems.

Since late 1998, a variety of free services have started that allow you to create a private mailing list with no special software and no special skills. Check first to see if there is a list

DARCY PATTISON's first book, The River Dragon (Lothrop, Lee & Shepard), was an American Booksellers Association "Pick of the Lists." Her first novel, The Wayfinder (Greenwillow Books), is a fall 2000 release, followed by a new picture book in 2002, The Journey of Oliver K. Woodman (Harcourt Children's Books). Yes, Darcy has been dot.commed! Visit her website at www.darcypattison.com.

that will meet your needs. Each service provides slightly different options in regard to varying statistics on members, size limits, advertising, etc. Be sure to read their agreements carefully:

- www.onelist.com
- www.listbot.com
- www.communityware.com
- www.egroups.com

PROMOTION

Websites. Have you been "dot.commed" yet, as in www.darcypattison.com? Most options for promotional activities center around your own website, including an online bookstore through various associate programs.

First, you need to carefully assess the reason you want a website, what content you can provide and how often you can update it, and the costs of establishing and maintaining your site. For information on Web design, try www.webpagesthatsuck.com or other similar informational sites. You'll soon see the admonition that *content is king*. A website that just mimics your printed brochure will not receive much attention. Ask yourself, "Why would anyone want to visit my website over and over again?" If there's no reason for regular visits, then you may not want to bother with a website. For a successful website, you should build in content that will bring visitors back for repeat visits.

For example, Carol Purdy (www.snowcrest.net/kidpower/authors.html) maintains a list of authors who do school visits, making her website a resource for educators. Aaron Shephard (www.aaronshep.com) provides reader theater scripts and teacher's guides for most of his picture books, again making his website a resource for educators. My website, Fantastic Books, (http://members.aol.com/fantstkbks/) offers monthly reviews of new children's novels, and during the National Book Awards and Newbery/Caldecott Awards seasons, I host a Popular Poll for visitors to vote on these awards. To look over other children's writer's websites for ideas—both good and bad—the Society of Children's Book Writers and Illustrators (SCBWI) website (www.scbwi.org) provides links to member's homepages. A couple hours spent evaluating these sites—from the ones that are Web-inappropriate static brochures to the ones that take advantage of the Web's unique opportunities for interactivity—will save you lots of time and headaches later.

After deciding on the content of your website, you can begin designing it or contacting Web-design companies. Choose basic books about learning HTML and only add extra features such as animated gifs, javascripts, etc. if they are actually needed to enhance the content. Keep the website easy to read, easy to navigate. To evaluate Web design companies, ask for listings of their websites to visit first.

If you want to have your own domain (yourname.com), you'll have to register with Internic (www.internic.com), then work with your service provider to have them host the domain. If you don't want to pay your current service provider the extra money to host your domain, look for low-cost alternative services (such as www.register.com), who provide a link from your domain name to your current website, a sort of call-forwarding for your website. Picture book author Rick Walton chose this low cost option for his website: "I think your own domain is valuable. It's so much easier to remember www.rickwalton.com than users.itsnet.com/~rickwalton/."

A popular addition to writers' websites is a way to purchase their books. Many online bookstores have associate or affiliate programs that will pay commissions on books sold from referral links on your website. For more information, read John Kremer's article at www.bookmarket.com/booksales.html. Before signing up for any affiliate program, be sure to read the individual agreements carefully. Some online bookstores offering affiliate programs include www.amazon.com, www.barnesandnoble.com and www.cherryvalleybooks.com.

Other items frequently added to websites—depending on what audience they are trying to attract—are FAQs (Frequently Asked Questions), reviews of books, teacher's guides, biographical information, calendar of author visits/book tours, information on school visits or teacher in-services, favorite links, artwork from the book, or printable bookmarks or coloring pages. Verla Kay takes a technological stance by adding scheduled talks in a chat room hosted on her website www.mlode.com/~verlakay/. (See the Insider Report with Kay on page 180.) Again, browse through representative sites from links at the SCBWI website to see what is typical (www.scbwi.org).

Promotional ideas. Other online promotional activities include press releases, public mailing lists or your own e-newsletter. For general promotion ideas, look at www.bookpromotion.com.

Press releases should be prepared much the same as they are for print publications with a good lead, timely information or local hook. Look for listings of e-mail addresses for radio stations or newspapers in your state. For information on marketing to schools and libraries including databases for sending press releases, look here: www.Internet-monitor.com/marketing_resources.html.

Participating in public mailing lists is a good way to gain exposure. Develop a good "sig," or signature tag, that gives information about your books and/or your website. When you post appropriate comments or helpful information—which establishes you as an authority or someone with valid insights—be sure to use the sig which will lead people to your books and to you. Sometimes, when I post on a mailing list which has about 1,000 members, my website will receive over a hundred visitors in a single afternoon, or about ten percent of those who read my message. Experts in direct mail advertising consider a three to four percent response as good, so the ten percent response is excellent. Look here for information on mailing lists related to children's literature—where you'll run into librarians and teachers who will use your books with kids: www.asc.ucalgary.ca/~dkbrown/listserv.html.

One of the basic tenets of running a website is to capture names. You want to find out who is visiting your website and once they visit, you want them to return. A free monthly newsletter, giving updated information on your writing efforts, monthly reviews, or other timely information is a great excuse to ask for a visitor's name and e-mail address. Your newsletter should also direct them back to the website each month, or at the very least keep them interested in your work and promote name recognition. To manage the newsletter you can use the same software mentioned above for managing private mailing lists.

Any other promotional activity done in print can be translated to something comparable online. Some ideas include virtual school visits, chats on large services like AOL, author interviews for Amazon.com, etc. The more you learn about the Internet culture, the more ideas you'll have. Internet promotion should not replace regular promotional activities, but it can be an effective addition to your overall efforts.

EDITORS AND AGENTS

Three hours or three months—how soon do you want that answer from an editor? Queries, revisions, acceptances, encouragement and problem solving are a few of the ways writers are communicating with editors and agents online—fast!

Print magazine editors. Because of their short production schedules, e-mail queries and their follow-ups are more common among magazine editors than for book publishers. Often, a magazine editor needs an article within a short time frame and is willing to look at a query, make the assignment and receive the article all online. Only the check goes through snail mail! Check this market guide for e-mail addresses and guidelines for submission. Here are a couple of online sources for magazine guidelines:

- www.inkspot.com
- www.awoc.com/Guidelines.cfm
- www.writersdigest.com

E-zine editors or websites. The proliferation of websites and e-zines means more opportunities to sell your work. Nonfiction is the big seller online. Kelly Milner Halls, a full-time freelance author with six books and hundreds of articles under her belt, suggests this strategy for finding places to query: "It's a little like finding a needle in a haystack, but I spend a lot of time just surfing the Web, moving from link, to link, to link. It's not quite as big a waste of time as it might seem. Much of my net head investments begin as research for traditional assignments. If I'm researching camping for teens or the dinosaurs of Ohio, germs or the women of World War II, I often come across high quality, online publications. If I'm really impressed with the professional quality of a website, I'll search for an editorial e-mail address and ask if they consider freelance submissions. More and more often, editors who man the upscale publications say, 'Yes.' " (See Halls's article Writing For Boys: Is the Gender Barrier Real? on page 75.)

Content Exchange (www.content-exchange.com) lists writers who specialize in online work, including children's writers. Or look at the Top 100 Websites for kids (www.100hot.com/kids/) for regularly occurring features that will need a constant stream of articles.

Book editors. E-mail queries and submissions are rare for book publishers. Once a relationship is established with a book editor, though, e-mail has become a common way to stay in touch as you discuss the details of a contract or minor revisions, submit new material or just chat about the industry. The rule of thumb here is to let the editor send the first e-mail, then only use the address for business purposes. For advice on the use of regular mail versus e-mail with children's book publishers, see Wendy McClure's article, Let the Mail Prevail! A Guide to Etiquette, Status Calls and More at www.users.interport.net/~hdu/etiquet.htm. (See the sidebar interview with McClure, editor at Albert Whitman, in First Books on page 49)

Agents. Susan Cohen, agent for Writers House, says she resisted e-mail for a long time, but after finally giving in, she finds it invaluable. "It's better than playing telephone tag. I can answer e-mail when I have time and often get back to editors and authors faster than otherwise. I'm not as articulate on the phone, so I prefer to give some sort of written response, but letters are too slow. E-mail gives you a written record of comments or information about submissions that can be referred back to when needed. It's also great for giving gentle nudges to slow editors." Like most book editors, though, she doesn't accept unsolicited e-mail queries or submissions, preferring hard copies and regular mail for these. E-mail is reserved for her clients and conversations with editors.

Tips on using e-mail. Nick Cook, author of *Roller Coasters, or I Had So Much Fun I Almost Puked* (Carolrhoda), has used e-mail to communicate with a magazine editor. The first submission—query with clips—was in hard copy, but after that, everything from query to article was done by e-mail. One of his assignments started with problems. Cook's query was answered by the magazine editor, but "his acceptance of the article ended up in the cyber version of a dead letter office; since his previous nonresponse to my queries meant, "no thanks," I assumed it was the case here too." It wasn't until the editor wrote asking how the piece was going that Cook realized it had been assigned.

The problems didn't stop there. The same article was cursed because of network problems and Cook had to send it three times on three different days to meet a deadline. Because of this problem, Cook suggests knowing multiple ways to send e-mail. In other words, understand how to use different e-mail programs and how to telnet and use pure text mailers (such as PINE). A knowledge of the difference between different text/word processing formats is helpful, too, as editors often use different programs than the writers they are working with.

RESEARCH

Need a fact or opinion in a hurry to finish your article? Need to research publishers, editors, agents or the market in general? Somewhere on the World Wide Web, there's an answer that is only minutes away.

Publishing industry contacts and news. With frequent personnel changes at publishing houses, the Internet provides the most up-to-date information. There are several ways to keep track of children's publishing online. Start with the Children's Book Council (www.cbcbooks .org) listing of publishers, which includes editors' names, addresses and contact information. To keep track of changes at publishers, the Children's Writing Resource Center (www.write4kids.-com) maintains updated information on the listings in *Children's Writer's & Illustrator's Market*. Harold Underdown, editor for Charlesbridge Books, maintains the Purple Crayon site (www.inter port.net/~hdu/chchange.htm) where he lists editors who have moved houses. *Publishers Weekly* online (www.bookwire.com/pw) updates its features about children's books several times a month and includes information on publishing industry personnel changes.

Researching story ideas. Search engines are the obvious starting place for researching a story idea. For the basics, beginners can refer to these articles for tips on using search engines to locate specific information:

- www.i-net.com.au/tutorials/search/index.html
- www.delphi.com/navnet/faq/search.html
- docs.yahoo.com/docs/info/faq.html

But don't stop with search engines. Also use your network of friends. For example, most of the people quoted in this article are part of a private mailing list. Often when I need information, someone on our list has personal experience relating to the topic. After all, they come from Manitoba, Alaska, Florida, New York, Missouri, Texas, Germany, Australia, Italy and Korea, from backgrounds as journalists, dairy farmers, computer techs, teachers and politicians, from never-published to published-over-three-hundred-books. This vast collective experience often comes through for me.

When researching online, remember the Internet makes self-publishing easy, which means some websites may present a personal belief rather than facts. Always double-check your facts on multiple sites, or at least attribute the information to the author of the site.

And if all that isn't enough to get you started on the Internet, visit the Sandbaggers Website, the home of my e-mail critique group. (It's easier to maintain a website when there are six people contributing!) Kevin Cummings has prepared a special article for writers getting started on the Internet: Notes from the WWW: 28 Cool Online Activities for Children's Writers (www.sa ndbaggers.8m.com/notes.html).

Internet Gossip: Post With Caution

Quick communication, which can be a blessing if you're querying about an article, or making corrections on a manuscript, can also be a curse when *private* comments you've made online are deliberately forwarded to the wrong person.

Janni Lee Simner, author of the Phantom Rider series (Scholastic), and a veteran of the Internet, mailing lists, websites and bulletin boards, says, "One of the things I tend to keep in mind online is that, essentially, I'm in a large public place where lots of people are listening. I may be talking only to my friends, but really, I don't know who will overhear. I found that if you say something about someone, it will get back to them sooner or later. "So, even though I hope people won't repeat my words, I try to stick to saying things I'm okay with having repeated, which can be a fair amount. Still, I believe strongly in information sharing, and if I really do have a problem with a publisher or a contract, I want other people to know about it. One of our strengths is that we can share information. But I am careful, too, even while I really do think the best of everyone I'm talking to online. I assume that I don't really know who's listening—or even who, while otherwise well-intentioned, may be a close friend of someone I talk about and thus feel honor-bound to pass along my post."

—*Darcy Pattison*

Setting Writing Goals That Work!

BY TRACEY E. DILS

If you're like me, you are probably pretty good at setting goals. Meeting them, of course, is another matter entirely. Whether it has to do with losing weight, cleaning out my overflowing closet, or writing, I always seem to come up short of my expectations.

I've learned to live with the extra weight. I've learned to live with the overflowing closet. But I couldn't learn to live with coming up short when it comes to my writing goals. Writing is simply too important to me. It is not only my career; I need to write to stay balanced emotionally.

So I took a hard look at my writing and my life (ignoring my weight and my closet, of course) and decided to do something about it. The first thing I did was figure out why the goals I had set hadn't been met so that I could set new ones that were attainable. And once I did that, I hit upon a process for goal-setting that really worked. It's a process that may help you clarify and—most importantly—begin meeting your goals.

Start with a mission statement

My first revelation came when I realized I often failed to meet my writing goals because I hadn't really defined for myself why I was writing in the first place. I didn't have a sense of my mission as a writer. I had some of the same reasons you probably have for writing—and they all had to do with being published, the thrill of seeing my name in print, and the hope that I might someday be able to make a living at it. But those reasons really weren't the ones in my heart. There were more urgent ones—ones that spoke to my own need for creativity and my delight in and love and respect for children.

I decided that my next step would be to explore all the reasons that I write in general and the reasons I write for children in particular. I wrote down all the reasons I could think of on index cards. From these cards, I reasoned, I could create a list in order of priority that would serve as mission statements. Those mission statements would help guide my decisions about my work. Here is what appeared on the cards that found their way to the top of my list:

I want my writing to reflect my own struggle to understand and make sense of myself and the world around me.

This sounds like heady stuff, but it is, in truth, why I started writing in the first place, way back in fifth grade. Writing is the way I figure things out. I want everything I write to be part of that self-discovery process.

I want my writing to make young people feel powerful.

I'll never forget the books that made me feel powerful when I was a young reader. *The Boxcar Children* and *My Side of the Mountain* are just two of the books that made me feel as if I could do anything. I want the work I create for children to instill that same sense of power.

I want my writing to instill a love of reading in young readers.

TRACEY E. DILS *is the author of more than 25 books for young readers, including* Annabelle's Awful Waffle, Grandpa's Magic *and* Real Life Scary Places, *as well as* You Can Write Children's Books *(published by Writer's Digest Books). She is the recipient of several writing awards including the Ohioana Award in Children's Literature. A veteran editor of various publishing companies, she is currently executive editor at McGraw-Hill. A frequent guest author in elmentary schools and a popular speaker at writer's conferences, Dils lives in Columbus, Ohio, with her husband and two children.*

After all is said and done, this is my most important goal—and I would suggest that this might be yours as well. Reading not only opens up new worlds for children; it is essential to their well-being. In fact American Academy of Pediatricians has found that exposing children to books at birth actually stimulates brain development. The list goes on. And at the bottom of my pile I found a real surprise. The reason that I thought I wanted to write in the first place— to be published and see my name in print—was really my last priority:

I will seek an audience for my work, through publishing and promoting myself.

Your priorities may be far different than mine. You may be writing because you want to put down on paper the bedtime stories you tell your children at night or because you want to preserve family stories. You may be writing because of the sheer glory of it—and that can include the moment you see your name in print. But I suspect if you go through the exercise I did, you will have a clearer vision of why you are writing and how you feel about writing for children. You'll find out what your priorities are. And you will probably be surprised what you learn about yourself as a writer and as a creative being.

Use your mission statement to guide your goals

I typed up all my mission statements in list form and created a kind of "ten commandments" for myself which I keep propped next to my computer. Now I had a clearer sense of why I was doing what I was doing. My next task was more difficult; I had to figure out how I would get there.

When I took a hard look at my mission statements, I noticed they could be grouped naturally into categories:

- writing and producing material
- trying new genres
- submitting and publishing
- serving my readers and my fellow writers

Again, you may find that your categories are different than mine, but I suspect we share some of the same goal categories. Now it's time for the real work—to set goals under each of these categories.

Set realistic and specific goals

The second reason I had failed to meet my goals is that they weren't always the most reasonable goals, nor were they specific enough to measure. In order to really meet my goals, I needed to be realistic about my life and my situation. I knew, for instance, that I had long set a goal for myself of writing every day. I never met that one (nor did I ever reach the goal of wearing a size ten during my dieting days). And even if I had, it would not have mattered much since I had not set a goal for what I would have been writing. So when I created goals in each of these categories, I made sure my goals were both realistic and specific.

Let's start with my first category: to write and produce work. Under this category I determined that I would write a page of something every other day. This goal is in effect only when I don't have something under contract or am working on a project for a specific publisher. Once that happens, I turn up the heat a bit and set goals that are specific to that project—always having to do with page count instead of time. (For me, time is a little bit like counting calories. It's easy to cheat and fritter that time away without realizing it, just like it's easy to eat something without even worrying about how fattening it is.) Either way, I am now pleased to say I am usually attaining that goal—and I'm attaining it because it is reasonable, specific and in line with my mission statement.

Now let's consider the second category: to try something new. Most children's book writers want to create the next great picture book. That goal had been among mine as well. I was reluctant to try something else because it seemed like it was a waste of time. I discovered, though, that trying a new genre was good for the business. (After all, picture books are a very hard category to break into.) I also found it was a good way to stretch my creative muscles.

Again, I was specific and reasonable about this goal. I decided in this calendar year I would try a biography (and I did, a biography of Samuel L. Jackson for Chelsea House publishers) and play around a bit with poetry. Next year, I want to write some nonfiction magazine articles, again something I've never really done routinely. While writing in these genres doesn't get me any closer to creating the next great picture book, I am finding that any writing I do—regardless of the genre—enhances me as a writer. It also provides titles to add to my list of credits.

The next category of goals—submitting and publishing—is one that has always been difficult for me. Submitting work means taking a risk—that dreadful risk of rejection. But it's also true that the more you submit, the easier it becomes. At the same time, of course, you are increasing your opportunities for publication through the simple law of averages.

I found a simple and obvious solution here. I set up a schedule for submitting my work. The first Tuesday of every month I commit to getting something in the mail. It may be only a query letter or a request for guidelines, but often it is an entire manuscript. The point is that one day of every month I am making contact with publishers. I'm not letting the fear of rejection or the need to run a story by my writer's group one more time stop me in my tracks. (Speaking of my writer's group, I have suggested that we submit work together on a regular basis—even walking to the post office together and then celebrating. It's a tradition we may start soon.)

I've come, finally, to my last category of goals: serving my readers and other writers. This goal comes from the mission I have defined for myself as a writer and as a human being. Put simply, I feel it's essential to become involved in the reading and writing community. For me, that means actively participating on a couple of different levels. The first is primarily professional: I speak at writer's conferences, offer manuscript critiques, and offer classes to those writers who are interested in learning how to write for children.

The second sounds altruistic on the surface: I work with young people in a variety of different settings—schools, community centers, libraries, even a teen parent program—to develop creative writing skills and to create enthusiasm for reading. While I recognize I am making a contribution to those organizations with which I work, in truth, the rewards I receive far outweigh what I've given. I learn so much. I observe a child learning to read, I share the triumph when a teen mother writes a poem about her baby, and I discover anew the power that comes from the written word. Quite simply, it makes me a better writer.

This category needs goals too and I've set modest ones: to serve my community through the written word four times a year. When all is said and done, it is the most powerful part of my writing life.

Review and assess

Goals are not meant to stand forever and I generally review my goal list and my mission statements every year, usually in the fall when "back-to-school" time signals a break in the routine. I cross some goals off my list, create new ones, and make adjustments to old goals, reassessing time frames and other specifics mentioned. And then I post them, along with my mission statements, next to my computer. They become a kind of conscience that keeps me in line. I also take great comfort in them once rejection comes calling. Knowing that I have stayed true to my mission statements takes a little of the sting out of rejection.

My closet still overflows and my scale will never point to the numbers I want. But somehow, it doesn't matter that much to me anymore. My writing life is under control. Through defining my mission and then setting realistic and specific goals, I'm making real progress. I still have days when I don't meet my goals because I simply feel lazy or a family disaster strikes and I have to put work aside. But I no longer have that feeling that I am always coming up short of my own expectations. When disaster, laziness or some other writing block hits, I let it pass. Then I read my mission statements, look over my goals, and get back to work.

And every once in awhile, when I run my fingers over my computer keyboard, I create something I know is magical and wonderful. I know then that I am living my mission.

Creating Balance: Secrets to Improve Your Writing & Illustrating Life

BY REVA SOLOMON

Most people think their writing and illustrating sits in a vacuum—hanging somewhere in limbo away from the rest of their lives. Have you ever considered that everything going on in your life is connected? It's not possible to isolate one part from the other.

When considering this concept, try looking at eight areas of your life: Career, Money, Health, Spirituality/Personal Growth, Personal Space or Environment, Significant Other, Fun & Recreation and Friends & Family. If one of these is non-existent or lacking, it absolutely affects all the others. So if we are talking about your career of writing or illustrating and you have no money coming in, or you are in poor health, these things are going to affect your creativity because your career focus will be out of balance worrying about these other areas of your life.

The idea is to have each area of your life at the optimum level of completeness so your life as a whole is in balance. When you are looking at your life as a whole, with all the pieces in place as best they can be, with no large gaps in any area, then you can proceed with your writing and illustrating with nothing else in the way. The difference you will find in the ability to create, without blocks, fears or procrastination will be astonishing.

Chart where you are

A great way to see this clearly is to take a piece of paper and draw a large circle. Divide the circle into eight wedges (think pieces of pie or a wagon wheel). Label each wedge on the outside of the circle with one of the eight areas of your life listed above. The circle represents your life. As you can see, all the wedges connect at the center of the circle, just as all areas of your life connect. Next assign an arbitrary number from one to ten (with ten being the highest) representing where you are today in each of these areas.

So if you are looking at career, let's say, and you are not where you want to be with this area of your life, you might assign that wedge with the number three. This means you probably want to look at your career and see how you can improve or change the work you have chosen.

In a perfect world, which of course doesn't exist, you would assign all your wedges tens. But since we are human, there probably will be a range of numbers on your circle. Next, compare the areas on the wheel which are similar. Did you assign a low number to both "Friends & Family" and maybe "Significant Other," but high numbers to "Career" and "Money"? How do these relate? What effect does your personal life have on your creative work? If you're spending a majority of your time worrying about another area of your life, your complete focus

REVA SOLOMON *is a writer and a personal and business success coach and lecturer. She is people editor for the Society of Children's Book Writers and Illustrators* Bulletin *and the former administrator for the SCBWI National Office. Her professional experience includes 20 years in the entertainment industry, including working as the director of development for Lin Oliver Productions in Los Angeles, specializing in children's film and television. Contact her at RSolomonPR@juno.com.*

can't be on your creative work. The idea is to strive to get closer to tens in all areas and create a more balanced life.

Create balance

If you're having trouble getting started writing or illustrating every time you sit at your desk, look around your house, studio or office. What do you see? Is your environment cluttered with piles everywhere? Do you have things that stimulate your creative juices where you work, such as plants or a vase of fresh flowers, or some of your favorite things? If you listen to music while you work (try it—I find it sets my mood and keeps me going) are your CDs and tapes organized or at least together in a general area so you don't have to spend hours digging in the back seat of your car or the bottom of your closet for your favorite tunes? Is your office or your studio set up in a comfortable way that allows you to have everything you need at your fingertips?

Look at what you are tolerating in your life—yes tolerating. Those pesky things you've been meaning to do that sit just on the edge of your consciousness and pop up just when you are on deadline or committed to finally writing or drawing for the first time; those things large and small that drain your energy and attention and distract you. Everything from getting the car washed to taking the pets for their shots; from cleaning out the hall closet to getting a massage? Get it? These pesky things lurking in the back of your mind take away from your creative objectives.

An interesting exercise to try is making a list of at least ten things you are tolerating in your life right now (I actually listed 60 things the first time I did this). Pick one thing from the list you can take care of easily right now. I guarantee if you begin to take care of these tolerations, your procrastination with your writing and illustrating will begin to slip away, your blocks will no longer exist, and you'll feel a sense of accomplishment as you cross things off your list. The writing and illustrating now has a place in your head that was previously filled with those tolerations you were thinking about!

Action = moving forward

Taking action—any action—creates a shift in your ability to move forward in your life, which means moving forward in your creative work.

Okay, here's a tough one to look at. Money. What could this possibly have to do with your creativity? You either have it or you don't, right? Wrong. Money is an emotional issue. Many of us bring a lot of old ideas attached to money. Feelings run deep with this subject and run the gamut from shame to exhilaration. What about all those credit cards maxed to the limit? Are you living on the edge with your money and figure you'll just "Scarlet O'Hara" this subject? (You know, "Fiddle-dee-dee, I'll think about it tomorrow!")

The idea of debt, lack of money, under earning, or living on the edge with money can gnaw at your mind from time-to-time, just enough to keep those creative juices clogged. If you are constantly thinking of other things in your life, rather than being able to stay in the moment and focus on your creative endeavors, you are making it more difficult for yourself and creating obstacles.

In a nutshell, here are ten steps to help get (and keep) your creative life on track:

1. Get rid of the tolerations in your life. Tolerations are the things draining you; things that gnaw away your mind.

2. Get rid of clutter. Off your desk, in your office, your home, the garage, your mind. With clutter in your life, there is no room for anything new to enter (like your writing or an offer from a publisher!).

3. Make H.A.L.T. a part of your life. Don't get too Hungry, Angry, Lonely or Tired. (If any of these dominate your day, there is no way you can write or draw.)

4. Let go of resentments. Towards people, places and things. Holding onto unresolved resentments keeps you stuck in anger and creates blocks in all areas of your life—especially the creative area which you use for writing.

5.   Make amends. Create a list of amends you need to make—to people alive or who have passed away; people you are still in contact with or those you no longer see. Don't forget those money amends. These can be done by letter, phone call or in person. Taking care of this will free you in ways you can't even imagine. Feeling good allows your creative juices to flow.

6.   Exercise! Even twenty minutes three times a week will help you feel better about yourself, not to mention contribute to your health. When those endorphins are jumping, your writing takes off!

7.   Let go of addictions. Although we hear how famous writers "suffered for their art," they also died from their addictions. What are some of yours you can't let go of? Sugar, alcohol, drugs, caffeine, food, sex, TV, procrastination, clutter, what? (If you can't do this alone, join a 12-step program, listed in the white pages of the phone book.)

8.   Eat healthier. It's been proven that there is a mind/body connection. You can see your writing improve just by changing what you eat. The fuel (food) you put in your body reflects the energy you have which is connected to how and what you write. Try it—eat healthier for a week. Cut out sugar and junk food—see what happens.

9.   Connect to Spirit. No matter what your religious beliefs (if any) you can connect to something greater than yourself whether you call that Spirit the Universe, a Higher Power or God. Being connected to that entity allows you to work from a higher plane and frees your writing because you are connected. The Spirit will bring your life in balance when connected with all the other work you are doing.

10. Create a support team. Ask for help. Just as a star athlete or celebrity has a team of people to help them with their career and their lives, you too can surround yourself with people to help you with your writing and illustrating. Think about the type of people who would be helpful to have on your team: a massage therapist for a weekly massage; a personal or business coach to help you set goals and take action to reach them; a therapist to work out old personal issues and get mentally healthy; a writers' or illustrators' group for support and camaraderie; a personal trainer to get physically in shape; a nutritionist to guide you with your food choices; a spiritual mentor or meditation leader to guide you.

Benefits of balance

When you have cleared up the clutter and distractions in your life, writing and illustrating will have a place to live and grow without any outside interference. A great rule for getting balance back in your life is "keep it simple." When you are coming from that place of simplicity and feel comfortable with each of the areas of your "life wheel," your can approach your writing and illustrating time in a way that is effortless.

As artists and creative people, we often don't want to look at taking care of ourselves. This is a good way to begin. Creativity is a gift and is something to be shared with others. By looking at other areas of your life, you might ask yourself the question, "How is this behavior or way of doing something serving me in my life today?" Then you will be able to come from a place of honesty and integrity in all areas of your life. When you can do this, your life will be more balanced; you will no longer struggle to spin plates in the air to live your life.

Creating balance can only lead to having more free time and more abundance in all areas of your life (not just with money). You'll be at peace with yourself and others, able to just "be you" no matter where you are or who you are with, connect to the Spirit of your choosing, and have a life that is happy, joyous and free. If you are in this place, your creativity will blossom and flourish and flow from a place inside you that is open and full of ideas. Why not try it? What have you got to lose? And, surprise! By letting go of some of these things that are holding you back, you might even get gifts you never dreamed of, which will allow you to give your creative gifts to the world.

Helpful Questions to Ask Yourself

1. What assumptions are your life based on now?
2. Are you juggling things in your life? How can you get in balance?
3. How do you present yourself to the world? Is this the way you want people to see you? What can you change to make yourself be that person?
4. How are you being of service to others? Your family? Your community? The world? Without caretaking, how could you reach out more?
5. What are you passionate about? How do you show it?
6. Are your needs getting met? Are you taking care of you, so you can be of help to others, or do you put yourself last?
7. Do you make time for fun in your life? How often? What is fun for you?
8. Do you stay stuck in the problem or try to go to the solution?
9. Do you have reserves in your life? Time, money, love, energy? How would your life be different if you had more than you needed?
10. How well do you know yourself? What are your bottom-line values?
11. Do you set boundaries in your life? If not, what are some you can create to take better care of you? (Remember "No" is a complete sentence!)
12. Are you in touch with your Spirit? What does that mean to you? (Meditating, praying or being in nature could be a start.)
13. What are you known for? If someone was asked to describe you, what would they say? Are you satisfied with that description? (You can change it if you are not happy with it.)
14. How aware are you of what goes on around you? Do you live in a vacuum or are you a part of the world you live in?
15. How are your communication skills? How could you improve them?
16. What are your goals? Do you set them in all areas of your life, or just your work? (Remember unless you write them down, they are not goals, but merely wishes!)
17. Are you a good listener? How could you change this?
18. Do you participate in your own life or are you a passive bystander? Do you want to change this? How can you become a participant?
19. Do you have enough love in your life? How do you express it to others? What are the various types of love you have created in your world?

—Reva Solomon

First Books

BY ANNE BOWLING & ALICE POPE

Getting published for the first time can be full of surprises. There's the initial surprise when the phone rings and it's an editor who wants to buy your manuscript. There's the surprise when you first see the illustrations that go with your text. There's the surprise at how kids react when you read your book to them at your first story time.

And each unique pairing of writer or illustrator with editor brings it's own surprising results as the individual visions of text and art become a book that, had it been accepted by another publisher on another day, would have turned out completely different.

Throughout the "first book" process everyone learns from the surprises, editors included. In this year's article, we offer an interview with an editor, Wendy McClure, who headed up her first book project for Albert Whitman, *Red Berry Wool*. She learned along the way, just as the book's illustrator Tim Coffey did working on his very first picture book assignment.

As subsequent publications happen, authors and illustrators get more comfortable with how things work and the process goes more smoothly. Nan Parson Rossiter, now at work on her third book as author/illustrator, has found that on her second and third projects she knew what to expect and was better able to balance her illustration schedule with her home life. She's the subject of this year's First Books Follow-Up. Here is her story and advice, along with McClure's, Coffey's and four first-time authors'. Read on and learn from them.

SONYA SONES
Stop Pretending: What Happened When My Big Sister Went Crazy (HarperCollins)

There's a theory in literature that good writing will find its audience, whether the book in question conforms to a genre or creates one of its own. Publication of Sonya Sones's first book, *Stop Pretending: What Happened When My Big Sister Went Crazy*—a collection of poems targeted at a young adult audience—bears that theory out.

The collection details Sones's sister's manic-depressive condition and its effects on the family. And despite its nontraditional format, *Stop Pretending* was snapped up by the first agent Sones approached, and by the next week was receiving bids from major publishers. "I told the agent he could represent my book on Monday afternoon, and by Friday morning, a bidding war was underway," Sones says. "I was truly in a state of euphoria."

Years of polishing her craft and networking among writers and editors preceded Sones's swift acceptance by HarperCollins. The California-based author began writing for children about seven years ago "by churning out some pretty bad verse," she says. Contacts Sones had made through the Society of Children's Book Writers and Illustrators (SCBWI) suggested she take some writing classes, which led her to UCLA and, specifically, a course on writing poetry for children taught by Myra Cohn Livingston. "If my teacher hadn't encouraged me to write about my sister's illness, I don't think I would have."

With a portion of the manuscript completed, Sones applied for and received a SCBWI Work-in-Progress Grant. "The grant was such a vote of confidence from the outside world, and it caused me to push on with renewed enthusiasm," she says. "In a word, I felt inspired." And it

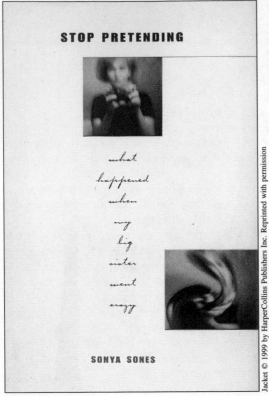

STOP PRETENDING

what
happened
when
my
big
sister
went
crazy

SONYA SONES

Stop Pretending, by Sonya Sones, is a collection of poetry for a YA audience based on the author's experience when her older sister was hospitalized for a mental breakdown and diagnosed as manic-depressive. Sones referred to her childhood journals to help her recreate the emotions she felt as a thirteen-year-old. "When I began writing *Stop Pretending*, it was extremely useful having my early journals to refer back to," she says. "Not only did they help me recall the details of the various incidents that took place, but they helped me remember how I really felt when they happened. I think having this access to my actual teenage voice helped me to create a more authentic one for my character."

was at an SCBWI conference that Sones (who calls herself a poster child for attending conferences) met her agent. "I've benefited from conferences in so many ways," she says. "I've gleaned loads of useful information from the various presentations. And I've made many new friends who have given me lots of sound advice on writing and the business of writing."

Sones also credits membership in two writers' groups with helping her develop her craft: "I'm deeply dependent on a constant flow of criticism when I'm working. Not only can I clearly see my work improving from week to week this way, but I thrive on the camaraderie and emotional support I get from these gatherings as well. I feel awfully fortunate to have such a terrific support system for my writing."

Sones began her collection of poems while studying writing at UCLA, and used the journals she'd kept as a teenager to recreate the autobiographical account. "When I began writing *Stop Pretending*, it was extremely useful having my early journals to refer back to," she says. "Not only did they help me recall the details of the various incidents that took place, but they helped me remember how I really felt when they happened. I think having this access to my actual teenage voice helped me to create a more authentic one for my character."

Despite its spare, emotionally-charged free verse format, *Stop Pretending* moves like a novel, not unlike Karen Hesse's 1998 Newbery Award-winner *Out of the Dust* (Scholastic). "Sister's in the psycho ward/and when I visit, I glance toward/the other patients' twisted faces,/quaking fingers,/frightened eyes,/wishing I could somehow break her out of here . . ./," reads a stanza from "Hospitalized." The poetry form works for the story, Sones says, because "the tale I've told is a painful one. Maybe telling the story with so few words adds to its power, because readers are called upon to fill in the emotional blanks with their own experiences of pain."

Sones's original manuscript consisted of 50 poems, which she estimates took her 2 years to write. Once it was accepted, her editor at HarperCollins wrote her a letter "asking lots of thought-provoking questions," Sones says. That letter led her to expand the original manuscript to almost double its original size in just a few months. "I was on such a roll that there were days when I wrote three or four poems in a matter of hours. I was constantly jotting down notes. Let's just say my family was very patient with me during this phase."

Now at work on a second volume of poems, a fictionalized account of a young teenager exploring first love, Sones has advice for writers still trying to break in. In addition to joining writers groups, attending conferences and taking classes on craft, Sones says: "Before you submit your work, research the different publishing houses to determine which of them would be most receptive to your particular manuscript. If you find a current book that has a similar feel to yours, call the publishing house to find out who edited the book. Then try submitting your manuscript to that editor. And don't get discouraged if your first attempts are rejected," she adds. "Just keep on writing and keep on getting better and better at what you do."

TIM COFFEY
Red Berry Wool (Albert Whitman & Co.)

Freelance artist Tim Coffey admits that when his illustrated poem "Sheep Leap" was first published in *Babybug*, he hoped a book publisher would spot his talent. "But I was very surprised when they actually did," he says. "It was just a few weeks after publication that Albert Whitman & Co. called with a potential book assignment. Houghton Mifflin called shortly after to ask if I would be interested in future projects. I am still receiving calls in response to that first appearance in *Babybug*."

When Coffey agreed to illustrate Robyn Eversole's *Red Berry Wool* for Albert Whitman, he realized a childhood dream. "I can remember being in first or second grade and wanting to be a book artist. I never lost my love of picture books," says the Massachusetts-based artist. Coffey carried that love through to college, where for his senior project he created a picture book with no text, "a story in only pictures. When I sent the finished product to publishers, I received some encouraging letters but no assignments."

After college, a "very humbling" job designing junk mail led Coffey to a position in the art department at Paramount Cards, where he enjoyed the security of a steady income illustrating greeting cards and freelancing his artwork for gift products. "I spent many nights and weekends working," Coffey says. "But after the book project came along, I realized it would be impossible for me to keep up that pace. It seemed like the perfect opportunity to strike out on my own."

Coffey brought a distinctive painting style to his first book project—bright greens and blues in outdoor scenes depicting Eversole's tale of a lamb who goes to great and sometimes dangerous lengths to improve the appearance of his wool. Coffey keeps his compositions simple, but adds interest with repeated patterns—creamy swirls in the sheep's wool, sweeping brushstrokes in the sky, and spiked textures in the grass and trees. "It can be very tedious," Coffey says of the process, which involves scratching patterns into dried gesso with handmade tools, and then layering the surface with thin acrylic washes.

Despite the painstaking nature of his technique, Coffey says the project was rewarding in the creative freedom Whitman's editors offered him: "I thought they would want strict control, especially since it was my first book. I was given a breakdown of the text. I supplied the initial rough sketches and ideas, and they provided art direction from there. They required some revisions to my sketches, but nothing so drastic as to change my vision of the finished product. There was a great deal of creative freedom."

While much of Coffey's current work has come to him as a result of the *Babybug* assignment, he still works as his own publicist. "I use my computer and color ink jet printer to print out

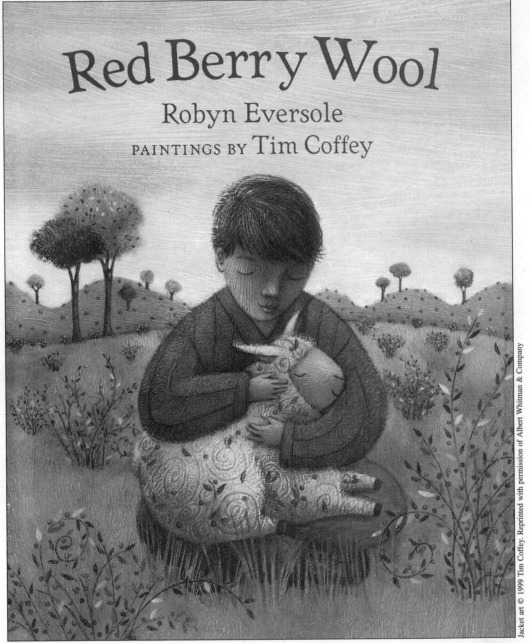

Tim Coffey's first picture book assignment, *Red Berry Wool*, gave the illustrator opportunity to showcase his unique, textured style featuring repeated patterns—creamy swirls in sheep's wool, sweeping brushstrokes in the sky, and spiked textures in the grass and trees. "It can be very tedious," Coffey says of the process, which involves scratching patterns into dried gesso with handmade tools, and then layering the surface with thin acrylic washes. His publisher chose to feature Coffey's *Red Berry Wool* cover illustration on the front of their fall 1999 catalog.

An Editor's 'First Book'

Editor Wendy McClure and illustrator Tim Coffey can thank a thoughtful editor-in-chief at Albert Whitman for a successful pairing on their first children's book project. "This was the first picture book for which I was to perform all the production duties," says McClure, who edited *Red Berry Wool*, which Coffey illustrated. "I think my editor saw this as a good opportunity for me to learn the ropes, so she assigned the book to me. And since I loved the story, I was happy."

Coffey's soft, textured acrylic paintings came to the attention of Whitman's art director through an illustrated poem, "Sheep Leap," he had published in *Babybug*. Although McClure said she knew of illustrators who needed a lot of direction on their first book projects, the relationship was a positive learning experience for both editor and illustrator: "Once, Tim had some questions about things like measurements and trim size—pretty technical stuff—and he admitted to feeling new to all these things," McClure says. "I wanted to put him at ease, but found I was at a loss for words, because I realized I was pretty much a novice, too. But the art director was experienced, and could answer Tim's questions."

Because the dramatic line of the *Red Berry Wool* story shifts several times, pacing the illustrations was a challenge, McClure says. But she and Coffey shared input on several dummy layouts, and found a rhythm that worked. "Tim helped us see what moments in the story were important," McClure says. "Perhaps it would have been easier if we'd simply given him a list of drawing instructions, but then the interpretation would have been that much more limited."

Here McClure shares an editor's perspective on the first book experience, and offers her advice for first-time writers and illustrators.

How did you acquire *Red Berry Wool*?

We knew from the start that we wanted to do the book—it's simple, like a fable, but with unusually funny and rich dimensions. However, by being distinctive, it also defied the kinds of categories that are sometimes helpful for selling books—it wasn't a holiday book or an historical story or a book about the first day of school. We had something memorable on our hands, but we worried about a way to lead people to its first page. Then one day, our art director showed us Tim's piece in *Babybug*. We were attracted to the style to begin with, and of course the sheep made us think of Robyn's story! We sent him a copy of the manuscript. Within days, Tim had sent us a sketch of the cover, and we were thrilled. Suddenly, we'd found the means for presenting this really great story.

Were there any particular challenges working with a first-time illustrator on the project?

The biggest challenge actually came after the paintings were finished. Sometimes an artist's work needs certain accommodations during production—maybe we need to watch for color problems at press time, for example. But since this was Tim's first book, we didn't know what to expect. And when we sent *Red Berry Wool* art off to the color separator to make the plates, some of the pre-press images turned out looking very different from the originals—we were all discovering for the first time that the camera could be a little harsh on some of Tim's textures. I panicked a bit, but as we discovered how to make adjustments, I realized that, like Tim, we were learning new things too, and we learned how to make Tim's work print beautifully.

Why do you feel his illustrations work so well with the story?

Often the first reaction people have to Robyn's story is that it's cute, but it's also very intelligent and evocative. Tim's work engages in much the same way—the shapes and figures are simple, but the textures keep you looking, thinking about how it all fits together. Then you step back and see how much depth it has. And just as the story is powered by repetitions and refrains, Tim's patterns are based on recurring motifs—his "woolly" spirals, for instance.

What did you learn as you worked on the project?

I learned a lot about storytelling through pictures. It got particularly hard when Tim's sketches were added to the mix. He had done a cliff scene that was really a breathtaking spread; I didn't want to touch it, but with time and a few more changes, it became clear that devoting two pages to this one scene would throw the rest of the book off balance. I'd always known that in theory, but to see it in action is another thing entirely. The work is bigger than your imagination, but you're part of it, and that's fun.

Do you have any advice to help writers and illustrators coming into their first publication?

Writers and illustrators just starting out need to prepare themselves for the long haul. For writers: nearly every author we publish also has an impressive record of near-misses—manuscripts that weren't quite right, earlier drafts, rejected queries. Give yourself as many chances as possible. And for illustrators: one of the best ways to showcase your work is through magazines in the children's market—don't ever neglect this area!

—Anne Bowling

After the publication of his poem "Sheep Leap" in an issue of *Babybug*, illustrator Tim Coffey was approached by several book publishers interested in future assignments, including Albert Whitman & Company, publisher of his first picture book *Red Berry Wool*, written by Robyn Eversole. "We were attracted to Tim's style to begin with, and of course, the sheep made us think of Robyn's story!" says Albert Whitman Editor Wendy McClure. "Suddenly, we'd found the means for presenting this really great story."

Text and art © 1998 Tim Coffey. Reprinted with permission

samples as needed," he says. "This way I can tailor my submissions for each company. I try to determine if they have a need for my style first, and when I do submit, I go all out." Coffey uses *Children's Writer's & Illustrator's Market* and *Artist's & Graphic Designer's Market* to review pay rates and rights purchased, and visits stores to check on the quality of the products prospective clients produce. The cost of ink jet paper, ink, postage and envelopes bring the price of his submission packages to between $2 and $15 each, Coffey says. "But I think art directors appreciate the presentation, and first impressions are extremely important."

Since publication of *Red Berry Wool*, Coffey has finished illustrations for Houghton Mifflin's school book division, and has signed a contract to illustrate an African folktale retold by Margaret Read McDonald for Albert Whitman. He has also picked up illustration assignments for *Ladybug* magazine. His advice to aspiring illustrators? "I recommend starting with magazines. So many great opportunities have come as a direct result of being published in *Babybug* and *Ladybug*. Art directors and editors occasionally refer to these magazines to find new talent," he says. "Also, having the ability to write can be an added advantage. I don't know if I would have landed an assignment as quickly as I did if *Babybug* had not been interested in publishing the poem that accompanied my submission."

Coffey adds: "Never give up. When I graduated from college, I sent out samples for a year and a half without a single significant bite. So I most definitely recommend starting with magazines."

BRENDA SHANNON YEE
Sand Castle (Greenwillow Books)

For picture book author Brenda Shannon Yee, getting published was the result of years of work with a bit of serendipity thrown in. Yee's first book *Sand Castle* was published by Greenwillow Books—but she hadn't submitted the manuscript to them.

Yee first began work on the manuscript for *Sand Castle* after the idea came to her while at the beach with her two daughters in August 1996. As the girls worked on building a sand castle, Yee watched several kids come up to join them in the construction. "They just seamlessly came up and started playing together. They were all strangers. Suddenly I realized, there's a story there," says Yee.

She didn't have a pen and paper with her at the beach, so Yee jogged to her car chanting the story line, found some paper and jotted it down. "By September, I had a draft of the story which I had revised several times. When I brought it to my critique group meeting, they said, 'Brenda, this is the one—this is going to get published.' That had never happened before."

So Yee took her manuscript to the Michigan SCBWI conference the following October. There she had a one-on-one critique with editor Harold Underdown, then working freelance. "He was really favorable, but he said it was missing a spark." She also read her manuscript at the conference open mike. Another editor in residence, Ana Cerro (then with Atheneum), approached Yee to tell her she liked the story. "I took a big gulp and said, 'Would you like to see it after I do revisions?'" Cerro said yes, but eventually rejected *Sand Castle*. "Ana said, 'I really love the story, I really love your writing—but the ending doesn't satisfy.'"

Where does Greenwillow fit into all this? "This is where the whole story gets silly," says Yee. After the comments from Cerro, Yee worked for five months revising the ending. "I so much wanted it to be perfect." Yee attended an SCBWI conference in Wisconsin and again submitted her story for critique. There were editors and published authors critiquing for the event, and Yee didn't know who would review her manuscript. Since it was a picture book, the manuscript was sent to Ava Weiss, art director at Greenwillow. Weiss was going to pass on the critiquing but decided to read Yee's manuscript anyway. She thought it was pretty good and

BY BRENDA SHANNON YEE
PICTURES BY THEA KLIROS

Jacket art © 1999 Thea Kliros. Reprinted with permission of Greenwillow Books

Brenda Shannon Yee's first book, *Sand Castle*, was sold through her attendance at a writer's conference, a surprise to the picture book author. "I went for the same reasons I go to any conference—not to be 'discovered,' " she says, "but rather to learn from other authors and enhance my understanding and knowledge of the market. By meeting editors and hearing about the books they edit and their publishing houses, I increase my professional knowledge and recharge my creative batteries."

showed it to an editor passing by her desk, who suggested she show it to editorial director Susan Hirschman.

Soon after, Yee got The Call. "It was a massive surprise. I had no clue my manuscript was there. And I had just decided to take a 15-minute siesta before the kids got home from school when the phone rang: 'Hello, this is Susan Hirschman from Greenwillow Books. I have your manuscript here, *Sand Castle*, and I'd like to buy it.'

"She was talking about advance, possible illustration date, and possible revisions, who might be the illustrator, royalites, boom, boom, boom, boom. I was furiously writing. At the end, she said, 'Do you have any questions?' I said, 'Yes, I do have one question. Could you tell me your name again?' I knew who Susan Hirschman was, and Greenwillow was absolutely my dream house. I just could not believe this was Susan Hirschman calling me."

This first publication certainly reinforced for Yee the importance of persistence, revision and attending conferences. She also knows that it's important to network and keep up relationships with editors, even as they move houses. This was reinforced by the acceptance of her second book by Ana Cerro, now at Orchard Books. Yee had planned to send *Sand Castle* back to Cerro with the revised ending when it was accepted by Greenwillow, "and I certainly wasn't going to tell Greenwillow no."

As soon as she had singed her contract with Greenwillow, Yee sent a letter to Cerro, who was still with Atheneum at the time. "I didn't want to lose that contact with Ana. I wrote her a sincere letter to tell her what happened and told her I would still like to work with her in the future, and I would be happy to send her something when I had a manuscript I thought would work for her."

Cerro, took a serious look at (but did not buy) another of Yee's manuscripts before Yee sent her the text of what will be her second published book *Hide and Seek* (scheduled for a fall 2000 release from Orchard). "This manuscript was very different from *Sand Castle* and what I'd sent Ana before. It's very short (about 60 words), very tight, and it rhymes."

Between school, library and bookstore appearances, Yee continues to submit manuscripts to Greenwillow, Orchard, and other houses, but contends that a first publication doesn't necessarily make subsequent acceptances easier to come by. "The fact that I'm published by Greenwillow has opened some doors for me with other editors. They know that Greenwilllow is not the easiest house to get in to. But it's not been a piece of cake getting something else published.

"The fact that you've been published may make publishers look at you a little more, but the writing's got to be there. And your manuscript has to be something that they're looking for, and it has to be something unlike something else they have on their list. The only thing an author can do is make sure she's sending in really well-written work. The fact that I've gotten a few books published doesn't make the writing any easier. I still fight; I fight for every word, every paragraph."

KATHLEEN KEELER
I Dare You: Stories to Scare You
(Scholastic/Cartwheel Books)

It's a bit of an understatement to say that Kathleen Keeler was ecstatic when her first book *I Dare You: Stories to Scare You* was accepted by Scholastic after 15 years of submitting manuscripts. "I should probably invent a completely new word for it, because I have never felt anything like it in my life." A beginning reader (for first- and second-graders) *I Dare You* is a fall 2000 Scholastic/Cartwheel Books release, part of Cartwheel's Hello Reader! series.

Through all those years of rejection, Keeler trudged on, kept writing, kept diligently researching the market, and tried to keep at least one manuscript circulating all the time. Her job as a children's librarian, she says, helped her stay upbeat "inspite of my manuscripts being rejected with horrifying regularity. Every day I see how ecstatically children love books. They grab them, they read them, they hug them close, and I've even seen toddlers kiss them! I often remember the children's joy when I write and try to have as much fun writing as they have reading."

As a librarian, Keeler knew that spooky beginning readers were perennially popular. "I suspected early on that this manuscript would be the one finally accepted for publication. I even reminded the Scholastic editor of the popularity of spooky readers in my query letter." (See Writing Effective Query Letters on page 20 for a look at Keeler's letter with comments from her editor.) Cartwheel accepted Keeler's manuscript solely on the basis of her query letter and the first story of her three-story collection. *I Dare You* was previously rejected by eleven publishers.

Before she submitted her story to Cartwheel, Keeler read as many books in their Hello Reader! series as she could get her hands on. "This convinced me even more that Cartwheel Books might be interested in my manuscript. I made sure to mention in my query letter that I felt my manuscript was appropriate for their Hello Reader! series. I knew from my market research," says Keeler, "that Cartwheel was publishing a lot of beginning readers, as opposed to some publishers who publish only one or two beginning readers a year. I predicted this would improve my odds."

Keeler actually began writing easy readers just a few years ago. Previously, she had devoted her writing time to picture book manuscripts. "I thought of myself solely as a picture book author for the first 13 years I was writing and would probably never have considered trying to write a reader if I hadn't had an idea I just couldn't get to work in picture book format," she says. "One day I was letting my mind wander with this idea and all of a sudden I realized that it might work as a beginning reader. It felt great and I knew immediately that I loved writing readers. I would certainly encourage all emerging children's writers not to pigeonhole themselves like I did."

The Hello Reader! series is for kids, preschool up to third grade, who are just learning to read on their own. They are high-interest stories that have been tested for vocabulary and sen-

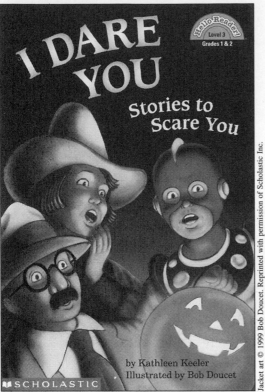

Jacket art © 1999 Bob Doucet. Reprinted with permission of Scholastic Inc.

Author Kathleen Keeler researched the market and submitted to publishers for 15 years before *I Dare You: Stories to Scare You* was accepted by Scholastic as part of their Cartwheel Books Hello Reader! series for beginning readers. Previously, Keeler had devoted her writing time to picture book manuscripts. "I thought of myself solely as a picture book author for the first 13 years I was writing and would probably never have considered trying to write a beginning reader if I hadn't had an idea I just couldn't get to work in picture book format," she says. "I would certainly encourage all emerging children's writers not to pigeonhole themselves like I did."

tence length. Keeler did not, however, worry about things like vocabulary when she wrote her story. "I was very familiar with easy readers, so I'm sure it was in my subconscious. I suspect any writer who consciously concentrates on vocabulary and sentence length would end up with a stilted, dry story."

Keeler's book will be released first in Scholastic's Lucky Book Club, then will likely be a trade title in bookstores, and may eventually end up as a selection in Scholastic Book Fairs. Keeler was a big fan of the Scholastic Book Club as a child, which made her acceptance by Cartwheel even more of a thrill. "I pored over my Scholastic book order form for hours on end and could barely concentrate on my school work any day the box of newly ordered books was delivered to my class," she says. "Scholastic is at least partially responsible for me becoming a writer in the first place."

As a first-time author, Keeler was pleasantly surprised at the amount of involvement she got to have in turning her manuscript into a book. She had input when her editor chose to change the title from Keeler's original *The Scare Dare*, and was even shown rough sketches of the art for her comments. "The whole process was a pleasure," she says.

Another surprise, though, was that throughout the editing process of *I Dare You*, Keeler changed editors twice. "I was on my third editor in nine months. I had read about the big turnover and restructuring in editorial staffs, but it still takes my breath away that there could be this many changes in this short of time," she says. "I just recently heard my book was being assigned to a new editor. I look forward to working with this editor, too, but it's hard to break ties with the second editor who shared one of the most significant periods of my life."

Keeler encourages pre-published writers to persevere as she did and to get as much market news as possible. To keep up-to-date on the children's publishing market, Keeler refers to *Chil-*

dren's Writer's & Illustrator's Market, subscribes to Children's Book Insider and Children's Writer, reads Publishers Weekly, looks at The Horn Book Guide, and refers the Society of Children's Book Writers and Illustrators annual market survey. She also highly recommends attending writer's conferences and networking.

She also advises writers not to "be shy or too demure. Sing your praises in your cover or query letter (in a professional way, of course)." She also believes in a having a number of manuscripts circulating, but doesn't let marketing cut into writing time. "I'm religiously careful to preserve writing time to work on new stories. If I'm not writing something new at the same time I am submitting manuscripts, the rejections are doubly devastating. My excitement over my new story ideas keeps me hopeful and enthusiastic in spite of receiving rejections."

D.H. FIGUEREDO
When This World Was New (Lee & Low Books)

Photo: Gabriela Figueredo

"My book is described as an immigration tale, but I didn't think I was writing a story about immigration," says D.H. Figueredo, author of *When This World Was New*. "I wanted to tell a story about my father and his relationship with me. To me, the story is about the bond between father and son."

Figueredo, who was born in Cuba and immigrated to the U.S. as a child, says his father was a natural storyteller. "On Saturdays back in the old country, he and I used to tour Old Havana, and he would tell me stories about pirates and ships and battles. One Saturday, we set out to find Hemingway and visited three bars the great writer frequented, but didn't get to see him. I think my wish to write emerged during those childhood excursions with my father."

It was an excursion with his own son that sparked the idea for Figueredo's first book *When This World Was New*. On the way home from seeing a production of *Peter Pan*, Figueredo and his son drove past open fields and farms covered with pure white snow, reminding the author of the story of the first time his father saw a snowfall. Figueredo's son suggested he put that story down on paper.

He worked on the story for three years, getting input and doing revisions. Figueredo sent a draft of his story to his friend Lyn Miller Lachman of the *Multicultural Review* for which he had written a number of articles on Latino literature and culture. She suggested a few changes to the story. On her advice, Figueredo rewrote his tale from the perspective of the child.

Figueredo ended up with the story of boy and his parents and their first moments in a new country, their anxiety and excitement, and seeing the magic of falling snow, "millions of white rose petals floating downward."

When he felt his story was ready to be sent to publishers, Figueredo decided to look into the publisher of one of his favorite books, *Baseball Saved Us*, by Ken Mochizuki. Lee & Low published this book, and after getting the publisher's catalog, reading about them in *Children's Writer's & Illustrator's Market* and checking several of their books out of the library, Figueredo decided they were right for his manuscript. "It was clear that Lee & Low was interested in exploring the multicultural experience and in presenting a view of American life through the eyes of a foreigner or someone who was not born in the U. S.," he says. "I was impressed by the quality of the illustrations and the absence of stereotypes in their stories. I fantasized that Lee & Low might be the right place for me."

It wasn't long before Figueredo's fantasy came to be. Two weeks after he sent it to Lee & Low, *When This World Was New* was accepted for publication.

As a first-time author, Figueredo was most surprised when he received the proofs of his book and saw the illustrations. "It was a beautiful book, but the characters by the illustrator didn't

Jacket art © 1999 Enrique Sanchez. Reprinted with permission of Lee & Low Books

First-time picture book author D.H. Figueredo's *When This World Was New* tells of a boy's trip with his parents from the Caribbean, and arrival to his new home in the U.S. The story emphasizes the boy's relationship with his father. "In reviews, the book was described as an immigration tale, but I wanted to tell a story about the bond between father and son," says Figueredo. His story, and his desire to write, were inspired by his own father, who Figueredo describes as a "natural story-teller."

look like me or my parents. I know now that this was rather silly on my part. Even though the illustrator had not met me, I still pictured me and my parents in the story," he says. "It took me a day or so to realize that my story had become the illustrator's story and he had as much to say about the event as I did. I think the story gained from Enrique Sanchez's vision."

When This World Was New has received several positive reviews. A *Booklist* reviewer said of the story: "True to a child's viewpoint, this picture book tells an elemental immigration story that is candid about both the hardship and the hope."

"I'm still getting over the fact that there are people out there reacting to my words and emotions and writing down those reactions," says Figueredo. "At the American Library Association conference, a reviewer came up to the Lee & Low booth and thanked me for writing this book. Can you believe it? I was happy but also embarrassed."

Figueredo enjoys more the reactions he's gotten from children and teachers. He's read *When This World Was New* at his local library, his daughter's school, and other schools in his area as well as other libraries and bookstores. "Some children said it was the best story they ever read. One college professor told me the book reminded her of her own journey to the U.S. Someone else cried at the end of my book. A neighbor told me that my story was similar to her father's even though her father had migrated from Poland. A teacher used it to tell students how beginning something new was always difficult."

When Figueredo addresses young readers, he tells them, "We all have stories to tell; they should write those stories and read them to family and friends." To writers working on becoming published, he says, "If an editor comments on your manuscript, study those comments and make changes to your work. Whatever you do, don't fall in love with your words, sentences and paragraphs. Do what's needed to make the story work."

First Books Follow-Up

Writer and illustrator Nan Parson Rossiter had her second children's book well under way when Dutton published her first, *Rugby & Rosie*, in 1997. "The story for *The Way Home* had been in my head for a long time," says Rossiter, who was featured in First Books in 1998, "I can remember talking over the story line with my husband even before *Rugby & Rosie* was finished." The poignant tale of a seeing-eye pup in training, *Rugby & Rosie* was good training for Rossiter—she has since had her second picture book published by Dutton, and is at work on a third.

Rossiter's first book was the story of Rosie, a golden retriever puppy who bonds during a year-long stay with a young boy, his family, and their Labrador named Rugby. Told in simple, engaging third-person narrative and set in the lush colors of a New England autumn, the award-winning *Rugby & Rosie* was called "a heart-tugging debut" by *Publishers Weekly*. Rossiter carried her distinctive palette of auburns, golds and russets through to *The Way Home*, the story of a young boy who nurtures an injured Canada goose back to health. Her third title will pick up a Labrador pup introduced briefly in *Rugby & Rosie*, and explore the relationship of faith developed between that guide dog and his blind master.

Some aspects of publishing do get easier with experience, Rossiter says. At one stage of work on her first title, Rossiter had to complete 21 paintings in little more than three months. But now, familiarity with production schedules helps her plan ahead for tight deadlines. The submission process, also, has gotten simpler: for her first book, Rossiter created color photo-copied dummies, which she sent unagented to one or two publishers at a time. After more than a dozen rejection letters, Rossiter found Dutton. Now, Dutton has asked to see Rossiter's new ideas first.

Here Rossiter takes time out to discuss how she manages to continue writing, painting and publishing as a full-time mother, and how her career has changed since publication of her first book.

What did you learn working on *Rugby & Rosie* that helped you as you completed your second book, *The Way Home*?

It prepared me a great deal for working on *The Way Home*. With that book, I knew that I wanted excellent reference material. It is difficult and frustrating to try to make things up. I knew, going into the project, that I wanted to be able to photograph my own reference material. This resulted in my husband and oldest son modeling for my characters. Overall, I believe knowing what to expect from each stage helped the most. Once the approvals of sketches start coming in, then, all of a sudden, there is a huge amount of work to be done! It is a little overwhelming, and I find it is best to simply take it one step at a time and be disciplined.

Has balancing the demands of work and your family gotten any easier? How do you manage it?

Definitely. Although I worked on the paintings for *The Way Home* again in the summer months, my newest endeavor will hopefully be completed during the school year. Since my boys are school-age now, I will have a little more time.

What inspired *The Way Home*?

I love to hear and watch Canada geese fly overhead. I also think it is amazing that they mate for life. These two things combined with the recollection of a local news story reflecting devotion in the wild sparked an idea for the story.

Both your books have similar themes of love, loss and renewal which work perfectly with your painting style. What's your next project, and will it have a similar feel?

I am just starting a new project which Dutton has agreed to publish. Called *True Blue*, it is about the black Lab puppy at the end of *Rugby & Rosie*. The story tells of the bonding that takes place between a guide dog and a blind person, and shares how the relationship of faith is developed. We hope to show a page of braille within the story.

What's your advice to authors and illustrators striving for publication?

On my drawing table I try to keep two clippings visible—although sometimes they do get buried. The first reads: "Perseverance is a great element of success. If you only knock long enough and loud enough at the gate, you are sure to wake somebody," (Henry Wadsworth Longfellow). The second is a verse from the Bible: "Do not be anxious about anything, but in everything, by prayer and petition, with thanksgiving, present your requests to God," (Philippians 4:6). These two things, prayer and perseverance, are the best advice I'm aware of.

—Anne Bowling

Jacket art © 1999 Nan Parson Rossiter

Author/illustrator Nan Parson Rossiter followed-up her first book *Rugby & Rosie* with *The Way Home* the warm story of a father, son and family dog and their relationship with a pair of Canada geese. Rossiter is currently working on a third project with Dutton called *True Blue*, a story about the bonding that takes place between a guide dog and a blind person.

Oh, the Places I've Been! Oh, the Places You Can Go! Preparing to Promote Your Children's Book

BY ESTHER HERSHENHORN

My author's copy of my first published picture book *There Goes Lowell's Party!* arrived at my door January 19, 1998, two months prior to its mid-March publication. Unfortunately, my publisher, Holiday House, didn't enclose readers in the book's padded mailer. No matter how far I gazed, too, through my front door window, not one lone child appeared on the horizon. I was an author, finally, after years of hard work. Yet I still had work to do for my book to reach readers.

I held and stroked my book like a first-time mother. Then I packed my bags and readied for the road. I'd been mentally scheduling my promotional tour for years. I knew places to go and people to see. I knew I'd need to show my book to the very same people who'd taught me my craft and introduced me to the industry: booksellers, librarians, teachers, reviewers, fellow writers and publishing professionals. They were the folks who would bring my book to children.

Let me tell you: Oh, the places I've been, traveling about, promoting my book! Let me tell you: Oh, the places you can go, once you're prepared to promote your book too!

Two rules of the road

Thinking about the trip was scary sometimes. For one thing, the word promote has its root in the Latin word promotus, "to move forward." I preferred the safety of my writing room and life. For another, my dictionary's first entry for promote stated "to help or encourage to exist or flourish." Help and encourage were ambiguous verbs. It was the "flourishing" part that pushed me out the door.

I put aside my fears, reviewed several colleagues' wise words and sought my publisher to specify my tasks. Actually, my publisher sought me. Diane Foote, Holiday House's director of marketing, wrote me soon after I signed my contract in 1996—two years before my book's publication. That's when I learned the Rules of the Road: 1) Work with your publisher. Your publisher, too, wants to see your book flourish. 2) Begin the process early.

It was my job to inform Holiday House of my interest, ability and availability to promote my book, to share local resources who could create promotional opportunities and to notify my publisher of such events. It's often the publisher who supplies books to sell at such events, if given a lead-time of four to six weeks.

ESTHER HERSHENHORN *wears many hats: writer, SCBWI Illinois Regional Advisor, newsletter editor, writing teacher and die-hard Cubs fan. Holiday House published her first book,* There Goes Lowell's Party! *in spring 1998. Future titles include* Fancy That *(Holiday House) and* Chicken Soup by Heart *(Simon & Schuster). Hershenhorn was surprised to learn that her happy ending was not seeing her first book in print—it was meeting, greeting and connecting with her readers, learning her story had touched hearts.*

There Goes Lowell's Party!

by Esther Hershenhorn

illustrated by Jacqueline Rogers

In Esther Hershenhorn's first book, *There Goes Lowell's Party!*, the title character fears rain will ruin the big family party planned for his birthday. Hershenhorn's story is weaved with weather proverbs signaling a downpour—red skies, low-flying geese, leaves showing their backs. The author sought interesting weather-related facts "from meteorology to American weather folklore to the Ozark tales and weather proverbs collected by folklorist Vance Randolph" after a *Chicago Tribune* headline reading "More Fact Than Fiction in Weather Proverbs" sparked her story idea.

I needed to listen to Holiday House, as well. They'd been publishing children's books for over 60 years. Their marketing department would submit my book to review journals, reading professionals, my local media and various award committees. They'd represent my book at trade shows and conferences, publicize it in catalogs and special outlets, consider it for additional advertising and promotional materials and coordinate my school, conference, bookstore, library and trade show appearances.

True, Holiday House is an independent, relatively small company, publishing 55 books each year. But it's also true that most trade children's book publishers are committed to promoting new titles and authors. Most publishers encourage new authors who are eager to join the process. Just remember that promotional support varies from house to house, from author to author, in dollars and substance.

Three homework assignments

I welcomed the opportunity to start my preparations early. I seldom left homework to the eve of its due date. My first written assignment was to create an author's bio—a reusable description to fit all promotional events. I described my book, my life, my publishing experiences—in under 200 words. I intentionally left room to reshape the material to match my audience. For instance,

I underscore my elementary education degree when speaking to teachers, my Illinois SCBWI Regional Advisor position when speaking to writers.

My second assignment was to compile a list of resource people—local and state children's book community folks—who would welcome a Holiday House courtesy copy, review copy, or at least, notification of *There Goes Lowell's Party!* I spun my Rolodex, queried colleagues and fingered through directories. My list included:

- my local children's librarian
- the director of my state library
- my local bookseller
- prominent booksellers in my area
- my local and area newspaper editors and book reviewers
- the head of my state's and district's education departments
- the director of my area's local book festival
- my local and area children's museums

Authors should also include resources for their books' specialized subject areas. In my case, I

Advice From a Director of Marketing

A few words about book reviews

Rest assured that your publisher will automatically send your book to the major review outlets for children's and young adult books: *Booklist, The Bulletin of the Center for Children's Books, The Horn Book, Kirkus Reviews, The New York Times Book Review, Publishers Weekly* and *School Library Journal.* Galleys or folded and gathered sheets (f & g's) are sent three to four months prior to publication, followed by finished books as soon as they become available.

These influential journals begin reviewing new books about one month before publication date and may continue throughout the publication season. Some (like *School Library Journal*) try to review every new book, favorably or otherwise; others (like *Booklist*) review only those books they feel they can recommend.

Your publisher will send you copies of major reviews. They will be delighted to share the joy of good (or starred!) reviews with you and can interpret the helpful criticism that comes along with any less-than-favorable ones. Others on your publisher's sample copy lists include magazines and newspapers, librarians and children's literature professors and school and library systems nationwide.

A few words about conventions

National conventions are a vital part of a publisher's promotion plans for your book. However, they are not necessarily the best promotional venue for the relatively new author, mostly because without an award-winning book or a speaking opportunity at the convention, it is very difficult to attract enough attention to make the trip worthwhile.

Publishers simply cannot take as many authors as they would like, nor can they take everyone who wants to go. In fact, the decision as to which authors to invite is not made by the publisher alone. The organizations (International Reading Asssociation, National Council of Teachers of English) themselves initiate many of the invitations to speak at their conferences. Most publishers also need time at the conventions to meet with and promote your book to the opinion makers and book buyers who attend, rather than hold constant autographings. Even if you are not present at national conventions, your book will be!

Have fun, and remember that you and your publisher share the same goal: To sell books!
—*Diane Foote, Holiday House*

During one stop on her promotional tour, author Esther Hershenhorn poses with a group of young readers (and her book *There Goes Lowell's Party!*) at a Palintine, Illinois Literary Fair in March, 1999. During her first year on the road as a published author, Hershenhorn attended a number of conferences, conventions and book fairs and appeared at schools, libraries and bookstores, getting the opportunity to meet kids, teachers, librarians and booksellers. "My scheduled stops reflect my publication's timing, my picture book's audience, my publisher's promotional efforts, my SCBWI connections, my years of networking, my geographical proximity to major and regional trade shows and conferences, my children's book community friendships and my singular good fortune," she says. "No two authors' itineraries can or should be the same."

added the names of those experts who'd helped me research my picture book's Ozark setting. I also added local meteorologists, since my book dealt with weather proverbs.

I abandoned my shyness to complete my third assignment: Tell everyone I know in both the real and virtual worlds—in person, by hand or fax, by word of mouth or e-mail—about my book's scheduled publication. And I do mean everyone, from my brother-in-law's cousin to my dental hygienist.

I also spread the word via professional newsletters, such as the SCBWI *Bulletin* and local chapter newsletters, listserv memberships, alumni magazines and former hometown newspapers. Networking flourished. Serendipity bloomed. Before I knew it, I'd accepted invitations to speak at many of the places I'd planned to visit anyway.

Two useful guidebooks

Of course, I still had questions that needed answers. Fortunately, I discovered two books that, when combined, told me everything I needed to know about promoting my children's book: Susan Salzman Raab's *An Author's Guide to Children's Book Promotion* (Raab Associates) and

Evelyn Gallardo's *How to Promote Your Children's Book: A Survival Guide* (Primate Productions). (See Helpful Books & Publications on page 348 for more information on these books.)

A publicist, Raab specializes in promoting children's books and authors. She understands how the various members of the children's book community work together to create a book's success. Raab's book suggests ways authors can reach the key decision makers (teachers, librarians, booksellers and reviewers), with special emphasis on media sources. Her directory gave me organizations to add to my resource list and helped me brainstorm even more opportunities. The guide is especially helpful to authors who self-publish or to those whose publishers offer minimal promotional support.

An author herself, Gallardo offers any-time promoters step-by-step instructions and a user-friendly manual. I consulted her book often, rereading her two-minute bookstore pitch or website suggestions or studying her bio, press kit and brochure samples. Her overview of school presentations was especially useful once I began my round of school visits. Gallardo's book helps make formidable tasks doable, from conference networking to book fair attendance.

Two important promotional tools

I couldn't wait to have my very own promotional postcard—a color reproduction of my picture book's cover. The 4×6 postcard proved an excellent investment. I used Modern Postcard, based on colleagues' recommendations. The California-based company walked and talked me through the ordering process. Thanks to early conversations with Diane Foote at Holiday House, I knew to obtain my illustrator Jacqueline Rogers's permission to reuse the art and to include

---

Names to Add to Your Rolodex

American Booksellers Association
560 White Plains Road
Tarrytown, NY 10591
(914) 631-7800
(800)637-0037
www.ambook.org

American Library Association
50 East Huron Street
Chicago, IL 60611
(312)944-6780
www.ala.org

Association of Booksellers for Children
4412 Chowen Ave., So. #303
Minneapolis, MN 55410
(800)421-1665

International Reading Association
800 Barksdale Road
P.O. Box 8139
Newark, DE 19714-8139
(302)731-1600
www.reading.org

Modern Postcard
1675 Faraday Ave.
Carlsbad, CA 92008
(800)959-8365
www.modernpostcard.com

Publishers Weekly
245 W. 17th St.
New York, NY 10011
(212)463-6758
www.bookwire.com

Society of Children's Book Writers
and Illustrators
8271 Beverly Blvd.
Los Angeles, CA 90048
(323)782-1010
www.scbwi.org

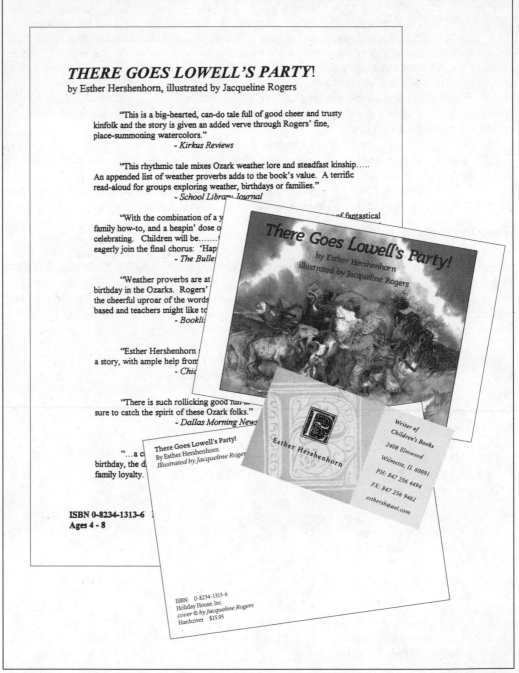

THERE GOES LOWELL'S PARTY!
by Esther Hershenhorn, illustrated by Jacqueline Rogers

"This is a big-hearted, can-do tale full of good cheer and trusty kinfolk and the story is given an added verve through Rogers' fine, place-summoning watercolors."
- *Kirkus Reviews*

"This rhythmic tale mixes Ozark weather lore and steadfast kinship..... An appended list of weather proverbs adds to the book's value. A terrific read-aloud for groups exploring weather, birthdays or families."
- *School Library Journal*

"With the combination of a y...........of fantastical family how-to, and a heapin' dose o................. celebrating. Children will be.......... eagerly join the final chorus: 'Hap............
- *The Bulle....*

"Weather proverbs are at.............. birthday in the Ozarks. Rogers'..... the cheerful uproar of the words....... based and teachers might like to.......
- *Bookli....*

"Esther Hershenhorn .... a story, with ample help from ....
- *Chic....*

"There is such rollicking good fun............ sure to catch the spirit of these Ozark folks."
- *Dallas Morning News....*

"...a c............. birthday, the d............. family loyalty.

ISBN 0-8234-1313-6
Ages 4 - 8

There Goes Lowell's Party!
By Esther Hershenhorn
Illustrated by Jacqueline Roger...

ISBN: 0-8234-1313-6
Holiday House, Inc.
cover © by Jacqueline Rogers
Hardcover $15.95

There Goes Lowell's Party!
by Esther Hershenhorn
illustrated by Jacqueline Rogers

Esther Hershenhorn

Writer of
Children's Books
2408 Elmwood
Wilmette, IL 60091
PH: 847 256 4494
FX: 847 256 9462
esthersh@aol.com

As part of her promotional efforts, Esther Hershenhorn invested in postcards featuring the cover illustration for her book *There Goes Lowell's Party!* "I use the blank reverse side for book signing invitations, publication and bookstore appearance announcements or handouts with excerpts from book reviews," she says. "The cards are perfect for reader correspondence and come in handy if my book sells out at signings." Hershenhorn also assembled a group of quotes from positive reviews gathered from *School Library Journal*, *Booklist* and other publications. And she also couldn't wait to create her very own business cards.

ordering information, such as my book's ISBN number and price. Because my illustrator and I were friends (a rare happening), we shared the production costs and the finished product.

The postcards continue to serve me well. I use the blank reverse side for book signing invitations, publication and bookstore appearance announcements or handouts with excerpts from book reviews. The cards are perfect for reader correspondence and come in handy if my book sells out at signings.

I also couldn't wait to create my very own business card. I'd been saving effective cards for years while eyeballing the work of local SCBWI illustrators, to discover the perfect graphic designer. Whether memorable in shape, size, color, graphic image or wording, all business cards should contain your name, mail and e-mail addresses and phone and fax numbers.

Some last-minute instructions

For my promotional travels, the following items proved useful to pack: my smile, my sense of humor, my business cards and book. Luckily, I'd also packed reserves of faith, pluck and courage. Authors too have hang-ups and bang-ups.

For instance, I found myself noticeably idle for long stretches of time at my first public book signing at a Midwest children's literature conference. I'd been seated smack dab in the middle of a long row of tables of Newbery-winning authors and Caldecott-winning illustrators. I watched endless lines of attendees gather for hours to have their books signed by everyone but me.

At my first public speaking engagement to librarians and teachers, I was the last presenter in a long day of programs, scheduled right before dinner and the cocktail hour. I stood front and center, while stomachs growled and bodies shifted in their seats. My knees knocked as loudly as my thumping heart.

And pride, I learned, does indeed goeth before a fall. At my first well-publicized story time at a children's bookstore, the snaking lines of adults with children in tow, queued up since sunrise for the store's morning opening, weren't there for me. They were Beanie Baby collectors awaiting the day's delivery.

I recommend *Oh, the Places You'll Go!*, by Dr. Seuss, for times like the above, when you're scared right out of your pants or feel all alone. Dr. Seuss's words had cheered me on before. I had to keep moving to meet new folks who would make things happen so I could happen too.

At that first Midwest children's literature conference, I used my free time to help the event's bookseller discover my book and its birthday party tie-ins. She now recommends it for birthday presents. At that second conference, I greeted those shifting bodies enthusiastically and booked a spring's worth of school visits and library programs. And once the children arrived at that first story time venture, they sparked book-related birthday party games I now use successfully.

Some places to visit: a sample itinerary

What follows is my itinerary for my first year on the road as a first-time author, promoting my spring '98 picture book, *There Goes Lowell's Party!* From January through August, I met the folks who would bring my book to children. By September *There Goes Lowell's Party!* had reached my readers' hands.

My scheduled stops reflect my publication's timing, my picture book's audience, my publisher's promotional efforts, my SCBWI connections, my years of networking, my geographical proximity to major and regional trade shows and conferences, my children's book community friendships and my singular good fortune. No two authors' itineraries can or should be the same.

When your author's copy of your first published book arrives at your door, give it a hug, then ready for the road. Now you know: Oh, the places you can go!

January: Butler University Children's Literature Conference, Indianapolis, IN—presentation to writers: "One Writer's Journey"

Amazon.com website visit to create author's profile

February:	SCBWI-Illinois Networks Program, Chicago, IL—"Everything I Learned While Writing *There Goes Lowell's Party!*
	Local celebration of first (good!) review
March:	Northern Illinois University's Children's Literature Conference, DeKalb, IL—presentation to librarians and teachers: "The New Kid on the Block"
April:	The Book Stall, Winnetka, IL—personal book signing party
May:	BookExpo Author Signing, Chicago, IL
	Association of Booksellers for Children (ABC) dinner, Chicago, IL
	ABC/SCBWI Illinois Dessert Reception, Chicago, IL
	Printers Row Book Fair, Chicago, IL—reading and signing
June:	Vassar Publishing Institute Reunion, Poughkeepsie, NY
	American Library Association, Washington, DC—dinner and signing
July:	Picture book manuscript sale to Simon & Schuster (You're only as good as your very next book!)
August:	Picture book manuscript sale to Holiday House (You're still only as good as your very next book!)
	National SCBWI Conference, Los Angeles, CA—named 1998 Member of the Year
September:	Story Time Hours—local Illinois bookstores
October:	Illinois Authors Festival, Springfield, IL—dinner, signing and presentation "How To Write for Children"
	Former hometown school and library visits, Penn Wynne, PA
November:	Children's Book Week Events: Local library presentation to adults, Wilmette, IL—"One Writer's Journey"
	Chicago Public Library appearance, Chicago, IL
	Literacy Volunteers of America, Chicago, IL—pro bono reading
	Holiday Fair book signings, northern suburbs
December:	Home at last (!) to prepare for Illinois Young Authors Conference and upcoming school visits

For Illustrators: Super Self-Promotion Strategies

BY MARY COX

Just as an editor is vital to any writer's career, the most important person to a freelance illustrator's career is the art director, the individual who matches a writer's words with an illustrator's images. You have several options for introducing yourself and your work to that all-important person! These guidelines for creating effective direct mail pieces will help you impress the art directors you contact.

Great samples get an art director's attention. There are several options illustrators can choose when creating samples for self-promotion. Here are a few of them:

Postcards

If designed and planned well, a simple postcard is one of the most practical and effective ways to showcase your work to art directors. Art directors like postcards because they are easy to file or tack on cubicle walls or bulletin boards. If the art director likes what she sees, she can always call and ask to see your portfolio or a few more samples. Have your name, address and phone number printed on the front of the postcard beneath the image, or in the return address corner. Somewhere on the card should be printed your name, along with the word "Illustrator." (See Theresa Smythe's sample postcard, and the assignment it brought her on page 70.)

It is especially effective to send quarterly postcards (with a new image each time) to the same art directors. If you use one or two colors, you can keep the cost below $200 for about 500 postcards. A full-color card will cost a little more.

You can have postcards printed inexpensively at commercial printers like Modern Postcard (1-800-959-8365) and Copy Craft (1-800-794-5594). Your printing costs will be lower if you can give the printing company a longer deadline. See Nuts & Bolts for Illustrators on page 28 for suggestions about the type of images art directors like to see.

Promotional sheets

If you want to show more of your work on one sample, you can opt for an 8×12 color or black and white photocopy of your work. It is an inexpensive, yet very effective choice for a promotional piece. It's a great way to show many characters at once. (See samples by Meredith Johnson and Christine Tripp on pages 71 and 72 for examples.)

Query or cover letter

A query letter is a nice way to introduce yourself to art directors for the first time. One or two paragraphs stating you are available for freelance work is all you need. Keep your tone friendly and professional, and be sure to include your phone number, samples or tearsheets. If your forte is creative fonts or hand-printing, and you want to show this talent to the art director,

MARY COX *has been editor of* Artist's & Graphic Designer's Market *since the 1995 edition of the book and is a frequent contributor to other Writer's Digest Books titles. In the last few years she's seen thousands of self-promotional pieces from illustrators come across her desk; she often tacks the best ones to her office walls.*

it is OK to print your letter, otherwise type your query letter using an easy-to-read font. It's also a nice touch to send a letter on your own professional stationery. Illustrators can design letterhead incorporating a logo or an illustration (of course, be sure to include your name, address, phone, fax, e-mail and website).

Tearsheets

After you complete assignments, ask the art director if she can arrange to send you copies of any printed pages on which your illustration appears. If the art director agrees and sends you some tearsheets, you can then send those tearsheets to other art directors as samples. Tearsheets impress art directors because they are proof you are experienced and have met deadlines on previous projects. When *Chirp* magazine Art Director Tim Davin asked Theresa Smythe to create a polar bear in the style of her sample, Theresa asked him if she could get tearsheets when the magazine was published. Now, she sends those tearsheets to potential clients.

If you send 8×12 photocopies or tearsheets, do not fold them. It is more professional to send them flat, not folded, in a 9×12 envelope, along with a typed query letter, preferable on your own professional stationery.

Mailing samples is like sowing seeds

After your first mailing, there will be a period of time—often as long as three or four months—when you say to yourself, "Gee, what's the difference! I've sent out all these samples, but art directors aren't calling me." That "pins and needles" feeling is the norm. Perhaps the hardest part of your career launch is "pushing through" the time it takes your first few mailings to gain momentum. It will take time for those samples to start working. Look upon those weeks or months as the time it takes for seeds in a garden to start taking root so they can grow. Busy yourself by sending out more samples instead of waiting by the mailbox.

Theresa Smythe, whose sample appears on page 70, learned that lesson after submitting her samples to Tim Davin, art director of *Chirp* magazine. "Tim got my samples in February and called me in June and told me he'd had my sample up on his bulletin board for months waiting for the right assignment for me," says Smythe.

Send quarterly follow-up mailings

Direct mail is cumulative. You must send follow-up mailings on a regular basis. I recommend quarterly mailing. An art director might really like your style, but she may not have a project requiring that particular style at the moment. But six months from now she might have something that would fit your style perfectly. If she's misplaced or misfiled your sample, she may be waiting for another to get your contact information.

Holiday promotions make you a stand-out!

I advise every illustrator to send out holiday promotions. Why? Because the most professional illustrators do this as a matter of course. Everyone loves getting holiday cards, and they are more likely to be kept and displayed on bulletin boards than most cards. Use your imagination and come up with seasonal cards that get you remembered! Meredith Johnson, whose promotional sample appears on page 71, often adds colorful holiday stickers to existing black and white samples to instantly brighten them up and transform them into holiday promotions.

You don't need to send a portfolio when you first contact a publisher or magazine. But after art directors see your samples, they may want to see more. For more information on preparing your portfolio for viewing, see Nuts & Bolts for Illustrators on page 28.

These suggestions are the basics. After your first mailing, consider branching out. Think about launching a web page (see the sidebar on page 73) or advertising in an illustration sourcebook or directory (see the sidebar on page 69). Before you know it, your self-promotion will have paid off with book and magazine assignment just like Theresa Smythe, Christine Tripp and Meredith Johnson whose promotional pieces follow.

Picturebook: What a Great Idea!

In addition to sending out mailings, many illustrators take advantage of advertising in annual illustration directories, often called "source-books" in the industry. Sourcebook publishers charge illustrators a fee for advertising in their directories, which they distribute free to thousands of art directors across the country who refer to them when looking for illustrators. Directories are popular with mid-career illustrators who want to take their careers to the next level through advertising.

For years, illustrators and art directors have been familiar with industry sourcebooks such as *American Showcase, Workbook, Black Book Illustration* and *RSVP*. At last, children's book illustrators have their own sourcebook, called *Picturebook*. And it's becoming more and more popular with illustrators and art directors alike.

Cover art for the *Picturebook* 2k by Lori Lohstoeter.

Picturebook is the brainchild of illustrator Cyd Moore (*I Love You Stinky Face, Alice and Gretta: A Tale of Two Witches*). The idea came as Moore was getting ready to write a check out for her annual sourcebook ad in one of the more popular directories. Because she hadn't received any children's book publishing assignments as a result of her past sourcebook ads, she decided to call some art directors and find out if they ever looked at these directories. To her chagrin, art directors told her they didn't look in the directories for children's illustrators, because it was just too hard to sort out children's illustrators from the other styles in the books. "What if there was a sourcebook filled with just children's illustration?" Moore asked one of the art directors. The art director immediately answered, "That would make my job *so* much easier!"

Moore knew illustrators and art reps would welcome such a directory, too—especially if advertising costs could be kept lower than the established directories. Amy Gary, a book publisher/agent Moore had worked with on another project, helped get the book off the ground. An expert in both publishing and marketing, Gary recognized the need on both sides of the desk for such a resource and agreed to come on board as partner and co-editor. According to Moore, the partnership has been "the perfect match."

Since its first edition debuted in 1997, illustrators and art directors have watched the directory grow progressively thicker and more substantial every year. The book is distributed to more than 7,000 targeted producers of books, greeting cards, games, electronic media, animation, music and advertising for children. Cost of advertising in *Picturebook* begins at $1,450 for one-page at the early bird rate and $2,500 for a two-page layout. Rates include one free color separation, a listing of published works in the index, a copy of *Picturebook* and 1,000 reprints which illustrators can use as promotional samples. For more information about*Picturebook*, call (888)490-0100 or visit www.picture-book.com.

—*Mary Cox*

...CHILL OUT...

with

THERESA SMYTHE
ILLUSTRATION

4443 Babcock Avenue
Studio City, CA 91604
Booktoon@aol.com

818•505•9639

ALL IMAGES © THERESA SMYTHE

Theresa Smythe had these snowman postcards (bottom) printed to showcase her collage style to art directors. After sending an initial mailing in February, four months later she got a call from Tim Davin, art director of *Chirp*, a Toronto children's magazine. "Just when I was wondering if it was worth spending the extra postage to send promos internationally, I got two inquiries in the same week from Canada! The art director basically asked me to 'do exactly what you did in this postcard, but make the snowman a bear (partially shown above).'" Smythe said when she got the assignments she was so happy "I just wanted to shout it to the rooftops! Mailings really do work!" When Smythe, who had loved author A.A. Milne as a child, found out her artwork would accompany a Milne poem, she felt her life had come full circle.

Art directors respond to the charming postcards and self-mailers created by illustrator Meredith Johnson to showcase her work. She sends material in an envelope (top) which is also covered in her lively drawings. "This has turned out to be the best idea for getting attention," says Johnson. "Art directors tend to keep the samples in the envelope for their files. Because of the size of the drawing on the front, it's hard to lose in a full drawer of promo pieces." Along with her postcards (bottom) Johnson had 2,500 copies of a black and white folding piece cleverly printed with several illustrations. She uses stickers to add color and make them holiday-specific.

If designed well, a full page (8½×11) black and white or color laser print or photocopy works well as a promotional sample, and is an inexpensive alternative to having postcards printed. Above are two examples of promo sheets for illustrator Christine Tripp. Tripp sends the promo sheets along with a cover letter, reply letter and SASE to children's magazine and book art directors. "I do the lettering on PhotoImpact and print them out on a Lexmark 5700 printer," says Tripp. "It's wonderful to be able to produce these flyers myself, in any quantity desired, instead of the pricey alternative of taking the hard copy to a printer as I used to do. Tripp adds her e-mail and website address to the bottom of her samples. Read all about Tripp's website launch on page 73.

Illustrators Find Camaraderie—and Clients—Online

You don't have to be a computer nerd to chat with fellow illustrators or launch your own website. Canadian cartoonist and humorous illustrator Christine Tripp thought she was past the point of learning anything new, especially something as "frightening" as computers. "We had one at home," says Tripp, "but until a year ago, I didn't even know how to turn it on!" Through trial and error and with the support of illustrators she met online, Tripp went from being "computer illiterate" to launching her own website.

"When I first started sending out mailings, I seemed to be getting nowhere" until one day, while browsing Yahoo! a click on the word "cartoonists" led her to a friendly support group of fellow freelancers. "The group was a godsend, " says Tripp. "They really kept me going with both technical and marketing advice—saying 'Send here!' or 'Try this!' "

It was Tripp's online friends who encouraged her to launch a website. Now Tripp adds her website address (www.members.home.net/ctripp) to the bottom of query letters, samples and business cards. "That way art directors can check out more of my work at their leisure." Though clients are not "coming in droves" to her site, Tripp found one of her best ongoing clients "as a direct result of the site." It was a client she would never have dreamed of contacting—an Australian company that does sandblasting on garnet! Tripp's new client found her site while browsing the Web in search of a cartoonist. "That assignment alone pretty much paid for my entire year's connection fee for the site," says Tripp.

Children's illustrator Marty Jones (www.mjarts.com) uses her website to reinforce her other marketing efforts. "I live in Oregon, which has yet to become the 'heart' of the publishing industry. We're a long way from New York. Leaving my portfolio for a review isn't very practical at this distance. I send out mailers once or twice a year with a selection of illustrations from my portfolio, but space limitations mean I only send out two or three images in each mailing. My website portfolio has 32 images." Art directors who like Jones's mailers can review her portfolio on her website. "This scenario has happened at least three times in the last four months, bringing me work on four separate books." Jones also has links posted on a number of other websites, including the SCBWI website (www.scbwi.org), and has a tracker program so she can count the number of visitors to her site.

Like Tripp, Alison Slikker of Slikker Design adds her website address (www.slikkerdesign.com) to her business cards and other promotional material. "In addition to looking more professional, having my own domain name also saves a significant amount of money, time and paper." Adding images to her site is less expensive than sending out new promotional samples each time she has new work to show.

"Having a website is a very important factor in the illustration industry," says Slikker. "It is a less pressured way for art directors and publishers to see an illustrator's work on their own time, perhaps even in the comfort of their own home. They don't have to worry about the illustrator hovering over them, or calling requesting their opinions about a submitted portfolio."

Setting up your page

You don't have to learn "html" or some technical computer language to set up your page. Tripp found out just how easy it is to compose a website when she accidentally clicked on an icon in the bottom corner of Netscape Navigator and found the Composer software that came with her browser. "I never knew what that icon was for! Lo and behold it helped me compose a website without having any special skills. It doesn't always work the first time, but eventually it works."

Mary Jones created her website using MS Front Page Express, "a fairly simple program to use," says Jones. She scans her images herself using her own scanner, but recommends using your local copy center's resources if you don't have one.

While she has devoted a large amount of time to developing her site, Jones says the total cash outlay was less than the cost of creating and sending out one of her promotional mailings.

Registering with search engines

"The biggest challenge of having the website as your source of recognition is getting recognized amidst the millions of other pages flooding the Internet," says Slikker. Submitting your website to hundreds of search engines helps art directors find your site.

How do you register your site with search engines? "If you go to the bottom of most search engine home pages, you'll find a spot that says 'Add URL' and that's it," explains humorous illustrator Jim Hunt (www.jimhuntillustration.com). "Some search engines make it a little trickier to find their submission form, but once you get there most times it's simply a matter of typing in your URL address and 'click!' that's it. If your site is built in an efficient and substantive manner, it should do well. Some engines automatically 'spider' the site in (via computer), but sites like Yahoo! have a real living and breathing computer technician check your site."

Another way to make sure art directors find your site is by linking to one they visit regularly. Slikker recommends signing on with one of the online art directories that displays samples of many illustrators, such as www.artwanted.com or www.theispot.com. "Art directors can simply click on a link to your direct Web page to peruse more."

Whether or not you actually launch your own page, you should definitely join one of the many newsgroups of illustrators for comraderie and encouragement. Christine Tripp will never forget how they helped her keep going. "We freelancers work so much in isolation. That daily connection really breaks up the day—like having co-workers in an office. Until I found my online friends, I was about to give up freelancing and go find a job at Wal-Mart!"

—Mary Cox

Writing for Boys: Is the Gender Barrier Real?

BY KELLY MILNER HALLS

Drawing reluctant boys into the rewarding world of reading requires more than a little finesse. Writers who have mastered the task—like Chris Crutcher, Bruce Coville, James Proimos and David Lubar—wield words the way surgeons wield scalpels. As they cut and carve for the good of the story, the masculine sparks they throw off are not lost on their readers.

But ask 1998 NCTE Intellectual Freedom Award recipient Chris Crutcher (*Ironman, Staying Fat for Sarah Byrnes*) if he writes "for boys," and a shadow descends even before he has a chance to reply. If he says yes, is he shutting out readers who happen to be girls? Is he contributing to a gender barrier that really shouldn't have to exist?

The answer, according to Crutcher, is yes. "All labels do some disservice because they are exclusionary," he says. Crutcher doesn't deny, and is pleased, that his books appeal to boys, and he understands why. "Boys who don't generally read like my stories, probably because they were written by an ex-boy who didn't generally like to read himself," he says.

Award winning author Bruce Coville (*Jeremy Thatcher, Dragon Hatcher; My Teacher is an Alien*) says boys seem to like reading about other boys. "So everybody put us, as authors, in little boxes. They keep our books where they seem to fall on the bell curves," he says.

Newcomer David Lubar (*Hidden Talents, Accidental Monsters*) admits, "by the time kids are reading our books they have usually been molded into gender roles."

But it's the "boys only" implication that gives Crutcher pause, "because," he says, "as many girls like my books as do boys."

Coville validates Crutcher's point. "People are so busy watching where most kids fall, they forget that some land outside of the curve; that the girl who is a tomboy and the boy who likes more feminine things are real too," he says.

Therein lies the rub, says picture book wizard, James Proimos (*Joe's Wish, The Loudness of Sam*). "The flaw is in thinking that boys only like books about boys and that girls only like books about girls. *George and Martha*, for instance, was a very successful book featuring hippos," he says, "but I have never heard it said that it was primarily read by hippopotami."

Does that mean authors who consistently create stories male readers love don't necessarily write them expressly for boys? "I don't know anyone who thinks like that before he or she starts a story," Crutcher says of the gender-specific mind set. "I guess I believe most authors write like I do—choose the plot and the characters and let the story go where it goes."

"We're raised differently," Lubar says of men and women. "Our brains are different. Our perceptions are different. Our hormones are different. Whether you draw your definition from science or the Bible, there are differences. Any attempt to deny that is well intentioned but essentially wrong. But I still think the best authors write just for themselves."

KELLY MILNER HALLS *is a full-time freelance writer based in Spokane, Washington. She is a regular contributor to the* Chicago Tribune, *the* Atlanta Journal Constitution, *the* Denver Post, Highlights for Children, Fox Kids, Guideposts for Kids, curiocity for kids, Guideposts for Teens, Teen People, FamilyFun, Parenting Teens *and many other publications. Her latest picture book,* I Bought a Baby Chicken, *is a spring 2000 release from Boyds Mills Press. E-mail Halls at kmhwrites@aol.com.*

Illustration © 1999 Michael Hussar. Reprinted with permission of Harcourt Inc.

Author Bruce Coville, sees a problem with gender issues in books for young readers. "The popular idea is that boys don't read, so books for boys won't make money," he says. "That means publishers won't take chances on the books boys might like, so boys can't find anything they want to read. It's a self-fulfilling prophecy." *Odder Than Ever*, a collection of short stories for young adults by the award-winning and beloved author, is a follow-up to Coville's *Oddly Enough* collection. Both books offer "wildly strange tales, each odder than its fellow, and each as moving as it is funny."

So what determines how a book will be categorized and why? "If the characters in a book are guys, if the plot involves guy stuff—explosions, body odors, or mindless risk taking—it's natural to shelve the book in the testosterone section," Lubar says.

Proimos agrees. "My books are seen as appealing to boys because they feature boys or men. My first book, *Joe's Wish*, is about a grandfather/grandson relationship. And my second book, *The Loudness of Sam*, is about a boy with a big mouth (although it does heavily feature his female Aunt Tillie and a duck that may or may not be a girl)."

According to Lubar, marketing also plays a part in determining whether or not a book will appeal to a boy. "Sometimes it's as simple as the cover design," he says. "As a boy, I would never have been caught dead carrying around a book with a pink cover."

"Exactly," Proimos says. "If the marketing of the book makes it clear that the publisher is saying, 'This is for girls,' then a boy won't pick it up. In fact, he's pretty much being told not to."

Coville sees the gender issue as something even deeper than characterization or marketing. And he sees the problem as two-fold. "First, the popular idea is that boys don't read, so books for boys won't make money," he says. "That means publishers won't take chances on the books boys might like, so boys can't find anything they want to read. It's a self-fulfilling prophecy."

The next barrier, according to Coville, is a matter of example. "Boys are trying to figure out how to be 'guys' in their elementary, middle school and high school years," he says. "And they're just not seeing role models—men willing to pick up good books and say reading is cool."

Society's disrespect for children, says Coville, works against providing masculine examples. "We live in a culture that despises children because children essentially have no power. When we raise men to crave power and the stepping stones to power, working with children is seen as something weak," he says.

As a result, Coville estimates 90 percent of the people teaching children to read, most of the people writing, editing and publishing books for kids, and the majority of librarians responsible for selecting the books to which young readers have access are women.

That feminine dominance, according to Coville, affects the reading material made available to kids. "What that means is the kind of storytelling energy that appeals to most boys is harder to get into print," Coville says. "Between me and my audience stands the good taste patrol."

Coville freely admits, "Boys are not always 'tasteful.' " In support of Coville's premise, Proimos gets overwhelmingly supportive fan mail about his illustration of a dog passing wind. Lubar has imagined monsters even a mother couldn't love. And Crutcher's colorful use of locker room humor is considered second to none.

But when it comes to bringing these awkward truths to editorial light, Crutcher, Coville, Lubar and Proimos are among the chosen few. "That's because we seem to have decided it's more important to make our kids tasteful than it is to get them literate," Coville says. "I maintain if you get them literate, it's much easier to teach them to be tasteful down the road."

Even so, Coville backs Crutcher's "not exclusively for boys" stance. "I like books that have farts and boogers," he says, "so I'm seen as a 'boy's writer.' But the really weird thing is that I frequently hear the other side of this argument too."

Like Crutcher, critics have called Coville's female characters strong and delightfully real. "So that brings up an odd question," he says. "If 90 percent of the people responsible for books for young readers are women, why are people saying to me, we appreciate your presentations of girls?"

According to Crutcher, the answer is simple. "I don't think it's our job as writers to decide who should read our books," he says. "I think if we just send up the best stories we can write, represent all the characters as best we can, the readers will find them. And that's how we'll know we're on the right track."

Proimos agrees. "If the books are great and current and relevant to kids, boys or girls, they will read them."

"People say girls like to read about relationships," Coville says, "what happens between

In his first novel for young adults, David Lubar tells the story or Martin Anderson, a misfit who's been "kicked out of every school he's ever attended." In *Hidden Talents* Martin falls in with five other rejects of the system at the last school that will take him, and each uncovers "a remarkable hidden talent." Of boy-aimed books, Lubar says, "If the characters in a book are guys, if the plot involves guy stuff—explosions, body odors or mindless risk-taking—it's natural to shelve it in the testosterone section."

Art © Brian Romero. Reprinted with permission of Tor Books.

"My books are seen as appealing to boys because they feature boys or men," says picture book illustrator and author James Proimos. *The Loudness of Sam*, his second book, "is about a boy with a big mouth," he says, "although it does heavily feature his female Aunt Tillie and a duck that may or may not be a girl." Proimos's first book, the acclaimed *Joe's Wish* is about a grandfather/grandson relationship.

Author Chris Crutcher is pleased that his novels like *Ironman*, the story of high school triathlete-in-training Bo Brewster, appeal to boys. "Boys who generally don't like to read like my books," he says, "probably because they were written by an ex-boy who didn't generally like to read himself."

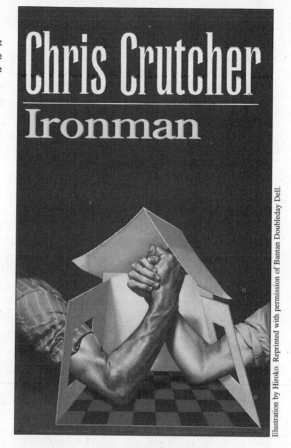

Illustration by Hiroko. Reprinted with permission of Bantam Doubleday Dell.

friends, but not so much about physical action. They say boys like to read about adventure, physical action, but shallow characterization. But I think the best book for both audiences is the one that finds the sweet spot in the middle."

Lubar states it more simply, "Even chocolate lovers like a scoop of vanilla once in a while."

GENDER ISSUES IN MAGAZINES

While book authors struggle with the concept of gender assignment, magazine editors can afford to take a more aggressive stance, thanks to subscription and reader demographics. Clearly, boys read *Boys' Life*. So Articles Editor Michael Goldman can comment with conviction on what young male readers like. Action, he says, is the perfect two-syllable summation.

"We find the key to good writing is to provide readers with solid, concrete action anecdotes full of meaty nuggets of information," he says. "It might be cliché, but the saying 'show, don't tell' is a rule that all writers—especially writers for the youth market—must follow. If we can draw a reader in with a solid action lead that pertains to his own life experiences, the battle is already half won."

Celebrity features, according to *Fox Kids* Editor Scott Russell are another sure fire hit. "Kids are starstruck," he says. "But it's a two-sided coin because if you devote a spread to a singer, the kid who likes that music is going to love it and the kid who hates that music is going to hate the whole issue because of it."

New launch archaeology magazine *Dig*'s Editor, Steve Hanks, says "yuck and muck" is another way to hedge your bets when it comes to boy appeal. "Anything gory and gross is also totally cool."

Regardless of subject matter, Russell says the best articles are visually stimulating. "Focus groups have shown that boys are drawn to artwork, particularly that of action and adventure. Breaking writing down into small paragraphs and disguising it as illustration/photo captions can get the information across without boring your reader into flipping to the next page."

True, Goldman says, but never sacrifice genuine substance. "Too often—much too often—youth writers tend to write down to their audience," he says, "turning the material into preachy drivel instead of a solid tale. The writer's job is to entertain and inform (we get back to show, don't tell) not to impose his or her moral messages on the articles."

Editors of these boy-friendly magazines (and in fact, of all magazines) wish submitting authors would study the markets before they put queries or manuscripts into the mail. "I get a lot of long semi-fiction articles about cats," Russell says. "Or 500-word stories on the nocturnal habits of opossums. Our readers want information they can share with their friends right away—small digestible bits of information that should be funny, entertaining and enlightening in a cool, hip way. It doesn't hurt if it's violent (let me amend that . . . action-oriented), gross, or just ludicrous."

Are boy readers really so far removed from girl readers? "I, personally, have not studied this issue enough to give an honest answer," Goldman says. "Besides, as an editor at *Boys' Life*, I don't necessarily have to deal with that" (he says with a grin).

Because *Fox Kids* has a 60:40 boy-to-girl reader ratio, it's a topic more at the forefront for Russell. "In general," he says, "boys want more action. They want it bigger, louder and in-your-face. As much as one might like to think to the contrary, stereotypes of boys and girls are surprisingly accurate."

Editors of boy-friendly magazines like *Dig* and *Boys' Life* have a good understanding of what appeals to young male readers. "We find the key is to provide readers with solid, concrete action anecdotes full of meaty nuggets of information," says *Boys' Life* Editor Michael Goldman. "Yuck and muck is also effective," says Steve Hanks, *Dig*'s editor. "Anything gory and gross is totally cool."

Dig Editor Hanks says, "For the most part, I don't detect much difference, although I think girls have more patience than boys to read longer stories."

Are some subjects "taboo" when it comes to writing for boys? "Too many to list, actually," Goldman says. "As a publication of the Boy Scouts of America, we screen our topics carefully to make sure they fit with the goals and values of the BSA. No violence (as in video games), athletes or other stars with black marks in their backgrounds, no dangerous activities, etc."

Surprisingly, Hanks avoids stories about kids. "Within the field of coverage for my magazine, about archaeology and paleontology, nothing would really be out of bounds in terms of subject, except for too many pieces where kids are the subject of the story. I don't think kids particularly care to read stories about other kids doing things unless the kids in the stories are celebrities."

Russell echoes Goldman. "There is a list of 'off limits' topics as long as a June day at our office," he says. "There is an entire department (Board of Standards and Practices) which deals with this exclusively. But aside from the things we 'can't' print, we 'won't' print anything that even comes close to being described as 'boring.' "

A Writer's Challenge

I know for a fact that there are boys who like poetry. I've gotten fan letters from them. I'm convinced that there are boys who'd rather read a story about a girl who has heart surgery than a monster who rips out people's hearts. I've talked with them. I'm positive there are girls who like books where people burp and fart. I'm one of them.

We all know that it's a mistake to stereotype people and their tastes, and that, furthermore, tastes overlap. An amusement at flatulence does not preclude a taste for haiku, and vice versa. A samurai in Japan was often a poet and a flower-arranger, as well as a fierce warrior. No one would have called him a sissy.

Pretty words, but the fact of the matter is the majority of boys really do like action, I can hear some folks telling me. Guys care a lot less about character development than hardware. If that is true (and I can't grant that it is since many of the boys I know from ages 9 to 81 care a great deal about well-developed characters), how did it get that way? Are boys innately programmed to like cars and robots and girls to appreciate horses and dolls, or are they taught to be interested in those things, and only those things?

If parents, teachers, librarians, bookstore clerks, publishing houses, magazine editors and, yes, even writers, continue to create and deem certain books as "boy books," how will we get boys and girls to expand their predilections? Are writers writing, publishers publishing for the market, or are they—we—in fact, creating the market? And if the latter, how can we change the situation? How can we encourage boys to read and, more importantly, enjoy a good love story or girls to get a lot out of a technical science fiction novel?

Rosanne Cerny, Coordinator of Children's Services for the Queens Borough Public Library says, "It starts with boys who do not see male role models reading. The boys who do, and who become readers themselves, will read a wide variety." Jennifer Armstrong, whose non-fiction book *Shipwreck at the End of the World* is a hit with boys and girls alike, says, "Much of book selection has to do with packaging—trim size, cover design. As an author these things are out of my hands, but they are often a significant factor in book selection by boys and girls."

Rosanne Cerny agrees, "A lot depends on packaging. Boys seem to be more self-conscious of what they think people will think about what they're reading than girls. Too many children's books have prissy packaging, and even more have unappealing covers—witness how the paperback publishers change things."

Walter Mayes, performer/book advocate/author of *Valerie and Walter's Lively, Opinionated Guide to the Best Children's Books*, goes further. When asked how to effect change in reading habits, he suggests "pediatricians making reading part of a well-child check up. Ministers and other religious leaders encouraging from the pulpit—not just the Bible, either. Sports stars making appearances at libraries. Product placement in movies and TV. Images of reading put before the masses in ways that foster an identification with it. A concerted effort by the publishing industry, the education community and the libraries to combine forces and do an ad campaign that reaches kids. Hip, cool, irreverent—it will take time and money."

And what can we authors do as part of this campaign? We can keep writing fiction that we care about, muscular fiction (and the heart is a muscle) that keeps us and our readers on their toes. Rosanne Cerny says, "There are a lot of authors who have done a good job at writing fiction for boys or that appeal to both genders . . . but I think the reason boys aren't reading much of it is because parents, teachers and often librarians just assume boys won't read fiction, so they don't even offer it."

I issue a challenge to writers, publishers, educators, parents and other interested parties to develop and share strategies that popularize thoughtful, deeper stories as boy-friendly, that make poetry a must-read for the cool, that hand girls a good sports novel and celebrate their enjoyment of it. I challenge everyone to march behind Walter Mayes's banner: "We have to change the culture. We have to make it cool to read."

—*Marilyn Singer, author*

Poetry & Plastic Laundry Baskets

BY KRISTINE O'CONNELL GEORGE

When I first started writing poetry for children, I'd sometimes receive an early morning phone call from my dear, but very opinionated friend, Mary. I'd answer and hear, "Kristine! Are you still writing poetry?" When I answered, "Yes," Mary would sigh loudly and say, "What am I going to do with you?" Mary wrote a lucrative mystery series for young readers and was constantly trying to "convert" me from writing poetry to writing mystery novels. She was certain I'd never sell poetry.

Well, I kept writing poetry. Why? Because I love poetry. Just as Mary adored devising those devious plot twists, I thrive on the nuance and music of poetry—those subtle surprises that make a poem memorable. Poetry is my way of celebrating life and of trying to capture the essence of things that astonish me.

I stored my poetry in a laundry basket. Blue plastic. A standard issue K-Mart laundry basket. I wrote and rewrote and rewrote again. I revised my poems as many as 15—or even 30—times. I piled poetry in this basket for six years until my first collection was accepted. Then, I treated myself to a file cabinet.

I still have my laundry basket. I look at it and remember that it took approximately four and a half feet of paper to produce one slim book. Hundreds of poems were whittled down to the 60-odd I submitted for what became the collection of 28 poems in my first book, *The Great Frog Race*.

Yet, every single poem in that basket was worthwhile—even if the poem was lousy. Because in the process of filling this basket, I learned volumes about writing poetry. I learned that poetry is an art form like music or oil painting. It is a discipline and it is a craft. Poetry takes practice. Very few of us are "natural-born poets," and contrary to popular myth, the "muse" rarely delivers a perfect poem to your doorstep. Or if she does, she's misplaced my address!

Perhaps you are already familiar with the craft of poetry. I wasn't. I began my poetry exploration in classes with Myra Cohn Livingston, the noted poet and anthologist. She introduced me to the mysteries of iambic pentameter, trochee and cinquain. The amount of homework Myra assigned was staggering, yet it was from those grueling weekly assignments that I learned the importance of writing consistently—every day if possible.

I've taken a while to sneak up on it, but here is the first advice I'll offer: Study poetry. Read "how to" books. Take classes. Learn the forms, the rhythms, and the structure of poetry. In the sidebar on page 89, I've listed a few of my favorite "how to" books, and you can find others on my website: www.kristinegeorge.com.

Read poetry aloud. Poetry is an oral art form; it comes alive when you read it aloud. I'm a firm believer that the more poetry you hear, the better your own poetry will become. Immerse yourself in poetry. Record your favorite poems on tape and listen to them in the car. Listen to

KRISTINE O'CONNELL GEORGE *was the recipient of both the 1998 Lee Bennett Hopkins Poetry Award and the International Reading Association's 1998 Promising Poet Award for* The Great Frog Race and Other Poems, *and the Golden Kite Award for* Old Elm Speaks: Tree Poems. *Her poetry collections have received critical acclaim including starred reviews, NTCE Notable,* Booklist *Editors' Choice and* School Library Journal *"Best Books." George has served as a poetry consultant for PBS "Storytime" television show, conducts teacher in-services, and speaks at conferences on her poetry and innovative ways to use poetry in the classroom. Visit her website at www.kristinegeorge.com.*

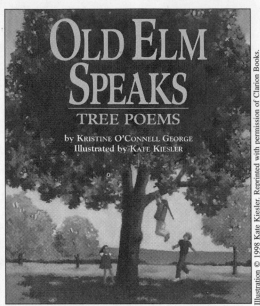

When Kristine O'Connell George started writing poetry, she collected her work in a blue plastic laundry basket. Now her poems are collected in books—her first two are *The Great Frog Race and Other Poems* and *Old Elm Speaks: Tree Poems*. George's poetry has been praised by reviewers in everything from *Publishers Weekly* and *The Horn Book* to the *Boston Globe*. Her work was recognized with a 1998 Lee Bennett Hopkins Poetry Award for *The Great Frog Race* and a 1999 Golden Kite Award from the Society of Children's Book Writers and Illustrators for *Old Elm Speaks*.

poetry in the morning while you're brushing your teeth or before you go to bed at night. Snuggle up with a child and read poetry.

By studying the craft of poetry, reading and listening to as much poetry as possible, and of course, writing lots of poetry, something wondrous will happen. You'll begin to discover your own "voice."

I'm convinced that having a distinctive "voice" is the key to being published. You—and only you—see the world in your own unique way. You may discover that you like to write poetry for teenagers or for the very young child. Particular topics will intrigue you more than others. They can even be quirky. I happen to write poetry about oddball subjects such as garden hoses, monkey wrenches and old metal buckets. I even see poetry in tadpoles:

> *Polliwogs*
>
> *Come see*
> *what I found!*
> *Chubby commas,*
> *Mouths round,*
> *Plump babies,*
> *Stubby as toes.*
> *Polliwogs!*
> *Tadpoles!*
>
> *Come see*
> *What I found!*
> *Frogs-in-waiting—*
> *Huddled in puddles,*
> *Snuggled in mud.*

"Polliwogs" from *The Great Frog Race and Other Poems*. Text copyright © 1997 by Kristine O'Connell George.

Award-Winning Poets and Poetry Books

Newbery Medal

1998 Karen Hesse, *Out of the Dust*

1989 Paul Fleischman, *Joyful Noise: Poems for Two Voices*

1982 Nancy Willard, *A Visit to William Blake's Inn: Poems for Innocent and Experienced Travelers*

National Council of Teachers of English (NCTE) Award for Excellence in Children's Poetry

This prestigious award honors a poet for a body of work. Check out the website for their thoughtful and well-written criteria of excellence in children's poetry. (www.ncte.org/elem/poetry)

1997 Eloise Greenfield

1994 Barbara Juster Esbensen

1991 Valerie Worth

1988 Arnold Adoff

1985 Lilian Moore

1982 John Ciardi

1981 Eve Merriam

1980 Myra Cohn Livingston

1979 Karla Kuskin

1978 Aileen Fischer

1977 David McCord

International Reading Association (IRA) / Lee Bennett Hopkins Promising Poet Award

Lee Bennett Hopkins founded and funds this award which is given every three years. (www.-reading.org/about/whatwedo/awards/Lee.html)

1998 Kristine O'Connell George

1995 Deborah Chandra

Lee Bennett Hopkins Poetry Award

Lee Bennett Hopkins also established this award to honor children's poetry. It is administered by the Penn State College of Education and University Libraries. (http://is124.ce.psu.edu/C&I/childrensliterature/)

1999 Angela Johnson, *The Other Side: Shorter Poems*

1999 Constance Levy, *A Crack in the Clouds* (Honor Book)

1998 Kristine O'Connell George, *The Great Frog Race and Other Poems*

1997 David Bouchard, *Voices from the Wild: An Animal Sensagoria*

1996 Barbara Juster Esbensen, *Dance with Me*

1995 Douglas Florian, *Beast Feast*

1994 Nancy Wood, *Spirit Walker*

1993 Ashley Bryan, *Sing to the Sun*

Claudia Lewis Poetry Award

Administered by the Children's Book Committee at Banks Street College of Education. (www.bnkst.edu/bookcom/awardlist.html)

1998 Catherine Clinton, *I, Too, Sing America: Three Centuries of African American Poetry*

1997 Liz Rosenberg, *The Invisible Ladder: An Anthology of Contemporary American Poems for Young Readers*

Reviewers' Choice Poetry

By reading the works of the following contemporary poets and anthologists, you will begin to get a sense of the current market for children's poetry. Many of these poets have published two or more titles and received awards or "starred" or "pointer" reviews from review sources such as *Booklist*, *Kirkus*, *Publishers Weekly* or *School Library Journal*.

Frank Asch	Mary Ann Hoberman	Neil Philip
Deborah Chandra	Paul Janeczko	Jack Prelutsky
Rebecca Kai Dotlich	Tony Johnston	Liz Rosenberg
Paul Fleischman	X. J. Kennedy	Cynthia Rylant
Ralph Fletcher	Karla Kuskin	Alice Schertle
Douglas Florian	Constance Levy	Marilyn Singer
Kristine O'Connell George	J. Patrick Lewis	James Stevenson
Lee Bennett Hopkins	Lilian Moore	Nancy Willard
Mel Glenn	Naomi Shihab Nye	Jane Yolen
Joan Graham	Ann Whitford Paul	

Multicultural poets

These exciting poets write poignantly about growing up as a member of a minority group or present the flavors of different cultures to young readers.

Alma Flor Ada	Eloise Greenfield	Walter Dean Myers
Arnold Adoff	Nikki Grimes	Gary Soto
Francisco X. Alarcon	Monica Gunning	Joyce Carol Thomas
Ashley Bryan	Angela Johnson	Janet S. Wong
Lucille Clifton	Pat Mora	

Perhaps the lowly polliwog isn't your "thing," and perhaps you don't have a special net under your kitchen sink for catching tadpoles. Spend time discovering "your thing." What amazes and enchants you? What do you care passionately about? Look over the poetry you've written. What emotions or topics keep bubbling up? It's your individual passions and enthusiasm—your "slant" on the world—that will make your poetry unique. Don't be afraid to try innovative topics for your poems. Dig deep. Be bold. This is all part of finding your "voice."

Poetry for children encompasses newborns to teenagers. It includes everything from simple rhymed books for toddlers to young adult poetry that addresses meaty issues such as death and divorce to entire novels written in free verse. When I tell someone I write poetry for children, I often get a blank look. They wonder: Humorous poetry like Jack Prelutsky? Shel Silverstein? Rhymed picture books like Dr. Seuss? Well, not exactly.

When you begin to look beyond the well-known poets for children, you'll quickly discover the amazing diversity of children's poetry. This wealth of variation translates into an opportunity for you and your unique voice. Read what's currently being published. Many new writers I meet have read very little children's poetry, assuming not much has changed since their own childhood. Nothing could be further from the truth. Children's poetry is a dynamic, exciting and constantly evolving genre.

I listed many poets in the above sidebar in the hope you'll take time to read them. Not only can you learn much from these writers, but reading widely will also help you understand the market. I hope you'll be excited by the many different poetic voices. Editors are looking for poetry collections that feature distinctive and exciting new voices. Why not yours?

Next, take a close look at recently published poetry collections. You'll notice that most poetry collections are written around a theme, and I think your chances for acceptance improve if your collection has a unifying theme.

Themes for poetry collections vary widely: nature and wildlife, bedtime, sports, personal experiences and many other topics. I really can't explain how I stumbled on the theme of trees for *Old Elm Speaks: Tree Poems*, or even my own pet for *Little Dog Poems*, but clearly these are topics I care deeply enough about to use as a theme for an entire poetry collection. Find a theme that excites you and use it to unite your poems.

Okay. You have written a laundry basket worth of poems. You have several poems you're quite proud of, but you are still working toward a full collection. What to do? Consider anthologies and magazines as possible markets for your poems. Study magazines to discover which ones accept poetry for children and write for the guidelines of these magazines. Consider writing to anthologists (care of their publishers if you don't have an address), and send along two or three of your strongest poems as samples. Ask if they have plans for a new anthology and if you might submit work to them. Many poets such as Rebecca Kai Dotlich jump-started their careers by submitting their poetry to magazines and anthologies.

Now, for a brief word about rhymed picture books or "rhyming stories," since I'm often asked about them. I know you've heard editors don't want to see rhymed picture books. So, how to explain the popularity of *Bringing the Rain to Kapiti Plain*, *Chicka Chicka Boom Boom* or *Goodnight Moon*? If you study publishers' catalogs you'll spot rhymed picture books by Nancy White Carlston, Mary Ann Hoberman, Verla Kay, Bill Martin, Jr., Ann Whitford Paul, Judy Sierra, Anastasia Suen, Nancy Van Laan and of course, Dr. Seuss. (See the Insider Report with Verla Kay, on page 180 and Anastasia Suen, on page 202.)

Read these books and you'll see why an editor said, *Yes!* The rhymes are smooth and logical, and the text has a clear rhythm and cadence. The topic is innovative and original, and the books are a joy to read aloud.

If you have a gift for rhyme and a strong sense of rhythm, by all means write rhymed picture books. Rhymed picture books *are* being published. Even though a good rhymed picture book is fiendishly difficult to write, children adore them.

Now, for my last bit of wisdom: Please don't get discouraged. Write poetry because you love it, not because you hope to see your name in print. Be good to yourself. Honor yourself as a writer. Don't be cheap like I was—buy a file cabinet for your poetry! Join writers' organizations such as the Society of Children's Book Writers and Illustrators. Participate in a critique group so you can share your poetry, and get feedback from others who are equally passionate about writing poetry.

One of the first poems I wrote for *Old Elm Speaks: Tree Poems* reminds me of the time we must invest to achieve our goals.

> *Old Elm Speaks*
>
> *It is as I told you, Young Sapling.*
>
> *It will take*
> *autumns of patience*
> *before you snag*
> *your*
> *first*
> *moon.*

"Old Elm Speaks" from *Old Elm Speaks: Tree Poems*. Text copyright © 1998 by Kristine O'Connell George.

Little Dog Poems

by Kristine O'Connell George

Illustrated by June Otani

Little Dog Poems, the third poetry collection by Kristine O'Connell George, offers, in verse, a romp through the day of a little girl and her Little Dog. George feels that every poet sees the world in her own way, and these visions contribute to a poet's unique voice. "I happen to write poetry about oddball subjects such as garden hoses, monkey wrenches and old metal buckets," she says. "Spend some time discovering 'your thing.' What amazes and enchants you? What do you care about passionately? Don't be afraid to try innovative topics for your poems. Dig deep. Be bold. This is all part of finding your voice."

That's it! If you find, as I do, that poetry is a powerful magic that has you under its spell, you'll keep writing—filling the equivalent of your own laundry basket. You'll read voraciously. You'll immerse yourself in the sounds of poetry. And, when you see your first poem in print, you'll feel as if you "snagged a moon." You'll celebrate. (No one cheered more loudly than my friend Mary when my first poem was accepted.) Then, you'll return to that quiet, contemplative and patient place to do what you love most: Write poetry.

Books on Writing and Writing Poetry

Several of the books shown below were written for young writers or elementary teachers (marked with an *) but would also be helpful to adults writing children's poetry. Also listed are books that will help familiarize you with the field of children's poetry.

Breathing In, Breathing Out: Keeping a Writer's Notebook, by Ralph Fletcher (Heinemann)

Children's Literature in the Elementary School (Chapter 8), by Charlotte Huck, Susan Hepler, Janet Hickman and Barbara Z. Kiefer (Brown & Benchmark)

*Easy Poetry Lessons that Dazzle and Delight, by David L. Harrison and Bernice E. Cullinan (Scholastic Professional)

*How to Write Poetry, by Paul B. Janeczko (Scholastic)

In the Palm of Your Hand: The Poet's Portable Workshop, by Steve Kowit (Tilbury House)

A Jar of Tiny Stars: Poems by NCTE Award-Winning Poets, by Bernice E. Cullinan, editor (Boyds Mills)

*Knock at a Star: A Child's Introduction to Poetry, by Dorothy and X. J. Kennedy (Little Brown)

Pass the Poetry, Please!, by Lee Bennett Hopkins (Harper)

The Poet's Handbook, by Judson Jerome (Writer's Digest Books)

The Place My Words Are Looking For: What Poets Say About and Through Their Work, by Paul Janeczko (Atheneum)

PoemCrazy: Freeing Your Life With Words, by Susan Goldsmith Wooldrige (Crown)

*Poem-Making: Ways to Begin Writing Poetry, by Myra Cohn Livingston (HarperCollins)

*Poetry from A to Z: A Guide for Young Writers, by Paul Janeczko (Atheneum)

A Poetry Handbook, by Mary Oliver (Harcourt Brace)

Rules for the Dance: A Handbook for Writing and Reading Metrical Verse, by Mary Oliver (Houghton Mifflin)

Novels that integrate poetry:

The Bat-Poet, by Randall Jarrell (HarperCollins)

For YOUR Eyes Only!, by Joanne Rocklin (Scholastic)

Jazmin's Notebook, by Nikki Grimes (Dial)

The Mouse of Amherst, by Elizabeth Spires (Farrar Straus)

From Ponyboy to *The Puppy Sister:* S.E. Hinton on Her Writing Life

BY ANNE BOWLING

"I really have to become my narrator, and I think one of the keys to writing convincing characters is to feel the emotion. Your characters have got to be feeling an emotion you're familiar with and that you can convey convincingly."

Known to friends and colleagues more informally as Susie, S.E. Hinton is known by the reading public as the writer who broke new ground in young adult fiction with her gritty novel of adolescent alienation *The Outsiders* (Viking). Published in 1967 to little critical notice, the slender volume has remained in print for more than 30 years, its enduring popularity based primarily on the power of the emotions it explores. Hinton followed publication of *The Outsiders* with 4 more young adult novels—which garnered 20 national awards among them—and 4 film adaptations of her books. Most recently, she has moved into writing for a younger audience, with publication of *Big David, Little David* (Doubleday, 1994) and *The Puppy Sister* (Delacorte, 1995).

S.E. Hinton

Because she has come to be a writer so closely identified with alienated youths, it may be a lot to ask that readers change their expectations of Hinton from switchblade rumbles in parking lots to grade-school practical jokes. But for a writer who has always drawn on life experiences for her stories, and has taken her craft with her from the angst of adolescence into parenthood, the transition makes perfect sense.

"Actually, I didn't find the transition difficult at all," Hinton says with characteristic, unassuming frankness. "Any time I try to write something, I try to put my mind in the mind of a character. In *The Puppy Sister*, the character was a puppy, so I switched genre and species in one fell blow. But it was just easy to picture. I just kind of wondered what the dog was thinking."

An avid reader since first grade, Hinton had already written 2 novels before she penned *The*

ANNE BOWLING *is production editor for* Writer's Market, *a frequent contributor and editor of Writer's Digest Books titles, and a contributing editor for* Fiction Writer *magazine. Among the authors she's interviewed for* Fiction Writer *are Jay McInerney, Alice McDermott, Terry McMillan and Anna Quindlan. Bowling and her three children are avid consumers of books for young readers and often contribute ideas to* Children's Writer's & Illustrator's Market.

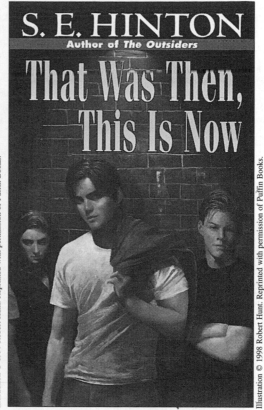

As a 16-year-old, S.E. Hinton penned her now classic *The Outsiders*; she wrote *That Was Then, This Is Now*, her second book, while in college after a period of writer's block. "My boyfriend, now my husband, was saying, 'I don't care if you never get published again, but you've got to start writing again. Enough of this gloom and doom stuff. Write two pages a day,'" says Hinton. "I was careful with *That Was Then*—I was thinking, 'I'm not going to make the mistakes I did in *The Outsiders*.' I did two pages, but they were hard. I didn't put down a word that I didn't want, and when I had a stack about the size of a book I sent it off."

Outsiders at age 16. "It wasn't an overnight success," Hinton says. "It got some attention because I was so young, but the success of it built over the years. It was definitely a word-of-mouth book." The word-of-mouth notoriety that made *The Outsiders* such a must-read was also what froze Hinton when, as a student at the University of Tulsa, she tried to write her second book. "I couldn't write," she recalls. "I was in college, and I was reading good writers, and I was seeing everything that was wrong with *The Outsiders*." By 1971, she had published *That Was Then, This Is Now* (Viking).

Hinton followed that title with *Rumble Fish* (Delacorte, 1975) and *Tex* (Delacorte, 1979), and wrapped up her young adult writing with 1988's *Taming the Star Runner* (Delacorte), written when her son Nick was a toddler. So why does the writer hailed by *The New York Times Book Review* as having the "almost mythical status of being the grande dame of young adult novelists" suddenly drop her genre?

"One Christmas, my editor was visiting me and had come to try to inspire me," Hinton says. "We sat around all afternoon trying to get inspired to write a young adult novel and couldn't. So we ended up talking about our kids." That conversation led her to write *Big David, Little David*, the portrayal of a prank Hinton and her husband had played on Nick as a kindergartner.

A *Publishers Weekly* reviewer wrote: "Hinton shifts easily into picture book gear in this genuinely funny look at the unorthodox dilemma facing a likable youngster named Nick."

Inspiration for *The Puppy Sister* wasn't far behind. Based on Nick's relationship with his Australian shepherd puppy, Aleasha, the middle reader follows a year in their lives as Aleasha evolves not into a dog but a girl. The family tries to hide her transformation, often with hilarious results, in what a starred *Publishers Weekly* review called "a consistently witty . . . irresistable fantasy . . . as memorable in its genre as her classic *The Outsiders* is in YA literature."

As Hinton's newer titles sit on the bookshelves near Kevin Henkes, E.B. White and Shel Silverstein, *The Outsiders* continues to carry the word-of-mouth popularity that has made it resonate with a third generation of young readers. A recent visit to Amazon.com 33 years after that title was published shows 345 reviews tallied, and such reader kudos as: "Even though I was only 12 when I read it, I remember that it had a profound effect on me," "I think anyone from 10 to 100 should check it out," and "All I can say is S.E. Hinton, if you're reading this, *please* keep writing!"

Although she has been quoted as saying, "Writing is actually a lot easier than talking about writing," Hinton took time out to speak with us from her home in Tulsa. Here she discusses writing for both young adult and picture book audiences, and the keys to creating unforgettable characters.

How do you judge the overall quality of children's literature today? Do you think it has expanded to include more quality titles in, say, the last 20 years?

I think so. I think a lot of people are realizing that there's nothing demeaning about writing children's books, and frankly what would you rather have written—*Valley of the Dolls* or *Black Beauty*? I think there's a lot of clever, intelligent work out there for kids.

Where did you get your inspiration for *Big David, Little David*?

I told my editor about this trick my husband had played on my son Nick. When Nick came home from kindergarten the first day he said, "Dad, there's a kid in my class who has black hair like you, he wears glasses like you, and his name's David like you—is that you?" And my husband said, "Yeah, that's me. Every day I get little and go to school with you." Freaked Nick out.

And I have to admit I abetted this thing. Any time I'd pick Nick up at school and he would say, "Kelsey threw up," when we'd get home, I'd immediately run to the phone and call my husband. And David would come home and say, "Man, that was gross when Kelsey threw up." We just kept going with this, and it actually went on for well over a year. Finally Nick figured out he was being put on.

When I told that story to my editor, he looked like he was about to call child services or fall off the chair laughing. Then he said, "Write that up as a picture book," and it was a lot of fun to write.

Were you ever concerned that the premise of *The Puppy Sister*, a puppy turning into a girl, would make the manuscript difficult to sell?

No, because I'm an animal person. I'm more surprised that they don't turn into humans. My mind doesn't make the differentiation that strongly between humans and animals.

Another nice part about writing that book was that plot is always the hard thing for me, but I pictured this transformation taking place over the period of a year. So at the end of the book, Aleasha had spent her first year in dog years—she'd be seven—and also I had holidays and things to work around and hang plot points on. So it was pretty easy to do.

The idea for S.E. Hinton's first picture book *Big David, Little David* came from a real-life trick Hinton and her husband played on their son. "When Nick came home from kindergarten the first day he said, 'Dad, there's a kid in my class who has black hair like you, he wears glasses like you, and his name's David like you—is that you?' My husband said, 'Yeah, that's me. Every day I get little and go to school with you.' Freaked Nick out. It actually went on for well over a year. Finally Nick figured out he was being put on."

How was writing for younger children different from writing for young adults?

I wasn't thinking about the audience, which I try never to do. You start feeling them looking over your shoulder, and you start thinking you're going to make a mistake. I've never thought "Oh, kids would like this, I'll stick this in." I especially don't make that mistake when I'm writing for young adults.

I have to write a story the way I see it and take the consequences. You never can completely get the audience out of your mind once you've been published, and after *The Outsiders*, I found that very difficult to deal with. But since then, I think I've gotten pretty good at it.

After *The Outsiders* was published, you struggled with a long period of writer's block before finishing *That Was Then, This Is Now*. Based on that experience, how do you recommend writers get past their dry spells?

Get the right boyfriend. I was in college and I was reading good writers, but at that time, I couldn't write. I was seeing everything that was wrong with *The Outsiders*; I was feeling the pressure of, "What is she going to do next?" and, "She wrote this well when she was 15, and she's going to have a masterpiece." And I knew I didn't have no masterpiece.

My boyfriend, who is now my husband, was saying, "I don't care if you never get published again, but you've got to start writing again. Enough of this gloom and doom stuff." He said, "Write two pages a day. Nobody's ever dropped dead of two pages." And he'd come over to take me out, and if I hadn't done my two pages we wouldn't go out. So that was a great motivation for writing. And I was so careful with *That Was Then*—I was thinking, "I'm not going to make the mistakes I did in *The Outsiders*." I did two pages, but they were hard. I didn't put down a word that I didn't want, and when I had a stack about the size of a book I sent it off.

So I'm very proud of it. I think it's a better book than *The Outsiders*, but I don't think it has the same emotional impact. So from then on, I tried to get emotional commitment with artistic control in the same book.

You were 15 when you started writing *The Outsiders*, and wrote 4 full drafts for the next year and a half before you had the manuscript. Did you have a mentor at that time, or was someone guiding your revisions?

No. I love to write. Actually, *The Outsiders* was the third book I had written; it was just the first one I had tried to publish. The first two ended up in drawers somewhere—I used characters from them later in other books, but I certainly didn't go back and rework them. Everybody's got to practice.

When I was writing *The Outsiders*, I would go to school and say, "Well, I'm writing a book, and this has happened so far, and what should happen next?," 'cause I'd get stuck. Someone would say, "Oh, make the church burn down." And I'd say, "That sounds good, I'll make the church burn down." I was just doing it because I liked doing it.

Because there was very little being published at that time for young adults that included such violent content and emotional depth, were you concerned at all that the book was really pushing the envelope?

No, I wasn't. One reason I wrote it was I wanted to read it. I couldn't find anything that dealt realistically with teenage life. I've always been a good reader, but I wasn't ready for adult books, they didn't interest me, and I was through with all the horse books. If you wanted to read about your peer group, there was nothing to read except "Mary Jane Goes to the Prom" or "Billy Joe Hits a Home Run"—just a lot of stuff I didn't see any relevance in.

I know I've been banned in places, but I've gotten so many letters from kids who say, "After reading your books, I realize how stupid violence is." I've never had a kid write me and say, "I read your book, got all hopped up and ran out and beat up someone."

In retrospect, how do you regard your writing ability at the time you worked on *The Outsiders*?

When I do glance at it again, I'm kind of surprised by that, too. But from grade school on, I knew I wanted to be a writer, and I read all the time, and I practiced, and the only way you're going to be a writer is to read all the time and then do it. So I was doing the right things.

I feel differently about *The Outsiders* than I do my other books. I'm really proud of it because it's done a lot of good—much more than my personal capacity for doing good could ever be—and I'm really pleased with it that way. I almost don't even think of myself as having anything to do with it. It was almost kind of like it was supposed to be out there, and I was just the way it got there.

While you were writing, were you consciously concerned with elements like, plot, pacing, characterization, dialogue?

Oh no, no, no. I tell people to try to not ever think that. Because that'll freeze you up so badly. So much of my writing is done in subconsciousness; I keep working on a way to take a nap and find a chapter done. But don't think about what you're doing, just keep your story going. Years later somebody's going to write you a letter and tell you what you wrote about. So don't worry about that part of it.

S.E. Hinton's first foray into middle readers is *The Puppy Sister*, the story of a boy and his dog—who slowly, over the course of a year, transforms into a girl. "I'm an animal person," says Hinton. "I'm surprised that they don't turn into humans." *The Puppy Sister* stars Nick and Aleasha, characters based on Hinton's son and her family's Australian shepherd. *Publishers Weekly* calls it "consistently witty . . . irresistible fantasy."

The Puppy Sister

★"This irresistible fantasy can take its place alongside *Stuart Little* and *Babe the Gallant Pig*."
—*Publishers Weekly*, Starred

S. E. Hinton
Illustrated by Jacqueline Rogers

Illustration © Jacqueline Rogers. Reprinted with permission of Bantam Doubleday Dell.

What's the key to writing convincingly from a variety of points of view—adolescent boys, a puppy who becomes human? You seem to not have much problem transcending these boundaries.

I know I'm a character writer, and I have to know everything about my character. And although I can say, "Don't base your characters on yourself," I guess Ponyboy's the closest character to myself I've ever written. He's very much like I was at that age, almost to the physical description.

With your other characters, you have to know their astrological signs, you have to know what they eat for breakfast, and so on. That doesn't have to come out in the book, you just have to know it anyway in defining your character. But on the other hand, no matter how well you think you're imagining somebody, or even basing it on somebody you know, the writer is still the filter that the character goes through, so the character is still some aspect of yourself. So, yes, I can say Ponyboy is just like me, but somewhere Dallas is like me, and somewhere Rusty James is like me, because I was their interpreter.

How do you develop your characters? I read that Tex McCormick is your favorite—could you use him as an example?

Tex is actually somebody who appeared in my earliest works—he appeared in Old West stories, he appeared in modern Westerns, he was somebody I really had been germinating for a long, long time. One reason I started writing about him when I did was I was finishing *Rumble Fish*, which had been very depressing. And at the end of that book, I felt like I had been beating my head against a stone wall, and I just wanted to be somebody happy for a change. And Tex, bless his heart, was just determined to be happy, and had such a generous heart, that it was a really nice experience inhabiting a character like that.

What pitfalls should authors writing for the young adult market beware of?

I think the most common trap is the idea that the writer is going to take a problem and write about it: you're going to take divorce, date rape, or drugs and write about it, instead of thinking you're going to take Travis, and write about him, or Rusty James, and write his story.

I think the problems are incidental to the characters. One reason *The Outsiders* is still selling as well as it ever has, including the year the movie came out, is the kids identify with those emotions. The names of the groups change, the uniforms change, but the emotions remain the same. If you've got ten kids in a school, they're going to divide up into the "in" group and the "out" group.

You seem to be most comfortable with the first-person point of view. What are its advantages?

I prefer first. I feel like the next book will definitely be first person. One of the most fun things about writing is you get to be somebody else. I compare it a lot to acting, because I've been around a lot of actors, and I feel what I do is a lot like what they do. You can know the whole screenplay but when you're in there you're in your part.

Star Runner was different, because my little boy was four years old when I wrote it, and I didn't have the emotional energy to do a first-person narration. I couldn't be that focused. So I thought I'd try third-person narration just to give me a little bit of distance, I think I can do that, and do it well, but I knew I didn't have the emotions to spare for a first-person narration.

You've said "I have a very good memory—I remember exactly what it was like to be a teenager who nobody listened to or paid attention to, or wanted around." Do you still remember, and do you intend to pick up young adult writing again?

I'd like to do young adult again. I still have a very good memory, and right now I've got somebody in the house reinforcing that memory all the time.

Did your son like *The Outsiders?*

I think so. But he was pretty closed-mouthed about it. I got the feeling he felt like, "It's okay, Mom, but you're no Tolkein." I notice he did not rush out and read the other ones. He read *Big David, Little David* and edited *Puppy Sister* for me. He went through the manuscript and made changes, and came back with some suggestions.

I know I've got at least one more teen novel in me, but I'm not ready to sit down and hash it out. Right now I'm doing some stuff that will probably never see the light of day, and I'm just trying to remember what it was like for writing to be fun. After awhile, if that's the way you're earning your living, it's not quite as much fun as it used to be. But since I'm working on stuff that I really, honestly never expect to get published, it's getting to be fun again.

Markets
Book Publishers

There's no magic formula for getting published. It's a matter of getting the right manuscript on the right editor's desk at the right time. Before you submit it's important to learn publishers' needs, see what kind of books they're producing and decide which publishers your work is best suited for. *Children's Writer's & Illustrator's Market* is but one tool in this process. To help you narrow down the list of possible publishers for your work, we've included several indexes at the back of this book. **The Subject Index** lists book and magazine publishers according to their fiction and nonfiction needs or interests. **The Age-Level Index** indicates which age groups publishers cater to. **The Photography Index** indicates which markets buy photography for children's publications. **The Poetry Index** lists publishers accepting poetry.

If you write contemporary fiction for young adults, for example, and you're trying to place a book manuscript, go first to the Subject Index. Locate the fiction categories under Book Publishers and copy the list under Contemporary. Then go to the Age-Level Index and highlight the publishers on the Contemporary list that are included under the Young Adults heading. Read the listings for the highlighted publishers to see if your work matches their needs.

Remember, *Children's Writer's & Illustrator's Market* should not be your only source for researching publishers. Here are a few other sources of information:

- The Society of Children's Book Writers and Illustrators (SCBWI) offers members an annual market survey of children's book publishers. (Members send a SASE with $3 postage. SCBWI membership information can be found at www.scbwi.org.)
- The Children's Book Council website (www.cbcbooks.org) gives information on member publishers.
- If a publisher interests you, send a SASE for submission guidelines *before* submitting. For a searchable database of over 1,150 publishers' guidelines, visit www.writersdigest.com.
- Check publishers' websites. Many include their complete catalogs which you can browse. Web addresses are included in many publishers' listings.
- Spend time at your local bookstore to see who's publishing what. While you're there, browse through *Publishers Weekly*, *The Horn Book* and *Riverbank Review*.

SUBSIDY AND SELF-PUBLISHING

Some determined writers who receive rejections from royalty publishers may look to subsidy and co-op publishers as an option for getting their work into print. These publishers ask writers to pay all or part of the costs of producing a book. We strongly advise writers and illustrators to work only with publishers who pay them. For this reason, we've adopted a policy not to include any subsidy or co-op publishers in *Children's Writer's & Illustrator's Market* (or any other Writer's Digest Books market books).

If you're interested in publishing your book just to share it with friends and relatives, self-publishing is a viable option, but it involves a lot of time, energy and money. You oversee all book production details. Check with a local printer for advice and information on cost. See the sidebar that follows for information on self-publishing from author Charles Ferry.

Whatever path you choose, keep in mind that the market is flooded with submissions, so it's important for you to hone your craft and submit the best work possible. Competition from thousands of other writers and illustrators makes it more important than ever to research publishers before submitting—read their guidelines, look at their catalogs, check out a few of their titles and visit their websites.

ADVICE FROM INSIDERS

For insight and advice on getting published from a variety of perspectives, be sure to read the Insider Reports in this section. Subjects include educational publisher **Larry Rood** of Gryphon House (page 124); Harcourt editorial director **Allyn Johnston** (page 130); young adult novelist **Francesca Lia Block** (page 136); **Jacqueline Briggs Martin**, author of 1999 Caldecott winner *Snowflake Bentley* (page 140); author of historical nonfiction **Brandon Marie Miller** (page 152); picture book author/illustrator **Paul Brett Johnson** (page 166); picture book author **Verla Kay** (page 180); series writing team **Marcia Thornton Jones** and **Debbie Dadey** (page 190); and prolific author and poet **Anastasia Suen** (page 202).

A Self-Published Author Shares His Experience

Charles Ferry published four young adult books with Houghton Mifflin: *Up in Sister Bay*, *O Zebron Falls!*, *Raspberry One* (ALA Best Book), and *One More Time!* (optioned for film). Then 61 mainstream publishers rejected *Binge*, his powerful novel about how alcohol destroys young lives, and Ferry published it himself.

Binge immediately won plaudits unprecedented for a self-published YA title, including major honors from The National Council of Teachers of English and the New York Public Library. *Binge* was the first self-published book in the history of the American Library Association to win a Best Book citation, and the editors of *Something About the Author*, in their write-up of Ferry, called *Binge* a breakthrough book which legitimized self-publishing and encouraged other authors to self-publish. Ferry, who continues to write in unflinching detail for young adults, has this advice for writers contemplating publishing their own work:

On self-publishing fiction

I self-published because I wrote a novel too realistic for mainstream children's publishers. And I recommend self-publishing to other writers, but sensibly. About 6,000 titles are self-published annually in this country, most of them nonfiction. Trying to crack the national market with a self-published novel is incredibly difficult and expensive. (*Binge* is unique in many ways.) So what I recommend is this: Don't aim to be a small fish in a big pond. Aim to be a big fish in a small pond. Self-publish your novel or picture book locally and market it locally, regionally, perhaps statewide.

I frequently cite the case of the poet Max Ellison. He published his poetry in a single hardcover volume titled *The Underbark*. He then marketed it himself by appearing in schools, colleges and libraries. He was so successful that the governor of Michigan named him Poet Laureate. So if you self-publish with your feet on the ground, you can be pretty hot stuff. Even if your book flops commercially, it will be an important event in your life, for your family and for your community.

On making money from self-publishing

With a traditional publisher, my author's royalty on a $8.95 paperback like *Binge* would be 6%, or 54¢. In self-publishing, I'm left with 89¢. Here are the numbers: Baker & Taylor and Ingram

Book Company, the major national wholesalers, get a 55% discount and free shipping. (Bear in mind, the wholesaler only fills orders; it's up to the publisher to create demand.) That leaves $4.03. Subtract from that postage ($1.24), mailer (50¢), and the cost of the book ($1.40), or a total of $3.14, and that leaves 89¢.

I published *Binge* on May 1, 1992. When sales were 5,713 (and the first edition will soon be sold out at 7,567 books), I had taken a total of $2,500 in profits. I spent the rest just in keeping my little company going. Now, that is the performance of a highly honored book, self-published by an established, award-winning author. And the experts tell me that this is a remarkable performance, that *Binge* has had a pivotal impact on the publishing industry. Maybe so, but it isn't putting food on my table. So why do I keep hanging in there? Quite simply, I am on a mission. *Binge* is changing lives.

On book promotion

With *Binge*, I was undercapitalized. I had no reserve to print more books, so when large orders began to come in, I had to borrow money. Because of a low budget, I sought out inexpensive promotion opportunities. For instance, I bought a one-year schedule of large ads in *VOYA* magazine (circulation 4,500), but that was only marginally effective. I spent $2,500 on a flyer to be delivered to 10,000 libraries with the new editions of *Children's Books in Print*, but that produced only a few sales because most librarians throw advertising away. So what I should have done instead of running a lot of ads in small publications was spend that money for one or two big ads in important magazines, like *Booklist, School Library Journal* and *The New York Times*.

It's a matter of plugging along. A high school in Baton Rouge is considering purchasing several hundred copies of *Binge* because a woman I met on a flight to Dallas told them about the book. In fact, the most effective thing I did with *Binge* was mailing news and updates to my select list of persons in the publishing and teaching fields. That's because *Binge* is not a bookstore title. I appear at Barnes & Noble now and then, but when I do, it's a bore; I rarely sign a book. Schools and libraries are my market. Kids are my greatest fans.

On the rewards of writing

In America, 95% of all books published (about 100,000 per year) earn their authors less than $5,000. But I have learned that true wealth is invisible. You can't see love. You can't see joy. You can't see the warmth that fills your heart when you find out that one of your books has touched the life of some young reader, for example, a 13-year-old boy who wrote me, "*Raspberry One* changed the way I feel about war and life and death, or another boy who extended his hand and simply said, "Thank you for writing *Binge*."

In the 23 years that I have been publishing for young adults, my books, with all of their honors, have earned me less than $30,000. That figures out to about $1,300 per year. A good plumber makes that much in a week. But my books touch lives. I am one of the wealthiest people in America.

—Anna Olswanger

ABINGDON PRESS, The United Methodist Publishing House, 201 Eighth Ave. S., Nashville TN 37203. (615)749-6384. Fax: (615)749-6512. **Acquisitions:** Peg Augustine, children's book editor. Estab. 1789. "Abingdon Press, America's oldest theological publisher, provides an ecumenical publishing program dedicated to serving the Christian community—clergy, scholars, church leaders, musicians and general readers—with quality resources in the areas of Bible study, the practice of ministry, theology, devotion, spirituality, inspiration, prayer, music and worship, reference, Christian education and church supplies."

Fiction: Picture books, middle readers, young readers, young adults/teens: multicultural, religion, special needs.
Nonfiction: Picture books, middle readers, young readers, young adults/teens: religion. Does not want to see animal stories.
How to Contact/Writers: Query; submit outline/synopsis and 1 sample chapter. Reports on queries in 3 months; mss in 6 months.
Illustration: Uses color artwork only. Reviews ms/illustration packages from artists. Query with photocopies only. Samples returned with SASE; samples not filed.
Photography: Buys stock images. Wants scenics, landscape, still life and multiracial photos. Model/property release required. Uses color prints. Submit stock photo list.
Terms: Pays authors royalty of 5-10% based on retail price. Work purchased outright from authors ($100-1,000).

ACROPOLIS BOOKS, 747 Sheridan Blvd., #1-A, Lakewood CO 80214.
● No longer publishing children's books.

ADVOCACY PRESS, P.O. Box 236, Santa Barbara CA 93102. (805)962-2728. Fax: (805)963-3580. Division of The Girls Incorporated of Greater Santa Barbara. Book publisher. Editorial Contact: Ruth Vitale, curriculum specialist. Publishes 2-4 children's books/year.
Fiction: Picture books, young readers, middle readers: adventure, animal, concepts in self-esteem, contemporary, fantasy, folktales, gender equity, multicultural, nature/environment, poetry. "Illustrated children's stories incorporate self-esteem, gender equity, self-awareness concepts." Published *Nature's Wonderful World in Rhyme* (birth-age 12, collection of poems); *Shadow and the Ready Time* (32-page picture book). "Most publications are 32-48 page picture stories for readers 4-11 years. Most feature adventures of animals in interesting/educational locales."
Nonfiction: Middle readers, young adults: careers, multicultural, self-help, social issues, textbooks.
How to Contact/Writers: "Because of the required focus of our publications, most have been written in-house." Reports on queries/mss in 1-2 months. Include SASE.
Illustration: "Require intimate integration of art with story. Therefore, almost always use local illustrators." Average about 30 illustrations per story. Reviews ms/illustration packages from artists. Submit ms with dummy. Contact: Ruth Vitale. Reports in 1-2 months. Samples returned with SASE.
Terms: Authors paid by royalty or outright purchase. Pays illustrators by project or royalty. Book catalog and ms guidelines for SASE.
Tips: "We are not presently looking for new titles."

AFRICA WORLD PRESS, P.O. Box 1892, Trenton NJ 08607. (609)844-9583. Fax: (609)844-0198. E-mail: awprsp@africanworld.com. Website: www.africaworld.com. Book publisher. **Manuscript Acquisitions:** Kassahun Checole. **Art Acquisitions:** Kassahun Checole, editor. Publishes 5 picture books/year; 15 young reader and young adult titles/year; 8 middle readers/year. Books concentrate on African and African-American life.
Fiction: Picture books, young readers: adventure, concept, contemporary, folktales, history, multicultural. Middle readers, young adults: adventure, contemporary, folktales, history, multicultural.
Nonfiction: Picture books, young readers, middle readers, young adults: concept, history, multicultural. Does not want to see self-help, gender or health books.
How to Contact/Writers: Query; submit outline/synopsis and 2 sample chapters. Reports on queries in 30-45 days; mss in 3 months. Will consider previously published work.
Illustration: Works with 10-20 illustrators/year. Reviews ms/illustration packages from artists. Query. Illustrations only: Query with samples. Reports in 3 months.
Terms: Pays authors royalty based on retail price. Pays illustrators by the project or royalty based on retail price. Book catalog available for SAE; ms and art guidelines available for SASE.

ALADDIN PAPERBACKS, 1230 Avenue of the Americas, 4th Floor, New York NY 10020. Paperback imprint of Simon & Schuster Children's Publishing Children's Division. Vice President/Editorial Director: Ellen Krieger. **Manuscript Acquisitions:** Stephen Fraser, executive editor. **Art Acquisitions:** Steve Scott, art director. Publishes 130 titles/year.
● Aladdin publishes primarily reprints of successful hardcovers from other Simon & Schuster imprints. They accept query letters with proposals for middle grade and young adult series, beginning readers and commercial nonfiction.

**FOR EXPLANATIONS OF THESE SYMBOLS,
SEE THE INSIDE FRONT AND BACK COVERS OF THIS BOOK**

ALYSON PUBLICATIONS, INC., P.O. 4371, Los Angeles CA 90078. (323)860-6065. Fax: (323)467-0173. Book publisher. **Acquisitions:** Editorial Department. Publishes 1 (projected) picture book/year and 3 (projected) young adult titles/year. "Alyson Wonderland is the line of illustrated children's books. We are looking for diverse depictions of family life for children of gay and lesbian parents."
Fiction: All levels: adventure, animal, contemporary, fantasy, history, humor, multicultural, nature/environment, science fiction. Young readers and middle readers: suspense, mystery. Teens: anthology.
Nonfiction: Teens: concept, social issues. "We like books that incorporate all racial, religious and body types, as well as dealing with children with gay and lesbian parents—which all our books must deal with. Our YA books should deal with issues faced by kids growing up gay or lesbian." Published *Heather Has Two Mommies*, by Lesléa Newman; and *Daddy's Wedding*, by Michael Willhoite.
How to Contact/Writers: Submit outline/synopsis and sample chapters (young adults); submit complete ms (picture books/young readers). Reports on queries/mss within 3 months. Include SASE.
Illustration: Works with 2 illustrators/year. Reviews mss/illustration packages from artists. Illustrations only: Submit "representative art that can be *kept on file*. Good quality photocopies are OK." Reports only if interested. Samples returned with SASE; samples kept on file.
Terms: Pays authors royalty of 8-12% based on wholesale price. "We *do* offer advances." Pays illustrators by the project (range: $25-100). Pays photographers per photo (range: $50-100). Book catalog and/or ms guidelines free for SASE.
Tips: "We only publish kids' books aimed at the children of gay or lesbian parents."

AMERICAN BIBLE SOCIETY, 1865 Broadway, New York NY 10023-7505. Fax: (212)408-1305. E-mail: americanbible.org. Website: www.americanbible.org. Book publisher. Estab. 1816. **Manuscript Acquisitions:** Barbara Bernstengel. **Art Acquisitions:** Christina Murphy, assistant director. Publishes 1-2 picture books/year; 1 young reader/year; 1 youth activity/year; and 1 young adult/year. Publishes books with spiritual/religious themes based on the Bible. "The purpose of the American Bible Society is to provide the Holy Scriptures to every man, woman and child in a language and form each can easily understand, and at a price each can easily afford. This purpose is undertaken without doctrinal note or comment." Please do not call. Submit all sample submissions, résumés, etc. for review via mail.
Nonfiction: All levels: activity books, multicultural, religion, self-help, reference, social issues and special needs. Multicultural needs include innercity lifestyle; African-American, Hispanic/Latino, Native American, Asian; mixed groups (such as choirs, classrooms, church events). "Unsolicited manuscripts will be returned unread! We prefer published writing samples with résumés so we can contact copywriters when an appropriate project comes up." Recently published *Experience Jesus Today*, a 248-page Bible storybook with prayers, discussion questions and background information, full color (ages 7-11).
How to Contact/Writers: All mss developed inhouse. Query with résumé and writing samples. Contact: Barbara Bernstengel. Unsolicited mss rejected. No credit lines given.
Illustration: Works with 2-3 illustrators/year. Reviews ms/illustration packages from artists. Contact: Christina Murphy via mail. Illustrations only: Query with samples; if interested, a personal interview will be arranged to see portfolio; send "résumés, tearsheets and promotional literature to keep; slides will be returned promptly." Reports on queries within 1 month. Samples returned; samples sometimes filed. Book catalog free on written request.
Photography: Contact: Christina Murphy via mail. Buys stock and assigns work. Looking for "nature, scenic, multicultural, intergenerational people shots." Model/property releases required. Uses any size b&w prints; 35mm, 2¼×2¼ and 4×5 transparencies. Photographers should query with samples first. If interested, a personal interview will be set up to see portfolio; provide résumé, promotional literature or tearsheets.
Terms: Photographers paid by the project (range: $800-5,000); per photo (range $100-400). Credit line given on most projects. Most photos purchased for one-time use. Factors used to determine payment for ms/illustration package include "nature and scope of project; complexity of illustration and continuity of work; number of illustrations." Pays illustrators $200-1,000/illustration; based on fair market value. Sends 2 complimentary copies of published work to illustrators. ABS owns all publication rights to illustrations and mss.
Tips: Illustrators and photographers: "Submit in a form that we can keep on file, if we like, such as tearsheets, postcards, photocopies, etc."

ATHENEUM BOOKS FOR YOUNG READERS, 1230 Avenue of the Americas, New York NY 10020. (212)698-2715. Website: www.simonsays.com/kidzone. Imprint of Simon & Schuster Children's Publishing Division. Book publisher. Vice President/Associate Publisher and Editorial Director: Jonathan Lanman. Estab. 1960.
Manuscript Acquisitions: Send queries with SASE to: Jonathan Lanman, vice president, editorial director, associate publisher; Anne Schwartz, editorial director of Anne Schwartz Books; Marcia Marshall, executive editor; Caitlyn Dlouhy, senior editor. **Art Acquisitions:** Ann Bobco. Publishes 15-20 picture books/year; 4-5 young readers/year; 20-25 middle readers/year; and 10-15 young adults/year. 10% of books by first-time authors; 50% from agented writers. "Atheneum publishes original hardcover trade books for children from pre-school age through young adult. Our list includes picture books, chapter books, mysteries, biography, science fiction, fantasy, middle grade and young adult fiction and nonfiction. We do not, however, publish textbooks, coloring or activity books, greeting cards, magazines or pamphlets or religious publications. Anne Schwartz Books is a

highly selective line of books within the Atheneum imprint. The lists of Charles Scribner's Sons Books for Young Readers have been folded into the Atheneum program."

- Atheneum does not accept unsolicited manuscripts. Send query letter only. Starting September 1, 1999, Richard Jackson joined Atheneum, where he heads his own imprint. Look to industry publications for more information.

How to Contact/Writers: Query only for all mss, regardless of length. Send letters with SASE to one of our editors at the above address. Reports on queries in 1 month; requested mss in 3 months. Publishes a book 18-24 months after acceptance. Will consider simultaneous queries from previously unpublished authors and those submitted to other publishers, "though we request that the author let us know it is a simultaneous query."

Illustration: Works with 40-50 illustrators/year. Send art samples, résumé, tearsheets to Ann Bobco, Design Dept. 4th Floor, 1230 Avenue of the Americas, New York NY 10020. Samples filed. Reports on art samples only if interested.

Terms: Pays authors in royalties of 8-10% based on retail price. Pays illustrators royalty of 5-6% or by the project. Pays photographers by the project. Sends galleys and proofs to authors; proofs to illustrators. Original artwork returned at job's completion. Ms guidelines for #10 SAE and 1 first-class stamp.

A/V CONCEPTS CORP., 30 Montauk Blvd., Oakdale NY 11769. (516)567-7227. Fax: (516)567-8745. Educational book publisher. **Manuscript Acquisitions:** Laura Solimene, editor. **Art Acquisitions:** President: Phil Solimene, president. Publishes 6 young readers/year; 6 middle readers/year; 6 young adult titles/year. 20% of books by first-time authors. Primary theme of books and multimedia is classic literature, math, science, language arts, self esteem.

Fiction: Middle readers: hi-lo. Young adults: hi-lo, multicultural, special needs. "We hire writers to adapt classic literature."

Nonfiction: All levels: activity books. Young adults: hi-lo, multicultural, science, self help, textbooks. Average word length: middle readers—300-400; young adults—500-950.

How to Contact/Writers: Fiction: Submit outline/synopsis and 1 sample chapter. Reports on queries in 1 month.

Illustration: Works with 4-6 illustrators/year. Reviews ms/illustration packages from artists. Submit ms with 3-4 pieces of final art. Illustrations only: Query with samples. Reports in 1 month. Samples returned with SASE; samples filed.

Photography: Submit samples.

Terms: Work purchased outright from authors (range $50-1,000). Pays illustrators by the project (range: $50-1,000). Pays photographers per photo (range: $25-250). Ms and art guidelines available for 9×12 SASE.

AVON BOOKS/BOOKS FOR YOUNG READERS (Avon Camelot, Avon Tempest and Avon hardcover), 1350 Avenue of the Americas, New York NY 10019. (212)261-6800. Fax: (212)261-6895. Website: www.avonbooks.com. A division of The Hearst Corporation. Book publisher. Elise Howard, editor-in-chief. **Acquisitions:** Ruth Katcher, senior editor and Abigail McAden, associate editor. Art Director: Russell Gordon. Publishes 12 hardcovers, 25-30 middle readers/year, 20-25 young adults/year. 10% of books by first-time authors; 80% of books from agented writers.

Fiction: Middle readers: comedy, contemporary, problem novels, sports, spy/mystery/adventure. Young adults: contemporary, problem novels, romance. Average length: middle readers—100-150 pages; young adults—150-250 pages. Avon does not publish preschool picture books.

Nonfiction: Middle readers: hobbies, music/dance, sports. Young adults: "growing up." Average length: middle readers—100-150 pages; young adults—150-250 pages. Recent publications: *Ragweed*, by Avi (ages 8-12); *The Key to the Indian*, by Lynne Reid Banks (ages 8-12); *Smack*, by Melvin Burgess (ages 12 and up).

How to Contact/Writers: "Please send for guidelines before submitting." Fiction/nonfiction: Submit outline/synopsis and 3 sample chapters. Reports on mss in 2-3 months. Publishes a book 18-24 months after acceptance. Will consider simultaneous submissions.

Illustration: Will not review ms/illustration packages.

Terms: Pays authors in royalties of 6% based on retail price. Average advance payment is "very open." Book catalog available for 9×12 SAE and 4 first-class stamps; ms guidelines for #10 SASE.

Tips: "We have four young readers imprints: Avon Camelot, books for the middle grades; Avon Flare and Avon Tempest, young adults; and Avon hardcover. Our list includes both individual titles and series, with the emphasis on high quality recreational reading—a fresh and original writing style; identifiable, three-dimensional characters; a strong, well-paced story that pulls readers in and keeps them interested." Writers: "Make sure you really know what a company's list looks like before you submit work. Is your work in line with what they usually do? Is

THE SUBJECT INDEX, located in the back of this book, lists book publishers and magazines according to the fiction and nonfiction subjects they seek.

your work appropriate for the age group that this company publishes for? Be aware of what's in your bookstore (but not what's in there for too long!)" Illustrators: "Submit work to art directors and people who are in charge of illustration at publishers. This is usually not handled entirely by the editorial department. Do *not* expect a response if no SASE is included with your material."

☑ Ⓐ **BANTAM DOUBLEDAY DELL, Books for Young Readers**, imprints of Random House, Inc., 1540 Broadway, New York NY 10036. (212)354-6500. Website: www.randomhouse.com. Book publisher. Vice President/Publisher: Craig Virden. Vice President/Deputy Publisher/Editor-in-Chief: Beverly Horowitz. **Manuscript Acquisitions:** Michelle Poploff, editorial director, paperbacks; Françoise Bui, executive editor, series; Wendy Lamb, executive editor; Karen Wojtyla, senior editor, Lauri Hornik, editor, hardcovers. **Art Acquisitions:** Patrice Sheridan, art director. Publishes 16 picture books/year; 35 middle reader hardcover books/year; 35 young adult hardcover titles/year. 10% of books by first-time authors; 70% of books from agented writers. "Bantam Doubleday Dell Books for Young Readers publishes award-winning books by distinguished authors and the most promising new writers."
Fiction: Picture books: adventure, animal, contemporary, fantasy, humor. Young readers: animal, contemporary, humor, fantasy, sports, suspense/mystery. Middle readers: adventure, animal, contemporary, humor, easy-to-read, fantasy, sports, suspense/mystery. Young adults: adventure, contemporary issues, humor, coming-of-age, suspense/mystery. Published *A Traitor Among the Boys*, by Phyllis Reynolds Naylor; *The Ink Drinker*, by Eric Sanvoisin; and *The Wreckers*, by Iain Lawrence.
Nonfiction: "Bantam Doubleday Dell Books for Young Readers publishes a very limited number of nonfiction titles."
How to Contact/Writers: Submit through agent; accepts queries from published authors. "All unsolicited manuscripts returned unopened with the following exceptions: Unsolicited manuscripts are accepted for the Delacorte Press Prize for a First Young Adult Novel contest (see Contests & Awards section) and the Marguerite de Angeli Prize for a First Middle Grade Novel contest (see Contests & Awards section)." Reports on queries in 6-8 weeks; mss in 3 months.
Illustration: Number of illustrations used per fiction title varies considerably. Reviews ms/illustration packages from artists. Query first. Do not send originals. "If you submit a dummy, please submit the text separately." Reports on ms/art samples only if interested. Cannot return samples; samples filed. Illustrations only: Submit tearsheets, résumé, samples that do not need to be returned. Original artwork returned at job's completion.
Terms: Pays authors advance and royalty. Pays illustrators advance and royalty or flat fee.

◨ **BARRONS EDUCATIONAL SERIES**, 250 Wireless Blvd., Hauppauge NY 11788. (516)434-3311. Fax: (516)434-3723. Book publisher. Estab. 1945. "Barrons tends to publish series of books, both for adults and children." **Acquisitions:** Grace Freedson, managing editor/director of acquisitions. Publishes 20 picture books/year; 20 young readers/year; 20 middle reader titles/year; 10 young adult titles/year. 25% of books by first-time authors; 25% of books from agented writers.
Fiction: Picture books: animal, concept, multicultural, nature/environment. Young readers: Adventure, multicultural, nature/environment, suspense/mystery. Middle readers: adventure, horror, multicultural, nature/environment, problem novels, suspense/mystery. Young adults: horror, problem novels. Recently published *Sports Success: Winning Women in Soccer*, by Marlene Targ Brill; *Word Wizardry*, by Margaret and William Kenda.
Nonfiction: Picture books: concept, reference. Young readers: how-to, reference, self help, social issues. Middle readers: hi-lo, how-to, reference, self help, social issues. Young adults: how-to, self help, social issues.
How to Contact/Writers: Fiction: Query. Nonfiction: Submit outline/synopsis and sample chapters. "Submissions must be accompanied by SASE for response. E-mailed or faxed proposals are not accepted." Reports on queries in 1 month; mss in 6-8 months. Publishes a book 1 year after acceptance. Will consider simultaneous submissions.
Illustration: Works with 10 illustrators/year. Reviews ms/illustration packages from artists. Query first; 3 chapters of ms with 1 piece of final art, remainder roughs. Illustrations only: Submit tearsheets or slides plus résumé. Reports in 3-8 weeks.
Terms: Pays authors in royalties of 10-16% based on wholesale price or buys ms outright for $2,000 minimum. Pays illustrators by the project based on retail price. Sends galleys to authors; dummies to illustrators. Book catalog, ms/artist's guidelines for 9×12 SAE.
Tips: Writers: "We are predominately on the lookout for preschool storybooks and concept books. No YA fiction/romance or novels." Illustrators: "We are happy to receive a sample illustration to keep on file for future consideration. Periodic notes reminding us of your work are acceptable." Children's book themes "are becoming much more contemporary and relevant to a child's day-to-day activities."

◪ **BEACH HOLME PUBLISHERS**, 2040 W. 12th Ave., Suite 226, Vancouver, British Columbia V6J 2G2 Canada. (604)733-4868. Fax: (604)733-4860. E-mail: bhp@beachholme.bc.ca. Website: www.beachholme.bc.ca. Book publisher. **Manuscript Acquisitions:** Joy Gugeler, managing editor. **Art Acquisitions:** Joy Gugeler. Publishes 4 young adult titles/year and 6 adult literary titles/year. 40% of books by first-time authors. "We publish primarily regional historical fiction. We publish young adult novels for children aged 8-12. We are particularly interested in works that have a historical basis and are set in the Pacific Northwest, or northern Canada. Include ideas for teachers guides or resources and appropriate topics for a classroom situation if applicable."

● Beach Holme *only* accepts work from Canadian writers.

Fiction: Young adults: contemporary, folktales, history, multicultural, nature/environment, poetry. Multicultural needs include themes reflecting cultural heritage of the Pacific Northwest, i.e., first nations, Asian, East Indian, etc. Does not want to see generic adventure or mystery with no sense of place. Average word length: middle readers—15-20,000; young adults/teens—30,000-40,000. Recently published *Shabash!*, by Ann Walsh (ages 8-12, young adult fiction); *White Jade Tiger*, by Julie Lawson (ages 10+, young adult fiction); and *Finders Keepers*, by Andrea Spalding (ages 8-12, young adult fiction).

How to Contact/Writers: Fiction: Submit outline/synopsis and 3 sample chapters. Reports on queries/mss in 1-2 months. Publishes a book 6 months-1 year after acceptance. Will consider simultaneous submissions (if specified).

Illustration: Works with 3 illustrators/year. Reports on submissions in 1-2 months if interested. Samples returned with SASE; samples filed. Originals returned at job's completion.

Terms: Pays authors 10-12% royalty based on retail price. Offers advances (average amount: $500). Pays illustrators by the project (range: $500-1,000). Pays photographers by the project (range: $100-300). Sends galleys to authors. Book catalog available for 9×12 SAE and 3 first-class Canadian stamps; ms guidelines available with SASE.

Tips: "Research what we have previously published to familiarize yourself with what we are looking for. Please, be informed."

BEECH TREE BOOKS, 1350 Avenue of the Americas, New York NY 10019.
● Beech Tree Books was dissolved due to the HarperCollins/Morrow merger.

BENCHMARK BOOKS, Imprint of Marshall Cavendish, 99 White Plains Rd., Tarrytown NY 10591. (914)332-8888. Fax: (914)332-1888. Manuscript Acquisitions: Joyce Stanton and Kate Nunn. Publishes 90 young reader, middle reader and young adult books/year. "We look for interesting treatments of primarily nonfiction subjects related to elementary, middle school and high school curriculum."

Nonfiction: Most nonfiction topics should be curriculum related. Average word length for books: 4,000-20,000. All books published as part of a series.

How to Contact/Writers: Nonfiction: submit complete ms or submit outline/synopsis and 1 or more sample chapters. Reports on queries and mss in 3 months. Publishes a book 2 years after acceptance. Will consider simultaneous submissions.

Photography: Buys stock and assigns work.

Terms: Pays authors royalty based on retail price or buys work outright. Offers advances. Sends galleys to authors. Book catalog available. All imprints included in a single catalog.

THE BENEFACTORY, One Post Rd., Fairfield CT 06430. (203)255-7744. Fax: (203)255-6200. Book publisher. Estab. 1990. **Acquisitions:** Cindy Germain, production manager. Publishes 6-12 picture books/year with the Humane Society of the United States; 6-12 picture books/year with The National Wildlife Federation. 50% of books by first-time authors. The Benefactory publishes "classic" true stories about real animals, through licenses with the Humane Society of the United States and National Wildlife Federation. Each title is accompanied by a read-along audiocassette and a plush animal. A percentage of revenues benefits the HSUS or NWF. Target age for NWF titles: 4-7; for HSUS titles: 5-10.

Nonfiction: Picture books: nature/environment; young readers: animal, nature/environment. Average word length: HSUS titles: 1,200-1,500; NWF titles: 700-800. Recently published *Chessie, the Travelin' Man*, written by Randy Houk, illustrated by Paula Bartlett (ages 5-10, picture book); *Condor Magic*, written by Lyn Littlefield Hoopes, illustrated by Peter C. Stone (ages 5-10, picture book); and *Caesar: On Deaf Ears*, written by Loren Spiotta-DiMare, illustrated by Kara Lee (ages 5-10, picture book).

How to Contact/Writers: Reports on queries in 3 weeks; ms in 6 months. Publishes a book 1 year after acceptance. Will consider simultaneous submissions. Send SASE for writer's guidelines.

Illustration: Works with 6-8 illustrators/year. Uses color artwork only. Reviews ms/illustration packages from artists. Query or send ms with dummy. Illustrations only: Send résumé, promo sheet and tearsheets to be kept on file. Reports in 6 months. Samples returned with SASE; samples filed. Send SASE for artist guidelines.

Terms: Pays authors royalty of 3-5% based on wholesale price. Offers advances (Average amount: $5,000). Pays illustrators royalty of 3-5% based on wholesale price. Sends galleys to authors; dummies to illustrators. Originals returned to artist at job's completion. Book catalog available for 8 1/2×11 SASE; ms and art guidelines available for SASE.

BETHANY HOUSE PUBLISHERS, 11400 Hampshire Ave. S., Minneapolis MN 55438-2455. (612)829-2500. Website: www.bethanyhouse.com. Book publisher. **Manuscript Acquisitions:** Rochelle Glöege, Natasha

---

VISIT THE WRITER'S DIGEST WEBSITE at www.writersdigest.com for hot new markets, daily market updates, writers' guidelines and much more.

Sperling. **Art Acquisitions:** Cathy Engstrom. Publishes 2 young readers/year; 18 middle-grade readers/year; and 16 young adults/year. Bethany House Publishers is a non-profit publisher seeking to publish imaginative, excellent books that reflect an evangelical worldview without being preachy. Publishes picture books under Bethany Backyard imprint.

Fiction: Series for early readers, middle readers, young adults: historical and contemporary adventure, history, humor, multicultural, suspense/mystery, religion, sports and current issues. Young adult: romance. Does not want to see poetry or science fiction. Average word length: early readers—6,000; young readers—20,000; young adults—40,000. Published *Too Many Secrets*, by Patricia H. Rushford (young adult/teens, mystery series); *The Ghost of KRZY*, by Bill Myers (middle-graders, mystery/humor series); and *The Mystery of the Dancing Angels*, by Elspeth Campbell Murphy (young readers, mystery series).

Nonfiction: Young readers, middle readers, young adults: religion/devotional, self-help, social issues. Published *Can I Be a Christian Without Being Weird?*, by Kevin Johnson (early teens, devotional book); and *Hot Topics, Tough Questions*, by Bill Myers (young adult/teen, Biblically based advice).

How to Contact/Writers: Fiction/Nonfiction: Query. Reports on queries in 2 months; mss in 4 months. Picture Books: does not accept unsolicited mss, query only. Publishes a book 12-18 months after acceptance. Will consider simultaneous submissions.

Illustration: Works with 12 illustrators/year. Reviews illustration samples from artists. Illustrations only: Query with samples. Reports in 2 months. Samples returned with SASE.

Terms: Pays authors royalty based on net sales. Pays illustrators by the project. Pays photographers by the project. Sends galleys to authors. Book catalog available for 11 × 14 SAE and 5 first-class stamps.

Tips: "Research the market, know what is already out there. Study our catalog before submitting material. We look for an evangelical message woven delicately into a strong plot and topics that seek to broaden the reader's experience and perspective."

BEYOND WORDS PUBLISHING, INC., 20827 N.W. Cornell Rd., Hillsboro OR 97124-1808. (503)531-8700. Fax: (503)531-8773. E-mail: beyondword.com. Website: www.beyondword.com. Book publisher. Director, Children's Division: Michelle Roehm. **Acquisitions:** Marianne Monson. Publishes 6-10 picture books/year and 2 nonfiction teen books/year. 50% of books by first-time authors. "Our company mission statement is 'Inspire to Integrity,' so it's crucial that your story inspires children in some way. Our books are high quality, gorgeously illustrated, meant to be enjoyed as a child and throughout life."

Fiction: Picture books: adventure, animal, contemporary, fantasy, feminist, folktales, history, multicultural, nature/environment, spiritual. "We are looking for authors/illustrators; stories that will appeal and inspire." Average length: picture books—32 pages. Recently published *Turtle Songs*, by Margaret Wolfson, illustrated by Karla Sachi (ages 5-10, South Pacific myth).

Nonfiction: Picture books, young readers: biography, history, multicultural, nature/environment. *The Book of Goddesses*, by Kris Waldherr (all ages, multicultural historic reference); and *Girls Know Best* (compilation of 38 teen girls' writing—ages 7-15).

How to Contact/Writers: Fiction: Submit complete ms. Nonfiction: Submit outline/synopsis. Reports on queries/mss in 6 months. Will consider simultaneous submissions and previously published work.

Illustration: Works with 4-6 illustrators/year. Reviews ms/illustration packages from artists. Submit ms with 2-3 pieces of final art. "No originals please!" Illustrations only: Send résumé, promo sheet, "samples—no originals!" Reports in 6 months only if interested. Samples returned with SASE; samples filed.

Photography: Works on assignment only.

Terms: Sends galleys to authors; dummies to illustrators. Book catalog for SAE; ms and artist's guidelines for SASE.

Tips: "Please research the books we have previously published. This will give you a good idea if your proposal fits with our company."

BLUE SKY PRESS, 555 Broadway, New York NY 10012. (212)343-6100. Website: www.scholastic.com. Book publisher. Imprint of Scholastic Inc. **Acquisitions:** Bonnie Verberg. Publishes 10 picture books/year; 4 middle readers/year. 5% of books by first-time authors. Publishes hardcover children's fiction and nonfiction including high-quality novels and picture books by new and established authors.

• Blue Sky is currently not accepting unsolicited submissions. Blue Sky title *No, David!*, written and illustrated by David Shannon, won a 1999 Caldecott Honor Award.

Fiction: Picture books: adventure, animal, concept, contemporary, fantasy, folktales, history, humor, multicultural, nature/environment, poetry. Young readers: adventure, contemporary, fantasy, folktales, history, humor, multicultural, nature/environment, poetry. Young adults: adventure, anthology, contemporary, fantasy, history, humor, multicultural, poetry. Multicultural needs include "strong fictional or themes featuring non-white characters and cultures." Does not want to see mainstream religious, bibliotherapeutic, adult. Average length: picture books—varies; young adults—150 pages. Recently published *To Every Thing There Is a Season*, illustrated by Leo and Diane Dillon (all ages, picture book); and *Bluish*, by Virginia Hamilton; *No David!*, by David Shannon; *The Adventures of Captain Underpants*, by Dav Pilkey; *The Heavenly Village*, by Cynthia Rylant.

How to Contact/Writers: "Due to large numbers of submissions, we are discouraging unsolicited submissions—send query (don't call!) only if you feel certain we publish the type of book you have written." Fiction: Query (novels, picture books). Reports on queries in 6 months. Publishes a book 1-3 years after acceptance;

depending on chosen illustrator's schedule. Will not consider simultaneous submissions.

Illustration: Works with 10 illustrators/year. Uses both b&w and color artwork. Reviews illustration packages "only if illustrator is the author." Submit ms with dummy. Illustrations only: Query with samples, tearsheets. Reports only if interested. Samples returned with SASE. Original artwork returned at job's completion.

Terms: Author's royalty varies by project—usually standard trade rates. Offers variable advance. Pays illustrators standard royalty based on retail price.

Tips: "Read currently published children's books. Revise—never send a first draft. Find your own voice, style, and subject. With material from new people we look for a theme or style strong enough to overcome the fact that the author/illustrator is unknown in the market."

BOINGO BOOKS, INC., 12720 Yardley Dr., Boca Raton FL 33428. **Acquisitions:** Lisa McCourt, creative director. Packages books for major children's book publishers. Averages 10 titles/year.

Fiction/Nonfiction: Recently published *I Miss You, Stinky Face,* by Lisa McCourt, illustrated by Cyd Moore; *The Candy Counting Book,* by Lisa McCourt.

How to Contact/Writers: Not accepting unsolicited mss. "To check for a change in our submission status, send a #10 SASE to the above address."

Illustration: Works with 10 illustrators/year. Send samples, résumé, promo sheet, client list. Samples are filed unless illustrator has included a SASE and "requested the return of the materials." Contact: Lisa McCourt.

Photography: Buys photos from freelancers. Contact: Lisa McCourt. Works on assignment only. Submit résumé, client list, samples or promo pieces.

Terms: All contracts negotiated separately; offers variable advance.

BOYDS MILLS PRESS, 815 Church St., Honesdale PA 18431. (800)490-5111. Fax: (717)253-0179. Imprint: Wordsong (poetry). Book publisher. **Manuscript Acquisitions:** Beth Troop. **Art Acquisitions:** Tim Gillner. 5% of books from agented writers. Estab. 1990. "We publish a wide range of quality children's books of literary merit, from preschool to young adult."

Fiction: All levels: adventure, contemporary, history, humor, multicultural, poetry. Picture books: animal. Young readers, middle readers, young adult: problem novels, sports. Middle readers, young adults: problem novels, sports. Multicultural themes include any story showing a child as an integral part of a culture and which provides children with insight into a culture they otherwise might be unfamiliar with. "Please query us on the appropriateness of suggested topics for middle grade and young adult. For all other submissions send entire manuscript." Does not want to see talking animals, coming-of-age novels, romance and fantasy/science fiction. Recently published *Kat's Surrender* (novel).

Nonfiction: All levels: nature/environment, science. Picture books, young readers, middle readers: animal, multicultural. Does not want to see reference/curricular text. Recently published *Lost Treasure of the Inca*, by Peter Lourie (nonfiction, ages 8 and up); *Coyote*, by Stephen Swinburne (nonfiction); and *Wild Country*, by David Harrison (poetry, ages 9 and up).

How to Contact/Writers: Fiction/Nonfiction: Submit complete ms or submit through agent. Query on middle reader, young adult and nonfiction. Reports on queries/mss in 1 month.

Illustration: Works with 25 illustrators/year. Reviews ms/illustration packages from artists. Submit complete ms with 1 or 2 pieces of art. Illustrations only: Query with samples; send résumé and slides. Reports back only if interested. Samples returned with SASE. Samples filed. Originals returned at job's completion.

Photography: Assigns work.

Terms: Authors paid royalty or work purchased outright. Offers advances. Illustrators paid by the project or royalties; varies. Photographers paid by the project, per photo, or royalties; varies. Mss/artist's guidelines available for #10 SASE.

Tips: "Picture books—with fresh approaches, not worn themes—are our strongest need at this time. Check to see what's already on the market before submitting your story."

BRIGHT LAMB PUBLISHERS, P.O. Box 844, Evans GA 30809. (706)863-2237. Fax: (706)863-9971. E-mail: brightlamb@aol.com. Website: www.brightlamb.com. Book publisher. Estab. 1995. **Contact:** Acquisitions Editor. "We publish books with product concepts or gift items to coincide with the storyline." Publishes 3 picture books/year; 3 young readers/year. 50% of books by first-time authors.

● Bright Lamb is not currently accepting mss.

Illustration: Works with 3 illustrators/year. Reviews ms/illustration packages from artists. Send ms with dummy. Illustrations only: Query with samples; send résumé, client list and tear sheets to be kept on file. Reports back only if interested.

Terms: Pays authors royalty based on wholesale price. Pays illustrators royalty based on wholesale price. Book

THE AGE-LEVEL INDEX, located in the back of this book, lists book publishers and magazines according to the age-groups for which they need material.

catalog available for 4×7 SASE and 2 first-class stamps; ms guidelines available for SASE.
Tips: "Study our catalog before submitting."

☑ **BRIGHT RING PUBLISHING, INC**, P.O. Box 31338, Bellingham WA 98228-3338. (360)734-1601 or (800)480-4278. Fax: (360)676-1271. E-mail: maryann@brightring.com. Website: www.brightring.com/books. Estab. 1985. **Acquisitions:** MaryAnn Kohl. Publishes 1 young reader title/year. 50% of books by first-time authors. "Bright Ring Publishing is *not* looking for picture books, juvenile fiction, poetry, manuals or coloring books. We are highly interested in creative activity/resource books for adults to use with children, or for children to use independently. We prefer books that match our own successful style for pre-school through elementary school (ages 3-12) and must work equally well for a parent and child at home or a teacher and children at school." See examples at our website.
Nonfiction: Young readers and middle readers: activity books involving art ideas, hobbies, cooking, how-to, multicultural, music/dance, nature/environment, science. "No picture books, no poetry, no stories of any kind and no coloring books." Average length: "about 125 ideas/book. We are moving into only recipe-style resource books in any variety of subject areas—useful with children 2-12. Interested in integrated art with other subjects." Recently published SCRIBBLE ART: *Independent Creative Art Experiences for Children*; MUDWORKS: *Creative Clay, Dough, and Modeling Experiences*; and SCIENCE ARTS: *Discovering Science Through Art Experiences* (all by Mary Ann Kohl); and *Discovering Great Artists: Hands-on Art for Children in the Styles of the Great Masters* (1997).
How to Contact/Writers: Nonfiction: write for guidelines; submit complete ms. Reports on queries in 2 weeks; mss in 6 weeks. Publishes a book 1 year after acceptance. Will consider simultaneous submissions.
Illustration: Works with 2 illustrators/year. Prefers to review "black line (drawings) for text." Reviews ms/illustration packages from artists. "Query first." Write for guidelines. Illustrations only: Query with samples; send tearsheets and "sample of ideas requested after query." Reports in 1 month.
Terms: Pays authors in royalties of 3-5% based on net sales. Work purchased outright (range: $500-2,000). Pays illustrators $500-2,000. Also offers "free books and discounts for future books." Book catalog, ms/artist's guidelines for business-size SAE and 33¢ postage.
Tips: "We cannot accept book ideas which require unusual packaging such as attached toys or unique binding or paper. Please look at one of our books to familiarize yourself with our style before submitting. We are very specific."

Ⓐ **BROWNDEER PRESS**, 9 Monroe Pkwy., Suite 240, Lake Oswego OR 97035-1487. (503)697-1017. Imprint of Harcourt Brace & Co. **Manuscript Acquisitions:** Linda Zuckerman, editorial director. Publishes 12 titles/year.
• Browndeer only accepts mss from agents, previously published authors, and SCBWI members.
Fiction: Picture books, young readers: adventure, animal, fantasy, folktales, humor, multicultural, nature/environment, poetry.
Nonfiction: Picture books: music/dance, nature/environment.
How to Contact/Writers: For picture books send complete ms with cover letter listing publishing credits or résumé; for longer fiction and nonfiction send cover letter, outline/synopsis and 3 sample chapters. Include SASE with all submissions. Reports on queries/mss in 3 months.
Illustration: Works with 9 illustrators/year. Send samples with SASE. Reports on artist's queries/submissions in 3 months. Originals returned at job's completion.
Terms: Pay authors royalty. Pay illustrators royalty for books; flat fee for book jackets. Send SASE for writer's and artist's guidelines.

CANDLEWICK PRESS, 2067 Massachusetts Ave., Cambridge MA 02140. (617)661-3330. Fax: (617)661-0565. E-mail: bigbear@candlewick.com. Children's book publisher. Estab. 1991. **Manuscript Acquisitions:** Liz Bickenll, editor-in-chief; Amy Ehrlich, editor-at-large; Mary Lee Donovan, executive editor; Gale Pryor, editor. **Art Acquisitions:** Ann Stott, associate director; Anne Moore, senior book designer; Chris Paul, art director; and Julie Bushway, senior book designer. Publishes 175 picture books/year; 5 middle readers/year; and 5 young adult titles/year. 5% of books by first-time authors. "Our books are truly for children, and we strive for the very highest standards in the writing, illustrating, designing and production of all of our books. And we are not averse to risk."
• Candlewick Press is not accepting queries or unsolicited mss at this time.
Fiction: Picture books, young readers: animal, concept, contemporary, fantasy, folktales, history, humor, multicultural, nature/environment, poetry. Middle readers, young adults: animal, anthology, contemporary, fantasy, history, humor, multicultural, poetry, science fiction, sports, suspense/mystery.
Nonfiction: Picture books: activity books, concept, biography, geography, nature/environment. Young readers: activity books, biography, geography, nature/environment.
Illustration: Works with 20 illustrators/year. "We prefer to see a variety of the artist's style." Reviews ms/illustration packages from artists. "General samples only please." Illustrations only: Submit résumé and portfolio to the attention of Design Dept. Reports on samples in 4-6 weeks. Samples returned with SASE; samples filed.
Terms: Pays authors royalty of 2.5-10% based on retail price. Offers advances. Pays illustrators 2.5-10% royalty

based on retail price. Sends galleys to authors; dummies to illustrators. Photographers paid 2.5-10% royalty. Original artwork returned at job's completion.

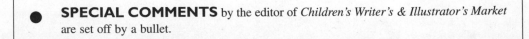 **CAROLRHODA BOOKS, INC.**, Division of the Lerner Publishing Group, 241 First Ave. N., Minneapolis MN 55401. (612)332-3344 or (800)328-4929. Fax: (612)332-7615. Website: www.lernerbooks.com. Imprint of Lerner. Book publisher. Estab. 1969. **Acquisitions:** Rebecca Poole, submissions editor. Accepts fiction and nonfiction for readers K through grade 6. List includes picture books, biographies, nature and science titles, multicultural and introductory geography books and fiction for beginning readers.

How to Contact/Writers: Submissions are accepted in the months of March and October only. Submissions received in any month other than March or October will be returned unopened to the sender. The Lerner Publishing Group does not publish alphabet books, puzzle books, songbooks, textbooks, workbooks, religious subject matter or plays. A SASE is required for all submissions. Please allow 2-6 months for a response.

CARTWHEEL BOOKS, Imprint of Scholastic Inc., 555 Broadway, New York NY 10012. (212)343-6100. Fax: (212)343-4437. Website: www.scholastic.com. Book publisher. Vice President/Editorial Director: Bernette G. Ford. **Manuscript Acquisitions:** Liza Baker. **Art Acquisitions:** Edie Weinberg, art director. Publishes 25-30 picture books/year; 30-35 easy readers/year; 15-20 novelty/concept books/year. "With each Cartwheel list, we strive for a pleasing balance among board books and novelty books, hardcover picture books and gift books, nonfiction, paperback storybooks and easy readers. Cartwheel seeks to acquire 'novelties' that are books first; play objects second. Even without its gimmick, a Cartwheel novelty book should stand along as a valid piece of children's literature. We want all our books to be inviting and appealing, and to have inherent educational and social value. We believe that small children who develop personal 'relationships' with books and grow up with a love for reading, become book consumers, and ultimately better human beings."

● See Writing Effective Query Letters on page 20 for query tips from Editor Liza Baker. Also see First Books on page 45 for an interview with Cartwheel author Kathleen Keller on her book *I Dare You: Stories to Scare You.*

Fiction: Picture books: adventure, animal, anthology, concept, contemporary, fantasy, folktales, history, humor, multicultural, nature/environment, poetry, science fiction, sports, suspense/mystery. Young readers: adventure, animal, concept, contemporary, fantasy, folktales, history, humor, multicultural, nature/environment, poetry, science fiction. Does not want to see too much of picture books; fantasy; folktales; history; nature. Average work length: picture books—1-3,000; young readers—100-3,000.

Nonfiction: Picture books, young readers: animal, biography, concept, history, multicultural, nature/environment, sports. "Most of our nonfiction is either written on assignment or is within a series. We do not want to see any arts/crafts or cooking." Average word length: picture books—100-3,000; young readers—100-3,000.

How to Contact/Writers: Cartwheel Books is no longer accepting unsolicited mss; query. All unsolicited materials will be returned unread. Fiction/nonfiction: For previously published or agented authors, submit complete ms. Reports on queries in 1-2 months; mss in 3-6 months. Publishes a book 18-24 months after acceptance. Will consider simultaneous submissions; electronic submissions via disk or modem; previously published work.

Illustration: Works with 100 illustrators/year. Reviews ms/illustration packages from artists. Send ms with dummy. Illustrations only: Query with samples; arrange personal portfolio review; send promo sheet, tearsheets to be kept on file. Reports in 2 months. Samples returned with SASE; samples filed.

Photography: Buys stock and assigns work. Uses photos of kids, families, vehicles, toys, animals. Submit published samples, color promo piece.

Terms: Pays authors royalty of 2-8% based on retail price or work purchased outright for $600-5,000. Offers advances (Average amount: $3,000). Pays illustrators by the project (range: $2,000-10,000); royalty of 1-3% based on retail price; flat fee; or advance against royalties. Photographers paid by the project (range: $250-10,000); per photo (range: $250-500); or royalty of 1-3% of wholesale price. Sends galley to authors; dummy to illustrators. Originals returned to artist at job's completion. Book catalog available for 9 × 12 SAE and 2 first-class stamps; ms guidelines for SASE.

Tips: "Know what types of books we do. Check out bookstores or catalogs to see where your work would 'fit' best."

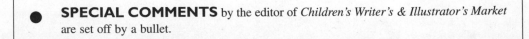 **CHARLESBRIDGE**, 85 Main St., Watertown MA 02472. (617)926-0329. Fax: (617)926-5720. E-mail: tradeeditorial@charlesbridge.com. Website: www.charlesbridge.com. Book publisher. Estab. 1980. Publishes 80% nonfiction, 20% fiction titles, picture books and board books. Publishes nature, science, multicultural social studies and fiction picture books and board books. Charlesbridge also has an educational division. Contact: Trade Editorial Department, submissions editor.

Fiction: Picture books: "Strong, realistic stories with enduring themes." Considers the following categories:

● **SPECIAL COMMENTS** by the editor of *Children's Writer's & Illustrator's Market* are set off by a bullet.

adventure, concept, contemporary, folktales, health, history, humor, multicultural, nature/environment, special needs, religion, sports, suspense/mystery. Recently published: *The Ugly Vegetables*, by Grace Lin.
Nonfiction: Picture books: animal, biography, careers, concept, geography, health, history, multicultural, music/dance, nature/environment, religion, science, social issues, special needs, hobbies, sports. Average word length: picture books—1,500. Recently published: *Turn of the Century*, by Ellen Jackson, illustrated by Jan Davey Ellis; and *COW*, by Jules Older, illustrated by Lyn Severance; and *Shockers of the Sea*, by Caroline Arnold, illustrated by Crista Forest.
How to Contact/Writers: Send ms and SASE. Exclusive submissions only. Reports on queries/mss in 2 months. Prefer full ms.
Illustration: Works with 5-10 illustrators/year. Uses color artwork only. Illustrations only: Query with samples; provide résumé, tearsheets to be kept on file. "Send no original artwork, please." Reports back only if interested. Samples returned with SASE; samples filed. Originals returned at job's completion.
Terms: Pays authors in royalties or work purchased outright. Pays illustrators by the project. Ms/art guidelines available for SASE. Exclusive submissions only.
Tips: Wants "books that have humor and are factually correct. Concerning educational material, we want to integrate the reading of good stories with instructional material."

CHICAGO REVIEW PRESS, 814 N. Franklin St., Chicago IL 60610. (312)337-0747. Fax: (312)337-5985. E-mail: publish@ipgbook.com. Website: www.ipgbook.com. Book publisher. Estab. 1973. **Manuscript Acquisitions:** Cynthia Sherry, executive editor. **Art Acquisitions:** Joan Sommers, art director. Publishes 3-4 middle readers/year and "about 4" young adult titles/year. 50% of books by first-time authors; 30% of books from agented authors. "Chicago Review Press publishes high-quality, nonfiction, educational activity books that extend the learning process through hands-on projects and accurate and interesting text. We look for activity books that are as much fun as they are constructive and informative."
Nonfiction: Picture books, young readers, middle readers and young adults: activity books, arts/crafts, multicultural, history, nature/environment, science. "We're interested in hands-on, educational books; anything else probably will be rejected." Average length: young readers and young adults—175 pages. Recently published *Shakespeare for Kids*, by Margie Blumberg and Colleen Aagesen (ages 9 and up); *Civil War for Kids*, by Janice Herbert (ages 9 and up); and *Bite-Sized Science*, by John H. Falk and Kristi Rosenberg, illustrated by Bonnie Matthews (ages 3-8).
How to Contact/Writers: Enclose cover letter and no more than table of contents and 1-2 sample chapters. Send for guidelines. Reports on queries/mss in 1-2 months. Publishes a book 1-2 years after acceptance. Will consider simultaneous submissions and previously published work.
Illustration: Works with 6 illustrators/year. Uses primarily b&w artwork. Reviews ms/illustration packages from artists. Submit 1-2 chapters of ms with corresponding pieces of final art. Illustrations only: Query with samples, résumé. Reports back only if interested. Samples returned with SASE.
Photography: Buys photos from freelancers ("but not often"). Buys stock and assigns work. Wants "instructive photos. We consult our files when we know what we're looking for on a book-by-book basis." Uses b&w prints.
Terms: Pays authors royalty of 7½-12½% based on retail price. Offers advances ("but not always") of $500-1,500. Pays illustrators by the project (range varies considerably). Pays photographers by the project (range varies considerably). Original artwork "usually" returned at job's completion. Book catalog/ms guidelines available for $3.
Tips: "We're looking for original activity books for small children and the adults caring for them—new themes and enticing projects to occupy kids' imaginations and promote their sense of personal creativity. We like activity books that are as much fun as they are constructive. Please write for guidelines so you'll know what we're looking for."

CHILDREN'S BOOK PRESS, 246 First St. #101, San Francisco CA 94105. (415)995-2200. Fax: (415)995-2222. E-mail: cbookpress@cbookpress.org. **Acquisitions:** Submissions Editor. Publishes 6-8 picture books/year. 50% of books by first-time authors. "Children's Book Press is a nonprofit publisher of multicultural and bilingual children's literature. We publish folktales and contemporary stories reflecting the traditions and culture of the emerging majority in the United States and from countries around the world. Our goal is to help broaden the base of children's literature in this country to include more stories from the African-American, Asian-American, Hispanic and Native American communities as well as the diverse Spanish-speaking communities throughout the Americas."
   ● Children's Book Press title, *i see the rhythm*, by Toyomi Igus, illustrated by Michelle Wood, won the 1999 Coretta Scott King Illustrator Award.
Fiction: Picture books, young readers: contemporary, folktales, history, multicultural, poetry. Average word length: picture books—800-1,600.
Nonfiction: Picture books, young readers: multicultural.
How to Contact/Writers: Submit complete ms to Submissions Editor. Reports on queries in 2-3 weeks; mss in 4 months. Publishes a book 1 year after acceptance. Will consider simultaneous submissions.
Illustration: Works with 4-5 illustrators/year. Uses color artwork only. Reviews ms/illustration packages from artists. Send ms with 3 or 4 color photocopies. Illustrations only: Send slides. Reports only of interested. Samples returned with SASE.

Terms: Pays authors and illustrators royalty of 3-8% based on wholesale price. Original artwork returned at job's completion. Book catalog available; ms guidelines available for SASE.

Tips: "Vocabulary level should be approximately third grade (eight years old) or below. Keep in mind, however, that many of the young people who read our books may be nine, ten, or eleven years old or older. Their life experiences are often more advanced than their reading level, so try to write a story that will appeal to a fairly wide age range. We are especially interested in humorous stories and original stories about contemporary life from the multicultural communities mentioned above by writers *from* those communities."

CHINA BOOKS & PERIODICALS, 2929 24th St., San Francisco CA 94110. (415)282-2994. Fax: (415)282-0994. E-mail: info@chinabooks.com. Website: www.chinabooks.com. Book publisher, distributor, wholesaler. Estab. 1960. **Acquisitions:** Greg Jones, editor. Publishes 1 picture book/year; 1 middle readers/year; and 1 young adult title/year. 50% of books by first-time authors. Only publishes books about China and Chinese culture. Recently published *Sing Chinese! Popular Children's Songs & Lullabies*, by Ma Baolin and Cindy Ma (children—adults/song book); and *The Moon Maiden and Other Asian Folktales*, by Hua Long (children to age 12/folktales). "China Books is the main importer and distributor of books and magazines from China, providing an ever-changing variety of useful tooks for travelers, scholars and others interested in China and Chinese culture."

Fiction: All levels: animal, anthology, folktales, history, multicultural, nature/environment.

Nonfiction: All levels: activity books, animal, arts/crafts, cooking, how-to, multicultural, music/dance, reference, textbooks. Recently published *West to East: A Young Girl's Journey to China*, by Qian Gao (young adult nonfiction travel journal).

How to Contact/Writers: Fiction/Nonfiction: Query. Reports on queries and mss in 2 months. Publishes a book 1 year after acceptance. Will consider simultaneous submissions, electronic submissions via disk or modem, previously published work.

Illustration: Works with 4-5 illustrators/year. Reviews ms/illustration packages from artists. Query. Illustrations only: Query with samples. Send résumé, promo sheet, tearsheets. Reports in 1 month only if interested. Samples returned with SASE; samples filed.

Terms: Pays authors 4-10% royalty based on wholesale price or work purchased outright. Pays illustrators and photographers by the project (range $400-1,500) or royalty based on wholesale price. Sends galleys to authors; dummies to illustrators. Originals returned to artist at job's completion. See website for guidelines.

CHRISTIAN ED. PUBLISHERS, P.O. Box 26639, San Diego CA 92196. (619)578-4700. Book publisher. Senior Editor: Dr. Lon Ackelson. Managing Editor: Carol Rogers. Publishes 80 Bible curriculum titles/year. "We publish curriculum for children and youth, including program and student books (for youth) and take-home papers (for children)—all handled by our assigned freelance writers only."

Fiction: Young readers: contemporary. Middle readers: adventure, contemporary, suspense/mystery. "We publish fiction for Bible club take-home papers. All fiction is on assignment only."

Nonfiction: Publishes Bible curriculum and take-home papers for all ages. Recently published *All-Stars for Jesus*, by Treena Herrington and Letitia Zook, illustrated by Beverly Warren (Bible club curriculum for grades 4-6); and *Honeybees Classroom Activity Sheets*, by Janet Miller and Wanda Pelfrey, illustrated by Aiko Gilson and Terry Walderhaug (Bible club curriculum for ages 2-3).

How to Contact/Writers: Fiction/Nonfiction: Query. Reports on queries in 4-5 weeks. Publishes a book 1 year after acceptance. Send SASE for guidelines.

Illustration: Works with 6-7 illustrators/year. Uses primarily b&w artwork. Query; include a SASE; we'll send an application form. Contact: Carol Rogers, managing editor. Reports in 3-4 weeks. Samples returned with SASE.

Terms: Work purchased outright from authors for 3¢/word. Pays illustrators by the project (range: $300-400/book). Book catalog available for 9 × 12 SAE and 4 first-class stamps; ms and art guidelines available for SASE.

Tips: "Read our guidelines carefully before sending us a manuscript or illustrations. All writing and illustrating is done on assignment only and must be age-appropriate (preschool-6th grade)."

CHRISTIAN PUBLICATIONS, INC., 3825 Hartzdale Dr., Camp Hill PA 17011. (717)761-7044. Fax: (717)761-7273. E-mail: editors@cpi-horizon.com. Website: www.cpi-horizon.com. Managing Editor: David Fessenden. **Manuscript Acquisitions:** George McPeek. **Art Acquisitions:** Marilynne Foster. Imprints: Christian Publications, Horizon Books. Publishes 1-2 young adult titles/year. 50% of books by first-time authors. The missions of this press are promoting participation in spreading the gospel worldwide and promoting Christian growth.

Fiction: "Not accepting unsolicited fiction."

Nonfiction: Young adults: religion. Does not want to see evangelistic/new Christian material. "Children and teens are too often assumed to have a shallow faith. We want to encourage a deeper walk with God." Average word length: young adults—25,000-40,000 words. Recently published *Grace and Guts to Live for God*, by Les Morgan (Bible study on Hebrews, 1 and 2 Peter); and *Holy Moses! And other Adventures in Vertical Living*, by Bob Hostetler. (Both are teen books which encourage a deeper commitment to God. Both illustrated by Ron Wheeler.) "Not accepting unsolicited material for age levels lower than teenage."

How to Contact/Writers: Nonfiction: Submit outline/synopsis and 2 sample chapters (including chapter one). Reports on queries in 6 weeks, mss in 2 months. Publishes a book 8-16 months after acceptance. Will consider simultaneous submissions, electronic submissions via disk or modem ("a one page, please").

Illustration: Works with 1-3 illustrators/year. Query with samples. Contact: Marilynne Foster, promotions coordinator. Reports back only if interested. Samples returned with SASE; samples filed.

Terms: Pays authors royalty of 5-10% based on retail price. Offers advances. Pays illustrators by the project. Sends galleys to authors; dummies to illustrators (sometimes). Originals returned to artist at job's completion (if requested). Ms guidelines available for SASE.

Tips: "Writers: Only opportunity is in teen market, especially if you have experience working with and speaking to teens. Illustrators: Show us a few samples."

CHRONICLE BOOKS, 85 Second St., San Francisco CA 94105. (415)537-3730. Fax: (415)537-4420. Book publisher. **Acquisitions:** Victoria Rock, associate publisher, children's books; Amy Novesky. Publishes 35-60 (both fiction and nonfiction) books/year; 5-10 middle readers, young adult nonfiction titles/year. 10-25% of books by first-time authors; 20-40% of books from agented writers.

Fiction: Picture books: animal, folktales, history, multicultural, nature/environment. Young readers: animal, folktales, history, multicultural, nature/environment, poetry. Middle readers: animal, history, multicultural, nature/environment, poetry, problem novels. Young adults: multicultural needs include "projects that feature diverse children in everyday situations." Recently published *Old Velvet*, by Mary Whitcomb; *Frank Was a Monster Who Wanted to Dance*, by Keith Graves; *Penguin Dreams*, by J.otto Seibold and Vivian Walsh.

Nonfiction: Picture books: animal, history, multicultural, nature/environment, science. Young readers: animal, arts/crafts, cooking, geography, history, multicultural and science. Middle readers: animal, arts/crafts, biography, cooking, geography, history, multicultural and nature/environment. Young adults: biography and multicultural. Recently published *Story Painter: The Life of Jacob Lawrence*, by John Duggleby; *Seven Weeks on an Iceberg*, by Keith Potter (Doodlezoo series).

How to Contact/Writers: Fiction/Nonfiction: Submit complete ms (picture books); submit outline/synopsis and 3 sample chapters (for older readers). Reports on queries/mss in 4-18 weeks. Publishes a book 1-3 years after acceptance. Will consider simultaneous submissions, as long as they are marked "multiple submission." Will not consider submissions by fax or e-mail. Must include SASE.

Illustration: Works with 15-20 illustrators/year. Wants "unusual art, graphically strong, something that will stand out on the shelves. Either bright and modern or very traditional. Fine art, not mass market." Reviews ms/ illustration packages from artists. "Indicate if project *must* be considered jointly, or if editor may consider text and art separately." Illustrations only: Submit samples of artist's work (not necessarily from book, but in the envisioned style). Slides, tearsheets and color photocopies OK. (No original art.) Dummies helpful. Résumé helpful. "If samples sent for files, generally no response—unless samples are not suited to list, in which case samples are returned. Queries and project proposals responded to in same time frame as author query/proposals."

Photography: Purchases photos from freelancers. Works on assignment only. Wants nature/natural history photos.

Terms: Generally pays authors in royalties based on retail price "though we do occasionally work on a flat fee basis." Advance varies. Illustrators paid royalty based on retail price or flat fee. Sends proofs to authors and illustrators. Book catalog for 9 × 12 SAE and 8 first-class stamps; ms guidelines for #10 SASE.

Tips: "Chronicle Books publishes an eclectic mixture of traditional and innovative children's books. We are interested in taking on projects that have a unique bent to them—be it in subject matter, writing style, or illustrative technique. As a small list, we are looking for books that will lend our list a distinctive flavor. Primarily we are interested in fiction and nonfiction picture books for children ages infant-8 years, and nonfiction books for children ages 8-12 years. We are also interested in developing a middle grade/YA fiction program, and are looking for literary fiction that deals with relevant issues. Our sales reps are witnessing a resistance to alphabet books. And the market has become increasingly competitive. The '80s boom in children's publishing has passed, and the market is demanding high-quality books that work on many different levels."

CLARION BOOKS, 215 Park Ave. S., New York NY 10003. (212)420-5889. Fax: (212)420-5855, Website: www.hmco.com/trade/. Imprint of Houghton Mifflin Company. Book publisher. Estab. 1965. **Manuscript Acquisitions:** Dinah Stevenson, editorial director; Michele Coppola, editor; Virginia Buckley, contributing editor. **Art Acquisitions:** Joann Hill.

● Clarion's list is full through 2001. Do not send timely material. See Writing Effective Query Letters on page 20 for query tips from Clarion Editorial Director Dinah Stevenson. See Poetry & Plastic Laundry Baskets on page 83 to hear from Clarion author Kristine O'Connell George.

How to Contact/Writers: Fiction: Send complete mss. Nonfiction: query. Must include SASE. Will accept simultaneous submission if informed.

Illustration: Send samples (no originals).

Terms: Pays illustrators royalty; flat fee for jacket illustration.

CLEAR LIGHT PUBLISHERS, 823 Don Diego, Santa Fe NM 87501. (505)989-9590. Fax: (505)989-9519. Book publisher. **Acquisitions:** Harmon Houghton, publisher. Publishes 4 middle readers/year; and 4 young adult titles/year.
Nonfiction: Middle readers and young adults: multicultural, American Indian only.
How to Contact/Writers: Fiction/Nonfiction: Submit complete ms. Will consider simultaneous submissions. Reports in 3 months.
Illustration: Reviews ms/illustration packages from artists. Submit ms with dummy.
Terms: Pays authors royalty of 10% based on wholesale price. Offers advances (average amount: up to 50% of expected net sales). Sends galleys to authors.
Tips: "We're looking for authentic American Indian art and folklore."

COMPASS PRODUCTIONS, 211 E. Ocean Blvd., #360, Long Beach CA 90802. (562)432-7613. Fax: (562)495-0445. **Acquisitions:** Dick Dudley, vice president. Book packager/producer.
Fiction: Pop-up and novelty books: adventure, fantasy, humor, juvenile, mystery, religious. Recently published *Wake Up Night*, by Alyssa Capucilli (pop-up).
Nonfiction: "All our books are pop-up and novelty books". Subjects: animals, concept, education, recreation, regional, religion. Recently published *The Eurpsville Pop-ups*, by Eurpsville.
How to Contact/Writers: Fiction/Nonfiction: Query with SASE. Reports in 6 weeks.
Terms: Produces hardcover originals. Pays 2-8% royalty on wholesale price for total amount of books sold to publisher. Offers $2,000 advance for idea/text.
Tips: "Keep in mind our books are *pop-up*, *dimensional*, or novelty *only*! Short verse, couplets or short nonfiction text for 6-7 spreads per book."

☑ **CONCORDIA PUBLISHING HOUSE**, 3558 S. Jefferson Ave., St. Louis MO 63118. (314)268-1187. Fax: (314)268-1329. Website: cphmall.com. Book publisher. **Manuscript Acquisitions:** Rachel Hoyer, Jane Wilke. **Art Acquisitions:** Ed Luhmann, art director. "Concordia Publishing House produces quality resources which communicate and nurture the Christian faith and ministry of people of all ages, lay and professional. These resources include curriculum, worship aids, books, multimedia products and religious supplies. We publish approximately 100 quality children's books each year. Most are fiction, with some nonfiction, based on a religious subject. We boldly provide Gospel resources that are Christ-centered, Bible-based and faithful to our heritage."
Fiction: Picture books: concept, poetry, contemporary, religion. Young readers, middle readers, young adults: concept, contemporary, humor, religion, suspense/mystery. Young adults: romance. "All books must contain explicit Christian content." Recently published *Daddy Promises*, by Kerry Arquette (picture book for ages 4-9); *Undercover Bible Stories*, by Patti Hoffman (novelty for ages 4-7); and *Aloha Cure*, by Theresa Kelly (youth fiction, ages 10-14).
Nonfiction: Picture books, young readers, middle readers: activity books, arts/crafts, religion. Young adults: religion.
How to Contact/Writers: Fiction: Submit complete ms (picture books); submit outline/synopsis and sample chapters (novel-length). May also query. Reports on queries in 1 month; mss in 3 months. Publishes a book 18 months after acceptance. Will consider simultaneous submissions. "No phone queries."
Illustration: Works with 50 illustrators/year. Illustrations only: Query with samples. Contact: Ed Luhmann, art director. Reports back only if interested. Samples returned with SASE; samples filed. Originals not returned at job's completion.
Terms: Pays authors in royalties based on retail price or work purchased outright ($500-2,500). Sends galleys to author. Ms guidelines for 1 first-class stamp and a #10 envelope. Pays illustrators by the project ($1,000).
Tips: "Do not send finished artwork with the manuscript. If sketches will help in the presentation of the manuscript, they may be sent. If stories are taken from the Bible, they should follow the Biblical account closely. Liberties should not be taken in fantasizing Biblical stories."

☑ **COTEAU BOOKS LTD.**, 401-2206 Dewdney Ave., Regina, Sasketchewan S4R 1H3 Canada. (306)777-0170. E-mail: coteau@coteau.unibase.com. Thunder Creek Publishing Co-op Ltd. Book publisher. Estab. 1975. **Acquisitions:** Barbara Sapergia, acquisitions editor; Geoffrey Ursell, publisher. Publishes 3-4 juvenile and/or young adult books/year, 12-14 books/year. 10% of books by first-time authors. "Coteau Books publishes the finest Canadian fiction, poetry, drama and children's literature, with an emphasis on western writers."
● Coteau Books publishes Canadian writers and illustrators only; mss from the U.S. are returned unopened.
Fiction: Young readers, middle readers, young adults: adventure, contemporary, fantasy, history, humor, multicultural, nature/environment, science fiction, suspense/mystery. "No didactic, message pieces, nothing religious. No picture books. Material should reflect the diversity of culture, race, religion, creed of humankind—we're looking for fairness and balance." Recently published *Angels in the Snow*, by Wenda Young (ages 11-14); *Bay Girl*, by Betty Dorion (ages 8-11); and *The Intrepid Polly McDoodle*, by Mary Woodbury (ages 8-12).
Nonfiction: Young readers, middle readers, young adult: biography, history, multicultural, nature/environment, social issues.
How to Contact/Writers: Fiction: Submit complete ms to acquisitions editor Barbara Sapergia. Include SASE

or send up to 20-page sample by e-mail, as an attached file, in the Mime protocol. Reports on queries in 3-4 months; mss in 3-4 months. Publishes a book 1-2 years after acceptance. Send for guidelines.

Illustration: Works with 1-4 illustrators/year. Illustrations only: Submit nonreturnable samples. Reports only if interested. Samples returned with SASE; samples filed.

Photography: "Very occasionally buys photos from freelancers." Buys stock and assigns work.

Terms: Pays authors in royalties based on retail price. Pays illustrators and photographers by the project. Sends galleys to authors; dummies to illustrators. Original artwork returned at job's completion. Book catalog free on request with 9 × 12 SASE.

Tips: "Truthfully, the work speaks for itself! Be bold. Be creative. Be persistent! There is room, at least in the Canadian market, for quality novels for children, and at Coteau, this is a direction we will continue to take."

COUNCIL OAK BOOKS, 1350 E. 15th St., Tulsa OK 74120.
- No longer publishing children's books.

CROCODILE BOOKS, 46 Crosby St., Northampton MA 01060. (413)582-7054. Fax: (413)582-7057. E-mail: interpg@aol.com. Imprint of Interlink Publishing Group, Inc. Book publisher. **Acquisitions:** Pam Thompson, associate publisher. Publishes 4 picture books/year. 25% of books by first-time authors.
- Crocodile does not accept unsolicited mss.

Fiction: Picture books: animal, contemporary, history, spy/mystery/adventure.

Nonfiction: Picture book: history, nature/environment.

Terms: Pays authors in royalties. Sends galleys to author; dummies to illustrator.

CROSSWAY BOOKS, Good News Publishers, 1300 Crescent, Wheaton IL 60187-5800. (630)682-4300. Fax: (630)682-4785. Book Publisher. Estab. 1938. Editorial Director: Marvin Padgett. **Acquisitions:** Jill Carter. Publishes 3-4 picture books/year; and 1-2 young adult titles/year. "Crossway Books is committed to publishing books that bring Biblical reality to readers and that examine crucial issues through a Christian world view."

Fiction: Picture books: religion. Middle readers: adventure, contemporary, history, humor, religion, Christian realism. Young adults: contemporary, history, humor, religion, Christian realism. Does not want to see horror novels, romance or prophecy novels. Not looking for picture book submissions at present time. Recently published *Lewis & Clark Squad Series*, by Stephen Bly (middle reader, mystery suspense); *Noah*, by Mary Rice Hopkins, illustrated by Wendy Francisce (preschool-8, picture book); and *I'll Be with You Always*, by Jane Eareckson Tada, illustrated by Craig Nelson (young reader, fiction).

How to Contact/Writers: Fiction: Query with outline/synopsis and up to 2 sample chapters. Reports on queries/mss in 6-8 weeks. Publishes a book 12-18 months after acceptance. Will consider simultaneous submissions.

Illustration: Works with 3-4 illustrators/year. Reviews ms/illustration packages from artists. Query. Illustrations only: Query with samples; provide résumé, promo sheet and client list. Reports on artists' queries/submissions in 6-8 weeks. Samples returned with SASE; samples filed. Originals returned at job's completion.

Terms: Pays authors royalty based on wholesale price. Pays illustrators by the project. Sends galleys to authors; dummies to illustrators. Book catalog available; ms guidelines available for SASE.

CROWN PUBLISHERS (CROWN BOOKS FOR CHILDREN), 201 E. 50th St., New York NY 10022. (212)940-7742. Website: www.randomhouse.com/kids. Imprint of Random House, Inc. See Random House listing. Book publisher. Publisher: Simon Boughton. **Manuscript Acquisitions:** Crown BFYR Editorial Dept. **Art Acquisitions:** Isabel Warren-Lynch, art director. Publishes 20 picture books/year; 10 nonfiction titles/year. 5% of books by first-time authors; 70% of books from agented writers.

Fiction: Picture books: animal, humor, nature/environment. Young readers: history, nature/environment. Does not want to see fantasy, science fiction, poetry. Average word length: picture books—750. Recently published: *My Little Sister Ate One Hare*, by Bill Grossman; and *Me on the Map*, by Joan Sweeney.

Nonfiction: Picture books, young readers and middle readers: activity books, animal, biography, careers, health, history, hobbies, music/dance, nature/environment, religion, science, sports. Average word length: picture books—750-1,000; young readers—20,000; middle readers—50,000. Does not want to see ABCs. Recently published: *Rosie the Riviter*, by Penny Coleman (ages 9-14); and *Children of the Dust Bowl*, by Jerry Stanley (9-14 years, middle reader).

How to Contact/Writers: Fiction/nonfiction: Submit query letter. Reports on queries/mss in 3-4 months if SASE is included. Publishes book approximately 2 years after acceptance. Will consider simultaneous submissions.

MARKET CONDITIONS are constantly changing! If you're still using this book and it is 2001 or later, buy the newest edition of *Children's Writer's & Illustrator's Market* at your favorite bookstore or order directly from Writer's Digest Books.

Illustration: Works with 20 illustrators/year. Reviews ms/illustration packages from artists. "Submit double-spaced, continuous manuscripts; do not supply page-by-page breaks. One or two photocopies of art are fine. *Do not send original art.* Dummies are acceptable." Reports in 2 months. Illustrations only: Submit photocopies, portfolio or slides with SASE; provide business card and tearsheets. Contact: Isabel Warren-Lynch, Art Director. Original artwork returned at job's completion.

Terms: Pays authors royalty based on retail price. Advance "varies greatly." Pays illustrators by the project or royalty. Sends galleys to authors; proofs to illustrators. Book catalog for 9 × 12 SAE and 4 first-class stamps. Ms guidelines for 4½ × 9½ SASE; art guidelines available by calling (212)940-7600.

CSS PUBLISHING, 517 S. Main St., P.O. Box 4503, Lima OH 45802-4503. (419)227-1818. Fax: (419)222-4647. E-mail: acquisitions@csspub.com. Website: www.csspub.com. Book publisher. Imprints include Fairway Press and Express Press. **Manuscript Acquisitions:** Thomas Lentz. **Art Acquisitions:** Scott Swiebel. Publishes books with religious themes. "We are seeking material for use by clergy, Christian education directors and Sunday school teachers for mainline Protestant churches. Our market is mainline Protestant clergy."

Fiction: Picture books, young readers, middle readers, young adults: religion, religious poetry and humor. Needs children's sermons (object lesson) for Sunday morning worship services; dramas for Advent, Christmas or Epiphany involving children for church services; activity and craft ideas for Sunday school or mid-week services for children (particularly pre-school and first and second grade). Does not want to see secular picture books. Published *That Seeing, They May Believe*, by Kenneth Mortonson (lessons for adults to present during worship services to pre-schoolers-third graders); *What Shall We Do With This Baby?*, by Jan Spence (Christmas Eve worship service involving youngsters from newborn babies-high school youth); and *Miracle in the Bethlehem Inn*, by Mary Lou Warstler (Advent or Christmas drama involving pre-schoolers-high school youth and adult.)

Nonfiction: Picture books, young readers, middle readers, young adults: religion. Young adults only: social issues and self help. Needs children's sermons (object lesson) for Sunday morning workship services; dramas for Advent, Christmas or Epiphany involving children for church services; activity and craft ideas for Sunday school or mid-week services for children (particularly pre-school and first and second grade). Does not want to see secular picture books. Published *Mustard Seeds*, by Ellen Humbert (activity/bulletins for pre-schoolers-first graders to use during church); and *This Is The King*, by Cynthia Cowen.

How to Contact/Writers: Reports on queries in 2 weeks; mss in 1-3 months. Publishes a book 9 months after acceptance. Will consider simultaneous submissions.

Terms: Work purchased outright from authors. Ms guidelines and book catalog available for SASE.

MAY DAVENPORT, PUBLISHERS, 26313 Purissima Rd., Los Altos Hills CA 94022-4539. (415)948-6499. Fax: (650)947-1373. E-mail: robertd@whidbeynet.com. Website: www.maydavenportpublishers.com. Independent book producer/packager. Estab. 1976. **Acquisitions:** May Davenport, editor/publisher. Publishes 1-2 picture books/year; and 2-3 young adult titles/year. 99% of books by first-time authors. Seeks books with literary merit. "We like to think that we are selecting talented writers who have something humorous to write about today's unglued generation in 30,000-50,000 words for teens and young adults in junior/senior high school before they become tomorrow's 'functional illiterates.' We are interested in publishing literature that teachers in middle and high schools can use in their Language Arts, English and Creative Writing courses. There's more to literary fare than the chit-chat Internet dialog and fantasy trips on television with cartoons or humanoids." This publisher is overstocked with picture book/elementary reading material.

Fiction: Young adults (15-18): contemporary, humorous fictional literature for use in English courses in junior-senior high schools in US. Average word length: 40,000-60,000. Recently published *Boudreau of de Bayou*, by Philip Stonecipher (for ages 5-8); *Windriders*, by Blake Grant (for ages 12 and up); and *Magda Rose*, by Paul Luria (for ages 12 and up).

Nonfiction: Teens: humorous. Published *Just a Little off the Top*, by Linda Ropes (essays for teens).

How to Contact/Writers: Fiction: Query. Reports on queries/mss in 2-3 weeks. "We do not answer queries or manuscripts which do not have SASE attached." Publishes a book 6-12 months after acceptance.

Illustration: Works with 1-2 illustrators/year. "Have enough on file for future reference." Reports only if interested. Samples returned with SASE; samples filed. Originals returned at job's completion.

Terms: Pays authors royalties of 15% based on retail price; negotiable. Pays "by mutual agreement, no advances." Pays illustrators by the project (range: $175-350). Book catalog, ms guidelines free on request with SASE.

Tips: "Create stories to enrich the non-reading 12-and-up readers. They might not appreciate your similies and metaphors and may find fault with your alliterations with the letters of the alphabet, but show them how you do it with memorable characters in today's society. Just project your humorous talent and entertain with more than two sentences in a paragraph."

DIAL BOOKS FOR YOUNG READERS, Penguin Putnam Inc., 345 Hudson St., New York NY 10014. Website: www.penguinputnam.com. Publisher: Nancy Paulsen. **Acquisitions:** Submissions Coordinator. Publishes 30 picture books/year; 5 young reader titles/year; 8 middle reader titles/year; and 5 young adult titles/year.

• Dial prefers submissions from agents and previously published authors. Dial title *A Long Way From Chicago*, by Richard Peck, won the 1999 Newbery Honor Award. Dial title *Jazmin's Notebook*, by Nikki Grimes, won a 1999 Coretta Scott King Author Honor Award.

Fiction: Picture books: adventure, animal, contemporary, folktales, history, nature/environment, poetry, religion, sports, suspense/mystery. Young readers: contemporary, easy-to-read, fantasy, folktales, history, nature/environment, poetry, sports, mystery/adventure. Middle readers, young adults: animal, contemporary, folktales, history, nature/environment, poetry, religion, sports, mystery/adventure. Published *A Long Way From Chicago*, by Richard Peck (ages 9-12, middle reader); *Brothers of the Knight*, by Debbie Allen (ages 5 and up, picture book); and *Parts*, by Tedd Arnold (ages 3-8, picture book).

Nonfiction: Will consider query letters for submissions of outstanding literary merit. Picture books: animals, biography, history, nature/environment, sports. Young readers: animals, biography, history, nature/environment, sports. Middle readers: biography, history. Young adults: biography, contemporary. Recently published *Thanks to My Mother*, by Schoschana Rabinovici (ages 12 and up, YA) and *Handmade Counting Book*, by Laura Rankin (ages 3-8, picture book).

How to Contact/Writers: Prefers agented material (but will respond to queries that briefly describe the ms and the author's writing credits with a SASE). "We do not supply specific guidelines, but we will send you a recent catalog if you send us a 9×12 SASE with four 33¢ stamps attached. Questions and queries should only be made in writing. We will not reply to anything without a SASE."

Illustration: To arrange a personal interview to show portfolio, send samples and a letter requesting an interview. Art samples should be sent to Ms. Toby Sherry and will not be returned without a SASE. "No phone calls please. Only artists with portfolios that suit the house's needs will be interviewed."

Terms: Pays authors and illustrators in royalties based on retail price. Average advance payment "varies."

DK INK, Imprint of Dorling Kindersley Publishing, Inc., 95 Madison Ave., New York NY 10016. (212)213-4800. Fax: (212)213-5240. Website: www.dk.com. Book publisher. Estab. 1997. Publishes 40-50 titles/year; first list included 20 titles. **Acquisitions:** Neal Porter, publisher; Melanie Kroupa, senior editor. "DK Ink is a distinctive imprint consisting primarily of picture books and fiction for children and adults, created by authors and illustrators you know and respect as well as exciting new talents. The main goal of these books is to edify, entertain and encourage kids to think about the human condition."

Fiction: Looking for picture books, middle readers and young adult material. Recently published: *Like, Likes, Like*, by Chris Raschka (picture book); *The Islander*, by Cynthia Rylant; *Voices in the Park*, by Anthony Browne (picture book).

Nonfiction: Nonfiction titles under DK Ink will have a distinctively differnent look from DK Publishing nonfiction titles.

How to Contact/Writers: Fiction: Submit complete ms. Nonfiction: Submit outline/sysnopsis and sample chapters. Reports in 8-10 weeks.

Illustration: Submit samples to Art Director.

Terms: Pays authors royalty; offers advance. Pays illustrators royalty or flat fee, depending on assignment.

N A DOG-EARED PUBLICATIONS, P.O. Box 620863, Middletown WI 53562-0863. Phone/fax: (608)831-1410. E-mail: field@dog-eared.com. Website: www.dog-eared.com. Book publisher. Estab. 1977. **Art Acquisitions:** Nancy Field, publisher. Publishes 2-3 middle readers/year. 1% of books by first-time authors. "Dog-Eared Publications create action-packed nature books for children. We aim to turn young readers into environmentally aware citizens and to foster a love for science and nature in the new generation."

Nonfiction: Middle readers: activity books, animal, nature/environment, science. Average word length varies. Recently published *Leapfrogging Through Wetlands*, by Margaret Anderson, Nancy Field and Karen Stephenson, illustrated by Michael Magdak (middle readers, activity book); *Ancient Forests*, by Margaret Anderson, Nancy Field and Karen Stephenson, illustrated by Nancy Field and Sharon Toruik (middle readers, activity book); *Discovering Wolves*, by Nancy Field and Corliss Karassov, illustrated by Cary Hunkel (activity book).

How to Contact/Writers: Nonfiction: Query or submit outline/synopsis. Reports on queries/mss in 1 month. Will consider electronic submissions via disk or modem.

Illustration: Only interested in agented material. Works with 2-3 illustrators/year. Reviews mss/illustration packages from artists. Submit query and a few art samples. Contact: Nancy Field, publisher. Illustrations only: Query with samples. Contact: Nancy Field, publisher. Reports only if interested. Samples not returned; samples filed.

Photography: Works on assignment only.

Terms: Pays authors royalty based on wholesale price. Offers advances (amount varies). Pays illustrators royalty based on wholesale price. Sends galleys to authors. Originals returned to artist at job's completion. Brochure available for SASE and 1 first-class stamp. Brochure available on website.

A DORLING KINDERSLEY PUBLISHING, INC., (formerly DK Publishing, Inc.), 95 Madison Ave., New York NY 10016. (212)213-4800. Fax: (212)689-1799. Website: www.dk.com. **Acquisitions:** Beth Sutinis, submissions editor. Imprint: DK Ink. Publishes 30 picture books/year; 30 young readers/year; 10 middle readers/year; and 5 young adult titles/year.

● DK works with previously published authors or agented authors only.

Fiction: Picture books: animal, contemporary, folktales, nature/environment. Middle readers: adventure, anthology, contemporary, fantasy, folktales, history, humor, sports, suspense/mystery. Young adult: adventure, contemporary, fantasy, problem novels. Average page count: picture books, middle readers: 32 pages. Recently published:

Eyewitness Classics: Black Beauty, by Anna Sewell, illustrated by Victo Ambrus (for young readers); and *Cybermama*, by Alexandre Jardin (for middle readers).

Nonfiction: Picture books: animal, concept, nature/environment. Middle readers: activity books, geography, history, nature/environment, reference, science, sports. Young adults: biography, careers, history, reference, science, social issues, sports. Average page count: picture books, middle readers: 32 pages; young readers: 128 pages. Recently published *Children Just Like Me: Our Favorite Stories*, by Jamila Gavin (for all ages); and *Stephen Biesty's Cross-Sections Castle* (for ages 8 and up).

How to Contact/Writers: Only interested in agented material. "Due to high volume, we are unable to accept unsolicited mss at this time. We will review policy in the future."

Illustration: Only interested in agented material. Uses color artwork only. Reviews ms/illustration packages from artists. Query with printed samples. Illustrations only: Query with samples. Send résumé and promo sheet. Reports back only if interested. Samples filed.

Photography: Buys stock and assigns work. Uses color prints. Submit cover letter, résumé, published samples, color promo piece.

Terms: Pays authors royalty. Offers advances. Book catalog available for 10×13 SASE and $3 first-class postage.

Tips: "Most of our projects are generated in London where authors and illustrators are solicited."

DOWN EAST BOOKS, P.O. Box 679, Camden, ME 04843-0679. (207)594-9544. Fax: (207)594-7215. E-mail: msteere@downeast.com. Book publisher. Senior Editor: Karin Womer. **Acquisitions:** Alice Devine, associate editor, Michael Steere. Publishes 1-2 young middle readers/year. 70% of books by first-time authors. "As a small regional publisher Down East Books specializes in non-fiction books with a Maine or New England theme. Down East Books' mission is to publish superbly crafted books which capture and illuminate the astonishing beauty and unique character of New England's people, culture and wild places; the very aspects that distinguish New England from the rest of the United States."

Fiction: Picture books, middle readers, young readers, young adults: animal, adventure, history, nature/environment. Young adults: suspense/mystery. Recently published *Moose, of Course!*, by Lynn Plourde, illustrated by Jim Sollers.

Nonfiction: Picture books, middle readers, young readers, young adults: animal, history, nature/environment. Recently published *Do Sharks Ever . . .?*, by Nathalie Ward, illustrated by Tessa Morgan.

How to Contact/Writers: Fiction/Nonfiction: Query. Reports on queries/mss in 1-2 months. Publishes a book 6-18 months after acceptance. Will consider simultaneous and previously published submissions.

Illustration: Works with 2-3 illustrators/year. Reviews ms/illustration packages from artists. Query. Illustrations only: Query with samples. Reports in 1-2 months. Samples returned with SASE; samples filed sometimes. Originals returned at job's completion.

Terms: Pays authors royalty (7-12% based on retail price). Pays illustrators by the project or by royalty (7-10% based on retail price). Sends galleys to authors; dummies to illustrators. Original artwork returned at job's completion. Book catalog available. Ms guidelines available for SASE.

DUTTON CHILDREN'S BOOKS, Penguin Putnam Inc., 375 Hudson St., New York NY 10014. (212)366-2600. Website: www.penguinputnam.com. Book publisher. **Acquisitions:** Lucia Monfried, editor-in-chief. **Art Acquisitions:** Sara Reynolds, art director. Publishes approximately 60 picture books/year; 4 young reader titles/year; 10 middle reader titles/year; and 8 young adult titles/year. 10% of books by first-time authors.

● Turn to First Books on page 45 to read about Dutton author/illustrator Nan Parson Rossiter and her book *The Way Home*. Dutton is temporarily not accepting new manuscripts.

Fiction: Picture books: adventure, animal, folktales, history, multicultural, nature/environment, poetry. Young readers: adventure, animal, contemporary, easy-to-read, fantasy, pop-up, suspense/mystery. Middle readers: adventure, animal, contemporary, fantasy, history, multicultural, nature/environment, suspense/mystery. Young adults: adventure, animal, anthology, contemporary, fantasy, history, multicultural, nature/environment, poetry, science fiction, suspense/mystery. Recently published *The Puddle Pail*, by Elisa Kleven (picture book); *The Iron Ring*, by Lloyd Alexander (novel); and *HIV Positive*, by Bernard Wolf (photo essay).

Nonfiction: Picture books: animal, history, multicultural, nature/environment. Young readers: animal, history, multicultural, nature/environment. Middle readers: animal, biography, history, multicultural, nature/environment. Young adults: animal, biography, history, multicultural, nature/environment, social issues. Recently published *Chile Fever: A Celebration of Peppers*, by Elizabeth King (ages 7-10, photo essay); and *Part of Me Died, Too: Stories of Creative Survival Among Bereaved Children and Teenagers*, by Virginia Lynn Fry (ages 10 and up).

How to Contact/Writers: Query (for longer books), or submit complete ms (if picture book). Publishes a book 12-18 months after acceptance. Will consider simultaneous submissions.

Illustration: Works with 40-60 illustrators/year. Reviews ms/illustration packages from artists. Query first. Illustrations only: Query with samples; send résumé, portfolio, slides—no original art please. Reports on art samples in 2 months. Original artwork returned at job's completion.

Photography: Will look at photography samples and photo-essay proposals.

Terms: Pays authors royalties of 4-10% based on retail price. Book catalog, ms guidelines for SASE with 8 first-class stamps. Pays illustrators royalties of 2-10% based on retail price unless jacket illustration—then pays by flat fee.

Tips: "Avoid topics that appear frequently. In nonfiction, we are looking for history, general biography, science and photo essays for all age groups." Illustrators: "We would like to see samples and portfolios from potential illustrators of picture books (full color), young novels (b&w) and jacket artists (full color)." Foresee "even more multicultural publishing, plus more books published in both Spanish and English."

☑ **E.M. PRESS, INC.**, P.O. Box 4057, Manassas VA 20108. (540)349-9958. E-mail: empress2@erols.com. Website: www.empressinc.com. Book publisher. **Acquisitions:** Beth Miller, publisher/editor. "E.M. Press has narrowed its focus to manuscripts of local interest (Virginia, Maryland, D.C.); manuscripts by local authors; nonfiction manuscripts; and children's books. We're now publishing illustrated children's books." 50% of books by first-time authors.
Fiction: Children, young adults: folk tales, nature/environment, special needs. Recently published *How Will They Get That Heart Down Your Throat? A Child's View of Transplants*, by Karen Walton (educates children regarding "recycling" life); and *The Relationship*, by John H. Hyman (story of a summer in the lives of two young boys—one white, one "colored"—in rural, 1940s North Carolina).
Nonfiction: Children, young adults: animal, arts/craft, health, history, multicultural, music/dance, nature/environment, religion, self-help, social issues. Recently published *Santa's New Reindeer*, by Judie Schrecker; *Virginia's Country Stores: A Quiet Passing*, by Joseph E. Morse (illustrated history of the origins of the old community store).
How to Contact/Writers: Query with outline/synopsis and SASE for novel-length work and complete ms for shorter work. Reports on ms/queries in 3 months. Publishes a book 18 months after acceptance. Will consider simultaneous submissions.
Illustration: Works with 4 children's illustrators/year. Illustration packages should be submitted to Beth Miller, publisher. Reports back in 3 months. Samples returned with SASE; samples kept on file. Original artwork returned at job's completion.
Terms: "We've used all means of payment from outright purchase to royalty." Offers varied advances. Sends galleys to authors. Book catalog for SASE.
Tips: "Present the most professional package possible. The market is glutted, so you must find a new approach."

EERDMAN'S BOOKS FOR YOUNG READERS, an imprint of Wm. B. Eerdmans Publishing Company, (formerly Wm. B. Eerdmans Publishing Company), 255 Jefferson Ave. SE, Grand Rapids MI 49503. (616)459-4591. Book publisher. **Manuscript Acquisitions:** Judy Zylstra, children's book editor. **Art Acquisitions:** Gayle Brown. Publishes 10-12 picture books/year; and 3-4 middle readers/year.
Fiction: Picture books, middle readers: parables, religion, retold Bible stories, child or family issues, historical fiction, art/artists.
Nonfiction: All levels: biography, religion.
How to Contact/Writers: Fiction/Nonfiction: Query with sample chapters (novels) or submit complete ms (picture books). Reports on queries in 3-6 weeks; mss in 8 weeks.
Illustration: Works with 10-12 illustrators/year. Reviews ms/illustration packages from artists. Reports on ms/art samples in 1 month. Illustrations only: Submit résumé, slides or color photocopies. Samples returned with SASE; samples filed.
Terms: Pays authors and illustrators royalties of 5-7% based on retail price. Sends galleys to authors; dummies to illustrators. Original artwork returned at job's completion. Book catalog free on request; ms and/or artist's guidelines free on request with SASE.
Tips: "We are looking for material that will help children build their faith in God and explore God's world. We accept all genres."

☑ **ENSLOW PUBLISHERS INC.**, Box 398, 40 Industrial Rd., Berkeley Heights NJ 07922-0398. Website: www.enslow.com. Estab. 1978. **Acquisitions:** Brian D. Enslow, vice president. Publishes 100 middle reader titles/year; and 100 young adult titles/year. 30% of books by first-time authors.
Nonfiction: Young readers, middle readers, young adults: animal, biography, careers, health, history, hobbies, nature/environment, social issues, sports. Average word length: middle readers—5,000; young adult—18,000. Published *Louis Armstrong*, by Patricia and Fredrick McKissack (grades 2-3, biography); and *Lotteries: Who Wins, Who Loses?*, by Ann E. Weiss (grades 6-12, issues book).
How to Contact/Writers: Nonfiction: Send for guidelines. Query. Reports on queries/mss in 2 weeks. Publishes a book 18 months after acceptance. Will not consider simultaneous submissions.
Illustration: Submit résumé, business card or tearsheets to be kept on file.

A SELF-ADDRESSED, STAMPED ENVELOPE (SASE) should always be included with submissions within your own country. When sending material to other countries, include a self-addressed envelope (SAE) and International Reply Coupons (IRCs).

Terms: Pays authors royalties or work-purchased outright. Sends galleys to authors. Book catalog/ms guidelines available for $2, along with an 8½×11 SAE and $1.67 postage.

■ **EVAN-MOOR EDUCATIONAL PUBLISHERS**, 18 Lower Ragsdale Dr., Monterey CA 93940-5746. (408)649-5901. Fax: (408)649-6256. E-mail: editorial@evan-moor.com. Website: www.evan-moor.com. Book publisher. **Manuscript Acquisitions:** Marilyn Evans, editor. **Art Acquisitions:** Joy Evans, production director. Publishes 30-50 books/year. Less than 10% of books by first-time authors. " 'Helping Children Learn' is our motto. Evan-Moor is known for high-quality educational materials written by teachers for use in the classroom and at home. We publish teacher resource and reproducible materials in most all curriculum areas and activity books (language arts, math, science, social studies). No fiction or nonfiction literature books."
Nonfiction: Nonfiction: Published late 1998, early 1999: *Play and Learn Series*, by Jill Norris, illustrated by Cindy Davis (6 books for parents); *Science Works for Kids* (10 80-page science units for grades 1-3); *Teaching and Learning with the Computer Series* (6 books providing lessons to teach skills using the computer); *Making Books with Pockets* (12-book series, one for each month, with cross-curricular projects; for teachers and parents of children in gradess PreK-6).
How to Contact/Writers: Query or submit complete ms. Reports on queries in 2 months; mss in 3 months. Publishes a book 12-18 months after acceptance. Will consider simultaneous submissions if so noted. Send SASE for submission guidelines.
Illustration: Works with 6-8 illustrators/year. Uses b&w artwork primarily. Illustrations only: Query with samples; send résumé, tearsheets. Contact: Joy Evans, production director. Reports only if interested. Samples returned with SASE; samples filed.
Terms: Work purchased outright from authors, "dependent solely on size of project and 'track record' of author." Pays illustrators by the project (range: varies). Sends galleys to authors. Artwork is not returned. Book catalog available for 9×12 SAE; ms guidelines available for SASE.
Tips: "Writers—know the supplemental education or parent market. (These materials are *not* children's literature.) Tell us how your project is unique and what consumer needs it meets. Illustrators—you need to be able to produce quickly, and be able to render realistic and charming children and animals." A number of subject areas are of ongoing interest. They include: interdisciplinary/cross-curricular units; science and math materials which emphasize "real-world," hands-on; learning and critical thinking/problem solving skills; materials related to cultural diversity, global awareness; geography materials; assessment materials; and materials for parents to use with their children at home.

EXCELSIOR CEE PUBLISHING, P.O. Box 5861, Norman OK 73070-5861. (405)329-3909. Fax: (405)329-6886. Book publisher. Estab. 1989. **Manuscript Acquisitions:** J.C. Marshall.
How to Contact/Writers: Nonfiction: Query or submit outline/synopsis. Reports on queries in 1 month. Publishes a book 1 year after acceptance. Will consider simultaneous submission.

FACTS ON FILE, 11 Penn Plaza, New York NY 10001. (212)967-8800. Book publisher. Editorial Director: Laurie Likoff. **Acquisitions:** Frank Darnstadt, science and technology/nature; Nicole Bowen, American history and studies; Anne Savarese, language and literature; Mary Kay Linge, world studies; Jim Chambers, arts and entertainment. Estab. 1941. "We produce high-quality reference materials for the school library market and the general nonfiction trade." Publishes 25-30 young adult titles/year. 5% of books by first-time authors; 25% of books from agented writers; additional titles through book packagers, co-publishers and unagented writers.
Nonfiction: Middle readers, young adults: animal, biography, careers, geography, health, history, multicultural, nature/environment, reference, religion, science, social issues and sports.
How to Contact/Writers: Nonfiction: Submit outline/synopsis and sample chapters. Reports on queries in 8-10 weeks. Publishes a book 10-12 months after acceptance. Will consider simultaneous submissions. Sends galleys to authors. Book catalog free on request. Send SASE for submission guidelines.
Tips: "Most projects have high reference value and fit into a series format."

■ **FARRAR, STRAUS & GIROUX INC.**, 19 Union Square W., New York NY 10003. (212)741-6900. Fax: (212)633-2427. Book publisher. Imprint: Frances Foster Books. Children's Books Editorial Director: Margaret Ferguson. **Acquisitions:** Frances Foster, publisher, Frances Foster Books; Beverly Reingold, executive editor; Wesley Adams, senior editor; Elizabeth Mikesell, associate editor. Estab. 1946. Publishes 30 picture books/year; 15 middle reader titles/year; and 15 young adult titles/year. 10% of books by first-time authors; 20% of books from agented writers.
  ● Farrar title *Holes*, by Louis Sachar, won the 1999 Newbery Medal, the 1999 Boston-Globe-Horn Book Award for fiction and the 1999 National Book Award (juvenile category). Farrar title *The Trolls*, by Polly Horvath, won a 1999 Boston Globe-Horn Book Honor Award for fiction. Farrar title *Tibet: Through the Red Box*, by Peter Sis, received a Boston Glove-Horn Book Special Citation and a Caldecott Honor Award in 1999. Farrar title *Snow*, written and illustrated by Uri Shulevitz, won a 1999 Caldecott Honor Award.
Fiction: All levels: all categories. "Original and well-written material for all ages." Published *Belle Prater's Boy*, by Ruth White (ages 10 up).
Nonfiction: All levels: all categories. "We publish only literary nonfiction."
How to Contact/Writers: Fiction/Nonfiction: Query with outline/synopsis and sample chapters. Do not fax

submissions or queries. Reports on queries in 6-8 weeks; mss in 1-3 months. Publishes a book 18 months after acceptance. Will consider simultaneous submissions.

Illustration: Works with 30-60 illustrators/year. Reviews ms/illustration packages from artists. Submit ms with 1 example of final art, remainder roughs. Do not send originals. Illustrations only: Query with tearsheets. Reports back in 1-2 months. Samples returned with SASE; samples sometimes filed.

Terms: "We offer an advance against royalties for both authors and illustrators." Sends galleys to authors; dummies to illustrators. Original artwork returned at job's completion. Book catalog available for 9×12 SAE and $1.87 postage; ms guidelines for 1 first-class stamp.

Tips: "Study our catalog before submitting. We will see illustrator's portfolios by appointment. Don't ask for criticism and/or advice—it's just not possible. Never send originals. Always enclose SASE."

☑ **THE FEMINIST PRESS**, 365 Fifth Ave., New York NY 10016. Website: www.feministpress.org. Estab. 1970. Acquisitions Editor: Amanda Hamlin. Publishes 4 middle readers/year; 1 young adult title/year. "We are a nonprofit, tax-exempt, education publishing organization interested in changing the curriculum, the classroom and consciousness."

Fiction: Middle readers, young adult: multicultural. Average word length: 20,000-30,000. Recently published *Families*, by Meredith Tax, illustrated by Maryln Hafner (ages 4-8); *Carly*, by Annegert Fuchshuber (ages 5 and up); *The Lilith Summer*, by Hadley Irwin (ages 10 and up); and *Josephina Hates Her Name*, by Diana Engel.

Nonfiction: Middle readers and young adults: biography, multicultural and social issues. Average word length: middle readers—20,000; young adult—30,000. Recently published *Aung San Su Kyi: Standing Up for Democracy in Burma*, by Bettina Ling (ages 10 and up); *Mamphela Ramphele: Challenging Apartheid in South Africa*, by Judith Harlan (ages 10 and up); and *Ela Bhatt: Uniting Women in India*, by Jyotsna Screenivasan (ages 10 and up).

How to Contact/Writers: Fiction: query. Nonfiction: submit complete ms. Reports on queries in 1 months; mss in 3 months. Publishes a book 18 months after acceptance. Will consider simultaneous submissions and previously published work.

Photography: Buys stock and assigns work. Contact: Dayna Navaro, production/design manager. Model/property releases required. Uses color and b&w prints. Submit published samples.

Terms: Pays authors royalty of 10% based on wholesale price. Offers advances (average amount $250). Pays illustrators and photographers by the project. Originals returned to artist at job's completion. Book catalog available for 8½×11 SAE and 4 first-class stamps. All imprints included in single catalog. Catalog available on website. Writer's guidelines available for SASE.

▓ ☜ **FENN PUBLISHING CO.**, 34 Nixon Rd., Bolton, Ontario L7E-1W2 Canada. Phone/fax: (905)951-6600. E-mail: jfenn@hbfenn.com. Website: wwwhbfenn.com. Estab. 1982. Specializes in Christian and multicultural material. **Acquisitions:** C. Jordan Fenn, publisher. Publishes 35 books/year.

Fiction: Picture books: adventure, animal, folktales, multicultural, religion, sports. Young readers: adventure, animal, folktales, multicultural, religion. Middle readers: adventure, animal, health, history, multicultural, religion, special needs, sports. Young adults: adventure, animal, contemporary, folktales, health, history, multicultural, nature/environment, religion, science fiction, sports.

Nonfiction: Picture books, young readers, middle readers, activity books, animal, arts/crafts, geography, health, history, hobbies, how-to, multicultural, nature/environment, religion.

How to Contact/Writers: Fiction/Nonfiction: Query or submit complete ms. Reports on queries/mss in 2 months.

Illustration: Reviews ms/illustration packages from artists. Contact: C. Jordan Fenn, publisher. Reports back only if interested. Samples not returned or filed.

FIESTA CITY PUBLISHERS, Box 5861, Santa Barbara CA 93150-5861. (805)733-1984. E-mail: fcooke3924 @aol.com. Book publisher. **Acquisitions:** Ann Cooke, president. Publishes 1 middle reader/year; 1 young adult/year. 25% of books by first-time authors. Publishes books about cooking and music or a combination of the two. "We are best known for children's and young teens' cookbooks and musical plays."

Fiction: Young adults: history, humor, musical plays.

Nonfiction: Young adult: cooking, how-to, music/dance, self-help. Average word length: 30,000. Does not want to see "cookbooks about healthy diets or books on rap music." Published *Kids Can Write Songs, Too!* (revised second printing), by Eddie Franck; *Bent-Twig*, by Frank E. Cooke, with some musical arrangements by Johnny Harris (a 3-act musical for young adolescents).

How to Contact/Writers: Query. Reports on queries in 3-4 days; on mss in 1 month. Publishes a book 1 year after acceptance. Will consider simultaneous submissions.

Illustration: Works with 1 illustrator/year. Will review ms/illustrations packages (query first). Illustrations only: Send résumé. Samples returned with SASE; samples filed.

Terms: Pays authors 5-10% royalty based on retail price.

Tips: "Write clearly and simply. Do not write 'down' to young adults (or children). Looking for self-help books on current subjects, original and unusual cookbooks, and books about music, or a combination of cooking and music." Always include SASE.

⬛ FIREFLY BOOKS LTD., 3680 Victoria Park Ave., Willowdale, Ontario M2H 3K1 Canada. (416)499-8412. Fax: (416)499-8313. Book publisher and distributor.
- Firefly Books Ltd. does not accept unsolicited mss.

FIRST STORY PRESS, Imprint of Rose Book Group, 1800 Business Park Dr., Suite 205, Clarksville TN 37040. (931)572-0806. Fax: (931)552-3200. Publisher/Editor in Chief: Judith Pierson. Contact: Acquisitions Editor. Publishes 4 books/year. 50% of books by first-time authors. Publishes books on multicultural, grandparent and quilt themes.
Fiction: Picture books. Average word length: picture books—700-1,500. Recently published *The Much Too Loved Quilt*, by Rachel Waterstone.
How to Contact/Writers: Fiction: Submit complete ms. Send hard copy. Reports on queries/mss in 3 months.
Illustration: Works with 3 illustrators/year. Reviews ms/illustration packages from artists. Send ms with dummy. Contact: Editor. Illustrations only: Send résumé, promo sheet and tearsheets to be kept on file. Contact: Editor. Reports only if interested. Samples returned with SASE; samples filed.
Terms: Pays authors royalty of 4-5% based on retail price or work purchased outright. Offers advances. Pays illustrators royalty of 4-5% based on retail price. Originals returned to artist. Ms guidelines available for SASE.
Tips: "SASE is always required. Do not send original artwork. Guidelines available—send SASE. Take a look at our books. We do not send out catalogs."

Ⓐ ⬛ FITZHENRY & WHITESIDE LTD., 195 Allstate Pkwy., Markham, Ontario L3R 4T8 Canada. (905)477-9700. Fax: (905)477-9179. Book publisher. President: Sharon Fitzhenry; Children's Publisher: Gail Winskill. Publishes 8 picture books/year; 8 early readers and early chapter books/year; 5 middle readers/year; 7 young adult titles/year. 10% of books by first-time authors. Publishes fiction and nonfiction—social studies, visual arts, biography, environment. Emphasis on Canadian authors and illustrators, subject or perspective.
- Fitzhenry & Whiteside no longer accepts unsolicited manuscripts. They prefer to work with agents.
How to Contact/Writers: Fiction/Nonfiction: **Accepts agented material only.** Publishes a book 12-18 months after acceptance. Will consider simultaneous submissions.
Illustration: Works with 15 illustrators/year. Reviews ms/illustration packages from artist. Submit outline and sample illustration (copy). Illustrations only: Query with samples and promo sheet. Reports in 3 months. Samples returned with SASE; samples filed if no SASE.
Photography: Buys photos from freelancers. Buys stock and assigns work. Captions required. Uses b&w 8×10 prints; 35mm and 4×5 transparencies. Submit stock photo list and promo piece.
Terms: Pays authors royalty of 10%. Offers "respectable" advances for picture books, 5% to author, 5% to illustrator. Pays illustrators by the project and royalty. Pays photographers per photo. Sends galleys to authors; dummies to illustrators.
Tips: "We respond to quality."

ⓝ FOREST HOUSE PUBLISHING COMPANY, INC., P.O. Box 738, Lake Forest IL 60045. (847)295-8287. Fax: (847)295-8201. Estab. 1989. **Acquisitions:** Dianne L. Spahr, president. Imprint: HTS Books. Published 44 titles in 1998. "We are not accepting any unsolicited manuscripts, until 2000."

FORWARD MOVEMENT PUBLICATIONS, 412 Sycamore St., Cincinnati OH 45202. (513)721-6659. Fax: (513)721-0729. E-mail: forwardmovement@msn.com. Website: www.forwardmovement.org. Contact: Sally B. Sedgwick, assistant director.
Fiction: Middle readers and young adults: religion and religious problem novels, fantasy and science fiction.
Nonfiction: Religion.
How to Contact/Writers: Fiction/Nonfiction: Query. Reports in 1 month.
Illustration: Query with samples. Samples returned with SASE.
Terms: Pays authors honorarium. Pays illustrators by the project.
Tips: "Forward Movement is now exploring publishing books for children and does not know its niche. We are an agency of the Episcopal Church and most of our market is to mainstream Protestants."

FRANKLIN WATTS, Sherman Turnpike, Danbury CT 06816. (203)797-3500. Subsidiary of Grolier Inc. Book publisher.
- See listing for Grolier Publishing (Children's Press and Franklin Watts).

FREE SPIRIT PUBLISHING, 400 First Ave. N., Suite 616, Dept. CWI, Minneapolis MN 55401-1730. (612)338-2068. Fax: (612)337-5050. E-mail: help4kids@freespirit.com. Website: www.freespirit.com. Book publisher. **Acquisitions:** Caryn Pernu. Publishes 15-20 titles/year for children and teens, teachers and parents. "We believe passionately in empowering kids to learn to think for themselves and make their own good choices."
- Free Spirit no longer accepts fiction or story book submissions.
Nonfiction: "Free Spirit Publishing specializes in SELF-HELP FOR KIDS® and SELF-HELP FOR TEENS®, with an emphasis on self-esteem and self-awareness, stress management, school success, creativity, friends and family, social action, and special needs (i.e., gifted and talented, children with learning differences). We prefer books written in a natural, friendly style, with little education/psychology jargon. We need books in our areas of

emphasis and prefer titles written by specialists such as teachers, counselors, and other professionals who work with youth." Recently published *What on Earth Do You Do When Someone Dies*, by Trevor Romain; *Too Old for This, Too Young for That: Your Guide to the Middle-School Years*, by Karen Unger and Harriet Mosatche, Ph.D.

How to Contact/Writers: Send query letter or proposal. Reports on queries/mss in 3 months. "If you'd like materials returned, enclose a SASE with sufficient postage." Write or call for catalog and submission guidelines before sending submission. Accepts queries only by e-mail. Submission guidelines available online.

Illustration: Submit samples to acquisitions editor for consideration. If appropriate, samples will be kept on file and artist will be contacted if a suitable project comes up. Enclose SASE if you'd like materials returned.

Photography: Submit samples to acquisitions editor for consideration. If appropriate, samples will be kept on file and photographer will be contacted if a suitable project comes up. Enclose SASE if you'd like materials returned.

Terms: Pays authors in royalties based on wholesale price. Offers advance. Pays illustrators by the project. Pays photographers by the project or per photo.

Tips: "Prefer books that help kids help themselves or that help adults help kids help themselves; that complement our list without duplicating current titles; and that are written in a direct, straightforward manner."

FREESTONE, Peachtree Publishers, 494 Armour Circle NE, Atlanta GA 30324-4088. (404)876-8761. Fax: (404)875-2578. Website: www.peachtree-online.com. Estab. 1997. **Manuscript Acquisitions:** Sarah Smith (children's, young adult). Art Acquisitions: Loraine Balesik (all). Publishes 3-4 young adult titles/year. Peachtree Jr. publishes 5 juvenile titles/year (ages 8-12) and Peachtree Publishers, Ltd. publishes 10 books a year. "We look for very good stories that are well-written, and written from the author's experience and heart with a clear application to today's young adults. We feel teens need to read about issues that are relevant to them, rather than reading adult books."

• Freestone is an imprint of Peachtree Publishers. See the listing for Peachtree for submission information.

FRONT STREET BOOKS, 20 Battery Park Ave., #403, Ashville NC 28801. (828)236-3097. Fax: (828)236-3098. E-mail: roxburgh@frontstreetbooks.com. Website: www.frontstreetbooks.com. Book publisher. Estab. 1995. **Acquisitions:** Stephen Roxburgh, publisher; Nancy Zimmerman, associate publisher. Publishes 10-15 titles/year. "We are a small independent publisher of books for children and young adults. We do not publish pablum: we try to publish books that will attract, if not addict, children to literature and art books that are a pleasure to look at and a pleasure to hold, books that will be revelations to young minds."

• See Front Street's website for submission guidelines and their complete catalog. Front Street focuses on fiction, but will publish poetry, anthologies, nonfiction and high-end picture books. They are not currently accepting unsolicited picture book manuscripts.

Fiction: Recently published: *Oh No, It's Robert*, by Barbara Seuling, illustrated by Paul Brewer (humor for ages 7-10); *Broken Chords*, by Barbara Snow Gilbert (coming of age story for ages 12 and up); and *Mop to the Rescue*, by Martine Schapp, illustrated by Alex de Wolf (picture book about a bumbling sheepdog for ages 4-8).

How to Contact/Writers: Fiction: Submit cover letter and complete ms if under 30 pages; submit cover letter, one or two sample chapters and plot summary if over 30 pages. Nonfiction: Submit detailed proposal and sample chapters. Poetry: Submit no more than 25 poems. Include SASE with submissions if you want them returned. "It is our policy to consider submissions in the order in which they are received. This is a time-consuming practice and we ask you to be patient in awaiting our response."

Illustration "If you are the artist or are working with an artist, we will be happy to consider your project." Submit ms, dummy and a sample piece of art "rendered in the manner and style representative of the final artwork."

Terms: Pays royalties.

FRONT STREET/CRICKET BOOKS, Imprint of Carus Publishing Company, 332 S. Michigan, Suite 1100, Chicago IL 60604. Website: www.cricketbooks.net. Imprint estab. 1999; Company estab. 1973. **Manuscript Acquisitions:** Laura Tillotson. **Art Acquisitions:** John Grandits. Publishes 5 young readers/year; 5 middle readers/year; 2 young adult/year. 50% of books by first time authors. "For 25 years we've published the best children's literary magazines in America, and we're looking for the same high-quality material for our book imprint."

Fiction: Young readers, middle readers, young adult/teen: adventure, animal, contemporary, fantasy, history, multicultural, humor, sports, suspense/mystery, science fiction, problem novels. Recently published *Casebook of a Private (Cat's) Eye*, by Mary Stolz, illustrated by Pam Levy (middle grade); *Oh No, It's Robert*, by Barbara Seuling, illustrated by Paul Brewer (ages 7-10); *Two Suns in the Sky*, by Miriam Bat-Ami (ages 12 and up).

How to Contact/Writers: Fiction: submit complete ms. Reports on queries in 2 months; mss in 10-12 weeks. Publishes a book 18 months after acceptance. Will consider simultaneous submissions.

Illustration: Works with 4 illustrators/year. Uses color and b&w. Illustration only: submit samples, tearsheets. Contact: John Grandits, art director. Reports back only if interested. Samples returned with SASE; sample filed.

Terms: Authors paid royalty of 7-10% based on retail price. Offers advances. Illustrators paid royalty of 3% based on retail price. Sends galleys to authors; dummies to illustrators. Originals returned to artist at job's completion. Writer's guidelines available for SASE. Catalog available at website.

Tips: "At this time we are only considering chapter book and middle-grade submissions. No nonfiction or picture books. Study *Cricket* and *Spider* magazines to get an idea of our approach and to learn more of what we're looking for."

FULCRUM KIDS, Imprint of Fulcrum Publishing, 350 Indiana St., Suite 350, Golden CO 80401-5093. (303)277-1623. Fax: (303)279-7111. E-mail: fulcrum@fulcrum-resources.com. Website: www.fulcrum-resources .com. Estab. 1984. Specializes in nonfiction and educational material. **Manuscript Acquisitions:** Suzanne I. Barchers, editorial director. Publishes 4 middle readers/year. 25% of books by first-time authors. "Our mission is to make teachers' and librarians' jobs easier using quality resources."

Nonfiction: Middle readers: activity books, multicultural, nature/environment. Recently published *America's Mountains*, by Marianne Wallace (nature, ages 8-12); *Why the Leopard Has Spots: Dan Stories from Liberia*, written by Won-Ldy Paye and Met Lippert, illustrated by Ashley Bryan (multicultural, ages 8-12 yrs.); and *Cucumber Soup*, by Vickie Leigh Krudwig, illustrated by Craig MacFarland Brown (nature/counting, ages 3-6).

How to Contact/Writers: Submit complete ms or submit outline/synopsis and 2 sample chapters. Reports on queries in 2-3 weeks; mss in 1-2 months. Publishes a book 12-18 months after acceptance. Will consider simultaneous submissions.

Illustration: Works with 4 illustrators/year. Reviews ms/illustration packages from artists. Send ms with dummy or submit ms with 3 pieces of final art. Send résumé, promotional literature and tearsheets. Contact: Suzanne Barchers, editorial director. Reports back only if interested. Samples not returned; samples filed.

Photography: Works on assignment only.

Terms: Pays authors royalty based on wholesale price. Offers advances (Average amount: $1,500). Pays illustrators by the project (range: $300-2,000) or royalty based on wholesale price. Sends galleys to authors; dummies to illustrators. Originals returned to artist at job's completion. Book catalog available for 9 × 12 SAE and 3 first-class stamps; ms guidelines available for SASE. Catalog available on website.

Tips: "Research our line first. We are emphasizing science and nature nonfiction. We look for books that appeal to the school market and trade. Be sure to include SASE."

LAURA GERINGER BOOKS, 1350 Avenue of the Americas, New York NY 10019. (212)261-6500. Imprint of HarperCollins Publishers. **Manuscript Acquisitions:** Laura Geringer, publisher and senior vice president. **Art Acquisitions:** Harriett Barton, art director. Publishes 10-12 picture books/year; 2-4 young adult titles/ year.

Fiction: All levels: all subjects. Average word length: picture books—250-1,200. Recently published *Jazper*, by Richard Egielski (ages 3-7, picture book); *Zoe Rising*, by Pam Conrad (ages 10 and up, middle grade fiction); and *Vanishing*, by Bruce Brooks; and *Rolie Polie Olie*, by William Joyce (ages 4-8, picture book).

How to Contact/Writers: Submit complete ms. Reports on queries in 2-4 weeks; mss in 3-4 months. Publishes a book 1-3 years after acceptance. Will consider simultaneous submissions.

Illustration: Works with 15-20 illustrators/year. Reviews ms/illustration packages from artists. Submit complete package. Illustrations only: Query with samples; submit portfolio for review; provide résumé, business card, promotional literature or tearsheets to be kept on file. Reports in 2-3 months. SASE for return of samples; samples kept on file.

Terms: Pays advance and royalties to be negotiated. Sends galleys to authors; proofs to illustrators. Original artwork returned at job's completion. Book catalog available for 9 × 11 SASE; ms/artist's guidelines available for SASE.

Tips: "Write about what you *know* and care about. Don't try to guess our needs. Don't write down to children. We are looking for fresh and original material with a strong sense of style and expression; whether it be comic or tragic, it should be deeply felt."

GIBBS SMITH, PUBLISHER, P.O. Box 667, Layton UT 84041. (801)544-9800. Fax: (801)544-5582. Imprint: Gibbs Smith Junior. Book publisher. Editorial Director: Madge Baird. **Acquisitions:** Suzanne Taylor, children's book editor. Publishes 2-3 books/year. 50% of books by first-time authors. 50% of books from agented authors.

Fiction: Picture books: adventure, contemporary, humor, multicultural, nature/environment, suspense/mystery, western. Average word length: picture books—1,000. Recently published *Bullfrog Pops!*, by Rick Walton, illustrated by Chris McAllister (ages 4-8); and *The Magic Boots*, by Scott Emerson, illustrated by Howard Post (ages 4-8).

Nonfiction: Middle readers: activity, arts/crafts, cooking, how-to, nature/environment, science. Average word length: up to 10,000. Recently published *Hiding in a Fort*, by G. Lawson Drinkard, illustrated by Fran Lee (ages 7-12); and *Sleeping in a Sack: Camping Activities for Kids*, by Linda White, illustrated by Fran Lee (ages 7-12).

"PICTURE BOOKS" are for preschoolers to 8-year-olds; "Young readers" are for 5- to 8-year-olds; "Middle readers" are for 9- to 11-year-olds; and "Young adults" are for ages 12 and up. Age ranges may vary slightly from publisher to publisher.

How to Contact/Writers: Fiction/Nonfiction: Submit several chapters or complete ms. Reports on queries and mss in 8-10 weeks. Publishes a book 1-2 years after acceptance. Will consider simultaneous submissions. Ms returned with SASE.

Illustration: Works with 2-3 illustrators/year. Reviews ms/illustration packages from artists. Query. Submit ms with 3-5 pieces of final art. Illustrations only: Query with samples; provide résumé, promo sheet, slides (duplicate slides, not originals). Reports back only if interested. Samples returned with SASE; samples filed.

Terms: Pays authors royalty of 4 7½% based on wholesale price or work purchased outright ($500 minimum). Offers advances (average amount: $2,000). Pays illustrators by the project or royalty of 4-5% based on wholesale price. Sends galleys to authors; color proofs to illustrators. Original artwork returned at job's completion. Book catalog available for 9×12 SAE and postage. Ms guidelines available.

Tips: "We target ages 5-11."

DAVID R. GODINE, PUBLISHER, 9 Hamilton Place, Boston MA 02108. (617)451-9600. Fax: (617)350-0250. Book publisher. Estab. 1970. Publishes 1 picture book/year; 1 young reader title/year; 1 middle reader title/year. 10% of books by first-time authors; 75% of books from agented writers. "We publish books that matter for people who care."

- This publisher is no longer considering unsolicited mss of any type.

Fiction: Picture books: adventure, animal, contemporary, folktales, nature/environment. Young readers: adventure, animal, contemporary, folk or fairy tales, history, nature/environment, poetry. Middle readers: adventure, animal, contemporary, folk or fairy tales, history, mystery, nature/environment, poetry. Young adults/teens: adventure, animal, contemporary, history, mystery, nature/environment, poetry. Recently published *The Empty Creel*, by Geraldine Pope (Paterson Prize winning book with vinyl-cut illustrations).

Nonfiction: Picture books: alphabet, animal, nature/environment. Young readers: activity books, animal, history, music/dance, nature/environment. Middle readers: activity books, animal, biography, history, music/dance, nature/environment. Young adults: biography, history, music/dance, nature/environment.

How to Contact/Writers: Query. Reports on queries in 2 weeks. Reports on solicited ms in 2 weeks (if not agented) or 2 months (if agented). Publishes a book 2 years after acceptance.

Illustration: Only interested in agented material. Works with 4-6 illustrators/year. Reviews ms/illustration packages from artists. "Submit roughs and one piece of finished art plus either sample chapters for very long works or whole ms for short works." Illustrations only: "After query, submit slides, with one full-size blow-up of art." Reports on art samples in 2 weeks. Original artwork returned at job's completion. "Almost all of the children's books we accept for publication come to us with the author and illustrator already paired up. Therefore, we rarely use freelance illustrators." Samples returned with SASE; samples filed (if interested).

Terms: Pays authors in royalties based on retail price. Number of illustrations used determines final payment for illustrators. Pay for separate authors and illustrators "differs with each collaboration." Illustrators paid by the project. Sends galleys to authors; dummies to illustrators. Originals returned at job's completion. Book catalog available for SASE.

Tips: "Always enclose a SASE. Keep in mind that we do not accept unsolicited manuscripts and that we rarely use freelance illustrators."

GOLDEN BOOKS, 888 Seventh Ave., New York NY 10106-4100. (212)547-6700. Imprint of Golden Books Family Entertainment Inc. **Editorial Directors:** Didre Arico, trade publishing; Lori Haskins, Road to Reading; Sharon Shavers Gayle, Gold Key Paperbacks. **Art Acquisitions:** Paula Darmofal, executive art director. 100% of books from agented authors.

- Golden Books is not currently accepting submissions (manuscripts or queries).

Fiction: They publish board books, novelty books, picture books, workbooks, series (mostly mass market).

GREENE BARK PRESS, P.O. Box 1108, Bridgeport CT 06601-1108. (203)372-4861. Fax: (203)371-5856. E-mail: greenebark@aol.com. Website: www.bookworld.com/greenebark. Book publisher. **Acquisitions:** Michele Hofbauer; associate publisher. Thomas J. Greene, publisher. Publishes 4-6 picture books/year. 40% of books by first-time authors. "We publish quality hardcover picture books for children. Our books and stories are selected for originality, imagery and colorfulness. Our intention is to capture a child's attention; to fire-up his or her imagination and desire to read and explore the world through books."

Fiction: Picture books, young readers: adventure, fantasy, humor. Average word length: picture books—650; young readers—1,400. Recently published *Excuse Me, Are you a Dargon?*, written and illustrated by Rhett Ransom Pennell (for aages 3 to 8); *The Monster Encyclopedia*, by Dave Branson, illustrated by Tom Bartimole (for ages 3-8); and *A Pumpkin Story*, written and illustrated by Markio Shinju (for ages 3 to 8).

How to Contact/Writers: Reports on queries in 1 month; ms in 2-4 months. Publishes a book 18 months after acceptance. Will consider simultaneous submissions. Prefer to review complete mss with illustrations.

Illustrations: Works with 1-2 illustrators/year. Uses color artwork only. Reviews ms/illustration packages from artists. Submit ms with 3 pieces of final art (copies only). Illustrations only: Query with samples. Reports in 2 months only if interested. Samples returned with SASE; samples filed. Originals returned at job's completion.

Terms: Pays authors royalty of 10-12% based on wholesale price. Pays illustrators by the project (range: $1,500-3,000) or 5-7½% royalty based on wholesale price. No advances. Send galleys to authors; dummies to illustrators.

insider report

Tapping into children's natural desire for learning

Larry Rood and his wife Leah started Gryphon House in 1971 with a typewriter, an adding machine and a few boxes of children's books. They paid $125/month to rent space in a Washington, D.C., fourth-floor walk-up office where the roof leaked when it rained. ("There is no such thing as the 'good old days,'" Rood says.) They didn't publish, but distributed preschool children's picture books to child care centers and preschools. In 1979 they published their first two activity books, which they kept in print for 15 years. A small family company, Gryphon House now publishes 8 books a year for parents and early childhood teachers and has a backlist of over 65 books.

Larry Rood

How is Gryphon House different from other publishers of books for parents and teachers?
We publish books of active, hands-on, creative learning activities which teachers and parents can share with young children. We try to include activities that are easy to do, but which also reflect good pedagogy and the best current information about how children learn and grow. We think it's important that learning experiences respect children's individuality and tap into their natural desire for learning.

Are there disadvantages to being a publisher outside New York City?
I don't think there are any particular disadvantages, aside from the lack of good bagels. You need a good source of freelance and part-time help, and any fair-sized metropolitan area can provide that. It might be tough to run a publishing company in a truly remote corner of the globe, I suppose, but with the advent of the electronic miracles, location becomes less and less important. We travel to New York twice a year to attend our distributor's sales conference and meet the reps, but that's the only event requiring our bodily presence in New York.

Have you changed as a publisher since you founded Gryphon House?
You mean besides the gray hair? When we started, I thought we were publishing books. Don't misunderstand, that's the thing we do. But what we really are is a complicated and wonderful pattern of relationships with the people who work at Gryphon House and our authors, customers, distributors and suppliers. This web of interconnectedness is what makes Gryphon House work. And the trick is to maximize the communication between the various people involved and to make clear to everyone his or her importance and value. Every role is indispensable. You cannot publish without people to read the books, people to write them, people to open the mail and people to pack the books in boxes. I have a special reverence for book packers.

Do you go out looking for new writers?

We sure do. We constantly search the literature in our field, which means we read the journals of the major professional associations and the independent journals *Early Childhood Today, Early Childhood News* and *Report on Preschool Programs.* We check the Web and attend workshops at conferences sponsored by the National Association for the Education of Young Children, the Association for Childhood Education International, the Southern Early Childhood Association and the International Reading Association. We see what new things people are talking about at these conferences and what sessions and meetings have the best "draw."

What's the best way for a writer to approach you?

We do NOT want to receive manuscripts. We prefer query letters, but will accept proposals. Our manuscript guidelines are available on our website (www.gryphonhouse.com) by clicking on "About Us." It will tell you what we want to know about you and your book. The reason we prefer this approach—queries and not manuscripts—is that we want to have some input on how you organize and present your material. We prefer to be involved from the beginning.

Making Make-Believe, which offers instructions for fun and easy-to-make costumes and props for play, games, dress-up and more, is an example of Gryphon House's line of activity books and teacher resources. The company's goal is "to provide teachers and parents with the best materials available to aid in the development and education of young children" through books offering "creative, participatory learning experiences." Visit their website (www.gryphonhouse.com) to learn more about the company and its titles.

What do you look for in a cover letter?

We want to know that you are knowledgeable in the subject matter. In addition to a résumé or curriculum vitae, if you are not well known, send us a couple of samples of your published writing, say, from a periodical or newsletter. Of course, if you have written previous books, let us know that. Our real question is, "Can we sell this book in quantities beyond our wildest dreams?" Anything you can tell us to help answer this question will be useful.

Is it more important to you that your authors be good writers or good educators in the field?

We require both. Authors must have an innovative, useful and easily accessible approach to their subject matter. They must also have material that teachers want.

What's the best way for illustrators to approach you?

They should send us their promotional pieces and a description of their previously published work. We keep these on file and go through them when we need a new illustrator.

Does the editor-author relationship ever go wrong?

At Gryphon House we have nifty editor-author relationships; many of our authors are repeat authors and have been writing for us for years. But, having said that, we have occasionally had problems. From our point of view, these come about when an author doesn't understand the publishing process and how a real-life business operates. An editor may be working on several books at once, and a first-time author may expect an immediate response to daily phone calls. Also, it takes time to move from manuscript to printed books in the store, but the new author assumes that once the manuscript is in, the book should emerge immediately. In addition to demands on the editor's time, there are issues around advertising and publicity. If, upon publication, the book is not as successful as the first-time author envisioned, he or she feels it's the publisher's fault. All of this is why one successful, mid-size trade publisher I know refuses to publish first-time authors.

What's the editor's responsibility in the author-editor relationship?

It's important for editors to assure authors that the manuscript they have sweated blood over is in good hands. Publishing, if done well, is a personal process. This mostly has to do with the bond the editor establishes with the author. I was recently in a roomful of editors from small publishing houses and they all agreed that the act of submitting a manuscript contains within it an element of vulnerability. A good editor recognizes this and treats the author-editor relationship as a human relationship.

What do you want to leave as your legacy in the publishing world?

Years ago I was in a workshop lead by publisher David Godine. I will never forget what he said: "Fifty years from now, no one will remember whether you were profitable or ran a good business. You will be known by the books you publish." I think that's the legacy most serious independent publishers want to leave. It's certainly mine.

—Anna Olswanger

Book catalog available for $2.00 fee which includes mailing. All imprints included in a single catalog. Ms and art guidelines available for SASE.

Tips: "As a guide for future publications do not look to our older backlist. Please no telephone, e-mail or fax queries."

GREENHAVEN PRESS, P.O. Box 289011, San Diego CA 92128-9011. (619)485-7424. Website: www.greenha ven.com. Book publisher. Estab. 1970. **Acquisitions:** David Haugen, managing editor. Publishes 100 young adult titles/year. 35% of books by first-time authors. "Greenhaven continues to print quality nonfiction for libraries and classrooms. Our well known opposing viewpoints series is still highly respected by students and librarians in need of material on controversial social issues. In recent years, Greenhaven has also branched out with a new series covering historical and literary topics."
- Greenhaven accepts no unsolicited mss. All writing is done on a work-for-hire basis.

Nonfiction: Middle readers: biography, controversial topics, history, issues. Young adults: biography, history, nature/environment. Other titles "to fit our specific series." Average word length: young adults—15,000-25,000.

How to Contact/Writers: Query only.

Terms: Buys ms outright for $1,500-3,000. Offers advances. Sends galleys to authors. Book catalog available for 9×12 SAE and 65¢ postage.

Tips: "Get our guidelines first before submitting anything."

GREENWILLOW BOOKS, 1350 Avenue of the Americas, New York NY 10019. (212)261-6500. Imprint of William Morrow & Co. Book publisher. Editor-in-Chief: Susan Hirschman. **Manuscript Acquisitions:** Submit to Editorial Department. **Art Acquisitions:** Ava Weiss, art director. Publishes 50 picture books/year; 5 middle readers books/year; and 5 young adult books/year. "Greenwillow Books publishes picture books, fiction for young readers of all ages, and nonfiction primarily for children under seven years of age. We hope you will read many children's books (especially those on our list), decide what you like or don't like about them, then write the story *you* want to tell (not what you think we want to read), and send it to us!"
- Turn to First Books on page 45 to read about Greenwillow author Brenda Shannon Yee and her book *Sand Castle*.

Fiction: Will consider all levels of fiction; various categories.

Nonfiction: Will consider nonfiction for children under seven.

How to Contact/Writers: Submit complete ms. "If your work is illustrated, we ask to see a typed text, rough dummy, and a *copy* of a finished picture. Please do not send original artwork with your submission." Do not call. Reports on mss in 10-12 weeks. Publishes a book 18-24 months after acceptance. Will consider simultaneous submissions.

Illustration: Reviews ms/illustration packages from artists. Illustrations only: Query with samples, résumé.

Terms: Pays authors royalty. Offers advances. Pays illustrators royalty or by the project. Sends galleys to authors. Book catalog available for 9×12 SAE with $2.20 postage (no cash); ms guidelines available for SASE.

Tips: "You need not have a literary agent to submit to us. We accept—and encourage—simultaneous submissions to other publishers and ask only that you so inform us. Because we receive thousands of submissions, we do not keep a record of the manuscripts we receive and cannot check the status of your manuscript. We do try to respond within ten weeks' time."

GROLIER PUBLISHING, (Children's Press and Franklin Watts), 90 Sherman Turnpike, Danbury CT 06816. (203)797-3500. Book publisher. Vice President/Publisher: John Selfridge. **Manuscript Acquisitions:** Mark Friedman, executive editor. **Art Acquisitions:** Marie Greco, art director. Science: Melissa Stewart. Publishes more than 400 titles/year. 5% of books by first-time authors; very few titles from agented authors. Publishes informational (nonfiction) for K-12; picture books for young readers, grades 1-3.

Fiction: Publishes 1 picture book series, Rookie Readers, for grades 1-2. Does not accept unsolicited mss.

Nonfiction: Photo-illustrated books for all levels: animal, arts/crafts, biography, careers, concept, geography, health, history, hobbies, how-to, multicultural, nature/environment, science, social issues, special needs, sports. Average word length: young readers—2,000; middle readers—8,000; young adult—15,000.

How to Contact/Writers: Fiction: Does not accept fiction proposals. Nonfiction: Query; submit outline/synopsis, résumé and/or list of publications, and writing sample. SASE required for response. Reports in 2-3 months. Will consider simultaneous submissions. Contact: Mark Friedman, executive editor. No phone or e-mail queries; will not respond to phone inquiries about submitted material.

Illustration: Works with 15-20 illustrators/year. Uses color artwork and line drawings. Illustrations only: Query with samples or arrange personal portfolio review. Contact: Marie Greco, art director. Reports back only if interested. Samples returned with SASE. Samples filed. Do not send originals. No phone or e-mail inquiries; contact only by mail.

Photography: Purchases photos from freelancers. Contact: Caroline Anderson, Photo Manager. Buys stock and assigns work. Model/property releases and captions required. Uses color and b&w prints; 2¼×2¼, 35mm transparencies, images on CD-ROM. Photographers should send cover letter and stock photo list.

Terms: Pays authors royalty based on net or work purchased outright. Pays illustrators at competitive rates. Photographers paid per photo. Sends galleys to authors; dummies to illustrators.

GROSSET & DUNLAP, INC./PRICE STERN SLOAN, (212)951-8700. Imprint of The Putnam & Grosset Group.
● Grosset & Dunlap/Price Stern Sloan does not accept unsolicited submissions.

GRYPHON HOUSE, P.O. Box 207, Beltsville MD 20704-0207. (301)595-9500. Fax: (301)595-0051. E-mail: kathyc@ghbooks.com. Book publisher. **Acquisitions:** Kathy Charner, editor-in-chief.
Nonfiction: Parent and teacher resource books—activity books, textbooks. Recently published *500 Five Minute Games*, by Jackie Silberg; *Global Art*, by MaryAnn Kohl and Jean Potter; *Count on Math*, by Pam Schiller; and *The Complete Resource Book*, by Pam Schiller.
How to Contact/Writers: Query. Submit outline/synopsis and 2 sample chapters. Reports on queries/mss in 3 months. Publishes a book 18 months after acceptance. Will consider simultaneous submissions, electronic submissions via disk or modem.
Illustration: Works with 3-4 illustrators/year. Uses b&w artwork only. Reviews ms/illustration packages from artists. Submit query letter with table of contents, introduction and sample chapters. Illustrations only: Query with samples, promo sheet. Reports back in 2 months. Samples returned with SASE; samples filed.
Photography: Buys photos from freelancers. Buys stock and assigns work. Submit cover letter, published samples, stock photo list.
Terms: Pays authors royalty based on wholesale price. Offers advances. Pays illustrators by the project. Pay photographers by the project or per photo. Sends galleys to authors. Original artwork returned at job's completion. Book catalog and ms guidelines available for SASE.
Tips: "Send a SASE for our catalog and manuscript guidelines. Look at our books, then submit proposals that complement the books we already publish or supplement our existing books. We are looking for books of creative, participatory learning experiences that have a common conceptual theme to tie them together. The books should be on subjects that parents or teachers want to do on a daily basis."

GULLIVER BOOKS, 15 E. 26th St., New York NY 10010. (212)592-1000. Imprint of Harcourt Brace & Co.
Acquisitions: Elizabeth Van Doren, editorial director, Anne Davies, senior editor. Publishes 25 titles/year.
● Gulliver only accepts mss submitted by agents, previously published authors, or SCBWI members.
Fiction: Emphasis on picture books. Also publishes middle grade and young adult.
Nonfiction: Publishes nonfiction.
How to Contact/Writers: Fiction/Nonfiction: Query or send ms for picture book.

HACHAI PUBLISHING, 156 Chester Ave., Brooklyn NY 11218-3020. (718)633-0100. Fax: (718)633-0103. E-mail: info@hachai.com. Website: www.hachai.com. Book publisher. **Manuscript Acquisitions:** Devorah Leah Rosenfeld, submissions editor. Publishes 3 picture books/year; 3 young readers/year; 1 middle reader/year. 75% of books published by first-time authors. "All books have spiritual/religious themes, specifically traditional Jewish content. We're seeking books about morals and values; the Jewish experience in current and Biblical times; and Jewish observance, Sabbath and holidays."
● Hachai Publishing's *Nine Spoons: A Chanukah Story*, by Marci Stillerman, won the AJL Sydney Taylor Award.
Fiction: Picture books and young readers: contemporary, history, religion. Middle readers: adventure, contemporary, problem novels, religion. Does not want to see animal stories, romance, problem novels depicting drug use or violence. Recently published *As Big As An Egg*, by Rachel Sandman, illustrated by Chana Zakashanskaya (ages 3-6, picture book); and *Red, Blue, and Yellow Yarn*, by Miriam Kosman, illustrated by Valeri Gorbachev (ages 3-6, picture book).
Nonfiction: Published *My Jewish ABC's*, by Draizy Zelcer, illustrated by Patti Nemeroff (ages 3-6, picture book); *Nine Spoons* by Marci Stillerman, illustrated by Pesach Gerber (ages 5-8).
How to Contact/Wrtiers: Fiction/Nonfiction: Submit complete ms. Reports on queries/mss in 6 weeks.
Illustration: Works with 4 illustrators/year. Uses primary color artwork, some b&w illustration. Reviews ms/illustration packages from authors. Submit ms with 1 piece of final art. Contact: Devorah Leah Rosenfeld, submissions editor. Illustrations only: Query with samples; arrange personal portfolio review. Reports in 6 weeks. Samples returned with SASE; samples filed.
Terms: Work purchased outright from authors for $800-1,000. Pays illustrators by the project (range: $2,000-3,500). Book catalog, ms/artist's guidelines available for SASE.
Tips: "Write a story that incorporates a moral . . . not a preachy morality tale. Originality is the key. We feel Hachai is going to appeal to a wider readership as parents become more interested in positive values for their children."

HAMPTON ROADS PUBLISHING COMPANY, INC., 134 Burgess Lane, Charlottesville VA 22902. (804)296-2772. Fax: (804)296-5096. E-mail: hrpc@hrpub.com. Website: www.hrpub.com. Estab. 1989. **Manuscript Acquisitions:** Robert Friedman. **Art Acquisitions:** Jane Hagaman. Publishes 3 picture books/year. 60% of books by first-time authors. Mission Statement: "to work as a team to seek, create, refine and produce the best books we are capable of producing, which will impact, uplift and contribute to positive change in the world; to promote the physical, mental, emotional and financial well-being of all its staff and associates; to build the

"The story, the publisher and the editor of this book made it one of the great challenges and joys of a very long art career," says Pesach Gerber of his work on *Nine Spoons: A Chanukah Story*, by Marci Stillerman. The book was especially challenging to illustrate because of its young audience and its troubling subject matter, the persistence of faith in a Nazi concentration camp. Hachai Publishing chose Gerber for the project because "we felt he could successfully convey the bleak atmosphere of a Nazi camp without frightening young children for whom the book is designed." Gerber used watercolor, gouache and colored pencil in his illustrations. Because his art career is broad and not limited to illustration, Gerber advises artists who want to illustrate for children to "learn all the art basics needed for any other field. Study the works of other illustrators and then work even harder at developing your imagination."

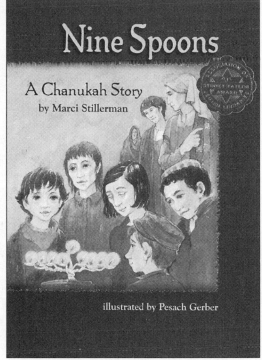

company into a powerful, respected and prosperous force in publishing in the region, the nation and the world in which we live."

Fiction: Picture books, young readers, middle readers, young adult titles: metaphysical and spiritual. Average word length: picture books—100-200; young readers—1,000-5,000; middle readers—500-4,000. Recently published *Star Babies*, by Mary Summer Rain (preschool-age 8); *The Little Soul*, by Neale Donald Walsch (ages 7-12); *OBO*, by Robert Anderson (preschool-age 8); *Herman's Magical Universe*, by Becky McCarley.

Nonfiction: Picture books, young readers, middle readers, young adult titles: metaphysical and spiritual. Average word length: picture books—100-200; young readers—1,000-5,000; middle readers—500-4,000. Recently published *Mountains, Meadows and Moonbeams*, by Mary Summer Rain (ages 5-8).

How to Contact/Writers: Fiction/nonfiction: submit complete ms. Reports on queries in 3-4 weeks; mss in 2-3 months. Publishes a book 6-12 months after acceptance. Will consider simultaneous submissions.

Illustration: Works with 2-3 illustrators/year. Reviews ms/illustration packages from artists. Submit ms with 2-3 pieces of final art (copies). Contact: Robert Friedman, president. Illustration only: query with samples. Contact: Jane Hagaman, art director. Reports in 1 month. Samples returned with SASE; samples not filed.

Terms: Pays authors royalty of 10-20% based on retail price. Offers advances (average amount: $1,000). Pays illustrators by the project (range: $250-1,000). Occasionally pays by royalty based on retail price. Sends galleys to authors. Original returned to artist at job's completion. Book catalog available for SASE. Writer's guidelines available for SASE.

Tips: "Please familiarize yourself with our mission statement and/or the books we publish. Preferably send manuscripts that can be recycled rather than returned. If there is no SASE, they will be recycled."

HARCOURT, INC., 525 B St., Suite 1900, San Diego CA 92101-4495. (619)231-6616. Children's Books Division includes: Harcourt Brace Children's Books (Allyn Johnston, editorial director), Gulliver Books (Elizabeth Van Doren, editorial director), Browndeer Press (Linda Zuckerman, editorial director), Silver Whistle Books (Paula Wiseman, editorial director), Voyager Paperbacks, Odyssey Paperbacks, and Red Wagon Books. Book publisher. **Art Acquisitions:** Art Director. Publishes 50-75 picture books/year; 5-10 middle reader titles/year; 10 young adult titles/year. 20% of books by first-time authors; 50% of books from agented writers. "Harcourt, Inc. owns some of the world's most prestigious publishing imprints—which distinguish quality products for the juvenile, educational and trade markets worldwide."

● The staff of Harcourt's children's book department is no longer accepting unsolicited manuscripts. Only query letters from previously published authors and mss submitted by agents will be considered.

insider report

Following editorial passion in a sales-driven publishing world

I thought about librarianship, and I thought about writing, but the moment I discovered there was such a thing as an editor, I realized I had been coming to it my whole life.

—Allyn Johnston
Editorial Director, Harcourt, Inc.

Allyn Johnston

. . . Her editorial history

I started my publishing career as a marketing assistant at Clarion Books in 1985. Then I worked as an editorial assistant at Harcourt, an editor at Putnam, and—back at Harcourt—an editor, senior editor, executive editor and now editorial director. Among the people I work with are Debra Frasier, Mem Fox, Cynthia Rylant, Lois Ehlert, Douglas Florian, Dav Pilkey, Theodore Taylor, Mary Lyn Ray, Jane Dyer, Jeanette Winter and Keith Baker.

. . . What her day is like

My day officially starts at 8:30 and goes to 5:00, but I'm fortunate in that I've been at Harcourt long enough that, to some extent, I can shape my day. I don't have to sit at my desk with my feet in place every minute; I often work at a little coffee shop in the mornings before coming into the office. But usually I have to be here, and it can be a juggle. I present books at sales conferences, talk to the marketing people, write catalog copy. And as an editorial director, I'm not only doing my books, I'm responsible for overseeing what other editors do, too. So it's hard to get the calm time to think and do the editorial work that brought me into the field to begin with. That intimate thinking time is the hardest to keep sacred.

. . . Why she signs up a book

I think about whether the book is going to matter, if people are going to read it and have an emotional reaction. Will it make them laugh or cry? Will it make them feel nervous, tense or excited? The books that cause readers to have an emotional reaction are the hardest books to write, and they are the rarest, but they are the ones that last.

. . . Advantages of being outside New York

It opens up my mind, but I'm from California so I admit to being biased. I find I'm able to relax more into the work here, instead of worrying about what people in other houses are doing. And because Harcourt is where it is, I can't just go down the street if I've had a bad day and look for a job elsewhere. I've made a commitment to being here, and I make it work.

. . . The pressures of economics on children's book publishing

At Harcourt it used to be just the editor and publisher talking about whether we should sign up a book, but in the last two years we have started having acquisition meetings where everybody is involved. It helps us to be more educated before we make hard and fast decisions. Something obvious to a sales or marketing person might not have crossed the mind of the author or editor. But if an editor stands up for something that others aren't quite getting, we're willing to back it. We still follow editorial passion. We're also better now about smaller print runs, which means we don't have huge inventories of books sitting in the warehouse. There is nothing worse than being the editor of a book that gets remaindered. So when you're signing up a book, first of all you think, "What's it going to be like to present this at a sales conference?" And then you think, "Will it have legs and sell, or will we be talking about remaindering it in the next two years?"

. . . What new writers should know about publishing

I wish new writers would educate themselves about what books are already out there, and what makes them have staying power. I'm always speaking at writing conferences and telling people to read books. I'm shocked at how few people do.

Illustration © Arthur Howard. Reprinted with permission of Harcourt, Inc.

A "fun spin on discovering hidden talents," dog lovers of all ages will enjoy *Cosmo Zooms*, written and illustrated by Arthur Howard and created under Harcourt Editorial Director Allyn Johnston's watch. Cosmo, the book's canine protagonist, finds something he's really good at—skateboarding! Howard's adorable watercolor paintings give life to an endearing group of dogs residing on Pumpkin Lane along with Cosmo, like Elvis (a hound who's a loud howler) and Puddles (a Saint Bernard who can "drool eleven hours in a row without stopping").

. . . What surprises new writers

New writers are surprised at how long it takes to find an illustrator for a picture book, how long it takes for the art to come in, and how long it takes to manufacture the book. Some writers and illustrators are overwhelmed when they realize how many books they are competing against. I've talked to people who have just had a book published, and three months later they feel let down because the world didn't stop when their book came out.

. . . What established writers should know about publishing

A lot of established writers aren't interested in doing anything to promote their books, but I wish they understood how tough it is to get books out in the world. Everything is celebrity-driven these days. Also, a lot of writers don't seem to know that their editor is trying to do well by them. Sometimes their first thought is, "She's not paying attention," instead of thinking about all the other demands on an editor's time.

. . . What authors should do to promote their books

Sometimes a book doesn't warrant a ton of promotion. Maybe it's a quiet first book. And if it's, say, a straight bedtime story without an educational hook, we can't do a teachers' guide the way we can for a concept book. But we love it when people want to go out and speak to schools, and we have a person in the office who helps arrange author appearances. We are kind of tense when authors go off on their own and promote their book without connecting with the house, though. They will set up appearances and fail to have the books ordered, or the materials they print up to give away aren't professional. That doesn't represent the book, author or publisher well, so we want to be involved."

. . . The importance of teachers

The retail market is crowded and libraries seem to have less money for books, but teachers—who are passionate about books—spend their own money. They want to know about different books, and they want suggestions about how to use them, so we have been consciously trying to connect with teachers directly through the Internet and making our authors available to them.

. . . Being a mother and editor

As an editor, I have always been drawn to books similar to the ones that spoke to me as a child. I was never off doing esoteric or academic children's books, but I have welcomed the experience of having my son to read to, and seeing every day what works, what doesn't. It's like a little in-house laboratory. Long picture book texts don't fly with him (or with the parent reading to him!), and the really trashy mass market books don't hold his attention. But sometimes he likes books that I've not responded to, and I've learned from having to stick with reading them. One thing I used to go around saying all the time was, "I don't want to see rhyming books." For the most part, when people write in rhyme, they succumb to it and let the rhyme control the story. But since I've had my son, I realize that you can really engage a child with good rhyme, so I'm much more open to it.

. . . Her legacy to children's book publishing

I want to publish books that go into the heart of a family and into the most private moments between parents and their children. I was one of those shy kids at the edges of things, and books were a place for me to get an emotional connection with a wider world. I could experience all these other lives, just from reading. I like to imagine the books I've worked on as being present in the lives of children the way books were for me.

—*Anna Olswanger*

Illustration © Jane Dyer. Reprinted with permission of Harcourt, Inc.

Allyn Johnston works with a number of well-known and beloved authors, Mem Fox among them. Fox's board book *Time for Bed*, illustrated by Jane Dyer, is a pre-slumber tale in lilting rhyme. Harcourt's line offers more than a dozen bedtime books including six new (Fall 1999) titles comprising their "Read to me Before I Go to Sleep" program, like Fox's *Sleepy Bears* (illustrated by Kerry Argent), *Hush Little Baby*, a folk song illustrated by Marla Frazee, and *I Hate to Go to Bed*, written and illustrated by Katie Davis.

Fiction: All levels: Considers all categories. Average word length: picture books—"varies greatly"; middle readers—20,000-50,000; young adults—35,000-65,000. Recently published *Home Run*, by Robert Burleigh, illustrated by Mike Wimmer (ages 6-10, picture book/biography); *Cast Two Shadows*, by Ann Rinaldi (ages 12 and up; young adult historical fiction); *Tell Me Something Happy Before I Go to Sleep*, by Joyce Dunbar, illustrated by Debi Glliori (ages 4-8, picture book).

Nonfiction: All levels: animal, biography, concept, history, multicultural, music/dance, nature/environment, science, sports. Average word length: picture books—"varies greatly"; middle readers—20,000-50,000; young adults—35,000-65,000. Recently published *Lives of the Presidents*, by Kathleen Krull; illustrated by Kathryn Hewitt (ages 8-12, illustrated nonfiction).

How to Contact/Writers: Only interested in agented material. Fiction: Query or submit outline/synopsis. Nonfiction: Submit outline/synopsis. Reports on queries/mss in 6-8 weeks.

Illustration: Works with 150 illustrators/year. Reviews ms/illustration packages from artists. "For picture book ms—complete ms acceptable. Longer books—outline and 2-4 sample chapters." Send one sample of art; no original art with dummy. Illustrations only: Submit résumé, tearsheets, color photocopies, color stats all accepted. "Please DO NOT send original artwork or transparencies." Samples are not returned; samples filed. Reports on art samples only if interested.

Photography: Works on assignment only.

Terms: Pays authors and illustrators in royalty based on retail price. Pays photographers by the project. Sends galleys to authors; dummies to illustrators. Original artwork returned at job's completion. Book catalog available for 8×10 SAE and 4 first-class stamps; ms/artist's guidelines for business-size SASE. All imprints included in a single catalog.

Tips: "Become acquainted with Harcourt Brace's books in particular if you are interested in submitting proposals to us."

✓ 🏆 HARPERCOLLINS CHILDREN'S BOOKS, 1350 Avenue of the Americas, New York NY 10019. (212)261-6500. Website: www.harpercollins.com. Book publisher. Editor-in-Chief: Kate Morgan Jackson. **Art Acquisitions:** Harriett Barton, art director. Imprints: Laura Geringer Books, Michael diCapua Books, Joanna Cotler Books.

● HarperCollins is not accepting unsolicited manuscripts not addressed to a specific editor. Harper title *Monster*, by Walter Dean Myers, won a 1999 Boston Globe-Horn Book Honor Award for fiction. Harper title *William Shakespeare & the Globe*, written and illustrated by Aliki, won a 1999 Boston Globe-Horn Book Honor Award for nonfiction. Harper title *The Owl and the Pussycat*, written by Edward Lear, illustrated by James Marshall, won a Boston Globe-Horn Book Honor Award for picture books. Harper title *I Have Heard of a Land*, by Joyce Carol Oates, illustrated by Floyd Cooper, won a 1999 Coretta Scott King Illustrator Honor Award. Turn to First Books on page 45 to read about HarperCollins author Sonya Sones and her book *Stop Pretending: What Happened When My Big Sister Went Crazy*.

Fiction: Picture books: adventure, animal, anthology, concept, contemporary, fantasy, folktales, hi-lo, history, multicultural, nature/environment, poetry, religion. Middle readers: adventure, hi-lo, history, poetry, suspense/mystery. Young adults/teens: fantasy, science fiction, suspense/mystery. All levels: multicultural. "Artists with diverse backgrounds and settings shown in their work."

Nonfiction: Picture books: animal, arts/crafts, biography, geography, multicultural, nature/environment. Middle readers: how-to.

Illustration: Works with 100 illustrators/year. Reports only if interested. Samples returned with SASE; samples filed only if interested.

How to Contact/Writers: Nonfiction: Query.

Terms: Ms and art guidelines available for SASE.

HARVEST HOUSE PUBLISHERS, 1075 Arrowsmith, Eugene OR 97402-9197. (541)343-0123. Fax: (541)342-6410. Book publisher. Publishes 1-2 picture books/year and 2 young reader titles/year. 2-5% of books by first-time authors. Books follow a Christian theme.

● Harvest House no longer accepts unsolicited children's manuscripts.

Illustration: Works with 2-3 illustrators/year. Reviews ms/illustration packages from artists. Submit copies (do not send originals) of art and any approximate rough sketches. Send résumé, tearsheets. Submit to color design coordinator. Reports on art samples in 6-8 weeks. Samples returned with SASE; samples filed.

Terms: Pays authors in royalties of 10-15%. Average advance payment: "negotiable." Pays illustrator: "Sometimes by project." Sends galleys to authors; sometimes sends dummies to illustrators. SASE for book catalog.

✓ 📁 HAYES SCHOOL PUBLISHING CO. INC., 321 Pennwood Ave., Wilkinsburg PA 15221-3398. (412)371-2373. Fax: (800)543-8771. E-mail: chayes@hayespub.com. Website: www.hayespub.com. **Acquisitions:** Mr. Clair N. Hayes. Estab. 1940. Produces folders, workbooks, stickers, certificates. Wants to see supplementary teaching aids for grades K-12. Interested in all subject areas. Will consider simultaneous and electronic submissions.

How to Contact/Writers: Query with description or complete ms. Reports in 5-6 weeks. SASE for return of submissions.

Illustration: Works with 3-4 illustrators/year. Reports in 5-6 weeks. Samples returned with SASE; samples filed. Originals not returned at job's completion.

Terms: Work purchased outright. Purchases all rights.

☑ **HEALTH PRESS**, P.O. 1388, Santa Fe NM 87504. (505)474-0303 or (800)643-2665. Fax: (505)424-0444. E-mail: hlthprs@trail.com. Website: www.healthpress.com. Book publisher. **Acquisitions:** Contact Editor. Publishes 4 young readers/year; 4 middle readers/year. 100% of books by first-time authors.

Fiction: Young readers, middle readers: health, special needs. Average word length: young readers—1,000-1,500; middle readers—1,000-1,500. Recently published *Pennies, Nickels and Dimes*, by Elizabeth Murphy.

Nonfiction: Young readers, middle readers: health, special needs.

How to Contact/Writers: Submit complete ms. Reports in 1 month. Publishes a book 9 months after acceptance. Will consider simultaneous submissions.

Terms: Pays authors royalty. Sends galleys to authors. Book catalog available.

HENDRICK-LONG PUBLISHING COMPANY, P.O. Box 25123, Dallas TX 75225. Fax: (214)352-4768. E-mail: hendrick-long@worldnet.att.net. Book publisher. Estab. 1969. **Acquisitions:** Joann Long, vice president. Publishes 1 picture book/year; 4 young reader titles/year; 4 middle reader titles/year. 20% of books by first-time authors. Publishes fiction/nonfiction about Texas of interest to young readers through young adults/teens.

Fiction: Middle readers: history books on Texas and the Southwest. No fantasy or poetry. Recently published *Molasses Cookies*, by Janet Kaderli, illustrated by Patricia Arnold (K-5); and *Terror from the Sea*, by Martha Tannery Jones (grades 3-5).

Nonfiction: Middle, young adults: history books on Texas and the Southwest, biography, multicultural. Recently published *Lone Star Justice: A Biography of Justice Tom C. Clark* (grades 9-12).

How to Contact/Writers: Fiction/Nonfiction: Query with outline/synopsis and sample chapter. Reports on queries in 1-4 weeks; mss in 2 months. Publishes a book 18 months after acceptance. No simultaneous submissions. Include SASE.

Illustration: Works with 2-3 illustrators/year. Uses primarily b&w interior artwork; color covers only. Illustrations only: Query first. Submit résumé or promotional literature or photocopies or tearsheets—no original work sent unsolicited. Reports back only if interested.

Terms: Pays authors in royalty based on selling price. Advances vary. Pays illustrators by the project or royalty. Sends galleys to authors; dummies to illustrators. Ms guidelines for 1 first-class stamp and #10 SAE.

Tips: "Material **must** pertain to Texas or the Southwest. Check all facts about historical firgures and events in both fiction and nonfiction. Be accurate."

◖ **HIGHSMITH PRESS**, P.O. Box 800, Ft. Atkinson WI 53538-0800. (920)563-9571. (920)563-4801. E-mail: hpress@highsmith.com. Website: www.hpress.highsmith.com. Imprints: Highsmith Press, Alleyside Press, Upstart Books. Book publisher. **Acquisitions:** Donald J. Sager, publisher. Highsmith Press publishes library, professional books. Alleyside Press and Upstart Books publishes reading activity materials, storytelling aids, and library/study skills instructional resources for youth PreK-12 grade.

Nonfiction: All levels: reading activity books, library skills, reference, study skills. Multicultural needs include storytelling resources. Young adults: careers. Average length: 64-120 pages. Published *Researching Events*, by Maity Schrecengost (ages 8-11, study skills); *Toddle on Over*, by Robin Davis (ages 2-4, activity book); and *The Teen's Guide to the World Wide Web*, by Mimi Mandel (ages 13-18, reference).

How to Contact/Writers: Query or submit complete ms or submit outline/synopsis. Reports on queries/mss in 6 weeks. Publishes a book 6 months after acceptance. Will consider simultaneous submissions.

Illustration: Works with 6-12 illustrators/year. Reports in 1 month. Samples returned with SASE; samples filed. Originals returned at job's completion.

Terms: Pays authors royalty of 10-12% based on wholesale price. Pays illustrators by the project; varies considerably. Offers advances. Sends galleys to authors. Book catalog available for 9 × 12 SAE and 2 first-class stamps; ms guidelines available for SASE.

Tips: "Review our catalog and ms guidelines to see what we publish. Our complete catalog and current guidelines can be found at our website on the Internet (address above), as well as a list of projects for which we are seeking authors. We are seeking ms which help librarians and teachers to stimulate reading and how to use the Internet for instructional purposes."

HINTERLAND PUBLISHERS, Box 198, Sandy Hook, Manitoba R0C 2W0 Canada. (204)389-3842. Fax: (204)339-3635. E-mail: hinterland@gatewest.net. Website: www.hinterland.mb.ca. Book publisher. **Acquisitions:** Norma Norton, managing director. Publishes 4 picture books/year. 100% of books by first-time authors.

Fiction: Picture books: adventure, contemporary, multicultural. For multicultural fiction, needs First Nation's contemporary (realistic) fiction. Does not want to see material on legends. Average word length: picture books—1,000-2,000. Recently published *The Moons of Goose Island*, written by Don K. Philpot, illustrated by Margaret Hessian (ages 6-12, contemporary realistic fiction).

How to Contact/Writers: Fiction: Query only.

Illustration: Query or send ms with dummy. Illustrations only: Query with samples; send résumé and portfolio

insider report

Challenging subject matter appeals to YA and adult audience

Fairies, witches and genies—sounds like the makings of a child's fairy tale, right? But what about a boy-crazy fairy who smokes? Or a witch who is a member of a Jane Mansfield cult? Or a genie who grants a wish so a teenage girl can live with her gay best friend and his lover? While books with such fantastical characters wouldn't be targeted at young children, deciding whether to market them to an adult or a YA audience poses a problem for their writer Francesca Lia Block and her publisher HarperCollins.

Block's books, *I Was a Teenage Fairy*, *Girl Goddess #9*, *The Hanged Man* and her collection *Dangerous Angels*, are lyrical tapestries of life in modern-day Los Angeles, magical realism, '80s punk subculture and Greek mythology. Because she appeals to a wide range of readers, determining her audience has been a

Francesca Lia Block

difficult task since her first book, *Weetzie Bat*, was published in 1989. The first of her popular series, it was marketed as a YA novel. But Block says, "As much as I love my young audience, I did not write *Weetzie Bat* for that audience. I was thinking more of people in their early twenties."

In her early twenties herself when she wrote the book, Block says she used writing as a cure for homesickness while studying English Literature at Berkeley. "I would tell myself these stories as I was walking home from class. *Weetzie* was something I was doing for myself—a healing thing, taking me back to Los Angeles and the people I missed."

After college, Block gave her manuscript to a friend who sent it to Charlotte Zolotow at HarperCollins. "I was thrilled," says Block, "I loved her books as a girl, and she's known for taking great risks successfully in the publishing of children's books." Still with HarperCollins, Block's current editor is Joanna Cotler, who worked on her latest book, *Violet & Claire*, as well as a book of modern fairy tales due out next year, with the working title *Charm*.

According to Block, working with these two prominent editors has been invaluable for her career. "They are brilliant editors," she says. "They really understand me in a deep, personal way. Joanna is wonderful because she encourages me to write whatever comes out. From there we figure out how to make it work."

For example, Block's novel *The Hanged Man*, which deals with sexual abuse and eating disorders, presented a challenge to her editors. "It was definitely a dark, difficult subject for a YA book," says Block. "But Joanna said, 'I like this book. I want to try it. Let's just see what happens.' She took that chance even though it was ahead of the times for YA publishing. It didn't do as well as some of my other books, but it's gotten my highest praise from readers of almost any book. You can get away with *Weetzie Bat* for 14-year-olds, but *The Hanged Man* is definitely for someone a little older or a very mature teenager." Her readers' acclaim added to her editor's support resulted in *The Hanged Man's* recent re-release in paperback.

Because bookstores often have a separate YA section, adults receive less exposure to her books. "People at readings come up to me to say I would never have read you if you hadn't been recommended to me by a friend," says Block. Sensing her frustration, HarperCollins came up with a solution to this marketing dilemma. They repackaged her five Weetzie Bat novels in *Dangerous Angels*, a single collection. "We wanted the thickness and the great cover," explains Block. "I don't think it would have made the *Los Angeles Times* Bestseller List if it was strictly a YA book. I try not to think of how marketing can affect sales too much because it takes me away from the reason I'm writing. At the same time, I want to reach the full audience, in particular the audience I intended *Weetzie Bat* for."

Nevertheless teens are drawn to phrases like "lanky lizards" and "slinkster cool" which inspire a feeling of confidance between Block and her readers. Young readers also relate easily to her characters like Witch Baby, who Block describes as "an anti-heroine who tears everything apart in order to bring it back together again" and Weetzie Bat who is "a sweet, maternal character who makes her own mistakes."

Still, critics of Block's books claim she writes material that is inappropriate for teenagers. Such critiques reflect another difficulty of marketing books originally written for adults to teens, but Block believes her young readers are capable of handling subjects like sex, drugs

Penned by the author called "one of the coolest people in L.A." by *Buzz* magazine, Francesca Lia Block's saga about "the punk pixie flower child" Wheetzie Bat and her contemporaries was published in a single collection by HarperCollins called *Dangerous Angels*. (The title comes from a quote in *Wheetzie Bat*: "Love is a dangerous angel."). The sophisticated, ethereal jacket and thickness of the collection, consisting of five novels, are meant to appeal to an adult audience who may not have come across Block's books shelved among young adult titles. The publisher even created a *Dangerous Angels* reading group guide.

Reprinted with permission of HarperCollins Publishers

and abuse. "As a writer of literature, I'm afraid to censor myself too much. I want to produce a story that is as true and meaningful as I can make it and then let my editors decide how to place it. Librarians, teachers, parents, and the kids themselves can also help decide what is appropriate. Kids are exposed to so much more now. I think the YA market has changed to meet their needs and interests. I believe it is better for a curious young person to read about difficult subjects than to seek them out in real life."

The written response to Block's work proves that her YA readers are not only capable of handling mature topics, they need books out there that deal with the real issues present in their daily lives. "The fan mail I receive brings me back to the real reason I'm writing—to express my feelings and to touch people," says Block. "The best thing is getting letters from kids feeling that it's okay to be gay or like one from a woman who read *The Hanged Man* and said it changed her life by helping her deal with issues of abuse and seek therapy. And when I think about that stuff, I stop worrying about where the books are in the store. It doesn't really matter."

—*Donya Dickerson*

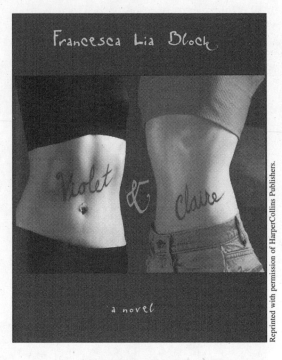

Reprinted with permission of HarperCollins Publishers.

"The elements of the story—fairies, overnight fame, arts, sex and drugs, glamorous parties, and of course, the heady Los Angeles setting—are classic Block," says a starred *Publishers Weekly* review of Francesca Lia Block's latest novel, *Violet & Clare*. "The combination, however, is fresh and arresting, and her fans will applaud it. . . . Shedding a transformative light onto the often complex nature of close friendship, Block's writing is as lush and luminous, as hip and wise as ever."

to be kept on file. Reports in 6 weeks. Samples returned with SASE. Must have proper postage for Canada (International Reply Coupon).

Terms: Pays authors royalty of 10-25% based on retail price. Pays illustrators royalty of 10-25% based on retail price. Sends galleys to authors; dummies to illustrators. Originals returned to artist at job's completion.

Tips: "Quality is a top consideration at Hinterland Publishers. Stories must be fresh, thoughtful and imaginative. Stylistically, a writer must demonstrate an excellent command of the English language. Stories told in a literary style will receive special attention."

HODDER CHILDREN'S BOOKS, Hodder Headline PLC, 338 Euston Rd., London NW1 3BH England. (0171)873-6000. Fax: (0171)873-6229. Book publisher. **Manuscript Acquisitions:** Margaret Conroy (audio), Kate Burns (picture books), Isabel Boissier (fiction) Anne Clark (nonfiction). **Art Acquisitions:** Claire Bond. Publishes 12 picture books/year; 24 young readers/year; 50 middle readers; 6 young adult titles/year; and series fiction.

Fiction: Young readers and middle readers: adventure, animal, contemporary, fantasy, humor, science fiction and suspense/mystery. Young adults: adventure, contemporary, fantasy, science fiction, sports, suspense/mystery, horror. Average word length: picture books—1,000; read alones (6-8 years) 2,000-4,000; story books (7-9 years) 8,000-12,000; novels (8 and up) 20,000-50,000.

Nonfiction: Picture books: animal. Young readers: activity books, humor. Middle readers: activity books. Young adults: activity books, animal, health, history, hobbies, how-to, reference, science. self-help, social issues. Average word length: picture books—1,000; young readers—5,000; middle readers—15,000; young adults—20,000. Recently published *Kit's Wilderness*, by David Almond; *The Great Pet Sale*, by Mick Inkpen; and *Wise Guides*.

How to Contact/Writers: Fiction: Submit outline/synopsis and 3 sample chapters addressed to the readers. Reports on queries in 1 month if SAE enclosed; mss in 6-8 weeks if SAE enclosed. Publishes a book 12-18 months after acceptance. Will consider simultaneous submissions.

Illustration: Works with 80 illustrators/year. Uses both b&w and color artwork. Reviews ms/illustration packages from authors. Submit ms with dummy. Contact: Children's Editor. Illustrations only: query with photocopied samples. Reports in 1 month only if interested. Samples returned with SASE; samples filed.

Photography: Buys photos from freelancers. Contact: Children's Art Dept. Buys stock and assigns work. Submit cover letter.

Terms: Pays authors 4-10% royalty based on retail price or work purchased outright. Pays illustrators by the project or royalty. Pays photographers by the project. Original artwork returned at job's completion. Sends galleys to authors. Ms guidelines available.

Tips: "Write from the heart. Don't patronize your reader. Do your research—read the finest writers around, see where the market is. We're looking for something original with a clear sense of the first reader."

HOLIDAY HOUSE INC., 425 Madison Ave., New York NY 10017. (212)688-0085. Fax: (212)421-6134. Book publisher. Estab. 1935. Vice President/Editor-in-Chief: Regina Griffin. **Acquisitions:** Associate Editor. Publishes 35 picture books/year; 3 young reader titles/year; 10 middle reader titles/year; and 3 young adult titles/year. 20% of books by first-time authors; 10% from agented writers.

Fiction: All levels: adventure, contemporary, ghost, historical, humor, school. Picture books, middle readers, young adults. Recently published *A Child's Calendar*, by John Updike, illustrated by Trina Schart Hyman; *I Was a Third Grade Science Project*, by M.J. Asch; and *Darkness Over Denmark*, by Ellen Levine.

> • See Oh, the Places I've Been! Oh, the Places You Can Go! Preparing to Promote Your Children's Book on page 59 for advice from Holiday House author Esther Hershenhorn and Holiday House Director of Marketing Diane Foote.

Nonfiction: All levels: animal, biography, concept, contemporary, geography, historical, math, nature/environment, science, social studies.

How to Contact/Writers: Send queries only to Associate Editor. Reports on queries in 2 months. "If we find your book idea suited to our present needs, we will notify you by mail. Once a ms has been requested, the writers should send in the exclusive submission, with a S.A.S.E., otherwise the ms will not be returned."

Illustration: Works with 35 illustrators/year. Reviews ms illustration packages from artists. Send ms with dummy. Do not submit original artwork or slides. Color photocopies or printed samples are preferred. Reports back only if interested. Samples returned with SASE or filed.

Terms: Pays authors and illustrators an advance against royalties. Originals returned at job's completion. Book catalog, ms/artist's guidelines available for a SASE.

Tips: "Fewer books are being published. It will get even harder for first timers to break in."

HENRY HOLT & CO., INC., 115 W. 18th St., New York NY 10011. (212)886-9200. Book publisher. **Manuscript Acquisitions:** Laura Godwin, editor-in-chief/associate publisher of Books for Young Readers dept.; Nina Ignatowicz, executive editor; Marc Aronson, senior editor, Christy Ottaviano, senior editor. **Art Acquisitions:** Martha Rago, art director. Publishes 20-40 picture books/year; 4-6 chapter books/year; 10-15 middle grade titles/year; 8-10 young adult titles/year. 8% of books by first-time authors; 40% of books from agented writers. "Henry Holt and Company Books for Young Readers is known for publishing quality books that feature imaginative authors and illustrators. We tend to publish many new authors and illustrators each year in our effort to develop and foster new talent."

insider report

Sharing the beauty of snowflakes—the reward is in the writing

Jacqueline Briggs Martin, author of the 1999 Caldecott award-winning *Snowflake Bentley*, has written 12 children's books, many of which celebrate the natural world. Her love of words is as evident in her writing as her love of the environment, and she encourages all writers to first become great readers. Her own writing inspirations include Maurice Sendak, William Steig, Barbara Cooney, Rosemary Wells, Steven Kellogg, Nancy Willard and Donald Hall. Here Martin shares the details of her writing life, keys to effective research and her tactics for finding publishers without an agent.

Jacqueline Briggs Martin

What influences in your life made you want to write books for children?

I have always loved the sounds of words. I grew up on a dairy farm and remember being particularly aware of the names of our registered Holsteins. (One of our cows, Riverflat Blanche Wisconsin, showed up in my book *Good Times on Grandfather Mountain*.) I've always loved hearing stories. As a child, I also enjoyed sitting on the edge of an adult conversation and listening to the stories. And I love sharing stories.

When our two children were young my husband and I lived in the country in a rented Iowa farmhouse. There were not many close neighbors to visit with or many close children to play with Sarah and Justin while my husband was at his job. So Justin, Sarah and I spent our days together playing and reading books. We read many books each day and one day I decided I wanted to write books for children—books that parents and children might enjoy as we had enjoyed the books of others.

How did you turn that desire into reality?

I bought a new tablet, a new pen and began to write while Sarah and Justin were napping. When they grew too old to nap I decided to get up early (and I do mean early—4:00 a.m.) so I could do my writing before they were awake. I wrote for about two years before any publishing house showed an interest in my work.

How do you balance your writing life with your family life?

In the early days of my writing life, and for many years, I balanced my writing life and my family life by separating them. My writing life occurred early in the day, before my family life began. If I had one or two hours of writing time each day that was enough. I was then ready for whatever else the day might contain.

Our children are now adults and live in their own places and it is in some ways harder for me to balance my writing life and my family life. Perhaps this is because I want more time to research and to write and perhaps it's because my writing life has become more complicated. For the most part, I try to do writing and research during the morning and attend to the other details of my professional and personal life during the afternoon.

Your books have been published by several different publishers and you don't have an agent. How do you select and approach publishers with your work?
I look at publishers' lists and try to choose a publisher that will be interested in a particular

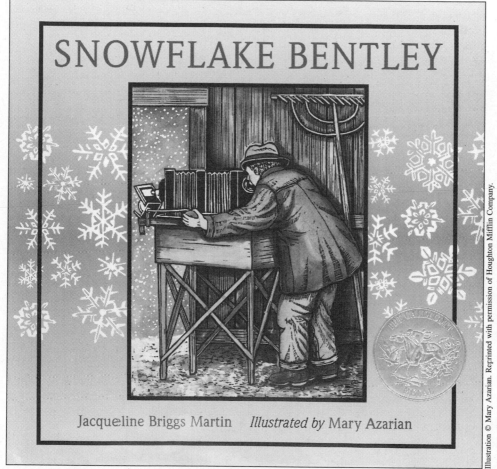

SNOWFLAKE BENTLEY

Jacqueline Briggs Martin   *Illustrated by* Mary Azarian

Jacqueline Briggs Martin shares the inspiring tale of Wilson Bentley, the first person to photograph snowflakes, in the Caldecott Medal-winning *Snowflake Bentley*, illustrated by Mary Azarian. Martin, who has often written stories relating to the natural world, first heard of Wilson "Snowflake" Bentley through an article appearing in *Cricket* in 1979. "[My children and I] were fascinated with the story of his life. Wilson Bentley became like a distant relative to our family," Martin says. Finally, on a snowy day, one of her children suggested she write about him. "I thought, 'Why don't I?' So I began to research his life."

work. When I was looking for a publisher for *Green Truck Garden Giveaway*, with its unusual format of story accompanied by extensive sidebars, I sent the manuscript to Virginia Duncan at Four Winds (later Simon & Schuster) because she had published another book with a story and nonfiction sidebars. *The Finest Horse in Town* (HarperCollins, 1992) is set in the past. When I wrote it in the late '80s, there were not a lot of picture books set in the past. But I knew Harper had published *Sarah, Plain and Tall*, and thought they might be interested. And they were.

How did you find a publisher for your first book?

I had looked at Lothrop, Lee & Shepard's catalog and knew they published books similar in tone to the books I was writing at the time. I sent them a manuscript for a Halloween story. They wrote back and said they had recently published some Halloween stories and weren't looking for more. They did ask that I send them additional work. I didn't have any additional work on hand, but as soon as I had finished the manuscript for *Bizzy Bones and Uncle Ezra*, I mailed it to them. Lothrop, Lee & Shepard published three Bizzy Bones books—*Bizzy Bones and Uncle Ezra*, *Bizzy Bones and Moosemouse* and *Bizzy Bones and the Lost Quilt*.

Many of your books deal with environmental themes. How did this become a focus for you?

When I was a child, I loved walking the lanes, fields and woods of our farm. I still love being in the outdoors. I love the surprises that happen outdoors: seeing a butterfly skim past and land on a flower; hearing a cardinal call from a nearby bush; coming upon a heron standing like a statue in shallow water waiting for lunch. Because these experiences are so important to me, they naturally find their way into my work.

How did you first learn of Wilson Bentley, and what made you decide to tell the story of his life in a children's book?

I first learned of Wilson Bentley in an article published in *Cricket* magazine in 1979. I was instantly drawn to him because of our similar backgrounds. He spent his life on a farm in Vermont. I grew up on a farm in Maine. I loved the story of his life—that he was so determined to share the beauty of snowflakes with others that he worked in obscurity for many years and worked with little financial reward. His reward was definitely in the work.

Because we all were fascinated with the story of his life, Wilson Bentley became like a distant relative to our family. We would often mention him when it snowed in Iowa and we looked for copies of his photographs in old books that we came across at garage sales. One snowy Christmas morning when Justin and Sarah had reached college age we were out walking. We talked about how Wilson Bentley would love the snow that was falling around us. Then either Sarah or Justin said, "Mom why don't you write about Snowflake Bentley?" And I thought, "Why don't I?" So after Christmas I began to research his life.

How has *Snowflake Bentley's* Caldecott Medal affected your life and career?

First, my life is much busier now, but I am learning to manage that. Having the Caldecott Medal attached to one's book is a wonderful thing because it means the book will have a much wider audience. I am glad thousands of readers will become acquainted with the story of Wilson Bentley's life.

Such an award is accompanied by challenges, though. I think the challenge for my future writing will be for me to forget about medals and awards and focus on making each work at hand as good as it can be for itself. I will try hard to keep my focus on the story because in fact, my career goals have not changed. I still hope to write stories that children and parents will enjoy and remember, stories they will carry with them for all their lives.

Although your books sound like stories, they are very much based on historical or contemporary fact and even include how-to sections and other educational information. How did you devise this successful structure and how have your readers reacted to it?

With the *Green Truck Garden Giveaway*, which is about giving away gardens, I wanted the book itself to be the gift of a garden. I hoped readers who wanted to grow a marigold or a radish after reading the story would have the information to do so. So I included the gardening information along with the text. I think growing trees is wonderful work and included instructions for sprouting and planting acorns in *Button, Bucket, Sky* for the same reason.

Often in researching a story I find information so interesting I want to include it (as in *Washing the Willow Tree Loon*) somewhere in the book. The information on healing plants in *Grandmother Bryant's Pocket* helps to make a connection from Sarah Bryant's time to our own. We still find dandelions. We still see great mullein, or velvet dock, growing along our roadsides.

I think readers find this information interesting. Often it works to make the stories meaningful to an audience older than the typical picture book audience. I sometimes wish I had included more of this information, such as instructions for making a pocket, in *Grandmother Bryant's Pocket*, but I don't ever want the story to be a vehicle for nonfiction information. It should always work the other way—the additional information extends the story, connects the reader to the story in another way. With *Snowflake Bentley*, my editor, Ann Rider, and I wanted the story to be spare and accessible to younger children. But in cutting the story to a thousand words we lost many of the wonderful details of Wilson Bentley's life. The sidebars were a way of putting the information back into the book so it would be there when readers were ready for it.

How do you research your books?

I love doing the research for my books. It is always exciting to learn something new. I go to primary sources when I can. For *Snowflake Bentley* I read all of Wilson Bentley's published articles on snow crystals and snow storms that I could find. I read other people's accounts of him. I read a magazine article containing an extensive interview with him. And I visited his home town of Jericho, Vermont, saw his camera, his black tray and several of his original photographs. I also saw his house and the attached shed where he took the photographs of snow crystals. I always learn much more than I can use in my stories. But I think all that I have learned helps me choose and shape what will eventually be in the story.

The millennium is upon us. Have you set any writing goals for the immediate future?

The coming of the millenium is a significant event in our minds—we are watching the closing of another thousand years of our recorded time. But I think our hearts will be much as they were. We will still respond to good stories. So my goal is simple, but difficult—to write stories that will last, that will live in readers' hearts and minds for years to come.

—*Megan Lane*

● Holt title *Breaking Ground, Breaking Silence: The Story of New York's African Burial Ground*, by Joyce Hansen and Gary McGowan, won a 1999 Coretta Scott King Author Honor Award.

Fiction: Picture books: animal, anthology, concept, folktales, history, humor, multicultural, nature/environment, poetry, special needs, sports. Middle readers: adventure, contemporary, history, humor, multicultural, special needs, sports, suspense/mystery. Young adults: contemporary, multicultural, problem novel, sports.

Nonfiction: Picture books: animal, arts/crafts, biography, concept, geography, history, hobbies, multicultural, music dance, nature/environment, sports. Middle readers, young readers, young adult: biography, history, multicultural, sports.

How to Contact/Writers: Fiction/Nonfiction: Submit complete ms. Reports on queries in 6 weeks; mss in 3-4 months. Will not consider simultaneous or multiple submissions.

Illustration: Works with 50-60 illustrators/year. Reviews ms/illustration packages from artists. Random samples OK. Illustrations only: Submit tearsheets, slides. Do *not* send originals. Reports on art samples in 1 month. Samples returned with SASE; samples filed. If accepted, original artwork returned at job's completion.

Terms: Pays authors/illustrators royalty based on retail price. Sends galleys to authors; proofs to illustrators.

HOUGHTON MIFFLIN CO., Children's Trade Books, 222 Berkeley St., Boston MA 02116-3764. (617)351-5000. Fax: (617)351-1111. Website: www.hmco.com. Book publisher. Vice President and Publisher: Anita Silvey. **Manuscript Aquisitions:** Amanda Sullivan, submissions coordinator. Kim Keller, assistant managing editor; Ann Rider, Margaret Raymo, senior editors; Amy Flynn, associate editor; Eden Edwards, Sandpiper Paperback editor; Matilda Welter, contributing editor; Walter Lorraine, Walter Lorraine Books, editor. **Art Acquisitions:** Bob Kosturko, art director. Averages 60 titles/year. Publishes hardcover originals and trade paperback reprints and originals. Imprints include Clarion Books. "Houghton Mifflin gives shape to ideas that educate, inform, and above all, delight."

● Houghton title *Snowflake Bentley*, by Jacqueline Briggs Martin, illustrated by Mary Azarian, won the 1999 Caldecott Medal. Houghton title *The Top of the World: Climbing Mt. Everest*, by Steve Jenkins, won the 1999 Boston Globe-Horn Book Award for Nonfiction.

Fiction: All levels: all categories except religion. "We do not rule out any theme, though we do not publish specifically religious material." *Blunder of the Rogues*, by Tim Egan (ages 4-8, picture book); *When JFK Was My Father*, by Amy Gordon (ages 10-14, novel); and *Three Stories You Can Read to Your Cat*, by Sara Swan Miller, illustrated by True Kelley (ages 7-10, early readers).

Nonfiction: All levels: all categories except religion. Recently published *Top of the World*, by Steve Jenkins (ages 6-10; picture book); *Once a Wolf*, by Stephen Swinburne (ages 4-8, photo); *Life and Times of the Peanut*, by Charles Micucci (ages 5-8, illustrated).

How to Contact/Writers: Fiction: Submit complete ms. Nonfiction: Submit outline/synopsis and sample chapters. Always include SASE. Response within 3 months.

Illustration: Works with 60 illustrators/year. Reviews ms/illustration packages from artists. Ms/illustration packages or illustrations only: Query with samples (colored photocopies are fine); provide tearsheets. Reports in 6-8 weeks. Samples returned with SASE; samples filed if interested.

Terms: Pays standard royalty based on retail price; offers advance. Illustrators paid by the project and royalty. Ms and artist's guidelines available for SASE.

HUNTER HOUSE PUBLISHERS, P.O.Box 2914, Alameda CA 94501-0914. Fax: (510)865-4295. E-mail: acquisitions@hunterhouse.com. Book publisher. **Manuscript Acquisitions:** Jeanne Brondino. **Art Acquisitions:** Jinni Fontana, art director. Publishes 0-1 titles for teenage women/year. 50% of books by first-time authors; 5% of books from agented writers.

Nonfiction: Young adults: health, multicultural, self help (self esteem), social issues. "We emphasize that all our books try to take multicultural experiences and concerns into account. We would be interested in a social issues or self-help book on multicultural issues." Books are therapy/personal growth-oriented. Does *not* want to see books for young children; fiction; illustrated picture books; autobiography. Published *Turning Yourself Around: Self-Help Strategies for Troubled Teens*, by Kendall Johnson, Ph.D.; *Safe Dieting for Teens*, by Linda Ojeda, Ph.D.

How to Contact/Writers: Query; submit overview and chapter-by-chapter synopsis, sample chapters and statistics on your subject area, support organizations or networks and marketing ideas. "Testimonials from professionals or well-known authors are crucial." Reports on queries in 1 month; mss in 3 months. Publishes a book 18 months after acceptance. Will consider simultaneous submissions.

Illustration: Works with 1 illustrator/year. Reports back only if interested. Samples returned with SASE; samples filed.

Photography: Purchases photos from freelancers. Buys stock images.

Terms: Payment varies. Sends galleys to authors. Book catalog available for 9 × 12 SAE and $1.25 postage; ms guidelines for standard SAE and 1 first-class stamp.

Tips: Wants therapy/personal growth workbooks; teen books with solid, informative material. "We do few children's books. The ones we do are for a select, therapeutic audience. No fiction! Please, no fiction."

HUNTINGTON HOUSE PUBLISHERS, P.O. Box 53788, Lafayette LA 70505. (318)237-7049. Fax: (318)237-7060. Book publisher. **Acquisitions:** Mark Anthony, publisher. Publishes 6 young readers/year. 30% of books by first-time authors. "Most books have spiritual/religious themes."
Fiction: Picture books, young readers, middle readers, young adults: all subjects. Does not want to see romance or multicultural. Average word length: picture books—12-50; young readers—100-300; middle readers—4,000-15,000; young adults/teens—10,000-40,000. Published *Greatest Star of All*, by Greg Gulley and David Watts (ages 9-11, adventure/religion).
Nonfiction: Picture books: animal, religion. Young readers, middle readers, young adults/teens: biography, history, religion. No nature/environment, multicultural. Average word length: picture books—12-50; young readers—100-300; middle readers—4,000-15,000; young adult/teens—10,000-40,000. Published *To Grow By Storybook Readers*, by Marie Le Doux and Janet Friend (preschool to age 8, textbook) *High on Adventure*, by Steve Arrington (young adult).
How to Contact/Writers: Fiction/Nonfiction: Query. Submit outline/synopsis, table of contents and proposal letter. One or two sample chapters are optional. Send SASE. Reports if interested in 2-3 months. Publishes a book 8 months after acceptance. Will consider simultaneous submissions.
Illustration: Works with 2 illustrators/year. Reviews ms/illustration packages from artists. Query; submit ms with dummy. Contact: Kathy Doyle, managing editor. Reports in 1 month. Illustrations only: Query with samples; send résumé and client list. Reports in 2-3 months. Samples returned with SASE; samples filed. Original artwork returned at job's completion.
Photography: Buys photos from freelancers. Contact: Managing Editor. Buys stock images. Model/property releases required. Submit cover letter and résumé to be kept on file.
Terms: Contracts negotiable. Pays authors royalty of 10% based on wholesale price. Pays illustrators by the project (range: $50-250) or royalty of 10% based on wholesale price. Sends galleys to authors; dummies to illustrators. Manuscript guidelines available on website.

HYPERION BOOKS FOR CHILDREN, 114 Fifth Ave., New York NY 10011. (212)633-4400. Fax: (212)633-4833. Website: www.disney.com/DisneyBooks/. An operating unit of Walt Disney Publishing Group, Inc. Book publisher. **Manuscript Acquisitions:** Katherine Tegen, editorial director. **Art Acquisitions:** Ken Geist, publisher and creative director. 10% of books by first-time authors. Publishes various categories.
- Hyperion title *Dance*, by Bill T. Jones, illustrated with photos by Susan Kuklin, won a 1999 Boston Globe-Horn Book Honor Award for picture books. Hyperion title *Duke Ellington*, by Andrea Davis Pinkney, illustrated by Brian Pinkney, won a 1999 Caldecott Honor Award and a 1999 Coretta Scott King Illustrator Honor Award.

Fiction: Picture books, young readers, middle readers, young adults: adventure, animal, anthology (short stories), contemporary, fantasy, folktales, history, humor, multicultural, poetry, science fiction, sports, suspense/mystery. Middle readers, young adults: commercial fiction. Recently published *Sons of Liberty*, by Adele Griffin (ages 10 and up); McDuff series by Rosemary Wells (ages 2-5); and *Zoom Broom*, by Margie Palatini (ages 5-9).
Nonfiction: All trade subjects for all levels.
How to Contact/Writers: Only interested in agented material.
Illustration: Works with 100 illustrators/year. "Picture books are fully illustrated throughout. All others depend on individual project." Reviews ms/illustration packages from artists. Submit complete package. Illustrations only: Submit résumé, business card, promotional literature or tearsheets to be kept on file. Reports back only if interested. Original artwork returned at job's completion.
Photography: Works on assignment only. Publishes photo essays and photo concept books. Provide résumé, business card, promotional literature or tearsheets to be kept on file.
Terms: Pays authors royalty based on retail price. Offers advances. Pays illustrators and photographers royalty based on retail price or a flat fee. Sends galleys to authors; dummies to illustrators. Book catalog available for 9×12 SAE and 3 first-class stamps; ms guidelines available for SASE.

IDEALS CHILDREN'S BOOKS, an imprint of Hambleton-Hill Publishing, Inc., 1501 County Hospital Rd., Nashville TN 37218-2501. Book publisher. **Acquisitions:** Bethany Snyder. Publishes 20-30 picture books/year.
- Ideals Children's Books only accepts manuscripts from members of the Society of Children's Book Writers and Illustrators (SCBWI), agented authors, and/or previously published book authors (submit with a list of writing credits) All others will be returned unread provided a SASE has been enclosed.

Fiction: Picture books: adventure, concept, contemporary, folktales, history, humor, multicultural, nature/environment, religion, sports, suspense/mystery. Average word length: picture books—200-1,200. Recently published *Molly*, by Joseph Bonsall, illustrated by Erin M. Mauterer (ages 5-8); *The Littlest Tree*, by Charles Tazewell, illustrated by Karen A. Jerome (all ages); and *Arianna and the Strawberry Tea*, by Maria Fasal Faulconer, illustrated by Katy Keek Arnsteen (ages 5-9).
How to Contact/Writers: Prefers to see complete ms rather than queries. Reports in 3-6 months. Publishes a book 18-24 months after acceptance. Must include SASE for response.
Illustration: Works with 15-20 illustrators/year. Uses color artwork only. Editorial reviews ms/illustration packages from artists. Submit ms with 1 color photocopy of final art and remainder roughs. Illustrations only: Submit

résumé and tearsheets showing variety of styles. Reports on art samples only if interested. "No original artwork, please." Samples returned with SASE, but prefers to keep them on file.

Terms: "All terms vary according to individual projects and authors/artists." Ms guidelines/artist guidelines for business envelope and 1 first-class stamp.

Tips: "Searching for strong storylines with realistic characters as well as 'fun for all kids' kinds of stories. We are not interested in young adult romances. We do not publish chapter books. We are not interested in alphabet books or anthropomorphism." Illustrators: "Be flexible in contract terms—and be able to show as much final artwork as possible."

☑ ILLUMINATION ARTS, P.O. Box 1865, Bellevue WA 98009. (425)644-7185. Fax: (425)644-9274. E-mail: liteinfo@illumin.com. Website: www.illumin.com. Book publisher. Estab. 1987. "All of our books are inspirational/spiritual. We specialize in children's picture books, but our books are designed to appeal to all readers, including adults." **Acquisitions:** Ruth Thompson, editorial director. "We publish high quality children's picture books with enduring inspirational and spiritual values. We are so selective and painstaking in every detail that our company has established a reputation for producing fine quality books. Additionally we are known for our outstanding artwork."

Fiction: Average word length: picture books—1,500-3,000. Recently published *The Bonsai Bear*, by Bernard Libster, illustrated by Aries Cheung; *Dragon* written and illustrated by Jody Bergsma; and *To Sleep With the Angels*, by H. Elizabeth Collins, illustrated by Judy Kuuisto.

How to Contact/Writers: Fiction: Submit complete ms. Reports on queries in 1 month. Publishes a book 2 years after acceptance. Will consider simultaneous submissions.

Illustration: Works with 2 illustrators/year. Uses color artwork only. Reviews ms/illustration packages from artists. Query or send ms with dummy. Illustrations only: Query with samples; send résumé and promotional literature to be kept on file. Contact: Ruth Thompson, editorial director. Reports in 1 week. Samples returned with SASE or filed.

Terms: Pays authors royalty based on wholesale price. Sends galleys to authors; dummies to illustrators. Originals returned to artist at job's completion. Book fliers available for SASE.

Tips: "Follow our guidelines. Expect considerable editing. Be patient. The market is tough. We receive 10-15 submissions a week and publish two-three books a year."

☑ IMPACT PUBLISHERS, INC., P.O. Box 6016, Atascadero CA 93423-6016. (805)466-5917. Fax: (805)466-5919. E-mail: info@impactpublishers.com. Website: www.impactpublishers.com. Estab. 1970. Nonfiction publisher. **Manuscript Acquisitions:** Melissa Froehner, children's editor. **Art Acquisitions:** Sharon Skinner, art director. Imprints: Little Imp Books, Rebuilding Books, The Practical Therapist Series. Publishes 1 young reader/year; 1 middle reader/year; and 1 young adult title/year. 50% of books by first-time authors. "Our purpose is to make the best human services expertise available to the widest possible audience."

Nonfiction: Young readers, middle readers, young adults: self-help. Recently published *Cool Cats, Calm Kids*, by Mary Williams, illustrated by Dianne O'Quinn Burke (ages 7-12, relaxation and stress management).

How to Contact/Writers: Nonfiction: Query or submit complete ms, cover letter, résumé. Reports on queries in 8-10 weeks; mss in 10-12 weeks. Will consider simultaneous submissions or previously published work.

Illustration: Works with 1 or less illustrator/year. Uses b&w artwork only. Reviews ms/illustration packages from artists. Query. Contact: Children's Editor. Illustrations only: query with samples. Contact: Sharon Skinner, production manager. Reports back only if interested. Samples returned with SASE; samples filed. Originals returned to artist at job's completion.

Terms: Pays authors royalty of 10-12%. Offers advances. Pays illustrators by the project. Sends galleys to authors. Book catalog available for #10 SAE with 2 first-class stamps; ms guidelines available for SASE. All imprints included in a single catalog.

◖ INCENTIVE PUBLICATIONS, INC., 3835 Cleghorn Ave., Nashville TN 37215-2532. (615)385-2934. Fax: (615)385-2967. E-mail: incentiv@nashville.net. Website: www.nashville.net/~incentiv. Estab. 1970. "Incentive publishes developmentally appropriate instructional aids for tots to teens." **Acquisitions:** Jennifer Janke. Approximately 20% of books by first-time authors. "We publish only educational resource materials (for teachers and parents of children from pre-school age through high school). We publish *no fiction*. Incentive endeavors to produce developmentally appropriate research-based educational materials to meet the changing needs of students, teachers and parents. Books are written by teachers for teachers for the most part."

FOR EXPLANATIONS OF THESE SYMBOLS,
SEE THE INSIDE FRONT AND BACK COVERS OF THIS BOOK

Nonfiction: Black & white line illustrated books, young reader, middle reader: activity books, arts/craft, multicultural, science, health, how-to, reference, animal, history, nature/environment, special needs, social issues, supplemental educational materials. "Any manuscripts related to child development or with content-based activities and innovative strategies will be reviewed for possible publication." Recently published *Character Education*, by John Deidel and Marion Lyman-Mercereau (grades K-12).

How to Contact/Writers: Nonfiction: Submit outline/synopsis, sample chapters and SASE. Usually reports on queries/mss in 1 month. Reports on queries in 4-6 weeks; mss in 6-8 weeks. Typically publishes a book 18 months after acceptance. Will consider simultaneous submissions.

Illustration: Works with 2-6 illustrators/year. Reports back in 2-4 weeks if reply requested (send SASE). Samples returned with SASE; samples filed. Need 4-color cover art; b&w line illustration for content.

Terms: Pays authors in royalties (5-10% based on wholesale price) or work purchased outright (range: $500-1,000). Pays illustrators by the project (range: $200-1,500). Pays photographers by the project. Original artwork not returned. Book catalog and ms and artist guidelines for SAE and $1.78 postage.

Tips: Writers: "We buy only educational teacher resource material that can be used by teachers and parents (home schoolers). Please do not submit fiction! Incentive Publications looks for a whimsical, warm style of illustration that respects the integrity and age of the child. We work primarily with local artists, but not exclusively."

☑ Ⓐ ☺ **JALMAR PRESS**, P.O. Box 1185, Torrance CA 90505. (310)816-3085. Fax: (310)816-3092. E-mail: blwjalmar@worldnet.att.net. Website: www.jalmarpress.com. Subsidiary of B.L. Winch and Associates. Book publisher. Estab. 1971. **Acquisitions:** Bradley Winch, publisher; Cathy Zippi, manager. Does not publish children's picture books or books for young readers. 10% of books by first-time authors. Publishes self-esteem (curriculum content related), character education, drug and alcohol abuse prevention, peaceful conflict resolution, stress management, whole-brain learning, accelerated learning and emotional intelligence materials for counselors, teachers, and other care givers. "Our goal is to empower children to become personally and socially responsible through activities presented by teachers, counselors and other caregivers that allow them to experience being both successful and responsible."

• Jalmar's catalog is found on their website. Jalmar is now the exclusive distributor for Innerchoice Publishing's entire line of school counselor-oriented material (K-12).

Fiction: All levels: self-concept, self-esteem. Does not want to see "children's fiction books that have to do with cognitive learning (as opposed to affective learning) and autobiographical work." Published *Hilde Knows: Someone Cries for the Children*, by Lisa Kent, illustrated by Mikki Macklen (child abuse); and *Scooter's Tail of Terror: A Fable of Addiction and Hope*, by Larry Shles (ages 5-105). "All submissions must teach (by metaphor) in the areas listed above."

Nonfiction: All levels: activity books, social issues, self-help. Does not want to see autobiographical work. Published *Esteem Builders Program*, by Michele Borba, illustrated by Bob Burchett (for school use—6 books, tapes, posters).

How to Contact/Writers: Only interested in agented material. Fiction/Nonfiction: Submit complete ms. Reports on queries in 1 month; mss in 6 months. Publishes a book 12-18 months after acceptance. Will consider simultaneous submissions.

Illustration: Works with 2 illustrators/year. Reports in 1 week. Samples returned with SASE; samples filed.

Terms: Pays authors 7½-15% royalty based on net receipts. Average advance varies. Pays illustrators by the project on a bid basis. Pays photographers per photo on a bid basis. Book catalog/ms guidelines free on request.

Tips: Wants "thoroughly researched, tested, practical, activity-oriented, curriculum content and grade/level correlated books on self-esteem, peaceful conflict resolution, stress management, emotional intelligence, and whole brain learning and books bridging self-esteem to various 'trouble' areas, such as 'at risk,' 'dropout prevention,' etc. Illustrators—make artwork that can be reproduced. Emotional intelligence is becoming a 'hot' category."

JEWISH PUBLICATION SOCIETY, 1930 Chestnut St., Philadelphia PA 19103. (215)564-5925. Fax: (215)564-6640. Editor-in-Chief: Dr. Ellen Frankel. Children's Editor: Bruce Black. Book publisher. All work must have Jewish content.

Fiction: Picture books, young readers, middle readers and young adults: adventure, contemporary, folktales, history, mystery, problem novels, religion, romance, sports. Recently published *A Coat for the Moon and Other Jewish Tales*, by Howard Schwartz and Barbara Rush, illustrated by Michael Iofin (folktales, ages 8 and up); *The Cross by Day, The Mezuzzah by Night*, by Deborah Spector Siegel (historical fiction ages 12 and up).

Nonfiction: Picture books: biography, history, religion. Young readers, middle readers, young adults: biography, history, religion, sports. Recently published *The Kids Catalog of Bible Treasures*, by Chaya Burstein (Bible, ages 8-12).

How to Contact/Writers: Fiction/Nonfiction: Query or submit outline/synopsis and sample chapters. Will consider simultaneous submissions (please advise). Reports on queries/mss in 6-8 weeks.

Illustration: Works with 3-4 illustrators/year. Will review ms/illustration packages. Query first or send 3 chapters of ms with 1 piece of final art, remainder roughs. Illustrations only: Query with photocopies; arrange a personal interview to show portfolio.

Terms: Pays authors and illustrators flat fees or royalties based on net. Reports back only if interested. Samples returned with SASE. Orginals returned at job's completion.

Tips: "Don't worry about the market. Write what you feel most passionately about, the subject which stirs your soul. Most of all, keep writing!"

N JUST US BOOKS, INC., 356 Glenwood Ave., East Orange NJ 07017. (201)676-4345. Fax: (201)677-7570. Imprint of Afro-Bets Series. Book publisher; "for selected titles" book packager. Estab. 1988. Vice President/Publisher: Cheryl Willis Hudson. **Acquisitions:** Allyson Sherwood, submissions manager. Publishes 4-6 picture books/year; "projected 6" young reader/middle reader titles/year. 33% of books by first-time authors. Looking for "books that reflect a genuinely authentic African or African-American experience. We try to work with authors and illustrators who are from the culture itself."
   • Just Us Books is not accepting new mss until further notice.
Fiction: Middle readers: adventure, contemporary, easy-to-read, history, multicultural (African-American themes), romance, suspense/mystery. Average word length: "varies" per picture book; young reader—500-2,000; middle reader—5,000. Wants African-American themes. Gets too many traditional African folktales. Recently published *Glo Goes Shopping* (picture book); *Dear Corinne: Tell Somebody*, by Mari Evans (middle readers).
Nonfiction: Middle readers, biography (African-American themes). Recently published *In Praise of Our Fathers and Our Mothers: A Black Family Treasury by Outstanding Authors and Artists.*
How to Contact/Writers: Fiction/Nonfiction: Query or submit outline/synopsis for proposed title. Reports on queries/ms in 3-4 months "or as soon as possible." Publishes a book 12-18 months after acceptance. Will consider simultaneous submissions (with prior notice).
Illustration: Works with 10 illustrators/year. Reviews ms/illustration packages from artists ("but prefers to review them separately"). "Query first." Illustrations only: Query with samples; send résumé, promo sheet, slides, client list, tearsheets; arrange personal portfolio review. Reports in 2-3 weeks. Samples returned with SASE; samples filed. Original artwork returned at job's completion "depending on project."
Photography: Purchases photos from freelancers. Buys stock and assigns work. Wants "African-American and multicultural themes—kids age 10-13 in school, home and social situations."
Terms: Pays authors royalty and some work for hire depending on project. Pays illustrators by the project or royalty, or flat fee based on project. Sends galleys to authors; dummies to illustrators. Book catalog for business-size SAE and 78¢ postage; ms/artist's guidelines for business-size SAE and 78¢ postage.
Tips: "Multicultural books are tops as far as trends go. There is a great need for diversity and authenticity here. They will continue to be in the forefront of children's book publishing until there is more balanced treatment on these themes industry wide." Writers: "Keep the subject matter fresh and lively. Avoid 'preachy' stories with stereotyped characters. Rely more on authentic stories with sensitive three-dimensional characters." Illustrators: "Submit 5-10 good, neat samples. Be willing to work with an art director for the type of illustration desired by a specific house and grow into larger projects."

☑ KAEDEN BOOKS, P.O. Box 16190, Rocky River OH 44117-6190. (216)356-0030. Fax: (440)356-5081. E-mail: books@kaeden.com. Website: kaeden.com. Book publisher. **Acquisitions:** Creative Vice President. Publishes 40 young readers/year. 50% of books by first-time authors. "Kaeden Books produces high quality, prereader, emergent and early reader books for classroom and reading program educators."
Fiction: Young readers: adventure, animal, concept, contemporary, health, history, humor, multicultural, nature/environment, science fiction, sports, suspense/mystery. Average word length: picture books—20-150 words; young readers—20-150 words. Recently published *The Big Fish*, by Joe Yukish, illustated by Kate Salley Palmer; *Sammy Gets A Ride*, by Karen Evans and Kathleen Urmston, illustrated by Gloria Gedeon; and *Time for a Bath*, by Jan Mader, illustrated by Karen Maizel.
Nonfiction: Young readers: activity books, animal, biography, careers, geography, health, history, hobbies, how-to, multicultural, music/dance, nature/environment, religion, science, sports. Multicultural needs include group and character diversity in stories and settings. Average word length: picture books—20-150 words; young readers—20-150 words.
How to Contact/Writers: Fiction/nonfiction: Query or submit complete ms. Do not send original transcripts. Reports on mss in 6-12 months. Will consider simultaneous submissions, electronic submissions via disk or modem.
Illustration: Works with 30 illustrators/year. Reviews ms/illustration packages from artists. Query. Submit art samples in color. Can be photocopies or tearsheets. Illustrations only: Query with samples. Send résumé, promo sheet, tearsheets, photocopies of work, preferably in color. Reports only if interested. Samples are filed.
Terms: Work purchased outright from authors. "Royalties to our previous authors." Offers negotiable advances. Pays illustrators by the project (range: $50-150/page). Book catalog available for 8½×11 SAE and 2 first-class stamps.
Tips: "Our books are written for emergent and fluent readers to be used in the educational teaching environment. A strong correlation between text and visual is necessary along with creative and colorful juvenile designs."

◆ KAMEHAMEHA SCHOOLS PRESS, 1887 Makuakane St., Honolulu HI 96817. (808)842-8880. Fax: (808)842-8875. E-mail: kspress@ksbe.edu. Website: www.ksbe.edu/pubs/KSPress/catalog.html. Estab. 1933. Specializes in educational and multicultural material. **Manuscript Acquisitions:** Henry Bennett. "Kamehameha Schools Press publishes in the areas of Hawaiian history, culture, language and studies."

Cool Melons—Turn to Frogs! is an introduction to haiku and the life of Issa, Japan's premier haiku poet. Illustrating the haiku of Issa had long been a dream of Kazuko Stone, a native of Japan. "I wanted to introduce American children to traditional Japanese images and feeling through haiku," she says. Her expressive watercolor and colored pencil images "delicately mirror the mood and subject of each poem," says Thomas Low of Lee & Low Books. The publisher specializes in multicultural literature for children and makes an effort to discover and work with artists and writers of color, he explains.

Nonfiction: Middle readers, young adults: biography, history, multicultural, Hawaiian folklore. Recently published *Voyage from the Past*, by Julie Stewart Williams, illustrated by Robin Yoko Burningham (Polynesian explorers and canoe voyaging).

How to Contact/Writers: Query. Reports on queries in 6-8 weeks; mss in 2-3 months. Publishes a book 12-18 months after acceptance.

Illustration: Uses b&w artwork only. Illustrations only: Query with samples. Reports back only if interested. Samples not returned.

Terms: Work purchased outright from authors. Pays illustrators by the project. Sends galleys to authors. Book catalog available for #10 SASE and 1 first-class stamp. All imprints included in a single catalog. Catalog available on website.

Tips: "Writers and illustrators *must* be knowledgeable in Hawaiian history/culture and be able to show credentials to validate their proficiency. Greatly prefer to work with writers/illustrators available in the Honolulu area."

KAR-BEN COPIES, INC., 6800 Tildenwood Lane, Rockville MD 20852-4371. (301)984-8733. Fax: (301)881-9195. E-mail: karben@aol.com. Website: www.karben.com. Book publisher. Estab. 1975. **Manuscript Acquisitions:** Madeline Wikler, vice president. Publishes 5-10 picture books/year; 20% of books by first-time authors. All of Kar-Ben Copies' books are on *Jewish themes for young children* and families.

Fiction: Picture books, young readers: adventures, concept, contemporary, fantasy, folktales, history, humor, multicultural, religion, special needs, suspense/mystery; *must be* on a Jewish theme. Average word length: picture books—2,000. Recently published *Once Upon a Shabbos*, by Jacqueline Jules; *Baby's Bris*, by Susan Wilkowski; and *The Magic of Kol Nidre*, by Bruce Siegel.

Nonfiction: Picture books, young readers: activity books, arts/crafts, biography, careers, concept, cooking, history, how-to, multicultural, religion, social issues, special needs; must be of Jewish interest. Average word length: picture books—2,000. Published *Jewish Holiday Games for Little Hands*, by Ruth Brinn; *Tell Me a Mitzvah*, by Danny Siegel; and *My First Jewish Word Book*, by Roz Schanzer.

How to Contact/Writers: Fiction/nonfiction: Submit complete ms. Reports on queries/mss in 3-6 weeks. Publishes a book 1 year after acceptance. Will consider simultaneous submissions. "Story should be short, no more than 3,000 words."

Illustration: Works with 6-8 illustrators/year. Prefers "four-color art in any medium that is scannable." Reviews ms/illustration packages from artists. Submit whole ms and sample of art (no originals). Illustrations only: Submit tearsheets, photocopies, promo sheet or anything representative that does *not* need to be returned. "Submit samples which show skill in children's book illustration." Enclose SASE for response. Reports on art samples in 3-6 weeks.

Terms: Pays authors in royalties of 8% based on net sales or work purchased outright (range: $500-2,000). Offers advance (average amount: $1,000). Pays illustrators royalty of 8% based on net sales or by the project (range: $500-3,000). Sends galleys to authors. Original artwork returned at job's completion. Book catalog free on request. Ms guidelines for 9×12 SAE and 2 first-class stamps.

Tips: Looks for "books for young children with Jewish interest and content, modern, non-sexist, not didactic. Fiction or nonfiction with a *Jewish* theme—can be serious or humorous, life cycle, Bible story, or holiday-related."

KEY PORTER BOOKS, 70 The Esplanade, Toronto, Ontario M5E 1R2 Canada. (416)862-7777. Fax: (416)862-2304. Book publisher. **Manuscript Acquisitions:** Susan Renouf, editor-in-chief. Publishes 4 picture books/year; and 4 young readers/year. 30% of books by first-time authors.

Fiction: Young readers, middle readers, young adult: animal, anthology, concept, health, multicultural, nature/environment, science fiction, special needs, sports, suspense/mystery. Does not want to see religious material. Average word length: picture books—1,500; young readers—5,000.

Nonfiction: Picture books: animal, history, nature/environment, reference, science. Middle readers: animal, careers, history, nature/environment, reference, science and sports. Average word length: picture books—1,500; middle readers—15,000. Recently published *How on Earth: A Question and Answer Book About How Animals & Plants Live*, by Ron Orenstein (ages 8-10, nature/environment); *Super Skaters: World Figure Skating Stars*, by Steve Milton (ages 8 and up, sports); and *The Seven Chairs*, by Helen Lanteigne (ages 4-8).

How to Contact/Writers: Only interested in agented material from Canadian writers; *no unsolicited mss.*

Photography: Buys photos from freelancers. Buys stock and assigns work. Captions required. Uses 35mm transparencies. Submit cover letter, résumé, duplicate slides, stock photo list.

KINGFISHER, Imprint of Larousse Kingfisher Chambers, 95 Madison Ave., New York NY 10016. (212)686-1060. Fax: (212)686-1082. "Kingfisher is a distinctive imprint of LKC, known for its high-quality nonfiction and its growing list of children's picture books."

● Kingfisher is not currently accepting unsolicited mss. They are only accepting submissions from agents and published authors.

Fiction: Recently published *Baby Bill and Little Lil*, by Sue Heap; *A Baby For Grace*, by Ian Whybren, illustrated by Christian Birmingham; and *Great Girl Stories*, compiled by Rosemary Sandberg (all picture books).

Nonfiction: Recently published *How the Future Began: Communications*, by Anthony Wilson; *The Kingfisher Young People's Book of Space*, by Martin Redfern; and *The Best Book of Sharks*, by Clair Llewellyn.

How to Contact/Writers: Only interested in agented material.

Illustration: Only interested in agented material.

Terms: Book catalog available for 9×12 SASE and 5 first-class stamps.

ALFRED A. KNOPF BOOKS FOR YOUNG READERS, 29th Floor, 201 E. 50th St., New York NY 10022. (212)751-2600. Website: www.randomhouse.com/kids. Imprint of Random House, Inc. Book publisher. Estab. 1915. Publishing Director: Simon Boughton. **Acquisitions:** send mss to Knopf Editorial Department. 90% of books published through agents. "Knopf is known for high quality literary fiction and is willing to take risks with writing styles. It publishes for children ages 5 and up."

Fiction: All levels: considers all categories.

Nonfiction: All levels: animal, arts/crafts, biography, history, how to, multicultural, music/dance, nature/environment, science, self help, sports.

How to Contact/Writers: Fiction/nonfiction: "We read agented material immediately. We will read queries from nonagented authors and then, possibly, request ms." Publishes a book 12-18 months after acceptance. Will consider simultaneous submissions. All mss must be accompanied by a SASE. Reports on queries/mss in 6 months.

Illustration: Reviews ms/illustration packages from artists through agent only. Illustration only: Contact: Art Director. Reports back only if interested. Samples returned with SASE; samples filed.

Terms: Pays authors in royalties. Pays illustrators and photographers by the project or royalties. Original artwork returned at job's completion. Book catalog and ms guidelines free on request with 9×12 SASE and 4 first-class stamps.

LEE & LOW BOOKS, INC., 95 Madison Ave., New York NY 10016-7801. (212)779-4400. Website: www.leeandlow.com. Book publisher. Estab. 1991. **Acquisitions:** Philip Lee, publisher; Louise May, senior editor. Publishes 10-12 picture books/year. 50% of books by first-time authors. Lee & Low publishes only picture books with multicultural themes. "Our goal is to discover new talent and produce books that reflect the multicultural society in which we live."

● Lee & Low Books is dedicated to publishing culturally authentic literature. The company makes a special effort to work with writers and artists of color and encourages new voices. *Elizabeti's Doll*, by Stephanie Stuve-Bodeen, won the Ezra Jack Keats New Writer Award in 1999. Turn to First Books on page 45 to read about Lee & Low author D.H. Figueredo and his book *When This World Was New*.

Fiction: Picture books: concept. Picture books, young readers: anthology, contemporary, history, multicultural, poetry. "We are not considering folktales, animal stories and chapter books." Picture book, middle reader: contemporary, history, multicultural, nature/environment, poetry, sports. Average word length: picture books—1,000-1,500 words. Recently published *Night Golf*, by William Miller, illustrated by Cedric Lucas (ages 6 and up, picture book); and *When This World Was New*, by D.H. Figueredo, illustrated by Enrique O. Sanchez (ages 3-10, picture book).

Nonfiction: Picture books: concept. Picture books, middle readers: biography, history, multicultural, science and sports. Average word length: picture books—1,500. Recently published *Cool Melons Turn to Frogs!*; *The Life and Poems of Issa*, story and Haiku translations by Mathew Gollub, illustrated by Kazuko G. Stone (ages 4 and up, picture book).

How to Contact/Writers: Fiction/Nonfiction: Submit complete ms. Reports in 2-4 months. Publishes a book 12-24 months after acceptance. Will consider simultaneous submissions.

Illustration: Works with 10-12 illustrators/year. Uses color artwork only. Reviews ms/illustration packages from artists. Submit ms with dummy. Illustrations only: Query with samples, résumé, promo sheet and tearsheets. Reports only if interested. Samples returned with SASE; samples filed. Original artwork returned at job's completion.

Photography: Buys photos from freelancers. Works on assignment only. Model/property releases required. Submit cover letter, résumé, promo piece and book dummy.

Terms: Pays authors royalty. Offers advances. Pays illustrators royalty plus advance against royalty. Photographers paid royalty plus advance against royalty. Sends galleys to authors; proofs to illustrators. Book catalog available for 9 × 12 SAE and $1.43 postage; ms and art guidelines available for SASE and 33¢ postge.

Tips: "We strongly urge writers to familiarize themselves with our list before submitting. Materials will only be returned with SASE."

LEGACY PRESS, Imprint of Rainbow Publishers, P.O. Box 261129, San Diego CA 92196. (619)271-7600. Book publisher. Estab. 1997. **Acquisitions:** Christy Allen, editor. Publishes 3 young readers/year; 3 middle readers/year; 3 young adult titles/year. Published nonfiction, Bible-teaching books. "We publish growth and development books for the evangelical Christian—from a non-denominational viewpoint—that may be marketed primarily through Christian bookstores."

Nonfiction: Young readers, middle readers, young adults: reference, religion. Recently published *God & Me!* (3-books series of devotionals for girls ages 2-12); *Gotta Have God* (3-book series of devotionals for boys ages 2-12) both illustrated by Aline Heiser.

How to Contact/Writers: Nonfiction: Submit outline/synopsis and 3-5 sample chapters. Reports on queries in 6 weeks; on ms in 3 months. Publishes a book 18 months after acceptance. Will consider simultaneous submissions; electronic submissions via disk or modem; previously published work.

Illustration: Works with 5 illustrators/year. Reviews ms/illustration packages from artists. Submit ms with 5-10 pieces of final art. Illustrations only: Query with samples to be kept on file. Reports in 6 weeks. Samples returned with SASE.

Terms: Pays authors royalty or work purchased outright. Offers advances. Pays illustrators by the project. Sends galley to authors. Book catalog available for business size SASE; ms guidelines for SASE.

Tips: "Get to know the Christian bookstore market. We are looking for innovative ways to teach and encourage children about the Christian life. No fiction, please."

LERNER PUBLICATIONS CO., 241 First Ave. N., Minneapolis MN 55401. (612)332-3344. Fax: (612)332-7615. Website: www.lernerbooks.com. Book publisher. Estab. 1959. **Manuscript Acquisitions:** Jennifer Zimian, submissions. Accepts primarily nonfiction for readers of all grade levels. List includes titles encompassing nature, geography, natural and physical science, current events, ancient and modern history, world art, special interest, sports, world cultures, and numerous biography series, as well as some YA and middle grade fiction.

How to Contact/Writers: Submissions are accepted in the months of March and October **only**. The Lerner Publishing Group does not publish alphabet books, puzzle books, song books, textbooks, workbooks, religious subject matter or plays. Work received in any month other than March or October will be returned unopened. A SASE is required for authors who wish to have their materials returned. Please allow 2-6 months for a response. No phone calls please.

ARTHUR LEVINE BOOKS, 555 Broadway, New York NY 10012. (212)343-6100. Imprint of Scholastic Inc.
 ● This publisher is not accepting submissions until 2001.

[N] [□] [♥] LIGHTWAVE PUBLISHING, Lightwave Publishing Inc., P.O. Box 160, Maple Ridge, British Columbia V3X-7G1 Canada. (604)462-7890. Fax: (604)462-8208. E-mail: mikal@lightwavepublishing.com. Website: www.lightwavepublishing.com. Estab. 1991. Independent book producer specializing in Christian material. **Manuscript Acquisitions:** Christie Bowler. **Art Acquisitions:** Terry Van Roon, art director. Publishes over 30 titles/year. "Our mission is helping parents pass on their Christian faith to their children."

Fiction: Picture books: religion, adventure, concept. Young readers: concept, religion. Middle readers: adventure, religion. Young adults: religion.

Nonfiction: Picture books, young readers: activity books, concept, religion. Middle readers, young adults: concept, religion. Average word length: young readers—2,000; middle readers—20,000; young adults—30,000. Recently published *I Want to Know About the Ten Commandments*, by R. Osborne and K. Christie Bowler (ages 8-12, religion, teaching); *Your Child and The Christian Life*, by R. Osborne with Christie Bowler (family, religion, teaching); *101 Questions Children Ask About Prayer*, by R. Osborne et al (ages 8-12, Q&A religion, teaching).

Just what the teacher ordered: Historical nonfiction is big market for classrooms, libraries

"Teachers are clamoring for good nonfiction they can use in their classrooms. Librarians want nonfiction for their students doing reports. Publishers want nonfiction that is exciting and different. Kids love nonfiction. There are nonfiction picture books; there's nonfiction at every level because kids are interested in the entire world around them. It's a huge market," says author Brandon Marie Miller.

Miller was a stay-at-home mom with two young girls, when she decided to put her history degree and her love of research to work and delve into the world of children's nonfiction writing. "*Cobblestone* magazine had just started. I didn't know anything about how to submit," she says. "So I got the *Writer's Market*, read the articles and sent for the magazine's guidelines and theme

Brandon Marie Miller

list." The first article she proposed, a piece on cowboy wardrobes called "Dressed for the Occasion," was accepted.

After the acceptance of two or three more article queries, Miller began getting assignments from *Cobblestone*. "I was getting four or five assignments a year. Once you get your foot in the door, you build a relationship with an editor and things happen."

Miller's *Cobblestone* editor eventually recommended her to both Lerner Publications and Harcourt (for work on their educational publications). She's had several books published in Lerner's People's History series including *Buffalo Gals: Women of the Old West; Just What the Doctor Ordered: The History of American Medicine*; and *Dressed for the Occasion: What Americans Wore 1620-1970* (which happens to have the same title as her very first article). Her books have been honored with, among others, a Scientific American Young Readers Book Award, a Society of School Librarians International Award and two International Reading Association Awards.

Miller spends about six or seven months researching a topic before she actually begins writing a book. "But if you do good research and stay organized, the writing part is easy. You've got all your quotes, anecdotes, stories and facts. It's just a matter of putting them together. I can write my first draft of a book in about a month." Others interested in writing nonfiction, whether for a book or a magazine, can learn from Miller's research and writing methods:

Start broad

I start at the library and search by subject. I find a couple of recent books and read them to get a broad idea about my subject. I've found it really helpful to look at footnotes, bibliographies, acknowledgements, preface—they point you to other sources. If you start seeing the same author popping up, that's a really good source to go to. Read everything.

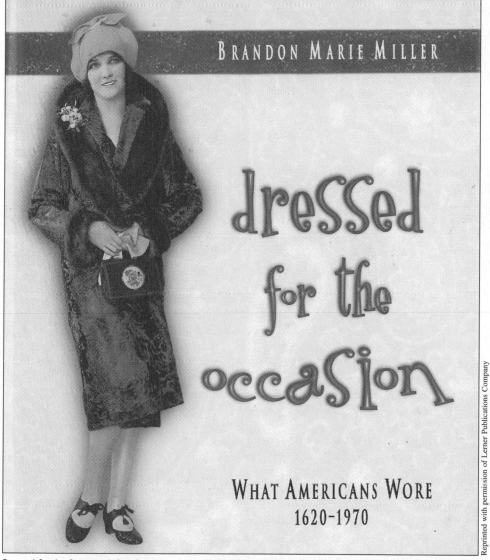

BRANDON MARIE MILLER

dressed for the occasion

WHAT AMERICANS WORE
1620-1970

Reprinted with permission of Lerner Publications Company

Dressed for the Occasion: What Americans Wore 1620-1970 is Brandon Marie Miller's third and latest book in Lerner's People's History series. *Dressed*, which got a starred review in *School Library Journal*, offers readers grades six to nine a fashion tour covering everything from corsets and powdered wigs to bell bottoms and Beatles haircuts. Miller often brings book-related props when she visits classrooms to talk about her books. "For my fashion talk, I have a hoop skirt, an old flat iron, fans, a tape measure (so when I talk about leg-o-mutton sleeves I can show the kids how wide they were), and a tri-corn hat I got in Williamsburg. Props help keep the kids interested."

Use primary sources

When you're researching history, it's important to look for primary sources. I love to read journals and diaries. Also look for old newspapers, paintings, photographs and catalogs. In *Dressed for the Occasion* there are reproductions of old Sears Roebuck catalogs. I've also referred to old advertisements, popular songs and period literature.

Narrow down your topic

When you start researching a topic, you begin with a broad base, but then you have to focus. You can't write an 800-word article on the Civil War, for example. But you can write a great piece on Civil War nurses, soldier's uniforms, the biography of a general—there are thousands of topics you could come up with just on the Civil War. Everyone's going to bring something different to a topic. You don't always have to think, "This topic has been done a lot." You can always take a topic in a new direction. That's what an editor is looking for.

Go where your research takes you

With *Buffalo Gals*, the editor at Lerner contacted me. She got my name from the editor at *Cobblestone*. I made a list of some topics and we decided a book about women of the Old West would be interesting. The next two books grew out of *Buffalo Gals*. I have three pages in *Buffalo Gals* on medicine and three pages on fashion. So the ideas for *Just What the Doctor Ordered* and *Dressed for the Occasion* grew out of that research.

Be organized

I use an index card system. I keep a numbered master bibliography with all the books I refer to. I write the bibliography number of the book I'm using on an index card, then copy information onto the card. I limit each card to a single topic or idea. When I'm done, I organize my big stack of cards into piles according to subject. This is how my chapters start taking shape. Everyone has her own system—the cards work for me. When I begin to write, I'm essentially flipping through the cards for each chapter and assembling the information.

Using an outline helps you from getting stuck because you always know where you should go next. It helps you set up a theme for the book. In nonfiction, there's a thread; there's a storyline. That's what really sets good nonfiction apart from a textbook. Remember that an outline is never written in stone. For *Just What the Doctor Ordered*, I ended up with a whole new first chapter on Native American medicine. In my outline, it was just a small part of another chapter, but I found so much information on it—it became a great way to start the book.

Don't pass up quirky facts

Kids find quirky facts fascinating—they love juicy details and can see humor in things. For instance, in *Dressed for the Occasion* I mention that women used to actually nibble on arsenic wafers which were advertised to "make your complexion pale and translucent." Women were actually poisoning themselves for fashion.

In *Buffalo Gals*, a little girl talks about her mother coming up in their wagon, seeing her one-room house made of sod, and bursting into tears. Kids get the humor in that—that her husband dragged her thousands of miles across the West and said, "Here's your new home, honey, made of dirt!"

Right now I'm working on a book about growing up in Colonial America. When he was growing up, George Washington made himself a list of civil behavior. He wrote the list to remind himself how to behave like a gentleman—how to walk, how to eat, that you don't spit or pick fleas off yourself. When I've mentioned that in schools, kids love it, because all of a sudden George Washington, instead of being the guy in the powdered wig, is a kid trying to teaches himself to behave in a society where manners were so important.

Enjoy your research

I've been assigned topics I thought weren't the least bit interesting. But when you start doing research, you will find something interesting—there's something interesting about everything. I enjoy the research process. I love getting into all the personal stuff. In a way, I think to do good research you have to be really nosey—the kind of person who, if you could, would go into someone's room and read her diary. And here you get to do it. I've even read collections of love letters—like the ones Henry IIX wrote to Anne Boleyn three years before he had her beheaded. It can be hard to stop researching and start writing.

Write about what interests you

You can't catch a trend. Write about what you like. Children's nonfiction is wide open when it comes to topics. If you're interested in cooking, write an article about the history of a type of food. If you have tips on how a teenager can organize her bedroom, that's a great article. You can explore science topics, holidays, careers—the possibilities are endless.
   —Alice Pope

How to Contact/Writers: Fiction/Nonfiction: Only interested in writers who will work for hire. Query. Reports on queries in 6 weeks; mss in 2 months. Publishes book 8 months after acceptance.
Illustration: Works with 5-10 illustrators/year. Reviews ms/illustration packages from artists. Submit ms "any way the artist wants to." Contact: Terry Van Roon, art director. Reports back only if interested. Samples not returned; samples filed.
Photography: Buys stock and assigns work. Model/property releases required. Uses color prints and digital.
Terms: Work purchased outright from authors. Amount varies. Pays illustrators by the project. Amount varies. Pays photographers by the project. Amount varies. Book catalog available for SASE. Writer's guidelines available for SASE. Catalog available on website.
Tips: "We only do work-for-hire writing and illustrating. We have our own projects and ideas then find writers and illustrators to help create them. No royalties. Interested writers and illustrators are welcome to contact us. Please don't put U.S. stamps on SASE."

LINNET BOOKS, Imprint of The Shoe String Press Inc., 2 Linsley St., North Haven CT 06473-2517. (203)239-2702. Fax: (203)239-2568. E-mail: sspbooks@aol.com. Estab. 1952. Specializes in nonfiction, educational material, multicultural material. **Manuscript Acquisitions:** Diantha C. Thorpe. **Art Acquisitions:** Sanna Stanley, production manager. Imprints: Linnet Books, Linnet Professional Publications, Archon Books—Diantha C. Thorpe, acquisitions for all. Publishes 8-10 middle readers/year.
Nonfiction: Young readers: activity books, animal. Middle readers: animal, biography, geography, history, multicultural, music/dance, nature/environment, reference, science. Young adults: animal, biography, geography, history, multicultural, nature/environment, reference. Recently published *The Round Book: Rounds Kids Love to Sing*, by Margaret Read MacDonald (all ages); *Angelina Grimké: Voice of Abolition*, by Ellen H. Todras (junior high, high school); *The New African Americans*, by Brent Ashalranner (middle school).
How to Contact/Writers: Nonfiction: Query or submit outline/synopsis and 3 sample chapters. Reports on queries in 4-6 weeks; mss in 3-4 months. Publishes a book 9-12 months after acceptance. Will consider simultaneous submissions "only if, when we indicate serious interest, the author withdraws from other publishers."
Illustration: Works with 2 illustrators/year. Uses b&w artwork only. Illustrations only: Query with samples. "We keep on file—send only disposable ones."
Photography: Buys stock. "We keep work on file but generally our authors are responsible for photo illustrations." Uses 5×7 glossy b&w prints. Send "anything that tells us what you specialize in."

Terms: Pays authors variable royalty. Offers advances. Sends galleys to authors; dummies to illustrators. Book catalog available for 9×12 SASE.

🅰 LITTLE, BROWN AND COMPANY, Three Center Plaza, Boston MA 02108. (617)227-0730. Website: www.LittleBrown.com. Book publisher. Estab. 1873. Editorial Director: Maria Modugno. Editor: Megan Tingley. Art Director: Sheila Smallwood. **Art Acquisitions:** Adrienne Wetmore. Estab. 1837. Publishes 50% picture books/year; 5% young reader titles/year; 30% middle reader titles/year; 15% young adult titles/year.

• Little, Brown does not accept unsolicited mss.

Fiction: Picture books: adventure, animal, contemporary, fantasy, folktales, history, humor, multicultural, nature/environment. Young adults: contemporary, health, humor, multicultural, nature/environment, suspense/mystery. Multicultural needs include "any material by, for and about minorities." Average word length: picture books—1,000; young readers—6,000; middle readers—15,000-25,000; young adults—20,000-40,000. Recently published *Tinker and Tom and the Star Baby*, by David McPhail (ages 4-8, picture book); *Miss Mary Mack*, by Mary Ann Hoberman (ages 4-8, picture book); and *Romance of the Snob Squad*, by Julie Anne Peters (ages 10 and up, young adult fiction).

Nonfiction: Picture books: nature/environment, sciences. Middle readers: arts/crafts, biography, history, multicultural, nature, self help, social issues, sports. Young adults: multicultural, self-help, social issues. Average word length: picture books—2,000; young readers—4,000-6,000; middle readers—15,000-25,000; young adults—20,000-40,000. Recently published *Exploring the Deep, Dark Sea*, by Gail Gibbons (ages 4 and up, nonfiction); and *The Girl's Guide to Life*, by Catherine Dee (ages 10 and up, nonfiction).

How to Contact/Writers: Only interested in agented material. Fiction: Submit complete ms. Nonfiction: Submit cover letter, previous publications, a proposal, outline and 3 sample chapters. Do not send originals. Reports on queries in 2 weeks. Reports on mss in 2 months.

Illustration: Works with 40 illustrators/year. Illustrations only: Query art director with samples; provide résumé, promo sheet or tearsheets to be kept on file. Reports on art samples in 6-8 weeks. Original artwork returned at job's completion.

Photography: Works on assignment only. Model/property releases required; captions required. Publishes photo essays and photo concept books. Uses 35mm transparencies. Photographers should provide résumé, promo sheets or tearsheets to be kept on file.

Terms: Pays authors royalties based on retail price. Pays illustrators and photographers by the project or royalty based on retail price. Sends galleys to authors; dummies to illustrators. Artist's and writer's guidelines for SASE.

Tips: "Publishers are cutting back their lists in response to a shrinking market and relying more on big names and known commodities. In order to break into the field these days, authors and illustrators research their competition and try to come up with something outstandingly different."

LITTLE FRIEND PRESS, 28 New Driftway, Scituate MA 02066. (781)545-1025. Estab. 1994. **Manuscript Acquisitions:** Lynne Finnegan. Publishes 2-3 picture books/year. 50% of books by first-time authors. "Several years ago a grandmother knit her grandson a special sweater that had a secret pocket knit inside. In that pocket she placed a Little Friend that stimulated the imagination of her grandson and established Little Friend Press. We are committed to providing a variety of merchandise and books to enhance the enjoyment and imagination that inspired the original Little Friend concept."

Fiction: Average word length: picture books—24-32 pages. Recently published *The Wishing Star*, by Diane R. Houghton (ages 3-7, rewards of friendship, picture book); *Aliens Took My Child*, by Mr. Hendersen (ages 3-7, humorous account of a toddler's busy day, picture book); and *What's Behind The Bump?* by Mr. Hendersen (ages 3-7, a child's perception of a mother's pregnancy).

Nonfiction: Average word length: picture books—24-32 pages. Recently published *My Little Friend Goes to School*, by Evelyn M. Finnegan (ages 3-7, account of first day nursery/kindergarten).

How to Contact/Writers: Fiction/Nonfiction: Submit complete ms. Reports on queries in 2-4 weeks; mss in 3-6 months. Publishes a book 1 year after acceptance. Will consider simultaneous submissions.

Illustration: Works with 2-3 illustrators/year. Uses color artwork only. Reviews ms/illustration packages from artists. Send résumé, promotional literature and tearsheets. Contact: Lynne Finnegan. Reports back only if interested. Samples kept on file.

Terms: Pays authors royalty. Pays illustrators by the project or royalty. Sends galleys to authors; dummies to illustrators. Originals returned to artist at job's completion. Book catalog available. Writer's guidelines for SASE. All imprints included in a single catalog.

🔻 LOBSTER PRESS, 1250 René-Lévesque Blvd. W., Suite 2200, Montréal, Quebec H3B 4W8 Canada. (514)989-3121. Fax: (514)989-3168. E-mail: tompkins@lobsterpress.com. Website: www.lobsterpress.com. Estab. 1997. **Acquisitions:** Kathy Tompkins (fiction); Bob Kirner (nonfiction). Publishes 4 picture books/year; 4 young readers/year. Encourages books by first-time authors.

Fiction: Picture books, young readers, middle readers: adventure, contemporary, health, history, multicultural, special needs, sports, suspense/mystery. Average word length: picture books—200-1,000. Recently published *from Poppa*, by Anne Carter, illustrated by Kasia Charko; *How Cold Was It?*, by Jane Barclay, illustrated by Janice Donato; *Pizza Party*, by Susan and Michael Johnston, illustrated by Susan Johnston.

Nonfiction: Young readers, middle readers and adults/teens: animal, biography, careers, geography, health, history, hobbies, how-to, multicultural, nature/environment, references, science, self-help, social issues, sports, travel. Average word length: middle readers—40,000. Recently published *The Lobster Kids' Guide to Exploring Montréal*, by John Symon; *The Lobster Kids' Guide to Exploring Ottawa-Hull*, by John Symon.

How to Contact/Writers: Fiction: submit complete ms. Nonfiction: submit complete ms or submit outline/synopsis and 2 sample chapters. Reports on queries in 1 month; mss in 6 months. Publishes a book 18 months after acceptance.

Illustration: Works with 5 illustrators/year. Uses color artwork only. Reviews ms/illustration packages from artists. Query with samples. Contact: Kathy Tompkins, acquisitions editor. Illustrations only: query with samples. Contact: Kathy Tompkins, acquisitions editor. Samples not returned; samples kept on file.

Terms: Pays authors 5-10% royalty based on retail price. Offers advances (average amount: $750-1,000). Pays illustrators by the project (range: $1,000-2,000) or 2-10% royalty based on retail price. Originals returned to artist at job's completion. Writer's and artist's guidelines available for SASE.

Tips: "Do not send manuscripts or samples registered mail or with fancy envelopes or bows and ribbons—everything is received and treated equally. Please do not call and ask for an appointment. We do not meet with anyone unless we are going to use their work."

N LORENZ BOOKS, Imprint of Anness Publishing, Inc., 27 W. 20th St., Suite, 504, New York NY 10011. (212)807-6739 or (800)354-9657. Fax: (212)807-6813. E-mail: wfanness@aol.com. Book publisher. Estab. 1996. **Acquisitions:** Shannon Ryan, editorial manager. Publishes 10 picture books/year; 15 young readers/year; 15 middle readers/year; 15 young adult/year. 10% of books by first-time authors. "Lorenz books creates unique titles that are valuable educational tools for kids of all ages. Very young children will be enthralled by bright, stimulating first word, concept and picture books, and older kids can learn about ancient cultures and civilizations, wildlife, machines and the environment through hands-on projects and lavishly illustrated text."

Fiction: Picture books: adventure, animal, anthology, concept, folktales, health, history, nature/environment. Young readers: animal, anthology, concept, folktales, history, nature/environment, religion. Middle readers, Young adults: animal, anthology, folktales, history, nature/environment, religion. Average word length: picture books—100-1,000; young readers—500-2,000; middle readers—1,000-2,000; young adults—1,000-10,000. Recently published *The Gummi Bear Counting Book*, by Lindley Boegehord (ages 6 months-2, board book); *Step Into Ancient Japan*, by Fiona MacDonald (ages 8-12, ancient Japanese culture).

Nonfiction: Picture books: activity books, animal, arts/crafts, concept, geography, history, how-to, music/dance, nature/environment, reference, religion, science. Young readers, middle readers, young adults: activity books, animal, arts/crafts, concept, cooking, geography, history, hobbies, how-to, music/dance, nature/environment, reference, religion, science. Average word length: picture books—100-1,000; young readers—500-2,500; middle readers—1,000-3,000; young adults—1,000-10,000. Recently published *Investigations: Space*, by Ian Graham (illustrated project book); *Nature Watch: Big Cats*, by Rhonda Klevansky (illustrated fact book); *Outdoor Activities For Kids*, by Clare Bradley and Cecilia Fitzsimons (young, middle readers, project book).

How to Contact/Writers: Fiction: Query or submit outline/synopsis. Nonfiction: Query or submit outline/synopsis and 1-2 sample chapters. Reports on queries in 1-2 weeks; mss in 4-6 weeks. Publishes a book 8 months after acceptance. Will consider simultaneous submissions and previously published work.

Illustration: Works with 3 illustrators/year. Reviews ms/illustration packages from artists. Query or submit ms with 1 piece of final art. Contact: Shannon Ryan, editorial manager. Illustrations only: Query with samples; send résumé. Contact: Shannon Ryan, editorial, manager. Reports in 1 month only if interested. Samples returned with SASE.

Photography: Buys stock and assigns work. Contact: Shannon Ryan, editorial manager. Uses photos of animals, nature, object/series of objects, styled foods, gardens, crafts, craft materials, art supplies. Uses color prints and 35mm transparencies. Submit cover letter and résumé.

Terms: Contact office for payment terms. Sends galleys to authors; dummies to illustrators. Originals returned to artist at job's completion. Guidelines available upon request.

Tips: "The market is fairly competitive, but we are open to all submissions and suggestions."

A LOTHROP, LEE & SHEPARD BOOKS, 1350 Avenue of the Americas, New York NY 10019. **Manuscript Acquisitions:** Susan Pearson, editor-in-chief; Melanie Donovan, senior editor; Jaïva Placide, editorial assistant. **Art Acquisitions:** Golda Laurens, art director. Publishes 30 total titles/year. "Lothrop, Lee & Shepard publishes original hardcover trade books for children from pre-school age through young adult. Our list includes picture books, biographies, humor, history, middle grade and young adult fiction, and nonfiction for all age groups. Although we don't currently have the staff to review unsolicited material, we are eager to see agented manuscripts and manuscripts by already published authors."

   • Lothrop was dissolved due to the HarperCollins/Morrow merger.

Fiction: Picture books, young readers, middle readers: animal, history, poetry. Middle readers, young adults: folktales. All levels: multicultural. Recently published *The Secret Knowledge of Grown-Ups*, written and illustated by David Wisniewski (full-color picture book for ages 7 and up); *So Many Bunnies: A Bedtime ABC & Counting Book*, by Rick Walton, illustrated by Paige Miglio Blair (full-color picture book for ages 2 and up).

Nonfiction: All levels: biography, history, multicultural, nature/environment. Recently published *African Beginnings*, by James Haskins and Kathleen Benson, illustrated by Floyd Cooper (full-color picture book for all ages);

A World of Words: An ABC of Quotations, by Tobi Tobias, illustrated by Peter Malone (full-color picture book for all ages).

How to Contact/Writers: Fiction: Send complete mss for fiction and picture books. Nonfiction: Query with proposal. Enclose SASE with submissions.

Illustration: Works with 25-30 illustrators/year. Editorial reviews ms/illustration packages from artists. Illustrations only: Query with samples. Submit portfolio for review—to arrange for drop-off, contact Golda Laurens, art director, at (212)261-6096. "Do not send original art." Reports back only if interested. Samples returned with SASE; samples kept on file.

Photography: Purchases photos from freelancers. Buys stock and assigns work.

Terms: Payment terms vary with project. Royalties/advances negotiated.

Tips: Currently seeking unique picture books and imaginative fiction. Does not want books written to fill a special need instead of from the writer's experience and personal conviction. Also does not want film scripts, cartoon merchandising ideas or pedantic books. Work should come from the heart.

LOWELL HOUSE JUVENILE/ROXBURY PARK JUVENILE, 2020 Avenue of the Stars, Suite 300, Los Angeles CA 90067. (310)552-7555. Fax: (310)552-7573. Book publisher, independent book producer/packager. **Manuscript Acquisitions:** Michael Artenstein, editor-in-chief, Roxbury Park Juvenile; Brenda Pope-Ostrow, editorial director, Lowell House Juvenile. **Art Acquisitions:** Brenda Pope-Ostrow and Bret Perry. Publishes 2-4 picture books/year; 30 young readers/year; 60 middle readers/year; 5 young adult titles/year. 25% of books by first-time authors. Lowell House Juvenile is best known for its trade workbooks, especially The Gifted & Talented series and its many science titles. Roxbury Park Juvenile specializes in middle grade fiction, and sports, science, and classics for midgraders and young adults.

- Lowell House does not accept mss. Instead they generate ideas inhouse then find writers to work on projects.

Fiction: Middle readers, young adults: adventure, anthology, contemporary, nature/environment, problem novels, multicultural, suspense, sports. Recently published *Qwan: the Showdown*, by A.L. Kim, cover art by Richard Kirk (ages 13 and up action novel); *Rafters*, by Nilsson Honnelly (ages 7-10, an adventure novel); *Classic Ghost Stories*; illustrated by Barbara Kiwak (ages 13 and up, collection of short scary stories); and *Shadows*, by Jonathan Schmidt (ages 10-14).

Nonfiction: Picture books, young readers: activity books, educational, arts/crafts. Middle readers: activity books, arts/crafts, social issues, multicultural, concept, cooking, geography, health, history, hobbies, reference, religion, science, sports. Young adult/teen: multicultural, reference, science, social issues, sports. Recently published *The Ultimate Soccer Almanac*, by Dan Woog (ages 10 and up); *Gifted & Talented Word Workbook for Preschoolers*, by Martha Cheney, illustrated by Kara Kaminski (ages 3-5); *101 Things Every Kid Should Know About Science*, by Samantha Beres (ages 8-12).

How to Contact/Writers: Reports on queries/mss in 1 month.

Illustration: Works with 75 illustrators/year. Send samples to give a feel for style. Include sample drawings with kids in them. Illustrations only: arrange personal portfolio review; send promo sheet, portfolio, tearsheets. Reports back only if interested. Samples returned with SASE; files samples.

Photography: Buys stock and assigns work. "We're not looking for more photographers at this time."

Terms: Payment decided on project-by-project basis. Authors are paid $1,000-5,000 for outright purchase. Illustrators paid by the project ($100-1,000). Photographers paid by the project ($50-1,000).

Tips: "Send art: lots of drawings of kids, samples to keep on file. Don't be afraid to send b&w art—never see enough junior-high aged kids! Editorial: We are interested in writing samples to lead to future jobs, but we do not accept manuscripts, preferring to generate ideas ourselves."

LOYOLA PRESS, 3441 N. Ashland, Chicago IL 60657. (773)281-1818. Fax: (773)281-0885. E-mail: editors@loyolapress.com. Book publisher. Estab. 1912. **Manuscript Acquisitions:** Helen Ranck, editorial assistant. **Art Acquisitions:** Leslie Uriss, production manager. Publishes 5 picture books/year. "Loyola Press serves faith formation and education in the Jesuit tradition,"

Fiction: Picture books: religion. Average word length—500-1,000.

Nonfiction: Picture books: religion. Average word length—500-1,000. Recently published *A Child's Book of Celtic Prayers*, by Joyce Denham and Helen Cann; *St. Francis Celebrates Christmas*, by Mary Walsh and Helen Caswell; *Do The Angles Watch Close By?* by Mary Joslin and Danuta Mayer.

How to Contact/Writers: Fiction/nonfiction: Submit complete ms. Reports on queries/mss in 2-3 months. Publishes a book 18 months after acceptance. Will consider simultaneous submissions and electronic submissions via disk or modem.

Illustrations: Reviews ms/illustration packages from artists. Submit ms with dummy. Contact: Helen Ranck, editorial assistant. Illustrations only: Query with samples. Contact: Leslie Uriss, production manager. Reports only if interested. Samples returned with SASE; samples filed.

Terms: Originals returned at job's completion. Book catalog available for 9 × 12 SASE and 4 first-class stamps; writer's guidelines available for SASE.

Tips: "We originate very few children's titles, but we would like to get acquainted with more illustrators. Potential writers and illustrators should be aware that we are a religion book publisher in the Catholic tradition but that our books are all written and designed for the general trade."

THE LUTTERWORTH PRESS, Imprint of James Clarke & Co. Ltd., P.O. Box 60, Cambridge England CB1 2NT. (01223)350865. Fax: (01223)366951. E-mail: publishing@lutterworth.com. Website: www.lutterworth.c om. Book publisher. **Acquisitions:** Adrian Brink, managing director.
Fiction: Picture books, young readers, middle readers and young adults: adventure, animal, folktales, health, history, nature/environment, religion. Recently published *The Thought That Counts*, by Y.Y. Ovezell, illustrations by Robin Laurie; *What Is God Like*, by Marie Agnès Goudzat, illustrated by Ulises Wensell; *Carol Corsa and Mickey Morgan*, by Claire Rosemary Yane, illustrated by Robert Hutchison.
Nonfiction: Picture books, young readers, middle readers and young adults: activity books, animal, arts/crafts, history, nature/environment, religion, science.
How to Contact/Writers: Fiction/Nonfiction: Submit outline/synopsis and 1 or 2 sample chapters. Reports on queries in 2 weeks; ms in 6 months.
Illustration: Reviews ms illustration packages from authors. Submit ms with color or b&w copies of illustration. Illustration only: Query with samples. Reports in 2-3 weeks. Samples returned with SASE; samples filed.
Photography: "Occasionally" buys photos from freelancers. Send résumé and samples. Works on assignment only.
Terms: Royalty negotiable. Book catalog available for SAE.

MAGINATION PRESS, 750 First Street NE, Washington DC 20002. Website: www.maginationpress.com. Book publisher. **Acquisitions:** Darcie Conner Johnston, managing editor. Publishes up to 15 picture books and young reader titles/year. "We publish books dealing with the psycho/therapeutic treatment or resolution of children's serious problems and psychological issues, many written by mental health professionals."
● Magination Press is an imprint of the American Psychological Association.
Fiction: Picture books, young readers, middle readers, young adult/teens: concept, health, mental health, multicultural, special needs. Recently published *My Grandma's the Mayor*, by Marjorie Pellegrino (ages 6-12); *The Very Lonely Bathtub*, by Ann Rasmussen (ages 3-7); *I Don't Know Why . . . I Guess I'm Shy*, by Barbara Cain (ages 4-8).
Nonfiction: Picture books, young readers: concept, health, mental health, multicultural, psychotherapy, self-help, social issues, special needs.
How to Contact/Writers: Fiction/nonfiction: Submit complete ms or query. Reports on queries/mss in 3-6 months. Materials returned only with a SASE. Publishes a book 12-18 months after acceptance.
Illustration: Works with 10-15 illustrators/year. Reviews ms/illustration packages. Will review artwork for future assignments. We keep all samples on file.
How to Contact/Illustrators: Illustrations only: Query with samples. Original artwork returned at job's completion.
Terms: Pays authors 5-15% in royalties based on receipts minus returns. Pays illustrators by the project. Book catalog and ms guidelines on request with SASE.

Ⓝ MAVAL PUBLISHING, INC., Imprint of Editora Maval, 567 Harrison St., Denver CO 80206. (303)320-1035. Fax: (303)320-1546. E-mail: maval@maval.com. Website: www.maval.com. Book publisher. Estab. 1991.
Acquisitions: George Waintrub, manager. Publishes 5 picture books/year; 3 young readers; 2 middle readers. 50% of books by first-time authors.
Fiction: Picture books: adventure, animal, anthology, concept, contemporary, fantasy, folktales, health, history, multicultural, nature/environment, sports. Young readers: adventure, animal, anthology, concept, contemporary, fantasy, health, history, multicultural, nature, environment. Middle readers: adventure, animal, anthology, contemporary, fantasy, health, history, multicultural, nature/enviroment.
Nonfiction: Picture books: adventure, animal, anthology, concept, contemporary, fantasy, folktales, health, history, multicultural, nature/environment, sports. Young readers: adventure, animal, anthology, concept, contemporary, fantasy, health, history, multicultural, nature/environment. Middle readers: adventure, animal, anthology, contemporary, fantasy, health, history, multicultural, nature/enviroment.
How to Contact/Writers: Fiction/Nonfiction: Submit outline/synopsis and 1-2 sample chapters. Reports on queries/mss in 2-3 months. Publishes a book 6-12 months after acceptance. Will consider simultaneous submissions and previously published work.
Illustration: Works with 2 illustrators/year. Reviews ms/illustration packages from artists. Submit manuscript with 1-2 pieces of final art. Contact: George Waintrub, manager. Illustrations only: Query with samples. Contact: George Waintrub, manager. Reports in 1-2 months. Samples not returned.
Photography: Buys stock.
Terms: Pays authors royalty of 7.5-25% based on retail price. Pays illustrators royalty of 7.5-25%. Book catalog

MARKET CONDITIONS are constantly changing! If you're still using this book and it is 2001 or later, buy the newest edition of *Children's Writer's & Illustrator's Market* at your favorite bookstore or order directly from Writer's Digest Books.

and writer's guidelines available for SASE. All imprints included in a single catalog. Catalog available on website.

☑ **McCLANAHAN BOOK COMPANY INC.**, 23 W. 26th St., New York NY 10010. (212)725-1515. Fax—editorial: (212)684-2785; art: (212)684-2785. E-mail: HighQ@McClanahanBook.com. Book publisher. CEO: Susan McClanahan. **Manuscript Acquisitions:** Kenn Goin, editorial director. **Art Acquisitions:** Dawn Beard, senior art director. Publishes 90 picture books/year. Publishes "affordable, high quality mass market, with educational value, including activity books, concept storybooks, workbooks, nonfiction, baby/toddler concept books and novelty books.

Fiction: Mainly baby and toddler concept books, also nature, animal, history and sports. No single-title fiction. Recently published *Know-It-All®* (series).

Nonfiction: Activity, concept, novelty, interactive. Picture books: career, arts/crafts, biography, history, nature, reference, science and sports. Recently published: *High Q™ Projects for Preschoolers*.

How to Contact/Writers: Query only. Reports on queries in 1 months. Ms guidelines available with SASE. Assignments to writers for projects originated inhouse.

Illustration: Works with up to 15 illustrators/photographers a year. Send samples, which will be returned with SASE and/or filed. Reports in 1 month.

Terms: Usually pays writers and illustrators/photographers on work-for-hire basis (flat fee by project). May pay small royalty for certain project originated by writer or artist. Artists' originals returned after job's completion.

✓**MARGARET K. McELDERRY BOOKS**, 1230 Sixth Ave., New York NY 10020. (212)698-2761. Fax: (212)698-2796. Website: www.simonsays.com/kidzone. Imprint of Simon & Schuster Children's Publishing Division. Editor at Large: Margaret K. McElderry. **Manuscript Acquisitions:** Emma Dryden, executive editor. **Art Acquisitions:** Ann Bobco, art director. Publishes 10-12 picture books/year; 2-4 young reader titles/year; 8-10 middle reader titles/year; and 5-7 young adult titles/year. 10% of books by first-time authors; 33% of books from agented writers. "Margaret K. McElderry Books publishes original hardcover trade books for children from preschool age through young adult. This list includes picture books, easy-to-read books, fiction and non-fiction for eight to twelve-year-olds, poetry, fantasy and young adult fiction. The style and subject matter of the books we publish is almost unlimited. We do not publish textbooks, coloring and activity books, greeting cards, magazines and pamphlets or religious publications."

● Margaret K. McElderry Books is not currently accepting unsolicited mss. Send queries only for picture books. Send queries and 3 sample chapters for middle grade and young adult projects; also looking for strong poetry.

Fiction: Young readers: adventure, contemporary, fantasy, history. Middle readers: adventure, contemporary, fantasy, mystery. Young adults: contemporary, fantasy, mystery, poetry. "Always interested in publishing humorous picture books and original beginning reader stories. We see too many rhymed picture book manuscripts which are not terribly original or special." Average word length: picture books—500; young readers—2,000; middle readers—10,000-20,000; young adults—45,000-50,000. Recently published *King of Shadows*, by Susan Cooper; *My Bear and Me*, by Barbara Maitland and Lisa Flather; *One, Two, Three Jump*, by Penelope Lively and Jan Ormerod.

Nonfiction: Young readers, young adult teens, biography, history. Average word length: picture books—500-1,000; young readers—1,500-3,000; middle readers—10,000-20,000; young adults—30,000-45,000. Recently published *Is There Life on Mars?*, by Dennis B. Fradir.

How to Contact/Writers: Fiction/nonfiction: Submit query and sample chapters with SASE; may also include brief résumé of previous publishing credits. Reports on queries in 2-3 weeks; mss in 3-4 months. Publishes a book 18 months after contract signing. Will consider simultaneous submissions (only if indicated as such).

Illustration: Works with 20-30 illustrators/year. Query with samples; provide promo sheet or tearsheets; arrange personal portfolio review. Contact: Ann Bobco, art director. Reports on art samples in 2-3 months. Samples returned with SASE or samples filed.

Terms: Pays authors royalty based on retail price. Pay illustrators royalty based on retail price. Pays photographers by the project. Sends galleys to authors; dummies to illustrators. Original artwork returned at job's completion. Ms guidelines free on request with SASE.

Tips: "We're looking for strong, original fiction. We are always interested in picture books for the youngest age reader."

☑ Ⓐ **MEADOWBROOK PRESS**, 5451 Smetana Dr., Minnetonka MN 55343. (612)930-1100. Fax: (612)930-1940. E-mail: meadowpr@bitsream.net. Book publisher. **Manuscript Acquisitions:** Joseph Gredler, submissions editor. **Art Acquisitions:** Joe Gagne, art director. Publishes 1-2 middle readers/year; and 2-4 young readers/year. 20% of books by first-time authors; 10% of books from agented writers. Publishes children's activity books, gift books, humorous poetry anthologies and story anthologies.

● Meadowbrook does not accept unsolicited children's picture books or novels. They are primarily a nonfiction press. The publisher offers specific guidelines for various types of submissions (such as Newfangled Fairy Tales, poetry and Girls to the Rescue anthologies). Be sure to specify the type of project you have in mind when requesting guidelines.

Fiction: Young readers and middle readers: anthology, folktales, humor, multicultural, poetry. "Poems and short stories representing people of color encouraged." Published *The New Adventures of Mother Goose*; *Girls to the*

Rescue (short stories featuring strong girls, for ages 8-12); and *A Bad Case of the Giggles* (children's poetry anthology).

Nonfiction: Young readers, middle readers: activity books, arts/crafts, cooking, hobbies, how-to, multicultural, self help. Multicultural needs include activity books representing traditions/cultures from all over the world, and especially fairy tale/folk tale stories with strong, multicultural heroines and diverse settings. "Books which include multicultural activities are encouraged." Average word length: varies. Recently published *Pick-a-Party Cookbook*, by Penny Warner; *Free Stuff for Kids* (activity book); and *Kids' Holiday Fun* (activity book).

How to Contact/Writers: Fiction/Nonfiction: Query or submit outline/synopsis or submit complete ms with SASE. Reports on queries/mss in 2-3 months. Publishes a book 1-2 years after acceptance. Send a business-sized SASE and 2 first-class stamps for free writer's guidelines and book catalog before submitting ideas. Will consider simultaneous submissions.

Illustration: Only interested in agented material. Works with 2-3 illustrators/year. Reviews ms/illustration packages from artists. Submit ms with 2-3 pieces of final art. Illustrations only: Submit résumé, promo sheet and tearsheets. Reports back only if interested. Samples not returned; samples filed.

Photography: Buys photos from freelancers. Buys stock and assigns work. Model/property releases required. Submit cover letter.

Terms: Pays authors in royalties of 5-7½% based on retail price. Offers average advance payment of $2,000-4,000. Pays for illustrators: $100-25,000; ¼-¾% of total royalties. Pays photographers per photo ($250). Originals returned at job's completion. Book catalog available for 5 × 11 SASE and 2 first-class stamps; ms guidelines and artists guidelines available for SASE.

Tips: "Illustrators and writers should send away for our free catalog and guidelines before submitting their work to us. Also, illustrators should take a look at the books we publish to determine whether their style is consistent with what we are looking for. Writers should also note the style and content patterns of our books. For instance, our children's poetry anthologies contain primarily humorous, rhyming poems with a strong rhythm; therefore, we would not likely publish a free-verse and/or serious poem. I also recommend that writers, especially poets, have their work read by a critical, objective person before they submit anywhere. Also, please correspond with us by mail before telephoning with questions about your submission. We work with the printed word and will respond more effectively to your questions if we have something in front of us."

MEGA-BOOKS, INC., 240 E. 60th St., New York NY 10022. (212)355-6200. Fax: (212)355-6303. **President:** John Craddock. **Acquisitions:** Rusty Fisher. Book packager/producer. Produces trade paperback and mass market paperback originals and fiction and nonfiction for the educational market. Works with first-time authors, established authors and unagented writers.
   • Mega-Books does not accept unsolicited mss.

Fiction: Young adult: mystery. Recently published Nancy Drew and Hardy Boys series; Pocahontas and The Lion King books (Disney).

How to Contact/Writers: Submit résumé, publishing history and clips.

Terms: Work purchased outright for $3,000 and up. Offers average 50% advance.

Tips: "Please be sure to obtain a current copy of our writers' guidelines before writing."

MERIWETHER PUBLISHING LTD., 885 Elkton Dr., Colorado Springs CO 80907-3557. Fax: (719)594-9916. E-mail: meriwthpub@aol.com. Book publisher. Estab. 1969. Executive Editor: Arthur L. Zapel. **Manuscript Acquisitions:** Ted Zapel, educational drama; Rhonda Wray, religious drama. "We do most of our artwork in-house; we do not publish for the children's elementary market." 75% of books by first-time authors; 5% of books from agented writers. "Our niche is drama. Our books cover a wide variety of theatre subjects from play anthologies to theatrecraft. We publish books of monologs, duologs, short one-act plays, scenes for students, acting textbooks, how-to speech and theatre textbooks, improvisation and theatre games. We also publish some general humor trade books. Our Christian books cover worship on such topics as clown ministry, storytelling, banner-making, drama ministry, children's worship and more. We also publish anthologies of Christian sketches. We do not publish works of fiction or devotionals."

Fiction: Middle readers, young adults: anthology, contemporary, humor, religion. "We publish plays, not prose-fiction."

Nonfiction: Middle readers: activity books, how-to, religion, textbooks. Young adults: activity books, drama/theater arts, how-to church activities, religion. Average length: 250 pages. Recently published *Perspectives*, by Mary Krell-Oishi (a book of scenes for teenage actors); and *Fool of the Kingdom*, by Philip Noble (a book on clown ministry).

How to Contact/Writers: Nonfiction: Query or submit outline/synopsis and sample chapters. Reports on queries in 2 weeks; mss in 6-8 weeks. Publishes a book 6-12 months after acceptance. Will consider simultaneous submissions.

Illustration: Works with 2 illustrators/year. Reviews ms/illustration packages from artists. Query first. Illustrations only: Query with samples; send résumé, promo sheet or tearsheets. Reports on art samples in 6-8 weeks. Samples returned with SASE. Samples kept on file. Originals returned at job's completion.

Terms: Pays authors in royalties of 10% based on retail or wholesale price. Outright purchase $200-1,000. Pays for illustrators by the project (range: $50-2,000); royalties based on retail or wholesale price. Book catalog for SAE and $2 postage; ms guidelines for SAE and 1 first-class stamp.

Tips: "We are currently interested in finding unique treatments for theater arts subjects: scene books, how-to books, musical comedy scripts, monologues and short plays for teens."

☑ **MILKWEED EDITIONS**, 430 First Ave. North, Suite 668, Minneapolis MN 55401-1743. (612)332-3192. Fax: (612)332-6248. Website: www.milkweed.org. Book Publisher. Estab. 1980. **Manuscript Acquisitions:** Emilie Buchwald, publisher; Elizabeth Fitz, manuscript coordinator. **Art Acquisitions:** Beth Olson. Publishes 3-4 middle readers/year. 25% of books by first-time authors. "Milkweed Editions publishes with the intention of making a humane impact on society, in the belief that literature is a transformative art uniquely able to convey the essential experiences of the human heart and spirit. To that end, Milkweed Editions publishes distinctive voices of literary merit in handsomely designed, visually dynamic books, exploring the ethical, cultural, and esthetic issues that free societies need continually to address."
Fiction: Middle readers: adventure, animal, contemporary, fantasy, humor, multicultural, nature/environment, suspense/mystery. Does not want to see anthologies, folktales, health, hi-lo, picture books, poetry, religion, romance, sports. Average length: middle readers—90-200 pages. Recently published *The Ocean Within*, by V.M. Caldwell (contemporary, nature); *No Place*, by Kay Haugaard (multicultural).
How to Contact/Writers: Fiction: Submit complete ms. Reports on mss in 2-6 months. Publishes a book 1 year after acceptance. Will consider simultaneous submissions.
Illustration: Works with 2-4 illustrators/year. Reviews ms/illustration packages from artists. Query; submit ms with dummy. Illustrations only: Query with samples; provide résumé, promo sheet, slides, tearsheets and client list. Samples filed or returned with SASE; samples filed. Originals returned at job's completion.
Terms: Pays authors royalty of 7½% based on retail price. Offers advance against royalties. Illustrators contracts are decided on an individual basis. Sends galleys to authors. Book catalog available for $1.50 to cover postage; ms guidelines available for SASE. Must include SASE with ms submission for its return.

▢ **THE MILLBROOK PRESS**, 2 Old New Milford Rd., Brookfield CT 06804. (203)740-2220. Fax: (203)775-5643. Book publisher. Estab. 1989. **Manuscript Acquisitions:** Laura Ondek, manuscript coordinator. **Art Acquisitions:** Judie Mills, art director. Publishes 20 picture books/year; 40 young readers/year; 50 middle readers/year; and 10 young adult titles/year. 10% of books by first-time authors; 20% of books from agented authors. Publishes nonfiction, concept-oriented/educational books. Publishes under Twenty-First Century Books imprint also.
Fiction: Picture books: concept. Young adults: history.
Nonfiction: All levels: animal, arts/craft, biography, cooking, geography, how-to, multicultural, music/dance, nature/environment, reference, science. Picture books: activity books, concept, hi-lo. Middle readers: hi-lo, social issues, sports. Young adults: careers, social issues. No poetry. Average word length: picture books—minimal; young readers—5,000; middle readers—10,000; young adult/teens—20,000. Published *Dandelion Adventures*, by Patricia L. Kite (grades PreK-1, picture book); *Love and Marriage Around the World*, by Carol Gelber (grades 4-6, history); and *Our Changing Constitution*, by Isobel V. Morin (grades 7 and up, history).
How to Contact/Writers: Query with outline/synopsis and 1 sample chapter. Reports on queries/mss in 1 month.
Illustration: Work with 75 illustrators/year. Reviews ms/illustration packages from artists. Query; submit 1 chapter of ms with 1 piece of final art. Illustrations only: Query with samples; provide résumé, business card, promotional literature or tearsheets to be kept on file. Samples returned with SASE; samples filed. Reports back only if interested.
Photography: Buys photos from freelancers. Buys stock and assigns work.
Terms: Pays author royalty of 5-7½% based on wholesale price or work purchased outright. Offers advances. Pays illustrators by the project, royalty of 3-7% based on wholesale price. Sends galleys to authors. Manuscript and artist's guidelines for SASE. Book catalog to 9×11 SASE.

☑ **MIRACLE SOUND PRODUCTIONS, INC.**, 1560 W. Bay Area Blvd., Suite 110, Friendswood TX 77546-2668. (281)286-4575. Fax: (281)286-0009. E-mail: imsworldwd@aol.com. Website: www.storyangel.c om. Book publisher. **Acquisitions:** Trey Boring, director of special projects. Estab. 1997. Publishes 2 young readers/year. 100% of books by first-time authors. Miracle Sound Productions is best known for "positive family values in multimedia products."
Fiction: Young readers. Average word length: young readers—500. Recently published *CoCo's Luck*, by Warren Chaney and Don Boyer (ages 3-8, Read-A-Long book and tape).
Illustration: Only interested in agented material. Works with 1 illustrator/year. Uses color artwork only. Reviews ms/illustration packages from artists. Submit ms with dummy. Contact: Trey W. Boring, director, special projects. Illustrations only: Send résumé and portfolio to be kept on file.
Photography: Works on assignment only. Contact: Trey W. Boring, director, special projects.
Terms: Payment negotiable for authors, illustrators and photographers.

MITCHELL LANE PUBLISHERS, INC., 17 Matthew Bathon Court, Elkton MD 21921-3669. (410)392-5036. Fax: (410)392-4781. E-mail: mitchelllane@dpnet.net. Website: www.angelfire.com/biz/mitchelllane/index.html. Book publisher. **Acquisitons:** Barbara Mitchell, president. Publishes 20 young adult titles/year. "We publish authorized multicultural biographies of role models for children and young adults."
Nonfiction: Young readers, middle readers, young adults: biography, multicultural. Average word length: 4,000-

50,000 words. Recently published *Shania Twain*, by Jim Gallagher; *Brandy*; and *Salma Hayek* (all real-life reader biographies for grades 3-8); and *Latinos in Baseball* (ages 11 and up).

How to Contact/Writers: Nonfiction: Query or submit outline/synopsis and 3 sample chapters. Reports on queries only if interested. Publishes a book 18 months after acceptance.

Illustration: Works with 2-3 illustrators/year. Reviews ms/illustration packages from artists. Query; arrange portfolio review, including color copies of work. Illustration only: query with samples; arrange personal portfolio review; send résumé, portfolio, slides, tearsheets. Reports back only if interested. Samples not returned; samples filed.

Photography: Buys stock images. Needs photos of famous and prominent minority figures. Captions required. Uses b&w prints. Submit cover letter, résumé, published samples, stock photo list.

Terms: Pays authors 5-10% royalty based on wholesale price or work purchased outright for $250-2,000. Pays illustrators by the project (range: $40-250). Sends galleys to authors.

Tips: "Most of our assignments are work-for-hire. Submit résumé and samples of work to be considered for future assignments."

☑ Ⓐ MONDO PUBLISHING, One Plaza Rd., Greenvale NY 11548. (516)484-7812. Fax: (516)484-7813. Website: www.mondopub.com. Book publisher. **Acquisitions:** Gina Shaw, senior editor. Publishes 60 picture and chapter books/year. 10% of books by first-time authors. Publishes various categories. "Our motto is 'creative minds creating ways to create lifelong readers.' We publish for both educational and trade markets, aiming for the highest quality books for both."

• Mondo Publishing only accepts agented material.

Fiction: Picture books, young readers, middle readers: adventure, animal, contemporary, fantasy, folktales, history, humor, multicultural, nature/environment, poetry, sports. Multicultural needs include: stories about children in different cultures or about children of different backgrounds in a U.S. setting. Recently published *My Lucky Hat*, by Kevin O'Malley (ages 5-9); *Hairy Tuesday*, by Uri Orlev (ages 6-10); and *Twiddle Twins* series by Howard Goldsmith (ages 6-10, adventure chapter books).

Nonfiction: Picture books, young readers, middle readers: animal, biography, geography, how-to, multicultural, nature/environment, science, sports. Recently published *Touch the Earth*, by Jane Baskwill (ages 6-10); and *Thinking About Ants*, by Barbara Brenner (ages 5-10, animals).

How to Contact/Writers: Accepting mss from agented or previously published writers only. Fiction/ Nonfiction: Query or submit complete ms. Reports on queries in 1 month; mss in 6 months. Will consider simultaneous submissions. Mss returned with SASE. Queries must also have SASE.

Illustration: Works with 40 illustrators/year. Reviews ms/illustration packages from illustrators. Illustration only: Query with samples, résumé, portfolio. Reports only if interested. Samples returned with SASE; samples filed.

Photography: Occasionally uses freelance photographers. Buys stock images. Uses mostly nature photos. Uses color prints, transparencies.

Terms: Pays authors royalty of 2-5% based on wholesale/retail price. Offers advance based on project. Pays illustrators by the project (range: 3,000-9,000), royalty of 2-4% based on retail price. Pays photographers by the project or per photo. Sends galleys to authors depending on project. Originals returned to artists at job's completion. Book catalogs available for 9 × 12 SASE with $3.20 postage.

Tips: "Prefer illustrators with book experience or a good deal of experience in illustration projects requiring consistency of characters and/or setting over several illustrations. Prefer manuscripts targeted to trade market plus crossover to educational market."

MOREHOUSE PUBLISHING CO., 4775 Linglestown Rd., Harrisburg PA 17112. (717)541-8130. Fax: (717)541-8136. Website: www.morehousegroup.com. Book publisher. Estab. 1884. Publisher: Harold Rast. **Manuscript Acquisitions:** Debra Farrington, editorial director. **Art Acquisitions:** Christine Finnegan, managing editor. Publishes 4 picture books/year. 25% of books by first-time authors. "Morehouse is a publisher and provider of books, church curricula, church resources materials and communications services for the Episcopal Church and other mainline church groups and organizations."

Fiction: Picture Books: spirituality, religion. Wants to see new and creative approaches to theology for children. Recently published *Jenny's Prayer*, by Annette Griessman, illustrated by Mary Anne Lard.

Nonfiction: Picture Books: religion and prayers.

How to Contact/Writers: Fiction/nonfiction: Submit ms (1,500 word limit). Reports on mss in 2-4 weeks. Publishes a book 2 years after acceptance.

Illustration: Works with 2-3 illustrators/year. Reviews ms/illustration packages from artists. Submit 3 chapters of ms with 1 piece of final art. Illustrations only: Submit résumé, tearsheets. Reports on art samples in 2 weeks. Samples returned with SASE; samples filed.

Terms: Pays authors royalty based on net price. Offers modest advance payment. Pays illustrators royalty based on net price. Sends galleys to authors. Book catalog free on request if SASE ($2 postage) is supplied.

Tips: "Morehouse Publishing seeks books that wrestle with important theological questions in words and story that children can understand."

MORGAN REYNOLDS PUBLISHING, 620 S. Elm St., Suite 384, Greensboro NC 27406. (910)275-1311. Fax: (336)275-1152. Website: www.morganreynolds.com. **Acquisitions:** John Riley, editor. Book publisher. Publishes 12 young adult titles/year. 50% of books by first-time authors.

 • Morgan Reynolds has added two new series: Makers of the Media and Women in Sciences, directed toward the YA reader.

Nonfiction: Middle readers, young adults/teens: biography, history, multicultural, social issues, sports. Multicultural needs include Native American, African-American and Latino subjects. Average word length: 12,000-20,000. Recently published *Tiger Woods*, by Aaron Boyd; *Myra Bradwell: First Woman Lawyer*, by Nancy Whitelaw; and *The Ordeal of Olive Oatman: A True Story of the American West*, by Margaret Rau.

How to Contact/Writers: Prefers to see entire ms. Query; submit outline/synopsis with 3 sample chapters. Reports on queries in 1 month; mss in 2 months. Publishes a book 9 months after acceptance. Will consider simultaneous submissions.

Illustration: Works with 2 illustrators/year. Reports only if interested. Samples returned with SASE. Originals returned at job's completion.

Terms: Pays authors negotiated price. Offers advances. Sends galleys to authors. Book catalog available for business-size SAE with 1 first-class stamp; ms guidelines available for SASE.

Tips: "We are open to suggestions—if you have an idea that excites you send it along. Recent trends suggest that the field is open for younger, smaller companies. Writers, especially ones starting out, should search us out."

MORROW JUNIOR BOOKS, 1350 Avenue of the Americas, New York NY 10019.

 • Morrow Junior was dissolved due to the HarperCollins/Morrow merger.

MOUNT OLIVE COLLEGE PRESS, 634 Henderson St., Mount Olive NC 28365. (919)658-2502. Book publisher. Estab. 1990. **Acquisitions:** Pepper Worthington, editor. Publishes 1 middle reader/year. 85% of books by first-time authors.

Fiction: Middle readers: animal, humor, poetry. Average word length: middle readers—3,000 words.

Nonfiction: Middle readers: nature/environment, religion, self help. Average word length: middle readers—3,000 words.

How to Contact/Writers: Submit complete ms or outline/synopsis and 3 sample chapters. Reports on queries in 6-12 months. Publishes a book 1 year after acceptance.

Illustration: Uses b&w artwork only. Submit ms with 50% of final art. Contact: Pepper Worthington, editor. Reports in 6-12 months if interested. Samples not returned.

Terms: Payment negotiated individually. Book catalog available for SAE and 1 first-class stamp.

☑ TOMMY NELSON, Imprint of Thomas Nelson, Inc., P.O. 24100, Nashville TN 37214. (615)889-9000. Fax: (615)902-3330. Book publisher. **Acquisitions:** Laura Minchew, acquisitions editor. Publishes 15 picture books/year; 20 young readers/year; and 25 middle readers/year. Evangelical Christian publisher.

Fiction: Picture books: concept, humor, religion. Young readers: adventure, concept, humor, religion. Middle readers: adventure, humor, religion, sports, suspense/mystery. Young adults: adventure, problem novels, religion, sports, suspense/mystery. Recently published *A Child's Garden of Verse*, by Thomas Kinkad (family); *Hey, That's Not What the Bible Says*, by Bill Ross (ages 3-7).

Nonfiction: Picture books, young readers: activity books, religion, self help. Middle readers, young adults: reference, religion, self help. Recently published *My Faith Journal*, by Karen Hill, illustrated by Bobby Gombert (ages 6-12); *Genesis For Kids*, by Rick Osbqurne (ages 8-14); and *The Children's Bible Story Book*, retold by Anne Degraff (ages 3-11).

How to Contact/Writers: Does not accept unsolicited mss, queries or proposals.

Illustration: Query with samples. Reports back only if interested. Samples filed. Contact: Karen Phillips, art director.

Terms: Pays authors royalty of 5% based on wholesale price or work purchased outright. Offers advances of $1,000 and up. Pays illustrators by the project or royalty.

Tips: "Know the CBA market—and avoid preachiness."

NEW HOPE, Imprint of Woman's Missionary Union, P.O. Box 12065, Birmingham AL 35202-2065. (205)991-8100. Website: www.newhopepubl.com. Book publisher. **Acquisitions:** Leslie Caldwell, editorial specialist; Jennifer Law. **Art Acquisitions:** Rachael Crutchfield (New Hope Publishers). Publishes 2-3 picture books/year; 1-

**FOR EXPLANATIONS OF THESE SYMBOLS,
SEE THE INSIDE FRONT AND BACK COVERS OF THIS BOOK**

2 young readers/year; and 1-2 middle readers/year. 75% of books by first-time authors. "Our goal is to equip and motivate children and adults to share the hope of Christ."

Fiction: All levels: multicultural, religion. Multicultural fiction must be related to Christian concepts. Recently published *Joy's Discovery*, written and illustrated by Jane Chu (picture book, preschool).

Nonfiction: All levels: multicultural, religion. Multicultural nonfiction must be related to Christian concepts, particularly women reaching beyond themselves to share the hope of Christ.

How to Contact/Writers: Submit complete ms. Reports on queries in 6 weeks; mss in 3 months. Publishes a book 2 years after acceptance. Will consider simultaneous submissions.

Illustration: Works with 3-4 illustrators/year. Reviews ms/illustration packages from artists. Send ms with dummy. Illustrations only: query with samples (color copies). Reports back only if interested. Samples not returned; samples filed.

Photography: Buy stock already on file. Model/property releases required.

Terms: Pays authors royalty of 5-10% based on retail price or work purchased outright (depends on length). Pays illustrators by the project, or by royalty. Sends galleys to author. Originals returned to artist at job's completion, if requested. Book catalog available for 10×12 SAE and 3 first-class stamps; ms guidelines for SASE.

Tips: "Obtain the catalog first to see the kinds of material we publish."

NORTH WORD PRESS, Creative Publishing International, 5900 Green Oak Dr., Minnetonka MN 55343. (612)936-4700. Fax: (612)932-0380. Estab. 1985. Publishes 2-3 picture books/year; 4-6 middle readers/year. 60% of books by first time authors.

Nonfiction: Picture books, middle readers: animal, nature/environment. Average word length: picture books—900; middle readers—3,000. Recently published *Foxes for Kids*, by Shuler (ages 8-12); *Children of the Earth . . . Remember*, by Schimmel (all ages); and *Wildflowers, Blooms & Blossoms*, by Burns (ages 8-12).

How to Contact/Writers: Nonfiction: query or submit complete ms. Reports on queries and ms in 3 months. Publishes a book 1 year after acceptance. Will consider simultaneous submissions and previously published work.

Illustration: Works with 2-3 illustrators/year. Uses color artwork only. Reviews ms/illustration packages from artists. Query or submit ms with 4-5 pieces of final art. Contact: acquisitions editor. Illustrations only: query with samples. Reports in 3 months. Samples returned with SASE; samples kept on file.

Photography: Buys stock. Contact: photo researcher. Uses nature and wildlife images. Model/property releases required; captions required. Uses 35mm, 2¼×2¼ and 4×5 color transparencies. Submit cover letter, résumé, dupe sample, slides and stock photo list.

Terms: Purchases transcripts or pays authors royalty based on wholesale price. Offers advances. Pays illustrators by the project. Pays photographer by the project or by the photo. Sends galleys to authors; dummies to illustrators. Originals returned to artist at job's completion. Book catalog available for 9×12 SAE and 7 first-class stamps; ms and art guidelines available for SASE. All imprints included in a single catalog.

NORTH-SOUTH BOOKS, 1123 Broadway, Suite 800, New York NY 10010. (212)463-9736. Website: www.northsouth.com. **Acquisitions:** Marc Cheshire, president, publisher and art director. U.S. office of Nord-Süd Verlag, Switzerland. Publishes 75 titles/year; 25 acquired through U.S. office.

Fiction: Picture books.

Nonfiction: Publishes nonfiction occasionally.

How to Contact/Writers: Only interested in agented material.

Illustration: Uses artists for picture book illustration.

Terms: Pays authors and illustrators advance and royalties.

THE OLIVER PRESS, INC., Charlotte Square, 5707 W. 36th St., Minneapolis MN 55416-2510. (612)926-8981. Fax: (612)926-8965. E-mail: queries@oliverpress.com. Website: www.oliverpress.com. Book publisher. **Acquisitions:** Denise Sterling, Pete Pawelski. Publishes 8 young adult titles/year. 10% of books by first-time authors. "We publish collective biographies of people who made an impact in one area of history, including science, government, archaeology, business and crime. Titles from The Oliver Press can connect young adult readers with their history to give them the confidence that only knowledge can provide. Such confidence will prepare them for the lifelong responsibilities of citizenship. Our books will introduce students to people who made important discoveries and great decisions."

Nonfiction: Middle reader, young adults: biography, history, multicultural, social issues, history of science and technology. "Authors should only suggest ideas that fit into one of our existing series. We would like to add to our Innovators series on the history of technology." Average word length: young adult—20,000 words. Recently published *You Are the Juror*, by Nathan Aaseng (ages 10 and up, history); *Women Who Led Nations*, by Joan Axelrod-Contrada (ages 10 and up, collective biography); *Communications: Sending the Message*, by Thomas Streissgath (ages 10 and up, collective biography); and *Puritans, Pilgrims, and Merchants: Founders of the Northeastern Colonies*, by Kieran Doherty (ages 10 and up, collective biography).

How to Contact/Writers: Nonfiction: Query with outline/synopsis. Reports in 6 months. Publishes a book approximately 1 year after acceptance.

Photography: Buys photos from freelancers. Buys stock images. Looks primarily for photos of people in the news. Captions required. Uses 8×10 b&w prints. Submit cover letter, résumé and stock photo list.

Terms: Pays authors negotiable royalty. Work purchased outright from authors (fee negotiable). Pays photogra-

insider report

Chasing dreams on the pages of picture books

Although award-winning children's author and illustrator Paul Brett Johnson showed an early aptitude for writing, he did not set out to be a writer. His passion was making pictures. "I sometimes think I was born with a box of crayons in my hand," he says. It was not until he attended college at the University of Kentucky, where he dropped a theater major and switched to art education, that he realized the symbiotic possibilities of combining pictures and words.

After taking courses in children's literature, he decided to try his hand at writing and illustrating children's books. However, when he submitted to publishers, he says, "My efforts were met with resounding rejections. Nonetheless, a seed had been planted—although it took 20 years to germinate and bloom."

Paul Brett Johnson

After spending several unfulfilled years in the work force, Johnson simply decided to get out of the rat race and "quit the real world." He did what most of us only dream of—he left his job, followed his heart, and opened his own art studio in an abandoned garage. "Amazingly," he says, "I managed to make a living, although, at first, it was a meager one. But happily and somewhat less frugally, I'm still chasing dreams 25 years later, never having punched a clock in all that time."

His perseverance and commitment to his craft and dreams have resulted in an award-winning career. He has illustrated 14 books, 8 of which he has also written, including *The Cow Who Wouldn't Come Down*, his signature piece, which won the Kentucky Bluegrass Award. *A Perfect Pork Stew* also won the Kentucky Student Choice Award. "I find that a bit overwhelming, especially when you consider that all recently published books are eligible—not only those by Kentucky authors," he says. "In a sense, the Student Choice Awards are more affirming than committee awards. It means you are connecting with kids and not all children's books do that." Johnson feels children's literature should do more than just encourage reading, skill-building and be entertaining, it should offer "the developing individual some insight into—or help build awareness of—self, environment and community."

Johnson visits approximately 15 schools a year, giving students an overview of the writing, illustrating and publishing process. But, he feels it's also important to move children to think creatively. "For my own part I find these encounters invaluable in terms of keeping in touch with my audience and assessing which story elements work and which ones don't." Often he will ask the children to be editors of a work-in-progress. They are eager with their replies. "Rarely are they shy about giving their opinions."

Johnson says there are a myriad of ideas out there, and he doesn't experience any difficulties tapping into them. He looks to life, experiences, personal history, current events and

Bright, bold watercolor illustrations help tell the story of *The Pig Who Ran a Red Light*, Paul Brett Johnson's sequel to his Kentucky Bluegrass Award-winning *The Cow Who Wouldn't Come Down*. In this tale, a pig named George can't quit imitating a very talented cow named Gertrude who can fly and drive a tractor. This leads to trouble for George, but Miss Rosemary, who lives on the farm with them, sneakily solves the problem. Johnson is working on a second companion book to *The Cow Who Wouldn't Come Down*.

newspaper stories. But "ideas are not in and of themselves stories," he says. "The challenge comes in recognizing which idea holds the potential for a story and then pulling the story out of the idea." Travel is also a fertile source of inspiration, allowing Johnson to observe different configurations of land, sky and people. His Appalachian roots supply him with a rich abundance of material, either through the retelling of folktales or the creation of his own original tall tales.

Being an illustrator, as well as a writer, is beneficial for Johnson when he creates his own work. "Whenever I write a story, in my mind's eye, I am working on the pictures as well. As the writing process continues, I subconsciously start writing toward these 'mind' pictures." Thus, he is conceiving mentally a relationship between word and picture. When he illustrates another writer's work, he doesn't have that advantage. "I must first internalize the story and try to make it my own. That takes time. The whole process seems more of a challenge."

Johnson's own style in writing and illustrating is eclectic, ranging from Russian folktales like *A Perfect Pork Stew* to *Farmers' Market*, a story about a young farm girl's experience at a city farmers' market. He attributes this approach to having "admired many writers and illustrators from different eras and schools. I have borrowed from one here and another there, but no one individual served as a role model."

When submitting, Johnson suggests writers target submissions and take the time to investigate which houses publish their type of story. "Unfortunately there is no magic shortcut to getting published. The odds are formidable." Johnson says there are far too few editors, looking at too many manuscripts. He advises writers to get themselves noticed. "If your story sounds like something you've read before, it's dead on arrival. But if you can manage to breathe freshness into your subject, you may catch the eye of an editor." That vigor and originality is best achieved "by giving your own unique sound to the language itself—otherwise known as voice."

Illustration © Paul Brett Johnson. Reprinted with permission of Orchard Books.

After traveling to Russia and observing an "incredibly rich folk heritage," author/artist Paul Brett Johnson longed to illustrate a tale from "that fascinating part of the world." But Johnson found all his favorite Russian stories had been done over and over. "What was there to do except concoct my own tale?" he says. "I started with a couple of stock characters from Russian lore. I added a pinch of tall tale, a bit of swapping motif, and a good dose of the sillies." The resulting picture book, *A Perfect Pork Stew*, won the Kentucky Student Choice Award.

To hone skills, try working with a writing group. This experience has been helpful to Johnson in two ways. "Analyzing others' work is great exercise for sharpening my critical thinking skills, which helps me become a better judge of my own work. Secondly, as I'm working on a piece, there comes a point when objectivity seems to take a vacation. Fresh eyes can see things about my work that I sometimes miss."

Johnson is excited about and is now working on the illustrations for his retelling of a southern "Jack Tale." Jack Tales are an American version of a European story cycle featuring the same heroic Jack who climbed the beanstalk and duped that ol' giant. He's hoping this book will be the first in a series, and he is looking forward to completing the second sibling to the *Cow Who Wouldn't Come Down*. Although Johnson says he may some day try his hand at writing chapter books or novels, he plans to always continue creating picture books, his true love.

—Pamala Shields

phers per photo (negotiable). Sends galleys to authors upon request. Book catalog and ms guidelines available for SASE.

Tips: "Authors should read some of the books we have already published before sending a query to The Oliver Press. Authors should propose collective biographies for one of our existing series."

ORCA BOOK PUBLISHERS, P.O. Box 5626 Station B, Victoria, British Columbia V8R 6S4 Canada. (604)380-1229. Fax: (604)380-1892. Book publisher. Estab. 1984. Publisher: R. Tyrrell. **Acquisitions:** Ann Featherstone, children's book editor. Publishes 10 picture books/year; 4 middle readers/year; and 4 young adult titles/year. 25% of books by first time authors. "We only consider authors who are Canadian or who live in Canada."

• Orca no longer considers nonfiction.

Fiction: Picture books: animals, contemporary, history, nature/environment. Middle readers: contemporary, history, nature/environment, problem novels. Young adults: adventure, contemporary, history, multicultural, nature/environment, problem novels, suspense/mystery. Average word length: picture books—500-2,000; middle readers—20,000-35,000; young adult—25,000-45,000. Published *Tall in the Saddle*, by Anne Carter, illustrated by David McPhail (ages 4-8, picture book); *Me and Mr. Mah*, by Andrea Spalding, illustrated by Janet Wilson (ages 5 and up, picture book); and *Alone at Ninety Foot*, by Katherine Holubitsky (young adult).

How to Contact/Writers: Fiction: Submit complete ms if picture book; submit outline/synopsis and 3 sample chapters. Nonfiction: Query with SASE. "All queries or unsolicited submissions should be accompanied by a SASE." Reports on queries in 6-8 weeks; mss in 1-3 months. Publishes a book 18-24 months after acceptance.

Illustration: Works with 8-10 illustrators/year. Reviews ms/illustration packages from artists. Submit ms with 3-4 pieces of final art. "Reproductions only, no original art please." Illustrations only: Query with samples; provide résumé, slides. Reports in 6-8 weeks. Samples returned with SASE; samples filed.

Terms: Pays authors royalty of 5% for picture books, 10% for novels, based on retail price. Offers advances (average amount: $2,000). Pays illustrators royalty of 5% minimum based on retail price and advance on royalty. Sends galleys to authors. Original artwork returned at job's completion if picture books. Book catalog available for legal or 8½×11 manila SAE and $2 first-class postage. Ms guidelines available for SASE. Art guidelines not available.

Tips: "American authors and illustrators should remember that the U.S. stamps on their reply envelopes cannot be posted in any country outside of the U.S."

ORCHARD BOOKS, 95 Madison Ave., New York NY 10016. (212)951-2600. Website: www.grolier.com. Imprint of Grolier, Inc. Book publisher. President and Publisher: Judy V. Wilson. **Manuscript Acquisitions:** Sarah Caguiat, editor; Ana Cerro, editor. **Art Acquisitions:** Art Director. "We publish between 60 and 70 books yearly including fiction, poetry, picture books, and some nonfiction." 10-25% of books by first-time authors.

• Orchard is not accepting unsolicited mss; query letters only. Orchard title *The Other Side: Shorter Poems*, by Angela Johnson, won a 1999 Coretta Scott King Author Honor Award.

Fiction: All levels: animal, anthology, contemporary, fantasy, folktales, history, humor, multicultural, nature/environment, poetry, science fiction, sports, suspense/mystery. Recently published *One Seal*, by John Stadler; *The Pig Who Ran a Red Light*, by Paul Brett Johnson; and *Wolf!* by Becky Bloom.

Nonfiction: Picture books, young readers: animal, history, multicultural, nature/environment, science, social issues. "We rarely publish nonfiction." Recently published *While You're Waiting for the Food to Come*, by Eric Mully; and *Mighty Boy*, by Carol Sonenklar.

How to Contact/Writers: Query only with SASE.

Illustration: Works with 40 illustrators/year. Art director reviews ms/illustration portfolios. Submit "tearsheets or photocopies or photostats of the work." Reports on art samples in 1 month. Samples returned with SASE. No disks or slides, please.

Terms: Most commonly an advance against list royalties. Sends galleys to authors; dummies to illustrators. Original artwork returned at job's completion. Book catalog free on request with 8½×11 SASE with 4 oz. postage.

Tips: "Read some of our books to determine first whether your manuscript is suited to our list."

✓ ▢ OTTENHEIMER PUBLISHERS, 5 Park Center Court, Suite 300, Owings Mills MD 21117-5001. (410)902-9100. Fax: (410)902-7210. Imprints: Dream House, Halo Press. Independent book producer/packager. Estab. 1896. **Manuscript Acquisitions:** Cathy Drinkwater Better, editorial director. **Art Acquisitions:** Andrew P. Murphy, art director. Publishes 2 picture books/year; 30 early readers/year. 20% of books by first-time authors. "We publish series; rarely single-tile ideas. Early learning, religious, Beatrix Potter, activity books. We do lots of novelty formats and always want more ideas for inexpensive and creative packaging concepts. We are sticker book and pop-up book experts."

Nonfiction: Picture books: activity books, animal, concept, early learning novelty formats, geography, nature/environment, reference, religion. Recently published *My Bible Alphabet Block Pop-Up Book* (ages 3-6); *Wonders of Nature* (ages 3-6); and *Classic Christmas Sticker Books* (ages 3-6).

How to Contact/Writers: Fiction (very rarely): Query. Nonfiction: Submit complete ms. Reports on queries/mss in 6-8 weeks. Publishes a book 6 months to 1 year after acceptance. Will consider simultaneous submissions; previously published work.

Illustration: Works with 8 illustrators/year. Reviews ms/illustration packages from artists. Query. Illustrations only: Send promo sheet and tearsheets to be kept on file. Reports back only if interested. Samples returned with SASE; samples kept on file.

Photography: Buys stock images.

Terms: Pays authors royalty of 5-10% based on wholesale price or work purchased outright for $200-1,000. Offers advances. Pays illustrators by the project (range: $200-16,000). Sends galleys to authors. Originals returned to artist at job's completion. Ms guidelines for SASE.

Tips: "Don't submit single stories; we want series concepts for early learners, ages three to seven."

OUR CHILD PRESS, P.O. Box 74, Wayne PA 19087-0074. (610)964-0606. Fax: (610)964-0938. Book publisher. **Acquisitions:** Carol Hallenbeck, president. 90% of books by first-time authors.

Fiction/Nonfiction: All levels: adoption, multicultural, special needs. Published *Don't Call Me Marda*, written and illustrated by Sheila Kelly Welch; *Is That Your Sister?* by Catherine and Sherry Burin; and *Oliver: A Story About Adoption*, by Lois Wichstrom.

How to Contact/Writers: Fiction/Nonfiction: Query or submit complete ms. Reports on queries/mss in 6 months. Publishes a book 6-12 months after acceptance.

Illustration: Works with 1 illustrator/year. Uses primarily b&w artwork. Reviews ms/illustration packages from artists. Ms/illustration packages and illustration only: Query first. Submit résumé, tearsheets and photocopies. Reports on art samples in 2 months. Samples returned with SASE; samples kept on file.

Terms: Pays authors in royalties of 5-10% based on wholesale price. Pays illustrators royalties of 5-10% based on wholesale price. Original artwork returned at job's completion. Book catalog for business-size SAE and 52¢ postage.

Tips: "Won't consider anything not related to adoption."

✓ ▢ OUR SUNDAY VISITOR, INC., 200 Noll Plaza, Huntington IN 46750. (219)356-8400. Fax: (219)359-9117. E-mail: jlindsey@osv.commdubriel@osv.com. Website: www.osv.com. Book publisher. **Acquisitions:** Jacquelyn M. Lindsey, Michael Dubruiel. Art Director: Eric Schoenig. Publishes primarily religious, educational, parenting, reference and biographies. OSV is dedicated to providing books, periodicals and other products that serve the Catholic Church.

● Our Sunday Visitor, Inc., is publishing only those children's books that tie in to sacramental preparation. Contact the acquisitions editor for manuscript guidelines and a book catalog.

Nonfiction: Picture books, middle readers, young readers, young adults. Recently published *I Am Special*, by Joan and Paul Plum, illustrated by Andee Most (3-year-old activity book).

How to Contact/Writers: Query, submit complete ms, or submit outline/synopsis, and 2-3 sample chapters. Reports on queries in 2 months; mss in 1 month. Publishes a book 18-24 months after acceptance. Will consider simultaneous submissions, electronic submissions via disk or modem, previously published work.

Illustration: Reviews ms/illustration packages from artists. Contact: Jacquelyn Lindsey or Michael Dubruiel, acquisitions editors. Illustration only: Query with samples. Contact: Aquisitions Editor. Reports only if interested. Samples returned with SASE; samples filed. Original artwork returned at job's completion.

Photography: Buys photos from freelancers. Contact: Acquisitions Editor.

Terms: Pays authors royalty of 10-12% net. Pays illustrators by the project (range: $200-1,500). Sends galleys to authors; dummies to illustrators. Book catalog available for SASE; ms guidelines available for SASE.

Tips: "Stay in accordance with our guidelines."

N: THE OVERMOUNTAIN PRESS, P.O. Box 1261, Johnson City TN 37605. (423)926-2691. Fax: (423)929-2464. E-mail: archer@planetc.com. Website: www.overmtn.com. Estab. 1970. Specializes in regional history trade books. **Manuscript Acquisitions:** Elizabeth L. Wright, senior editor. Publishes 4 picture books/year; 2 young readers/year; 2 middle readers/year. 50% of books by first-time authors. "We are primarily a publisher of southeastern regional history, and we have recently published several titles for children. Children's books about southern Appalachia are of special interest."

Fiction: Picture books: animal, folktales, history, nature/environment, religion. Young readers, middle readers: animal, folktales, history, nature/environment, religion, suspense/mystery. Average word length: picture books—800-1,000; young readers—5,000-10,000; middle readers—20-30,000. Recently published *Bloody Mary: The Mystery of Amanda's Magic Mirror*, by Patrick Bone (young, middle reader); *Zebordee's Miracle*, by Ann G. Cooper, illustrated by Adam Hickam (pre-elementary, picture book); and *Appalachian ABCs*, by Francie Hall, illustrated by Kent Oehm (pre-elementary, picture book).

Nonfiction: Picture books, young readers, middle readers: animal, biography (regional), history (regional), nature/environment, religion. Average word length: picture books—800-1,000; young readers—5,000-10,000; middle readers—20-30,000. Recently published *Ten Friends: A Child's Story About the Ten Commandments*, written and illustrated by Gayla Dowdy Seale (preschool-elementary, picture book).

How to Contact/Writers: Fiction/Nonfiction: Submit outline/synopsis and 2 sample chapters. Reports on queries in 2 months; mss in 6 months. Publishes book 1 year after acceptance. Will consider simultaneous submissions and previously published work.

Illustration: Works with 4 illustrators/year. Uses color artwork only. Reviews ms/illustration packages from artists. Send ms with dummy with at least 3 color copies of sample illustrations. Illustrations only: Send résumé. Reports back only if interested. Samples not returned; samples filed.

Terms: Pays authors royalty of 5-15% based on wholesale price. Pays illustrators royalty of 5-10% based on wholesale price or by author/illustrator negotiations (author pays). Sends galleys to authors; dummies to illustrators. Originals sometimes returned to artist at job's completion. Book catalog available for 8½×11 SAE and 4 first-class stamps; ms guidelines available for SASE. All imprints included in a single catalog. Catalog available on website.

Tips: "Because we are fairly new in the children's market, we will not accept a manuscript without complete illustrations. We are compiling a database of freelance illustrators which is available to interested authors. Please call if you have questions regarding the submission process or to see if your product is of interest. The children's market is HUGE! If the author can find a good local publisher, he or she is more likely to get published. We are currently looking for authors to represent our list in the new millenium. We are slowly expanding our list and broadening our horizons in regard to children's titles."

RICHARD C. OWEN PUBLISHERS, INC., P.O. Box 585, Katonah NY 10536. (914)232-3903. Fax: (914)232-3977. Website: www.rcowen.com. Book publisher. **Acquisitions:** Janice Boland, children's books editor/art director. Publishes 20 picture story books/year. 90% of books by first-time authors. We publish "child-focused books, with inherent instructional value, about characters and situations with which five-, six-, and seven-year-old children can identify—books that can be read for meaning, entertainment, enjoyment and information. We include multicultural stories that present minorities in a positive and natural way. Our stories show the diversity in America."

Fiction: Picture books, young readers, middle readers: adventure, animal, anthology, contemporary, folktales, hi-lo, humor, multicultural, nature/environment, poetry, science fiction, sports, suspense/mystery. Does not want to see holiday, religious themes, moral teaching stories. "No talking animals with personified human characteristics, jingles and rhymes, alphabet books, stories without plots, stories with nostalgic views of childhood, soft or sugar-coated tales. No stereotyping." Average word length: 40-100 words. Recently published *Digging to China*, by Katherine Goldsby, illustrated by Viki Woodworth; *The Red-Tailed Hawk*, by Lola Schaefer, illustrated by Stephen Taylor; and *Dogs at School*, by Suzanne Hardil, illustrated by Jo-Ann Friar.

Nonfiction: Picture books, young readers, middle readers: animals, careers, hi-lo, history, how-to, music/dance, geography, multicultural, nature/environment, science, sports. Multicultural needs include: "Good stories respectful of all heritages, races, cultural—African-American, Hispanic, American Indian." Wants lively stories. No "encyclopedic" type of information stories. Average word length: 40-100 words. Recently published *New York City Buildings*, by Ann Mace, photos by Tim Holmstron.

How to Contact/Writers: Fiction/nonfiction: Submit complete ms. "*Must* request guidelines first with #10 SASE." Reports on mss in 2-9 months. Publishes a book 2-3 years after acceptance. Will consider simultaneous submissions.

Illustration: Works with 20 illustrators/year. Uses color artwork only. Illustration only: Send color copies/reproductions or photos of art or provide tearsheets; do not send slides. Must request guidelines first. Reports in 2-9 months if interested; samples filed.

Photography: Buys photos from freelancers. Contact: Janice Boland, art director. Wants photos that are child-oriented; candid shots; not interested in portraits. "Natural, bright, crisp and colorful—of children and of interesting subjects and compositions attractive to children. If photos are assigned, we buy outright—retain ownership and all rights to photos taken in the project." Sometimes interested in stock photos for special projects. Uses 35mm, 2¼×2¼, color transparencies.

Terms: Pays authors royalties of 5% based on wholesale price or outright purchse (range: $50-500). Offers no advances. Pays illustrators by the project (range: $50-2,800). Pays photographers by the project (range: $50-2,000) or per photo ($100-150). Original artwork returned 12-18 months after job's completion. Book brochure, ms/artists guidelines available for SASE.

Tips: Seeking "stories (both fiction and nonfiction) that have charm, magic, impact and appeal; that children living in today's society will want to read and reread; books with strong storylines, child-appealing language, action and interesting, vivid characters. Write for the ears and eyes and hearts of your readers—use an economy of words. Visit the children's room at the public library and immerse yourself in the best children's literature."

N: OWL BOOKS, Imprint of Greey de Pencier Books, 70 The Esplanade, 4th Floor, Toronto, Ontario M5E 1R2 Canada. (416)971-5275. Fax: (416)971-5294. Book publisher. Estab. 1976. Publishing Director: Sheba Meland. **Manuscript Acquisitions:** Submissions Editor. **Art Acquisitions:** Art Director; Photo Editor. Estab. 1976. Publishing Director: Sheba Meland. Publishes 2 picture books/year; 3 young readers, middle readers/year. 10% of books by first-time authors. Publishes nature, science and children's crafts and hobbies. "We give preference to work by Canadian writers living in Canada or the U.S."

Fiction: Picture books, young readers: animal, concept, humor, nature/environment. Does not want to see "cliché environmental stories." Average word length: picture books—1,000; young readers—2,000. Recently published *Wild in the City*, written and illustrated by Jan Thornhill (ages 5-10, picturebook/nature); and *Dragon in the Rocks*, written and illustrated by Marie Day (ages 5-10, picturebook/biography).

Nonfiction: Picture books, young readers, middle readers: animal, arts/crafts, concept, hobbies, how-to, nature/environment, science. Average word length: picture books—1,000-1,500; young readers—2,000-3,500; middle readers—7,500-10,000. Recently published *Cyber Surfer: The Owl Kid's Guide to the Internet*, by Nyla Ahmad (ages 8-12, science/tech); *Wow Canada! Exploring This Land from Coast to Coast* (ages 9-12, adventure/travel); and *Family Tree Detective* (ages 9-12, activity book).

How to Contact/Writers: Fiction: Submit complete ms. Nonfiction: Submit outline/synopsis and 2 sample chapters. Reports on queries/mss in 3 months. Publishes a book 18 months after acceptance.

Illustration: Uses color artwork only. Reviews ms/illustration packages from artists. Send ms with dummy and 3 pieces of final art.

Photography: Buys stock images. Uses photos of nature, science, children. Model/property release required; captions required. Uses 35mm, 2¼×2¼, color transparencies. Submit cover letter, résumé, published samples, client list, stock photo list.

Terms: Pays authors royalties based on retail price, outright purchase. Offers advances. Pays illustrators royalty or by the project. Pays photographers by the project or per photo. Sends galleys to authors; dummies to illustrators. Book catalog available for SAE and 6 first-class stamps.

Tips: "We are affiliated with *Owl* and *Chickadee* magazines. We publish mainly nonfiction, and look for innovative ideas, top-notch research, and an understanding of what children want in an information or activity book. Read some Owl Books for an appreciation of our approach!"

PACIFIC VIEW PRESS, P.O. Box 2657, Berkeley CA 94702. (510)849-4213. Fax: (510)843-5835. E-mail: PVP@sirius.com. Book publisher. **Acquisitions:** Pam Zumwalt, president. Publishes 1-2 picture books/year. 50% of books by first-time authors. "We publish unique, high-quality introductions to Asian cultures and history for children 8-12, for schools, libraries and families. Our children's books focus on hardcover illustrated nonfiction. We look for titles on aspects of the history and culture of the countries and peoples of the Pacific Rim, especially China, presented in an engaging, informative and respectful manner. We are interested in books that all children will enjoy reading and using, and that parents and teachers will want to buy."

Nonfiction: Young readers, middle readers: Asia-related multicultural only. Recently published *Kneeling Carabao and Dancing Giants: Celebrating Filipino Festivals*, by Rena Krasno, illustrated by Ileana C. Lee (ages 8-12, nonfiction on festivals and history of Philippines); and *Made in China: Ideas and Inventions from Ancient China*, by Suzanne Williams, illustrated by Andrea Fong (ages 10-12, nonfiction on history of China and Chinese inventions).

How to Contact/Writers: Query with outline and sample chapter. Reports in 3 months.

Illustration: Works with 2 illustrators/year. Reports back only if interested. Samples returned with SASE.

Terms: Pays authors royalty of 8-12% based on wholesale price. Pays illustrators by the project (range: $2,000-5,000).

Tips: "We welcome proposals from persons with expertise, either academic or personal, in their area of interest. While we do accept proposals from previously unpublished authors, we would expect submitters to have considerable experience presenting their interests to children in classroom or other public settings, and to have skill in writing for children."

MARKET CONDITIONS are constantly changing! If you're still using this book and it is 2001 or later, buy the newest edition of *Children's Writer's & Illustrator's Market* at your favorite bookstore or order directly from Writer's Digest Books.

PARENTING PRESS, INC., P.O. Box 75267, Seattle WA 98125. (206)364-2900. Fax: (206)364-0702. E-mail: office@parentingpress.com. Website: www.parentingpress.com. Book publisher. Estab. 1979. Publisher: Carolyn Threadgill. **Acquisitions:** Elizabeth Crary. Publishes 4-5 books/year for parents or/and children and those who work with them. 40% of books by first-time authors. "Parenting Press publishes educational books for children in story format—no straight fiction. Our company publishes books that help build competence in parents and children. We are known for practical books that teach parents and can be used successfully by parent educators, teachers, and educators who work with parents. We are interested in books that help people feel good about themselves because they gain skills needed in dealing with others. We are particularly interested in material that provides 'options' rather than 'shoulds.' "

● Parenting Press's guidelines are available on their website.

Fiction: Picture books: concept. Publishes social skills books, problem-solving books, safety books, dealing-with-feelings books that use a "fictional" vehicle for the information. "We rarely publish straight fiction." Recently published *I Can't Wait, I Want It, My Name Is Not Dummy*, by Elizabeth Crary, illustrations by Marina Megale (ages 3-8, social skill building); *Telling Isn't Tattling*, by Kathryn Hammerseng, illustrations by Dave Garbot (ages 4-12, personal safety); and 4 toddler board books on expressing feelings.

Nonfiction: Picture books: health, social skills building. Young readers: health, social skills building books. Middle readers: health, social skills building. No books on "new baby; coping with a new sibling; cookbooks; manners; books about disabilities (which we don't publish at present); animal characters in anything; books that tell children what they should do, instead of giving options." Average word length: picture books—500-800; young readers—1,000-2,000; middle readers—up to 10,000. Published *Kids to the Rescue*, by Maribeth and Darwin Boelts (ages 4-12).

How to Contact/Writers: Query. Reports on queries/mss in 3 months, "after requested." Publishes a book 18 months after acceptance. Will consider simultaneous submissions.

Illustrations: Works with 3 illustrators/year. Reviews ms/illustration packages from artists. "We do reserve the right to find our own illustrator, however." Query. Illustrations only: Submit "résumé, samples of art/drawings (no original art); photocopies or color photocopies okay." Reports only if interested. Samples returned with SASE; samples filed, if suitable.

Terms: Pays authors royalties of 5-8% based on wholesale price. Pays illustrators (for text) by the project; 3-5% royalty based on wholesale price. Pays illustrators by the project ($500-3,000). Sends galleys to authors; dummies to illustrators. Book catalog/ms/artist's guidelines for #10 SAE and 1 first-class stamp.

Tips: "Make sure you are familiar with the unique nature of our books. All are aimed at building certain 'people' skills in adults or children. Our publishing for children follows no trend that we find appropriate. Children need nonfiction social skill-building books that help them think through problems and make their own informed decisions."

PAULIST PRESS, 997 Macarthur Blvd., Mahwah NJ 07430. (201)825-7300. Fax: (201)825-8345. Website: www.paulistpress.com. Book publisher. Estab. 1865. **Acquisitions:** Therese Johnson Borchard, editor. Publishes 9-11 picture books/year; 8-10 young reader titles/year; and 3-4 middle reader titles/year. 80% of books by first-time authors; 30% of books from agented writers. "Our goal is to produce books that 'heal with kid-appeal,' 'share the goodness,' and delight in diversity."

Fiction: Picture books, young readers, middle readers and young adults: interested mainly in books providing an accessible introduction to basic religious and family values, but not preachy. Recently published *I Hate Goodbyes*, by Kathleen Szaj, illustrated by Mark A. Hicks; Walking With God series: *Spirit!, Yes, I Can!, Imagine!* and *Where Is God?*, by Heidi Bratton; *Elizabeth, Who is NOT a Saint*, by Kathleen Szaj, illustrated by Mark A. Hicks; and *Little Blessings*, by Sally Ann Conan, illustrated by Kathy Rogers.

Nonfiction: All levels: biography, concept, multicultural, religion, self help, social issues.

How to Contact/Writers: Fiction/nonfiction: Submit complete ms. Reports on queries/mss in 6-8 months. Publishes a book 12-16 months after acceptance.

Illustration: Works with 10-12 illustrators/year. Editorial reviews all varieties of ms/illustration packages from artists. Submit complete ms with 1 piece of final art (photocopy only) remainder roughs. Illustrations only: Submit résumé, tearsheets. Reports on art samples in 6-8 months.

Photography: Buys photos from freelancers. Works on assignment only. Uses inspirational photos.

Terms: Pays authors royalty of 6-8% based on retail price. Offers average advance payment of $500. Pays illustrators by the project (range: $50-100) or royalty of 2-6% based on retail price. Pays photographers by the project (range: $25-150; negotiable). Factors used to determine final payment: color art, b&w, number of illustrations, complexity of work. Pay for separate authors and illustrators: Author paid by royalty rate; illustrator paid by flat fee, sometimes by royalty. Sends galleys to authors; dummies to illustrators. Original artwork returned at job's completion, "if requested by illustrator."

Tips: "We cannot be responsible for unsolicited manuscripts. Please send copies, not originals. We try to respond to all manuscripts we receive—please understand if you have not received a response within six months the manuscript does not fit our current publishing plan. We look for authors who diligently promote their work."

PEACHTREE PUBLISHERS, LTD., 494 Armour Circle NE, Atlanta GA 30324. (404)876-8761. Fax: (404)875-2578. Website: www.peachtree-online.com. Book publisher. Imprints: Peachtree Jr. and Freestone. Estab. 1977. **Acquisitions:** Helen Harriss. Publishes 20 titles/year.

Fiction: Picture books: adventure, animal, concept, history, nature/environment. Young readers: adventure, animal, concept, history, nature/environment, poetry. Middle readers: adventure, animal, history, nature/environment, sports. Young adults: fiction, mystery, adventure. Does not want to see science fiction, romance.
Nonfiction: Picture books: adventure, animal, fiction, mystery, nature/environment. Young readers, middle readers, young adults: animal, biography, nature/environment. Does not want to see sports, religion.
How to Contact/Writers: Fiction/Nonfiction: Submit complete ms. Reports on queries in 2-3 months; mss in 4 months. Publishes a book 1-1½ years after acceptance. Will consider simultaneous and previously published submissions.
Illustration: Works with 8 illustrators/year. Illustrations only: Query with samples, résumé, slides, color copies to keep on file. Reports back only if interested. Samples returned with SASE; samples filed.
Terms: Ms guidelines for SASE, or call for a recorded message.

PELICAN PUBLISHING CO. INC., P.O. Box 3110, Gretna LA 70054-3110. (504)368-1175. E-mail: office@pelicanpub.com. Website: www.pelicanpub.com. Book publisher. Estab. 1926. **Manuscript Acquisitions:** Nina Kooij, editor-in-chief. **Art Acquisitions:** Tracey Clements, production manager. Publishes 10 young readers/year and 3 middle reader titles/year. 10% of books from agented writers. "Pelican publishes hardcover and trade paperback originals and reprints. Our children's books (illustrated and otherwise) include history, holiday, bilingual, sports, folklore and textbooks."
Fiction: Young readers: folktales, history, multicultural. Middle readers: Louisiana history. Multicultural needs include stories about African-Americans, Irish-Americans, Jews, Asian-Americans, Cajuns and Hispanics. Does not want animal stories, general Christmas stories, "day at school" or "accept yourself" stories. Maximum word length: 1,100 young readers; middle readers—40,000. Recently published *Jolie Blonde and the Three Héberts: A Cajun Twist to an Old Tale*, by Sheila Hébert Collins.
Nonfiction: Young readers: biography, history. Middle readers: Louisiana biography, history. Recently published *The Governor of Louisiana*, by Miriam G. Reeves (ages 8-12, biography).
How to Contact/Writers: Fiction/Nonfiction: Query. Reports on queries in 1 month; mss in 3 months. Publishes a book 9-18 months after acceptance.
Illustration: Works with 8 illustrators/year. Reviews ms/illustration packages from artists. Query first. Illustrations only: Query with samples (no originals). Reports only if interested. Samples returned with SASE; samples kept on file.
Terms: Pays authors in royalties; buys ms outright "rarely." Sends galleys to authors. Illustrators paid by "various arrangements." Book catalog and ms guidelines available for SASE.
Tips: "No anthropomorphic stories, pet stories (fiction or nonfiction), fantasy, poetry, science fiction or romance. Writers: Be as original as possible. Develop characters that lend themselves to series and always be thinking of new and interesting situations for those series. Give your story a strong hook—something that will appeal to a well-defined audience. There is a lot of competition out there for general themes. We look for stories with specific 'hooks' and audiences, and writers who actively promote their work."

PENGUIN PUTNAM INC., 345 Hudson St., New York NY 10014. See listings for Dial Books for Young Readers, Dutton Children's Books, Philomel Books, Puffin Books, G.P. Putnam's Sons and Viking Children's Books.

PERFECTION LEARNING CORPORATION, Cover to Cover, 10520 New York, Des Moines IA 50322. (515)278-0133. Fax: (515)278-2980. E-mail: acquisitions@plconline.com. Website: www.perfectionlearning.com. Book publisher, independent book producer/packager. **Manuscript Acquisitions:** S. Thies (K-12), Terry Ofner (curriculum). **Art Acquisitions:** Randy Messer, art director. Publishes 20 early chapter books/year; 40-50 middle readers/year; 25 young adult titles/year.
 • Perfection Learning Corp. publishes *all* hi-lo children's books on a variety of subjects.
Fiction: All levels: adventure, animal, contemporary, fantasy, folktales, history, humor, multicultural, nature/environment, poetry, problem novels, science fiction, special needs, sports, suspense/mystery. Average word length: early chapter books—4,000; middle readers—10,000-14,000; young adults: 10,000-30,000. Recently published *Holding the Yellow Rabbit*; and *Prairie Meeting*.
Nonfiction: All levels: activity, animal, biography, careers, geography, health, history, hobbies, multicultural, nature/environment, science, self-help, social issues, special needs, sports. Multicultural needs include stories, legends and other oral tradition narratives by authors who are of the culture. Does not want to see ABC books. Average word length: early chapter books—4,000; middle readers—10,000-14,000; young adults—10,000-14,000.
How to Contact/Writers: Fiction/Nonfiction: Submit complete ms. Reports on queries in 1 month; mss in 4 months. Publishes a book 18 months after acceptance.
Illustration: Works with 15-20 illustrators/year. Illustration only: Query with samples; send résumé, promo sheet, client list, tearsheets. Contact: Randy Messer, art director. Reports only if interested. Samples returned with SASE; samples filed.
Photography: Buys photos from freelancers. Contact: Randy Messer, art director. Buys stock and assigns work. Uses children. Uses color or up to 8×10 b&w glossy prints; 2¼×2¼, 4×5 transparencies. Submit cover letter, client list, stock photo list, promo piece (color or b&w).

Terms: Pays authors "depending on going rate for industry." Offers advances. Pays illustrators by the project. Pays photographers by the project. Original artwork returned on a "case by case basis."

Tips: "Our materials are sold through schools for use in the classroom. Talk to a teacher about his/her needs."

☑ PHILOMEL BOOKS, Penguin Putnam Inc., 345 Hudson St., New York NY 10014. (212)414-3610. Website: www.penguinputnam.com. Putnam Books. Book publisher. Estab. 1980. **Manuscript Acquisitions:** Patricia Gauch, editorial director; Alison Keehn, assistant editor; Michael Green, senior editor. **Art Acquisitions:** Gina Casquarelli, design assistant. Publishes 18 picture books/year; 2 middle-grade/year; 2 young readers/year; 4 young adult/year. 5% of books by first-time authors; 80% of books from agented writers. "We look for beautifully written, engaging manuscripts for children and young adults."

• Philomel Books is not accepting unsolicited manuscripts.

Fiction: All levels: adventure, animal, anthology, contemporary, fantasy, folktales, hi-lo, history, humor, poetry, sports, multicultural. Middle readers, young adults: problem novels, science fiction, suspense/mystery. No concept picture books, mass-market "character" books, or series. Average word length: 1,000 for picture books; 1,500 young readers; 14,000 middle readers; 20,000 young adult.

Nonfiction: Picture books, young readers, middle readers: hi-lo. "Creative nonfiction on any subject." Average word length: 2,000 for picture books; 3,000 young readers; 10,000 middle readers.

How to Contact/Writers: Not accepting unsolicited mss. Fiction: Submit outline/synopsis and first two chapters. Nonfiction: Query. Reports on queries in 3 months; mss in 4 months.

Illustration: Works with 20-25 illustrators/year. Reviews ms/illustration packages from artists. Query with art sample first. Illustrations only: Query with samples. Send résumé and tearsheets. Reports on art samples in 1 month. Original artwork returned at job's completion. Samples returned with SASE, or kept on file.

Terms: Pays authors in royalties. Average advance payment "varies." Illustrators paid by advance and in royalties. Sends galleys to authors; dummies to illustrators. Book catalog, ms guidelines free on request with SASE (9×12 envelope for catalog).

Tips: Wants "unique fiction or nonfiction with a strong voice and lasting quality. Discover your own voice and own story—and persevere." Looks for "something unusual, original, well-written. Fine art. The genre (fantasy, contemporary, or historical fiction) is not so important as the story itself, and the spirited life the story allows its main character. We are also interested in receiving adolescent novels, particularly novels that contain regional spirit, such as a story about a young boy or girl written from a Southern, Southwestern or Northwestern perspective."

⬛ PHOENIX LEARNING RESOURCES, 12 W. 31st St., New York NY 10001-4415. (212)629-3887. (212)629-5648. E-mail: john@phoenixlr.com. Website: www.phoenixlr.com. Book publisher. Executive Vice President: John A. Rothermich. Publishes 20 textbooks/year. Publisher's goal is to provide proven skill building materials in reading, language, math and study skills for today's student, grades K-adult.

Nonfiction: Middle readers, young readers, young adults: hi-lo, textbooks. Recently published *Reading for Concepts*, Third Edition.

How to Contact/Writers: Nonfiction: Submit outline/synopsis. Reports on queries in 2 weeks; mss in 1 month. Will consider simultaneous submissions and previously published work.

Photography: Buys stock. Contact: John A. Rothermich, executive vice president. Uses color prints and 35mm, 2¼×2¼, 4×5 transparencies. Submit cover letter.

Terms: Pays authors royalty based on wholesale price or work purchased outright. Pays illustrators and photographers by the project. Sends galleys to authors. Book catalog available for SASE.

Tips: "We look for classroom tested and proven materials."

THE PLACE IN THE WOODS, "Different" Books, 3900 Glenwood Ave., Golden Valley MN 55422-5302. (612)374-2120. Book publisher. **Acquisitions:** Roger Hammer, publisher/editor; Kathryn Smitley, special editor. Publishes 2 elementary-age titles/year and 1 middle readers/year; 1 young adult titles/year. 100% of books by first-time authors. Books feature primarily diversity/multicultural storyline and illustration.

Fiction: All levels: adventure, animal, contemporary, fantasy, folktales, hi-lo, history, humor, poetry, multicultural, special needs.

Nonfiction: All levels: hi-lo, history, multicultural, special needs. Multicultural themes must avoid negative stereotypes. "Generally, we don't publish nonfiction, but we would look at these."

How to Contact/Writers: Fiction/Nonfiction: Submit complete ms. Reports on queries/mss in 1 month with SASE. "No multiple or simultaneous submissions. Please indicate a time frame for response."

Illustration: Works with 2 illustrators/year. Uses primarily b&w artwork only. Reviews ms/illustration packages from authors. Query; submit ms with dummy. Contact: Roger Hammer, editor. Illustration only: Query with samples. Reports in 1 week. Include SASE. "We buy all rights."

Photography: Buys photos from freelancers. Works on assignment only. Uses photos that appeal to children. Model/property releases required; captions required. Uses any b&w prints. Submit cover letter and samples with SASE.

Terms: Work purchased outright from authors ($50-250). Pays illustrators by the project (range: $10-500). Pays photographers per photo. For all contracts, "initial payment repeated with each printing." Original artwork not returned at job's completion. Guidelines available for SASE.

PLAYERS PRESS, INC., P.O. Box 1132, Studio City CA 91614-0132. (818)789-4980. Book publisher. Imprints: Showcase Publishing; Gaslight Productions; Health Watch Books. Estab. 1965. Vice President/Editorial: Robert W. Gordon. **Manuscript Acquisitions:** Attention: Editor. **Art Acquisitions:** Attention: Art Director. Publishes 7-25 young readers dramatic plays and musicals/year; 2-10 middle readers dramatic plays and musicals/year; and 4-20 young adults dramatic plays and musicals/year. 35% of books by first-time authors; 1% of books from agented writers.

Fiction: Picture books, middle readers, young readers, young adults: history. Young adults: health, suspense/mystery. Recently published *Tower of London*, a play by William Hezlep; *Punch and Judy*, a play by William-Alan Landes; and *Silly Soup!*, by Carol Kerty (a collection of short plays with music and dance).

Nonfiction: Picture books, middle readers, young readers, young adults. "Any children's nonfiction pertaining to the entertainment industry, performing arts and how-to for the theatrical arts only." Needs include, activity, arts/crafts, careers, history, how-to, music/dance, reference and textbook. Published *Stagecrafter's Handbook*, by I.E. Clark; and *New Monologues for Readers Theatre*, by Steven Porter. Recently published *Assignments in Musical Theatre Acting & Directing*, by Jacque Wheeler and Halle Laughlin (how-to on teaching or learning to a musical theater actor or director); and *Theatre for Children in the United States: A History*, by nellie McCaslin (complete history of children's theater from the turn of the century through 1996).

How to Contact/Writers: Fiction/nonfiction: Submit plays or outline/synopsis and sample chapters of entertainment books. Reports on queries in 2-4 weeks; mss in 1-12 months. Publishes a book 10 months after acceptance. No simultaneous submissions.

Illustration: Works with 2-6 illustrators/year. Use primarily b&w artwork. Illustrations only: Submit résumé, tearsheets. Reports on art samples in 1 week only if interested. Samples returned with SASE; samples filed.

Terms: Pays authors royalties based on wholesale price. Pay illustrators by the project (range: $5-5,000). Pays photographers by the project (up to 1,000); royalty varies. Sends galleys to authors; dummies to illustrators. Book catalog and ms guidelines available for SASE.

Tips: Looks for "plays/musicals and books pertaining to the performing arts only. Illustrators: send samples that can be kept for our files."

PLAYSKOOL BOOKS, 345 Hudson St., New York NY 10014. (212)414-3700. Fax: (212)414-3397. Website: www.penguin.com. Book publisher. Division of Dutton Children's Books. **Manuscript Acquisitions:** Lucia Monfried, editor-in-chief. **Manuscript/illustration packages:** Lucia Monfried. **Art acquisitions:** Rick Farely, art director.Published 20 picture books/year. 5% by first-time authors. "We publish books for preschoolers that emphasize play and learning."

● Playskool is temporarily not accepting new manuscripts.

Fiction: Picture books: animal, concept, contemporary, humor, multicultural, novelty. Does not want to see folktales. Recently published: *My First Toolbox*; *My Photo Book About Me*, illustrated by Angie Sage; and *Mr. Potato Head's Costume Party: A Mix and Match Book* (all novelty books for ages 2-5).

Nonfiction: Picture Books: activity books, animal, concept. Recently published: *Seeing Shapes*, photographed by Sandra Lousada (concept board book for ages 2-5).

How to Contact/Writers: Submit complete ms. Reports in 2 months. Published a book 1 year after acceptance. Will consider simultaneous submissions.

Illustration: Works with 12-20 illustrators/year. Uses color artwork only. Reviews ms/illustration packages from artists. Send ms with dummy. Illustrations only: send tearsheets. Reports in 1 month. Samples returned with SASE; samples filed.

Photography: Buys stock images. Contact: Rick Farley, art director or Susan Van Metre, editor. Looking for photos of animals and children. Uses color prints and 35mm transparencies. Send color promo piece.

Terms: Work purchased outright from authors; fee negotiable. Pays illustrators and photographers by the project; negotiable. Sends galleys to authors; dummies to illustrators. Original artwork returned at job's completion. Book catalog availab e for 9 × 12 SAE with 3 first-class stamps. All imprints included in a single catalog. Ms guidelines available for SASE.

Tips: "We are only interested in manuscripts and art appropriate for preschool age children."

PLEASANT COMPANY PUBLICATIONS, 8400 Fairway Place, Middleton WI 53562-0998. (608)836-4848. Fax: (608)836-1999. Website: www.americangirl.com. Book publisher. Editorial Director: Judy Woodburn. **Manuscript Acquisitions:** Jennifer Hirsch, submissions editor; Jodi Evert, executive editor, fiction; Michelle Watkins, director, American Girl Library. **Art Acquisitions:** Jane Varda, art director. Imprints: The American Girls Collection, American Girl Library, Bitty Baby Collection, History Mysteries, AG Fiction. Publishes 8-20 middle readers/year. 40% of books by first-time authors. Publishes fiction and nonfiction for girls 7 and up. "Pleasant Company's mission is to educate and entertain girls with high-quality products and experiences that build self-esteem and reinforce positive social and moral values."

● Pleasant Company publishes *American Girl* magazine.

Fiction: Middle readers: adventure, animal, contemporary, fantasy, history, suspense/mystery. Recently published *Changes for Josefina*, by Valerie Tripp, illustrated by Jean-Paul Tibbles (ages 7-12, historical fiction); *Ceiling of Stars*, by Ann Howard Creel (ages 10 and up, contemporary fiction); *Smuggler's Treasure*, by Sarah Masters Buckey (ages 10 and up, historical fiction/mystery).

Nonfiction: Middle readers: activity books, arts/crafts, cooking, history, hobbies, how-to, self-help, sports.

Recently published *The Care and Keeping of You*, by Valerie Lee Schaefer, illustrated by Norm Bendell (ages 8 and up, self-help); *Ooops! The Manners Guide for Girls*, by Nancy Holyoke, illustrated by Debbie Tilley (ages 8 and up, self-help); and *Josefina's Cookbook, Pleasant Company* (ages 7-12, cooking).
How to Contact/Writers: Fiction/nonfiction: Query or submit entire ms. Reports on queries/mss in 2 months. Will consider simultaneous submissions.
Illustration: Works with 10 illustrators/year. Reviews ms/illustration packages from artists. Illustrations only. Query with samples. Reports back only if interested. Samples returned with SASE; copies of samples filed.
Photography: Buys stock and assigns work. Submit cover letter, published samples, promo piece.
Terms: Pays authors royalty or work purchased outright. Pays illustrators by the project. Pays photographers by the project. Sends galleys to authors; dummies to illustrators. Originals returned to artist at job's completion. Book catalog available for 8½ × 11 SAE and 4 first-class stamps. All imprints included in a single catalog.

N: POLAR BEAR & CO., P.O. Box 311, Brook St., Solon ME 04979. (207)643-2795. E-mail: polarbear@skow.net. **Manuscript Acquisitions:** Alex duHoux. **Art Acquisitions** Emily duHoux, art editor. Publishes 1 middle reader/year; 4 young adult titles/year. 50% of books by first-time authors. "Our mission is to rebuild America's cultural heritage with nature's democratic mythology in words and art."
Fiction: Middle readers: folktales, multicultural, nature/environment, poetry. Young adults: adventure, contemporary, fantasy, folktales, multicultural, nature/environment, poetry, problem novels, science fiction, suspense/mystery, mythology. Average word length: middle readers—10,000; young adults—25,000-50,000. Recently published *Manitou, A Mythological Journey In Time*, by Ramona duHoux (novel); *Stage 3, Emily duHoux Adventure* (ages 12 and up, detective novel); *One Dream, Bet Shoshannah Pecora* (young adult problem novel).
Nonfiction: Young adults: nature/enviroment.
How to Contact/Writers: Fiction: Submit outline/synopsis and 1 sample chapter. Nonfiction: Query. Reports on queries in 2 weeks; mss in 1month. Publishes a book 1 year after acceptance. Will consider simultaneous submissions.
Illustration: Works with 2 illustrators/year. Uses b&w artwork only. Reviews ms/illustration packages from artists. Send ms with dummy. Contact: Ramona duHoux, publisher. Illustrations only: Send résumé, slides.
Photography: Contact Ramona duHoux, publisher. Send cover letter, résumé. published samples, slides, portfolio. Uses photos that will go with poetry. Model/property releases required. Uses color or b&w prints, 8 × 10 and matte; 35mm and 4 × 5 transparencies.
Terms: Pays authors royalty. "We work on an individual basis." Pays illustrators by the project and on an individual basis. Pays photographers by the project and on an individual basis. Originals returned at job's completion.

✓ PONTALBA PRESS, 4417 Dryades St., New Orleans LA 70115. (888)436-3724. Fax: (504)822-6028. E-mail: wayne@pontalbapress.com. Website: www.pontalba.press.com. Estab. 1996. Manuscript and Art Acquisitions: Christian Allman. Publishes 1 picture book/year; 2 young readers/year. 50% of books by first-time authors. "We publish work by both established and new authors and focus on titles and subjects that have mainstream appeal but are often overlooked or ignored by mainstream publishers."
Fiction: History, suspense/mystery. Young readers: folktales, history. Middle readers: folktales, multicultural, nature/environment. Young adult: adventure, history, humor, nature/environment. Recently published *12th Night: Mother Goose Visits Lapland*.
Nonfiction: Middle readers: history. Young adults: biography. Recently published *Wake Up, Wise Up, Win*, by L.F. Zimerman (teens-adult); *Unlock Your Possibilities*, by Rita Losee (teens-adult).
How to Contact/Writers: Fiction: query, submit outline/synopsis or submit outline/synopsis and 3 sample chapters. Nonfiction: submit outline/synopsis and 3 sample chapters. Reports on queries in 6-8 weeks; mss in 2-3 months. Publishes a book 6 months after acceptance. Will consider electronic submissions via disk or modem and previously published work.
Illustration: Works with 2 illustrators/year. Reviews ms/illustration packages from artists. Submit ms with 3 pieces of final art. Contact: Christian Allman, marketing/editorial director. Illustrations only: query with samples or send portfolio, client list and tearsheets. Contact: Christian Allman. Reports in 2-3 months. Samples returned with SASE.
Photography: Works on assignment only. Contact: Christian Allman. Uses all types of photos, but especially dramatic people photos. Captions required. Uses color prints and 4 × 5 transparencies. Submit cover letter, client list and published samples.
Terms: Pays authors negotiated royalty. Pays illustrators by the project (range: $1,000-3,000). Sends galleys to authors. Originals returned to artist at job's completion. Book catalog available for SAE with 4 first-class stamps; ms and art guidelines available for SASE. All imprints included in a single catalog. Catalog available on website.
Tips: "Be specific and complete with your queries. We give preference to brief synopses and full manuscripts and authors who have at least a basic understanding about how and to whom to market their work."

N: PORTUNUS PUBLISHING CO., 316 Midvalley Center #270, Carmel CA 93923. (888)450-5021. Fax: (831)622-0681. E-mail: service@portunus.net. Website: www.portunus.net. Book publisher. Estab. 1995. **Manuscript Acquisitions:** Sandra Delay. **Art Acquisitions:** Wyatt Portz, portfolio review manager. Publishes 3-5 picture books/year. 60% of books by first-time authors. "Motivated by a deep love for people, we at Portunus

Publishing Co. produce beautifully illustrated and compelling children's storybooks. We want our books to nourish heart and mind, so that each child can acquire the understanding and skills necessary to make a unique, positive contribution to the world. We hope to inspire kids to reach their fullest potential by teaching, entertaining and encouraging them to think about important issues facing people everywhere—including, of course, themselves."

Fiction: Picture books, young readers: concept, contemporary, fantasy, humor, multicultural, nature/environment, special needs. Average word length: picture books—1,200. Recently published *The Wizard and King Whifflegroan*, written and illustrated by Sheila Bailey (ages 5-9); *Wolf Songs*, by Faye Raya-Norman, illustrated by Richard Ziehler-Martin (ages 5-9); *Mending Peter's Heart*, by Maureen Wittbold, illustrated by Larry Salk (ages 5-9).

How to Contact/Writers: Fiction: Submit complete manuscript. Reports on mss in 3 months.

Illustration: Works with 3-5 illustrators/year. Use color artwork only. Reviews ms/illustration packages from artists. Submit ms with 2-3 good color copies of art. Contact: Sandra Delay, acquisitions editor. Illustrations only: send promo sheet, tearsheets. Contact: Wyatt Portz, art acquisitions editor. Reports in 2 months. Samples returned with SASE; samples filed.

Terms: Pays authors royalty of 5-10% based on wholesale price. Offers advances (amount varies). Pays illustrators royalty of 5-10% based on wholesale price. Originals returned at job's completion. Book catalog and writer's guidelines available for SASE. All imprints included in a single catalog. Catalog available on website.

Tips: "The intentions and themes of our books are serious, so if you want to use humor, treat a serious theme in a humorous way. Look at the *The Wizard and King Whifflegroan*, as an example."

☑ PRIDE & IMPRINTS, 7419 Ebbert Dr. SE, Port Orchard WA 98367. Website: www.pride-imprints.com. **Acquisitions:** Ms. Cris Newport, senior editor. Publishes trade paperback originals and reprints. Publishes 10 titles/year. 50% of books from first-time authors; 50% from unagented writers. Pride & Imprints consists of the following imprints: Little Blue Works—Children's titles and young adult novels released in paper and on multimedia CD-ROM; Pride—Cutting-edge fiction. Publishes genre fiction and poetry primarily in paper and on multimedia CD-ROM; RAMPANT Gaming—Role-playing and other games for ages 14 and up; and Arts Ex Machine—Theatre, film and other arts. "Pride & Imprints publishes work that is revolutionary in content. In order to understand what we mean by this, please read several of our books from the different imprints. We do not publish work that is racist, homophobic, sexist or graphically violent in content. All of our authors and artists should expect to be proactive in marketing their work. If you do not wish to read from and/or sign your books and/or artwork, you should not submit work to us."

Fiction: All levels and categories. Published *Caruso the Mouse*, by Landis Emond, illustrated by Susie Lester; *The Garden Stories*, by Carmen Alexander, illustrated by Stacey Roswell (Multimedia CD-ROM); and *Tonight I Heard the Ghost Cat*, by Jennifer Anna, illustrated by Patrick Dengate.

Nonfiction: All levels and categories.

How to Contact/Writers: Write for submission guidelines before submitting. However, "we are not accepting submissions/queries for New York until September, 2000. Read several of our titles in the genre you are writing in. Visit our website."

Illustration: Works with 10 illustrators/year. Write for submission guidelines before sending material.

Photography: Buys photos from freelancers. Query first.

Terms: Pays 10-15% royalty based on wholesale price. Will consider simultaneous submissions. Artists and photographers are paid up to $1,000 for covers only. All other work is paid on royalty basis. Royalty payment is 10% of gross monies received."

Tips: Be sure to request submission guidelines. "We reserve the right to destroy any submissions that deviate from our format."

PROMETHEUS BOOKS, 59 John Glenn Dr., Amherst NY 14228-2197. Fax: (716)564-2711. E-mail: slmpbbo oks@aol.com. Website: www.PrometheusBooks.com. Book publisher. Estab. 1969. **Acquisitions:** Steven L. Mitchell, editor-in-chief. **Art Acquisitions:** Jacqueline Cooke. Publishes 1-2 titles/year. 40% of books by first-time authors; 50% of books from agented writers. "We hope more books will be published that focus on real issues children face and real questions they raise. Our primary focus is to publish children's books with alternative viewpoints: humanism, free thought, skepticism toward the paranormal, moral values, critical reasoning, human sexuality, and independent thinking based upon science and reasoning. Our niche is the parent who seeks informative books based on these principles. We are dedicated to offering customers the highest-quality books. We are also committed to the development of new markets both in North America and throughout the world."

Nonfiction: All levels: sex education, moral education, critical thinking, nature/environment, science, self help, skepticism, social issues. Average word length: picture books—2,000; young readers—10,000; middle readers—20,000; young adult/teens—60,000. Recently published *All Families Are Different*, by Sol Gordon (social issues, ages 4 and up); *It's Up to You, What Do You Do*, by S.M. Humphrey (decision making, ages 6 and up); *Bringing UFOs Down to Earth*, by P. Klass (skepticism, ages 9 and up); and *Little Feelings*, by J.S. Bartan (self-help, ages 3-8).

How to Contact/Writers: Submit complete ms with sample illustrations (b&w). Reports on queries in 1-3 weeks; mss in 1-2 months. Publishes a book 12-18 months after acceptance. SASE required for return of ms/ proposal.

Illustration: Works with 1-2 illustrators/year. "We will keep samples in a freelance file, but freelancers are rarely used." Reviews ms/illustration packages from artists. "Prefer to have full work (manuscript and illustrations); will consider any proposal." Include résumé, photocopies.

Terms: Pays authors royalty of 5-15% based on wholesale price. "Author hires illustrator; we do not contract with illustrators." Pays photographers per photo (range: $50-100). Sends galleys to author. Book catalog is free on request.

Tips: "Book should reflect secular humanist values, stressing nonreligious moral education, critical thinking, logic, and skepticism. Authors should examine our book catalog to learn what sort of manuscripts we're looking for."

PUFFIN BOOKS, Penguin Putnam Inc., 345 Hudson St., New York NY 10014-3657. (212)366-2000. Website: www.penguinputnam.com. Imprint of Penguin Putnam Inc. **Acquisitions:** Sharyn November, senior editor; Joy Peskin, associate editor. Publishes trade paperback originals (very few) and reprints. Publishes 175-200 titles/year. Receives 300 queries and mss/year. 1% of books by first-time authors; 5% from unagented writers. "Puffin Books publishes high-end trade paperbacks and paperback originals and reprints for preschool children, beginning and middle readers, and young adults."

Fiction: Picture books, young adult novels, middle grade and easy-to-read grades 1-3. "We publish mostly paperback reprints. We publish few original titles." Recently published *The Ear, the Eye, and the Arm*, by Nancy Farmer (Puffin novel).

Nonfiction: Biography, children's/juvenile, illustrated book, young children's concept books (counting, shapes, colors). Subjects include education (for teaching concepts and colors, not academic), women in history. " 'Women in history' books interest us." Reviews artwork/photos. Send color photocopies. Recently published *Rachel Carson: Pioneer of Ecology*, by "Fadlinski" (history); *Grandma Moses*, by O'Neill Ruff (history).

How to Contact/Writers: Fiction: Submit complete picture book ms or 3 sample chapters with SASE. Nonfiction: Submit 5 pages of ms with SASE. "It could take up to 5 months to get response." Publishes book 1 year after acceptance. Will consider simultaneous submissions, if so noted.

Terms: Pays royalty. Offers advance (varies). Book catalog for 9×12 SASE with 7 first-class stamps; send request to Marketing Department.

G.P. PUTNAM'S SONS, Penguin Putnam Inc., 345 Hudson St., New York NY 10014. (212)366-2000. Website: www.penguinputnam.com. Book publisher. **Manuscript Acquisitions:** Kathy Dawson, senior editor; Susan Kochan, editor. **Art Acquisitions:** Cecilia Yung, art director, Putnam and Philomel. Publishes 22 picture books/year; 13 middle readers/year; and 2 young adult titles/year. 5% of books by first-time authors; 50% of books from agented authors.

• Putnam has published two Caldecott Medal winners, *Mirette on the High Wire*, by Emily Arnold McCully and *Officer Buckle and Gloria*, by Peggy Rathmann. Their books are frequently nominated for state awards, and have won several awards such as the Christopher Award, the Carter G. Woodwon Award and the Jane Addams Peace Award, for nonfiction books on social issues.

Fiction: Picture books: animal, concept, contemporary, humor, multicultural, special needs. Young readers: adventure, contemporary, history, humor, multicultural, special needs, suspense/mystery. Middle readers: adventure, contemporary, history, humor, multicultural, problem novels, special needs, sports, suspense/mystery. Young adults: contemporary, history, problem novels, special needs. "Multicultural books should reflect different cultures accurately but unobtrusively." Regarding special needs, "stories about physically or mentally challenged children should portray them accurately and without condescension." Does not want to see series, romances. Very little fantasy. Average word length: picture books—200-1,500; middle readers—10,000-30,000; young adults—40,000-50,000. Recently published *Raising Sweetness*, by Diane Stanley, illustrated by Brian Karas (ages 4-8); and *Amber Brown Sees Red*, by Paula Danziger (ages 7-10).

Nonfiction: Picture books: animal, concept, nature/environment. Subject must have broad appeal but inventive approach. Average word length: picture books—200-1,500. Recently published *Bridges are to Cross*, by Philemon Sturges, illustrated by Giles Laroche (all ages, 32 pages).

How to Contact/Writers: Fiction/nonfiction: Query with outline/synopsis and 3 sample chapters. Unsolicited picture book mss only. Reports on queries in 2-3 weeks; mss in 4-10 weeks. Publishes a book 2 years after acceptance. Will consider simultaneous submissions on queries only.

Illustration: Works with 40 illustrators/year. Reviews ms/illustration packages from artists. Ms/illustration packages and illustration only: Query. Reports back only if interested. Samples returned with SASE; samples filed.

Terms: Pays authors royalty based on retail price. Pays illustrators by the project or royalty based on retail price. Sends galleys to authors. Original artwork returned at job's completion. Books catalog and ms and artist's guidelines available for SASE.

Tips: "Study our catalogs and get a sense of the kind of books we publish, so that you know whether your project is likely to be right for us."

RAGWEED PRESS, P.O. Box 2023, Charlottetown, Prince Edward Island C1A 7N7 Canada. (902)566-5750. Fax: (902)566-4473. E-mail: editor@ragweed.com. Book publisher. **Contact:** Managing Editor. Publishes 1 picture book/year; 2 young adult titles/year. 20% of books by first-time authors.

• Ragweed accepts work from Canadian authors only.

insider report

Bringing history to life in 'cryptic rhyme'

It's Tuesday night, just before nine o'clock. The crowd begins to gather, each person trying to find a good spot for the featured workshop speaker. There's a spirit of camaraderie, a bit of chit-chat. But mostly you'll find serious, professional writers who return week after week to share market information, discuss craft and learn from each other in an open, supportive setting.

These loyal writers call it "Tuesday Night Chat." Informally, many refer to "going to Verla's."

The host at this cyber salon is Verla Kay, the author of seven picture books, including 1999's *Iron Horses* and *Gold Fever* (both published by G.P. Putnam's Sons). Despite a typically insane schedule of writing, researching, school visits (which often include a gold panning demonstration) and promoting her books,

Verla Kay

Kay makes a point of helping novice and veteran writers. She's used the Internet, e-mail, her author website (www.mlode.com~verlakay/), message boards, regular article contributions to online magazines and chat rooms to share her experience. The result is a growing list of grateful writers as well as faithful readers anticipating each new book.

Kay's first book, *Gold Fever*, strikes it rich with a short, colorful tale following one man during the 1849 gold rush. Her second book, *Iron Horses*, chronicles (in 200 words) the amazing story of the Transcontinental Railroad. Steeped in history but told in rhyme, Kay has filled a niche of bringing colorful history to life for children. She coined the phrase "cryptic rhyme" to describe her style of writing—and it's a term that's caught on with reviewers and readers alike.

Forthcoming books by Verla Kay include *Covered Wagons/Bumpy Trails*; *Tattered Sails*; *Homespun Sarah*; *Broken Feather* (all from Putnam); and *Rough, Tough Charley* (Millbrook Press).

How do you describe your "cryptic rhyme" style of writing?
When I started writing verses like this, I didn't have any way to describe it to people, so I coined my own term for it. I call it "cryptic rhyme" because I write short, clipped, descriptive verses that paint vivid, concise pictures. Much is left to the imagination of the reader, who has to fill in the gaps. Hence the term cryptic—verses with hidden meanings. Many others have written in a similar style—they just didn't name it.

How do you structure rhyme while also shaping the story?
I start out writing in rhyme and then mold the verses into a story. With *Iron Horses*, I couldn't get a story line to "work." I'd written close to 150 verses for it, but I didn't have a story. Finally, in desperation, I gave up and decided to write the story in prose. I got it about a third

of the way done. Then I realized, as I read the prose, "Hey! I have a verse that says this. And I have a verse that says that, too! Hey! I can do this in verse." And *Iron Horses* was born.

We all know the maxim "it takes a long time to write short." Can you comment on your experience writing concise stories?
It's taken me two to five years to get each of my stories "just right." I will work on one verse or line or even one word for months to get it right. For instance, it took me six months to find two words in the first stanza of *Gold Fever*. Until I found "dashing" and "snicker" for that verse, it simply didn't have the flavor of the time period and the urgency that I wanted to convey to the reader. Since there are so few words in my stories, it is imperative that each one carries a lot of weight, that each word builds an image in the reader's mind.

What inspires your interest in history? How do you select your topics?
I tend to gravitate towards what I know best, which is my local area, California and the West. This is where I was born and grew up and it's where I've lived most of my life. A few years ago, my husband and I moved to the foothills of the Sierra Nevada mountains in the middle of

VERLA KAY ◆ MICHAEL McCURDY

Illustration © 1999 Michael McCurdy. Reprinted with permission of G.P. Putnam's Sons.

"Piercing whistles,/ Shrieking wheels./ Hot steam hissing,/ High-pitched squeals./ Huffing, puffing,/ Smoking stacks./ Screeching, stopping,/ End of tracks." So begins Verla Kay's *Iron Horses*. In fewer than 200 words, Kay recounts the building of the transcontinental railroad in her signature "cryptic rhyming" style. Kay's spare text is complemented by the strong, bold scratchboard illustrations of Michael McCurdy. The text, together with the art, offers vivid images of the process of stretching the Union Pacific and Central Pacific Railroads across the U.S. in the 1860s. Kay included an author's note in *Iron Horses* giving specifics on the railroad-building race.

the Motherlode Gold Country. Our love for gold panning, and the history that surrounds us, have been a constant inspiration to my writing.

I think about the history of the United States and what events occurred that might be of interest to younger children. Then I try to think of a strong story line that I can use within that time period. When it clicks, I seriously begin writing. As I mentioned, each story has taken me from two to five years to "get right." They don't come fast.

How did you research and validate your forthcoming book, Broken Feather?

Broken Feather was written to open children's eyes to the beauty and serenity of the Nez Perce tribe and how much their lives were changed by the coming of the white men. In order to make sure that what I "tell" to the children is historically and culturally accurate, I contacted a man at the tribal museum in Idaho and asked if he would be willing to fact check my story before I sent it to my editor. He pointed out that things like tee-pees, pow-wows and peace pipes were not a "normal part of their lives." After restructuring the story, I sent it off and it was purchased just a short time later.

What type of pre-release promotion have you done for your books?

My website was created in February 1998 (a year before *Gold Fever* was released) after an argument with my teenage son who was going to create a website for me. I got mad, and in the tradition of the Little Red Hen I said "Fine, then. I'll do it myself!" And I did. Four days later, I had my website up and running. Now, I thank him profusely for making me so mad, because I could never be doing what I'm doing with it if I wasn't doing it myself. I credit my website, the chat room and the weekly writing workshops that take place there for a lot of the interest in my books. It's been a wonderful thing to be able to share so much information with so many other writers.

—Linda Johns

Fiction: Young readers: adventure, multicultural, suspense/mystery. Middle readers, young adults: adventure, anthology, contemporary, history, multicultural. Average word length: picture books—1,000-24 pages (full color illustration); middle readers: 96 pages; young adults: 256 pages. Recently published *At the Edge: A Book of Risky Stories*, collected by Dan Yashinsky (for ages 12 and up).

How to Contact/Writers: Fiction: Submit complete ms. Reports on queries/mss in 5-6 months. Publishes a book 6 months from final ms, "up to 2 years before editorial process is completed." Will consider simultaneous submissions.

Illustration: Works with 1-2 illustrators/year. Uses color artwork only. Reviews illustration packages from artists. Query with samples. Contact: Managing Editor. Samples returned with SASE if requested; samples filed.

Terms: Pays authors/illustrators royalty of 5-10% based on retail price. Sends galleys to authors. Original artwork returned at job's completion. Book catalog available for 9×12 SAE and 2 first-class stamps Canadian or IRC; ms and art guidelines available for SASE.

Tips: "Submit in writing—phone calls won't get results. We do look at everything we receive and make our decision based on our needs. Be patient."

RAINBOW BOOKS, (formerly Rainbow Publishers), P.O. Box 261129, San Diego CA 92196. (619)271-7600. Fax: (619)578-4795. Book publisher. Estab. 1979. **Acquisitions:** Christy Allen, editor. Publishes 5 young readers/year; 5 middle readers/year; and 5 young adult titles/year. 50% of books by first-time authors. "Our mission is to publish Bible-based, Christ-centered materials that contribute to and inspire spiritual growth and development."

Nonfiction: Young readers, middle readers, young adult/teens: activity books, arts/crafts, how-to, reference, religion. Does not want to see traditional puzzles. Recently published *Hands-On Nature*, by various authors, illustrated by Chuck Galey (series of 5 books for age 2 through grade 6); *Big Puzzles for Little Hands*, by Carla Williams, illustrated by Chuck Galey (series of 4 books for preschoolers).

How to Contact/Writers: Nonfiction: Submit outline/synopsis and 3-5 sample chapters. Reports on queries in

6 weeks; mss in 3 months. Publishes a book 18 months after acceptance. Will consider simultaneous submissions, electronic submissions via disk and previously published work.

Illustration: Works with 2-5 illustrators/year. Reviews ms/illustration packages from artists. Submit ms with 2-5 pieces of final art. Illustrations only: Query with samples. Reports in 6 weeks. Samples returned with SASE; samples filed.

Terms: Pays authors royalty of 4% and up based on wholesale price or work purchased outright (range: $500 and up). Pays illustrators by the project (range: $300 and up). Sends galleys to authors. Book catalog available for 10 × 13 SAE and 2 first-class stamps; ms guidelines available for SASE.

Tips: "Our Rainbow imprint carries reproducible books for teachers of children in Christian ministries, including crafts, activities, games and puzzles. Our Legacy imprint (new in '97) handles nonfiction titles for children and adults in the Christian realm, such as Bible story books, devotional books, and so on. Please write for guidelines and study the market before submitting material."

RAINTREE STECK-VAUGHN, Imprint of Steck-Vaughn, 466 Southern Blvd., Chatham NJ 07928. (973)514-1525. Fax: (973)514-1612. Book publisher. Publishing Directors: Frank Sloan and Walter Kossmann. Art Director Joyce Spicer (Steck-Vaughn, 4515 Seton Center Pkwy., Suite 30, Austin TX 78759.) Publishes 30 young readers/year; 30 middle readers/year; 20 young adults/year.
   • Raintree Steck-Vaughn publishes strictly nonfiction titles.

Nonfiction: Picture books, young readers, middle readers: animal, biography, geography, health, history, multicultural, nature/environment, science, sports. Young adults: biography, careers, geography, health, history, sports. Average page length: young readers—32; middle readers—48; young adults: 64-78. Recently published: *Indian Nation* series (Indian tribes); *Science at Work* series (science); *House Divided* series (Civil War period history).

How to Contact/Writers: Nonfiction: query. Reports on queries/mss in 3-4 months.

Illustration: Contact Joyce Spicer at above Texas address.

Photography: Contact Joyce Spicer at above Texas address.

Terms: Pays authors royalty or flat fee. Offers advance. Sends galleys to authors. Book catalog available for 9 × 12 SAE and $3 first-class postage. Ms guidelines available for SASE.

Tips: "Request a catalog so you're not proposing books similar to those we've already done. Always include SASE."

Ⓐ ⬛ **RANDOM HOUSE BOOKS FOR YOUNG READERS,** 201 E. 50th St., New York NY 10022. (212)572-2600. Random House, Inc. Book publisher. Estab. 1935. "Random House Books aims to create books that nurture the hearts and minds of children, providing and promoting quality books and a rich variety of media that entertain and educate readers from 6 months to 12 years." Vice President/Publishing Director: Kate Klimo. Vice President/Associate Publishing Director: Cathy Goldsmith. **Acquisitions:** Easy-to-Read Books (step-into-reading and picture books): Heidi Kilgras, senior editor. Nonfiction: Alice Jonaitis, senior editor. First Stepping Stones and middle grade fiction: Mallory Loehr, assistant publishing director. Fantasy & Science Fiction: Alice Alfonsi, senior editor. Baby & Toddler Books: Shana Corey. 100% of books published through agents; 2% of books by first-time authors.
   • Random House accepts only agented material.

Fiction: Picture books: animal, easy-to-read, history, sports. Young readers: adventure, animal, easy-to-read, history, sports, suspense/mystery. Middle readers: adventure, history, sports, suspense/mystery.

Nonfiction: Picture books: animal. Young readers: animal, biography, hobbies. Middle readers: biography, history, science, hobbies, sports.

How to Contact/Writers: Fiction/Nonfiction: Submit through agent only. Publishes a book 12-18 months after acceptance. Will consider simultaneous submissions.

Illustration: Reviews ms/illustration packages from artists through agent only.

Terms: Pays authors in royalties; sometimes buys mss outright. Sends galleys to authors. Book catalog free on request.

☑ **RED DEER PRESS,** (formerly Red Deer College Press), 56th Ave. and 32nd St., Box 5005, Red Deer, Alberta T4N 5H5 Canada. (403)342-3321. Fax: (403)357-3639. E-mail: vicki.mix@rdc.ab.ca. Imprints: Northern Lights Books for Children, Northern Lights Young Novels. Book publisher. Estab. 1975. **Acquisitions:** Peter Carver, children's editor. Publishes 2 picture books/year; 2 young adult titles/year. 50% of books by first-time authors. Red Deer Press is known for their "high-quality international children's program that tackles risky and/ or serious issues for kids."

Fiction: Picture books, young readers: adventure, contemporary, fantasy, folktales, history, humor, multicultural,

THE SUBJECT INDEX, located in the back of this book, lists book publishers and magazines according to the fiction and nonfiction subjects they seek.

nature/environment, poetry; middle readers, young adult/teens: adventure, contemporary, fantasy, folktales, hi-lo, history, humor, multicultural, nature/environment, problem novels, suspense/mystery. Recently published *The Strongest Man This Side of Cremona*, written and illustrated by Georgia Graham (ages 4-8); *The Taker's Key*, by Martine Bates (ages 9-16); and *On Tumbledown Hill*, by Tim Wynne-Jones, illustrated by Dusan Petricia (ages 4-8).

How to Contact/Writers: Fiction/Nonfiction: Query or submit outline/synopsis. Reports on queries in 6 months; ms in 6-8 months. Publishes a book 18 months after acceptance. Will consider simultaneous submissions.

Illustration: Works with 2-4 illustrators/year. Illustrations only: Query with samples. Reports back only if interested. Samples not returned; samples filed.

Photography: Buys stock and assigns work. Model/property releases required. Submit cover letter, résumé and color promo piece.

Terms: Pays authors royalty (negotiated). Offers advances (negotiated). Pays illustrators and photographers by the project or royalty (depends on the project). Sends galleys to authors. Originals returned to artist at job's completion. Guidelines not available.

Tips: "Red Deer Press is currently not accepting children's manuscripts unless the writer is an established Canadian children's writer with an original project that fits its publishing program. Writers, illustrators and photographers should familiarize themselves with RD Press's children's publishing program."

RED WHEELBARROW PRESS, INC., P.O. Box 33143, Austin TX 78764. (512)441-4191. E-mail: publisher@rwpress.com. Website: www.rwpress.com. Estab. 1997. Trade book publisher specializing in fiction (with slant) and educational material. **Manuscript Acquisitions:** L.C. Sajbel, publisher. Publishes 1-2 young readers/year. 100% of books by first-time authors. "Red Wheelbarrow Press is in business to publish distinctive literature for a niche market composed of readers interested in new authors and in sophisticated, enjoyable fiction, nonfiction and poetry."

Fiction: Young readers: concept. Young readers, middle readers: adventure, contemporary, folktales, history, humor, multicultural, poetry, suspense/mystery. Recently published *The Ambitious Baker's Batter*, written/illustrated by Wendy Seese (ages 5-11 humorous poetry picture book).

Nonfiction: "We have not yet published nonfiction yet, but we're open to it."

How to Contact/Writers: Fiction: Query, submit complete ms or submit outline/synopsis and 3 sample chapters. Nonfiction: Query. Reports on queries in 4-6 weeks; mss in 6-8 weeks. Publishes a book 1 year after acceptance.

Illustration: Works with 1-2 illustrators/year. Send ms with dummy. Contact: L.C. Sajbel, publisher. Samples returned with SASE; samples filed if requested by artist.

Terms: Pays authors royalty of 8-12% based on retail price. Pays illustrators royalty of 5-10%. Sends galleys to authors; dummies to illustrators. Originals returned to artist at job's completion. Ms guidelines available for SASE.

Tips: "Submissions accepted only between January and April. Check our up-to-date guidelines on our website. We are looking for a fresh approach and for stories or works that appeal to ages 5-12. Work that teaches a concept or a moral without appearing didactic is of interest to us; we want our books to teach children to think and to imagine. The more 'layers' a story has, the more it appeals to our editor and to our readers. We want literature to be exciting for young audiences."

REIDMORE BOOKS INC., 18228-102 Ave., Edmonton, Alberta T5S 1S7 Canada. (780)444-0912. Fax: (780)444-0933. E-mail: reidmore@compusmart.ab.ca. Website: www.reidmore.com. Book publisher. **Acquisitions:** Leah-Ann Lymer, editorial director. Publishes 4 textbooks/year (grades 2-12). 25% of books by first-time authors.

● Reidmore Books does not publish fiction.

Nonfiction: Young readers: history. Middle readers, young adults/teens: geography, history, Canadian studies, textbooks. Does not want to see "material that is not directly tied to social studies curricula. No picture books, please." Recently published: *Finding Your Voice: You and Your Government*, by Flaig and Galvin (grades 5-6, social studies textbook).

How to Contact/Writers: Nonfiction: Query, submit outline/synopsis. Reports on queries in 1 month, mss in 8 months. Publishes a book 18 months after acceptance. Will consider simultaneous submissions.

Illustration: Works with 1 illustrator/year. Uses color artwork and b&w outlines. Illustration only: Query with samples. Contact: Leah-Ann Lymer, editorial director. Samples returned with SASE; samples filed.

Photography: Buys photos from freelancers. Buys stock images. Uses "content-rich photos, often geography-related." Photo captions required. Uses color prints and 35mm transparencies. Submit cover letter.

Terms: Pays authors royalty. Pays illustrators by the project. Pays photographers by the project or per photo. Sends galleys to authors. Book catalog available for 9 × 12 SAE and 2 first-class stamps.

Tips: "Mail, fax or e-mail queries. Please do not phone."

RISING MOON, (formerly Northland Publishing), P.O. Box 1389, Flagstaff AZ 86002-1389. (520)774-5251. Fax: (520)774-0592. E-mail: editorial@northlandpub.com. Website: www.northlandpub.com. Book publisher. **Manuscript Acquisitions:** Aimee Jackson, children's associate editor. **Art Acquisitions:** Jennifer Schaber, art director. Publishes 10-12 picture books/year; 2-3 middle-reader novels. 25% of books by first-time authors.

© Sibyl Graber Gerig

"Sam fiddled high, and he fiddled low. He fiddled fast, and he fiddled slow," wrote Mariana Dengler in *Fiddlin' Sam*. Artist Sibyl Graber Gerig took on the task of capturing Sam's music in watercolor illustrations. "The reviews of Sibyl's artwork have always been phenomenal. Everyone's first reaction to her art is usually awe," says Rising Moon's Aimee Jackson. A former Rising Moon art director saw a book Sibyl illustrated and began to offer her assignments. "Sibyl was trained as a medical illustrator, which could certainly explain her flawless technique with hands, especially, and people in general," Jackson says. "Her work is a good example of the high quality artwork we are seeking."

"Rising Moon is committed to publishing educational and entertaining books with contemporary, universal themes that all children, in all regions of the U.S., will enjoy. We are best known for our attention to illustrative style and design, as well as for our heart-warming multicultural tales."

Fiction: Picture books: humor, contemporary, multicultural, nature/environment, poetry. Middle readers: adventure, suspense/mystery. All levels: multicultural. "Multicultural needs include stories with characters/plots that have to do with multicultural Hispanic aspects. No religion, science fiction, anthology. Average word length: picture books—300-1,500; middle readers—20,000-30,000. Recently published *Fiddlin' Sam*, by Marianna Dengler, illustrated by Sibyl Graber Gerig (ages 5-8); *Missing in the Mountains*, by T.S. Fields (ages 8-12); *Twelve Lizards Leaping: A New 12 Days of Christmas*, by Jan Romero Stevens, illustrated by Christine May.

Nonfiction: Picture books: activity books, animal, nature/environment, sports. Young readers: activity books, arts/crafts, nature/environment, sports.

How to Contact/Writers: Submit complete ms for picture books; submit outline/synopsis and 3 sample chapters for middle readers. Reports on queries/mss in 3-6 months. Publication usually takes 2-3 years. Will consider simultaneous submissions if labelled as such. "We accept all unsolicited picture book submissions, but only agented submissions for juvenile novels."

Illustration: Works with 10 illustrators/year. Uses color artwork only. Reviews ms/illustration packages from artists. Submit ms with 3 pieces of final art (color copy). Illustrations only: Contact: art director with résumé, samples, promo sheet, slides, tearsheets. Samples returned with SASE; samples filed.

Terms: Pays authors royalty based on retail or wholesale price. Pays illustrators by the project or royalty based on retail or wholesale price. Sends galleys to authors; dummies to illustrators. Originals returned at job's completion. Catalog and writer's and artist's guidelines available for SASE.

Tips: "No phone, fax or e-mail queries or submissions. Follow standard submission guidelines carefully and research us by visiting our website (check SCBWI if unsure how to submit manuscripts). Accepts unsolicited picture books, but will only accept juvenile novels from previous, or agented authors. Especially looking for contemporary stories with humor and message."

RONSDALE PRESS, 3350 W. 21st Ave., Vancouver, British Columbia V6S 1G7 Canada. (604)738-4688. Fax: (604)731-4548. E-mail: ronhatch@pinc.com. Website: ronsdalepress.com. Book publisher. Estab. 1988. **Acquisitions:** Veronica Hatch, children's editor. Publishes 2 children's books/year. 80% of titles by first-time authors. "Ronsdale Press is a Canadian literary publishing house that publishes 8 to 10 books each year, two of which are children's titles. Of particular interest are books involving children exploring and discovering new aspects of Canadian history."

Fiction: Middle readers, young adults: adventure, animal, contemporary, fantasy, folktales, history, multicultural, nature/environment, poetry, problem novels. Average word length: Average word length: for middle readers and young adults 25,000. Recently published *Tangled in Time*, by Lynne Fairbridge (ages 8-15); *The Keeper of the Trees*, by Beverley Brenna (ages 8-12); and *The Ghouls' Night Out*, by Janice MacDonald, illustrated by Pamela Breeze Currie (ages 6-10).

Nonfiction: Middle readers, young adults: animal, biography, history, multicultural, social issues. Average word length: young readers—90; middle readers—90.

How to Contact/Writers: Fiction/Nonfiction: Submit complete ms. Reports on queries in 2 weeks; ms in 2 months. Publishes a book 1 year after acceptance. Will consider simultaneous submissions.

Illustrations: Works with 2 illustrators/year. Reviews ms/illustration packages from artists. Submit ms with dummy. Reports back in 2 weeks. Samples returned with SASE. Originals returned to artist at job's completion.

Terms: Pays authors royalty of 10-12% based on retail price. Pays illustrators royalty of 10-12% based on retail price. Sends galleys to authors; dummies to illustrators. Book catalog available for 8½ × 11 SAE and $1 postage; ms and art guidelines available for SASE.

Tips: "Ronsdale Press publishes well-written books that have a new slant on things or books that can take an age-old story and give it a new spin. We are particularly interested in novels for middle readers and young adults with a historical component that offers new insights into a part of Canada's history. We publish only Canadian authors."

THE ROSEN PUBLISHING GROUP INC., 29 E. 21st St., New York NY 10010. (212)777-3017. Fax: (212)253-6915. E-mail: rosened@erols.com. Book publisher. Estab. 1950. Publisher: Roger Rosen. **Manuscript Acquisitions:** Amy Haugesag, middle school; Erin M. Hovanec, young adult; Kristin Ward, juvenile; Michael Isaac, reference. Publishes 144 juvenile readers/year; 50 middle readers/year; and 100 young adults/year. 35% of books by first-time authors; 1% of books from agented writers. "We publish quality self-help/guidance books for children, middle readers, young adults and at-risk youth."

Nonfiction: Young readers: animal, concept, cooking, history, how-to, nature/environment, religion, science, sports. Middle readers: science, sports, careers, history. Young adult: careers, hi-lo, history, science, religion. All levels: biography, health, multicultural, self-help, social issues, special needs. No fiction. Average word length: juvenile—800; middle readers—8,000-30,000; young adults. Published *Body Talk: A Girl's Guide to What's Happening to Your Body*, by Victoria Shaw (9-13 years); *Coping with Discrimination and Prejudice*, by Mary-Bowman-Kruhm (13-18 years); and *Learning About Courage through the Life of Christopher Reeve*, by Jane Kelly Kosek (4-8 years).

How to Contact/Writers: Send queries with a résumé and clips rather than completed mss. Reports on queries in 2-4 months; mss in 4-6 months. Publishes a book 9 months after acceptance.

Photography: Buys photos from freelancers. Contact: Gregory Payan. Works on assignment only.

Terms: Pays authors in royalties of 6-10% based on wholesale price or work purchased outright for $1,000-1,500. Pays illustrators and photographers by the project. Book catalog free on request.

Tips: "Target your manuscript to a specific age group and reading level and write for established series published by the imprint you are approaching."

RUNESTONE PRESS, A Division of the Lerner Publishing Group, 241 First Ave., N., Minneapolis MN 55401. (612)332-3344 or (800)328-4929. Fax: (612)332-7615. Website: www.lernerbooks.com. Contact: Jennifer Zimian, submissions editor.

Nonfiction: Nonfiction for readers grades 5 and up. Newly revised editions of previously out of print books.

Recently published Buried Worlds (archaeology series and titles covering Medieval life, Jewish communities, Native Americans and daily life in ancient and modern world cities).
How to Contact/Writers: Submissions are accepted in the months of March and October only. The Lerner Publishing Group does not publish alphabet books, puzzle books, song books, text books, work books, religious subject matter or plays. Work received in any month other than March or October will be returned unopened. A SASE is required for return of materials. Reports in 2-6 months. No phone calls.

ST. ANTHONY MESSENGER PRESS, 1615 Republic St., Cincinnati OH 45210-1298. (513)241-5615. Fax: (513)241-0399. E-mail: stanthony@americancatholic.org. Website: www.AmericanCatholic.org. Book publisher. Managing Editor: Lisa Biedenbach. **Manuscript Acquisitions:** Katie Carroll. 25% of books by first-time authors. Imprints include Franciscan Communications (print and video) and Ikonographics (video). "Through print and electronic media marketed in North America and worldwide, we endeavor to evangelize, inspire and inform those who search for God and seek a richer Catholic, Christian, human life. We also look for books for parents and religious educators."
Fiction: Picture books, middle readers, young readers: religion.
Nonfiction: Picture books, young readers, middle readers, young adults: religion. "We like all our resources to

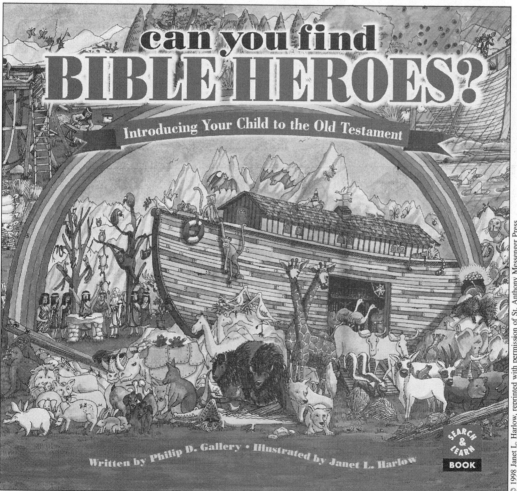

Another publisher recommended artist Janet Harlow and her writing partner to St. Anthony Messenger Press. The team's first book, *Can You Find Jesus*, won the 1997 Catholic Book Award's best children's book. This illustration is the cover of their second book, *Can You Find Bible Heroes?*, which won the same award in 1999. "The style is colorful and clever, giving a contemporary twist to a historic text," says St. Anthony's Lisa Biedenbach. "Bookstores love it and so do children. They love the way humor infuses the story and illustrations."

include anecdotes, examples, etc., that appeal to a wide audience. All of our products try to reflect cultural and racial diversity." Recently published *The Wind Harp and Other Angel Tales*, by Ethel Pochocki (middle to adult readers); *Can You Find Jesus? Introducing Your Child to the Gospel*, by Philip Gallery and Janet Harlow (ages 5-10); *God Is Calling* (family based catechetical program for ages 11-14 and under 10); and *Can You Find Bible Heroes? Introducing Your Child to the Old Testament*, by Philip Gallery and Janet Harlow (ages 5-10).

How to Contact/Writers: Query or submit outline/synopsis and sample chapters. Reports on queries in 1 month; mss in 2 months. Publishes a book 12-18 months after acceptance.

Illustration: Works with 2 illustrators/year. "We design all covers and do most illustrations in-house, unless illustrations are submitted with text." Reviews ms/illustration packages from artists. Query with samples, résumé. Contact: Mary Alfieri, art director. Reports on queries in 2-4 weeks. Samples returned with SASE; samples filed. Originals returned at job's completion.

Photography: Purchases photos from freelancers. Contact: Mary Alfieri, art director. Buys stock and assigns work.

Terms: Pays authors royalties of 10-12% based on net receipts. Offers average advance payment of $1,000. Pays illustrators by the project. Pays photographers by the project. Sends galleys to authors. Book catalog and ms guidelines free on request.

Tips: "Know our audience—Catholic. We seek popularly written manuscripts that include the best of current Catholic scholarship. Parents, especially baby boomers, want resources for teaching children about the Catholic faith for passing on values. We try to publish items that reflect strong Catholic Christian values."

ST. MARY'S PRESS, Christian Brothers Publications, 702 Terrace Heights, Winona MN 55987-1320. (507)457-7900 or (800)533-8095. Fax: (507)457-7990. Book publisher. "Our mission is to significantly advance the ministry of sharing the Good News among youth . . . employing all appropriate settings, means, and media." **Contact:** Steve Nagel.

Fiction: Young adults: history, mystery, science fiction, all topics that "both give insight into the struggle of teens to become healthy, hopeful adults and also shed light on Catholic experience, history or cultures."

How to Contact/Writers: Query with cover letter and sample chapter. Cover letter should include personal bio including background and experience; a tentative title; table of contents; date of availability for final ms; estimated word count; author's address, phone numbers and Social Security number. SASE. Simultaneous submissions are okay with notification.

Terms: Payment varies.

Tips: "Here are key questions to ask yourself before submitting: does my work further SMP's publishing program and mission? Am I clearly in touch with the needs of my audience? Has my book been critiqued by those who are qualified to do so? If you wish to learn more about us, call our toll free number and ask for a free catalog."

SCHOLASTIC INC., 555 Broadway, New York NY 10012. (212)343-6100. Website: www.scholastic.com. Estab. 1920. Senior Vice President and Publisher: Jean Feiwel. **Manuscript Acquisitions:** Scholastic Press: Elizabeth Szabla, editorial director; Blue Sky Press: Bonnie Verburg, editorial director; Trade Paperback: Craig Walker, vice president and editorial director; Cartwheel Books: Bernette Ford, vice president and editorial director; Arthur A. Levine Books: Arthur Levine; Scholastic Reference: Wendy Barrish, editorial director. **Art Acquisitions:** David Saylor, creative director. "We are proud of the many fine, innovative materials we have created—such as classroom magazines, book clubs, book fairs, and our new literacy and technology programs. But we are most proud of our reputation as 'The Most Trusted Name in Learning.' "

● Scholastic is not interested in receiving ideas for more fiction paperback series. They do not accept unsolicited mss.

Illustration: Works with 50 illustrators/year. Does not review ms/illustration packages.Illustrations only: send promo sheet and tearsheets.Reports back only if interested. Samples not returned. Original artwork returned at job's completion.

Terms: All contracts negotiated individually; pays royalty. Sends galleys to author; dummies to illustrators.

SCHOLASTIC PRESS, 555 Broadway, New York NY 10012. (212)343-6100. Book publisher. Imprint of Scholastic Inc. **Manuscript Acquisitions:** Dianne Hess, executive editor (picture book fiction/nonfiction); Lauren Thompson, senior editor (picture book fiction/nonfiction); Tracy Mack, senior editor (picture book, middle grade, YA). **Art Acquisitions:** David Saylor, Scholastic Press, Reference, Paperback; Edie Weinberg, Cartwheel Books. Publishes 37 picture books/year; 28 young adult titles/year. 1% of books by first-time authors.

● Scholastic Press title *Red-Eyed Tree Frog*, by Joy Cowley, illustrated with photos by Nic Bishop, won a 1999 Boston Globe-Horn Book Award for picture books.

Fiction: All levels: adventure, animal, anthology, concept, contemporary, fantasy, health, history, humor, multicultural, nature/environment, poetry, religion, science fiction, sports, suspense/mystery. Picture books: concept, folktales. Middle readers: folktales, problem novels, romance. Young adults: problem novels, romance. Multicultural needs include: strong fictional or nonfictional themes featuring non-white characters and cultures. Does not want to see mainstream religious, bibliotherapeutic, adult. Average word length: picture books—varies; young adults—150 pages. Recently published *Out of the Dust*, by Karen Hesse; *Rocking Horse Christmas*, by Mary Pope Osborne, illustrated by Ned Bittinger.

Nonfiction: All levels: animal, biography, history, multicultural, music/dance, nature/environment, science, social issues, sports. Picture books: concept. Multicultural needs "usually best handled on biography format." Average word length: picture book—varies; young adults—150 pages. Recently published *Women of Hope*, by Joyce Hansen.

How to Contact/Writers: Fiction: "Due to large numbers of submissions, we are discouraging unsolicited submissions by unpublished authors—send query (don't call!) only if you feel certain we publish the type of book you have written." Nonfiction: young adult titles: query. Picture books: submit complete ms. Reports in 1-3 months.

Illustrations: Works with 30 illustrators/year. Uses both b&w and color artwork. Contact: Editorial Submissions. Illustration only: Query with samples; send tearsheets. Reports only if interested. Samples returned with SASE. Original artwork returned at job's completion.

Photography: Buys photos from freelancers. Contact: Photo Research Dept. Buys stock and assigns work. Uses photos to accompany nonfiction. Model/property releases required; captions required. Submit cover letter, résumé, client list, stock photo list.

Terms: Pays authors by varying royalty (usually standard trade roles) or outright purchase (rarely). Offers variable advance. Pays illustrators by the project (range: varies) or standard royalty based on retail price. Pays photographers by the project or royalty. Sends galleys to authors.

Tips: "Read *currently* published children's books. Revise, rewrite, rework and find your own voice, style and subject. We are looking for authors with a strong and unique voice who can tell a great story and have the ability to evoke genuine emotion. Children's publishers are becoming more selective, looking for irresistable talent and fairly broad appeal, yet still very willing to take risks, just to keep the game interesting."

SIERRA CLUB BOOKS FOR CHILDREN, Imprint of Sierra Club Books, 85 Second St., San Francisco CA 94105. (415)977-5500. **Acquisitions:** Helen Sweetland, director. "Sierra Club Books for Children publishes books that offer responsible information about the environment to young readers, with attention to the poetry and magic in nature that so fascinated and inspired John Muir, the poet-philosopher who was the Sierra Club's founder." Publishes hardcover originals and trade paperback originals and reprints. Publishes 15 titles/year. Receives 100 queries/year. 2% of books from first-time authors; 10% from unagented writers. Pays 8-10% royalty on retail price. Advance varies. Publishes book an average of 2 years after acceptance of ms; works waiting for illustrators may take significantly longer. Reports in up to 1 year on queries. Book catalog for 9×12 SASE.

• Sierra Club Books for Children prefers agented submissions.

Nonfiction: Children's/juvenile. Subjects include nature/environment. Query. All unsolicited mss returned unopened.

Recent Nonfiction Title(s): *In Good Hands: Behind the Scenes at a Center for Orphaned and Injured Birds*, by Stephen R. Swinburne; and *Phantom of the Prairie: Year of the Black-footed Ferret*, by Jonathan London.

Fiction: Juvenile, nature/environment. Query. All unsolicited mss returned unopened.

Recent Fiction Title(s): *Desert Trip*, by Barbara A. Steiner; *The Empty Lot*, by Dale H. Fife; *The Snow Whale*, by Caroline Pitcher.

SILVER DOLPHIN BOOKS, Advantage Publishers Group, 5880 Oberlin Dr., Suite 400, San Diego CA 92121. (619)457-2500. Fax: (619)812-6476. Book publisher and distributor. Estab. 1982. "We create a lot of product for warehouse clubs." **Manuscript Acquisitions:** Product Manager, Silver Dolphin. **Art Acquisitions:** JoAnn Padgett, managing editor. Imprints: Silver Dolphin Books, Thunder Bay Press, Laurel Glen Publishing. Publishes 30 young readers/year; 60 middle readers/year.

Fiction: Young readers: animal, concept, health, history, multicultural, nature/environment. Middle readers: animal, health, history, multicultural, nature/environment. Recently published *Richard Scarry's 4 Busy Day Storybooks*.

Nonfiction: Young readers, middle readers: activity books, animal, arts/crafts, concept, geography, history, hobbies, how-to, music/dance, nature/environment, science, self help. Recently published *Let's Start Drawing*; *My First ABC*; *Cartoon Works: Bugs Bunny & Friends*.

How to Contact/Writers: Nonfiction: Submit outline/synopsis or complete ms. Reports in 8-10 weeks on queries; 10-12 weeks on mss. Will consider simultaneous submissions, electronic submissions via disk or modem, previously published work.

Illustration: Uses color artwork only. Reviews ms/illustration packages from artists. Send ms with dummy, include SASE for return. Contact: JoAnn Padgett, managing editor. Illustrations only: Send résumé, client list, tearsheets. Reports back only if interested. Samples not returned; samples filed.

Photography: Buys stock. Model/property releases required; captions required. Uses 35mm or 4×5 transparencies. Submit cover letter, résumé, client list, stock photo list.

Terms: Pays authors royalty of 10-15% based on wholesale price or purchased outright from authors (amount to be determined). Pays illustrators by the project or royalty. Pays photographers per photo (range: $50 and up). Sends galleys to authors; dummies to illustrators. Originals returned to artist at job's completion. Book catalog; writer's guidelines available for $8½ \times 11$ SASE.

SILVER MOON PRESS, 160 Fifth Ave., New York NY 10010. (212)242-6499. E-mail: mail@silvermoonpress.com. Website: www.silvermoonpress.com. Publisher: David Katz. **Acquisitions:** Karin Lillebo. Book publisher. Publishes 2 books for grades 4-6. 25% of books by first-time authors; 10% books from agented authors.

insider report

Collaborators don't drop hot potatoes (and become bestsellers)

Writing team Marcia Thornton Jones and Debbie Dadey's books have sold about 20 million copies since the publication of their first book, *Vampires Don't Wear Polka Dots* in 1990. From that first title three Scholastic series evolved: The Adventures of the Bailey School Kids, Triplet Trouble and The Bailey City Monsters.

The authors (Jones, a Lexington, Kentucky-based teacher and Dadey a former school librarian and

Marcia Thornton Jones   **Debbie Dadey**

mother of three living in the Chicago area) collaborate on stories using the "hot potato" method—taking turns writing chapters from an outline, and passing them back and forth through e-mail. "Just like with the game, it's important for neither one of us to drop 'the potato' by letting it sit on our desks too long."

The duos' upcoming books include *Dracula Doesn't Rock and Roll*, *The Bride of Frankenstein Doesn't Bake Cookies* and the first title in the new Writer's Digest Books Write for Kids series tentatively titled *Story Starters*. Jones and Dadey are also working on independent titles. (For more information about their books, check out these websites: www.baileykids.com; www.author-illustr-source.com/marciathorntonjones.htm; and www.shcolastic.com.)

Jones and Dadey collaborated on this interview as well. Read on to find out how their first book was pulled from the slush pile and eventually spawned a series. They also offer thoughts on working as a partnership, tips on writing dialogue for 9- to 12-year-old readers and share how it feels to be on the bestseller list.

The Adventures of the Bailey School Kids was not originally planned as a series by your publisher. How did it become one? How did your two subsequent series evolve?

After writing *Vampires Don't Wear Polka Dots*, we were hopeful that Scholastic would be interested in publishing another book highlighting the same characters. That wasn't the case. Our editor told us they weren't interested in a series. Instead of giving up, we decided to keep revising our story until it was so good the editor couldn't refuse it. That's just what happened.

We rewrote *Werewolves Don't Go To Summer Camp* three times before Scholastic decided to buy it. But, they told us, it was not a series. They called it a companion book to *Vampires Don't Wear Polka Dots*. That was fine with us. We decided that if they liked two books, maybe they'd like three. So we wrote *Santa Claus Doesn't Mop Floors*. Sure enough, they bought it. But, they repeated, it was not a series, just another companion book. We wrote two more books like that. After our fifth book, our editor called. She told us our books were doing well and was wondering if we'd be interested in writing four more books for our series. *Series?* we asked. She laughed and told us that if we ended up with ten books, then it was a series. So The Adventures of the Bailey School Kids became a series because we simply wouldn't give up.

Our other two series were created in a more typical manner. Our editor asked us to write a series for younger readers and to consider using triplets as the main characters. That's when we developed Triplet Trouble.

The Bailey City Monsters grew out of a single line of dialogue in one of the Super Specials written for The Adventures of the Bailey School Kids. Towards the end of the book, *Mrs. Jeepers' Batty Vacation*, a character the Bailey Kids believe may be a vampire tells them she may come to Bailey City to visit. Our editor read that line and thought it would be fun if a family of monsters moved to Bailey City, and she asked us if we'd be interested in writing a series about them. Of course we said yes. Bailey City Monsters was developed from there.

What are the pros and cons of a writing partnership?
For us, the pros of a writing partnership far outweigh the cons. Collaborating allows writers to share the secretarial responsibilities. We take turns marketing, keeping records and answer-

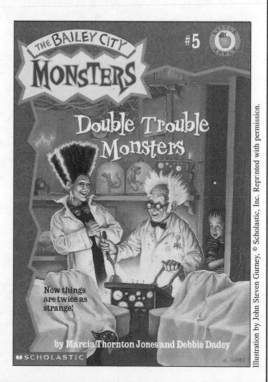

The curious kids of Bailey City fear a mad scientist is working with neighbor Hilda Hauntly on a secret formula to clone monsters in *Double Trouble Monsters*, part of Marcia Thornton Jones and Debbie Dadey's humorously hair-raising series The Bailey City Monsters, a spin-off of the team's The Adventures of the Bailey School Kids. Other Monsters titles include *Spooky Spells*, *Vampire Trouble* and *Howling at the Hauntleys*. Jones and Dadey's books have sold more than 20 million copies for Scholastic.

Illustration by John Steven Gurney. © Scholastic, Inc. Reprinted with permission.

ing fan mail. Using each other as a sounding board is another benefit. Knowing that your partner will help you flesh out an idea is a great help. Manuscripts are also made stronger through revision because there are two writers working to craft our stories. But one of the most important benefits to a writing partnership is that when one of us is discouraged, there is always a partner who understands and can help motivate the other writer. A partnership is a great way to remain disciplined and motivated. Of course, one con might be that not only do you share the work, but you share all the earnings, too.

We've been extremely fortunate. We've been working together for over a decade and we've never had a fight. That's because we've learned the value of compromise. Not only that, we've also learned that there is not a single right way to write. There are just different ways. But we have known writing partnerships that haven't worked because the writers just didn't see eye-to-eye.

How does it feel to have your books on bestseller lists? Why do you think they're so appealing to kids?

Knowing that kids are choosing to read our books is very important to us. We're both educators, and Marcia still teaches. We know the importance of providing books that kids want to read so they can become fluent and successful readers. Being on the bestseller list was a thrill, but it's even more thrilling when we get letters from students, teachers and parents telling us how our books really made a difference in their lives. You can't ask for much more than that.

One of the reasons we've been told our books are appealing is that we understand relationships between kids, and we show our characters interacting in realistic ways. Another reason is that our kids tend to end up in messes even though they try to be good. Lots of readers have told us they can really identify with that. But most readers tell us they find our books appealing because they're just fun.

Dialogue is key to moving your stories along. Any tips for writing good dialogue for 9- to 12-year-old readers?

Good dialogue has a natural sound to it. The only way to write good dialogue for 9- to 12-year-old readers is to listen to how they talk and then use the natural rhythms in the story. Another tip is to read your stories out loud, and *listen* to the sound of your words. If they don't ring true, then revisions are probably needed. We learned to write dialogue by speaking our stories out loud as we wrote them. We took turns being the characters and saying their lines. The dialogue became a natural growth from our storytelling.

How often do each of you do school visits? What kinds of presentations do you give? What reactions do you get from kids?

We visit schools often. Since we've both been teachers, we try to be flexible when giving presentations. Sometimes teachers ask us to conduct small writing workshops, but usually we're asked to talk to large groups about our writing process and how we work together. Included in our presentations are stories about individual books as well as how the illustrator worked on the pictures.

It's important to be able to relate to the kids using humor and storytelling. But kids will be kids, and they can get wiggly if you don't change the pace of the presentation. We include humor, puppets, readings and audience participation to keep our audience alert and interested.

Students, teachers and administrators are always positive. One of our favorite reactions came from a sixth-grade student who was overheard saying, "They're cool," as he left the room. One teacher told us her kids were so inspired after our presentation that they chose to skip recess so they could write. When you are better than recess, you know you've really made an impression!

What's your advice for writers striving for publication?
Never give up. If we had let those first rejections discourage us we never would have published three series. Instead, we kept trying different things.

Know your audience. Keep your audience in mind as you write. Writing is like having a conversation with someone. When you speak to people, you vary your vocabulary, voice and style in order to pique their interest. Do the same thing with your writing.

Write what you like to read. Reading is one of the best ways to learn how to write. It is through reading that we learn pace, dialogue and style. So read your favorite type of book, and then write the kind of book you'd like to read. That way, your joy will show through your writing.

Keep your mind open. Remember, there is no right way to write. There are different ways to write. Sometimes, another way of looking at something you've written could make your piece stronger. So if an editor or member of a critique group suggests changing something you've written, give it serious consideration.

Don't expect instant success. The unfortunate truth is, most writers receive many more rejections than acceptances. We have our own collection of rejection letters, but we consider each letter a type of success, because each rejection means we actually completed a project and at least tried to publish it. That's more than many wanna-be writers can say they've done.
—*Alice Pope*

"We publish books of entertainment and educational value and develop books which fit neatly into curriculum for grades 4-6. Silver Moon Press publishes mainly American historical fiction with a strong focus on the Revolutionary War and Colonial times. History comes alive when children can read about other children who lived when history was being made!"

Fiction: Middle readers: historical, multicultural and mystery. Average word length: 14,000. Recently published *A Message for General Washington*, by Vivian Schurfranz; and *A Secret Party in Boston Harbor*, by Kris Hemphill (both historical fiction, ages 8-12); *Treason Stops at Oyster Bay*, by Anna Leah Sweetzer.

How to Contact/Writers: Fiction: Query. Send synopsis and/or a few chapters, along with a SASE. Reports on queries in 2-4 weeks; mss in 1-2 months. Publishes a book 1-2 years after acceptance. Will consider simultaneous submissions, electronic submissions via disk or modem, previously published work.

Illustration: Works with 2-3 illustrators/year. Reviews ms/illustration packages from artists. Query. Illustrations only: Query with samples, résumé, client list. Reports only if interested. Samples returned with SASE; samples filed. Original artwork returned at job's completion.

Photography: Buys photos from freelancers. Buys stock and assigns work. Uses archival, historical, sports photos. Captions required. Uses color, b&w prints; 35mm, 2¼×2¼, 4×5, 8×10 transparencies. Submit cover letter, résumé, published samples, client list, promo piece.

Terms: Pays authors royalty or work purchased outright. Pays illustrators by the project, royalty. Pays photographers by the project, per photo, royalty. Sends galleys to authors; dummies to illustrators. Book catalog available for 8½×11 SAE and 77¢ postage.

SIMON & SCHUSTER BOOKS FOR YOUNG READERS, 1230 Avenue of the Americas, New York NY 10020. (212)698-7000. Fax: (212)698-2796. Website: www.simonsays.com/kidzone. Imprint of Simon & Schuster Children's Publishing Division. Vice President/Editorial Director: Stephanie Owens Lurie. **Manuscript Acquisitions:** David Gale, executive editor (middle grade and YA fiction); Rebecca Davis, editor (picture books, poetry, fiction); Kevin Lewis, senior editor (young picture books); Amy Hampton-Knight, associate editor (picture books, middle grade and YA fiction); John Rudolph, editorial assistant (picture books and fiction). **Art Acquisitions:** Paul Zakris, art director. Publishes 75 books/year. "We publish high-quality fiction and nonfiction for a variety of age groups and a variety of markets. Above all we strive to publish books that will offer kids a fresh perspective on their world."

• Simon & Shuster Books for Young Readers does not accept unsolicited manuscripts. Simon & Schuster title *Heaven*, by Angela Johnson, won the 1999 Coretta Scott King Author Award. Simon & Schuster title *The Bat Boy & His Violin*, by Gavin Curtis, illustrated by E.B. Lewis won a 1999 Coretta Scott King Illustrator Honor Award.

Fiction: Picture books: animal, concept. Middle readers, young adult: adventure, suspense/mystery. All levels: anthology, contemporary, history, humor, poetry, nature/environment. Recently published *Hitty: Her First Hundred Years* (an adaptation), by Rosemary Wells, illustrated by Susan Jeffers; *Moose's First Christmas*, by Lauren Thompson, illustrated by Buket Erdogan; and *Just Ella*, by Margaret Peterson Haddix.

Nonfiction: All levels: biography, history, nature/environment. Picture books: concept. "We're looking for innovative and accessible nonfiction for all age levels." Recently published *The Mary Celeste: An Unsolved Mystery from History*, by Jane Yolen and Heidi Elisabeth Yolen Stemple, illustrated by Roger Roth; and *To Every Seas*, written and illustrated by Jane Breskin Zalben.

How to Contact/Writers: Accepting query letters only. Reports on queries/mss in 1-2 months. Publishes a book 2-4 years after acceptance. Will consider simultaneous submissions.

Illustration: Works with 70 illustrators/year. Do not submit original artwork. Editorial reviews ms/illustration packages from artists. Submit query letter to Submissions Editor. Illustrations only: Query with samples; samples filed. Provide promo sheet, tearsheets. Reports only if interested. Originals returned at job's completion.

Terms: Pays authors royalty (varies) based on retail price. Pays illustrators or photographers by the project or royalty (varies) based on retail price. Original artwork returned at job's completion. Ms/artist's guidelines free on request.

Tips: "We're looking for picture books centered on a strong, fully-developed protagonist who grows or changes during the course of the story; YA novels that are challenging and psychologically complex; also imaginative and humorous middle-grade fiction. And we want nonfiction that is as engaging as fiction. Our imprint's slogan is 'Reading You'll Remember.' We aim to publish books that are fresh, accessible and family-oriented; we want them to have an impact on the reader."

SOUNDPRINTS, 353 Main Ave., Norwalk CT 06851-1552. (203)846-2274. Fax: (203)846-1776. E-mail: sndprnts@ix.netcom.com. Website: www.soundprints.com. Book publisher. Lines: Smithsonian's Backyard, Smithsonian Oceanic Collection, Smithsonian Odyssey and The Nature Conservancy series. **Manuscript Acquisitions:** Attn: Editorial Assistant. **Art Acquisitions:** Diane Hinze Kanzler, graphic designer. Publishes 16-20 picture books/year. "Soundprints publishes books about wildlife (including oceanic and backyard wildlife and habitats) and history created to educate while entertaining. Each book communicates information about its subject through an exciting storyline. At the same time, each book is based solidly in fact and all aspects must be supported by careful research. All titles are published with an audio and toy component. Each book is illustrated in full-color and contains a glossary and 'about the subject' paragraph to further explain to young children information in the text. All materials in Soundprints' books require the approval of curators and reviewers at the Smithsonian Institution and The Nature Conservancy. This curatorial review is a careful scrutiny that frequently necessitates changes in the text or art before approval will be granted."

Fiction: Picture books: animal, nature/environment. *No* fantasy or anthropomorphic animals. Young readers, middle readers: history, nature/environment. Average word length: picture books (grades PS-2)—800-1,000; (grades 2-5)—1,800-2,200. Recently published *Monarch Butterfly of Aster Way*, by Elizabeth Ring, illustrated by Katie Lee; *Tiger Territory*, by Ann Whitehead Nagda, illustrated by Paul Kratter; *Northern Refuge*, by Audrey Fraggalosch, illustrated by Crista Forest.

Nonfiction: Picture books, young readers: animal, history. "Soundprints books are fiction, but based in research, with an intent to teach."

How to Contact/Writers: Query. Reports on queries 2-3 weeks, mss in 4-6 weeks. Publishing time approximately 2 years. Will consider simultaneous submissions. "Do not send manuscripts without reading our guidelines first."

Illustration: Works with 8-10 illustrators/year. Uses color artwork only. Illustrations are usually full bleed 2-page spreads. Reviews ms/illustration packages from artists "if subject matter is appropriate." Query. Illustrations only: Query with samples; provide résumé, portfolio, promo sheet, slides. "If interest is generated, additional material will be requested." Reports back only if interested. Samples returned with SASE or filed.

Terms: Authors are paid $1,500-2,500 for outright purchase of work. Illustrators paid by the project ($5,000-8,000). Original artwork returned at job's completion. Book catalog for 8½×11 SAE and $1.05 postage; ms guidelines and artist guidelines for #10 SASE. "It's best to request both guidelines and catalog. Both can be sent in self-addressed envelope at least 8½×11 with $1.31 postage."

Tips: "We want books that educate children about the subject while capturing the interest of the reader/listener through an entertaining storyline. As of Spring 1998, Soundprints offers 14 titles in the Smithsonian Wild heritage collection, 15 titles in the Smithsonian's Backyard series, 15 titles in the Smithsonian Oceanic Collection 8 titles in the Smithsonian Odyssey series and 8 titles in The Nature Conservancy Series. Authors should read a few of the titles in the relevant series before submitting a manuscript. Soundprints has very specific guidelines for each line and it is unlikely that a manuscript written by an author who is not familiar with our books will be acceptable. It is also a good idea to verify in advance that Soundprints has not already published, or is not currently working on, a book on your chosen topic."

THE SPEECH BIN, INC., 1965 25th Ave., Vero Beach FL 32960. (561)770-0007. Fax: (561)770-0006. Book publisher. Estab. 1984. **Acquisitions:** Jan J. Binney, senior editor. Publishes 10-12 books/year. 50% of books by first-time authors; less than 15% of books from agented writers. "Nearly all our books deal with treatment of children (as well as adults) who have communication disorders of speech or hearing or children who deal with family members who have such disorders (e.g., a grandparent with Alzheimer's disease or stroke)."
  • The Speech Bin is currently overstocked with fiction.
Fiction: Picture books: animal, easy-to-read, fantasy, health, special needs. Young readers, middle readers, young adult: health, special needs.
Nonfiction: Picture books, young readers, middle readers, young adults: activity books, health, textbooks, special needs. Published *Chatty Hats and Other Props*, by Denise Mantione; *Holiday Hoopla: Holiday Games for Language & Speech*, by Michele Rost; and *Speech Sports*, by Janet M. Shaw.
How to Contact/Writers: Fiction/Nonfiction: Query. Reports on queries in 4-6 weeks; mss in 2-3 months. Publishes a book 10-12 months after acceptance. "Will consider simultaneous submissions *only* if notified; too many authors fail to let us know if manuscript is simultaneously submitted to other publishers! We *strongly* prefer sole submissions."
Illustration: Works with 4-5 illustrators/year ("usually inhouse"). Reviews ms/illustration packages from artists. Ms/illustration packages and illustration only: "Query first!" Submit tearsheets (no original art). SASE required for reply or return of material.
Photography: Buys stock and assigns work. Looking for scenic shots. Model/property releases required. Uses glossy b&w prints, 35mm or 2¼ × 2¼ transparencies. Submit résumé, business card, promotional literature or tearsheets to be kept on file.
Terms: Pays authors in royalties based on selling price. Pay illustrators by the project. Photographers paid by the project or per photo. Sends galleys to authors. Original artwork returned at job's completion. Book catalog for 5 first-class stamps and 9 × 12 SAE; ms guidelines for #10 SASE.
Tips: "No calls, please."

STANDARD PUBLISHING, 8121 Hamilton Ave., Cincinnati OH 45231. (513)931-4050. Fax: (513)931-0950. Book publisher. Estab. 1866. Director, Children's Publishing: Diane Stortz. **Manuscript Acquisitions:** Lise Caldwell, children's editor. **Art Acquisitions:** Coleen Davis, art director. Number and type of books varies yearly. Many projects are written inhouse. No juvenile or young adult novels. 25-40% of books by first-time authors; 1% of books from agented writers. "We publish well-written, upbeat books with a Christian perspective. Books are fun with relevancy in Christian education."
  • Standard publishes *LiveWire, Kidz Chat* and *Straight*, all listed in Magazines. Also see listing for Standard Publishing in the Greeting Cards, Puzzles & Games section. Standard is currently not accepting unsolicited mss due to backlog.
Fiction: Adventure, animal, contemporary, Bible stories. Average word length: board/picture books—400-1,000.
Nonfiction: Bible background, nature/environment, devotions. Average word length: 400-1,000. Recently published *Pattycake Devotions*, by Christine Tangiold, illustrated by Norma Garris (board books).
How to Contact/Writers: Reports in 6 weeks on queries, mss in 3 months.
Illustration: Works with 20 new illustrators/year. Illustrations only: Submit cover letter and photocopies. Reports on art samples only if interested. Samples returned with SASE; samples filed.
Terms: Pays authors royalties based on net price or work purchased outright (range varies by project). Pays illustrators (mostly) by project. Pays photographers by the photo. Sends galleys to authors on most projects. Book catalog available for $2 and 8½ × 11 SAE; ms guidelines for letter-size SASE.
Tips: "We look for manuscripts that help draw children into a relationship with Jesus Christ; help children develop insights about what the Bible teaches; make reading an appealing and pleasurable activity."

STEMMER HOUSE PUBLISHERS, INC., 2627 Caves Rd., Owings Mills MD 21117-9919. (410)363-3690. Fax: (410)363-8459. E-mail: stemmerhouse@home.com. Website: www.stemmer.com. Book publisher. Estab. 1975. **Acquisitions:** Barbara Holdridge, president. Publishes 1-3 picture books/year. "Sporadic" numbers

---

A SELF-ADDRESSED, STAMPED ENVELOPE (SASE) should always be included with submissions within your own country. When sending material to other countries, include a self-addressed envelope (SAE) and International Reply Coupons (IRCs).

of young reader, middle reader titles/year. 60% of books by first-time authors. "Stemmer House is best known for its commitment to fine illustrated books, excellently produced."

Fiction: Picture books: animal, folktales, multicultural, nature/environment. Middle readers: folktales, nature/environment. Does not want to see anthropomorphic characters. Published *How Pleasant to Know Mr. Lear: Poems by Edward Lear*, illustrated by Bohdan Butenko; and *The Marvelous Maze*, by Maxine Rose Schur, illustrated by Robin DeWitt and Patricia DeWitt-Grush.

Nonfiction: Picture books: animal, multicultural, nature. All level: animals, nature/environment. Multicultural needs include Native American, African. Recently published *A Duck in a Tree*, by Jennifer A. Loomis, photographs by the author; *The Bird Alphabet Encyclopedia Coloring Book*, by Julia Pinkham; *Ask Me If I'm a Frog*, by Ann Milton, illustrated by Jill Chambers.

How to Contact/Writers: Fiction/Nonfiction: Query or submit outline/synopsis and sample chapters. Reports on queries/mss in 2 weeks. Publishes a book 18 months after acceptance. Will consider simultaneous submissions. No submissions via e-mail.

Illustration: Works with 2-3 illustrators/year. Uses color artwork only. Reviews ms/illustration packages from artists. Query first with several photocopied illustrations. Illustrations only: Submit tearsheets and/or slides (with SASE for return). Reports in 2 weeks. Samples returned with SASE; samples filed "if noteworthy."

Terms: Pays authors royalties of 4-10% based on wholesale price. Offers average advance payment of $300. Pays illustrators royalty of 4-10% based on wholesale price. Pays photographers 4-10% royalty based on wholesale price. Sends galleys to authors. Original artwork returned at job's completion. Book catalog and ms guidelines for 9×12 SASE.

Tips: Writers: "Simplicity, literary quality and originality are the keys." Illustrators: "We want to see ms/illustration packages—don't forget the SASE!"

STODDART KIDS, *A Division of Stoddart Publishing Co. Ltd.* 34 Lesmill Rd., Toronto, Ontario M3B 2T6 Canada. (416)445-3333. Fax: (416)445-5967. E-mail: kelly.jones@ccmailgw.genpub.com. Book publisher. **Acquisitions:** Kathryn Cole, publisher. Publishes 15 picture books/year; 6 young readers/year; 6 young adults/year. 20% of books by first-time authors.

Fiction: Picture books: adventure, animal, contemporary, folktales, history, humor, multicultural. Young readers: contemporary, folktales, history. Young adult: contemporary, history, multicultural, suspense/mystery. Does not want to see science fiction. Average word length: picture books—800; young readers—38,000; young adult/teens—70,000. Recently published *Flags*, by Maxine Trottier and Paul Morin (ages 4-7, picture book); *Ahmek*, by Patrick Watson (ages 8-12, young reader); *Dahling if you Luv Me Would You Please Please Smile*, by Rukhsana Khan (ages 12 and up, young adult book); *Baby Dreams*, by Eugenie Fernandes (ages 2-5, picture book).

How to Contact/Writers: Fiction/Nonfiction: submit outline/synopsis only. Reports on queries in 3 weeks. Publishes a book 18 months after acceptance. Will consider simultaneous submissions.

Illustration: Works with 18 illustrators/year. Illustrations only: Send photocopied artwork only, SASE and query. Reports in 2 months. Samples returned with SASE; samples filed "if desirable."

Terms: Author and illustrator payments vary with project size and type. Sends galleys to authors. Originals returned to artist at job's completion. Book catalog available for large SASE and 2 first-class stamps.

Tips: "Stoddart Kids is interested in developing a strong Canadian publishing program and therefore encourages the submission of Canadian materials. However, topics that cover both American and Canadian markets are also welcome."

SUNBELT MEDIA, INC./EAKIN PRESS, P.O. Box 90159, Austin TX 78709. (512)288-1771. Fax: (512)288-1813. E-mail: eakinpub@sig.net. Website: www.eakinpress.com. Book publisher. Estab. 1978. President: Ed Eakin. Publishes 25 books for young readers/year. 50% of books by first-time authors; 5% of books from agented writers.

Fiction: Picture books: animal. Middle readers, young adults: history, sports. Average word length: picture books—3,000; young readers—10,000; middle readers—15,000-30,000; young adults—30,000-50,000. "90% of our books relate to Texas and the Southwest."

Nonfiction: Picture books: animal. Middle readers and young adults: history, sports. Recently published *Abuelito Eats With His Fingers*, by Janice Levy, illustrated by Layne Johnson.

How to Contact/Writers: Fiction/Nonfiction: Query. Reports on queries in 2 weeks; mss in 6 weeks. Publishes a book 18 months after acceptance. Will consider simultaneous submissions.

Illustration: Reviews ms/illustration packages from artists. Query. Illustrations only: Submit tearsheets. Reports on art samples in 2 weeks.

Terms: Pays authors royalties of 10-15% based on net to publisher. Pays for separate authors and illustrators: "Usually share royalty." Pays illustrators royalty of 10-15% based on wholesale price. Sends galleys to authors. Book catalog $1 available with SASE; writer guidelines available with SASE.

Tips: Writers: "Be sure all elements of manuscript are included—include bio of author or illustrator."

THROUGH THE BIBLE PUBLISHING, (formerly Treasure Learning Systems), 1133 Riverside, Suite B, Fort Collins CO 80524-3216. (970)484-8483. Fax: (970)495-6700. E-mail: andrea@throughthebible.com. Website: www.throughthebible.com. Book publisher. **Acquisitions:** Andrea Taylor, editor. "Through the Bible Publishing exists to assist the Church of Jesus Christ in fulfilling the Great Commission. We create, market and distribute

"Barbara's ability to animate facial expressions and physical movement while keeping the integrity of the animals made her the perfect artist for the project," says Kathryn Cole of Stoddart Kids. Barbara Spurll's lively watercolor images bring to life the story of *Emma and the Coyote*. "Spurll's artwork has been well-received all over the world, and Emma has become a favorite character for many young readers," Cole says. Cole made the initial contact with Spurll and Stoddart Kids has used the artist's work in many projects.

Writer/illustrator/choreographer/dancer/actor/etc. Remy Charlip is the creator of 26 children's books. *Peanut Butter Party*, with its watercolor illustrations, is Charlip's second book after a 12-year hiatus from children's publishing. Tricycle Press also recently reissued two Charlip classics, *Arm in Arm* and *Hooray for Me!* "With this, my first new Tricycle book, I feel I'm in a safe harbor and happy with my new Tricycle family," Charlip says.

Christian education resouces which feature excellence in biblical content, educational methodology and product presentation. Our primary responsibility is to serve the local and international Church."

Nonfiction: Bible study resources for elementary children ages 6-12, preschool (ages 2-5) and junior/senior high school (ages 13-18). Recently published *DiscipleLand* curriculum.

How to Contact/Writers: Query with writing sample and SASE. Freelance writers send résumé with samples of children's writing to acquisition editor.

Illustration: Freelance designers send résumé and samples to art director.

Terms: Freelance writers/illustrators work for hire contracts only.

Tips: "Our present interest is children's Bible curriculum. No fiction, please."

TILBURY HOUSE, PUBLISHERS, 2 Mechanic St., #3, Gardiner ME 04345. (207)582-1899. Fax: (207)582-8227. Book publisher. Publisher: Jennifer Elliott. Publishes 1-3 young readers/year.

Fiction: Young readers and middle readers: multicultural, nature/environment. Special needs include books that teach children about tolerance and honoring diversity.

Nonfiction: Young readers and middle readers: multicultural, nature/environment. Published *Talking Walls* and *Who Belongs Here?* both by Margy Burns Knight, illustrated by Anne Sibley O'Brien (grades 3-8); *Stone Wall Secrets*, by Kristine and Robert Thorson, illustrated by Gustav Moore; *Everybody's Somebody's*, by Cherie Mason, illustrated by Gustav Moore.

How to Contact/Writers: Fiction/Nonfiction: Submit outline/synopsis. Reports on queries/mss in 1 month. Publishes a book 1-2 years after acceptance. Will consider simultaneous submissions "with notification."

Illustration: Works with 1-2 illustrators/year. Illustrations only: Query with samples. Contact: J. Elliott, associate publisher. Reports in 1 month Samples returned with SASE. Original artwork returned at job's completion.

Photography: Buys photos from freelancers. Contact: J. Elliott, publisher. Works on assignment only.

Terms: Pays authors royalty. Pays illustrators/photographers by the project; royalty. Sends galleys to authors. Book catalog available for 6×9 SAE and 55¢ postage.

Tips: "We are primarily interested in children's books that teach children about tolerance in a multicultural society and honoring diversity. We are also interested in books that teach children about environmental issues."

TOR BOOKS, Forge, Orb, 175 Fifth Ave., New York NY 10010. E-mail: benjamin.yots@stmartins.com. Website: www.tor.com. Publisher, Middle Grade and Young Adult Division: Kathleen Doherty. Children's, Young Adult Editor: Jonathan Schmidt. Educational Sales Coordinator: Benjamin Yots. Publishes 5-10 middle readers/year; 5-10 young adults/year.

Fiction: Middle readers, young adult titles: adventure, animal, anthology, concept, contemporary, fantasy, folktales, health, history, humor, multicultural, nature/environment, problem novel, science fiction, special needs, sports, suspense/mystery. "We are interested and open to books which tell stories from a wide range of perspectives. We are interested in materials that deal with a wide range of issues." Average word length: middle readers—10,000; young adults—30,000-60,000. Published *Mind Quakes: Stories to Shatter Your Brain* and *Scorpions Shards*, by Neal Shusterman (ages 8 and up); and *From One Experience to Another*, edited by Helen and Jerry Weiss (ages 10 and up).

Nonfiction: Middle readers and young adult: activity books, geography, history, how-to, multicultural, nature/environment, science, social issues. Does not want to see religion, cooking. Average word length: middle readers—10,000-15,000; young adults—40,000. Published *Strange Unsolved Mysteries*, by Phyllis Rabin Emert; *Stargazer's Guide* (to the Galaxy), by Q.L. Pearce (ages 8-12, guide to constellations, illustrated).

How to Contact/Writers: Fiction/Nonfiction: Submit outline/synopsis and 3 sample chapters or complete ms. Reports on queries in 3 weeks; mss in 4-6 months.

Illustration: Works with 40 illustrators/year. Reviews ms/illustration packages from artists. Query with samples. Contact: Jonathan Schmidt. Reports only if interested. Samples returned with SASE; samples kept on file.

Terms: Pays authors royalty. Offers advances. Pays illustrators by the project. Book catalog available for 9 × 12 SAE and 3 first-class stamps. Submission guidelines available with SASE.

Tips: "Know the house your are submitting to, familiarize yourself with the types of books they are publishing. Get an agent. Allow him/her to direct you to publishers who are most appropriate. It saves time and effort."

TRADEWIND BOOKS, 2216 Stephens St., Vancouver, British Columbia V6K 3W6 Canada.(604)730-0153. Fax: (604)730-0154. E-mail: tradewindbooks@yahoo.com. Website: tradewindbooks.com. Estab. 1994. Trade book publisher. **Manuscript Acquisitions:** Michael Katz, publisher. **Art Acquisitions:** Carol Frank, art director. Publishes 3 picture books/year. 25% of books by first-time authors.

Fiction: Picture books: adventure, animal, multicultural, folktales. Average word length: 900 words. Recently published *Mr. Belinsky's Bagels*; *Mama God, Papa God*; and *Wherever Bears Be*.

Nonfiction: Picture books: animal and nature/environment.

How to Contact/Writers: Fiction: Submit complete ms. Will consider simultaneous submissions. Reports on queries in 3 weeks; mss in 6 weeks.

Illustration: Works with 3-4 illustrators/year. Uses color artwork only. Reviews ms/illustration packages from artists. Send ms with dummy. Illustrations only: Query with samples. Reports only if interested. Samples returned with SASE; samples filed.

Photography: Works on assignment only. Uses color prints.

Terms: Pays authors royalty of 7½% based on wholesale price. Offers advances against royalties. Pays illustrators royalty of 7½% based on wholesale price. Sends galleys to authors; dummies to illustrators. Originals returned to artist at job's completion. Book catalog available for 8 × 10 SAE and 3 first-class stamps. Catalog available on website.

TRANSWORLD PUBLISHERS LIMITED, 61-63 Uxbridge Rd., London W5 5SA England. Phone: (0181)579-2652. Fax: (0181)231-6737. E-mail: childrens.editorial@transworld-publishers.co.uk. Imprints are Doubleday, Picture Corgi (ages 3-6), Corgi Pups (ages 5-8), Young Corgi (ages 6-9), Corgi Yearling (ages 8-11), Corgi (ages 10+), Corgi Freeway (ages 11+) and Bantam Books (ages 10+). Book publisher. Publisher, Children's and Young Adult Publishing: Philippa Dickinson. Publishes 10 picture books/year; 12 young readers/year; 12 middle readers/year; and a few young adult titles/year.

Fiction: Picture books: adventure, animal, anthology, contemporary, fantasy, folktales, humor, multicultural, nature/environment, poetry, suspense/mystery. Young readers: adventure, animal, anthology, contemporary, fantasy, folktales, humor, multicultural, nature/environment, poetry, sports, suspense/mystery. Middle readers: adventure, animal, anthology, contemporary, fantasy, folktales, humor, multicultural, nature/environment, problem novels, romance, sports, suspense/mystery. Young adults: adventure, contemporary, fantasy, humor, multicultural, nature/environment, problem novels, romance, science fiction, suspense/mystery. Average word length: picture books—800; young readers—1,500-6,000; middle readers—10,000-15,000; young adults—20,000-45,000. Recently published *Pig-Heart Boy*, by Malorie Blackman (ages 8 and up, computer assisted adventure); *The Illustrated Mum*, by Jacqueline Wilson (ages 10 and up, contemporary); and *Mr. Ape*, by Dick King-Smith (ages 6-8, animal novel).

How to Contact/Writers: Submit outline/synopsis and 3 sample chapters to Children's Editorial. Reports on queries in 1 month; mss in 2 months. Will consider simultaneous and previously published submissions.

Illustration: Works with 50 illustrators/year. Reviews ms/illustration packages from artists. Submit ms with dummy. Contact: Penny Walker. Illustrations only: Query with samples. Reports in 1 month. Samples are returned with SASE (IRC).

Photography: Buys photos from freelancers. Contact: Tracy Hurst, art department. Buys stock images. Photo captions required. Uses color or b&w prints. Submit cover letter, published samples.

Terms: Pays authors royalty. Offers advances. Pays illustrators by the project or royalty. Pays photographers by the project or per photo. Sends galleys to authors; dummies to illustrators.

☑ TRICYCLE PRESS, Imprint of Ten Speed Press, P.O. Box 7123, Berkeley CA 94707. (510)559-1600. Fax: (510)524-1052. Website: www.tenspeed.com. Estab. 1971. **Acquisitions:** Nicole Geiger, editor. Publishes 8 picture books/year; 5 activity books/year; 3 young readers/year; 5 young adult/year. 30% of books by first-time authors. "Tricycle Press looks for something outside the mainstream; books that encourage children to look at the world from a different angle."

Fiction: Picture books, young readers, middle reader: adventure, animal, contemporary, folktales, history, multicultural, nature/environment. Picture books, young readers: concept. Middle readers: anthology. Average word length: picture books—1,200. Recently published *Hurry Granny Annie*, by Arlene Alda (ages 4-7, picture book); *Peanut Butter Party*, by Remy Charlip (ages 6-12, picture book); *Frog Girl*, by Paul Owen Lewis (ages 6-9, picture book); *Never Let Your Cat Make Lunch for You*, by Lee Harris, illustrated by Debbie Tilley (ages 4-7, picture book).

Nonfiction: Picture books, middle readers, young readers: activity books, animal, arts/crafts, concept, cooking, hobbies, how-to, nature/environment, science, self help, social issues. Young readers: activity books, arts/crafts, health, how-to, nature/environment, science, self help, social issues. Picture books, middle readers: concept, hobbies. Young adult: hobbies. Recently published *G is for Googol: A Math Alphabet Book*, by David M. Schwartz (ages 9 and up, picture book); *Honest Pretzels and 64 Other Amazing Recipes for Cooks Ages 8 & Up*, by Mollie Katzen (activity book); and *Divorce is Not the End of the World: Zoe's and Evan's Coping Guide for Kids*, by Zoe, Evan and Ellen Sue Stern (ages 9-14, self-help); *Pumpkin Circle: The Story of a Garden*, by George Levenson, photography by Shmuel Thaler (ages 5-8, nonfiction picture book).

How to Contact/Writers: Fiction: Submit complete ms for picture books. Submit outline/synopsis and 2-3 sample chapters for chapter book. "No queries!" Nonfiction: Submit complete ms. Reports on mss in 2-5 months. Publishes a book 1-2 years after acceptance. Welcomes simultaneous submissions and previously published work. Do not send original artwork; copies only, please.

Illustration: Works with 9 illustrators/year. Uses color and b&w. Reviews ms/illustration package from artists. Submit ms with dummy and/or 2-3 pieces of final art. Illustrations only: Query with samples, promo sheet, tearsheets. Contact: Nicole Geiger. Reports back only if interested. Samples returned with SASE; samples filed. Original artwork returned at job's completion unless work for hire.

Photography: Works on assignment only. Contact: Nicole Geiger. Uses 35mm transparencies. Submit samples.

Terms: Pays authors royalty. Offers advances. Pays illustrators by the project or royalty. Pays photographers royalty and by the project. Sends galleys to authors. Book catalog for 9×12 SASE ($1.01). Ms guidelines for SASE.

Tips: "We are looking for something a bit outside the mainstream and with lasting appeal (no one-shot-wonders). Lately we've noticed a sacrifice of quality writing for the sake of illustration."

Ⓐ TROLL COMMUNICATIONS, 100 Corporate Dr., Mahwah NJ 07430. (201)529-4000. Book publisher. **Acquisitions:** Marian Frances, editor.

● Troll Communications only accepts agented manuscripts and are not currently accepting unsolicited manuscripts; they are open to receiving samples from illustrators.

Fiction: Picture books: animal, contemporary, folktales, history, nature/environment, poetry, sports, suspense/mystery. Young readers: adventure, animal, contemporary, folktales, history, nature/environment, poetry, science fiction, sports, suspense/mystery. Middle readers: adventure, anthology, animal, contemporary, fantasy, folktales, health-related, history, nature/environment, poetry, problem novels, romance, science fiction, sports, suspense/mystery. Young adults: problem novels, romance and suspense/mystery.

Nonfiction: Picture books: activity books, animal, biography, careers, history, hobbies, nature/environment, sports. Young readers: activity books, animal, biography, careers, health, history, hobbies, music/dance, nature/environment, sports. Middle readers: activity books, animal, biography, careers, health, history, hobbies, music/dance, nature/environment, sports. Young adults: health, music/dance.

How to Contact/Writers: Currently not accepting unsolicited mss. Fiction: Query or submit outline/synopsis and 3 sample chapters. Nonfiction: Query. Reports in 4 weeks.

Illustration: Reviews ms/illustration packages from artists. Contact: Marian Frances, editor. Illustrations only:

**FOR EXPLANATIONS OF THESE SYMBOLS,
SEE THE INSIDE FRONT AND BACK COVERS OF THIS BOOK**

Query with samples; provide résumé, promotional literature or tearsheets to be kept on file. Reports in 4 weeks.
Photography: Interested in stock photos. Model/property releases required.
Terms: Pays authors royalty or work purchased outright. Pays illustrators by the project or royalty. Photographers paid by the project.

TROPHY BOOKS, 10 E. 53rd St., New York NY 10022. (212)207-7044. Fax: (212)207-7915. Subsidiary of HarperCollins Children's Books Group. Book publisher. **Acquisitions:** Ginee Seo, vice president/editorial director; Susan Rich, editor; Susan Chang, associate editor. Publishes 6-9 chapter books/year, 25-30 middle grade titles/year, 20 reprint picture books/year, 10-15 young adult titles/year.
 • Trophy is primarily a paperback reprint imprint. They publish a limited number of chapter book, middle grade and young adult manuscripts each year.

TURTLE BOOKS, 866 United Nations Plaza, Suite 525, New York NY 10017. (212)644-2020. Website: www.turtlebooks.com. Book Publisher. Estab. 1997. **Acquisitions:** John Whitman. "Turtle Books publishes only picture books for very young readers. "Our goal is to publish a small, select list of quality children's books each spring and fall season. As often as possible, we will publish our books in both English and Spanish editions."
Fiction: Picture books: adventure, animal, concept, contemporary, fantasy, folktales, hi-lo, history, humor, multicultural, nature/environment, religion, sports, suspense/mystery. Recently published: *The Legend of Mexicatl*, by Jo Harper, illustrated by Robert Casilla (the story of Mexicatl and the origin of the Mexican people); *Vroom, Chugga, Vroom-Vroom*, by Anne Miranda, illustrated by David Murphy (a number identification book in the form of a race car story); *The Crab Man*, by Patricia VanWest, illustrated by Cedric Lucas (the story of a young Jamaican boy who must make the difficult decision between making an income and the ethical treatment of animals); and *Prairie Dog Pioneers*, by Jo and Josephine Harper, illustrated by Craig Spearing (the story of a young girl who doesn't want to move, set in 1870s Texas).
How to Contact/Writers: Send complete ms. "Queries are a waste of time." Response time varies.
Illustrators: Works with 6 illustrators/year. Reports on artist's queries/submissions only if interested. Samples returned with SASE only.
Terms: Pays royalty. Offers advances.

TURTLE PRESS, P.O. Box 290206, Wethersfield CT 06129-0206. (860)529-7770. Fax: (860)529-7775. E-mail: editorial@turtlepress.com. Website: www.turtlepress.com. Estab. 1990. Publishes trade books. Specializes in nonfiction, multicultural material. **Manuscript Acquisitions:** Cynthia Kim. Publishes 1 young reader/year; 1 middle reader/year. 40% of books by first-time authors.
Fiction: Middle readers, young adults: multicultural, sports. Recently published *A Part of the Ribbon: A Time Travel Through Adventure the History of Korea*.
Nonfiction: Young readers, middle readers, young adults: multicultural, sports. Recently published *Martial Arts Training Diary for Kids* and *Everyday Warriors*.
How to Contact/Writers: Fiction/Nonfiction: Query. Nonfiction: Query. Reports on queries in 1 month; 2 months on mss. Publishes a book 12-18 months after acceptance. Will consider simultaneous submissions.
Photography: Buys stock.
Terms: Pays authors royalty of 8-12%. Offers advances against royalties of $1,000. Pays illustrators by the project. Sends galleys to authors. Book catalog available for 6×9 SAE and 3 first-class stamps; ms guidelines for SASE. All imprints included in a single catalog. Catalog available on website.
Tips: "We focus on martial arts and related cultures."

UAHC PRESS, 633 Third Ave., New York NY 10017. (212)650-4120. Fax: (212)650-4119. E-mail: press@uahc.org. Website: www.uahc.press.org. Book publisher. Estab. 1876. **Acquisitions:** Rabbi Hara Person, managing editor. Publishes 4 picture books/year; 4 young readers/year; 4 middle readers/year; 2 young adult titles/year. "The Union of American Hebrew Congregations Press publishes textbooks for the religious classroom, children's tradebooks and scholarly work of Jewish education import—no adult fiction."
Fiction: Picture books, young readers, middle readers, young adult/teens: religion. Average word length: picture books—150; young readers—500; middle readers—3,000; young adult/teens—20,000. Recently published *A Thousand and One Chickens*, written by Seymour Rossel, illustrated by Vlad Guzner (ages 10 and up, Jewish folktales); *The Mystery of the Coins*, written and illustrated by Chaya Burnstein (ages 10 and up, juvenile Jewish fiction); and *Rooftop Secrets*, by Lawrence Bush (ya, stories of anti-semitism).
Nonfiction: Picture books, young readers, middle readers, young adult/teens: religion. Average word length: picture books—150; young readers—500; middle readers—3,000; young adult/teens—20,000. Recently published *Tot Shabbat*, illustrated by Camille Kress (toddlers' board book); *Book of the Jewish Year*, by Stephen Wylen (ages 12 and up, Jewish holidays); and *The Number on My Grandfather's Arm*, by David Adler (ages 6 and up, Holocaust survival).
How to Contact/Writers: Fiction: Submit outline/synopsis and 2 sample chapters. Nonfiction: Submit complete ms. Reports on queries/ms in 2-4 months. Publishes a book 18 months after acceptance. Will consider simultaneous submissions.
Illustration: Works with 10 illustrators/year. Reviews ms/illustration packages from artists. Send ms with dummy. Illustrations only: Send portfolio to be kept on file. Reports in 2 months. Samples returned with SASE.

insider report

Tune out the 'voices' and make every word sing

As the oldest of seven children, Anastasia Suen has been reading and creating books for kids since she was a kid herself. The author of 27 books, including picture books, easy readers and basals, Suen, a teacher and poet, creates books that engage, entertain and educate children with words that sing. "I think of poetry as spoken music," says Suen. "Every word has to sing." Just read *Man on the Moon* (Viking), *Baby Born* (Lee & Low) or *Window Music* (Viking) to feel Suen's love of language. In addition to writing, Suen is a textbook consultant, past advisor and conference director for a Society of Children's Book Writers and Illustrators chapter, writing teacher at Southern Methodist University and children's book columnist for several publications. During an exciting month when she sold a new book a week to publishers, Suen took time to share her views on writing, publishing and finding your own voice.

Anastasia Suen

When did you first start writing? What helped you stay determined and keep writing while you waited to get published?
I wrote my first book when I was 11. I sold my first book the day after my 40th birthday. I had been writing for children almost forever by that point. I wrote for my baby sister when she was small. I wrote for my students when I worked full-time in the classroom. I kept writing because I had to. Over the years, I had several editors mentor me, sending rejection letters with helpful comments and encouragement. How could I quit? What if I gave up one book too soon? I knew I wanted a book with my name on it. I was not going to give up until that happened.

Do you participate in a writing group?
I am currently in several writing groups on the Web. My e-mail groups are not critique groups, however. We talk about writing. I have found when I'm in a critique group, I try to please everyone. It interfered with my process. I need to be free to throw everything in a story away and start over. Groups that talk about writing work better for me than groups that talk about specific manuscripts.

How did your textbook series come about? How is working with educational publishers different from working with trade publishers?
Networking is how all the textbook jobs have come to me. Textbooks are a team effort and writing for educational publishers is very different. They have very specific guidelines for each book. The topics are assigned, as are word counts, lines per page, formatting, etc. I also specify all of the art. It's like putting a puzzle together, creatively.

What are the most challenging aspects of writing picture books?

A picture book has to work on so many levels at the same time. Kids want the same books read to them over and over again. Can your story stand up to that, or will it be read once, and forgotten? That's why I write short books, making them parent- and child-friendly!

I constantly rewrite. I have drawers and drawers of books that aren't ready yet. Writing for me is not a linear process. I don't get an idea, write a book, mail it out and sell it. In-between all of that, a lot of other things are happening. Books are going in and out of the filing cabinet. Ideas are running around in my head. It takes time to write a book with layers, a book that works on more than one level. I have to let go and let my subconscious do the writing. That is why I can "write" a book in a day but it has actually taken me twenty years! Draft after draft with the kernel of the idea has gone in and out of the filing cabinet during that time. Some books I have published have five or six books inside them.

With short books, how do you keep your writing to the essential elements?

I love short books. I don't want to get caught up in the words, in long explanations, and have

by Anastasia Suen   Illustrated by Wade Zahares

Illustration © Wade Zahares. Reprinted with permission of Viking.

"Window music" is a wonderful railroad slang term for the scenery that races by during a train ride. Author Anastasia Suen's *Window Music* is a critically acclaimed picture book about the same. "As the journey progresses," says a starred review in *The Horn Book*, "the scenery becomes more fantastic, as if the observer has fallen into a vivid dream. Acting almost as background music, the short text underscores the actions and the ambiance of each spread. This is a book that understands the simultaneously exciting and hypnotic lure of trains."

everyone start wiggling on me. I think of poetry as spoken music. If the beat is off, the verses aren't even, the picture isn't clear, or the story doesn't build, I rewrite. I cut until I reach the very essence of the story, of the experience, until the words sing!

What has been the most difficult thing you have had to overcome as a writer?
The most difficult thing was to stop listening to other people's voices. I can't be a people pleaser and write at the same time. I try to please, and I lose my vision for the book in the process. I can't listen to any voices until the book is ready. After the book is ready, I send it out into the world, and it comes back again and again, because it hasn't found the right editor yet. More voices. After it finds the right editor and finally becomes a book, it meets the critics. More voices, and influential ones, too. If they don't like the book, wow! The bad news goes everywhere! There are also face-to-face encounters with the public. Not everyone will like your work, that's a fact, but some people feel the need to tell you all about it. Your private thoughts, ideas and dreams are there for all the world to see, and criticize. Ouch!

What advice do you have for children's writers starting out?
Read, read, read every children's book you can. Absorb the form, and write the kind of book you love best. Don't worry about the marketplace. Do one thing at a time. When you are writing, write. When you are editing, edit. When you are mailing, see what the competition is, and act wisely. Don't mail your book to 80 publishers at once. Send it to someone who will respect your work, and you.
—*Tricia Waddell*

Photography: Buys stock and assigns work. Uses photos with Jewish content. Prefer modern settings. Submit cover letter and promo piece.
Terms: Offers advances. Pays photographers by the project (range: $200-3,000) or per photo (range:$20-100). Book catalog free; ms guidelines for SASE.
Tips: "Look at some of our books. Have an understanding of the Reform Jewish community. We sell mostly to Jewish congregations and day schools.' "

UNITY HOUSE, (formerly Unity Books), 1901 NW Blue Pkwy., Unity Village MO 64065-0001. (816)524-3550, ext. 3190. Fax: (816)251-3552. Website: www.unityworldhq.org. Book publisher. Estab. 1896. Publishes "spiritual, metaphysical, new thought publications." **Manuscript Acquisitions:** Raymond Teague. Other imprints: Wee Wisdom. Publishes 1 picture book/year.
Fiction: All levels: religion. Recently published *I Turn to the Light*, by Connie Bowen (picture book); and *Adventures of the Little Green Dragon*, by Mari Prirette Ulmer, illustrated by Mary Maass (picture book anthology).
Nonfiction: All levels: religion.
How to Contact/Writers: Fiction/Nonfiction: Submit outline/synopsis and 1-3 sample chapters. Reports on queries/mss in up to 2 months. Publishes a book approximately 1 year after acceptance. Will consider simultaneous submission or previously self-published work. Writer's guidelines and catalog available upon request.
Illustration: Reviews ms/illustration packages from artists. Query. Contact: Raymond Teague, associate editor.
Terms: Pays authors royalty of 10-15% based on retail price or work purchased outright. Offers advances (Average amount: $1,500). Book catalog available.
Tips: "Read our Writer's Guidelines and study our catalog before submitting. All of our publications reflect Unity's spiritual teachings, but the presentations and applications of those teachings are wide open."

✓ VIKING CHILDREN'S BOOKS, Penguin Putnam Inc., 345 Hudson St., New York NY 10014-3657. (212)366-2000. Website: www.penguinputnam.com. **Acquisitions:** Judy Carey, associate editor, all types of fiction; Cathy Hennessy, assistant editor, middle-grade fiction; Jill Davis, senior editor, nonfiction; Melanie Cecka, editor, easy-to-read. **Art Acquisitions:** Denise Cronin, Viking Children's Books. Publishes hardcover originals. Publishes 80 books/year. Receives 7500 queries/year. 25% of books from first-time authors; 33% from unagented writers. "Viking Children's Books is known for humorous, quirky picture books, in addition to more traditional fiction and publishes the highest quality trade books for children including fiction, nonfiction, and novelty books for pre-schoolers through young adults." Publishes book 1-2 years after acceptance of artwork. Accepts simultaneous submissions.

Fiction: All levels: adventure, animal, anthology, contemporary, hi-lo, humor, multicultural, suspense/mystery, easy-to-read, history, poetry, religion, sports. Middle readers, young adults/teens: problem novels, fantasy, romance, science fiction. Recently published *The Awful Aardvarks Go to School*, by Reeve Lindbergh (picture book); *Virtual World*, by Chris Westwood (young adult novel); and *Seal Island School*, by Susan Bartlett (middle grade).

Nonfiction: Picture books: activity books, biography, concept. Young readers, middle readers, young adult: biography, history, reference, religion, science, sports. Middle readers: animal, biography, geography, hi-lo, history, hobbies, multicultural, music/dance, nature/environment, religion, science, social issues, sports. Young adult/teens: animal, biography, cooking, geography, hi-lo, history, multicultural, music/dance, nature/environment, reference, religion, science, social issues, sports.

Illustration: Works with 40 illustrators/year. Reports on artist's queries/submissions only if interested. Samples returned with SASE or samples filed. Originals returned at job's completion.

How to Contact/Writers: Picture books: submit entire ms and SASE. Novels: submit outline with 3 sample chapters and SASE. Nonfiction: query with outline, one sample chapter and SASE. Reports on queries/mss in 6-8 months.

Terms: Pays 2-10% royalty on retail price or flat fee. Advance negotiable.

Tips: Mistake often made is that "authors disguise nonfiction in a fictional format."

WALKER AND CO., 435 Hudson St., New York NY 10014. (212)727-8300. Fax: (212)727-0894. Division of Walker Publishing Co. Inc. Book publisher. Estab. 1959. **Manuscript Acquisitions:** Emily Easton, publisher; Masha Rand, editorial assistant. **Acquisitions:** Marlene Tungseth, art director. Publishes 16 picture books/year; 4-6 middle readers/year; 2-4 young adult titles/year. 5% of books by first-time authors; 65% of books from agented writers.

Fiction: Picture books: animal, history, multicultural. Young readers: contemporary, history, humor, multicultural. Middle readers: animal, contemporary, history, multicultural, humor. Young adults: contemporary and historical fiction. Recently published *Milkman's Boy*, by D. Hall; *Ethan Between Us*, by A. Myers (young adult); *Devil's Den*, by S. Pfeffer (middle grade).

Nonfiction: Young readers: animals. Middle readers: animal, biography, health, history, multicultural, reference, social issues. Young adults: biography, health, history, multicultural, reference, social issues, sports. Published *Bold and Bright Black and White Animals*, by D. Patent (picture book history); and *What's Going on Down There*, by K. Graville (young adult health). Multicultural needs include "contemporary, literary fiction and historical fiction written in an authentic voice. Also high interest nonfiction with trade appeal."

How to Contact/Writers: Fiction/nonfiction: Submit outline/synopsis and sample chapters; query for novels. Reports on queries/mss in 2-3 months. Send SASE for writer's guidelines.

Illustration: Works with 10-12 illustrators/year. Uses color artwork only. Editorial reviews ms/illustration packages from artists. Query or submit ms with 4-8 samples. Illustrations only: Tearsheets. "Please do not send original artwork." Reports on art samples only if interested. Samples returned with SASE.

Terms: Pays authors royalties of 5-10%; pays illustrators royalty or flat fee. Offers advance payment against royalties. Original artwork returned at job's completion. Sends galleys to authors. Book catalog available for 9×12 SASE; ms guidelines for SASE.

Tips: Writers: "Make sure you study our catalog before submitting. We are a small house with a tightly focused list. Illustrators: "Have a well-rounded portfolio with different styles." Does not want to see folktales, ABC books, genre fiction (mysteries, science fiction, fantasy). "Walker and Company is committed to introducing talented new authors and illustrators to the children's book field."

DANIEL WEISS ASSOCIATES, INC., 11th Floor, 33 W. 17th St., New York NY 10011. (212)645-3865. Fax: (212)633-1236. Independent book producer/packager. Estab. 1987. **Manuscript Acquisitions:** Jennifer Klein, editorial assistant. **Art Acquisitions:** Paul Matarazzo, art director (illustrations); Mike Rivilis, associate art director (ms/illustration packages). Publishes 30 young readers/year; 40 middle readers/year; and 70 young adults/year. 25% of books by first-time authors. "We do mostly series! We mainly publish middle grade and YA series and hire writers for books in these series. As a book packager, we work with the larger publishing houses."

Fiction: Middle readers: sports. Young adults: fantasy, romance. Recently published Svtt Senior Year #8; *Major Who*; Thoroughbred #34; *On The Track*.

Nonfiction: Young adults. Recently published *Ultimate Cheerleading Handbook Scene* series.

How to Contact/Writers: Send SASE for guidelines to write for series currently in production. No unsolicited mss.

Illustration: Works with 20 illustrators/year. Reviews ms/illustration packages from artists. Submit query. Illustrations only: Provide promo sheet. Reports in 2 months. Samples returned with SASE. Original artwork returned at job's completion.

Terms: Pays authors royalty on work purchased outright from authors. Offers advances. Pays illustrators by the project.

N WHAT'S INSIDE PRESS, P.O. Box 16965, Beverly Hills CA 90209. (323)965-7863. E-mail: whatsin@aol .com. Website: www.whatsinsidepress.com. Estab. 1998. Specializes in fiction. **Acquisitions:** Debbie Kirchen, president of creative affairs. Publishes 6 picture books/year; 5 young adult titles/year. 75% of books by first-time authors. "What's Inside Press, is dedicated to the creation and publication of quailty children's and young adult literature. We pride ourselves on the positive nature of our stories and activley seek material that embraces the joys and journeys of childhood."

Fiction: Picture books—average word length varies; young adults—35,000. Recently published *Kitty in the City*, by Kinsley Foster, illustrated by Kari McGaven; *Millie the Middle Child*, by Irene S. Blanchard; *Wild Abandon*, by Kinsley Foster.

How to Contact/Writers: Submit complete mss. Reports on mss in 2 months. Publishes a book 18 months after accpetance.

Illustration: Works with 5 illustrators/year. Uses color artwork only. Reviews ms/illustration packages from artists. Send ms with dummy. Contact: Debbie Kirchen, president of creative affairs. Illustrations only: Query with samples. Contact Debbie Kirchen, president of creative affairs. Reports in 2 weeks. Samples returned with SASE.

Photography: Buys stock and assigns work. Contact: Debbie Kirchen, president of creative affairs. Uses b&w prints. Submit cover letter and published samples.

Terms: Pays authors royalty of 15% based on retail price. Offers advances. Pays illustrators by the project (range varies). Sends galleys to authors; dummies to illustrators. Book catalog available for SASE; writer's, artist's and photographer's guidelines available for SASE.

Tips: "Take a chance and send us your stuff. We are always happy to provide writers and artists with guidance, even if we don't buy their work. Don't be intimidated or discouraged if you don't hear from us right away. The process takes time."

N WHISPERING COYOTE PRESS, INC., 7130 Alexander Dr., Dallas TX 75214. **Acquisitions:** Lou Alpert, editor/publisher. Publishes 8 picture books/year. 40% of books from first-time authors.

Fiction: Picture books: adventure, animal, contemporary, fantasy, hi-lo, history, humor, poetry. Does not want to see number, alphabet, death, handicap and holiday books. Average word length: picture books—under 1,500. Recently published *Row, Row Your Boat*, written and illustrated by Iza Trapani (4-8, picture book); and *Arctic Dreams*, by Carole Gerber, illustrated by Marty Husted.

How to Contact/Writers: Submit complete ms. Reports in 3 months. Publishes a book 1½-3 years after acceptance. Will consider simultaneous submissions. "Include SASE. If no SASE is included manuscript is destroyed *without* reading."

Illustration: Works with 10-15 illustrators/year. Uses color artwork only. Reviews ms/illustration packages from artists. Submit ms with dummy or 3-4 pieces of final art. Illustrations only: Submit color copies or a half dozen pieces for file. "Do not send originals." Reports back only if SASE is included. Samples returned with SASE; samples filed if instructed to do so by illustrator.

Terms: Pays authors royalty of 4-5% based on retail price. Offers advances. Pays illustrators royalty of 4-5%. Book catalog available for #10 SASE and 55¢ first-class postage. Ms and art guidelines available for SASE.

Tips: "Look at what we do before submitting. Follow the guidelines. I think publishers are doing fewer books and are therefore more selective in what they agree to publish. We are having more luck with shorter books with a sense of humor."

WHITECAP BOOKS, 351 Lynn Ave., North Vancouver, British Columbia V7J 2C4 Canada. (604)980-9852. E-mail: whitecap@pinc.com. Book publisher. **Acquisitions:** Robin Rivers, editorial director. Publishes 4 young readers/year; and 2 middle readers/year.

● Whitecap is publishing 2 children's picture books this year.

Fiction: Picture books for children 3-7.

Nonfiction: Young readers, middle readers: animal, nature/environment. Does not want to see text that writes down to children. Recently published *Welcome to the World of Wolves*, by Diane Swanson (ages 5-7); *Animals Eat the Weirdest Things*, by Diane Swanson (ages 8-11); and *Whose Feet Are These*, by Wayne Lynch (ages 5-7).

How to Contact/Writers: Nonfiction: Query. Reports on queries in 1 month; ms in 3 months. Publishes a book 6 months after acceptance. Will consider simultaneous submissions. Please send international postal voucher if submission is from US.

Illustration: Works with 1-2 illustrators/year. Reviews ms/illustration packages from artists. Query. Illustrations only: Query with samples—"never send original art." Contact: Robin Rivers. Samples returned with SASE with international postal voucher for Canada if requested.

Photography: Buys stock. "We are always looking for outstanding wildlife photographs." Uses 35mm transparencies. Submit cover letter, client list, stock photo list.

Terms: Pays authors a negotiated royalty or purchases work outright. Offers advances. Pays illustrators by the project or royalty (depends on project). Pays photographers per photo (depends on project). Originals returned to artist at job's completion unless discussed in advance. Ms guidelines available for SASE with international postal voucher for Canada.

Tips: "Writers and illustrators should spend time researching what's already available on the market. Whitecap specializes in nonfiction for children and adults. Whitecap fiction focuses on humorous events or extraordinary animals. Please review previous publications before submitting."

ALBERT WHITMAN & COMPANY, 6340 Oakton St., Morton Grove IL 60053-2723. (847)581-0033. Fax: (847)581-0039. Website: www.awhitmanco.com. Book publisher. Estab. 1919. **Manuscript Acquisitions:** Kathleen Tucker, editor-in-chief. **Art Acquisitions:** Scott Piehl, designer. Publishes 30 books/year. 15% of books by first-time authors; 15% of books from agented authors.

• Turn to First Books on page 45 to read about Albert Whitman, illustrator Tim Coffey and his book *Red Berry Wool*, by Robyn Eversole. First Books also features Albert Whitman editor Wendy McClure.

Fiction: Picture books, young readers, middle readers: adventure, animal, concept, contemporary, health, history, humor, multicultural, nature/environment, special needs. Middle readers: problem novels, suspense/mystery. "We are interested in contemporary multicultural stories—stories with holiday themes (except Christmas) and exciting distinctive novels. We publish a wide variety of topics and are interested in stories that help children deal with their problems and concerns. Does not want to see "religion-oriented, ABCs, pop-up, romance, counting." Published *Mr. Tanen's Ties,* by Maryann Cocca-Leffler; *Mei-Mei Loves the Morning,* by Margaret Holloway Tsub, illustrated by Cornelius Van Wright and Ying-Hwa Hu; and *No Time for Mother's Day,* by Laurie Halse Anderson, illustrated by Dorothy Donohue.

Nonfiction: Picture books, young readers, middle readers: animal, biography, concept, geography, health, history, hobbies, multicultural, music/dance, nature/environment, special needs. Middle readers: careers. Middle readers, young adults: biography, social issues. Does not want to see "religion, any books that have to be written in or fictionalized biographies." Recently published *Shelter Dogs,* by Peg Kehret; *I Have a Weird Brother Who Digested a Fly,* by Joan Hulub, illustrated by Patrick Girouard; and *The Riches of Oseola McCarty,* by Evelyn Coleman, illustrated by Daniel Minter.

How to Contact/Writers: Fiction/Nonfiction: Submit complete ms. Reports on queries in 6 weeks; mss in 3-4 months. Publishes a book 18 months after acceptance. Will consider simultaneous submissions "but let us know if it is one."

Illustration: Works with 30 illustrators/year. Uses more color art than b&w. Reviews ms/illustration packages from artists. Illustrations only: Query with samples. Send slides or tearsheets. Samples returned with SASE; samples filed. Originals returned at job's completion. Reports back in 2 months.

Photography: Publishes books illustrated with photos but not stock photos—desires photos all taken for project. "Our books are for children and cover many topics; photos must be taken to match text. Books often show a child in a particular situation (e.g., kids being home-schooled, a sister whose brother is born prematurely)." Photographers should query with samples; send unsolicited photos by mail.

Terms: Pays authors royalty. Offers advances. Pays illustrators and photographers royalty. Sends galleys to authors; dummies to illustrators. Original artwork returned at job's completion. Ms/artist's guidelines available for SASE, or on website. Book catalogs available with 9 × 12 SASE and $1.43 in postage.

Tips: "In both picture books and nonfiction, we are seeking stories showing life in other cultures and the variety of multicultural life in the U.S. We also want fiction and nonfiction about mentally or physically challenged children—some recent topics have been autism, asthma, diabetes. Look up some of our books first, to be sure your submission is appropriate for Albert Whitman & Co."

JOHN WILEY & SONS, INC., 605 Third Ave., New York NY 10158. (212)850-6206. Fax: (212)850-6095. Website: www.wiley.com. Book publisher. **Acquisitions:** Kate Bradford, editor. Publishes 18 middle readers/year; 2 young adult titles/year. 10% of books by first-time authors. Publishes educational, nonfiction: primarily history, science, and other activities.

Nonfiction: Middle readers: activity books, animal, arts/crafts, biography, cooking, geography, health, history, hobbies, how-to, nature/environment, reference, science, self help. Young adults: activity books, arts/crafts, health, hobbies, how-to, nature/environment, reference, science, self help. Average word length middle readers—20,000-40,000. Recently published: *Teresa Weatherspoon's Basketball for Girls* (ages 8 and up, sports); *Civil War Days,* in the American Kids in History series (ages 8-12, history/activity).

How to Contact/Writers: Query. Submit outline/synopsis, 2 sample chapters and an author bio. Reports on queries in 1 month; mss in 3 months. Publishes a book 1 year after acceptance. Will consider simultaneous and previously published submissions.

Illustration: Works with 6 illustrators/year. Uses primarily black & white artwork. Reviews ms/illustration packages from artists. Query. Illustrations only: Query with samples, résumé, client list. Reports back only if interested. Samples filed. Original artwork returned at job's completion. No portfolio reviews.

Photography: Buys photos from freelancers.

Terms: Pays authors royalty of 4-10% based on wholesale price, or by outright purchase. Offers advances. Pays illustrators by the project. Photographers pay negotiable. Sends galleys to authors. Book catalog available for SASE.

Tips: "We're looking for topics and writers that can really engage kids' interest—plus we're always interested in a new twist on time-tested subjects."

WILLIAMSON PUBLISHING CO., Box 185, Charlotte VT 05445. (802)425-2102. Fax: (802)425-2199. Website: www.williamsonbooks.com. Book publisher. Estab. 1983. **Manuscript Acquisitions:** Susan Williamson, editorial director. **Art Acquisitions:** Jack Williamson, publisher. Publishes 12-15 young readers titles/year. 50% of books by first-time authors; 10% of books from agented authors. Publishes "very successful nonfiction series (Kids Can!® Series—2,000,000 sold) on subjects such as nature, creative play, arts/crafts, geography. Successfully launched *Little Hands®* series for ages 2-6 and recently introduced the new *Kaleidoscope Kids*™ series (age 7 and up). Our mission is to help every child fulfill his/her potential and experience personal growth.

● Williamson won American Bookseller Pick of the List, Benjamin Franklin Awards for Best Nonfiction, juvenile; Best Fiction, juvenile; Best Multicultural. Also winner of Oppenheim Toy Award, Parents' Choice Awards.

Nonfiction: Picture books, young readers, middle readers, young adult/teens: hands-on activity books, arts/crafts, biography, careers, geography, health, history, hobbies, how-to, math, multicultural, music/dance, nature/environment, science, self-help, social issues. Picture books, middle readers: animal, concept. Does not want to see textbooks, poetry, fiction. "We are looking for books in which learning and doing are inseparable." Published *Gizmos and Gadgets*, by Jill Hauser, illustrated by Michael Kline (ages 6-12, exploring science); *Alphabet Art*, by Judy Press (ages 2-6, early learning skills); and *Ancient Greece!*, by Avery Hart and Paul Mantell, illustrated by Michael Kline (ages 7 and up, learning history through activities and experience).

How to Contact/Writers: Query with outline/synopsis and 2 sample chapters. Reports on queries in 4 months; mss in 4 months. Publishes book, "depending on graphics, about 1 year" after acceptance. Writers may send a SASE for guidelines.

Illustration: Works with 6 illustrator and 6 designers/year. "We're interested in expanding our illustrator and design freelancers." Uses primarily b&w artwork; some 2-color and 4-color. Reports only if interested. Samples returned with SASE; samples filed.

Photography: Buys photos from freelancers

Terms: Pays authors royalty based on wholesale price or purchases outright. Pays illustrators by the project. Pays photographers per photo. Sends galleys to authors. Book catalog available for 8½×11 SAE and 4 first-class stamps; ms guidelines available for SASE.

Tips: "We're interested in interactive learning books with a creative approach packed with interesting information, written for young readers ages 2-6 and 4-10. In nonfiction children's publishing, we are looking for authors with a depth of knowledge shared with children through a warm, embracing style. Our publishing philosophy is based on the idea that all children can succeed and have positive learning experiences. Children's lasting learning experiences involve participation."

WM KIDS, Imprint of White Mane Publishing Co., Inc., P.O. Box, 152, 63 W. Burel St., Shippensburg PA 17257. (717)532-2237. Fax: (717)532-7704. E-mail: collier@innernet.net. Book publisher. Estab. 1987. **Acquisitions:** Harold Collier. Publishes 10 middle readers/year. 50% of books are by first-time authors.

Fiction: Picture books, young readers, middle readers, young adults: history. Average word length: middle readers—30,000. Recently published *Shenandoah Autumn*, by Mauriel Joelyn (grades 5 and up); *House of Spies*, by Margaret W. Blair (grades 5 and up); *The Powder Monkey*, by Carol Campbell (grades 5 and up).

Nonfiction: Young readers, middle readers, young adults: history. Average word length: middle readers—30,000.

How to Contact/Writers: Fiction: Query. Nonfiction: Submit outline/synopsis and 2-3 sample chapters. Reports on queries in 1 month; mss in 3 months. Publishes a book 1 year after acceptance. Will consider simultaneous submissions.

Illustration: Works with 3 illustrators/year. Reviews ms/illustration packages from artists. Submit ms with 3 pieces of final art. Contact: Harold Collier, acquisitions editor. Reports in 1 month. Samples returned with SASE.

Photography: Buys stock and assigns work. Submit cover letter and portfolio.

Terms: Pays authors royalty of 7%. Pays illustrators by the project. Pays photographers by the project. Sends galleys for review. Originals returned to artist at job's completion. Book catalog and writer's guidelines available for SASE. All imprints included in a single catalog.

WOMAN'S MISSIONARY UNION, P.O. Box 830010, Birmingham AL 35283-0010. (205)991-8100. Fax: (205)995-4841. Website: www.wmu.com/wmu. Imprint: New Hope. **Acquisitions:** Jan Turrentine. Publishes 2 picture books/year; 5 middle readers/year; 3 young adult titles/year. 50% of books from first-time authors.

Fiction: All levels: multicultural, religion. Multicultural fiction must be related to mission/ministry.

Nonfiction: All levels: multicultural, religion. Materials must teach missions concepts, evangelism or ministry and outreach to persons without Christ; materials published with this imprint are for Christian concepts.

How to Contact/Writers: Fiction/nonfiction: Submit complete ms. Reports on queries in 3 months. Publishes a book 2 years after acceptance. Will accept simultaneous submissions. We accept children's and ethnic mss also.

Illustration: Works with 2-3 illustrators/year. Reviews ms/illustration packages from artists. Send ms with dummy. Illustrations only: Query with samples (color copies). Reports back only if interested. Samples filed.

Photography: Buys stock already on file. Model/property releases required.

Terms: Pays authors royalty of 7-10% (depends on length). Pays illustrators by the project. Sends galleys to authors. Originals returned to artist at job's completion. Book catalog available for 10×12 SAE and 3 first-class stamps. Ms guidelines available for SASE.

Tips: "Obtain the catalog first to see the kinds of material we publish."

WORLD BOOK, INC., 525 W. Monroe St., Chicago IL 60661. (312)258-3700. Fax: (312)258-3950. Website: www.worldbook.com. Book publisher. **Manuscript Acquisitions:** Paul A. Kobasa, product development director. **Art Acquisitions:** Roberta Dimmer, executive art director. World Book, Inc. (publisher of *The World Book Encyclopedia*), publishes reference sources and nonfiction series for children in the areas of science, mathematics, English-language skills, basic academic and social skills, social studies, history, and health and fitness. We publish print and nonprint material appropriate for children ages 3 to 14. WBT does not publish fiction, poetry, or wordless picture books."

Nonfiction: Young readers: activity books, animal, arts/crafts, careers, concept, geography, health, reference. Middle readers: activity books, animal, arts/crafts, careers, geography, health, history, hobbies, how-to, nature/environment, reference, science. Young adult: arts/crafts, careers, geography, health, history, hobbies, how-to, nature/environment, reference, science.

How to Contact/Writers: Nonfiction: Submit outline/synopsis only; no mss. Reports on queries/mss in 1-2 months. Unsolicited mss will not be returned. Publishes a book 18 months after acceptance. Will consider simultaneous submissions.

Illustration: Works with 10-30 illustrators/year. Illustrations only: Query with samples. Reports only if interested. Samples returned with SASE; samples filed "if extra copies and if interested."

Photography: Buys stock and assigns work. Needs broad spectrum; editorial concept, specific natural, physical and social science spectrum. Model/property releases required; captions required. Uses color 8×10 gloss and matte prints, 35mm, $2\frac{1}{4} \times 2\frac{1}{4}$, 4×5, 8×10 transparencies. Submit cover letter, résumé, promo piece (color and b&w).

Terms: Payment negotiated on project-by-project basis. Sends galleys to authors. Book catalog available for 9×12 SASE. Ms and art guidelines for SASE.

Magazines

Children's magazines are a great place for unpublished writers and illustrators to break into the market. Illustrators, photographers and writers alike may find it easier to get book assignments if they have tearsheets from magazines. Having magazine work under your belt shows you're professional and have experience working with editors and art directors and meeting deadlines.

But magazines aren't merely a breaking-in point. Writing, illustration and photo assignments for magazines let you see your work in print quickly, and the magazine market can offer steady work and regular paychecks (a number of them pay on acceptance). Book authors, illustrators and photographers may have to wait a year or two before receiving royalties from a project. The magazine market is also a good place to use research material that didn't make it into a book project you're working on. You may even work on a magazine idea that blossoms into a book project.

TARGETING YOUR SUBMISSIONS

It's important to know the topics typically covered by different children's magazines. To help you match your work with the right publications, we've included several indexes in the back of this book. The **Subject Index** lists both book and magazine publishers by the fiction and nonfiction subjects they're seeking. **If you're a photographer**, the **Photography Index** lists children's magazines that use photos from freelancers. Using these two indexes in combination, you can quickly narrow your search of markets that suit your work. For instance, if you photograph sports, compare the Magazine list in the Photography Index with the list under Sports in the Subject Index. Highlight the markets that appear on both lists, then read those listings to decide which magazines might be best for your work.

If you're a writer, use the Subject Index in conjunction with the **Age-Level Index** to narrow your list of markets. Targeting the correct age group with your submission is an important consideration. Most rejection slips are sent because a writer has not targeted a manuscript to the correct age. Few magazines are aimed at children of all ages, so you must be certain your manuscript is written for the audience level of the particular magazine you're submitting to. Magazines for children (just as magazines for adults) may also target a specific gender. For more on this topic, see Writing for Boys: Is the Gender Barrier Real? on page 75.

If you're a poet, refer to the new **Poetry Index** to find which magazines publish poems. For more information on writing poems for children see Poetry & Plastic Laundry Baskets on page 83.

Each magazine has a different editorial philosophy. Language usage also varies between periodicals, as does the length of feature articles and the use of artwork and photographs. Reading magazines *before* submitting is the best way to determine if your material is appropriate. Also, because magazines targeted to specific age groups have a natural turnover in readership every few years, old topics (with a new slant) can be recycled.

Since many kids' magazines sell subscriptions through direct mail or schools, you may not be able to find a particular publication at bookstores or newsstands. Check your local library, or send for copies of the magazines you're interested in. Most magazines in this section have sample copies available and will send them for a SASE or small fee.

Also, many magazines have submission guidelines and theme lists available for a SASE. (Visit www.writersdigest.com for a searchable database of more than 1,150 writers guidelines.)

Check magazines' websites, too. Many offer excerpts of articles, submission information and the editorial philosophy of the publication.

For advice straight from magazine editors, read the Insider Reports in this section with **Deborah Vetter**, editor of *Cicada*, the literary magazine for teens from the publishers of *Cricket* (page 220); and **Elizabeth Lindstrom**, editor of *Odyssey, Adventures in Science*, published by Cobblestone (page 244).

ADVOCATE, PKA'S PUBLICATION, PKA Publication, 301A Rolling Hills Park, Prattsville NY 12468. (518)299-3103. **Publisher**: Patricia Keller. Bimonthly tabloid. Estab. 1987. Circ. 12,000. "*Advocate* advocates good writers and quality writings. We publish art, fiction, photos and poetry. *Advocate*'s submitters are talented people of all ages who do not earn their livings as writers. We wish to promote the arts and to give those we publish the opportunity to be published through a for-profit means rather than in a not-for-profit way. We do this by selling advertising and offering reading entertainment."
  • Gaited Horse Association newsletter is now included in our publication. Horse oriented stories, poetry, art and photos are currently needed.

Fiction: Middle readers and young adults/teens: adventure, animal, contemporary, fantasy, folktales, health, humorous, nature/environment, problem-solving, romance, science fiction, sports, suspense/mystery. Looks for "well written, entertaining work, whether fiction or nonfiction." Buys approximately 42 mss/year. Average word length: 1,500. Byline given. Wants to see more humorous material, nature/environment and romantic comedy.
Nonfiction: Middle readers and young adults/teens: animal, arts/crafts, biography, careers, concept, cooking, fashion, games/puzzles, geography, history, hobbies, how-to, humorous, interview/profile, nature/environment, problem-solving, science, social issues, sports, travel. Buys 10 mss/year. Average word length: 1,500. Byline given.
Poetry: Reviews poetry any length.
How to Contact/Writers: Fiction/nonfiction: send complete ms. Reports on queries in 4-6 weeks/mss in 6-8 weeks. Publishes ms 2-18 months after acceptance.
Illustration: Uses b&w artwork only. Uses cartoons. Reviews ms/illustration packages from artists. Submit a photo print (b&w or color), an excellent copy of work (no larger than 8×10) or original. Illustrations only: "Send previous unpublished art with SASE, please." Reports in 2 months. Samples returned with SASE; samples not filed. Credit line given.
Photography: Buys photos from freelancers. Model/property releases required. Uses color and b&w prints. Send unsolicited photos by mail with SASE. Reports in 2 months. Wants nature, artistic and humorous photos.
Terms: Pays on publication. Acquires first rights for mss, artwork and photographs. Pays in copies. Original work returned upon job's completion. Sample copies for $4. Writer's/illustrator/photo guidelines for SASE.
Tips: "Artists and photographers should keep in mind that we are a b&w paper."

AIM MAGAZINE, America's Intercultural Magazine, P.O. Box 1174, Maywood IL 60153-8174. **Contact:** Ruth Apilado (nonfiction), Mark Boone (fiction). **Photo Editor:** Betty Lewis. Quarterly magazine. Circ. 8,000. Readers are high school and college students, teachers, adults interested in helping, through the written word, to create a more equitable world. 15% of material aimed at juvenile audience.
Fiction: Young adults/teens: adventure, folktales, humorous, history, multicultural, "stories with social significance." Wants stories that teach children that people are more alike than they are different. Does not want to see religious fiction. Buys 20 mss/year. Average word length: 1,000-4,000. Byline given.
Nonfiction: Young adults/teens: biography, interview/profile, multicultural, "stuff with social significance." Does not want to see religious nonfiction. Buys 20 mss/year. Average word length: 500-2,000. Byline given.
How to Contact/Writers: Fiction: Send complete ms. Nonfiction: Query with published clips. Reports on queries in 2 weeks; mss in 6 weeks. Will consider simultaneous submissions.
Illustration: Buys 6 illustrations/issue. Preferred theme: Overcoming social injustices through nonviolent means. Reviews ms/illustration packages from artists. Query first. Illustrations only: Query with tearsheets. Reports on art samples only if interested. Samples returned with SASE or filed. Original artwork returned at job's completion "if desired." Credit line given.
Photography: Wants "photos of activists who are trying to contribute to social improvement."
Terms: Pays on acceptance. Buys first North American serial rights. Pays $15-25 for stories/articles. Pays in contributor copies if copies are requested. Pays $25 for b&w cover illustration. Photographers paid by the project. Sample copies for $5.
Tips: "We need material of social significance, stuff that will help promote racial harmony and peace and illustrate the stupidity of racism."

AMERICAN CHEERLEADER, Lifestyle Publications LLC, 250 W. 57th St., Suite 420, New York NY 10107. (212)265-8890. Fax: (212)265-8908. E-mail: editors@americancheerleader.com. Website: www.americancheerleader.com. **Editor:** Julie Davis. Bimonthly magazine. Estab. 1995. Circ. 200,000. Special interest teen magazine for kids who cheer.
Nonfiction: Young adults: biography, interview/profile, careers, fashion, beauty, health, how-to, problem-solv-

ing, sports, cheerleading specific material. "We're looking for authors who know cheerleading." Buys 50 mss/year. Average word length: 200-1,000. Byline given.

How to Contact/Writers: Query with published clips. Reports on queries/mss in 3 months. Publishes ms 3 months after acceptance. Will consider electronic submission via disk or modem.

Illustration: Buys 6 illustrations/issue; 30-50 illustrations/year. Works on assignment only. Reviews ms/illustration packages from artists. Illustrations only: Query with samples; arrange portfolio review. Reports only if interested. Samples filed. Originals not returned at job's completion. Credit line given.

Photography: Buys photos from freelancers. Looking for cheerleading at different sports games, events, etc. Uses 35mm, 2¼×2¼ transparencies. Query with samples; provide résumé, business card, tearsheets to be kept on file. "After sending query, we'll set up an interview." Reports only if interested.

Terms: Pays on publication. Buy all rights for mss, artwork and photographs. Pays $100-1,000 for stories. Pays illustrators $50-200 for b&w inside, $100-300 for color inside. Pays photographers by the project $300-750; per photo (range: $25-100). Sample copies for $5.

Tips: "Authors: Absolutely must have cheerleading background. Photographers and illustrators must have teen magazine experience or high profile experience."

☑ **AMERICAN GIRL**, Pleasant Company, 8400 Fairway Place, P.O. Box 620986, Middleton WI 53562-0984. (608)836-4848. **Editor:** Kristi Thom. **Managing Editor:** Barbara Stretchberry. **Contact:** Editorial Dept. Assistant. Bimonthly magazine. Estab. 1992. Circ. 750,000. "For girls ages 8-12. We run fiction and nonfiction, historical and contemporary."

Fiction: Middle readers: contemporary, historical, multicultural, suspense/mystery, good fiction about anything. No preachy, moralistic tales or stories with animals as protagonists. Only a girl or girls as characters—no boys. Buys approximately 6 mss/year. Average word length: 1,000-2,300. Byline given.

Nonfiction: Any articles aimed at girls ages 8-12. Buys 3-10 mss/year. Average word length: 600. Byline sometimes given.

How to Contact/Writers: Fiction: Send complete ms. Nonfiction: Query with published clips. Reports on queries/mss in 6-12 weeks. Will consider simultaneous submissions.

Illustration: Works on assignment only.

Terms: Pays on acceptance. Buys first North American serial rights. Pays $500 minimum for stories; $300 minimum for articles. Sample copies for $3.95 and 9×12 SAE with $1.93 in postage (send to Editorial Department Assistant). Writer's guidelines free for SASE.

Tips: "Keep (stories and articles) simple but interesting. Kids are discriminating readers, too. They won't read a boring or pretentious story. We're looking for short (maximum 175 words) how-to stories and short profiles of girls for 'Girls Express' section, as well as word games, puzzles and mazes."

☑ **APPLESEEDS, The Magazine for Young Readers**, Cobblestone Publishing, 99 Perkins Point Rd., Newcastle MA 04553. E-mail: barbara_burt@posthavard.edu. **Editor:** Barbara Burt. Magazine published monthly except June, July and August. *Appleseeds* is a theme-based social studies magazine from Cobblestone Publishing for ages 7-10. Published 9 times/year.

● *Appleseeds* is aimed toward readers ages 5-8. Themes for 2000 include: Person of the Year: Jackie Robinson; Fiesta!; and American Places: San Diego. Contact them for complete theme list or visit their website.

How to Contact/Writers: Nonfiction: Query. Send SASE for submission guidelines and theme list.

Tips: See listings for *California Chronicles*, *Calliope*, *Cobblestone*, *Faces*, *Footsteps* and *Odyssey*.

☒ **Archaeology's DIG**, Archaeological Institute of America, 135 William St., New York NY 10038. (212)732-5154. Fax: (212)732-5707. E-mail: editor@dig.archaeology.org. Website: www.archaeology.org. Editor-in-Chief: Stephen Hawks. Art Director: Ken Feisel. Photo Editor: Jena Malone. Bimonthly magazine. Estab. 1999. Circ. 50,000. An archaeology magazine for kids ages 8-13. Publishes entertaining and educational stories about discoveries, dinosaurs, etc.

● See Writing for Boys: Is the Gender Barrier Real? to hear from *Archaeology's Dig* editor Steve Hanks.

Fiction: Middle readers, young adults: history. Buys 1-2 mss/year. Average word length: 700-1,500. Byline given.

Nonfiction: Middle readers, young adults: biography, games/puzzles, history, science, archaeology. Buys 15-20 mss/year. Average word length: 400-1,000. Byline given.

How to Contact/Writers: Fiction: Query with published clips. Send complete ms. Nonfiction: Query with published clips. Reports on queries/mss in 1 month. Publishes ms 2-3 months after acceptance. Will consider simultaneous submissions and electronic submission via disk or modem.

Illustration: Buys 10-15 illustrations/issue; 60-75 illustrations/year. Uses color artwork only. Works on assignment only. Reviews ms/illustration packages from artists. Query. Contact: Ken Feisel, art director. Illustrations only: Query with samples. Arrange portfolio review. Send tearsheets. Contact: Ken Feisel, art director. Reports in 2 months only if interested. Samples not returned; samples filed. Credit line given.

Photography: Uses anything related to archaeology, history, artifacts, dinosaurs and current archaeological events that relate to kids. Uses color prints and 35mm transparencies. Provide résumé, business card, promotional literature or tearsheets to be kept on file. Reports only if interested.

Terms: Pays on publication. Buys all rights for mss. Buys first North American rights for artwork and photos. Original artwork returned at job's completion. Pays 50¢-$1/word. Additional payment for ms/illustration packages and for photos accompanying articles. Pays illustrators $1,000-3,000 for color cover; $150-2,000 for color inside. Pays photographers by the project (range: $500-1,000). Pays per photo (range: $100-500).

Tips: "We are looking for writers who can communicate archaeological and paleontological concepts in a conversational style for kids. Writers should have some idea where photography can be located to support their work."

ASPCA ANIMALAND, 424 E. 92nd St., New York NY 10128. (212)876-7700, ext. 4441. Fax: (212)410-0087. Website: www.aspca.org. **Managing Editor:** Pune Dracker. **Art Director:** Al Braverman. Bimonthly magazine. For the young members of the ASPCA (ages 7-12). All topics related to animals.

Fiction: Young readers, middle readers: animal, history, problem-solving.

Nonfiction: Young readers, middle readers: careers, hobbies, nature/environment.

Illustration: Buys 5 illustrations/issue; 12 illustrations/year. Works on assignment only. Reviews ms/illustration packages from artists. Send ms with dummy. Illustrations only: "Please send a photocopy or tearsheet sample that we can hold on file for reference. We need dynamic, endearing, descriptive and imaginative images which communicate ideas or emotions. Off-beat, alternative techniques are always welcome. We are always in need of heart-warming portraits of cats (and kittens), dogs (and puppies). We have plenty of 'realistic wildlife' as well as single-cell pen and ink cartoons and do not need any of these." Samples returned with SASE or kept on file. Originals returned upon job's completion. Credit line given.

Photography: Looking for animal care and animal protection. Model/property releases required. Uses 8×10, glossy color/b&w prints; 35mm, 2¼×2¼ and 4×5 transparencies. Please send originals or dupes (35mm slides or any larger format transparency) of your work, a brief statement of the kind of photography you do or a résumé as well as a properly posted SASE. You may submit 10 slides of various images or all of the same subject."

BABYBUG, Carus Publishing Company, P.O. Box 300, Peru IL 61354. (815)224-6656. **Editor:** Paula Morrow. **Art Director:** Suzanne Beck. Published 10 times/year (every 6 weeks). Estab. 1994. "A listening and looking magazine for infants and toddlers ages 6 to 24 months, *Babybug* is 6 ¼×7, 24 pages long, printed in large type (26-point) on high-quality cardboard stock with rounded corners and no staples."

• After illustrator Tim Coffey's work appeared in *Babybug*, several book editors contacted him for assignments. Read about Coffey's first book (and see his illustration from *Babybug*) in First Books on page 45.

Fiction: Looking for very simple and concrete stories, 4-6 short sentences maximum.

Nonfiction: Must use very basic words and concepts, 10 words maximum.

Poetry: Maximum length 8 lines. Looking for rhythmic, rhyming poems.

How to Contact/Writers: "Please do not query first." Send complete ms with SASE. "Submissions without SASE will be discarded." Reports in 3 months.

Illustration: Uses color artwork only. Works on assignment only. Reviews ms/illustration packages from artists. "The manuscripts will be evaluated for quality of concept and text before the art is considered." Contact: Paula Morrow, editor. Illustrations only: Send tearsheets or photo prints/photocopies with SASE. "Submissions without SASE will be discarded." Reports in 12 weeks. Samples filed.

Terms: Pays on publication for mss; after delivery of completed assignment for illustrators. Buys first rights with reprint option or (in some cases) all rights. Original artwork returned at job's completion. Rates vary ($25 minimum for mss; $250 minimum for art). Sample copy for $5. Guidelines free for SASE.

Tips: "*Babybug* would like to reach as many children's authors and artists as possible for original contributions, but our standards are very high, and we will accept only top-quality material. Before attempting to write for *Babybug*, be sure to familiarize yourself with this age child." (See listings for *Cricket, Cicada, Ladybug, Muse* and *Spider*.)

 BLACK BELT FOR KIDS, Rainbow Publications, P.O. Box 918, Santa Clarita CA 91355-3466. (661)257-4066. Fax: (661)257-3028. **Articles Editor:** Douglas Jeffrey. Bimonthly. Special insert in *Karate/Kung Fu Illustrated* magazine. Estab. 1995. Circ. 35,000. "We publish instructional, inspirational and philosophical pieces written for children who study martial arts."

Nonfiction: Young readers, middle readers, young adults: sports, travel, martial arts. Does not want to see profiles written by parents about their own kid. Buys 10-15 mss/year. Average word length: 800-1,500. Byline given.

How to Contact/Writers: Nonfiction: Query. Reports on queries/mss in 1 month. Publishes ms 6 months after acceptance. Will consider electronic submissions via disk or modem.

Illustration: Reports in 1 month. Samples returned with SASE. Originals returned at job's completion. Credit line given.

Terms: Pays on publication. Buys all rights for mss. Pays $75-200 for articles. Pays illustrators $50-200 for color inside. Pays photographers per photo (range $50-150). Sample copies free for 9×12 SAE and 6 first-class stamps. Writer's guidelines free for SASE.

Tips: "Talk to us first. Make it fun."

BOYS' LIFE, Boy Scouts of America, 1325 W. Walnut Hill Lane, P.O. Box 152079, Irving TX 75015-2079. (214)580-2366. Website: www.bsa.scouting.org. **Editor-in-Chief:** J.D. Owen. **Managing Editor:** W.E. Butter-worth, IV. **Articles Editor:** Michael Goldman. **Fiction Editor:** Shannon Lowry. **Director of Design:** Joseph P. Connolly. **Art Director:** Elizabeth Hardaway Morgan. Monthly magazine. Estab. 1911. Circ. 1,300,000. *Boys' Life* is "a general interest magazine for boys 8 to 18 who are members of the Cub Scouts, Boy Scouts or Explorers; a general interest magazine for all boys."

● *Boys' Life* ranked number 31 on *Writer's Digest's* 1999 Fiction 50, the magazine's annual list of "50 best places to publish your short stories." See Writing for Boys: Is the Gender Barrier Real? to hear from *Boys' Life* editor Michael Goldman.

Fiction: Middle readers: adventure, animal, contemporary, fantasy, history, humor, problem-solving, science fiction, sports, spy/mystery. Does not want to see "talking animals and adult reminiscence." Buys 12 mss/year. Average word length: 1,000-1,500. Byline given.

Nonfiction: "Subject matter is broad. We cover everything from professional sports to American history to how to pack a canoe. A look at a current list of the BSA's more than 100 merit badge pamphlets gives an idea of the wide range of subjects possible. Even better, look at a year's worth of recent issues. Column headings are science, nature, earth, health, sports, space and aviation, cars, computers, entertainment, pets, history, music and others." Average word length: 500-1,500. Columns 300-750 words. Byline given.

How to Contact/Writers: Fiction: Send complete ms with SASE. Nonfiction: query with SASE for response. Reports on queries/mss in 6-8 weeks.

Illustration: Buys 5-7 illustrations/issue; 25-50 illustrations/year. Works on assignment only. Reviews ms/illustration packages from artists. "Query first." Illustrations only: Send tearsheets. Reports on art samples only if interested. Samples returned with SASE. Original artwork returned at job's completion.

Terms: Pays on acceptance. Buys first rights. Pays $750-1,500 for fiction; $150-1,500 for major articles; $150-400 for columns; $250-300 for how-to features. Pays illustrators $1,500-3,000 for color cover; $100-1,500 color inside. Sample copies for $3 plus 9×12 SASE. Writer's/illustrator's/photo guidelines available for SASE.

Tips: "We strongly urge you to study at least a year's issues to better understand the type of material published. Articles for *Boys' Life* must interest and entertain boys ages 8 to 18. Write for a boy you know who is 12. Our readers demand crisp, punchy writing in relatively short, straightforward sentences. The editors demand well-reported articles that demonstrate high standards of journalism. We follow *The New York Times* manual of style and usage. All submissions must be accompanied by SASE with adequate postage."

BOYS' QUEST, The Bluffton News Publishing and Printing Co., 103 N. Main St., Bluffton OH 45817. (419)358-4610. Fax: (419)358-5027. **Articles Editor:** Marilyn Edwards. **Art Submissions:** Becky Jackman. Bimonthly magazine. Estab. 1995. "*Boys' Quest* is a magazine created for boys from 6 to 13 years, with youngsters 8, 9 and 10 the specific target age. Our point of view is that every young boy deserves the right to be a young boy for a number of years before he becomes a young adult. As a result, *Boys' Quest* looks for articles, fiction, nonfiction, and poetry that deal with timeless topics, such as pets, nature, hobbies, science, games, sports, careers, simple cooking, and anything else likely to interest a young boy."

Fiction: Young readers, middle readers: adventure, animal, history, humorous, nature/environment, problem-solving, sports, jokes, building, cooking, cartoons, riddles. Does not want to see violence, teenage themes. Buys 30 mss/year. Average word length: 200-500. Byline given.

Nonfiction: Young readers, middle readers: animal, arts/crafts, biography, cooking, games/puzzles, history, how-to, humorous, math, problem-solving, science. Prefer photo support with nonfiction. Buys 30 mss/year. Average word length: 200-500. Byline given.

Poetry: Reviews poetry. Maximum length: 21 lines. Limit submissions to 6 poems.

How to Contact/Writers: All writers should consult the theme list before sending in articles. To receive current theme list, send a SASE. Fiction/Nonfiction: Query or send complete ms (preferred). Send SASE with correct postage. No faxed material. Reports on queries in 1-2 weeks; mss in 3 weeks (if rejected); 3-4 months (if scheduled). Publishes ms 3 months-3 years after acceptance. Will consider simultaneous submissions and previously published work.

Illustration: Buys 6 illustrations/issue; 36-45 illustrations/year. Uses b&w artwork only. Works on assignment only. Reviews ms/illustration packages from artists. Send ms with dummy. Illustrations only: Query with samples, arrange portfolio review. Send portfolio, tearsheets. Reports in 2 weeks. Samples returned with SASE; samples filed. Credit line given.

Photography: Photos used for support of nonfiction. "Excellent photographs included with a nonfiction story

"I'd never have dreamed my 'claim to fame' would be drawing hidden pictures, but they now appear in nearly a million magazines and newspapers weekly. The best part is I love doing them," says illustrator Liz Ball. This hidden picture drawing was published in *Boys' Quest* magazine. Ball had been doing hidden pictures for years for *Hopscotch* magazine and they naturally thought of her when they wanted to do a similar feature in their new magazine. "I do not have a rep and so far, I've not advertised in any sourcebooks," Ball explains. "I find new markets by reading *Children's Writer's & Illustrator's Market*, attending writing/art conferences, newsletters (SCBWI and *Children's Writer*), and checking the Internet. I also try to follow up with new material after a magazine has used my work—it often turns into a monthly assignment."

is considered very seriously." Model/property releases required. Uses b&w, 5×7 or 3×5 prints. Query with samples; send unsolicited photos by mail. Reports in 2-3 weeks.

Terms: Pays on publication. Buys first North American serial rights for mss. Buys first rights for artwork. Pays 5¢/word for stories and articles. Additional payment for ms/illustration packages and for photos accompanying articles. Pays $150-200 for color cover. Pays photographers per photo (range: $5-10). "*Boys' Quest*, as a new publication, is aware that its rates of payment are modest at this time. But we pledge to increase those rewards in direct proportion to our success. Meanwhile, we will strive to treat our contributors and their work with respect and fairness. That treatment, incidentally, will include quick decision on all submissions." Originals returned to artist at job's completion. Sample copies for $4. Writer's/illustrator's/photo guidelines free for SASE.

Tips: "We are looking for lively writing, most of it from a young boy's point of view—with the boy or boys directly involved in an activity that is both wholesome and unusual. We need nonfiction with photos and fiction stories—around 500 words—puzzles, poems, cooking, carpentry projects, jokes and riddles. Nonfiction pieces that are accompanied by black and white photos are far more likely to be accepted than those that need illustrations. We will entertain simultaneous submissions as long as that fact is noted on the manuscript." (See listing for *Hopscotch*.)

☑ **BREAD FOR GOD'S CHILDREN**, Bread Ministries, Inc., P.O. Box 1017, Arcadia FL 34265-1017. (941)494-6214. Fax: (941)993-0154. E-mail: bread@desoto.net. **Editor:** Judith M. Gibbs. Bimonthly magazine. Estab. 1972. Circ. 10,000 (US and Canada). "*Bread* is designed as a teaching tool for Christian families." 85% of publication aimed at juvenile market.

Fiction: Young readers, middle readers, young adult/teen: adventure, religious, problem-solving, sports. Looks for "teaching stories that portray Christian lifestyles without preaching." Buys approximately 20 mss/year. Average word length: 900-1,500 (for teens); 600-900 (for young children). Byline given.

Nonfiction: Young readers, middle readers: animal. All levels: how-to. "We do not want anything detrimental to solid family values. Most topics will fit if they are slanted to our basic needs." Buys 3-4 mss/year. Average word length: 500-800. Byline given.

Illustration: "The only illustrations we purchase are those occasional good ones coming with a story we accept."

How to Contact/Writers: Fiction/nonfiction: Send complete ms. Reports on mss in 3 weeks-6 months "if considered for use." Will consider simultaneous submissions and previously published work.

Terms: Pays on publication. Pays $10-50 for stories; $25 for articles. Sample copies free for 9×12 SAE and 5 first-class stamps (for 2 copies).

Tips: "We want stories or articles that illustrate overcoming by faith and living solid, Christian lives. Know our publication and what we have used in the past . . . know the readership . . . know the publisher's guidelines. Stories should teach the value of morality and honesty without preaching. Edit carefully for content and grammar."

🅝 **CALIFORNIA CHRONICLES, The Magazine That Makes California History Come Alive**, 555 DeHaro St., Suite 334, San Francisco CA 94107. Website: www.cobblestonepub.com. **Managing Editor:** Ashley Chase. Magazine published 5 times/year. Focuses on California history for ages 9-14.

● *California Chronicles* is theme based. Themes for 2000 include Hollywood and California statehood. See their website for more information or contact the magazine for guidelines and theme list.

Nonfiction: Middle readers: history. Average word length: 1,200.

How to Contact/Writers: Nonfiction: Query.

Tips: See listings for *Appleseeds, Calliope, Cobblestone, Faces, Footsteps* and *Odyssey*.

☑ **CALLIOPE, World History for Kids**, Cobblestone Publishing, Inc., 7 School St., Peterborough NH 03458. (603)924-7209. Website: www.cobblestonepub.com. **Managing Editor:** Lou Waryncia. **Art Director:** Ann Dillon. Magazine published 9 times/year. "*Calliope* covers world history (East/West) and lively, original approaches to the subject are the primary concerns of the editors in choosing material."

● See Writing Effective Query Letters on page 20 for query tips from *Calliope* editor Rosalie Baker.

Fiction: Middle readers and young adults: adventure, folktales, plays, history, biographical fiction. Material must relate to forthcoming themes. Word length: up to 800.

Nonfiction: Middle readers and young adults: arts/crafts, biography, cooking, games/puzzles, history. Material must relate to forthcoming themes. Word length: 300-800.

Poetry: Maximum line length: 100. Wants "clear, objective imagery. Serious and light verse considered."

How to Contact/Writers: "A query must consist of the following to be considered (please use nonerasable paper): a brief cover letter stating subject and word length of the proposed article; a detailed one-page outline explaining the information to be presented in the article; an extensive bibliography of materials the author intends to use in preparing the article; a self-addressed stamped envelope. Writers new to *Calliope* should send a writing sample with query. If you would like to know if your query has been received, please also include a stamped postcard that requests acknowledgment of receipt. In all correspondence, please include your complete address as well as a telephone number where you can be reached. A writer may send as many queries for one issue as he or she wishes, but each query must have a separate cover letter, outline, bibliography and SASE. Telephone queries are not accepted. Handwritten queries will not be considered. Queries may be submitted at any time, but queries sent well in advance of deadline *may not be answered for several months*. Go-aheads requesting material proposed in queries are usually sent five months prior to publication date. Unused queries will be returned approximately three to four months prior to publication date."

Illustration: Illustrations only: Send tearsheets, photocopies. Original work returned upon job's completion (upon written request).

Photography: Buys photos from freelancers. Wants photos pertaining to any forthcoming themes. Uses b&w/ color prints, 35mm transparencies. Send unsolicited photos by mail (on speculation).

Terms: Buys all rights for mss and artwork. Pays 20-25¢/word for stories/articles. Pays on an individual basis for poetry, activities, games/puzzles. "Covers are assigned and paid on an individual basis." Pays photographers per photo ($15-100 for b&w; $25-100 for color). Sample copy for $3.95 and SAE with $1.05 postage. Writer's/ illustrator's/photo guidelines for SASE. (See listings for *Footsteps, Appleseeds, Caliornia Chronicles, Cobblestone, Faces, Footsteps* and *Odyssey*.)

CAMPUS LIFE, Christianity Today, Inc., 465 Gundersen Dr., Carol Stream IL 60188. (630)260-6200. Fax: (630)260-0114. E-mail: cledit@aol.com. Website: www.campuslife.net. **Articles and Fiction Editor:** Chris Lutes. **Art Director:** Doug Johnson. Bimonthly magazine. Estab. 1944. Circ. 100,000. "Our purpose if to help Christian high school students navigate adolescence with their faith intact."

Fiction: Young adults: humorous, problem-solving. Buys 5-6 mss/year. Byline given.

Poetry: Reviews poetry.

How to Contact/Writers: Fiction/nonfiction: Query.

Illustration: Works on assignment only. Reviews illustration packages from artists. Contact: Doug Johnson, design director. Illustrations only: Query; send promo sheet. Contact: Doug Johnson, design director. Reports back only if interested. Credit line given.

Photography: Looking for photos depicting lifestyle/authentic teen experience. Model/property release required. Uses 8×10 glossy prints and 35mm, 2¼×2¼, 4×5 transparencies. Query with samples. Reports only if interested.

Terms: Pays on acceptance. Original artwork returned at job's completion. Writer's/illustrator's/photo guidelines for SASE.

CAREER WORLD, Curriculum Innovations Group, 900 Skokie Blvd., Suite 200, Northbrook IL 60062-4028. (847)205-3000. Fax: (847)564-8197. **Articles Editor:** Carole Rubenstein. **Art Director:** Carl Krach. Monthly (school year) magazine. Estab. 1972. A guide to careers, for students grades 7-12.

Nonfiction: Young adults/teens: education, how-to, interview/profile, career awareness and development. Byline given.

How to Contact/Writers: Nonfiction: Query with published clips and résumé. "We do not want any unsolicited manuscripts." Reports on queries in 2 weeks.

Illustration: Buys 5-10 illustrations/year. Works on assignment only. Reviews ms/illustration packages from artists. Ms/illustration packages and illustration only: Query; send promo sheet and tearsheets. Credit line given.

Photography: Purchases photos from freelancers.

Terms: Pays on publication. Buys all rights for ms. Pays $150 and up for articles. Pays illustrators by the project. Writer's guidelines free, but only on assignment.

⟨N⟩ CAREERS & COLLEGES, E.M. Guild, 989 Avenue of the Americas, New York NY 10018. (212)563-4688. (212)967-2531. Website: www.careersandcolleges.com. **Editorial Director:** Don Rauf. Magazine published 4 times during school year (September, November, January, March). Circ. 100,000. "*Careers & Colleges* provides juniors and seniors in high school with useful, thought-provoking, and hopefully entertaining reading on career choices, higher education and other topics that will help prepare them for life after high school. Content of the magazine includes career features, college (or other post-secondary education) features, coming-of-age columns, career profiles and celebrity interviews."

• *Careers & Colleges* has recently been redesigned.

Nonfiction: Young adults/teens: careers, college, health, how-to, humorous, interview/profile, personal development, problem-solving, social issues, sports, travel. Wants more celebrity profiles. Buys 20-30 mss/year. Average word length: 1,000-1,500. Byline given.

How to Contact/Writers: Nonfiction: Query. Reports on queries in 6 weeks. Will consider electronic submissions via disk or modem.

Illustration: Buys 8 illustrations/issue; buys 32 illustrations/year. Works on assignment only. Reviews ms/ illustration packages from artists. Query first. Illustrations only: Send tearsheets, cards. Reports on art samples in 3 weeks if interested. Original artwork returned at job's completion. Credit line given.

Terms: Pays on acceptance plus 30 days. Buys first North American serial rights. Pays $100-600 for assigned/ unsolicited articles. Additional payment for ms/illustration packages "must be negotiated." Pays $300-1,000 for color illustration; $200-700 for b&w/color inside illustration. Pays photographers by the project. Sample copy $2.50 with SAE and $1.25 postage; writer's guidelines free with SASE.

Tips: "We look for articles with great quotes, good reporting, good writing. Articles must be rich with examples and anecdotes, and must tie in with our mandate to help our teenaged readers plan their futures."

CARUS PUBLISHING COMPANY, P.O. Box 300, Peru IL 61354. See listings for *Babybug*, *Cicada*, *Cricket*, *Ladybug*, *Muse* and *Spider*.

CAT FANCY, The Magazine for Responsible Cat Owners, Fancy Publications, P.O. Box 6050, Mission Viejo CA 92690. (949)855-8822. Fax: (949)855-3045. Website: www.catfancy.com. Monthly magazine. Estab. 1965. Circ. 300,000. "Our magazine is for cat owners who want to know more about how to care for their pets in a responsible manner. We want to see 500-750-word articles showing children relating to or learning about cats in a positive, responsible way. We'd love to see more craft projects for children." 3% of material aimed at juvenile audience.

Fiction: Middle readers, young adults/teens: animal (all cat-related). Does not want to see stories in which cats talk. Buys 2 mss/year. Average word length: 750-1,000. Byline given. Never wants to see work showing cats being treated abusively or irresponsibly or work that puts cats in a negative light. Never use mss written from cats' point of view. Query first.

Nonfiction: Middle readers, young adults/teens: careers, arts/crafts, puzzles, profiles of children who help cats (all cat-related). Buys 3-9 mss/year. Average word length: 450-1,000. Byline given. Would like to see more crafts and how-to pieces for children.

Poetry: Reviews short poems only. "No more than five poems per submission please."

How To Contact/Writers: Fiction/nonfiction: Send query only. Reports on queries in 1-2 months. Publishes ms (juvenile) 4-12 months after acceptance. Send SASE for writer's guidelines.

Illustration: Buys 2-10 illustrations/year. "Most of our illustrations are assigned or submitted with a story. We look for realistic images of cats done with pen and ink (no pencil)." Illustration only: "Submit photocopies of work; samples of spot art possibilities." Samples returned with SASE. Reports in 1-2 months. Credit line given.

Photography: "Cats only, in excellent focus and properly lit. Send SASE for photo needs and submit according to them."

Terms: Pays on publication. Buys first North American serial rights. Buys one-time rights for artwork and photos. Originals returned to artist at job's completion. Pays $50-200 for stories; $75-400 for articles; $35-50 for crafts or puzzles; $20 for poems. Pays illustrators $50-200 for color inside. Photographers paid per photo (range: $35-200). Writer's/artist's/photo guidelines free for #10 SAE and 1 first-class stamp.

Tips: "Perhaps the most important tip we can give is: consider what 9- to 14-year-olds want to know about cats and what they enjoy most about cats, and address that topic in a style appropriate for them. Writers, keep your writing concise, and don't be afraid to try again after a rejection. Illustrators, we use illustrations mainly as spot art; occasionally we make assignments to illustrators whose spot art we've used before."

 CATHOLIC FAITH & FAMILY, Circle Media, 33 Rossotto Dr., Hamden CT 06514. (203)288-5600. Fax: (203)288-5157. E-mail: editor@twincircle.com. **Articles Editor:** Loretta G. Seyer. **Art Director:** Tom Brophy. Biweekly tabzine. Estab. 1965. Circ. 18,000. 5% of publication aimed at children.

Nonfiction: Buys hundreds of mss/year. Average word length: 450-2,000. Byline given.

How to Contact/Writers: Nonfiction: Send complete ms. Reports on queries in 2 months; mss in 6 months. Will consider electronic submission via disk or modem.

Illustration: Uses color artwork only. Reviews ms/illustration packages from artists. Query; send ms with dummy. Illustrations only: Query with samples. Contact: Loretta G. Seyer, editor. Reports in 3 months. Samples returned with SASE. Credit line given.

Photography: Needs photos depicting family-oriented activities. Uses color glossy prints and 35mm, 2¼×2¼, 4×5 or 8×10 transparencies. Query with samples; call. Reports in 3 months.

Terms: Pays on publication. Buys first North American rights. Buys one-time rights for artwork. Original artwork returned at job's completion. Pays $75-300 for articles. Pays illustrators $75-100 for color cover; $25-50 for color inside. Pays photographers per photo. Sample copies for SASE. Writer's/illustrator's/photo guidelines for SASE.

Tips: "We need photos of families—parents, kids, grandparents and combos for our publication. They should be showing a variety of emotions and activities."

CHILD LIFE, Children's Better Health Institute, P.O. Box 567, Indianapolis IN 46206. Parcels and packages: please send to 1100 Waterway Blvd., 46202. (317)636-8881. **Editor:** Lise Hoffman. **Art Director:** Phyllis Lybarger. Magazine published 8 times/year. Estab. 1921. Circ. 80,000. Targeted toward kids ages 9-11. Focuses on health, sports, fitness, nutrition, safety, general interests, and the nostalgia of *Child Life's* early days. "We publish jokes, riddles and poems by children." Kids should include name, address, phone number (for office use) and school photo. "No mass duplicated, multiple submissions."

"PICTURE-ORIENTED MATERIAL" is for preschoolers to 8-year-olds; "Young readers" are for 5- to 8-year-olds; "Middle readers" are for 9- to 11-year-olds; and "Young adults/teens" are for ages 12 and up. Age ranges may vary slightly from magazine to magazine.

• *Child Life* is no longer accepting manuscripts for publication. See listings for *Children's Digest, Children's Playmate, Humpty Dumpty's Magazine, Jack And Jill, Turtle Magazine* and *U*S*Kids*.

Tips: "We use kids' submissions from our age range—9 to 11. Those older or younger should try one of our sister publications: *Children's Digest, Children's Playmate, Humpty Dumpty's Magazine, Jack And Jill, Turtle Magazine, U*S*Kids*."

CHILDREN'S BETTER HEALTH INSTITUTE, 1100 Waterway Blvd., P.O. Box 567, Indianapolis IN 46206. See listings for *Child Life, Children's Digest, Children's Playmate, Humpty Dumpty's Magazine, Jack and Jill, Turtle* and *U*S* Kids*.

☑ **CHILDREN'S DIGEST**, Children's Better Health Institute, 1100 Waterway Blvd., Box 567, Indianapolis IN 46206. (317)634-1100. **Editor:** Mark Tipton. **Art Director:** Penny Rasdall. Magazine published 8 times/year. Estab. 1950. Circ. 110,000. For preteens; approximately 33% of content is health-related.
• *Children's Digest* would like to see more photo stories about current events and topical matters and more nonfiction in general. Currently not accepting unsolicited manuscripts.
Fiction: Adventure, humorous, mainstream, mystery. Stories should appeal to both boys and girls. "We need some stories that incorporate a health theme. However, we don't want stories that preach, preferring instead stories with implied morals. We like a light or humorous approach."
Nonfiction: Historical, craft ideas, health, nutrition, fitness and sports. "We're especially interested in factual features that teach readers about fitness and sports or encourage them to develop better health habits. We are *not* interested in material that is simply rewritten from encyclopedias. We try to present our health material in a way that instructs *and* entertains the reader."
Poetry: Accepts poetry.
How to Contact/Writers: *Currently not accepting unsolicited mss.*
Photography: State availability of full color or b&w photos. Model releases and identification of subjects required.
Terms: Pays on publication. Buys all rights. Pays up to 12¢/word for articles/stories. Pays $25 minimum for poetry.
Tips: See listings for *Children's Playmate, Children's Digest, Humpty Dumpty's Magazine, Jack and Jill, Turtle Magazine* and *U*S*Kids*.

CHILDREN'S PLAYMATE, Children's Better Health Institute, 1100 Waterway Blvd., Box 567, Indianapolis IN 46206. (317)636-8881. **Editor:** Terry Harshman. **Art Director:** Chuck Horsman. Magazine published 8 times/year. Estab. 1929. Circ. 135,000. For children ages 6-8 years; approximately 50% of content is health-related.
Fiction: Young readers: animal, contemporary, fantasy, folktales, history, humorous, science fiction, sports, suspense/mystery/adventure. Buys 25 mss/year. Average word length: 300-700. Byline given.
Nonfiction: Young readers: arts/crafts, biography, cooking, games/puzzles, health, history, how-to, humorous, safety, science, sports. Buys 16-20 mss/year. Average word length: 300-500. Byline given.
Poetry: Maximum length: 20-25 lines.
How to Contact/Writers: Fiction/nonfiction: Send complete ms. Reports on mss in 2-3 months.
Illustration: Works on assignment only. Reviews ms/illustration packages from artists. Query first.
Photography: Buys photos with accompanying ms only. Model/property releases required; captions required. Uses 35mm transparencies. Send completed ms with transparencies.
Terms: Pays on publication for illustrators and writers. Buys all rights for mss and artwork; one-time rights for photos. Pays 17¢/word for stories. Pays $275 for color cover illustration; $35-90 for b&w inside; $70-155 for color inside. Pays photographers per photo (range: $10-75). Sample copy $1.75. Writer's/illustrator's guidelines for SASE.
Tips: See listings for *Child Life, Children's Digest, Humpty Dumpty's Magazine, Jack and Jill, Turtle Magazine* and *U*S* Kids*.

CHIRP, The Owl Group, 179 John St., Suite 500, Toronto, Ontario M5T 3G5 Canada. E-mail: owl@owl.on.ca. Website: www.owl.on.ca. **Editor-in-chief:** Marybeth Leatherdale. **Creative Director:** Tim Davin. Published monthly during school year. Discovery magazine for children ages 2-6. "*Chirp* aims to introduce preschool non-readers to reading for pleasure about the world around them."
Fiction: Picture-oriented material: nature/environment, adventure, animal, multicultural, problem-solving, sports. Word length: 250 maximum.
Nonfiction: Picture-oriented material: fun, easy craft ideas, animal, games/puzzles, how-to, multicultural, nature/environment, problem-solving.
Poetry: Wants rhymes and poetry. Maximum length: 8 lines.
How to Contact/Writers: Query. Reports on queries/mss in 1 month.
Illustration: Uses approximately 15 illustrations/issue; 135 illustrations/year. Samples returned with SASE. Originals returned at job's completion. Credit line given.
Terms: Pays on acceptance. Buys all rights. Pays on publication. Pays writers $250 (Canadian); illustrators $150-650 (Canadian); photographers paid per photo $150-375 (Canadian). Sample copies available for $4 (Canadian).
Tips: "Chirp editors prefer to read completed manuscripts of stories and articles, accompanied by photographs

Listening to the buzz of a generation of teens

Teenagers are bugged by many aspects of the transitional period in life known as "young adulthood." With new privileges come responsibilities that carry even more restrictions. They juggle part-time jobs with schoolwork and relationships, while pop culture bombards them with messages persuading them to buy CDs, facial creams, the right clothes—anything and everything to fit in the right scene.

Deborah Vetter

For teenagers interested in reading, this may become a frustrating time because literature, the subject that once encouraged their imaginations and challenged them to learn and read more, becomes "required reading" for term papers and exams. Carus Publishing, creator of *Babybug*, *Ladybug*, *Muse*, *Spider* and *Cricket*, has synthesized a new species that promises to keep teens interested in literature with *Cicada*, a literary magazine for young adults.

Deborah Vetter, editor of *Cicada*, explains that the publication is unique because it's about literature with a genuine teen sensibility. "Unlike many other magazines for teens, it does not contain dating and makeup tips or interviews with movie stars. What it does have is a variety of witty, thought-provoking, well-written short stories, poems and essays both by adult authors and by teenagers themselves."

Cicada features fiction, poetry, essays, book reviews and short stories "presented in a sophisticated cartoon format." Vetter notes, "as with our younger 'bug' magazines, we hope to cover nearly all genres, from contemporary coming-of-age stories to historical fiction, mystery and detective stories, adventure, science fiction and fantasy, humor, personal experiences and so on."

Cicada was formed because of a concern Marianne Carus, editor-in-chief, had for *Cricket* readers who had outgrown the material and "wanted something more advanced for teenagers." Vetter also respects the opinions of her readers, takes advice from them and publishes their thoughts and ideas in a "Letters" section of *Cicada*, a point that should be noted by any author submitting to the publication.

Vetter suggests authors approach writing for young adults "from inside the teen psyche" in order to create protagonists readers can sympathize with. "To have a teenager railing bitterly against the unfairness of life because he or she can't go to the prom or can't borrow the car seems very trite. The teen comes across as a selfish, shallow person nobody could possibly like," she explains. "There has to be a certain logic to a protagonist's behavior so the reader can be on that character's side and understand what's going on underneath the surface."

Another recommendation Vetter offers is that authors "think in terms of writing for adults, but about experiences and situations that are relevant or interesting to teenagers." She points

May/June 1999

Cicada®

$7.95 $9.95 in Canada

The Cricket Magazine Group editor-in-chief Marianne Carus created *Cicada* to offer more advanced material to former *Cricket* readers who had outgrown the magazine. "Unlike many other magazines for teens, it does not contain dating and makeup tips or interviews with movie stars," says editor Deborah Vetter. "It does have a variety of witty, thought-provoking, well-written short stories, poems and essays by adult authors and by teenagers themselves. We hope to cover nearly all genres, from contemporary coming-of-age stories to historical fiction, mystery and detective stories, adventure, science fiction and fantasy, humor and personal experiences."

out that teenagers are interested in adult novels and want to be challenged by literary style and treatment of subject matter. "Another problem I'm seeing deals with clichés, most specifically the handsome brawny jock and the blond with the perfect bod and no brain. Avoid them."

Understanding that *Cicada* is literature for young adults brings up the concern of what is "appropriate" subject matter. An author may wonder what's too mature, or what's not mature enough, and for that same reason there have been some "alarmed" parents and some "twelve-year-olds who've found they're not quite ready for *Cicada*," Vetter says.

An example of this conflict came in the responses Vetter received after *Cicada* reprinted "I Had Seen Castles," a Cynthia Rylant story set during World War II. "We got letters from a handful of angry parents who called the story trash because of a few lines about a young, unmarried couple having sex before the boy went off to Europe to fight as a soldier in the war," recalls Vetter. At the same time, she received a letter from a college student who, due to the eye-opening atrocities Rylant portrays in the story's battle scenes, turned away from embracing violent images, "saying she now understood that 'people weren't meant to be blown open.'

"So, I find myself wondering who got the point of Rylant's story: the parents alarmed at a few lines about sex or the teenager who realized that war is a horrifying experience. Who is the more sophisticated reader?

"We are presenting high-quality literature, but it's going to be literature that often deals with some of the subjects we've considered 'taboo' in our younger magazines. These topics include war and violence, dating relationships, sex, drugs and domestic abuse." However, she adds, " The one topic we won't be addressing is teen suicide—it seems much too dangerous an issue."

While *Cicada* delves into some of the harsher realities of life, Vetter and her readers admit to a need for humor in their reading. "After reading the first few issues, one reader wrote, 'I think just maybe you are overestimating the angst of today's teenagers,' " says Vetter. "As you can probably guess, we're seeing a lot of angst-ridden stories, and we'd like to encourage authors to lighten up. Park death at the door, and explore human foibles. Snap your fingers at life's absurdities. While doing this, however, avoid the trivial and the superficial."

Besides the need for more stories that can bring a smile to her reader's faces, Vetter is searching for authors who can "explore less-obvious genres" such as mystery and adventure. "And our readers want them," she says. "One teenage boy even wrote plaintively to ask, 'Can't we have a story where the hero rides around having adventures and grows up at the same time?' " Teenagers are undoubtedly interested in growing up and Vetter would like to have some first-person experiences from adults on topics such as military, Peace Corps or college life, or a first "real" job. "It's intriguing to see what other people have learned, what insights they've gained, during their crucial years of 'growing-up'—a process that extends far beyond adolescence."

In addition, Vetter would like to feature some "300- to 700-word book reviews that provide thoughtful, in-depth commentary on adult or YA books" and also coordinate graphic novels or short stories in a "comix" format. *Cicada* uses black-and-white interior illustrations and full-color covers, notes Vetter. "We are always looking for new illustrators and fresh artistic styles."

Cicada also accepts submissions from its readers and treats them the same as adult authors. "Many of the submissions we receive from teenage authors are perceptive, funny, original and very well written," says Vetter. "We also want to nurture teen artists by publishing their work as spot illustrations throughout the issue. We respect our teen authors and artists and pay them at the same rate we pay our adult authors and illustrators."

For sophisticated young adults with a literature bug, there is a *Cicada* out there waiting for them to spread its pages and let it fly through their imaginations. For authors writing for young adults, there is a challenge to understand the buzz of a generation and be part of its song. Don't put a pin through your readers, simplifying their traits and categorizing them—watch them in their complicated, confused, exhilarating, foolhardy, beautiful flight and respect them for getting off the ground.

—*Eric Burdsall*

or suggestions of visual references where they are appropriate. All craft ideas should be based on materials that are found around the average household." See listings for *Chickadee* and *OWL*.

CICADA, Carus Publishing Company, P.O. Box 300, 315 Fifth St., Peru IL 61354. (815)224-6656. Fax: (815)224-6615. E-mail: CICADA@caruspub.com. Website: www.cicadamag.com. **Editor-in-Chief:** Marianne Carus. **Editor:** Deborah Vetter. **Senior Editor:** John D. Allen. **Senior Art Director:** Ron McCutchan. Bimonthly magazine. Estab. 1998. *Cicada* publishes fiction and poetry with a genuine teen sensibility, aimed at the high school and college-age market. The editors are looking for stories and poems that are thought-provoking but entertaining.
Fiction: Young adults: adventure, animal, contemporary, fantasy, history, humorous, multicultural, nature/environment, romance, science fiction, sports, suspense/mystery, stories that will adapt themselves to a sophisticated cartoon, or graphic novel format. Buys up to 60 mss/year. Average word length: about 5,000 words for short stories; up to 15,000 for novellas only—we run one novella per issue.
Nonfiction: Young adults: first-person, coming-of-age experiences that are relevant to teens and young adults (example-life in the Peace Corps). Buys 6 mss/year. Average word length: about 5,000 words. Byline given.
Poetry: Reviews serious, humorous, free verse, rhyming (if done well) poetry. Maximum length: up to 25 lines. Limit submissions to 5 poems.
How to Contact/Writers: Fiction/nonfiction: send complete ms. Reports on mss in 8-10 weeks. Publishes ms 1-2 years after acceptance. Will consider simultaneous submissions if author lets us know.
Illustration: Buys 20 illustrations/issue; 120 illustrations/year. Uses color artwork for cover; b&w for interior. Works on assignment only. Reviews ms/illustration packages from artists. Send ms with 1-2 sketches and samples of other finished art. Contact: Ron McCutchan, senior art director. Illustrations only: Query with samples. Contact: Ron McCutchan, senior art director. Reports in 6 weeks. Samples returned with SASE; samples filed. Credit line given.
Photography: Wants documentary photos (clear shots that illustrate specific artifacts, persons, locations, phenomena, etc., cited in the text) and "art" shots of teens in photo montage/lighting effects etc. Uses b&w 4×5 glossy prints. Submit portfolio for review. Reports in 6 weeks.
Terms: Pays on publication. Buys first rights for mss. Buys one-time, first publication rights for artwork and photographs. Pays up to 25¢/word for mss; up to $3/line for poetry. Pays illustrators $750 for color cover; $50-150 for b&w inside. Pays photographers per photo (range: $50-150). Sample copies for $8.50. Writer's/illustrator's/photo guidelines for SASE.
Tips: "Please don't write for a junior high audience. We're looking for good character development, strong plots, and thought-provoking themes for young people in high school and collge. Don't forget humor!" (See listings for *Babybug, Cricket, Ladybug, Muse* and *Spider*.)

CLASS ACT, Class Act, Inc., P.O. Box 802, Henderson KY 42419-0802. E-mail: classact@henderson.net. Website: www.henderson.net/~classact. **Articles Editor:** Susan Thurman. Monthly, September-May. Newsletter. Estab. 1993. Circ. 300. "We are looking for practical, ready-to-use ideas for the English/language arts classroom (grades 6-12)."
Nonfiction: Young adults/teens: games/puzzles, how-to. Does not want to see esoteric material; no master's theses; no poetry (except articles about how to write poetry). Buys 20 mss/year. Average word length: 200-2,000. Byline given.
How to Contact/Writers: Send complete ms. E-mail submissions and submissions on disk using Word encouraged. Reports on queries/mss in 1 month. Usually publishes ms 3-12 months after acceptance. Will consider simultaneous submissions. Must send SASE.
Terms: Pays on acceptance. Pays $10-40 per article. Buys all rights. Sample copy for $3 and SASE.
Tips: "We're only interested in language arts-related articles for teachers and students. Writers need to realize

teens often need humor in classroom assignments. In addition, we are looking for teacher-tested ideas that have already worked in the classroom. We currently have more puzzles than we need and are looking for prose rather than puzzles. Be clever. We've already seen a zillion articles on homonyms and haikus. If a SASE isn't sent, we'll assume you don't want a response."

COBBLESTONE PUBLISHING, INC., 7 School St., Peterborough NH 03458. See listings for *Appleseeds*, *California Chronicles*, *Calliope*, *Cobblestone*, *Faces*, *Footsteps* and *Odyssey*.

COBBLESTONE, Discover American History, Cobblestone Publishing Co., 30 Grove St., Suite C, Peterborough NH 03458. (603)924-7209. Fax: (603)924-7380. Website: www.cobblestonepub.com. **Editor:** Meg Chorlian. **Art Director:** Ann Dillon. **Managing Editor:** Denise L. Babcock. Magazine published 9 times/year. Circ. 36,000. "*Cobblestone* is theme-related. Writers should request editorial guidelines which explain procedure and list upcoming themes. Queries must relate to an upcoming theme. It is recommended that writers become familiar with the magazine (sample copies available)."

● At presstime, *Cobblestone* was revising their writers guidelines. See their website for updated information. Themes for 2000-2001 include: The White House. Jefferson Davis and the Panama Canal. Contact them for a complete theme list or visit their website.

Nonfiction: Middle readers (school ages 8-14): activities, biography, games/puzzles (no word finds), history (world and American), interview/profile, science, travel. All articles must relate to the issue's theme. Buys 120 mss/year. Average word length: 600-800. Byline given.

Poetry: Up to 100 lines. "Clear, objective imagery. Serious and light verse considered." Pays on an individual basis. Must relate to theme.

How to Contact/Writers: Fiction/nonfiction: Query. "A query must consist of all of the following to be considered: a brief cover letter stating the subject and word length of the proposed article, a detailed one-page outline explaining the information to be presented in the article, an extensive bibliography of materials the author intends to use in preparing the article, a self-addressed stamped envelope. Writers new to *Cobblestone* should send a writing sample with query. If you would like to know if your query has been received, please also include a stamped postcard that requests acknowledgment of receipt. In all correspondence, please include your complete address as well as a telephone number where you can be reached. A writer may send as many queries for one issue as he or she wishes, but each query must have a separate cover letter, outline, bibliography and SASE. Telephone queries are not accepted. Handwritten queries will not be considered. Queries may be submitted at any time, but queries sent well in advance of deadline *may not be answered for several months*. Go-aheads requesting material proposed in queries are usually sent five months prior to publication date. Unused queries will be returned approximately three to four months prior to publication date."

Illustration: Buys 4 color illustrations/issue; 36 illustrations/year. Preferred theme or style: Material that is simple, clear and accurate but not too juvenile. Sophisticated sources are a must. Works on assignment only. Reviews ms/illustration packages from artists. Query. CIllustrations only: Send photocopies, tearsheets, or other nonreturnable samples. "Illustrators should consult issues of *Cobblestone* to familiarize themselves with our needs." Reports on art samples in 2 weeks. Samples returned with SASE; samples not filed. Original artwork returned at job's completion (upon written request). Credit line given.

Photography: Photos must relate to upcoming themes. Send transparencies and/or color prints. Submit on speculation.

Terms: Pays on publication. Buys all rights to articles and artwork. Pays 20-25¢/word for articles/stories. Pays on an individual basis for poetry, activities, games/puzzles. Pays photographers per photo ($15-100 for b&w; $25-100 for color). Sample copy $4.95 with 7½×10½ SAE and 5 first-class stamps; writer's/illustrator's/photo guidelines free with SAE and 1 first-class stamp.

Tips: Writers: "Submit detailed queries which show attention to historical accuracy and which offer interesting and entertaining information. Study past issues to know what we look for. All feature articles, recipes, activities, fiction and supplemental nonfiction are freelance contributions." Illustrators: "Submit color samples, not too juvenile. Study past issues to know what we look for. The illustration we use is generally for stories, recipes and activities." (See listings for *Appleseeds*, *California Chronicles*, *Calliope*, *Faces*, *Footsteps* and *Odyssey*.)

✔ **COLLEGE BOUND MAGAZINE**, Ramholtz Publishing, Inc., 2071 Clove Rd., Staten Island NY 10304. (718)273-5700. Fax: (718)273-2539. E-mail: editorial@collegebound.net. Website: www.collegebound.net. **Articles Editor:** Gina LaGuardia. **Art Director:** Giulio Rammairone. Monthly magazine and website. Estab. 1987. Circ. 75,000 (regional); 750,000 (national). *College Bound Magazine* is written by college students for high school juniors and seniors. It is designed to provide an inside view of college life, with college students from around the country serving as correspondents. The magazine's editorial content offers its teen readership personal accounts on all aspects of college, from living with a roommate, choosing a major, and joining a fraternity or sorority, to college dating, interesting courses, beating the financial aid fuss, and other college-bound concerns. *College Bound Magazine* is published six times regionally throughout the tri-state area. Special issues include the Annual National Edition (published each February) and Fall and Spring California and Chicago issues. The magazine also has an award-winning World Wide Web site, *CollegeBound.NET*, at www.collegebound.net.

Nonfiction: Young adults: careers, college prep, fashion, health, how-to, interview/profile, problem-solving, social issues, college life. Buys 70 mss/year. Average word length: 400-1,100 words. Byline given.

How to Contact/Writers: Nonfiction: Query with published clips. Reports on queries in 5 weeks; mss in 5-6 weeks. Publishes ms 2-3 months after acceptance. Will consider electronic submission via disk or modem, previously published work (as long as not a competitor title).

Illustration: Buys 2-3 illustrations/issue. Uses color artwork only. Works on assignment only. Reviews ms/illustration packages from artists. Query. Contact: Giulio Rammarone, art director. Illustrations only: Query with samples. Reports in 2 months. Samples kept on file. Credit line given.

Terms: Pays on publication. Buys first North American serial rights, all rights or reprint rights for mss. Buys first rights for artwork. Originals returned if requested, with SASE. Pays $25-100 for articles 30 days upon publication. All contributors receive 2 issues with payment. Pays illustrators $25-125 for color inside. Sample copies free for #10 SASE and $3 postage. Writer's guidelines for SASE.

Tips: "Review the sample issue and get a good feel for the types of articles we accept and our tone and purpose."

CONTACT KIDS, (formerly *3-2-1 Contact*), Children's Television Workshop, One Lincoln Plaza, New York NY 10023. (212)595-3456.
 • *Contact Kids* uses a small amount of freelance material. They do not accept unsolicited manuscripts.

☑ **COUNSELOR**, Cook Communications Ministries, P.O. Box 36640, Colorado Springs CO 80936. (719)536-0100 or (800)708-5550. Fax: (719)533-3045. E-mail: burtonj@cookministries.org. **Editor:** Janice K. Burton. **Art Director:** Randy Maid. Newspaper distributed weekly; published quarterly. Estab. 1940. "Audience: children 8-10 years. Papers designed to present everyday living stories showing the difference Christ can make in a child's life. Must have a true Christian slant, not just a moral implication. Correlated with Scripture Press Sunday School curriculum."

Fiction: Middle readers: adventure, animal, contemporary, history, humorous, multicultural, nature/environment, problem-solving, religious, sports (all with a strong Christian context). "Appreciate well-written fiction that shows knowledge of our product. Suggest people write for samples." Buys approximately 12 mss/year. Average word length: 850. Byline given.

Nonfiction: Middle readers: animals, arts/crafts, biography, games/puzzles, geography, health, history, hobbies, how-to, humorous, interview/profile, multicultural, nature/environment, problem-solving, religion, science, social issues, sports (all with Christian context). Buys approximately 12 mss/year. Average word length: 300-350. Byline given.

How to Contact/Writers: Fiction/nonfiction: Send complete ms, hard copy and #10 SAE for reply. Reports on mss in 6-8 weeks. Publishes ms 1-2 years after acceptance ("we work a year in advance"). Will consider previously published work.

Illustrations: Buys approximately 1-2 illustrations/issue; 12-20 illustrations/year. Credit line given.

Terms: Pays on acceptance. Buys second (reprint) rights, one-time rights, or all rights for mss. Pays 7-10¢/word for stories or articles, depending on amount of editing required. Sample copies for #10 SAE and 1 first-class stamp. Writers guidelines for SASE.

Tips: "Send copy that is as polished as possible. Indicate if story is true. Indicate rights offered. Stick to required word lengths. Include Social Security number on manuscript. Write for tips for writers, sample copies and theme lists."

☑ **CRAYOLA KIDS: Family Time Fun**, Meredith Custom Publishing, 1716 Locust St., Des Moines IA 50309-3023. (515)284-3474. **Articles Editor:** Mary Heaton. **Art Director:** Bob Riley. Bimonthly magazine. Estab. 1994. Circ. 550,000. "The mission of *Crayola Kids: Family Time Fun*, is to enrich the lives of families with young children (ages 3-10) by encouraging creative fun and the joy of discovery through reading. Each bimonthly issue focuses on a single theme and features a full-length reprint of a previously published picture book (trade book) and related puzzles, crafts and activities."

Nonfiction: Picture-oriented material, young readers: animal, arts/crafts, games/puzzles, how-to, multicultural, nature/environment, science, travel. "Seasonal tie-ins are a plus. Best opportunities are in crafts and family activities." Does not want to see biographies. Buys 20-30 mss/year. Average word length: 250. Byline given.

How to Contact/Writers: Nonfiction: Query. Reports on queries in 6-8 weeks. Reports on mss in 2-3 months.

Illustration: Only interested in agented material.

Terms: Pays on acceptance. Buys all rights for mss. Pays $15-200 for articles. "Depends on subject, length, complexity, originality." Sample copies for $3.50 plus SASE (large enough to hold a magazine).

Tips: "We are interested in highly creative multicultural, nonsexist activities, visual puzzles, games and craft ideas related to the theme or seasonality of an issue. Submit a sample of a craft or a Polaroid shot of it. Tell us your story or activity idea and what's unique and fun about it. Convince us that kids will love reading it, doing it, or making it. Study the magazine. Query for theme list."

CRICKET MAGAZINE, Carus Publishing, Company, P.O. Box 300, Peru IL 61354. (815)224-6656. **Articles/Fiction Editor-in-Chief:** Marianne Carus. **Editor:** Deborah Vetter. **Senior Editor:** John D. Allen. **Art Director:** Ron McCutchan. Monthly magazine. Estab. 1973. Circ. 71,000. Children's literary magazine for ages 9-14.

Fiction: Middle readers, young adults/teens: adventure, animal, contemporary, fantasy, folk and fairy tales, history, humorous, multicultural, nature/environment, science fiction, sports, suspense/mystery. Buys 140 mss/year. Maximum word length: 2,000. Byline given.

Nonfiction: Middle readers, young adults/teens: animal, arts/crafts, biography, environment, experiments, games/puzzles, history, how-to, interview/profile, natural science, problem-solving, science and technology, space, sports, travel. Multicultural needs include articles on customs and cultures. Requests bibliography with submissions. Buys 40 mss/year. Average word length: 1,200. Byline given.

Poetry: Reviews poems, 1-page maximum length. Limit submissions to 5 poems or less.

How to Contact/Writers: Send complete ms. Do not query first. Reports on mss in 2-3 months. Does not like but will consider simultaneous submissions. SASE required for response.

Illustration: Buys 35 illustrations (14 separate commissions)/issue; 425 illustrations/year. Uses b&w and full-color work. Preferred theme or style: "strong realism; strong people, especially kids; good action illustration; no cartoons. All media, but prefer other than pencil." Reviews ms/illustration packages from artists "but reserves option to re-illustrate." Send complete ms with sample and query. Illustrations only: Provide tearsheets or good quality photocopies to be kept on file. SASE required for response/return of samples. Reports on art samples in 2 months.

Photography: Purchases photos with accompanying ms only. Model/property releases required. Uses color transparencies, b&w glossy prints.

Terms: Pays on publication. Buys first publication rights in the English language. Buys first publication rights plus promotional rights for artwork. Original artwork returned at job's completion. Pays up to 25¢/word for unsolicited articles; up to $3/line for poetry. Pays $750 for color cover; $75-150 for b&w, $150-250 for color inside. Pays $750 for color cover; $75-150 for b&w, $150-250 for color inside. Writer's/illustrator's guidelines for SASE.

Tips: Writers: "Read copies of back issues and current issues. Adhere to specified word limits. *Please* do not query." Illustrators: "Edit your samples. Send only your best work and be able to reproduce that quality in assignments. Put name and address on *all* samples. Know a publication before you submit—is your style appropriate?" (See listings for *Babybug*, *Cicada*, *Ladybug*, *Muse* and *Spider*.)

CRUSADER, Calvinist Cadet Corps, P.O. Box 7259, Grand Rapids MI 49510. (616)241-5616. Fax: (616)241-5558. **Editor:** G. Richard Broene. **Art Director:** Robert DeJonge. Magazine published 7 times/year. Circ. 13,000. "Our magazine is for members of the Calvinist Cadet Corps—boys aged 9-14. Our purpose is to show how God is at work in their lives and in the world around them. Our magazine offers nonfiction articles and fast-moving fiction—everything to appeal to interests and concerns of boys, teaching Christian values subtly."

Fiction: Middle readers, young adults/teens: adventure, humorous, multicultural, problem-solving, religious, sports. Buys 12 mss/year. Average word length: 900-1,500.

Nonfiction: Middle readers, young adults/teens: arts/crafts, games/puzzles, hobbies, how-to, humorous, interview/profile, problem-solving, science, sports. Buys 6 mss/year. Average word length: 400-900.

How to Contact/Writers: Fiction/nonfiction: Send complete ms. Reports on queries in 2-4 weeks; on mss in 1-2 months. Will consider simultaneous submissions.

Illustration: Buys 1 illustration/issue; buys 6 illustrations/year. Works on assignment only. Reviews ms/illustration packages from artists. Reports in 3-5 weeks. Samples returned with SASE. Originals returned to artist at job's completion. Credit line given.

Photography: Buys photos from freelancers. Wants nature photos and photos of boys.

Terms: Pays on acceptance. Buys first North American serial rights; reprint rights. Pays 4-5¢/word for stories/articles. Pays illustrators $50-200 for b&w/color cover or b&w inside. Sample copy free with 9×12 SAE and 4 first-class stamps.

Tips: "Our publication is mostly open to fiction; send SASE for a list of themes (available yearly in January). We use mostly fast-moving fiction that appeals to a boy's sense of adventure or sense of humor. Avoid preachiness; avoid simplistic answers to complicated problems; avoid long dialogue with little action. Articles on sports, outdoor activities, bike riding, science, crafts, etc. should emphasize a Christian perspective, but avoid simplistic moralisms."

THE CRYSTAL BALL, The Starwind Press, P.O. Box 98, Ripley OH 45167. (937)392-4549. **Articles/Fiction Editor:** Marlene Powell. Quarterly magazine. Estab. 1997. Circ. 1,000. Publishes science fiction and fantasy for young adults.

Fiction: Young adults: fantasy, folktale, science fiction. Buys 8-12 mss/year. Average word length: 1,500-5,000. Byline given.

Nonfiction: Young adults: biography, how-to, interview/profile, science. Buys 8-12 mss/year. Average word length: 1,000-3,000.

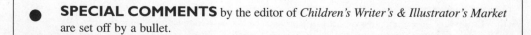

● **SPECIAL COMMENTS** by the editor of *Children's Writer's & Illustrator's Market* are set off by a bullet.

Poetry: Only publishes poetry by kids.
How to Contact/Writers: Fiction: send complete ms. Nonfiction: query. Reports on queries and mss in 2-3 months. Publishes ms 6-12 months after acceptance. Will consider previously published work if published in noncompeting market.
Illustration: Buys 6-10 illustrations/issue; 12-15 illustrations/year. Uses b&w camera ready artwork only. Works on assignment only. Reviews ms/illustration packages from artists. Send ms with dummy. Contact: Marlene Powell, editor. Illustrations only: query with samples. Contact: Marlene Powell, editor. Reports in 2-3 months if SASE enclosed. Samples kept on file. Credit line given.
Photography: Looking for photos to illustrate nonfiction pieces. Uses b&w, line shots or already screened. Reports in 2-3 months.
Terms: Pays on acceptance. Buys first North American serial rights for mss, artwork and photos. Original artwork returned at job's completion if requested. Pays $5-20 for stories and articles. Additional payment for photos accompanying article. Pays illustrators $5-20 for b&w inside and cover. Pays photographers per photo (range: $5-20). Sample copies for $3. Writer's/illustrator's guidelines for SASE.

N CURRENT HEALTH I, The Beginning Guide to Health Education, 900 Skokie Blvd., Suite 200, Northbrook IL 60062-4028. (847)205-3000. Fax: (847)564-8197. E-mail: crubenstein@glcomm.com. **Editor:** Carole Rubenstein. Published 8 times/year; monthly during school year September-May magazine. "For classroom use by students, this magazine is curriculum-specific and requires experienced educators/health writers who can write clearly and well at fifth grade reading level."
Nonfiction: Middle-grade readers: health. Buys 60-70 mss/year. Average word length: 1,000. Byline given.
How to Contact/Writers: Nonfiction: Query with published clips and résumé. Publishes ms 4-6 months after acceptance.
Illustration: Works on assignments only. Query with samples. Samples returned with SASE; samples filed. Originals returned at job's completion. Credit line given.
Terms: Pays on publication. Buys all rights. Pays $150, "more for longer features."
Tips: Needs material about drug education, nutrition, fitness and exercise, disease, psychology, first aid and safety. Articles are assigned to freelance writers on specific topics.

☑ DISCOVERIES, Children's Ministries, 6401 The Paseo, Kansas City MO 64131. (816)333-7000. Fax: (816)333-4439. E-mail: vfolsom@nazarene.org. **Editor:** Virginia Folsom. **Executive Editor:** Beula Postlewait. **Assistant Editor:** Kathleen M. Johnson. Weekly tabloid. "*Discoveries* is a leisure-reading piece for third and fourth graders. It is published weekly by WordAction Publishing. The major purpose of the magazine is to provide a leisure-reading piece which will build Christian behavior and values and provide reinforcement for Biblical concepts taught in the Sunday School curriculum. The focus of the reinforcement will be life-related, with some historical appreciation. *Discoveries'* target audience is children ages eight to ten in grades three and four. The readability goal is third to fourth grade."
Fiction: Middle readers: adventure, contemporary, humorous, religious. "Fiction—stories should vividly portray definite Christian emphasis or character-building values, without being preachy. The setting, plot and action should be realistic." 500 word maximum. Byline given.
Nonfiction: Game/puzzles, history (all Bible-related) and Bible "trivia."
How to Contact/Writers: Fiction: Send complete ms. Reports on queries/mss in 1 month.
Terms: Pays "approximately one year before the date of issue." Buys multi-use rights. Pays 5¢/word. Contributor receives 4 complimentary copies of publication. Sample copy free for #10 SASE with 1 first-class stamp. Writer's/artist's guidelines free with #10 SAE.
Tips: "*Discoveries* is committed to reinforcement of the Biblical concepts taught in the Sunday School curriculum. Because of this, the themes needed are mainly as follows: faith in God, obedience to God, putting God first, choosing to please God, accepting Jesus as Savior, finding God's will, choosing to do right, trusting God in hard times, prayer, trusting God to answer, importance of Bible memorization, appreciation of Bible as God's Word to man, Christians working together, showing kindness to others, witnessing." (See listing for *Power and Light*.)

DISCOVERY, The John Milton Society for the Blind, 475 Riverside Dr., Room 455, New York NY 10115. (212)870-3335. Fax: (212)870-3229. E-mail: dquigley@jmsblind.org. Website: www.jmsblind.org. **Assistant Editor**: Ingrid Peck. **Executive Director & Editor**: Darcy Quigley. Quarterly braille magazine. Estab. 1935. Circ. 2,000. "*Discovery* is a free Christian braille magazine for blind and visually impaired youth ages 8-18. 95% of material is stories, poems, quizzes and educational articles, reprinted from 20 Christian and other magazines for youth. Original pieces from individual authors must be ready to print with little or no editing involved. We cannot offer reprint fees. Christian focus."
Fiction: Young readers, middle readers, young adults/teens: all categories and issues pertaining to blind; adventure, animal, contemporary, fantasy, folktales, health, history, humorous, multicultural, nature/environment, problem solving, religious. Does not want stories in which blindness is described as a novelty. It should be part of a story with a larger focus. Buys less than 10 mss/year. Average word length: 1,500 words (maximum). Byline given.
Nonfiction: Young readers, middle readers, young adults/teens: animal, biography, careers, concept, cooking, games/puzzles, geography, health, history, hobbies, how-to, humorous, interview/profile, multicultural, nature/

environment, problem solving, religion, science, social issues. Also want inspirational stories involving visually impaired. Buys less than 10 mss/year. Average word length: 1,500 words (maximum). Byline given.

Poetry: Reviews poetry. Maximum length: 500 words.

How to Contact/Writers: Fiction/nonfiction: Send complete ms. Reports on queries/mss in 6-8 weeks. Publishes ms 3-12 months after acceptance. Will consider simultaneous submissions, previously published work.

Terms: Acquires reprint rights. Authors do not receive payment, only sample copy. Sample copies free with SASE.

Tips: "95% of the material in *Discovery* is reprinted from Christian and other periodicals for youth. Previously unpublished material must therefore be ready to print with little or no editing involved. Please send complete manuscripts or request our 'Writers' Guidelines' which includes a list of periodicals we reprint from."

☑ **DISCOVERY TRAILS**, Gospel Publishing House, 1445 Boonville Ave., Springfield MO 65802-1894. (417)862-2781. E-mail: discoverytrails@ag.org. Website: home.ag.org. **Articles Editor:** Sinda S. Zinn. **Art Director:** Dale Gehris. Quarterly take-home paper. Circ. 40,000. "*Discovery Trails* provides fiction stories that promote Christian living through application of biblical principles. Puzzles and activities are fun ways to learn more about God's Word and "bytes" of information are provided to inspire readers to be in awe of God's wonderful creation."

Fiction: Middle readers: adventure, animal, contemporary, humorous, nature/environment, problem-solving, religious, suspense/mystery. Buys 100 or less mss/year.

Nonfiction: Middle readers: animal, arts/crafts, how-to, humorous, nature/environment, problem-solving, religion. Buys 50-100 mss/year. Average word length: 200-500. Byline given.

Poetry: Reviews poetry. Limit submissions, at one time, to 2 poems.

How to Contact/Writers: Fiction/nonfiction: Send complete ms. Reports on queries in 2-4 weeks. Publishes ms 15-24 months after acceptance. Will consider simultaneous submissions or previously published work. Please indicate such.

Illustration: Buys 1 illlustration issue; 50-60 illustrations/year from assigned freelancers. Uses color artwork only. Works on assignment only. Send promo sheet, portfolio. Contact: Dale Gehris, art coordinator. Reports back only if interested. Samples returned with SASE; samples filed. Credit line given.

Terms: Pays on acceptance. Pays authors 7-10¢ per word. Buys first rights or reprint rights for mss. Buys reprint rights for artwork. Original artwork returned at job's completion. Sample copies for 6×9 SAE and 2 first-class stamps. Writer's guidelines for SASE.

DOLPHIN LOG, The Cousteau Society, 61 E. Eighth St., Box 112, New York NY 10003. (212)673-9097. Fax: (212)673-9183. **Editor:** Lisa Rao. Bimonthly magazine for children ages 7-13. Circ. 80,000. Entirely nonfiction subject matter encompasses all areas of science, natural history, marine biology, ecology and the environment as they relate to our global water system. The philosophy of the magazine is to delight, instruct and instill an environmental ethic and understanding of the interconnectedness of living organisms, including people. Of special interest are articles on ocean- or water-related themes which develop reading and comprehension skills.

Nonfiction: Middle readers, young adult: animal, games/puzzles, geography, interview/profile, nature/environment, science, ocean. Multicultural needs include indigenous peoples, lifestyles of ancient people, etc. Does not want to see talking animals. No dark or religious themes. Buys 10 mss/year. Average word length: 500-700. Byline given.

How to Contact/Writers: Nonfiction: Query first. Reports on queries in 3 months; mss in 6 months.

Illustration: Buys 1 illustration/issue; buys 6 illustrations/year. Preferred theme: Biological illustration. Reviews ms/illustration packages from artists. Illustrations only: Query; send résumé, promo sheet, slides. Reports on art samples in 8 weeks only if interested. Credit line given to illustrators.

Photography: Wants "sharp, colorful pictures of sea creatures. The more unusual the creature, the better." Submit duplicate slides only.

Terms: Pays on publication. Buys first North American serial rights; reprint rights. Pays $75-250 for articles. Pays $100-400 for illustrations. Pays $75-200/color photos. Sample copy $2.50 with 9×12 SAE and 3 first-class stamps. Writer's/illustrator's guidelines free with #10 SASE.

Tips: Writers: "Write simply and clearly and don't anthropomorphize." Illustrators: "Be scientifically accurate and don't anthropomorphize. Some background in biology is helpful, as our needs range from simple line drawings to scientific illustrations which must be researched for biological and technical accuracy."

☑ **DYNAMATH**, Scholastic Inc., 555 Broadway, New York NY 10012-3999. (212)343-6458. **Editor:** Matt Friedman. **Art Director:** Deb Dinger. Monthly magazine. Estab. 1981. Circ. 225,000. Purpose is "to make learning math fun, challenging and uncomplicated for young minds in a very complex world."

Nonfiction: Middle readers: animal, arts/crafts, cooking, fashion, games/puzzles, health, history, hobbies, how-to, humorous, math, multicultural, nature/environment, problem-solving, science, social issues, sports—all must relate to math and science topics.

How to Contact/Writers: Nonfiction: Query with published clips, send ms. Reports on queries in 1 month; mss in 6 weeks. Publishes ms 4 months after acceptance. Will consider simultaneous submissions.

Illustration: Buys 4 illustrations/issue. Illustration only: Query first; send résumé and tearsheets. Reports back on submissions only if interested. Credit line given.

Terms: Pays on acceptance. Buys all rights for mss, artwork, photographs. Originals returned to artist at job's completion. Pays $50-350 for stories. Pays artists $800-1,000 for color cover illustration; $100-800 for color inside illustration. Pays photographers $300-1,000 per project.
Tips: See listings for *Science World.*

☑ **FACES, People, Places & Cultures**, Cobblestone Publishing, Inc., 30 Grove St., Suite C, Peterborough NH 03458. (603)924-7209. Fax: (603)924-7380. E-mail: faces@cobblestonepub.com. Website: www.cobblestone pub.com. **Editor**: Elizabeth Crooker. **Managing Editor**: Lou Waryncia. **Art Director**: Ann Dillon. Magazine published 9 times/year (September-May). Circ. 15,000. *Faces* is a theme-related magazine; writers should send for theme list before submitting ideas/queries. Each month a different world culture is featured through the use of feature articles, activities and photographs and illustrations.

● Themes for *Faces* issues for 2000 include The Scots, Life in Reunified Germany and people and cultures of Iceland. Send for complete theme list before submitting.

Fiction: Middle readers, young adults/teens: adventure, folktales, history, multicultural, plays, religious, travel. Does not want to see material that does not relate to a specific upcoming theme. Buys 9 mss/year. Maximum word length: 800. Byline given.
Nonfiction: Middle readers and young adults/teens: animal, anthropology, arts/crafts, biography, cooking, fashion, games/puzzles, geography, history, how-to, humorous, interview/profile, nature/environment, religious, social issues, sports, travel. Does not want to see material not related to a specific upcoming theme. Buys 63 mss/year. Average word length: 300-800. Byline given.
Poetry: Clear, objective imagery; up to 100 lines. Must relate to theme.
How to Contact/Writers: Fiction/nonfiction: Query with published clips and 2-3 line biographical sketch. "Ideas should be submitted six to nine months prior to the publication date. Responses to ideas are usually sent approximately four months before the publication date."
Illustration: Buys 3 illustrations/issue; buys 27 illustrations/year. Preferred theme or style: Material that is meticulously researched (most articles are written by professional anthropologists); simple, direct style preferred, but not too juvenile. Works on assignment only. Roughs required. Reviews ms/illustration packages from artists. Illustrations only: Send samples of b&w work. "Illustrators should consult issues of *Faces* to familiarize themselves with our needs." Reports on art samples only if interested. Samples returned with SASE. Original artwork returned at job's completion (upon written request). Credit line given.
Photography: Wants photos relating to forthcoming themes.
Terms: Pays on publication. Buys all rights for mss and artwork. Pays 20-25¢/word for articles/stories. Pays on an individual basis for poetry. Covers are assigned and paid on an individual basis. Pays illustrators $50-300 for color inside. Pays photographers per photo ($25-100 for color). Sample copy $4.95 with 7½×10½ SAE and 5 first-class stamps. Writer's/illustrator's/photo guidelines free with SAE and 1 first-class stamp.
Tips: "Writers are encouraged to study past issues of the magazine to become familiar with our style and content. Writers with anthropological and/or travel experience are particularly encouraged; *Faces* is about world cultures. All feature articles, recipes and activities are freelance contributions." Illustrators: "Submit b&w samples, not too juvenile. Study past issues to know what we look for. The illustration we use is generally for retold legends, recipes and activities." (See listing for *Appleseeds, California Chronicles, Calliope, Cobblestone, Footsteps* and *Odyssey.*)

THE FLICKER MAGAZINE, Hillview Lake Publishing Co., P.O. Box 660544, Birmingham AL 35266-0544. (205)824-3311. Fax: (205)824-0151. E-mail: yellowhamr@aol.com. Website: www.flickermag.com. **Editor:** Ann Dorer. **Art Director:** Jimmy Bass. Bimonthly magazine. Estab. 1994. Circ. 7,000. "*The Flicker Magazine* is a publication that promotes balanced growth in all areas of life—physical, spiritual, social, mental and emotional. It includes nonfiction, fiction, poetry, interviews, etc." Target audience is 10- to 12-year olds.
Fiction: Middle readers: adventure, animal, contemporary, folktale, health, history, humorous, multicultural, nature/environment, problem-solving, religious, sports, travel. Does not want to see science fiction, fantasy or romance. Sees too much fantasy and didactic materials. Wants more humorous submissions. Buys 75-80 mss/year. Word length: 800-850. Byline given.
Nonfiction: Middle readers: arts/crafts, biography, concept, cooking, games/puzzles, geography, health, history, hobbies, how-to, humorous, multicultural, nature/environment, problem-solving, religion, science, social issues, sports, travel. Need how-to's. Buys 15-25 mss/year. Word length: 500 words or fewer. Byline given.
Poetry: Reviews poetry. Maximum length: 4-24 lines. Humorous preferred.
How to Contact/Writers: Fiction/Nonfiction: Send complete ms. Reports on queries/mss in 2-3 months. Will consider simultaneous submissions. Buys all rights.

A SELF-ADDRESSED, STAMPED ENVELOPE (SASE) should always be included with submissions within your own country. When sending material to other countries, include a self-addressed envelope (SAE) and International Reply Coupons (IRCs).

Illustration: Buys 5 illustrations/issue; 30 illustrations/year. Uses color artwork only. Works on assignment only. Reviews illustrations from artists. Contact: Jimmy Bass, art director. Send promo sheet and tearsheets. Reports back only if interested. Samples returned with SASE; samples filed. Credit line given.

Terms: Pays on publication. Buys all rights for mss, artwork and photos. Pays 10¢/word for stories; 10¢/word for articles; $25 for poems; $10 for jokes. Pays illustrators $50-250 for color inside. Pays photographers by the project (range: $50-200). Sample copies for $2.95. Writer's/illustrator guidelines and theme list free for SASE.

Tips: "If you are submitting illustrations, please do not send originals unless otherwise specified. The magazine usually has a central theme. Send SASE for guidelines. Remember our target audience is 10- to 12-year of age. Work needs to have kid appeal."

N ✓ FLORIDA LEADER, for high school students, Oxendine Publishing, Inc., P.O. Box 14081, Gainesville FL 32604-2081. (352)373-6907. Fax: (352)373-8120. E-mail: teresa@studentleader.com. Website: www.floridaleader.com. **Articles Editor**: Teresa Beard. **Art Director**: Jeff Riemersma. Published 3 times/year. Estab. 1992. Circ. 25,000. "Magazine features academic-major and career articles, current financial aid and admissions information, and stories on other aspects of college life for prospective college students." Audience includes ages 14-17. Aimed at the juvenile market.

Nonfiction: Young adult/teens: biography, careers, how-to, humorous, interview/profile, problem-solving, social issues, travel. Looking for "more advanced pieces on college preparation—academic skills, career exploration and general motivation for college." Buys 6-8 mss/year. Average word length: 800-1,000. 200-300 for columns.

How to Contact/Writers: Nonfiction: Query with published clips. Reports on queries in 3-5 weeks; mss in 3-5 weeks. Publishes ms 3-5 months after acceptance. Will consider simultaneous submissions, electronic submissions, previously published work.

Illustration: Buys 5 illustrations/issue; 20 illustrations/year. Uses color artwork only. Works on assignment only. Reviews ms/illustration packages from artists. Query. Illustrations only: query with samples; send résumé, promo sheet, tearsheets. Reports only if interested. Samples returned with SASE; samples filed. Credit line given.

Photography: Buys photos from freelancers. Buys photos separately. Works on assignment only. Model/property release required. Uses color prints and 35mm, 2¼ × 2¼, 4 × 5 transparencies. Query with samples. Reports only if interested.

Terms: Pays on publication. Buys first North American serial rights, reprint rights for mss. Buys first-time rights for artwork and photos. Originals returned at job's completion. Pays $35-75 for articles. Pays first-time or less experienced writers or for shorter items with contribution copies or other premiums. Pays illustrators $75 for color inside. Pays photographers by the project (range: $150-300). Sample copies for $3.50. Writer's guidelines for SASE.

Tips: "Query first and review past issues for style and topics."

Focus on the Family CLUBHOUSE; Focus on the Family CLUBHOUSE JR., Focus on the Family, 8605 Explorer Dr., Colorado Springs CO 80920. (719)531-3400. Fax: (719)531-3499. Website: www.family.org. **Editor:** Jesse Florea. **Art Director:** Timothy Jones. Monthly magazine. Estab. 1987. Combined circulation is 200,000. "*Focus on the Family Clubhouse* is a 24-page Christian magazine, published monthly, for children ages 8-12. Similarly, *Focus on the Family Clubhouse Jr.* is published for children ages 4-8. We want fresh, exciting literature that promotes biblical thinking, values and behavior in every area of life."

Fiction: Young readers, middle readers: adventure, contemporary, multicultural, nature/environment, religious. Middle readers: history, sports, science fiction. Multicultural needs include: "interesting, informative, accurate information about other cultures to teach children appreciation for the world around them." Buys approximately 6-10 mss/year. Average word length: *Clubhouse*, 500-1,400; *Clubhouse Jr.*, 250-1,100. Byline given on all fiction and puzzles.

Nonfiction: Young readers, middle readers: arts/crafts, cooking, games/puzzles, how-to, multicultural, nature/environment, religion, science. Young readers: animal. Middle readers, young adult/teen: interview/profile. Middle readers: sports. Buys 3-5 mss/year. Average word length: 200-1,000. Byline given.

Poetry: Wants to see "humorous or biblical" poetry for 4-8 year olds. Maximum length: 250 words.

How to Contact/Writers: Fiction/nonfiction: send complete ms. Reports on queries/mss in 4-6 weeks.

Illustration: Buys 8 illustrations/issue. Uses color artwork only. Works on assignment only. Reviews ms/illustration packages from artists. Submit ms with rough sketches. Contact: Tim Jones, art director. Illustrations only: Query with samples, arrange portfolio review or send tearsheets. Contact: Tim Jones, art director. Reports in 2-3 months. Samples returned with SASE; samples kept on file. Credit line given.

Photography: Buys photos from freelancers. Uses 35mm transparencies. Photographers should query with samples; provide résumé and promotional literature or tearsheets. Reports in 2 months.

Terms: Pays on acceptance. Buys first North American serial rights for mss. Buys first rights or reprint rights for artwork and photographs. Original artwork returned at job's completion. Additional payment for ms/illustration packages. Pays writers $100-300 for stories; $50-150 for articles. Pays illustrators $300-700 for color cover; $200-700 for color inside. Pays photographers by the project or per photo. Sample copies for 9 × 12 SAE and 3 first-class stamps. Writer's/illustrators/photo guidelines for SASE.

Tips: "Test your writing on children. The best stories avoid moralizing or preachiness and are not written *down* to children. They are the products of writers who share in the adventure with their readers, exploring the characters they have created without knowing for certain where the story will lead. And they are not always explicitly

Sue Ellen Brown earned $850 for this *Clubhouse Jr.* cover illustration. The magazine found her through her directory page in *Picturebook*. "I appear in one sourcebook every year," Brown explains. "I send some mailers—limited to targeted companies and those with whom I've worked in the past." Brown advises artists to "do what you love the way you love to work; believe. Read *The Artist's Way, Art & Fear* and any inspirational/practical books that truly inspire you."

Christian, but are built upon a Christian foundation (and, at the very least, do not contradict biblical views or values)."

N: FOOTSTEPS, The Magazine of African American History, 30 Grove St., Suite C, Peterborough NH 03458. (603)924-7204 or (800)821-0115. Fax: (608)924-7380. Website: www.cobblestonepub.com. **Editor:** Charles F. Baker. Magazine on African American history for readers ages 9-14.
- *Footsteps* is theme based. Themes for 2000 include Toussaint L'Ouverture and Haiti, Voluntary Immigration to the U.S. and American Negro Theatre (1930-1950). See their website for more information or contact them for complete theme list and guidelines.

Tips: See listings for *Appleseeds, California Chronicles, Calliope, Cobblestone, Faces* and *Odyssey*.

FOX KIDS MAGAZINE, (formerly *Totally Fox Kids Magazine*), Peter Green Design/Fox Kids Network, 4219 W. Burbank Blvd., Burbank CA 91505. (818)953-2210. Fax: (818)953-2220. E-mail: bananadog@aol.com. Website: www.foxkids.com. **Articles Editor:** Scott Russell. **Art Director:** Debra Hintz. Quarterly magazine. Estab. 1990. Circ. 4 million. Features "fun and hip articles, games and activities for Fox Kids Club members ages 6-13, promoting Fox Kids shows."
- See Writing for Boys: Is the Gender Barrier Real? to hear from *Fox Kids* editor Scott Russell.

Nonfiction: Young readers, middle readers, young adults/teens: animals, arts/crafts, concept, games/puzzles, how-to, humorous, science, nature/environment, sports. Middle readers, young adult: interview/profile, hobbies. Any material tied in to a Fox Kids Network show or one of our other features (no religious material). Buys 16 mss/year. Average word length: 100-300.

How to Contact/Writers: Nonfiction only: Query with published clips. Reports on queries/mss in 2-3 months. Publishes mss 2-6 months after acceptance. Will consider simultaneous submissions and electronic submissions via disk or modem.

Illustration: Buys 5 illustrations/issue. Uses color artwork only. Works on assignment only. Prefers "cartoon character work, must be *on model*." Reviews ms/illustration packages from artists. Query. Illustrations only: Send résumé, promo sheet, tearsheets. Reports only if interested. Samples returned with SASE; samples filed. Original work returned at job's completion. Credit line given.

Photography: Buys photos from freelancers. Uses a variety of subjects, depending on articles. Model/property release required. Uses color prints and 4×5 or 35mm transparencies. Query with résumé, business card, tearsheets. Reports only if interested.

Terms: Pays 30 days from acceptance. Buys all rights. Pays $100-400 for stories/articles. Additional payment for ms/illustration packages and for photos accompanying articles. Sample writer's guidelines for SASE.

Tips: "Practice. Read. Come up with some new and creative ideas. Our articles are almost always humorous. We try to give kids cutting-edge information. All of our articles are tied into Fox Kids shows."

THE FRIEND MAGAZINE, The Church of Jesus Christ of Latter-day Saints, 50 E. North Temple, Salt Lake City UT 84150-3226. (801)240-2210. **Editor:** Vivian Paulsen. **Art Director:** Richard Brown. Monthly magazine for 3-11 year olds. Estab. 1971. Circ. 350,000.

Fiction: Picture material, young readers, middle readers: adventure, animal, contemporary, folktales, history, humorous, problem-solving, religious, ethnic, sports, suspense/mystery. Does not want to see controversial issues, political, horror, fantasy. Average word length: 400-1,000. Byline given.

Nonfiction: Picture material, young readers, middle readers: animal, arts/crafts, biography, cooking, games/ puzzles, history, how-to, humorous, problem-solving, religious, sports. Does not want to see controversial issues, political, horror, fantasy. Average word length: 400-1,000. Byline given.

Poetry: Reviews poetry. Maximum length: 20 lines.

How to Contact/Writers: Fiction/nonfiction: Send complete ms. Reports on mss in 2 months.

Illustration: Illustrations only: Query with samples; arrange personal interview to show portfolio; provide résumé and tearsheets for files.

Terms: Pays on acceptance. Buys all rights for mss. Pays 9-11¢/word for unsolicited fiction articles; $25 and up for poems; $10 for recipes, activities and games. Contributors are encouraged to send for sample copy for $1.50, 9×11 envelope and 4 33¢ stamps. Free writer's guidelines.

Tips: "*The Friend* is published by The Church of Jesus Christ of Latter-day Saints for boys and girls up to twelve years of age. All submissions are carefully read by the *Friend* staff, and those not accepted are returned within two months when a self-addressed, stamped envelope is enclosed. Submit seasonal material at least eight months in advance. Query letters and simultaneous submissions are not encouraged. Authors may request rights to have their work reprinted after their manuscript is published."

GIRLS' LIFE, Monarch, 4517 Harford Rd., Baltimore MD 21214. (410)254-9200. Fax: (410)254-0991. Website: www.girlslife.com. **Senior Editor:** Kelly White. **Art Director:** Chun Kim. Bimonthly magazine. Estab. 1994. General interest magazine for girls, ages 9-15.

Nonfiction: Interview/profile, multicultural, nature/environment, new products, party ideas, skin care, social issues, sports, travel, health, hobbies, humorous. Buys appoximately 25 mss/year. Word length varies. Byline given. "No fiction!"

How to Contact/Writers: Nonfiction: Query with published clips or send complete ms on spec only. Reports

in 2 weeks. Publishes ms 3 months after acceptance. Will consider simultaneous submissions. No phone calls.
Illustration: Buys 4 illustrations/issue. Uses color artwork only. Works on assignment only. Reviews ms/illustration packages from artists. Send ms with dummy. Contact: Kelly White, senior editor. Illustration only: Query with samples; send tearsheets. Contact: Chun Kim, art director. Reports back only if interested. Samples returned with SASE; samples filed. Credit line given.
Photography: Buys photos from freelancers. Uses 35mm transparencies. Provide samples. Reports back only if interested.
Terms: Pays on publication. Original artwork returned at job's completion. Pays $500-800 for features; $150-350 for departments. Sample copies available for $5. Writer's guidelines for SASE.
Tips: "Don't call with queries. Make query short and punchy."

THE GOLDFINCH, Iowa History for Young People, State Historical Society of Iowa, 402 Iowa Ave., Iowa City IA 52240-1806. (319)335-3916. Fax: (319)335-3935. E-mail: mfrese@blue.weeg.uiowa.edu. **Editor**: Millie K. Frese. Quarterly magazine. Estab. 1975. Circ. 2,000. "The award-winning *Goldfinch* consists of 10-12 nonfiction articles, short fiction, poetry and activities per issue. Each magazine focuses on an aspect or theme of history that occurred in or affected Iowa."
Fiction: Middle readers, young adults/teens: historical fiction only, adventure, folktales, multicultural. "Study past issues for structure and content. Most manuscripts written inhouse." Average word length: 500-1,500. Byline given.
Nonfiction: Middle readers; young adults/teens: history, interview/profile, "all tied to an Iowa theme." Uses about 10 freelance mss/year. Average word length: 500-800. Byline given.
Poetry: Reviews poetry. No minimum or maximum word length; no maximum number of submissions. "All poetry must reflect an Iowa theme."
How to Contact/Writers: Fiction/nonfiction: Query with published clips. Reports on queries/mss in up to 2 months. Publishes ms 1 month-1 year after acceptance. Will consider electronic submissions via disk or modem.
Illustration: Buys 2-6 illustrations/issue; 8-24 illustrations/year. Works on assignment only. Prefers cartoon, line drawing. Illustrations only: Query with samples. Reports in up to 2 months. Samples returned with SASE. Credit line given.
Photography: Types of photos used vary with subject. Model/property releases required with submissions. Uses b&w prints; 35mm transparencies. Query with samples. Reports in 2-4 weeks.
Terms: Pays on publication. Buys all rights. Payment begins at $25 per article. Pays illustrators $250 for b&w cover; $10-50 b&w inside. Sample copy for $4. Writer's/illustrator's guidelines free for SASE. Pays photographers by the project (range varies).
Tips: "The editor researches the topics and determines the articles. Writers, most of whom live in Iowa, work from primary and secondary research materials to write pieces. The presentation is aimed at children 8-14. All submissions must relate to an upcoming Iowa theme. Please send SASE for our writer's guidelines and theme lists before submitting manuscripts. Upcoming topics: February, 2000, Folk Art; May 2000, A New Look at Immigration."

GUIDEPOSTS FOR KIDS, P.O. Box 638, Chesterton IN 46304. Fax: (219)926-3839. Website: www.gp4k.com. **Editor-in-Chief:** Mary Lou Carney. **Assistant Fiction Editor:** Ginjer Clarke. **Art Director**: Mike Lyons. **Photo Editor**: Julie Brown. Bimonthly magazine. Estab. 1990. Circ. 200,000. "*Guideposts for Kids* is published bimonthly by Guideposts for kids 7-12 years old (emphasis on upper end of that age bracket). It is a value-centered, direct mail magazine that is *fun* to read. It is *not* a Sunday school take-home paper or a miniature *Guideposts*."
● At presstime, *Guideposts for Kids* was looking for a new editor. Look to industry newsletters for news on who gets the position.
Fiction: Middle readers: adventure, animal, contemporary, fantasy, folktales, historical, humorous, multicultural, nature/environment, problem-solving, science fiction, sports, suspense/mystery. Multicultural needs include: Kids in other cultures—school, sports, families. Does not want to see preachy fiction. "We want real stories about real kids doing real things—conflicts our readers will respect; resolutions our readers will accept. Problematic. Tight. Filled with realistic dialogue and sharp imagery. No stories about 'good' children always making the right decision. If present at all, adults are minor characters and *do not* solve kids' problems for them." Buys approximately 10 mss/year. Average word length: 500-1,400. Byline given.
Nonfiction: Middle readers: animal, current events, games/puzzles, history, how-to, humorous, interview/profile, multicultural, nature/environment, problem-solving, profiles of kids, science, seasonal, social issues, sports. "Make nonfiction issue-oriented, controversial, thought-provoking. Something kids not only *need* to know but *want* to know as well." Buys 20 mss/year. Average word length: 200-1,300. Byline usually given.
How to Contact/Writers: Fiction: Send complete ms. Nonfiction: Query or send ms. Reports on queries/mss in 6 weeks.
Illustration: Buys 10 illustrations/issue; 60 illustrations/year. Uses color artwork only. Works on assignment only. Reviews ms/illustration packages from artists. Contact: Mike Lyons, art director. Illustration only: Query; send résumé, tearsheets. Reports only if interested. Credit line given.
Photography: Looks for "spontaneous, *real* kids in action shots."
Terms: Pays on acceptance. Buys all rights for mss. Buys first rights for artwork. "Features range in payment

from $300-450; fiction from $250-500. We pay higher rates for stories exceptionally well-written or well-researched. Regular contributors get bigger bucks, too." Additional payment for ms/illustration packages "but we prefer to acquire our own illustrations." Pays illustrators $400-800/page. Pays photographers by the project (range: $300-1,000) or per photo (range: $100-500). Sample copies for $3.25. Writer's guidelines free for SASE.
Tips: "Make your manuscript good, relevant and playful. No preachy stories about Bible-toting children. *Guideposts for Kids* is not a beginner's market. Study our magazine. (Sure, you've heard that before—but it's *necessary*!) Neatness *does* count. So do creativity and professionalism. SASE essential." (See listings for *Guideposts for Teens*.)

GUIDEPOSTS FOR TEENS, P.O. Box 638, Chesterton IN 46304. (219)929-4429. Fax: (219)926-3839. E-mail: gp4t@guideposts.org. **Editor-in-Chief:** Mary Lou Carney. **Editor:** Betsy Kohn. **Art Director:** Michael Lyons. **Photo Editor:** Julie Brown. Bimonthly magazine. Estab. 1998. "We are a value-centered magazine that offers teens advice, humor and true stories—lots of true stories. These first-person (ghostwritten) stories feature teen protagonists and are filled with action, adventure, overcoming adversity and growth—set against the backdrop of God at work in everyday life."
Nonfiction: Young adults: how-to, humorous, interview/profile, social issues, sports, true stories, most embarrassing moments. Average word length: 300-1,500. Byline sometimes given.
How to Contact/Writers: Nonfiction: Query. Reports on queries/mss in 4-6 weeks. Will consider simultaneous submissions or electronic submission via disk or modem. Send SASE for writer's guidelines.
Illustration: Uses color artwork only. Works on assignment only. Reviews ms/illustration packages from artists. Query. Contact: Michael Lyons, art director. Illustrations only: Query with samples. Reports back only if interested. Samples kept on file. Credit line given.
Photography: Buys photos separately. Wants location photography and stock; digital OK. Uses color prints; and 35mm, 2¼×2¼, 4×5 or 8×10 transparencies. Query with samples; provide web address. Reports back only if interested.
Terms: Pays on acceptance. Buys all rights for mss. Buys one-time rights for artwork. Original artwork returned at job's completion. Pays $300-500 for true stories; $100-300 for articles. Additional payment for photos accompanying articles. Pays illustrators $125-1,500 for color inside (depends on size). Pays photographers by the project (range: $100-1,000). Sample copies for $4.50 from: Guideposts, 39 Seminary Hill Rd., Carmel NY 10512. Attn: Special Handling.
Tips: "Language and subject matter should be current and teen-friendly. No preaching, please! For illustrators: We get illustrators from two basic sources: submissions by mail and submissions by Internet. We also consult major illustrator reference books. We prefer color illustrations, "on-the-edge" style. We accept art in almost any digital or reflective format." (See listing for *Guideposts for Kids*.)

HIGH ADVENTURE, Assemblies of God, 1445 Boonville Ave., Springfield MO 65802. (417)862-2781, Ext. 4181. Fax: (417)831-8230. E-mail: rangers@ag.org. Website: royalranger.ag.org. **Editor:** Marshall Bruner. Quarterly magazine. Circ. 86,000. Estab. 1971. Magazine is designed to provide boys ages 5-7 with worthwhile, enjoyable, leisure reading; to challenge them in narrative form to higher ideals and greater spiritual dedication; and to perpetuate the spirit of Royal Rangers through stories, ideas and illustrations. 75% of material aimed at juvenile audience.
Fiction: Buys 100 mss/year; adventure, humorous, problem solving, religious, sports, travel. Maximum word length: 1,000. Byline given.
Nonfiction: Articles: Christian living, devotional, Holy Spirit, salvation, self-help; biography; missionary stories; news items; testimonies, inspirational stories based on true-life experiences; arts/crafts, games/puzzles, geography, health, hobbies, how-to, humorous, nature/environment, problem solving, sports, travel.
How to Contact/Writers: Fiction/nonfiction: Send complete ms. Reports on queries in 6-8 weeks. Will consider simultaneous submissions. Will review ms/illustration packages.
Illustrations: Ms/illustration packages: Send complete ms with final art. Illustrations only: "Most of our artwork is done in-house." Buys 25 illustrations/year. Reports in 6-8 weeks. Samples returned with SASE.
Terms: Pays on acceptance. Buys first or all rights. Pays 3-5¢/word for articles; $18-25 for cartoons; $12-15 for puzzles, $2-3 for jokes. Sample copy free with 9×12 SASE. Free writer's/illustrator's guidelines for SASE.
Tips: Obtain writer's guidelines and themes list.

HIGHLIGHTS FOR CHILDREN, 803 Church St., Honesdale PA 18431. (717)253-1080. **Manuscript Coordinator:** Beth Troop. **Art Director:** Janet Moir McCaffrey. Monthly magazine. Estab. 1946. Circ. 2.8 million. "Our motto is 'Fun With a Purpose.' We are looking for quality fiction and nonfiction that appeals to children, encourages them to read, and reinforces positive values. All art is done on assignment."
 ● *Highlights* ranked number 7 on the 1999 *Writer's Digest*'s Fiction 50, the magazine's annual list of "50 best places to publish your short stories."
Fiction: Picture-oriented material, young readers, middle readers: adventure, animal, contemporary, fantasy, folktales, history, humorous, multicultural, problem-solving, sports. Multicultural needs include first person accounts of children from other cultures and first-person accounts of children from other countries. Does not want to see war, crime, violence. "We see too many stories with overt morals." Would like to see more suspense/ stories/articles with world culture settings, sports pieces, action/adventure and stories with children in contempo-

Illustrator Les Gray has been working with *Highlights for Children* for almost 20 years. "The artist has done several covers utilizing these same mouse characters," says *Highlights*. "He usually does one a year for us. This one is especially nice because it's a night scene." These mice on a merry-go-round were rendered in watercolor and colored pencil.

© 1999 *Highlights for Children*

rary settings. Buys 150 mss/year. Average word length: 400-800. Byline given.
Nonfiction: Picture-oriented material, young readers, middle readers: animal, arts/crafts, biography, careers, games/puzzles, geography, health, history, hobbies, how-to, interview/profile, multicultural, nature/environment, problem solving, science, sports. Multicultural needs include articles set in a country *about* the people of the country. "We have plenty of articles with Asian and Spanish settings. We also have plenty of holiday articles." Does not want to see trendy topics, fads, personalities who would not be good role models for children, guns, war, crime, violence. "We'd like to see more nonfiction for younger readers—maximum of 600 words. We still need older-reader material, too—600-900 words." Buys 75 mss/year. Maximum word length: 900. Byline given.
How to Contact/Writers: Send complete ms. Reports on queries in 1 month; mss in 4-6 weeks.
Illustration: Buys 25-30 illustrations/issue. Preferred theme or style: Realistic, some stylization, cartoon style acceptable. Works on assignment only. Reviews ms/illustration packages from artists. Illustrations only: photocopies, promo sheet, tearsheets, or slides. Résumé optional. Portfolio only if requested. Contact: Janet Moir McCaffrey, art director. Reports on art samples in 4-6 weeks. Samples returned with SASE; samples filed. Credit line given.
Terms: Pays on acceptance. Buys all rights for mss. Pays $100 and up for unsolicited articles. Pays illustrators $1,000 for color cover; $25-200 for b&w inside, $100-500 for color inside. Sample copies $3.95 and 9×11 SASE with 4 first-class stamps. Writer's/illustrator's guidelines free on request.
Tips: "Know the magazine's style before submitting. Send for guidelines and sample issue if necessary." Writers: "At *Highlights* we're paying closer attention to acquiring more nonfiction for young readers than we have in the past." Illustrators: "Fresh, imaginative work encouraged. Flexibility in working relationships a plus. Illustrators presenting their work need not confine themselves to just children's illustrations as long as work can translate to our needs. We also use animal illustrations, real and imaginary. We need party plans, crafts and puzzles—any activity that will stimulate children mentally and creatively. We are always looking for imaginative cover subjects. Know our publication's standards and content by reading sample issues, not just the guidelines. Avoid tired themes, or put a fresh twist on an old theme so that its style is fun and lively. We'd like to see stories with subtle messages, but the fun of the story should come first. Write what inspires you, not what you think the market needs."

HOPSCOTCH, The Magazine for Girls, The Bluffton News Publishing and Printing Company, 103 N. Main St., Bluffton OH 45817. (419)358-4610. **Editor**: Marilyn Edwards. **Contact**: Becky Jackman, editorial assistant. Bimonthly magazine. Estab. 1989. Circ. 14,000. For girls from ages 6-12, featuring traditional subjects—pets, games, hobbies, nature, science, sports, etc.—with an emphasis on articles that show girls actively involved in unusual and/or worthwhile activities."

Fiction: Picture-oriented material, young readers, middle readers: adventure, animal, history, humorous, nature/environment, science fiction, sports, suspense/mystery. Does not want to see stories dealing with dating, sex, fashion, hard rock music. Buys 30 mss/year. Average word length: 300-700. Byline given.

Nonfiction: Picture-oriented material, young readers, middle readers: animal, arts/crafts, biography, cooking, games/puzzles, geography, hobbies, how-to, humorous, math, nature/environment, science. Does not want to see pieces dealing with dating, sex, fashion, hard rock music. "Need more nonfiction with quality photos about a *Hopscotch*-age girl involved in a worthwhile activity." Buys 46 mss/year. Average word length: 400-700. Byline given.

Poetry: Reviews traditional, wholesome, humorous poems. Maximum word length: 300; maximum line length: 20. Will accept 6 submissions/author.

How to Contact/Writers: All writers should consult the theme list before sending in articles. To receive a current theme list, send a SASE. Fiction: Send complete ms. Nonfiction: Query, send complete ms. Reports on queries in 2 weeks; on mss in 2 months. Will consider simultaneous submissions.

Illustration: Buys illustrations for 6-8 articles/issue; buys 50-60 articles/year. "Generally, the illustrations are assigned after we have purchased a piece (usually fiction). Occasionally, we will use a painting—in any given medium—for the cover, and these are usually seasonal." Uses b&w artwork only for inside; color for cover. Review ms/illustration packages from artists. Query first or send complete ms with final art. Illustrations only: Send résumé, portfolio, client list and tearsheets. Reports on art samples with SASE in 2 weeks. Credit line given.

Photography: Purchases photos separately (cover only) and with accompanying ms only. Looking for photos to accompany article. Model/property releases required. Uses 5×7, b&w prints; 35mm transparencies. Black and white photos should go with ms. Should show girl or girls ages 6-12.

Terms: For mss: pays a few months ahead of publication. For mss, artwork and photos: buys first North American serial rights; second serial (reprint rights). Original artwork returned at job's completion. Pays 5¢/word and $5-10/photo. "We always send a copy of the issue to the writer or illustrator." Text and art are treated separately. Pays $150-200 for color cover. Photographers paid per photo (range: $5-15). Sample copy for $4. Writer's/illustrator's/photo guidelines free for #10 SASE.

Tips: "Remember we publish only six issues a year, which means our editorial needs are extremely limited. Please look at our guidelines and our magazine . . . and remember, we use far more nonfiction than fiction. If decent photos accompany the piece, it stands an even better chance of being accepted. We believe it is the responsibility of the contributor to come up with photos. Please remember, our readers are 6-12 years—most are 7-10—and your text should reflect that. Many magazines try to entertain first and educate second. We try to do the reverse of that. Our magazine is more simplistic, like a book to be read from cover to cover. We are looking for wholesome, non-dated material." (See listing for *Boys' Quest*.)

HUMPTY DUMPTY'S MAGAZINE, Children's Better Health Institute, 1100 Waterway Blvd., P.O. Box 567, Indianapolis IN 46206. (317)636-8881. Fax: (317)684-8094. **Editor:** Nancy S. Axelrad. **Art Director:** Rebecca Ray. Magazine published 8 times/year—Jan/Feb; Mar; April/May; June; July/Aug; Sept; Oct/Nov; Dec. *HDM* is edited for children ages 4-6. It includes fiction (easy-to-reads; read alouds; rhyming stories; rebus stories), nonfiction articles (some with photo illustrations), poems, crafts, recipes, and puzzles. Content encourages development of better health habits.

   • *Humpty Dumpty's* publishes material promoting health and fitness with emphasis on simple activities, poems and fiction.

Fiction: Picture-oriented stories: adventure, animal, contemporary, fantasy, folktales, health, humorous, multicultural, nature/environment, problem-solving, science fiction, sports. Does not want to see "bunny-rabbits-with-carrot-pies stories! Also, talking inanimate objects are very difficult to do well. Beginners (and maybe everyone) should avoid these." Buys 8-10 mss/year. Maximum word length: 300-400. Byline given.

Nonfiction: Picture-oriented articles: animal, arts/crafts, concept, games/puzzles, health, how-to, humorous, nature/environment, no-cook recipes, science, social issues, sports. Buys 6-10 mss/year. Prefers very short nonfiction pieces—200 words maximum. Byline given.

How to Contact/Writers: Send complete ms. Nonfiction: Send complete ms with bibliography if applicable. "No queries, please!" Reports on mss in 2-3 months. Send seasonal material at least 8 months in advance.

Illustration: Buys 13-16 illustrations/issue; 90-120 illustrations/year. Preferred theme or style: Realistic or cartoon. Works on assignment only. Illustrations only. Query with slides, printed pieces or photocopies. Contact: Rebecca Ray, art director. Samples are not returned; samples filed. Reports on art samples only if interested. Credit line given.

Terms: Writers: Pays on publication. Artists: Pays within 1-2 months. Buys all rights. "One-time book rights may be returned if author can provide name of interested book publisher and tentative date of publication." Pays up to 22¢/word for stories/articles; payment varies for poems and activities. 10 complimentary issues are provided to author with check. Pays $250 for color cover illustration; $35-90 per page b&w inside; $70-155 for color inside. Sample copies for $1.75. Writer's/illustrator's guidelines free with SASE.

Tips: Writers: "Study current issues and guidelines. Observe word lengths and adhere to requirements. Submit what you do best. Don't send your first, second, or even third drafts. Polish your piece until it's as perfect as you can make it." Illustrators: "Please study the magazine before contacting us. Your art must have appeal to three- to seven-year-olds." (See listings for *Child Life, Children's Digest, Children's Playmate, Jack and Jill, Turtle Magazine* and *U*S* Kids*.)

☑ **INSIGHT MAGAZINE**, Review & Herald Pub. Assoc., 55 W. Oak Ridge Dr., Hagerstown MD 21740. (301)393-4037. E-mail: insight@rhpa.org. Website: www.insightmagazine.org. **Articles Editor:** Lori Peckham. Weekly magazine. Estab. 1970. Circ. 20,000. "We print only true stories written about the author's or author's subject's teen years that portray a spiritual truth. We look for good story-telling elements such as a dramatic beginning, realistic dialogue, and believable, alive characters." This magazine is aimed at teens ages 14-19.

Nonfiction: Teens: animal, biography, concept, health, history, humorous, interview/profile, multicultural, religion, science, social issues, sports, travel, (all these topics must have a spiritual slant.) Buys 200-300 mss/year. Average word length: 500-1,500. Byline given.

How to Contact/Writers: Nonfiction: Send complete ms. Reports on mss in 6 weeks. Publishes ms 6 months after acceptance. Will consider simultaneous submissions, electronic submissions via disk or modem or previously published work.

Terms: Pays on acceptance. Buys first rights or one-time rights for mss. Pays $25-100 for stories.

N INTEEN, Urban Ministries, Inc., 1551 Regency Ct., Calumet City IL 60409. (708)868-7100, ext. 239. Fax: (708)868-7105. E-mail: unil551@aol.com. **Editor:** Katara A. Washington. **Art Acquisitions:** Larry Taylor. Quarterly magazine. Estab. 1970. "We publish Sunday school lessons for urban teens and features for the same group."

● Contact *Inteen* for guidelines. They work on assignment only—do not submit work.

Nonfiction: Young adults/teens: careers, games/puzzles, how-to, interview/profile, religion. "We make 40 assignments/year."

Terms: Pays $75-150 for stories.

JACK AND JILL, Children's Better Health Institute, 1100 Waterway Blvd., P.O. Box 567, Indianapolis IN 46206. (317)636-8881. **Editor:** Daniel Lee. **Art Director:** Andrea O'Shea. Magazine published 8 times/year. Estab. 1938. Circ. 360,000. "Write entertaining and imaginative stories *for* kids, not just *about* them. Writers should understand what is funny to kids, what's important to them, what excites them. Don't write from an adult 'kids are so cute' perspective. We're also looking for health and healthful lifestyle stories and articles, but don't be preachy."

Fiction: Young readers and middle readers: adventure, contemporary, folktales, health, history, humorous, nature, sports. Buys 30-35 mss/year. Average word length: 700. Byline given.

Nonfiction: Young readers, middle readers: animal, arts/crafts, cooking, games/puzzles, history, hobbies, how-to, humorous, interview/profile, nature, science, sports. Buys 8-10 mss/year. Average word length: 500. Byline given.

Poetry: Reviews poetry.

How to Contact/Writers: Fiction/nonfiction: Send complete ms. Reports on mss in 3 months.

Illustration: Buys 15 illustrations/issue; 120 illustrations/year. Reports back only if interested. Samples not returned; samples filed. Credit line given.

Terms: Pays on publication; minimum 17¢/word. Pays illustrators $275 for color cover; $35-90 fr b&w, $70-155 for color inside. Pays photographers negotiated rate. Sample copies $1.25. Buys all rights.

Tips: Publishes writing/art/photos by children. See listings for *Child Life, Children's Digest, Children's Playmate, Humpty Dumpty's Magazine, Turtle Magazine* and *U*S* Kids*.

JUMP, For Girls Who Dare to be Real, Weider, 21100 Erwin St., Woodland Hills CA 91367. Fax: (818)594-0972. E-mail: letters@jumponline.com. Website: www.jumponline.com. **Contact:** Elizabeth Sosa, editorial assistant. **Editor:** Kiru Berger. **Managing Editor:** Maureen Meyers. Monthly magazine for a female teen audience. Estab. 1997. Circ. 300,000.

Nonfiction: Young adults/teens: general interest, how-to, interview/profile, new product, personal experience. *Jump* columns include Busted! (quirky, bizarre and outrageous trends, news, quotes—6 items, 50 words each); The Dish (food and nutrition for teens—1,500 words); Jump On . . . In, Music, Sports, Body & Soul (small news and trend items on sports, health, music, etc.—6 items, 75 words each).

How to Contact/Writers: Nonfiction: Query with published clips. Reports on queries in 1 month. Publishes ms 4 months after acceptance. Will consider simultaneous submissions.

Terms: Pays on publications. Buys all rights. Pays 50¢-$1/word.

Tips: "Writers must read our magazine before submitting queries. We'll turn away queries that clearly show the writer isn't familiar with the content of the magazine."

KIDS' WALL STREET NEWS, Kids' Wall Street News, Inc., P.O. Box 1207, Rancho Santa Fe CA 92067. (760)591-7681. Fax: (760)591-3731. E-mail: info@kwsnews.com. Website: www.kwsnews.com. **Contact:** Kate Allen, editor-in-chief. Bimonthly magazine. Estab. 1996. *"Kids' Wall Street News* hopes to empower and educate America's youth so they will be better prepared for today and their future. This bimontly magazine covers world and business news, financial information, computer updates, the environment, adventure and much more."
Nonfiction: Young adults/teens: animal, biography, careers, finance, geography, health, history, interview/profile, nature/environment, science, social issues, sports, travel. Buys 130 mss/year. Average word length: 250-550. Byline given.
How to Contact/Writers: Nonfiction: Query with published clips. Reports on queries in 2-3 months. Will consider simultaneous submissions and electronic submission via disk or modem.
Terms: Pays on publication. Buys exclusive magazine rights for mss. Samples copies for 9 × 12 SAE and $1.70 postage (6 first-class stamps).
Tips: *"Kids' Wall Street News* generally assigns specific subject matter for articles. There is a heavy financial slant to the magazine."

KIDZ CHAT, Standard Publishing, 8121 Hamilton Ave., Cincinnati OH 45231. (513)931-4050. **Editor:** Gary Thacker. Weekly magazine. Circ. 55,000. *Kidz Chat* is a weekly take-home paper for boys and girls who are in grades 3 and 4. "Our goal is to reach these children with the truth of God's Word, and to help them make it the guide of their lives. Most of our features, including our stories, correlate with the Sunday school lesson themes. Send SASE for a quarterly theme list and sample copies of *Kidz Chat*."
• *Kidz Chat* ranked number 13 on *Writer's Digest*'s 1999 Fiction 50, the magazine's annual list of "50 best places to publish your short stories."
Fiction: Young readers, middle readers: adventure, animal, humorous, nature/environment, sports, suspense/mystery, travel, religious. Does not want to see fantasy or science fiction. Buys 52 mss/year. Maximum word length: 475. Byline given.
Nonfiction: Young readers, middle readers: animal, nature/environment, religious, science. Buys 50 mss/year. Average word length: 200-225. Byline given.
How to Contact/Writers: Fiction/nonfiction: Send complete ms. Reports on mss in 4-5 weeks after theme list deadline. Will consider simultaneous submissions (but prefers not to). "No queries or manuscript submissions via fax, please."
Terms: Pays on acceptance. Buys first rights, one-time rights, second serial, first North American rights for mss. Pays 3-7¢/word for unsolicited articles. Contributor copies given not as payment but all contributors receive copies of their articles. Sample copy and writer's guidelines free with #10 SASE and 1 first-class stamp.
Tips: "Write about current topics, issues that elementary-age children are dealing with. Children are growing up much more quickly these days than ever before. Send an SASE for sample copies, guidelines, and theme sheet. Be familiar with the publication for which you wish to write." (See listings for *Live Wire* and *Straight*.)

LADYBUG, the Magazine for Young Children, Carus Publishing Company, P.O. Box 300, Peru IL 61354. (815)224-6656. **Editor-in-Chief:** Marianne Carus. **Editor:** Paula Morrow. **Art Director:** Suzanne Beck. Monthly magazine. Estab. 1990. Circ. 130,000. Literary magazine for children 2-6, with stories, poems, activities, songs and picture stories.
Fiction: Picture-oriented material: adventure, animal, fantasy, folktales, humorous, multicultural, nature/environment, problem-solving, science fiction, sports, suspense/mystery. "Open to any easy fiction stories." Buys 50 mss/year. Average word length 300-850 words. Byline given.
Nonfiction: Picture-oriented material: activities, animal, arts/crafts, concept, cooking, humorous, math, nature/environment, problem-solving, science. Buys 35 mss/year.
Poetry: Reviews poems, 20-line maximum length; limit submissions to 5 poems. Uses lyrical, humorous, simple language.
How to Contact/Writers: Fiction/nonfiction: Send complete ms. Queries not accepted. Reports on mss in 3 months. Publishes ms up to 2 years after acceptance. Will consider simultaneous submissions if informed. Submissions without SASE will be discarded.
Illustration: Buys 12 illustrations/issue; 145 illustrations/year. Prefers "bright colors; all media, but use watercolor and acrylics most often; same size as magazine is preferred but not required." To be considered for future assignments: Submit promo sheet, slides, tearsheets, color and b&w photocopies. Reports on art samples in 3 months. Submissions without SASE will be discarded.
Terms: Pays on publication for mss; after delivery of completed assignment for illustrators. For mss, buys first publication rights; second serial (reprint rights). Buys first publication rights plus promotional rights for artwork. Original artwork returned at job's completion. Pays 25¢/word for prose; $3/line for poetry. Pays $750 for color (cover) illustration, $50-100 for b&w (inside) illustration, $250/page for color (inside). Sample copy for $4. Writer's/illustrator's guidelines free for SASE.
Tips: Writers: "Get to know several young children on an individual basis. Respect your audience. Wants less cute, condescending or 'preachy-teachy' material. Less gratuitous anthropomorphism. More rich, evocative language, sense of joy or wonder. Keep in mind that people come in all colors, sizes, physical conditions. Be inclusive in creating characters. Set your manuscript aside for at least a month, then reread critically." Illustrators: "Include examples, where possible, of children, animals, and—most important—action and narrative (i.e., several

"It's a delight to work with the editors of the Cricket Magazine Group," says Illustrator Robin Hansen. Her illustration for "Can You Say This?" was published in the April 1999 issue of *Ladybug*. Hansen sent a proposal for illustration and verse with a multicultural theme. "I sent in sample illustrations as I thought they might appear along with words," she explains. "I planned them in an action rhyme format, which I had done for *Ladybug* in the past." Hansen markets her talents by sending sample illustrations, scanned into her computer and output on photo quality paper, to markets she finds in *Children's Writer's & Illustrator's Market*. She advises aspiring illustrators to do what they love. "What makes you happy shows in your work. Have patience and persevere. Only send your best work, researching the market to see what is where. Draw constantly."

scenes from a story, showing continuity and an ability to maintain interest). (See listings for *Babybug*, *Cicada*, *Cricket*, *Muse* and *Spider*.)

☑ **LISTEN, Drug-Free Possibilities for Teens**, Health Connection, 55 West Oak Ridge Dr., Hagerstown MD 21740. (301)393-4020. Fax: (301)393-4055. E-mail: ajacobs@rhpa.org. **Editor:** Larry Becker. Monthly magazine, 9 issues. Estab. 1948. Circ. 50,000. *"Listen* offers positive alternatives to drug use for its teenage readers. Helps them have a happy and productive life by making the right choices."
Fiction: Young adults: health, humorous, problem-solving peer pressure. Buys 50 mss/year. Average word length: 1,000-1,200. Byline given.
Nonfiction: Young adults: biography, games/puzzles, hobbies, how-to, health, humorous, problem solving, social issues, drug-free living. Wants to see more factual articles on drug abuse. Buys 50 mss/year. Average word length: 1,000-1,200. Byline given.
How to Contact/Writers: Fiction/nonfiction: Query. Reports on queries in 6 weeks; mss in 2 months. Will consider simultaneous submissions, electronic submission via disk or e-mail and previously published work.
Illustration: Buys 8-10 illustrations/issue; 72 illustrators/year. Reviews ms/illustration packages from artists. Ms/illustration packages and illustration only: Query. Contact: Ed Guthero, designer. Reports only if interested. Originals returned at job's completion. Samples returned with SASE. Credit line given.
Photography: Purchases photos from freelancers. Photos purchased with accompanying ms only. Uses color and b&w photos; 35mm, 2¼×2¼. Query with samples. Looks for "youth oriented—action (sports, outdoors), personality photos."
Terms: Pays on acceptance. Buys exclusive magazine rights for ms. Buys one-time rights for artwork and photographs. Pays $50-200 for stories/articles. Pay illustrators $500 for color cover; $75-225 for b&w inside; $135-450 for color inside. Pays photographers by the project (range: $125-500); pays per photo (range: $125-500). Additional payment for ms/illustration packages and photos accompanying articles. Sample copy for $1 and 9×12 SASE and 2 first class stamps. Writer's guidelines free with SASE.
Tips: *"Listen* is a magazine for teenagers. It encourages development of good habits and high ideals of physical, social and mental health. It bases its editorial philosophy of primary drug prevention on total abstinence from alcohol and other drugs. Because it is used extensively in public high school classes, it does not accept articles and stories with overt religious emphasis. Four specific purposes guide the editors in selecting materials for *Listen*: (1) To portray a positive lifestyle and to foster skills and values that will help teenagers deal with contemporary problems, including smoking, drinking and using drugs. This is *Listen's* primary purpose. (2) To offer positive alternatives to a lifestyle of drug use of any kind. (3) To present scientifically accurate information about the nature and effects of tobacco, alcohol and other drugs. (4) To report medical research, community programs and educational efforts which are solving problems connected with smoking, alcohol and other drugs.

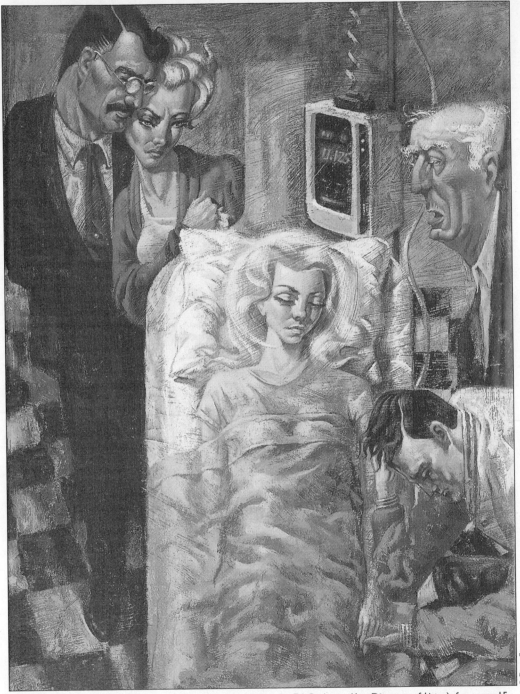

"I've been completing illustration commissions assigned to me by Ed Guthero, (Art Director of *Listen*), for some 15 years," says illustrator Perry Stewart. "Ed walked into my first illustration class in college and handed out two or three business cards." The illustration for the article "Dying Dreams" was created using acrylics on gessoed illustration board. "The paint consistency used was a range from very wet to very dry," Stewart explains. He promotes his work by mailing postcards three times a year, maintaining a website and advertising in source books. Stewart advises illustrators to "work very hard. Complete illustrations for yourself when you don't have assignments. Never do a shoddy job despite what you are being paid. Every painting has the potential to breed new work and new clients."

Articles should offer their readers activities that increase one's sense of self-worth through achievement and/or involvement in helping others. They are often categorized by three kinds of focus: (1) Hobbies. (2) Recreation. (3) Community Service.

LIVE WIRE, Standard Publishing Co., 8121 Hamilton Ave., Cincinnati OH 45231. (513)931-4050. Fax: (513)931-0950. E-mail: standardpub@attmail.com. Website: www.standardpub.com. **Articles Editor:** Carla J. Crane. **Art Director:** Sandy Wimmer. **Photo Editor:** Sandy Wimmer. Newspaper published quarterly in weekly parts. Estab. 1997. Circ. 40,000. "*Live Wire* is a weekly publication geared to preteens (10-12 year olds). 'who want to connect to Christ.' Articles are in a news brief format that feature current events and profiles. We publish true stories about kids, puzzles, activities, interview."

Nonfiction: Middle readers: animal, arts/crafts, biography, cooking, games/puzzles, religion, geography, health, history, how-to, humorous, interview/profile, multicultural, nature/environment, science, sports. Buys 50-70 mss/year. Average word length: 250-350. Byline given.

Poetry: Reviews poetry from preteens only. Limit submissions to 5 poems.

How to Contact/Writers: Nonfiction: Send complete ms. Reports on queries in 1-2 weeks; mss in 2-3 months. Ms published 1 year after acceptance. Accepts simultaneous submissions and previously published work.

Illustration: Buys 4 illustrations/issue; 200 illustrations/year. Uses color artwork only. Works on assignment only. Reviews ms/illustration packages from artists. Ms/illustration packages: query first.

Terms: Pays on acceptance. Buys first rights or reprint rights for mss. Buys full rights for artwork; one-time use for photos. Pays 3-7¢ per word for articles. Additional payment for photos accompanying articles. Pays illustrators $100-200 for color cover, $25-125 for color inside. Pays photographers per photo (range: $100-150). Writer's guidelines for SASE.

Tips: "Articles should be appealing and fun. Multicultural material should deal specifically with missionary families or kids." (See listings for *Kidz Chat* and *Straight*.)

MUSE, Carus Publishing, 332 S. Michagan Ave, Suite 1100, Chicago IL 60604. (312)939-1500. Fax: (312)939-8150. E-mail: muse@caruspub.com. Website: www.musemag.com. **Editor:** Diana Lutz. **Art Director:** John Grandits. **Photo Editor:** Carol Parden. Estab. 1996. Circ. 100,000. "The goal of *Muse* is to give as many children as possible access to the most important ideas and concepts underlying the principal areas of human knowledge. It will take children seriously as developing intellects by assuming that, if explained clearly, the ideas and concepts of an article will be of interest to them. Articles should meet the highest possible standards of clarity and transparency aided, wherever possible, by a tone of skepticism, humor, and irreverence."

● *Muse* is published in cooperation with the Cricket Magazine Group and *Smithsonian* magazine. The magazine changed frequency from 6 to 10 issues in 1999.

Nonfiction: Middle readers, young adult: animal, biography, history, interview/profile, math, multicultural, nature/environment, problem-solving, science, social issues. Buys 60-75 mss/year. Word length for articles: 500 words minimum. Work on commision only. "Each article must be about a topic that children can understand. The topic must be a 'large' one that somehow connects with a fundamental tennet of some discipline or area of practical knowledge. The topic and presentation must lead to further questioning and exploration; it must be open-ended rather than closed. The treatment of the topic must be of the competence one would expect of an expert in the field in which the topic resides. It must be interesting and hold the reader's attention, not because of the way it is written, but because of the compelling presentation of the ideas it describes."

How to Contact/Writers: Nonfiction: Query with résumé, writing samples, published clips, detailed story ideas and SASE. Will consider simultaneous submissions, electronic submissions via disk or modem or previously published work.

Illustration: Buys 6 illustrations/issue; 40 illustrations/year. Uses color artwork only. Works on assignment only. Reviews ms/illustration packages. Send ms with dummy. Illustrations only: Query with samples. Send résumé, promo sheet and tearsheets. Reports back only if interested. Samples returned with SASE. Credit line given.

Photography: Needs vary. Query with samples. Reports back only if interested.

Terms: Pays within 60 days of acceptance. Buys first publications rights; all rights for feature articles. Pays 50¢/word for assigned articles; 25¢/word for unsolicited manuscripts. Writer's guidelines and sample copy available for $5.

Tips: "*Muse* many on occasion publish unsolicited manuscripts, but the easiest way to be printed in *Muse* is to send a query. However, manuscripts may be submitted to the Cricket Magazine Group for review, and any that are considered suitable for *Muse* will be forwarded. Such manuscripts will also be considered for publication in *Cricket*, *Spider* or *Ladybug*." (See listing for *Babybug*, *Cricket*, *Ladybug* and *Spider*.)

☑ **MY FRIEND, The Catholic Magazine for Kids**, Pauline Books & Media, 50 St. Paul's Ave., Jamaica Plain, Boston MA 02130-3491. (617)522-8911. Fax: (617)541-9805. E-mail: myfriend@pauline.org. Website: www.pauline.org. **Articles/Fiction Editor:** Sr. Kathryn James, FSP. **Art Director:** Sister Regina Dick, FSP.

Monthly magazine. Estab. 1979. Circ. 12,000. "*My Friend* is a 32-page monthly Catholic magazine for boys and girls. Its' goal is to celebrate the Catholic Faith—as it is lived by today's children and as it has been lived for centuries. Its pages are packed with fun, learning, new experiences, information, crafts, global awareness, friendships and inspiration. Together with it's web-page KidStuff." *My Friend* provides kids and their families a wealth of information and contacts on every aspect of the Faith."

Fiction: Young readers, middle readers: adventure, Christmas, contemporary, humorous, multicultural, nature/environment, problem-solving, religious, sports, science fiction. Does not want to see poetry, animals as main characters in religious stories, stories whose basic thrust would be incompatible with Catholic values. Buys 50 mss/year. Average word length: 450-750. Byline given.

Nonfiction: Young readers, middle readers: games/puzzles, humorous, interview/profile, media literacy, nature/environment, problem-solving, religious, multicultural, social issues. Does not want to see material that is not compatible with Catholic values; no "New Age" material. Buys 10 mss/year. Average word length: 450-750. Byline given.

How to Contact/Writers: Fiction/nonfiction: Send complete ms. Reports on queries/mss in 2 months.

Illustration: Buys 8 illustrations/issue; buys 60-80 illustrations/year. Preferred theme or style: realistic depictions of children, but open to variety!

Terms: Pays on acceptance for mss. Buys first rights for mss; variable for artwork. Original artwork returned at job's completion. Pays $60-150 for stories/articles. Pays illustrators $250/color (cover); $50-150/b&w (inside); $75-175/color (inside). Pays photographers $15-250/photo. Sample copy $2.75 with 9×12 SAE and 4 first-class stamps. Writer's guidelines free with SAE and 1 first-class stamp.

Tips: Writers: "We are looking for fresh perspectives into a child's world that are imaginative, unique, challenging, informative, current and fun. We prefer articles that are visual, not necessarily text-based—articles written in 'windows' style with multiple points entry. Illustrators: Please contact us! For the most part, we need illustrations for fiction stories."

✔ NATIONAL GEOGRAPHIC WORLD, National Geographic Society, 1145 17th St. NW, Washington DC 20036-4688. (202)857-7000. Fax: (202)775-6112. **Editor:** Susan Tejada. **Art Director**: Ursula Vosseler. **Photo Editor**: Chuck Herron. Monthly magazine. Estab. 1975. Circ. 1.1 million.

Nonfiction: Young readers, middle readers, young adult/teens: animal, arts/crafts, biography, cooking, games/puzzles, geography, history, hobbies, how-to, interview/profile, multicultural, nature/environment, science, sports, travel. Middle readers, young adult/teens: social issues. "We do not review or buy unsolicited manuscripts, but do use freelance writers."

Illustration: Buys 100% of illustrations from freelancers. Works on assignment only. Query. Illustrations only: Query with samples. Reports in 2 months. Samples returned with SASE; samples filed. Credit line given.

Photography: Buys photos separately. Looking for active shots, funny, strange animal close-ups. Uses 35mm transparencies. Query with samples. Reports in 2 months.

Terms: Pays on acceptance. Buys all rights for mss and artwork. Originals returned to artist at job's completion. Writers get 3 copies of issue their work appears in. Pays photographers by the project. Sample copies for 9×12 SAE and 2 first-class stamps; photo guidelines available free for SASE.

Tips: "Most story ideas are generated in-house and assigned to freelance writers. Query with cover letter and samples of your writing for children or young adults. Keep in mind that *World* is a visual magazine. A story will work best if it has a very tight focus and if the photos show children interacting with their surroundings as well as with each other."

✔ NATURE FRIEND MAGAZINE, 2727 Press Run Rd., Sugarcreek OH 44681. (330)852-1900. Fax: (330)852-3285. **Articles Editor:** Marvin Wengerd. Monthly magazine. Estab. 1983. Circ. 9,000.

Fiction: Picture-oriented material, conversational.

Nonfiction: Picture-oriented material, animal, how-to, nature. No evolutionary material. Buys 100 mss/year. Average word length: 500. Byline given.

How to Contact/Writers: Nonfiction: Send complete ms. Reports on mss in 4 months. Will consider but must note simultaneous submissions.

Illustration: Buys approximately 8 illustrations/issue from freelancers; 96 illustrations/year. Reports on artist's submissions in 1 month. Works on assignment only. Credit line given.

Terms: Pays on publication. Buys one-time rights. Pays $15-75. Payment for illustrations: $15-80/b&w, $50-100/color inside. Two sample copies and writer's guidelines for $5 with 7½×10½ SAE and $1.47 postage. Writer's/illustrator's guidelines for $2.50.

Tips: Looks for "main articles, puzzles and simple nature and science projects. Needs conversationally-written stories about unique animals or nature phenomena. Please examine samples and writer's guide before submitting."

VISIT THE WRITER'S DIGEST WEBSITE at www.writersdigest.com for hot new markets, daily market updates, writers' guidelines and much more.

☑ **NEW MOON: The Magazine For Girls & Their Dreams**, New Moon Publishing, Inc., P.O. Box 3620, Duluth MN 55803-3620. (218)728-5507. Fax: (218)728-0314. E-mail: girl@newmoon.org. Website: www.newm oon.org. **Managing Editors:** Deb Mylin and Bridget Grosser. Bimonthly magazine. Estab. 1992. Circ. 25,000. *New Moon* is for every girl who wants her voice heard and her dreams taken seriously. *New Moon* portrays strong female role models of all ages, backgrounds and cultures now and in the past. 100% of publication aimed at juvenile market.

Fiction: Middle readers, young adults: adventure, animal, contemporary, fantasy, folktales, history, humorous, multicultural, nature/environment, problem-solving, religious, science fiction, sports, suspense/mystery, travel. Buys 3 mss/year from adults and 3 mss/year from girls. Average word length: 900-1,200. Byline given.

Nonfiction: Middle readers, young adults: animal, arts/crafts, biography, careers, cooking, games/puzzles, health, history, hobbies, humorous, interview/profile, math, multicultural, nature/environment, problem-solving, science, social issues, sports, travel, stories about real girls. Does not want to see how-to stories. Wants more stories about real girls doing real things written by girls. Buys 6 mss/year. Average word length: 600. Byline given.

How to Contact/Writers: Fiction/Nonfiction: Does not return or acknowledge unsolicited mss. Send only copies. Reports only if interested. Will consider simultaneous submissions and electronic submission and e-mail.

Illustration: Buys 6-12 illustrations/year from freelancers. *New Moon* seeks 4-color cover illustrations as well as b&w illustrations for inside. Reviews ms/illustrations packages from artists. Query. Submit ms with rough sketches. Illustration only: Query; send portfolio and tearsheets. Samples not returned; samples filed. Reports in 6 months only if interested. Credit line given.

Terms: Pays on publication. Buys all rights for mss. Buys one-time rights, reprint rights for artwork. Original artwork returned at job's completion. Pays 5-12¢/word for stories; 6-12¢/word for articles. Pays in contributor's copies. Pays illustrators $400 for color cover; $50-125 for b&w inside. Sample copies for $6.50. Writer's/cover art guidelines for SASE or available on website.

Tips: "Please refer to a copy of *New Moon* to understand the style and philosophy of the magazine. Writers and artists who understand our goals have the best chance of publication. We're looking for stories about real girls; women's careers, and historical profiles. We publish girls' and women's writing only." Publishes art/photos by girls.

☑ **ODYSSEY, Adventures in Science**, Cobblestone Publishing, Inc., 30 Grove St., Suite C, Peterborough NH 03458. (603)924-7209. Fax: (603)924-7380. E-mail: odyssey@cobblestonepub.com. Website: www.odyssey magazine.com. (Also see www.cobblestonepub.com.) **Editor:** Elizabeth E. Lindstrom. **Managing Editor:** Lou Waryncia. **Art Director:** Ann Dillon. Magazine published 9 times/year. Estab. 1979. Circ. 22,000. Magazine covers earth, science and technology, astronomy and space exploration for children ages 10-16. All material must relate to the theme of a specific upcoming issue in order to be considered.

● Themes for *Odyssey* issues in 2000 include Treasure Hunters: Exploring Shipwrecks; Decoding Iceland; and Eat Up! Eat Smart! Contact them for complete theme list before submitting.

Fiction: Middle readers and young adults/teens: science fiction, science, astronomy. Does not want to see anything not theme-related. Average word length: 900-1,200 words.

Nonfiction: Middle readers and young adults/teens: arts/crafts, biography, cooking, games/puzzles (no word finds), science (space). Don't send anything not theme-related. Average word length: 200-750, depending on section article is used in.

How to Contact/Writers: "A query must consist of all of the following to be considered (please use nonerasable paper): a brief cover letter stating the subject and word length of the proposed article; a detailed one-page outline explaining the information to be presented in the article; an extensive bibliography of materials the author intends to use in preparing the article; a SASE. Writers new to *Odyssey* should send a writing sample with query. If you would like to know if your query has been received, please also include a stamped postcard that requests acknowledgment of receipt. In all correspondence, please include your complete address as well as a telephone number where you can be reached. A writer may send as many queries for one issue as he or she wishes, but each query must have a separate cover letter, outline, bibliography, and SASE. Telephone queries are not accepted. Handwritten queries will not be considered. Queries may be submitted at any time, but queries sent well in advance of deadline *may not be answered for several months*. Go-aheads requesting material proposed in queries are usually sent five months prior to publication date. Unused queries will be returned approximately three to four months prior to publication date."

Illustration: Buys 3 illustrations/issue; 27 illustrations/year. Works on assignment only. Reviews ms/illustration packages from artists. Query. Contact: Beth Lindstrom, editor. Illustration only: Query with samples. Send tearsheets, photocopies. Reports in 2 weeks. Samples returned with SASE; samples not filed. Original artwork returned upon job's completion (upon written request).

Photography: Wants photos pertaining to any of our forthcoming themes. Uses b&w and color prints; 35mm transparencies. Photographers should send unsolicited photos by mail on speculation.

Terms: Pays on publication. Buys all rights for mss and artwork. Pays 20-25¢/word for stories/articles. Covers are assigned and paid on an individual basis. Pays photographers per photo ($15-100 for b&w; $25-100 for color). Sample copy for $3.95 and SASE with $1.05 postage. Writer's/illustrator's/photo guidelines for SASE. (See listings for *Appleseeds, California Chronicles, Calliope, Cobblestone, Faces* and *Footsteps*.)

insider report

Guiding the explorations of young science adventurers

Elizabeth Lindstrom never thought she'd be a science magazine editor. She has taught college-level writing, worked as a newspaper reporter and then features' editor, and has sold her paintings. Her husband has always viewed her as an "artsy" person. "But I've always loved science and remember winning prizes at science fairs as a child," says Lindstrom. "I think my journalism background—the ability to recognize a good story, analyze information quickly and present it to a specific audience—combined with my love of science and ease with it make me a good editor of *Odyssey*."

Odyssey, Adventures in Science is enjoyed by 10- to 16-year-olds with inquisitive minds and enthusiasm for science. Though the magazine concentrates on physical science and technology,

Elizabeth Lindstrom

issues are sprinkled with environmental and nature stories to provide a well-rounded exploration of the field. Lindstrom says the magazine is not afraid to tackle complex subjects such as genetics or the work of Stephen Hawking. "*Odyssey* always treats its readers with the respect they deserve as young science adventurers. We don't talk down to them," says Lindstrom. "In science, talking down to kids tends to simplify to the point that things seem to happen magically. It's best to include the necessary information in your explanations, but to diffract it by using good analogies that kids can relate to."

The best part of being senior editor (and also the hardest) is researching and planning an issue. Lindstrom says, "I love learning about new areas of science and talking with scientists who are always eager to convey their discoveries to young people. I wish I had more time for this part of the process. That's where my reporting background becomes helpful. I soak up information quickly and am able to analyze it and decide how to present it."

This talent for efficiently taking in data and dispensing it is key when working on four different issues simultaneously—especially when you're the magazine's lone in-house editor. Lindstrom nurtures each magazine from concept (what its theme will be) to completion (reading the page proofs). She does "thrash out" most tough decisions via e-mail with a dedicated contributing editor living in Hawaii. An extra hand comes from a consulting editor—a scientist specializing in work related to an issue's theme. Lindstrom selects this editor who sometimes pilots the issue but more often puts a stamp of approval on the finished product.

The content of *Odyssey* revolves around its theme list lodged in the back of Lindstrom's mind. She compiles the list by clipping articles, reading books, jotting down notes while watching TV, and asking lots of kids and adults (including *Odyssey*'s writers) what they think would make a good issue. "I try to include themes on astronomy, space science, technology, biology, mathematics, the environment, and a profile of a role model scientist each editorial year. Most importantly, I include only themes I can get excited about." Then she presents her list to a diverse panel including her husband, 12-year-old son and his friends, the managing editor, marketing director, publisher and *Odyssey*'s Advisory Board. (The Advisory Board consists of scientists from different disciplines plus a student advisor.) After gathering all the comments, Lindstrom finalizes the list, occasionally making changes through the year depending on new advances in science.

There are a few things Lindstrom wishes she could change about queries from writers. The principal faux pas is inappropriate material, the result of being unfamiliar with the magazine. Following that blunder are queries written in "choppy sentences and disjointed thoughts." When a mangled query is accompanied by a stellar writing sample, she automatically assumes the sample was rewritten by an editor. Lindstrom also warns, "Don't tell me you're going to write a 750-word piece and then give me an outline that explores the entire field of biotechnology. Do adequate research, but then find a good angle on the subject that enables you to write a focused, tight piece. Do begin your query with a title for your article and a lead paragraph that shows lively writing and focus. Follow this with an outline that, without fail, includes interviews, not just book or online research."

Potential writers should read *Odyssey*'s theme list and guidelines before submitting the best researched and written query they are capable of composing, says Lindstrom. A writer's age, marital status and number of children is not appropriate for a query. "Usually this information comes in the form of an apology for not having been published previously. One of my best writers is a Harvard-educated attorney, turned writer, who has three children at home. I learned all of this many months after she published her first story in *Odyssey*, which was the

Part of the Cobblestone family of magazines, *Odyssey, Adventures in Science* helps make issues relating to physical science and technology, as well as the environment and nature, accessible to curious young readers. The magazine is not afraid to tackle complex subjects such as genetics or the work of Stephen Hawking, says editor Elizabeth Lindtrom. "*Odyssey* always treats its readers with the respect they deserve as young science adventurers." *Odyssey*, which is designed to be used in the classroom, offers a website as a companion to the printed publication (www.odyssey-mag.com).

first children's magazine article she ever published. This now seasoned children's writer never fails to submit a query in the format I have described."

Articles explaining cutting-edge science as a story are forever in demand. Readers are eager for a science adventure "that unfolds as a narrative." Always welcome at the magazine are Q&A interviews with important, articulate scientists, educational activities kids will really want to do, and short (750-1,000 words) fiction stories about science targeted at 12 year olds. Lindstrom turns away articles that don't pertain to an upcoming theme, and multiple queries on the same obvious topic for a specific theme (e.g., "Major Discoveries in the 20th Century" for the millennium issue).

Lindstrom strives to make writers an important component of the magazine. "I think they sense they are and so take time for that extra interview, or to give me leads on the perfect photograph for their piece. They work on tight deadlines, and sometimes on last minute notice and then thank "me for letting them be a part of the issue. I just wish I had lots more writers like these special ones."

For Lindstrom, no extra effort is necessary to make science fun. "Science *is* fun. It's an ongoing adventure, and it needs to be presented that way. Let scientists talk about their work. Go out into the field with them. You'll be surprised how many show their own excitement. If you are a good researcher, interviewer and writer who has been afraid to try the science market, try it. It's a rich, rewarding area and good science writers have never been needed more."

—Tara Horton

ON COURSE, A Magazine for Teens, General Council of the Assemblies of God, 1445 Boonville Ave., Springfield MO 65802-1894. (417)862-2781. Fax: (417)866-1146. E-mail: oncourse@ag.org. **Editor:** Melinda Booze. **Art Director:** David Danielson. Quarterly magazine. Estab. 1991. Circ. 166,000. *On Course* is a religious quarterly for teens "to encourage Christian, biblical discipleship; to promote denominational post-secondary schools; to nurture loyalty to the denomination."

● *On Course* works on assignment only. Each issue focuses on a theme. Send for theme list along with writers guidelines. Send to Amber Weigand-Buckley, assistant editor. Accepts résumés and writing samples for publication's writer's file. Manuscripts not returned.

Fiction: Young adults: Christian discipleship, contemporary, humorous, multicultural, problem-solving, sports. Average word length: 1,000. Byline given.

Nonfiction: Young adults: careers, interview/profile, multicultural, religion, social issues, college life, Christian discipleship.

How to Contact/Writers: Works on assignment basis only.

Illustration: Buys 4 illustrations/issue; 16 illustrations/year. Uses color artwork only. Reviews ms/illustration packages from artists. Query. Illustration only: Query with samples or send résumé, promo sheet, slides, client list and tearsheets. Contact Melinda Booze, editor. Reports back only if interested. Originals not returned at job's completion. Credit line given.

Photography: Buys photos from freelancers. "Teen life, church life, college life; unposed; often used for illustrative purposes." Model/property releases required. Uses color glossy prints and 35mm or 2¼ × 2¼ transparencies. Query with samples; send business card, promotional literature, tearsheets or catalog. Reports only if interested.

Terms: Pays on acceptance. Buys first or reprint rights for mss. Buys one-time rights for photographs. Pays 10¢/word for stories/articles. Pays illustrators and photographers "as negotiated." Sample copies free for 9 × 11 SAE. Writer's guidelines for SASE.

OWL, The Discovery Magazine for Children, Bayard Press, 179 John St., Suite 500, Toronto, Ontario M5T 3G5 Canada. (416)971-5275. Fax: (416)971-5294. E-mail: owl@owlkids.com. Website: www.owlkids.com. **Editor:** Keltie Thomas. **Creative Director:** Tim Davin. **Photo Editor:** Katherine Murray. Monthly magazine. Circ. 110,000. "*OWL* helps children over eight discover and enjoy the world of science, nature and technology. We look for articles that are fun to read, that inform from a child's perspective, and that motivate hands-on interaction. *OWL* explores the reader's many interests in the natural world in a scientific, but always entertaining, way."

Nonfiction: Middle readers: animal, biology, games/puzzles, high-tech, humor, nature/environment, science, social issues, sports, travel. Especially interested in puzzles and game ideas: logic, math, visual puzzles. Does not want to see religious topics, anthropomorphizing. Buys 20 mss/year. Average word length: 500-1,500. Byline given.

How to Contact/Writers: Nonfiction: Query with published clips. Reports on queries/mss in 3-4 months.

Illustration: Buys 3-5 illustrations/issue; 40-50 illustrations/year. Uses color artwork only. Preferred theme or style: lively, involving, fun, with emotional impact and appeal. "We use a range of styles." Works on assignment only. Illustrations only. Send tearsheets and slides. Reports on art samples only if interested. Original artwork returned at job's completion.

Photography: Looking for shots of animals and nature. "Label the photos." Uses 2¼ × 2¼ and 35mm transparencies. Photographers should query with samples.

Terms: Pays on publication. Buys first North American and world rights for mss, artwork and photos. Pays $200-500 (Canadian) for assigned/unsolicited articles. Pays up to $650 (Canadian) for illustrations. Photographers are paid per photo. Sample copies for $4. Free writer's guidelines.

Tips: Writers: "*OWL* is dedicated to entertaining kids with contemporary and accurate information about the world around them. *OWL* is intellectually challenging but is never preachy. Ideas should be original and convey a spirit of humor and liveliness." (See listings for *Chickadee* and *Chirp*.)

✔ **POCKETS, Devotional Magazine for Children**, The Upper Room, 1908 Grand, P.O. Box 189, Nashville TN 37202-0189. (615)340-7333. Fax: (615)340-7267. E-mail: pockets@upperroom.org. Website: www.upperroo m.org/pockets. **Articles/Fiction Editor:** Lynn W. Gilliam. **Art Director**: Chris Schechner, Suite 207, 3100 Carlisle Plaza, Dallas TX 75204. Magazine published 11 times/year. Estab. 1981. Circ. 96,000. "*Pockets* is a Christian devotional magazine for children ages 6-12. Stories should help children experience a Christian lifestyle that is not always a neatly wrapped moral package but is open to the continuing revelation of God's will."

  ● *Pockets* ranked number 15 on the 1999 *Writer's Digest*'s Fiction 50, the magazine's annual list of "50 best places to publish your short stories."

Fiction: Picture-oriented, young readers, middle readers: adventure, contemporary, folktales, multicultural, nature/environment, problem-solving, religious. Does not want to see violence or talking animal stories. Buys 40-45 mss/year. Average word length: 800-1,400. Byline given.

Nonfiction: Picture-oriented, young readers, middle readers: cooking, games/puzzles, interview/profile, religion. Does not want to see how-to articles. "Our nonfiction reads like a story." Multicultural needs include: stories that feature children of various racial/ethnic groups and do so in a way that is true to those depicted. Buys 10 mss/year. Average word length: 800-1,400. Byline given.

How to Contact/Writers: Fiction/nonfiction: Send complete ms. "Prefer not to deal with queries." Reports on mss in 6 weeks. Will consider simultaneous submissions.

Illustration: Buys 40-50 illustrations/issue. Preferred theme or style: varied; both 4-color and 2-color. Works on assignment only. Illustrations only: Send promo sheet, tearsheets.

✔ **POWER AND LIGHT**, Children's Ministries, 6401 The Paseo, Kansas City MO 64131-1284. (816)333-7000. Fax: (816)333-4439. E-mail: mprice@nazarene.org. Website: www.nazarene.org. **Editor:** Matt Price. Weekly story paper. "*Power and Light* is a leisure-reading piece for fifth and sixth graders. It is published weekly by the Department of Children's Ministries of the Church of the Nazarene. The major purposes of *Power and Light* are to provide a leisure-reading piece which will build Christian behavior and values; provide reinforcement for Biblical concepts taught in the Sunday School curriculum. The focus of the reinforcement will be life-related, with some historical appreciation. *Power and Light*'s target audience is children ages 11-12 in grades 5 and 6."

Fiction: Middle readers, young adults: adventure, contemporary, humorous, multicultural, preteen issues, problem solving, religious. "Avoid fantasy, science fiction, abnormally mature or precocious children, personification of animals. Also avoid extensive cultural or holiday references, especially those with a distinctly American frame of reference. Our paper has an international audience. We need stories involving multicultural preteens in realistic settings dealing with realistic problems with God's help." Average word length: 500-700. Byline given.

Nonfiction: Middle readers, young adults: archaeological, biography, history, games/puzzles, how-to, interview/profile, problem-solving, multicultural, religion, social issues, travel. Multicultural needs include: ethnics and cultures—other world areas especially English-speaking.

How to Contact/Writers: Send complete ms. Reports on queries/mss in 2 months. Publishes ms 2 years after acceptance.

Photography: Buys "b&w archaeological/Biblical for inside use.

Terms: Pays on publication. "Payment is made approximately one year before the date of issue." Buys multiple use rights for mss. Purchases all rights for artwork and first/one-time rights for photographs. Pays 5¢/word for stories/articles. Writer's guidelines for SASE.

Tips: Writers: "Themes and outcomes should conform to the theology and practices of the Church of the Nazarene, Evangelical Friends, Free Methodist, Wesleyan and other Bible-believing Evangelical churches." We look for bright, colorful illustrations; concise, short articles and stories. Keep it realistic and contemporary. Request guidelines first!" (See listing for *Discoveries*.)

 **POWER STATION**, Scripture Press Publications, 4050 Lee Vance View, Colorado Springs CO 80918. (719)536-0100. Fax: (719)533-3045. E-mail: burtonj@cookministries.org. **Editor:** Jan Burton. **Art Director:** Randy Maid. Quarterly newspaper. Estab. 1999. "We are a Sunday School take-home paper for fifth and sixth graders. Our papers correlate with the Scripture Press Sunday School curriculum. The purpose of our papers is to show children how Bible truths relate to their everyday life experiences. We seek to disciple children in Christian living."

Fiction: Middle readers: adventure, history, humorous, multicultural (stories set in other countries or ethnic settings in the US), nature/environment, problem-solving, religious, sports. All stories must have Christian context. Buys 50 mss/year. Average word length: 800-850. Byline given.

Nonfiction: Middle readers: arts/crafts, biography, games/puzzles, history, hobbies, how-to, humorous, interview/profile, multicultural, nature/environment, problem-solving, religion, science, social issues, sports. Buys 50 mss/year. All must have Christian context. Average word length: 300-350. Byline given.

How to Contact/Writers: Fiction/nonfiction: send complete ms. Reports on mss in 1-2 months.

Terms: Pays on acceptance. Buys first North American serial rights, first rights, one-time rights, reprint rights or all rights. Pays 8-10¢/word for stories and articles depending on editing required. Additional payment for photos accompanying article. Sample copies free for SAE and 1 first-class stamp. Writer's guidelines free for SASE.

Tips: "Pay attention to the Writers Tips or Guidelines. Write for sample copies so you know the flavor of the papers. Send manuscripts in acceptable form. Proofread all submissions carefully. Be sure submissions have a Christian emphasis, moral slant. Stories need to show God's work in a child's life or situation."

RANGER RICK, National Wildlife Federation, 8925 Leesburg Pike, Vienna VA 22184. (703)790-4000. Website: www.nwf.org.
• Ranger Rick is no longer accepting unsolicited queries or manuscripts.

REACT MAGAZINE, The magazine that raises voices, Parade Publications, 711 Third Ave., New York NY 10017. (212)450-0900. Fax: (212)450-0978. **Editor:** Lee Kravitz. **Managing Editor:** Susan Byrne. **Executive Editor:** Nina Malkin. **Art Director:** Linda Rubes. **Photo Editor:** Margaret Kemp. Weekly magazine. Estab. 1995. Circ. 3.6 million. 100% publication aimed at teen market.

Nonfiction: Young adult: animal, entertainment, games/puzzles, health, hobbies, interview/profile, nature/environment, news, science, social issues, sports. Average word length: 250-600. Byline given.

How to Contact/Writers: Query with published clips.

Illustration: Works on assignment only. Illustration only: arrange portfolio review. Contact: Linda Rubes, art director. Credit given.

Photography: Query with résumé or credits. Arrange portfolio review. Reports only if interested.

Terms: Pays on acceptance. Buys all rights for mss, artwork and photographs. Pays writers by the project. Additional payment for photos accompanying articles. Pays photographers by the project. Writer's guidelines and sample issue for SAE and 80¢ postage.

Tips: "Do not submit work. Query with clips only."

 **READ**, Weekly Reader Corporation, 200 First Stamford Place, P.O. Box 120023, Stamford CT 06912-0023. Fax: (203)705-1661. E-mail: edread@weeklyreader.com. Website: www.weeklyreader.com. **Editor:** Suzanne Garchers. Magazine published 18 times during the school year. Language arts periodical for use in classrooms for students ages 12-16; motivates students to read and teaches skills in listening, comprehension, speaking, writing and critical thinking.

Fiction: Wants short stories, narratives and plays to be used for classroom reading and discussions. Middle readers, young adult/teens: adventure, animal, contemporary, fantasy, folktales, history, humorous, multicultural, nature/environment, problem solving, sports. Average word length: 1,000-2,500.

Nonfiction: Middle readers, young adult/teen: animal, games/puzzles, history, humorous, problem solving, social issues.

How to Contact: Reports on queries/mss in 6 weeks.

Illustration: Buys 2-3 illustrations/issue; 20-25 illustration jobs/year. Reports back only if interested. Samples returned with SASE. Credit line given.

Terms: Pays on publication. Rights purchased varies. Pays writers $200-1,000 for stories/articles. Pays illustrators $650-850 for color cover; $125-750 for b&w and color inside. Pays photographers by the project (range:

**FOR EXPLANATIONS OF THESE SYMBOLS,
SEE THE INSIDE FRONT AND BACK COVERS OF THIS BOOK**

$450-650); per photo (range: $125-650). Samples copies free for digest sized SAE and 3 first-class stamps.
Tips: "We especially like plot twists and surprise endings. Stories should be relevant to teens and contain realistic conflicts and dialogue. Plays should have at least 12 speaking parts for classroom reading. Avoid formula plots, trite themes, underage material, stilted or profane language, and sexual suggestion. Get to know the style of our magazine as well as our teen audience. They are very demanding and require an engaging and engrossing read. Grab their attention, keep the pace and action lively, build to a great climax, and make the ending satisfying and/or surprising. Make sure characters and dialogue are realistic. Do not use cliché, but make the writing fresh—simple, yet original."

☑ **SCIENCE WEEKLY**, Science Weekly Inc., P.O. Box 70638, Chevy Chase MD 20813. (301)680-8804. Fax: (301)680-9240. E-mail: sciencew@erols.com. **Editor:** Deborah Lazar. Magazine published 16 times/year. Estab. 1984. Circ. 200,000.
• *Science Weekly* uses freelance writers to develop and write an entire issue on a single science topic. Send résumé only, not submissions. Authors must be within the greater DC, Virginia, Maryland area. *Science Weekly* works on assignment only.
Nonfiction: Young readers, middle readers, (K-8th grade): science/math education, education, problem-solving.
Terms: Pays on publication. Prefers people with education, science and children's writing background. *Send résumé.* Samples copies free with SAE and 2 first-class stamps. Follow what is asked for by a publication when submitting materials—if it says résumé only, just send a résumé. If it says a specific locale only, don't send if you are outside of this area. It is a waste of your valuable time and the time of the publication to go through materials it cannot use.

SCIENCE WORLD, Scholastic Inc., 555 Broadway, New York NY 10012-3999. (212)343-6456. Fax: (212)343-6333. E-mail: scienceworld@scholastic.com. **Editor:** Mark Bregman. **Art Director:** Susan Kass. Magazine published biweekly during the school year. Estab. 1959. Circ. 350,000. Publishes articles in Life Science/Health, Physical Science/Technology, Earth Science/Environment/Astronomy for students in grades 7-10. The goal is to make science relevant for teens.
• *Science World* publishes a separate teacher's edition with lesson plans and skills pages to accompany feature articles.
Nonfiction: Young adults/teens: animal, concept, geography, health, nature/environment, science. Multicultural needs include: minority scientists as role models. Does not want to see stories without a clear news hook. Buys 20 mss/year. Average word length: 500-1,000. Byline sometimes given.
How to Contact/Writers: Nonfiction: Query with published clips. Reports on queries/mss in 2 weeks. Publishes ms 2 months after acceptance.
Illustration: Buys 2 illustrations/issue; 28 illustrations/year. Works on assignment only. Illustration only: Query with samples, tearsheets. Contact: Susan Kass, art director. Reports back only if interested. Samples returned with SASE; samples filed "if we use them." Credit line sometimes given.
Photography: Model/property releases required; captions required including background information. Provide résumé, business card, promotional literature or tearsheets to be kept on file. Reports back only if interested.
Terms: Pays on acceptance. Buys all right for mss/artwork. Originals returned to artist at job's completion. For stories/articles, pays $200. Pays photographers per photo. Sample copies free for 9×12 SAE and 2 first-class stamps. Writer's guidelines for SASE.

SEVENTEEN MAGAZINE, Primedia, 850 Third Ave., New York NY 10022. (212)407-9700. **Editor-in-Chief:** Patrice G. Adcroft. **Executive Editor:** Roberta Caploe, fiction. **Deputy Editor:** Tamara Glenny. **Art Director:** Florence Sicard. Monthly magazine. Estab. 1944. Circ. 2.5 million. "*Seventeen* is a young women's first fashion and beauty magazine."
• *Seventeen* ranked number 1 on *Writer's Digest*'s 1999 Fiction 50, the magazine's annual list of "50 best places to publish your short stories."
Fiction: "We consider all good literary short fiction." Buys 6-12 mss/year. Average word length: 800-4,000. Byline given.
Nonfiction: Young adults: animal, beauty, entertainment, fashion, careers, health, hobbies, how-to, humorous, interview/profile, multicultural, relationships, religion, social issues, sports. Buys 150 mss/year. Word length: Varies from 800-1,000 words for short features and monthly columns to 800-2,500 words for major articles. Byline given.
How to Contact/Writers: Fiction: Send complete ms. Nonfiction: Query with published clips or send complete ms. "Do not call." Reports on queries/mss in 6-12 weeks. Will consider simultaneous submissions.
Terms: Pays on acceptance. Pays $1/word. Strongly recommends requesting writers guidelines with SASE and reading recent issues of the magazine.

☑ **SHARING THE VICTORY**, Fellowship of Christian Athletes, 8701 Leeds, Kansas City MO 64129. (816)921-0909. Fax: (816)921-8755. Website: www.fca.org. **Articles/Photo Editor:** David Smale. **Art Director:** Frank Grey. Magazine published 9 times a year. Estab. 1982. Circ. 75,000. "Purpose is to present to coaches and athletes, and all whom they influence, the challenge and adventure of receiving Jesus Christ as Savior and Lord."

Nonfiction: Young adults/teens: interview/profile, sports. Buys 30 mss/year. Average word length: 500-1,000. Byline given.

Poetry: Reviews poetry. Maximum length: 50-75 words.

How to Contact/Writers: Nonfiction: Query with published clips. Reports in 6 weeks. Publishes ms 3 months after acceptance. Will consider simultaneous submissions, electronic submissions via disk or modem and previously published work. Writer's guidelines available on website.

Photography: Purchases photos separately. Looking for photos of sports action. Uses color, b&w prints and 35mm transparencies.

Terms: Pays on publication. Buys first rights and second serial (reprint) rights. Pays $50-200 for assigned and unsolicited articles. Photographers paid per photo (range: $50-100). Sample copies for 9×12 SASE and $1. Writer's/photo guidelines for SASE.

Tips: "Be specific—write short. Take quality photos that are useable." Wants interviews and features. Interested in colorful sports photos.

SKIPPING STONES, A Multicultural Children's Magazine, P.O. Box 3939, Eugene OR 97403. (541)342-4956. E-mail: skipping@efn.org. Website: www.nonviolence.org/skipping. **Articles/Photo/Fiction Editor:** Arun N. Toké. Bimonthly magazine. Estab. 1988. Circ. 3,000. "*Skipping Stones* is a multicultural, nonprofit children's magazine designed to encourage cooperation, creativity and celebration of cultural and ecological richness. We encourage submissions by minorities and under-represented populations."

● Send SASE for *Skipping Stones* guidelines and theme list for detailed descriptions of the topics they're looking for.

Fiction: Middle readers, young adult/teens: contemporary, meaningful, humorous. All levels: folktales, multicultural, nature/environment. Multicultural needs include: bilingual or multilingual pieces; use of words from other languages; settings in other countries, cultures or multi-ethnic communities.

Nonfiction: All levels: animal, biography, cooking, games/puzzles, history, humorous, interview/profile, multicultural, nature/environment, creative problem-solving, religion and cultural celebrations, sports, travel, social and international awareness. Does not want to see preaching or abusive language; no poems by authors over 18 years old; no suspense or romance stories for the sake of the same. Average word length: 500-750. Byline given.

How to Contact/Writers: Fiction: Query. Nonfiction: Send complete ms. Reports on queries in 1 month; mss in 4 months. Will consider simultaneous submissions; reviews artwork for future assignments. Please include your name on each page.

Illustration: Prefers color and/or b&w drawings, especially by teenagers and young adults. Will consider all illustration packages. Ms/illustration packages: Query; submit complete ms with final art; submit tearsheets. Reports back in 4 months. Credit line given.

Photography: Black & white photos preferred, but color photos with good contrast are welcome. Need children 7-17, international, nature, celebration.

Terms: Acquires first or reprint rights for mss and artwork; reprint rights for photographs. Pays in copies for authors, photographers and illustrators. Sample copies for $5 with SAE and 4 first-class stamps. Writer's/illustrator's guidelines for 4×9 SASE.

Tips: "We want material meant for children and young adults/teenagers with multicultural or ecological awareness themes. Think, live and write as if you were a child—naturally, uninhibited." Wants "material that gives insight on cultural celebrations, lifestyle, custom and tradition, glimpse of daily life in other countries and cultures. Photos, songs, artwork are most welcome if they illustrate/highlight the points. Translations are invited if your submission is in a language other than English. Upcoming themes will include cultural celebrations, living abroad, challenging disability, rewards and punishments, hospitality customs of various cultures, modern technology and its impact on human societies, life in the year 2000, cross-cultural communications, African, Asian and Latin American cultures, indigenous architecture, humor, international, creative problem solving and turning points in life."

[N] SMILE MAGAZINE, Mixx Entertainment, Inc., 746 W. Adams Blvd., Los Angeles CA 90089. (213)743-2519. Fax: (213)743-7189. E-mail: editorial@mixxonline.com. Website: www.smilegear.com. **Articles Editors:** Sydney Spiller or Susan Jaget. **Fiction Editor:** Livia Ching. **Art Director:** Rod Sampson. Photo Editor: Susan Jaget. Bimonthly magazine. Estab.1998. Circ. 20,000-50,000. "We foster a digital, cyberspace futuristic videogaming anime culture for 10-16 year old females."

Fiction: Buys 100-150 mss/year. Average word length: 100-1,000. Byline given.

Nonfiction: Middle readers, young adults: animal, arts/crafts, biography, career, concept, cooking, fashion, games/puzzles, geography, health, history, hobbies, how-to, humorous, interview/profile, math, multicultural, nature/environment, problem-solving, religion, science, social issues, sports, travel. Buys 50-100 mss/year. Average word length: 200-1,050. Byline given.

How To Contact/Writers: Only interested in agented material. Fiction/Nonfiction: Query with published clips. Send complete ms. Reports on queries/mss in 1 month. Will consider simultaneous submissions and electronic submissions via disk or modem.

Photography: Uses celebrity and interview photos. Captions required. Uses color prints and slides. Submit portfolio for review. Reports in 6 weeks only if interested.

Terms: Pays on publication. Buys exclusive magazine rights. Originals returned to artist at job's completion. Pays $100 per page for stories/articles.

Tips: "Think futuristic teen girl."

SOCCER JR., The Soccer Magazine for Kids, Triplepoint Inc., 27 Unquowa Rd., Fairfield CT 06430-5015. (203)259-5766. Fax: (203)256-1119. E-mail: soccerjrol@aol.com. **Articles/Fiction Editor:** Jill Schoff Bimonthly magazine. Estab. 1992. Circ. 120,000. *Soccer Jr.* is for soccer players 8-16 years old. "The editorial focus of *Soccer Jr.* is on the fun and challenge of the sport. Every issue contains star interviews, how-to tips, lively graphics, action photos, comics, games, puzzles and contests. Fair play and teamwork are emphasized in a format that provides an off-the-field way for kids to enjoy the sport."

Fiction: Middle readers, young adults/teens: sports (soccer). Does not want to see "cute," preachy or "moralizing" stories. Buys 3-4 mss/year. Average word length: 1,000-2,000. Byline given.

Nonfiction: Young readers, middle readers, young adults/teens: sports (soccer). Buys 10-12 mss/year.

How to Contact/Writers: Fiction/nonfiction: Send complete ms. Reports on mss in 4-6 weeks. Publishes ms 3-12 months after acceptance. Will consider simultaneous submissions.

Illustration: Buys 2 illustrations/issue; 20 illustrations/year. Works on assignment only. Illustrations only: Send samples to be filed. Samples not returned; samples kept on file. "We have a small pool of artists we work from but look for new freelancers occasionally, and accept samples for consideration." Credit line given.

Terms: Pays on acceptance. Buys first rights for mss. Pays $50-600 for stories. Pays illustrators $300-750 for color cover; $50-200 for b&w inside; $75-300 for color inside. Pays photographers per photo (range: $75-300). Sample copies for 9×12 SAE and 5 first-class stamps.

Tips: "We ask all potential writers to understand *Soccer Jr.*'s voice. We write to kids, not to adults. We request a query for any feature ideas, but any fiction pieces can be sent complete. All submissions, unless specifically requested, are on a speculative basis. Please indicate if a manuscript has been submitted elsewhere or previously published. Please give us a brief personal bio, including your involvement in soccer, if any, and a listing of any work you've had published. We prefer manuscripts in Microsoft Word, along with an attached hard copy." The magazine also accepts stories written by children.

SPIDER, The Magazine for Children, Carus Publishing Company, P.O. Box 300, Peru IL 61354. (312)939-1500. Website: www.cricketmag.com. **Editor-in-Chief:** Marianne Carus. **Associate Editor:** Laura Tillotson. **Art Director:** Tony Jacobson. Monthly magazine. Estab. 1994. Circ. 85,000. *Spider* publishes high-quality literature for beginning readers, primarily ages 6-9.

Fiction: Young readers: adventure, animal, contemporary, fantasy, folktales, history, humorous, multicultural, nature/environment, problem-solving, science fiction, sports, suspense/mystery. "Authentic, well-researched stories from all cultures are welcome. No didactic, religious, or violent stories, or anything that talks down to children." Average word length: 300-900. Byline given.

Nonfiction: Young readers: animal, arts/crafts, cooking, games/puzzles, geography, history, math, multicultural, nature/environment, problem-solving, science. "Well-researched articles on all cultures are welcome. Would like to see more games, puzzles and activities, especially ones adaptable to *Spider*'s takeout pages. No encyclopedic or overtly educational articles." Average word length: 300-800. Byline given.

Poetry: Serious, humorous, nonsense rhymes. Maximum length: 20 lines.

How to Contact/Writers: Fiction/nonfiction: Send complete ms. Reports on mss in 3 months. Publishes ms 3-4 years after acceptance. Will consider simultaneous submissions and previously published work.

Illustration: Buys 20 illustrations/issue; 240 illustrations/year. Uses color artwork only. "Any medium—preferably one that can wrap on a laser scanner—no larger than 20×24. We use more realism than cartoon-style art." Works on assignment only. Reviews ms/illustration packages from artists. Submit ms with rough sketches. Illustrations only: Send promo sheet and tearsheets. Reports in 6 weeks. Samples returned with SASE; samples filed. Credit line given.

Photography: Buys photos from freelancers. Buys photos with accompanying ms only. Model/property releases required; captions required. Uses 35mm or 2¼×2¼ transparencies. Send unsolicited photos by mail; provide résumé and tearsheets. Reports in 6 weeks.

Terms: Pays on publication for text; within 45 days from acceptance for art. Buys first, one-time or reprint rights for mss. Buys first and promotional rights for artwork; one-time rights for photographs. Original artwork returned at job's completion. Pays 25¢/word for stories/articles. Authors also receive 2 complimentary copies of the issue in which work appears. Additional payment for ms/illustration packages and for photos accompanying articles. Pays illustrators $750 for color cover; $200-300 for color inside. Pays photographers per photo (range: $25-75). Sample copies for $4. Writer's/illustrator's guidelines for SASE.

Tips: Writers: "Read back issues before submitting." (See listings for *Babybug, Cicada, Cricket, Click, Muse* and *Ladybug*.)

STANDARD PUBLISHING, 8121 Hamilton Ave., Cincinnati OH 45231. See listings for *Kidz Chat, Live Wire* and *Straight*.

STRAIGHT, Standard Publishing, 8121 Hamilton Ave., Cincinnati OH 45231. (513)931-4050. Fax: (513)931-0950. **Articles/Fiction Editor:** Heather Wallace. Magazine published quarterly in weekly parts. Circ. 25,000. *Straight* is a magazine designed for today's Christian teenagers.
  • *Straight* ranked number 27 on the 1999 *Writer's Digest* Fiction 50, the magazine's annual list of "50 best places to publish your short stories." At presstime, *Straight* was in the process of changing formats and changing names. Changes will be in effect in 2000.

Fiction: Young adults/teens: adventure, contemporary, health, humorous, multicultural, nature/environment, problem solving, religious, romance, sports. Does not want to see science fiction, fantasy, historical. "All should have religious perspective." Byline given.

Nonfiction: Young adults/teens: biography, careers, health, hobbies, how-to, humorous, interview/profile, multicultural, nature/environment, problem-solving, religion, social issues, sports. Does not want to see devotionals. Byline given.

Poetry: Reviews poetry from teenagers only.

How to Contact/Writers: Fiction/nonfiction: Query or send complete ms. Reports on queries in 1-2 weeks; mss in 1-2 months. Will consider simultaneous submissions.

Illustration: Uses color artwork only. Preferred theme or style: Realistic, cartoon (full-color only). Works on assignment only. Query first. Illustrations only: Submit promo sheets or tearsheets. Samples returned with SASE. Reports back only if interested. Credit line given.

Photography: Buys photos from freelancers. Looking for photos of contemporary, modestly dressed teenagers. Model/property release required. Uses 35mm transparencies. Photographer should request themes.

Terms: Pays on acceptance. Buys first rights and second serial (reprint rights) for mss. Buys full rights for artwork; one-time rights for photos. Writer's/illustrator's guidelines for business SASE.

Tips: "Remember we are a publication for Christian teenagers. Each fiction or nonfiction piece should address modern-day issues from a religious perspective. We are trying to become more racially diverse. Writers, illustrators and photographers should keep this in mind and submit more material with African-Americans, Hispanics, Asian-Americans, etc. as the focus. The main characters of all pieces should be contemporary teens who cope with modern-day problems using Christian principles. Stories should be uplifting, positive and character-building, but not preachy. Conflicts must be resolved realistically, with thought-provoking and honest endings. Nonfiction is accepted. We use articles on current issues from a Christian point of view and humor. Nonfiction pieces should concern topics of interest to teens, including school, family life, recreation, friends, part-time jobs, dating and music." This magazine publishes writing/art/photos by children. (See listings for *Kidz Chat* and *Live Wire*.)

☑ TEEN LIFE, Gospel Publishing House, 1445 Boonville Ave., Springfield MO 65802-1894. (417)862-2781, ext. 4370. Fax: (417)862-6059. E-mail: teenlife@ag.org. **Articles/Fiction Editor:** Tammy Bicket. **Art Director:** Sonny Carder. Quarterly magazine. Estab. 1920. Circ. 50,000. "Slant articles toward the 15- to 19-year-old teen. We are a Christian publication, so all articles should focus on the Christian's responses to life. Fiction should be realistic, not syrupy nor too graphic. Fiction should have a Christian slant also."
  • *Teen Life* is not currently accepting freelance writing.

Fiction: Young adults/teens: adventure, contemporary, history, humorous, multicultural, problem-solving, religious, romance, science fiction, sports (all with Christian slant). Also wants fiction based on true stories. Buys 50 mss/year. Average word length 700-1,500. Byline given.

Nonfiction: Young adults/teens: biography, careers, games/puzzles, history, how-to, humorous, interview/profile, multicultural, problem-solving, religion, social issues, sports, "thoughtful treatment of contemporary issues (i.e., racism, preparing for the future); interviews with famous Christians who have noteworthy stories to tell." Multicultural needs include: material on missions. Buys 50 mss/year. "Looking for more articles and fewer stories." Average word length: 1,000. Byline given.

How to Contact/Writers: Fiction/nonfiction: Send published samples for review.

Illustration: Buys 50-100 illustrations/issue, 200 illustrations/year. Uses color artwork only. Prefers to review youth-oriented styles. Art director will assign freelance art. Works on assignment only. Reviews ms/illustration packages from artists. Send portfolio. "We are Mac literate." Illustration only: arrange portfolio review or send promo sheet, slides, client list, tearsheets or on disk (Mac). Illustrations and design: "We are interested in looking at portfolios consisting of illustration and design work that is teen-oriented." Reports in 3-4 weeks. Samples returned with SASE. Originals returned to artist at job's completion. Credit line given.

Photography: Buys photos from freelancers. Wants "teen photos that look spontaneous. Ethnic and urban photos urgently needed." Uses color prints, 35mm, 2¼×2¼, 4×5 transparencies. Send unsolicited photos by mail.

Terms: Pays on acceptance. For mss, buys first North American serial rights, first rights, one-time rights, second

---

THE SUBJECT INDEX, located in the back of this book, lists book publishers and magazines according to the fiction and nonfiction subjects they seek.

serial (reprint rights), simultaneous rights. For artwork, buys one-time rights for cartoons; one-time rights for photos. Rights for illustrations negotiable. Pays $25-75 for stories; $25-100 for articles. Pays illustrators: $75-100 for color cover or $50-60 for color inside. Pays photographers $25-100. Sample copy free with 9 × 12 SASE for 3 first-class stamps. Writer's/photo guidelines for SASE.

Tips: "We want contemporary, real life articles, or fiction that has the same feel. Try to keep it teen-oriented—trendy, hip, interesting perspectives; current, topical situations that revolve around teens. We work on specific themes for each quarter, so interested writers should request current writers guidelines and topic list."

'TEEN MAGAZINE, Petersen Publishing Co., 6420 Wilshire Blvd., Los Angeles CA 90048-5515. (213)782-2950. **Editor:** Roxanne Camron. **Art Director:** Laurel Finnerty. Monthly magazine. Estab. 1957. Circ. 1,100,000. "We are a pure high school female audience. *'TEEN* teens are upbeat and want to be informed."
- *'TEEN* ranked number 33 on *Writer's Digest* Fiction 50, the magazine's annual list of "50 best places to publish your short stories."

Fiction: Young adults: contemporary, humorous, problem-solving, romance, suspense/mystery. Does not want to see "that which does not apply to our market—i.e., science fiction, history, religious, adult-oriented." Buys 12 mss/year. Length for fiction: 10-15 pages typewritten, double-spaced.

Nonfiction: Young adults: careers, cooking, health, multicultural, problem-solving, social issues, travel. Does not want to see adult-oriented, adult point of view." Buys 25 mss/year. Length for articles: 10-20 pages typewritten, double-spaced. Byline given.

How to Contact/Writers: Nonfiction: Query. Reports on queries in 3 weeks; mss in 3-4 weeks. Prefer submissions hard copy and disk. Fiction: Submit story.

Illustration: Buys 0-4 illustrations/issue. Uses various styles for variation. Uses a lot of b&w illustration. "Light, upbeat." Reviews ms/illustration packages from artists. "Query first." Illustrations only: "Want to see samples whether it be tearsheets, slides, finished pieces showing the style." Reports back only if interested. Credit line given.

Terms: Pays on acceptance. Buys all rights. Pays $100-400 for stories; $50-500 for articles. Pays $25-250/b&w inside; $100-400/color inside. Writer's/illustrator's guidelines free with SASE.

Tips: Illustrators: "Present professional finished work. Get familiar with magazine and send samples that would be compatible with the style of publication." There is a need for artwork with "fiction/specialty articles. Send samples or promotional materials on a regular basis."

TEENS ON TARGET, United Pentecostal Church International, 8855 Dunn Rd., Hazelwood MO 63042. (314)837-7300. **Articles Editors:** R.M. Davis and P.D.Buford. Weekly leaflet. Estab. 1994. Circ. 6,000.

Fiction: Young adults: religious. Buys 52-70 mss/year. Average word length: 1,200-1,600. Byline given.

Nonfiction: Young adults: religion. Buys 26-40 mss/year. Average word length: 1,200-1,600. Byline given.

How to Contact/Writers: Fiction/nonfiction: Send complete ms. Reports on mss in 3-12 months. Publishes ms 3-12 months after acceptance. Will consider simultaneous submissions or previously published work.

Illustration: Samples returned with SASE.

Terms: Pays on publication. Buys reprint rights for mss. Sample copies for #10 SASE and a first-class stamp.

TODAY'S CHRISTIAN TEEN, Marketing Partners Inc., P.O. Box 100, Morgantown PA 19543. (610)372-1111. Fax: (610)372-8227. E-mail: tcpubs@mkpt.com. Articles Editor: Elaine Williams. Publishes issues of interest to teenagers from a conservative biblical view.

Nonfiction: Young adults: health, religion, social issues. Buys 10 mss/year. Average word length: 800-1,100. Byline given.

How to Contact/Writers: Nonfiction: send complete ms. Reports on queries in 2 weeks; mss in 2-3 months. Publishes ms 1 year after acceptance. Will consider simultaneous submissions, electronic submissions via disk or modem and previously published work.

Terms: Pays on publication. Pays $75-150 for articles. Sample copies free for 9 × 12 SAE with 4 first-class stamps. Writer's guidelines for SASE.

Tips: "Make articles applicable to conservative teens with a biblical perspective—something they can use, not just entertainment."

TOGETHER TIME, WordAction Publishing Co., 6401 The Paseo, Kansas City MO 64131. (816)333-7000. Fax: (816)333-4439. E-mail: mhammer@nazarene.com. Website: www.nazarene.org or www.nphdirect.com. **Contact:** Melissa Hammer. Weekly magazine. Estab. 1981. Circ. 27,000. "*Together Time* is a story paper that correlates with the WordAction Sunday School Curriculum. Each paper contains a story, a poem, an activity and an article directed to the parents. It is designed to connect Sunday School learning with the daily living experiences and growth of children three and four years old. All submissions must agree with the theology and practices of the Nazarene and other holiness denominations."

Fiction: Picture-oriented material: religious. "We would like to see more realistic stories. We don't like them to seem staged. We also do not purchase stories that give life and feeling to inanimate objects." Buys 50 mss/year. Average word length: 100-150. Byline given.

Nonfiction: Picture-oriented material: arts/crafts.

Poetry: Reviews poetry. Maximum length: 8 lines. Limit submissions to 10 poems.

How to Contact/Writers: Fiction: Send complete ms. Reports on queries/mss in 1 month. Publishes ms 1 year after acceptance.

Illustration: Buys 52 illustrations/year. "We do assignment only and like both realistic and cartoon. Must be age-appropriate." Works on assignment. Reviews ms/illustration packages from artists. Illustration only: Query with samples. Send résumé, slides and tearsheets. Reports backs only if interested. Sample returned with SASE. Credit line given.

Photography: Buys photos from freelancers. Looks for outdoor or indoor pictures of 3- and 4-year-old children. Uses color and b&w prints; 35mm transparencies. Query with samples. Reports in 1 month.

Terms: Pays on publication. Buys all rights for mss. Buys all rights for artwork; multi-use rights for photographs. "Writers receive payment and contributor copies." Sample copies for #10 SAE and 1 first-class stamp. Writer's/illustrator's/photo guidelines for SASE.

Tips: "Make sure the material you submit is geared to three- and four-year-old children. Request a theme list with the guidelines and try to submit stories that correlate with specific issues."

TOUCH, GEMS Girls' Clubs, Box 7259, Grand Rapids MI 49510. (616)241-5616. Fax: (616)241-5558. E-mail: servicecenter@gemsgc.org. Website: www.gospelcom.net/gems. **Editor:** Jan Boone. **Managing Editor:** Carol Smith. Monthly (with combined May/June issue and July/August newsletter) magazine. Circ. 16,000. "*Touch* is designed to help girls ages 9-14 see how God is at work in their lives and in the world around them."

Fiction: Middle readers: adventure, animal, contemporary, health, history, humorous, multicultural, nature/environment, problem-solving, religious, sports. Does not want to see unrealistic stories and those with trite, easy endings. Buys 30 mss/year. Average word length: 400-1,000. Byline given.

Nonfiction: Middle readers: animal, arts/crafts, careers, cooking, fashion, games/puzzles, health, hobbies, how-to, humorous, nature/environment, multicultural, problem-solving, religious, social issues, sports, travel. Buys 9 mss/year. Average word length: 200-800. Byline given.

How to Contact/Writers: Send for annual update for publication themes. Fiction/nonfiction: Send complete ms. Reports on mss in 1 month. Will consider simultaneous submissions.

Illustration: Buys 3 illustrations/year. Prefers ms/illustration packages. Works on assignment only. Reports on submissions in 3 weeks. Samples returned with SASE. Credit line given.

Terms: Pays on publication. Buys first North American serial rights, first rights, second serial (reprint rights) or simultaneous rights. Original artwork not returned at job's completion. Pays $5-50 for stories; $20-50 for assigned articles; $5-30 for unsolicited articles. "We send complimentary copies in addition to pay." Pays $25-75 for color cover illustration; $25-50 for color inside illustration. Pays photographers by the project ($25-75 per photo). Writer's guidelines for SASE.

Tips: Writers: "The stories should be current, deal with adolescent problems and joys, and help girls see God at work in their lives through humor as well as problem-solving."

TURTLE MAGAZINE, For Preschool Kids, Children's Better Health Institute, 1100 Waterway Blvd., P.O. Box 567, Indianapolis IN 46206. (317)636-8881. **Editor:** Terry Harshman. **Art Director:** Bart Rivers. Monthly/bimonthly magazine published January/February, March, April/May, June, July/August, September, October/November, December. Circ. 300,000. *Turtle* uses read-aloud stories, especially suitable for bedtime or naptime reading, for children ages 2-5. Also uses poems, simple science experiments, easy recipes and health-related articles. All but 2 pages aimed at juvenile audience.

Fiction: Picture-oriented material: adventure, animal, contemporary, fantasy, folktales, health-related, history, holiday themes, humorous, multicultural, nature/environment, problem-solving, sports, suspense/mystery. "We need very simple experiments illustrating basic science concepts. Also needs action rhymes to foster creative movement. We no longer buy stories on 'generic' turtles because we now have PokeyToes, our own trade-marked turtle character." Do not want stories about monsters or scary things. Avoid stories in which the characters indulge in unhealthy activities like eating junk food. Buys 30 mss/year. Average word length: 150-300. Byline given.

Nonfiction: Picture-oriented material: animal, arts/crafts, cooking, games/puzzles, geography, health, multicultural, nature/environment, science, sports. Buys 24 mss/year. Average word length: 150-300. Byline given.

Poetry: "We're especially looking for short poems (4-8 lines) and slightly longer action rhymes to foster creative movement in preschoolers. We also use short verse on our back cover."

How to Contact/Writers: Fiction/nonfiction: "Prefer complete manuscript to queries." Reports on mss in 3 months.

Photography: Buys photos from freelancers with accompanying ms only.

Terms: Pays on publication. Buys all rights for mss/artwork; one-time rights for photographs. Pays up to 22¢/word for stories and articles (depending upon length and quality) and 10 complimentary copies. Pays $25 minimum for poems. Pays $30-70 for b&w inside. Sample copy $1.75. Writer's guidelines free with SASE.

Tips: "We're beginning to edit *Turtle* more for the very young preschooler (ages 2-5), so we're looking for stories and articles that are written more simply than those we've used in the past. Our need for health-related material, especially features that encourage fitness, is ongoing. Health subjects must be age-appropriate. When writing about them, think creatively and lighten up! Fight the tendency to become boringly pedantic. Nobody—not even young kids—likes to be lectured. Always keep in mind that in order for a story or article to educate preschoolers, it first must be entertaining—warm and engaging, exciting, or genuinely funny. Understand that vriting for *Turtle* is a difficu t chal. ge. Study the magazine to see if your manuscript is right for *Turtle*. Magazines have distinct persor alities ich can't be understood by only reading market listings. Here the trend is toward leaner, lighter writing. Ther will be a growing need for interactive activities. Writers might want to consider developing an activity to acc pany their concise manuscripts." (See listings for *Child Life, Children's Digest, Children's Playmate, Humpty umpty's Magazine, Jack and Jill* and *U*S* Kids*.)

☑ **TWIST**, Bauer Publishing Company, 270 Sylvan Ave., Englewood Cliffs NJ 07632. (201)569-6699. Fax: (201)569-4458. E-mail: twistmail@aol.com. **Articles Editors:** Jeannie Kim and Jena Hofstedt. **Art Director:** Lisa Mauro. Monthly magazine. Estab. 1997. Circ. 700,000. "We capture the energy, attitude and interests of young women today. We stress reality over fantasy and serve as a forum for the concerns and passions of our 14- to 19-year-old readers."
Nonfiction: Young teens: health, humorous, interview/profile, social issues, relationships/dating, "real life" experiences, quizzes. Average word length: 100-1,800. Byline given.
How to Contact/Writers: Nonfiction: query with published clips. Reports on queries in 1-4 weeks. Will consider simultaneous submissions.
Illustration: Buys 4 illustrations/issue. Uses color artwork only. Works on assignment only. Query; send promo sheet and tearsheets; "follow with a phone call." Contact: Lisa Mauro, creative director. Reports only if interested. Samples not returned; samples not filed.
Photography: Uses 35mm, 2¼×2¼ transparencies. Query with samples; provide promotional literature or tearsheets.
Terms: Pays on acceptance. Buys first North American serial rights. Pays $50 minimum and up to $1/word for articles. Pays illustrators $100-500 for color inside. Pays photographers by the project (range: $30/day up to $400); or per photo (range: $75 minimum). Sample copies not available. Writer's guidelines free for SASE.

☑ **U*S* KIDS**, Children's Better Health Institute, 1100 Waterway Blvd., P.O. Box 567, Indianapolis IN 46206. (317)636-8881. **Editor:** Nancy S. Axelrod. **Art Director:** Rebecca Ray. Magazine published 8 times a year. Estab. 1987. Circ. 250,000.
Fiction: Young readers: adventure, animal, contemporary, health, history, humorous, multicultural, nature/environment, problem-solving, sports, suspense/mystery. Buys limited number of stories/year. Average word length: 400. Byline given.
Nonfiction: Young readers: animal, arts/crafts, cooking, games/puzzles, health, history, hobbies, how-to, humorous, interview/profile, multicultural, nature/environment, science, social issues, sports, travel. Wants to see interviews with kids ages 5-10, who have done something unusual or different. Buys 30-40 mss/year. Average word length: 400. Byline given.
Poetry: Maximum length: 32 lines.
How to Contact/Writers: Fiction/nonfiction: Send complete ms. Reports on queries and mss in 2-3 months. Publishes ms 6 months after acceptance.
Illustration: Buys 8 illustrations/issue; 70 illustrations/year. Color artwork only. Works on assignment only. Reviews ms/illustration packages from artists. Query. Illustrations only: Send résumé and tearsheets. Reports back only if interested. Samples returned with SASE; samples kept on file. Does not return originals. Credit line given.
Photography: Purchases photography from freelancers. Looking for photos that pertain to children ages 5-10. Model/property release required. Uses color and b&w prints; 35mm, 2¼×2¼, 4×5 and 8×10 transparencies. Photographers should provide résumé, business card, promotional literature or tearsheets to be kept on file. Reports back only if interested.
Terms: Pays on publication. Buys all rights for mss. Purchases all rights for artwork. Purchases one-time rights for photographs. Pays 25¢/word minimum. Additional payment for ms/illustration packages. Pays illustrators $155/page for color inside. Photographers paid by the project or per photo (negotiable). Sample copies for $2.95. Writer's/illustrator/photo guidelines for SASE.
Tips: "Write clearly and concisely without preaching or being obvious." (See listings for *Child Life; Children's Digest, Children's Playmate, Humpty Dumpty's Magazine, Jack and Jill* and *Turtle Magazine*.)

☑ **W.O.W. (Wild Outdoor World)**, 44 N. Last Chance Gulch, Suites 16-20, P.O. Box 1249, Helena MT 59601. (406)449-9197. Fax: (406)442-9197. **Editorial Director:** Carolyn Zieg Cunningham. **Executive Editor:** Kay Morton Ellerhoff. **Design Editor:** Bryan Knaff. Publishes 5 issues/year. Estab. 1993. Circ. 100,000. "A magazine for young conservationists (age 8-12)." W.O.W. is distributed in fourth grade classrooms throughout the US.
Nonfiction: Middle readers: adventure (outdoor), animal, nature/environment, sports (outdoor recreation), travel (to parks, wildlife refuges, etc.). Average word length: 800 maximum. Byline given.
How to Contact/Writers: Fiction/nonfiction: Query. Reports in 6 months.
Illustration: Buys 2 illustrations/issue; 12-15 illustrations/year. Prefers work on assignment. Reviews ms/illustration packages from artists. Illustrations only: Query; send slides, tearsheets. Reports in 2 months. Samples returned with SASE; samples sometimes filed. Credit line given.
Photography: *Must* be submitted in 20-slide sheets and individual protectors, such as KYMAC. Looks for "children outdoors—camping, fishing, doing 'nature' projects." Model/property releases required. Photo captions

required. Uses 35mm transparencies. Does not accept unsolicited photography. Contact: Theresa Morrow Rush, photo editor. Reports in 2 months.

Terms: Pays 30-60 days after publication. Buys one-time rights for mss. Purchases one-time rights for photographs. Original work returned at job's completion. Pays $100-300 for articles; $50 for fillers. Pays illustrators variable rate for b&w inside; $250 color cover; $35-100 color inside. Pays photographers $50-100 for full inside; per photo (range: $50-100); $250 for cover photo. Sample copies for $3.95 and 8½×11 SAE. Writer's/illustrator's/photo guidelines for SASE.

Tips: "We are seriously overloaded with manuscripts and do not plan to buy very much new material in the next year."

WHAT! A MAGAZINE, What! Publishers Inc. 108-93 Lombard Ave., Winnipeg, Manitoba R3B 3B1 Canada. (204)985-8160. Fax: (204)943-8991. E-mail: l.malkin@m2ci.mb.ca. **Articles Editor:** Leslie Malkin. **Art Director:** Brian Kauste. Magazine published 5 times/year. Estab. 1987. Circ. 200,000. "Informative and entertaining teen magazine for both genders. Articles deal with issues and ideas of relevance to Canadian teens. The magazine is distributed through schools so we aim to be cool and responsible at the same time."

Nonfiction: Young adults (14 and up): biography, careers, concept, health, how-to, humorous, interview/profile, nature/environment, science, social issues, sports. "No cliché teen stuff. Also, we're getting too many heavy pitches lately on teen pregnancy, AIDS, etc." Buys 8 mss/year. Average word length: 675-2,100. Byline given.

How to Contact/Writers: Nonfiction: Query with published clips. Reports on queries/mss in 2 months. Publishes ms 2 months after acceptance.

Terms: Pays on publication plus 30 days. Buys first rights for mss. Pays $100-500 (Canadian) for articles. Sample copies when available for 9×12 and $1.45 (Canadian). Writer's guidelines free for SASE.

Tips: "Teens are smarter today than ever before. Respect that intelligence in queries and articles. Aim for the older end of our age-range (14-19) and avoid cliché. Humor works for us almost all the time."

WITH, The Magazine for Radical Christian Youth, Faith & Life Press, 722 Main, P.O. Box 347, Newton KS 67114. (316)283-5100. Fax: (316)283-0454. E-mail: deliag@gcmc.org. **Editor:** Carol Duerksen. Published 8 times a year. Circ. 5,800. Magazine published for teenagers, ages 15-18, in Mennonite, Brethren and Mennonite Brethren congregations. "We deal with issues affecting teens and try to help them make choices reflecting a radical Christian faith."

● *With* ranked number 42 on the 1999 *Writer's Digest*'s Fiction 50, the magazine's annual list of "50 best places to publish your short stories."

Fiction: Young adults/teens: contemporary, fantasy, humorous, multicultural, problem-solving, religious, romance. Multicultural needs include race relations, first-person stories featuring teens of ethnic minorities. Buys 15 mss/year. Average word length: 1,000-2,000. Byline given.

Nonfiction: Young adults/teens: first-person teen personal experience (as-told-to), how-to, humorous, multicultural, problem-solving, religion, social issues. Buys 15-20 mss/year. Average word length: 1,000-2,000. Byline given.

Poetry: Wants to see religious, humorous, nature. "Buys 1-2 poems/year." Maximum length: 50 lines.

How to Contact/Writers: Send complete ms. Query on first-person teen personal experience stories and how-to articles. (Detailed guidelines for first-person stories, how-tos, and fiction available for SASE.) Reports on queries in 2-3 weeks; mss in 3-6 weeks. Will consider simultaneous submissions.

Illustration: Buys 6-8 assigned illustrations/issue; buys 64 assigned illustrations/year. Uses b&w and 2-color artwork only. Preferred theme or style: candids/interracial. Reviews ms/illustration packages from artists. Query first. Illustrations only: Query with portfolio (photocopies only) or tearsheets. Reports back only if interested. Credit line given.

Photography: Buys photos from freelancers. Looking for candid photos of teens (ages 15-18), especially ethnic minorities. Uses 8×10 b&w glossy prints. Photographers should send unsolicited photos by mail.

Terms: Pays on acceptance. For mss buys first rights, one-time rights; second serial (reprint rights). Buys one-time rights for artwork and photos. Original artwork returned at job's completion upon request. Pays 6¢/word for unpublished manuscripts; 4¢/word for reprints. Will pay more for assigned as-told-to stories. Pays $10-25 for poetry. Pays $50-60 for b&w cover illustration and b&w inside illustration. Pays photographers per project (range: $120-180). Sample copy for 9×12 SAE and 4 first-class stamps. Writer's/illustrator's guidelines for SASE.

Tips: "We want stories, fiction or nonfiction, in which high-school-age youth of various cultures/ethnic groups are the protagonists. Stories may or may not focus on cross-cultural relationships. We're hungry for stuff that makes teens laugh—fiction, nonfiction and cartoons. It doesn't have to be religious, but must be wholesome.

Most of our stories would not be accepted by other Christian youth magazines. They would be considered too gritty, too controversial, or too painful. Our regular writers are on the *With* wavelength. Most writers for Christian youth magazines aren't." For writers: "Fiction and humor are the best places to break in. Send SASE and request guidelines." For photographers: "If you're willing to line up models and shoot to illustrate specific story scenes, send us a letter of introduction and some samples of your work."

WRITERS' INTL. FORUM, "For Those Who Write to Sell," Bristol Services Intl., P.O. Box 516, Tracyton WA 98393-0516. E-mail: services@bristolservicesintl.com. Website: www.bristolservicesintl.com. **Editor:** Sandra E. Haven. Estab. 1990. "Writing competitions held exclusively at our website." Up to 25% aimed at writers of juvenile literature. "We offer authors the unique chance of having a winning short story or essay published plus receiving a free professional critique. If published, author must agree to allow both the manuscript and our professional critique to be published at our website; includes writing lessons and markets information."
Fiction: Middle readers, young readers, young adults/teens: adventure, contemporary, fantasy, humorous, nature/environment, problem-solving, religious, romance, science fiction, suspense/mystery. "No experimental formats; no picture books; no poetry. No stories for children under age eight. We see too many anthropomorphic characters. We would like to see more mysteries, problem-solving and adventures." Maximum word length: 2,500. Byline and bio information printed.
How to Contact/Writers: Fiction: Reports on mss in 2 months. Publishes winning ms 2 months after competition results.
Terms: Prizes vary per competition. Latest competition awarded $250 top prize; other winners received magazine subscriptions and books such as *Children's Writer's & Illustrator's Market*.
Tips: "We want well-crafted stories with traditional plots which are written in clear language, have fully developed characters and an interesting storyline. Essays must have a tight focus, make a distinct point, and back up that point with specific facts and/or experiences. Always state the age group for which the children's manuscript is intended and be certain your material is suitable specifically for that audience."

YES MAG, Canada's Science Magazine for Kids, Peter Piper Publishing Inc., 4175 Francisco Place, Victoria, British Columbia V8N 6H1 Canada. Phone/fax: (250)477-5543. E-mail: shannon@yesmag.bc.ca. Website: www.yesmag.bc.ca. **Articles Editor:** Shannon Hunt. **Art/Photo Director:** David Garrison. Quarterly magazine. Estab. 1996. Circ. 15,000. "*YES Mag* is designed to make science accessible, interesting, exciting, and FUN. Written for children ages 8 to 14, *YES Mag* covers a range of topics including science and technology news, environmental updates, do-at-home projects and articles about Canadian students and scientists."
Nonfiction: Middle readers: animal, health, math, nature/environment, science. Buys 70 mss/year. Average word length: 250-1,250. Byline given.
How to Contact/Writers: Nonfiction: Query with published clips or send complete ms (on spec only). Reports on queries/mss in 3 weeks. Publishes ms 3 months after acceptance. Will consider simultaneous submissions, electronic submission via disk or modem, previously published work.
Illustration: Buys 2 illustrations/issue; 10 illustrations/year. Uses color artwork only. Works on assignment only. Reviews ms/illustration packages from artists. Query. Contact: David Garrison, art director. Illustration only: Query with samples. Contact: David Garrison, art director. Reports in 3 weeks. Samples filed. Credit line given.
Photography: "Looking for science, technology, nature/environment photos based on current editorial needs." Photo captions required. Uses color prints. Provide résumé, business card, promotional literature, tearsheets if possible. Reports in 3 weeks.
Terms: Pays on publication. Buys one-time rights for mss. Buys one-time rights for artwork/photos. Original artwork returned at job's completion. Pays $25-125 for stories and articles. Sample copies for $3.50. Writer's guidelines for SASE.
Tips: "We do not publish fiction or science fiction. Visit our web site for more information, sample articles and writers guidelines. We accept queries via e-mail. Articles relating to the physical sciences and mathematics are encouraged."

YM, 685 Third Ave., New York NY 10017. Fax: (212)499-1698. E-mail: diane@ym.com. **Editor:** Diane Salvatore. **Executive Editor:** Ellen Seidman. "*YM* is a national magazine for girls ages 12-24 to help guide them through the joys and challenges of young adulthood."
Nonfiction: "*YM* covers dating, psychology, entertainment, friendship, self-esteem, human interest and news trends. All articles should be lively and empowering and include quotes from experts and real teens. We do not publish fiction or poetry." Word length: 800-2,000 words.
How to Contact/Writers: Nonfiction: Query with SASE. (Write "query"on envelope.) Reports on queries in 4-6 weeks; mss in 1-2 months.
Terms: Pays on acceptance. Rates vary. Sample copies available for $2.50.

YOUNG SALVATIONIST, The Salvation Army, 615 Slaters Lane, P.O. Box 269, Alexandria VA 22314-1112. (703)684-5500. Fax: (703)684-5534. E-mail: ys@usn.salvationarmy.org. Website: publications.salvationarmyusa .org. Published 10 times/year. Estab. 1984. Circ. 50,000. **Managing Editor:** Tim Clark. "We accept material with clear Christian content written for high school age teenagers. *Young Salvationist* is published for teenage members of The Salvation Army, an evangelical part of the Christian Church that focuses on living the Christian life."

Fiction: Young adults/teens: contemporary, humorous, problem-solving, religious. Buys 10-11 mss/year. Average word length: 750-1,200. Byline given.

Nonfiction: Young adults/teens: religious—careers, concept, interview/profile, how-to, humorous, multicultural, problem-solving, social issues, sports. Buys 40-50 mss/year. Average word length: 750-1,200. Byline given.

How to Contact/Writers: Fiction/nonfiction: Query with published clips or send complete ms. Reports on queries/mss in 1 month. Will consider simultaneous submissions.

Illustrations: Buys 3-5 illustrations/issue; 20-30 illustrations/year. Reviews ms/illustration packages from artists. Send ms with art. Illustrations only: Query; send résumé, promo sheet, portfolio, tearsheets. Reports back only if interested. Samples returned with SASE; samples filed. Credit line given.

Photography: Purchases photography from freelancers. Looking for teens in action.

Terms: Pays on acceptance. Buys first North American serial rights, first rights, one-time rights or second serial (reprint) rights for mss. Purchases one-time rights for artwork and photographs. Original artwork returned at job's completion "if requested." For mss, pays 10-15¢/word; 10¢/word for reprints. Pays $60-150 color (cover) illustration; $60-150 b&w (inside) illustration; $60-150 color (inside) illustration. Pays photographers per photo (range: $60-150). Sample copy for 9×12 SAE and 4 first-class stamps. Writer's guidelines for #10 SASE.

Tips: "Ask for theme list/sample copy! Write 'up,' not down to teens. Aim at young *adults*, not children." Wants "less fiction, more 'journalistic' nonfiction."

☑ **YOUR BIG BACKYARD**, National Wildlife Federation, 8925 Leesburg Pike, Vienna VA 22184. (703)790-4515. Fax: (703)827-2585. E-mail: johnsond@nwf.org. **Articles/Fiction Editor:** Donna Johnson. **Art Director:** Tamara Tylenda. **Photo Editor:** Page Carr. Monthly magazine. Estab. 1980. Circ. 400,000. Purpose of the magazine is to educate young children (ages 3-6) about nature and wildlife in a fun, interactive and entertaining way. 90% of publication aimed at juvenile market (10% are parents' pages).

Fiction: Picture-oriented material: animal, fantasy, humorous, multicultural, nature/environment. Young readers: adventure, animal, humorous, multicultural, nature/environment. "We do not want fiction that does not involve animals or nature in some way." Buys 12 mss/year. Average word length: 200-1,000. Byline given.

Nonfiction: All mss written in-house.

Poetry: Reviews poetry. Buys 12-15 poems/year. Maximum length: 25 lines.

How to Contact/Writers: Fiction: Not accepting fiction or nonfiction stories. For poetry, send complete ms. Reports on queries/mss in 2 months. Publishes ms 4 months after acceptance. Will consider simultaneous submissions, electronic submission via disk or modem and previously published work.

Illustration: Buys 5 illustrations/issue 60 illustrations/year. Uses color artwork only. Reviews ms/illustration packages from artists. Send ms with dummy. Contact: Donna Johnson, art director. Illustrations only: Send promo sheet, portfolio, slides, tearsheets. Contact: Tammy Tylenda, art director. Reports back only if interested. Samples not returned; filed. Credit line given.

Photography: Wants animal photos. Uses 35mm transparencies. Send unsolicited photos by mail ("professional photographers only"). Reports in 2 months.

Terms: Pays on acceptance. Buys one-time rights, reprint rights for mss. Buys one-time rights for artwork and photographs. Original artwork returned at job's completion. Pays $250-750 for stories; $50-200 for articles. Additional payment for ms/illustration packages and for photos accompanying articles. Pays illustrators $200-500 for color inside. Pays photographers per photo (range: $200-600).

YOUTH CHALLENGE, United Pentecostal Church International, 8855 Dunn Rd., Hazelwood MO 63042. (314)837-7300. **Articles Editors:** R.M. Davis and P.D. Buford. Weekly leaflet. Estab. 1994. Circ. 4,500.

Fiction: Young adults: religious. Buys 52-70 mss/year. Average word length: 1,200-1,600. Byline given.

Nonfiction: Young adults: religion. Buys 26-40 mss/year. Average word length: 1,200-1,600. Byline given.

How to Contact/Writers: Fiction/nonfiction: send complete ms. Reports on mss in 3-12 months. Publishes ms 3-12 months after acceptance. Will consider simultaneous submissions.

Illustration: Samples returned with SASE.

Terms: Pays on publication. Buys reprint rights for mss. Sample copies for #10 SAE and 1 first-class stamp. Writer's guidelines for SASE.

YOUTH UPDATE, St. Anthony Messenger Press, 1615 Republic St., Cincinnati OH 45210. (513)241-5615. E-mail: carolann@americancatholic.org. Website: www.AmericanCatholic.org. **Articles Editor:** Carol Ann Morrow. **Art Director:** June Pfaff Daley. Monthly newsletter. Estab. 1982. Circ. 23,000. "Each issue focuses on one topic only. *Youth Update* addresses the faith and Christian life questions of young people and is designed to attract, instruct, guide and challenge its audience by applying the gospel to modern problems and situations. The students who read *Youth Update* vary in their religious education and reading ability. Write for average high school students. These students are 15-year-olds with a C+ average. Assume that they have paid attention to religious instruction and remember a little of what 'sister' said. Aim more toward 'table talk' than 'teacher talk.' "

Nonfiction: Young adults/teens: religion. Buys 12 mss/year. Average word length: 2,200-2,300. Byline given.

How to Contact/Writers: Nonfiction: Query. Reports on queries/mss in 2 months. Will consider computer printout and electronic submissions via disk.

Photography: Buys photos from freelancers. Uses photos of teens (high-school age) with attention to racial diversity and with emotion.

Terms. Pays on acceptance. Buys first North American serial rights for mss. Buys one-time rights for photographs. Pays $350-500 for articles. Pays photographers per photo ($50-75 minimum). Sample copy free with #10 SASE. Writer's guidelines free on request.

Tips: "Read the newsletter yourself—3 issues at least. In the past, our publication has dealt with a variety of topics including: dating, Lent, teenage pregnancy, baptism, loneliness, violence, confirmation and the Bible. When writing, use the *New American Bible* as translation. Interested in church-related topics."

☑ **ZILLIONS For Kids From Consumer Reports**, Consumers Union, 101 Truman Ave., Yonkers NY 10703-1057. (914)378-2551. Fax: (914)378-2985. **Articles Editor:** Karen McNulty. **Art Director:** Rob Jenter. Bimonthly magazine. Estab. 1980. Circ. 300,000. "*Zillions* is the *Consumer Reports* for kids (with heavy emphasis on fun!) We offer kids information on product tests, ads and fads, money smarts, and more."

• *ZILLIONS* works on assignment only. They do not accept unsolicited manuscripts; query first.

Nonfiction: Children/young adults: arts/crafts, careers, games/puzzles, health, hobbies, how-to, humorous, nature/environment, problem-solving, social issues, sports. "Will consider story ideas on kid money matters, marketing to kids and anything that educates kids to be smart consumers." Buys 10 mss/year. Average word length: 800-1,000.

How to Contact/Writers: Nonfiction: Query with résumé and published clips. "We'll contact if interested (within a few months probably)." Publishes ms 2 months after acceptance.

Terms: Pays on publication. Buys all rights for ms. Pays $1,000 for articles. Writer's guidelines for SASE.

Tips: "Read the magazine!"

Greeting Cards, Puzzles & Games

In this section you'll find companies that produce puzzles, games, greeting cards and other items (like coloring books, stickers and giftwrap) especially for kids. These are items you'll find in children's sections of bookstores, toy stores, departments stores and card shops.

Because these markets create an array of products, their needs vary greatly. Some may need the service of freelance writers for greeting card copy or slogans for buttons and stickers. Others are in need of illustrators for coloring books or photographers for puzzles. Artists should send copies of their work that art directors can keep on file—never originals. Carefully read through the listings to find companies' needs, and send for guidelines and catalogs if they're available, just as you would for book or magazine publishers.

If you'd like to find out more about the greeting card industry beyond the market for children, there are a number of resources to help you. The Greeting Card Association is a national trade organization for the industry. For membership information, contact the GCA at 1030 15th NW, Suite 870, Washington DC 20005. (202)393-1778. *Greetings Etc.* (Edgel Communications), is a quarterly trade magazine covering the greeting card industry. For information call (978)262-9611. Illustrators should check out *The Complete Guide to Greeting Card Design & Illustration*, by Eva Szela (North Light Books) and *Greeting Card Designs*, by Joanne Fink (PBC Intl. Inc.). For a complete list of companies, consult the latest edition of *Artist's & Graphic Designer's Market* (Writer's Digest Books). Writers should see *You Can Write Greeting Cards*, by Karen Ann Moore and *How to Write & Sell Greeting Cards, Bumper Stickers, T-shirts and Other Fun Stuff*, by Molly Wigand (both Writer's Digest Books).

[N] ABBY LOU ENTERTAINMENT, 1411 Edgehill Place, Pasadena CA 91103. (612)795-7334. Fax: (626)795-4013. E-mail: ale@full-moon.com. President: George LeFave. Estab. 1985. Animation production company and book publisher. "We are looking for top creative children's illustrators with classic artwork. We are a children's book publisher moving into greeting cards—nature illustrations with characters." Publishes greeting cards (Whispering Gardens), coloring books, puzzles, games, posters, calendars, books (Adventures in Whispering Gardens). 100% of products are made for kids or have kid's themes.

Writing: Needs freelance writing for children's greeting cards and other children's products. Makes 6 writing assignments/year. For greeting cards, accepts both rhymed and unrhymed verse ideas. Other needs for freelance writing include the theme of "Listen to your heart and you will hear the whispers." To contact, send cover letter, résumé, client list, writing samples. Reports in 2 weeks. Materials not returned; materials filed. For greeting cards, pays flat fee of $500, royalty of 3-10%; negotiable or negotiable advance against royalty. For other writing, pay is negotiated. Pays on acceptance. Buys one-time rights; negotiable. Credit line given.

Illustration: Need freelance illustration for children's greeting cards, posters and TV related property. Makes 12 illustration assignments/year. Prefers a "classical look—property that needs illustration is Adventures in Whispering Gardens and multidimentional entertainment property." Uses color artwork only. To contact send cover letter, published samples, slides, color photocopies and color promo pieces. Materials not returned; materials filed. For greeting cards and other artwork, pay is negotiable. Pays on acceptance or publication. Rights purchased are negotiable. Credit line given

Tips: "Give clear vision of what you want to do in the business and produce top quality, creative work."

[N] THE AVALON HILL GAME CO., 4517 Harford Rd., Baltimore MD 21214. (410)254-9200. Fax: (410)254-0991. Publisher/Editor-in-Chief: Karen Bokram. Senior Editor: Kelly White. Art Director: Chun Kim. Fashion Editor: Miki Hicks. Estab. 1994. Produces *Girl's Life* magazine for girls ages 9-14. *Girl's Life* is the official magazine of the Girl Scouts of America. 50% of material written and illustrated by freelancers. Buys 50 freelance projects/year; receives 500 submissions annually.

Writing: Makes 6 writing assignments/month; 36/year. To contact send cover letter, résumé, client list, writing samples to Senior Editor. No phone queries. Reports back only if interested. Prefers features on positive ways for modern girls to feel confident through community service, sports or quizzes. Pays on publication. Buys all rights. Credit line given.

Illustration: Makes 12 illustration assignments/month. Prefers styles pertaining to general interest topics for girls, no cartoons. To contact send cover letter, résumé, published samples, portfolio to Art Director. Reports in 1 month. Pays on acceptance. Buys all rights. Credit line given.

N **AVONLEA TRADITIONS, INC.**, 17075 Leslie St., Units 12-15, Newmarket, Ontario L3Y-8E1 Canada (905)853-1777. Fax: (905)853 1763. Website: www.avonlea-traditions.com. President: Kathryn Morton. Estab. 1988. Giftware importer and distributor. Designs, imports and distributes products related to Canada's most famous storybook, *Anne of Green Gables*, and other Canadian themes. Publishes greeting cards (blank), novelties, coloring books, quarterly newsletter, website.

Writing: Makes 2 writing assignments/month. Other needs for freelance writing include articles, puzzles, or anything to do with *Anne of Green Gables* and author L.M. Montgomery. To contact, send the proposed article, or outline. Reports back only if interested. Materials not returned; material filed. For other writing assignments, offers gift certificates redeemable for products. Pays on publication. Buys all rights. Credit line given.

Illustration: Needs freelance illustration for stationery and packaging for giftware. Makes 2-3 illustration assignments/month; 24/year. Prefers romantic, Victorian, storybook artwork. To contact, send color photocopies and promo pieces. Reports back only if interested. Materials not returned; materials filed. For other artwork, pays by the hour (range: $10-25). Pays on publication. Buys all rights. Credit line sometimes given.

Photography: Works on assignment only. Wants product photos. Uses transparencies. To contact, send portfolio and promo piece. Reports back only if interested. Materials not returned; material filed. Pays on usage. Buys all rights. Credit line sometimes given.

Tips: "We strongly prefer artists/writers who are Canadian. Also give preference to those located in the Toronto area. Submit seasonal material 6 months in advance."

THE BEISTLE COMPANY, P.O. Box 10, Shippensburg PA 17257. (717)532-2131. Fax: (717)532-7789. E-mail: beistle@mail.cvn.net. Website: www.beistle.com. Product Manager: C. Michelle Luhrs-Wiest. Estab. 1900. Paper products company. Produces decorations and party goods, posters—baby, baptism, birthday, holidays, educational, wedding/anniversary, graduation, ethnic themes, and New Year parties. 50% of products are made for kids' or have kids themes.

Illustration: Needs freelance illustration for decorations, party goods, school supplies, point-of-purchase display materials and gift wrap. Makes 100 illustration assignments/year. Prefers fanciful style, cute 4- to 5-color illustration in gouache and/or computer illustration. To contact, send cover letter, résumé, client list, promo piece. To query with specific ideas, phone, write or fax. Reports only if interested. Materials returned with SASE; materials filed. Pays by the project or by contractual agreement; price varies according to type of project. Pays on acceptance. Buys all rights. Artist's guidelines available for SASE.

Photography: Buys photography from freelancers. Buys stock and assigns work. Makes 30-50 assignments/year. Wants scenic landscapes and product still life displays. Uses 35mm, 2¼×2¼, 4×5 transparencies. To contact, send cover letter, résumé, slides, client list, promo piece. Reports only if interested. Materials returned if accompanied with SASE; materials filed. Pays on acceptance. Buys first rights. Credit line sometimes given—depends on project. Guidelines available for SASE.

Tips: Submit seasonal material 6 months in advance.

N **CONTEMPO COLOURS, INC.**, One Paper Place, Kalamazoo MI 49001. (616)349-2626. Fax: (616)349-2162. Website: www.contempocolours.com. Creative Director: Kathleen Pavlack. Estab. 1935. Paper products company. Produces paper party goods for all age markets. 40% of products are made for kids or have kids' themes.

Illustration: Needs freelance illustration for paper party goods. Prefers artwork submitted once a year on themes that are predetermined and are usually trend driven. Uses color artwork only. To contact, send cover letter and color promo pieces. To query with specific ideas, write to request disclosure form first. Reports back only if interested. Materials returned with SASE; materials filed. Payment varies by artist and design. Pays on manufacture of product. Buys exclusive product rights. Credit line sometimes given. Artist's guidelines available for SASE.

Tips: Submit seasonal material 6 months in advance.

A **CREATE-A-CRAFT**, P.O. Box 941293, Plano TX 75094-1293. Contact: Editor. Estab. 1967. Greeting card company. Produces greeting cards (Create-A-Card), giftwrap, games (Create-A-Puzzle), coloring books, calendars (Create-A-Calendar), posters, T-shirts, sweatshirts, stationery and paper tableware products for all ages.

Writing: Needs freelance writing for children's greeting cards and other children's products. Makes 5 writing assignments/year. For greeting cards, accepts both rhymed and unrhymed verse ideas. Other needs for freelance writing include rhymed and unrhymed verse ideas on all products. To contact send via recognized agent only. Reports back only if interested. Material not returned. For greeting cards pays depending on complexity of project. Pays on publication. Buys all rights. Writer's guidelines available for SASE and $2.50—includes sample cards.

Illustration: Works with 3 freelance artists/year. Buys 3-5 designs/illustrations/year. Primary age concentration is 4-8 year old market. Prefers artists with experience in cartooning. Works on assignment only. Buys freelance designs/illustrations mainly for greetings cards and T-shirts. Also uses freelance artists for calligraphy, P-O-P displays, paste-up and mechanicals. Considers pen & ink, watercolor, acrylics and colored pencil. Prefers humorous and "cartoons that will appeal to families. Must be cute, appealing, etc. No religious, sexual implications or off-beat humor." Produces material for all holidays and seasons. Contact only through artist's agent. Some samples are filed; samples not filed are not returned. Reports only if interested. Write for appointment to show portfolio of original/final art, final reproduction/product, slides, tearsheets, color and b&w. Original artwork is not returned. "Payment depends upon the assignment, amount of work involved, production costs, etc. involved in the project." Pays after all sales are tallied. Buys all rights. For guidelines and sample cards, send $2.50 and #10 SASE.

Tips: Submit 6 months in advance. "Demonstrate an ability to follow directions exactly. Too many submit artwork that has no relationship to what we produce. No phone calls accepted. Follow directions given. Do not ignore them. We do not work with anyone who does not follow them."

CREATIF LICENSING CORP., 31 Old Town Crossing, Mt. Kisco NY 10549. (914)241-6211. Fax: (603)372-5310. E-mail: creatif@usa.net. Website: www.members.aol.com/creatiflic. President: Paul Cohen. Estab. 1975. Gift industry licensing agency. Publishes greeting cards, puzzles, posters, calendars, fabrics, home furnishings, all gifts. 50% of products are made for kids or have kids' themes.

Illustration: Needs freelance illustration for children's greeting cards, all gift and home furnishings. Makes many illustration assignments/month. Uses both color and b&w artwork. To contact, send cover letter, résumé, client list, published samples, photocopies, portfolio, promo piece and SASE. Reports in 1 month. Materials returned with SASE; materials filed. For greeting cards, pays royalty and advance. For other artwork, pays royalty and advance. Pays on acceptance or publication. Artist's guidelines available for SASE. Submission guidelines posted on website. Does not accept images via e-mail.

Tips: Submit seasonal material 8-12 months in advance.

DESIGN DESIGN INC., P.O. Box 2266, Grand Rapids MI 49501. (616)774-2448. Fax: (616)774-4020. President: Don Kallil. Creative Director: Tom Vituj. Estab. 1986. Greeting card company. 5% of products are made for kids or have kids themes.

Writing: Needs freelance writing for children's greeting cards. Prefers both rhymed and unrhymed verse ideas. To contact, send cover letter and writing samples. Materials returned with SASE; materials not filed. For greeting cards, pays flat fee. Buys all rights or exclusive product rights; negotiable. No credit line given. Writer's guidelines for SASE.

Illustration: Needs freelance illustration for children's greeting cards and related products. To contact, send cover letter, published samples, color or b&w photocopies, color or b&w promo pieces or portfolio. Returns materials with SASE. Pays by royalty. Buys all rights or exclusive product rights; negotiable. Artist's guidelines available for SASE. Do not send original art.

Photography: Buys stock and assigns work. Looking for the following subject matter: babies, animals, dog, cats, humorous situations. Uses 4×5 transparencies or high quality 35mm slides. To contact, send cover letter with slides, stock photo list, color copies, published samples and promo piece. Materials returned with SASE; materials not filed. Pays royalties. Buys all rights or exclusive product rights; negotiable. Photographer's guidelines for SASE. Do not send original photography.

Tips: Seasonal material must be submitted 1 year in advance.

☑ **FAX-PAX USA, INC.**, 37 Jerome Ave., Bloomfield CT 06002. (860)242-3333. Fax: (860)242-7102. Editor: Stacey L. Savin. Estab. 1990. Buys 1 freelance project/year. Publishes art and history flash cards. Needs include US history, natural history.

Writing/Illustration: Buys all rights. Pays on publication. Cannot return material.

Tips: "We need concise, interesting, well-written 'mini-lessons' on various subjects including U.S. and natural history."

☑ **GALLERY GRAPHICS, INC.**, 2400 S. Hwy. 59, P.O. Box 502, Noel MO 64854-0502. (417)475-6191. Fax: (417)475-6494. E-mail: gginfo@gallery-graphics.com. Website: www.gallery-graphics.com. Marketing Director: Terri Galvin. Estab. 1979. Greeting card, paper products company. Specializes in products including prints, cards, calendars, stationery, magnets, framed items, books, flue covers and sachets. We market towards all age groups. Publishes reproductions of children's books from the 1800's. 10% of products are made for kids or have kid's themes.

Illustration: Needs freelance illustration for children's greeting cards, other children's products. Makes 8 illustration assignments/year. Prefers children, angels, animals in any medium. Uses color artwork only. To contact, send cover letter, published samples, photocopies (prefer color), promo pieces. Reports in 3 months. "We'll return materials at our cost. If artist can send something we can file, that would be ideal. I'll usually make copies." For greeting cards, pays flat fee of $100-700, or royalty of 5-7% for life of card. Pays on sales. Buys exclusive product rights. Credit line sometimes given.

Tips: "We've significantly increased our licensing over the last year. Most of these are set up on a 5% royalty basis. Submit various art subjects."

☑ GREAT AMERICAN PUZZLE FACTORY, INC., 16 S. Main St., S. Norwalk CT 06854. (203)838-4240. Fax: (203)838-2065. E-mail: gapfctad@aol.com. Website: www.greatamericanpuzzle.com. Contact: Art Director. Estab. 1976. Produces puzzles. 70% of products are made for kids or have kids' themes.

Illustration: Needs freelance illustration for puzzles. Makes over 20 freelance assignments/year. To contact, send cover letter, color photocopies and color promo pieces (no slides or original art) with SASE. Reports in 1 month. Artists guidelines available for SASE. Rights purchased vary. Buys all rights to puzzles. Pays on publication. Pay varies.

Photography: Needs local cityscapes for regional puzzles. "Photos that we have used have been of wildlife. We do occasionally use city skylines. These are only for custom jobs, though, and must be 4×5 or larger format."

Tips: Targets ages 4-12 and adult. "Go to a toy store and look at puzzles. See what is appropriate. No slides. Send color copies (3-4) for style. Looking for whimsical, fantasy and animal themes with a bright, contemporary style. Not too washy or cute. No people, babies, abstracts, landscapes or still life. We often buy reprint rights to existing work. Graphic, children's-book style work is ideal for puzzles." Submit seasonal material 1 year in advance.

HOW RICH UNLIMITED, LLC, (formerly Everything Gonzo!), P.O. Box 1322, Roslyn Heights NY 11577. (516)623-9477. Fax: (212)213-0055. E-mail: polygonzo@aol.com. Website: www.howrichunlimited.com. Owner: H.J. Fleischer. Toy designer, licensing agent and manufacturer. Designs, licenses, manufactures toys, gifts and related products. Manufactures novelties (educational, impulse, creative), puzzles, games; publishes booklets. 100% of products are made for kids or have kids' themes.

Illustration: Needs freelance illustration for toy concepts. Makes 100 illustration assignments/year. Uses both color and b&w artwork. To contact, send cover letter, résumé, published samples, portfolio, photocopies, promo pieces. To query with specific ideas, write to request disclosure form first. Reports only if interested. Materials returned with SASE; materials filed. For other artwork, pays by the hour($10); negotiable royalty. Pays on acceptance. Credit line sometimes given.

Photography: Buys photography from freelancers. Works on assignment only. Uses transparencies. To contact, send cover letter, published samples, portfolio, promo piece. Reports only if interested. Materials returned; materials filed. Pays on acceptance. Credit line sometimes given.

Tips: Submit seasonal material 6 months in advance. Concept submissions require prototype or detailed professionally presented illustrations. "Interested in unique toy/game/product concepts."

☒ INNOVA, P.O. Box 36, Redmond WA 98073. (206)746-7774. Fax: (206)451-3959. E-mail: kenj@liberty.sea net.com. Owner: Ken Jacobson. Estab. 1981. Paper products company and producer of educational and strategic games. Publishes coloring books, games, books. 10% of products are made for kids or have kids' themes.

Writing: To contact, send cover letter and writing samples. Reports in 3 months only if interested. Materials returned with SASE; materials filed. Payment is negotiated. Buys all rights. Credit line given.

Illustration: Makes 1-2 illustration assignments/year. To contact, send cover letter and published samples. Reports in 3 months. Materials returned with SASE. Payment is negotiated. Pays on publication. Buys all rights. Credit line given.

Photography: Buys stock and assigns work. To contact, send cover letter and published samples. Reports in 3 months. Material returned if accompanied with SASE; materials filed. Payment is negotiated. Buys all rights. Credit line given.

☑ INTERNATIONAL PLAYTHINGS, INC., 75 Lackawanna Ave., Parsippany NJ 07054-1712. (973)316-2500. Fax: (973)316-5883. E-mail: lindag@intplay.com. Website: www.intplay.com. Product Manager: Linda Golowko. Estab. 1968. Toy/game company. Distributes and markets children's toys, games and puzzles in specialty toy markets. 100% of products are made for kids or have kids' themes.

Illustration: Needs freelance illustration for children's puzzles and games. Makes 20-30 illustration assignments/year. Prefers fine-quality, original illustration for children's puzzles. Uses color artwork only. To contact, send published samples, slides, portfolio, or color photocopies or promo pieces. Reports in 1 month only if interested. Materials filed. For artwork, pays by the project (range: $500-2,000). Pays on publication. Buys one-time rights, negotiable.

Tips: "Mail correspondence only, please. No phone calls."

☑ JILLSON & ROBERTS GIFT WRAPPINGS, 5 Watson Ave., Irvine CA 92618. (949)859-8781. Art Director: Josh Neufeld. Estab. 1973. Paper products company. Makes gift wrap/gift bags. 20% of products are made for kids or have kids' themes.

Illustration: Needs freelance illustration for children's gift wrap. Makes 6-12 illustration assignments/year. Wants children/baby/juvenile themes. To contact, send cover letter. Reports in 1 month. Returns material with

SASE; materials filed. For wrap and bag designs, pays flat fee of $250. Pays on publication. Rights negotiable. Artist's guidelines for SASE.

Tips: Seasonal material should be submitted up to 3½ months in advance. "We produce two lines of gift wrap per year: one everyday line and one Christmas line. The closing date for everyday is June 30th and Christmas is September 15."

N MARCEL SCHURMAN COMPANY, Schurman Design, 101 New Montgomery St., 6th Floor, San Francisco CA 94105. Attn: Portfolio Submissions. Greeting card company. Publishes greeting cards, gift wrap, stationery, bags, journals and note cards. 20% of products are made for kids or have kids' themes.

Writing: Needs freelance writing for children's greeting cards. Makes 2-3 writing assignments/month; 50/year. For greeting cards, prefers unrhymed verse ideas. To query with specific ideas, write to request disclosure form first. Reports in 6 weeks. Materials returned with SASE; sometimes files material. For greeting cards, pays flat fee of $75-125 on acceptance. Writer's guidelines available for SASE.

Illustration: Needs freelance illustration for children's greeting cards. Makes 60 illustration assignments/month; 800/year. Uses color artwork only. To contact, send color photocopies. To query with specific ideas, send letter with or without samples. Reports in 1 month. Materials returned if accompanied by SASE; materials filed. For greeting cards pays a flat fee or royalty.

Photography: Buys photography from freelancers. Buys stock and assigns work. Uses 4×5 transparencies. To contact, send slides. Reports in 1 month. Materials returned with SASE or filed. Guidelines for SASE.

Tips: Submit seasonal ideas 6-8 months in advance.

N J.T. MURPHY COMPANY, 200 W. Fisher Ave., Philadelphia PA 19120. Greeting card company. Publishes greeting cards. 30% of products are made for kids or have kids' themes.

Writing: To contact, send writing samples. Materials returned with SASE. Pays on acceptance.

Illustration: Needs freelance illustration for children's greeting cards.

NOVO CARD PUBLISHERS, INC., 3630 W. Pratt Ave., Lincolnwood IL 60712. (847)763-0077. Fax: (847)763-0020. E-mail: novo@novocards.com. Contact: Marie Bubser, art production. Estab. 1926. Greeting card company. Company publishes greeting cards, note/invitation packs and gift envelopes for middle market. Publishes greeting cards (Novo Card/Cloud-9). 20% of products are made for kids or have kids' themes.

Writing: Needs freelance writing for children's greeting cards. Makes 400 writing assignments/year. Other needs for freelance writing include invitation notes. To contact send writing samples. To query with specific ideas, write to request disclosure form first. Reports back in 1 month only if interested. Materials returned only with SASE; materials filed. For greeting cards, pays flat fee of $2/line. Pays on acceptance. Buys all rights. Credit line sometimes given. Writer's guidelines available for SASE.

Illustration: Needs freelance illustration for children's greeting cards. Makes 1,000 illustration assignments/year. Prefers just about all types: traditional, humor, contemporary, etc. To contact, send published samples, slides and color photocopies. To query with specific ideas write to request disclosure form first. Reports in 1 month. Materials returned with SASE; materials filed. For greeting cards, pay negotiable. Pays on acceptance. Rights negotiable. Credit line sometimes given. Artist's guidelines available for SASE.

Photography: Buys stock and assigns work. Buys more than 100 stock images/year. Wants all types. Uses color and b&w prints; 35mm transparencies. To contact, send slides, stock photo list, published samples, paper copies acceptable. Reports in 1 month. Materials returned with SASE; materials filed. Pays negotiable rate. Pays on acceptance. Rights negotiable. Credit line sometimes given. Guidelines for SASE.

Tips: Submit seasonal material 10-12 months in advance. "Novo has extensive lines of greeting cards: everyday, seasonal (all) and alternative lives (over 24 separate lines of note card packs and gift enclosures). Our lines encompass all types of styles and images."

P.S. GREETINGS/FANTUS PAPER PRODUCTS, 5060 N. Kimberly Ave., Chicago IL 60630. (773)725-9308 or (800)334-2141. Fax: (773)725-9308. Website: www.psg-fpp.com. Art Director: Jennifer Dodson. Estab. 1950. Greeting card company. Publishes boxed and individual counter greeting cards. Seasons include: Christmas, every major holiday and everyday. 30% of products are made for kids or have kid's themes.

Writing: Needs freelance writing for children's greeting cards. Makes 10-20 writing assignments/year. To contact, send cover letter and writing samples. To query with specific idea, write to request disclosure form and submission guidelines first. Reports in 1 month. Material returned only with SASE. For greeting cards, pays flat fee/line. Pays on acceptance. Buys greeting card rights. Credit line given. Writer's guidelines free with SASE.

Illustration: Needs freelance illustration for children's greeting cards. Makes about 10-20 illustration assignments/year. Open to all mediums, all themes. To contact, send published samples, color promo pieces and color photocopies only. Reports in 1 month. Returns materials with SASE. For greeting cards, pays flat fee of $250-400. Pays on acceptance. Buys greeting card rights. Credit line given. Artist's guidelines free with SASE.

Photography: Buys photography from freelancers. Buys and assigns work. Buys 5-10 stock images/year. Makes 5-10 assignments/year. Wants florals, animals, seasonal (Christmas, Easter, valentines, etc.). Uses 35mm transparencies. To contact, send slides. Reports in 6 weeks. Materials returned with SASE; materials filed. Pays on acceptance. Buys greeting card rights. Credit line given. Photographer's guidelines free with SASE.

Tips: Seasonal material should be submitted 6 months in advance.

Taiwanese artist Chih-Wei Chang contacted Novo Card Publishers after reading their listing in the 1997 *Children's Writer's & Illustrator's Market*. His watercolor image of a young boy in a boat was used on the cover of a greeting card bearing the message "Distant moon above/ Bright stars below,/ Hold onto your dreams,/ Wherever you go." Chang does not work with a rep, though he hopes to find one. Instead he sends samples to potential clients. "I enjoy working with colors," he says. "For me, looking for the right color is like playing with a jigsaw puzzle."

PANDA INK, P.O. Box 5129, West Hills CA 91308-5129. (818)340-8061. Fax: (818)883-6193. Owner: Art/Creative Director: Ruth Ann Epstein. Estab. 1981. Greeting card company and producer of clocks, magnets, bookmarks. Produces Judaica—whimsical, metaphysical, general, everyday. Publishes greeting cards. 15% of products are made for kids or have kids' themes.

Writing: Needs freelance writing for children's greeting cards. Makes 1-2 writing assignments/year. For greeting cards, accepts both rhymed and unrhymed verse ideas. Looks for greeting card writing which is Judaica or metaphysical. To contact, send cover letter and SASE. To query with specific ideas, write to request disclosure form first. Reports in 1 month. Materials returned with SASE; materials filed. For greeting cards, pays flat fee of $3-20. Pays on acceptance. Rights negotiable. Credit line sometimes given.

Illustration: Needs freelance illustration for children's greeting cards, magnets, bookmarks. Makes 1 illustration assignment/year. Needs Judaica (Hebrew wording), metaphysical themes. Uses color artwork only. To contact, send cover letter. Query with specific ideas. Reports in 2 months. Materials returned with SASE; materials filed. Payment is negotiable. Pays on acceptance. Rights negotiable. Credit line sometimes given. Artist's guidelines available for SASE.

Tips: Submit seasonal material 1 year in advance. "Always send SASE."

:N: PEACEABLE KINGDOM PRESS, 707B Heinz Ave., Berkeley CA 94710. (510)644-9801. Fax: (510)644-9805. E-mail: artdog@pacbell.net. Website: www.pkpress.com. Editor, Creative Development: Gail Peterson. Creative Director: Suellen Ehnebuske. Estab. 1983. Produces posters, greeting cards, stickers, gift wrap and related products. Uses children's book illustrators exclusively but not necessarily targeted only to children. 98% of products are made for kids or have kids' themes.

Writing: Needs freelance writing for children's greeting cards. Makes approximately 300 writing assignments/year. To contact, send cover letter, client list, writing samples. Reports in 6-8 weeks. Materials not returned; materials filed. For greeting cards, pays a flat fee of $50.

Illustration: Needs freelance illustration for children's greeting cards and posters. Makes 50 illustration assignments/year. "For specific occasions—Christmas, Chanukah, Mother's and Father's Days, etc., we look for visually sophisticated work with a narrative element." To contact, send cover letter, slides, promo pieces, published books or f&g's and color photocopies. To query with specific ideas, submit 5×7 of same dimensions enlarged, vertical, plus ⅛, if full bleed color. Materials returned with SASE; materials not filed. Contact Molly Gauld or Gail Peterson, creative directors. Reports in 2 months. Pays on publication with advance. Pays 6% for 3 years or advance of $350 against 6% for 3 years. For other artwork, pays royalty of $350 against 6% for 3 years. Pays on publication. Buys first rights and reprint rights; negotiable for greeting cards. Buys rights to distribution worldwide. Artist's guidelines available for SASE.

Photography: Buys photos ocassionally. Buys 10 stock images/year. Wants zaney, wacky kids, pets and/or creations. Uses transparencies and 35mm. To contact send cover letter, slides, client list. Reports in 2 months. Materials returned with SASE. Pays royalty of $90. Pays on publication. Buys first rights and reprint rights; negotiable. Credit lines given.

Tips: "We only choose from illustrations that are from published children's book illustrators, or commissioned art by established children's book illustrators. Be a successful published children's book illustrator or almost one. Think of occasion-specific images. Submit seasonal and everyday greeting cards one year in advance."

PLUM GRAPHICS INC., P.O. Box 136, Prince St. Station, New York NY 10012. Phone/fax: (212)337-0999. Owner: Yvette Cohen. Estab. 1983. Greeting card company. Produces die-cut greeting cards for ages 5-105. Publishes greeting cards and message boards.

Writing: Needs freelance writing for greeting cards. Makes 4 writing assignments/year. Looks for "greeting card writing which is fun." To contact, send SASE for guidelines. Contact: Michelle Reynoso. Reports in 2 months. Materials returned with SASE; materials filed. For greeting cards, pays flat fee of $40. Pays on publication. Buys all rights. Writer's guidelines available for SASE.

Illustration: Needs freelance illustration for greeting cards. Makes 10-15 freelance illustration assignments/year. Prefers very tight artwork that is fun and realistic. Uses color artwork only. To contact, send b&w photocopies. Contact: Yvette Cohen. Reports only if interested. Materials returned with SASE; materials filed. For greeting cards, pays flat fee of $350-450 "plus $50 each time we reprint." Pays on publication. Buys exclusive product rights. Credit line given.

Tips: "Go to a store and look at our cards and style before submitting work."

POCKETS OF LEARNING LTD., 30 Cutler St., Suite 101, Warren RI 02885. (800)635-2994. Fax: (800)370-1580. Product Manager: Wendy Aylward. Estab. 1989. Educational soft toy company. Specializes in design, manufacture and distribution of high-quality educational cloth books, soft sculptures, wallhangings, travel bags and gifts. 100% of products are made for children ranging from birth to 6 years old.

Illustration: Needs freelance illustration for educational cloth toys. Makes 5 illustration assignments/year. "We introduce 20-30 new products per year, including cloth books, travel bags, soft sculpture and wallhangings." Uses both color and b&w artwork. To contact, send cover letter, slides, photocopies. To query with specific ideas, write to request disclosure form first. Pays on acceptance. Buys all rights.

PROMOTIONAL RESOURCES GROUP, P.O. Box 19235, University Blvd. at Essex Entrance Bldg. 2704 B-1, Topeka KS 66619-0235. (785)862-3707. Fax: (785)862-1424. E-mail: erics@prgnet.com. Art Director: Eric Scott. Estab. 1982. "We produce kids promotions for restaurants nation-wide. Includes sacks, cartons and toys." Produces kids' meal sacks, cartons, menus, activity books and toys. 100% of products are made for kids or have kids' themes.

Illustration: Needs freelance illustration for kids' meal sacks, cartons, menus, activity books and toys. Makes 10 illustration assignments/year. Submit ideas in color copy format. Reports back only if interested. Materials returned with SASE; materials filed. For other artwork, pays by the project (range: $250-2,000). Pays on acceptance. Buys all rights.

Tips: Submit materials 3 months in advance.

RECO INTERNATIONAL CORP., 138-150 Haven Ave., Pt. Washington NY 11050. (516)767-2400. Fax: (516)767-2409. E-mail: recoint@aol.com. Website: www.reco.com. President: Heio W. Reich. Estab. 1967. Collector's plate producer. 60% of products are made for kids or have kids' themes.

Writing: Needs freelance writing for children's greeting cards. Makes 40 writing assignments/year.

Illustration: Needs freelance illustration for collector's plates—children's subjects mainly, but also western, Indian, flowers, animals, fantasy and mystical. Makes 40 assignments/year. Uses color artwork only. To contact, send portfolio. Submit specific ideas. Reports in 1 month. Materials returned with SASE; materials filed. For greeting cards, pays flat fee and royalty. For other artwork, pays royalty and advance. Pays on acceptance. Buys exclusive product rights. Artist's guidelines available for SASE after review of portfolio.

Photography: Buys photos at times. Wants good art photos.

Tips: Submit seasonal material 12-18 months in advance (although rarely uses seasonal work).

RED FARM STUDIO, 1135 Roosevelt Ave., P.O. Box 347, Pawtucket RI 02862. (401)728-9300. Contact: Production Coordinator. Estab. 1949. Greeting card company. Publishes coloring books and paintables. 20% of products are made for kids or have kids' themes.

Illustration: Needs freelance illustration for children's traditional subject greeting cards, coloring books and paintables. Makes 1 illustration assignment/month; 6-12/year. Prefers "watercolor, realistic styles yet cute." For first contact, request art guidelines with SASE. Reports in 2-4 weeks. Returns materials with SASE. Appropriate materials are kept on file. "We work on assignment using ink line work (coloring books) or pencil renderings (paintables)." Buys all rights. Credit line given and artist may sign artwork. Artist's guidelines for SASE.

Tips: Majority of freelance assignments made during January-May/yearly. "Research companies before sending submissions to determine whether your styles are compatible."

RESOURCE GAMES, 2704 185th Ave. NE, Redmond WA 98052. (425)883-3143. Fax: (425)883-3136. Website: www.resourcegames.com. Owner: John Jaquet. Estab. 1987. Educational game manufacturer. Resource Games manufactures a line of high-quality geography theme board and card games for ages 6 and up. Publishes games. 100% of products made for kids or have kids' themes.

Tips: "We are always on the lookout for innovative educational games for the classroom and the home. If accepted, we enter into royalty agreements ranging from 5-10%."

SHULSINGER SALES, INC., 50 Washington St., Brooklyn NY 11201. (718)852-0042. Fax: (718)935-9691. President: Miriam Gutfeld. Estab. 1979. Greeting card, novelties and paper products company. "We are a Judaica company, distributing products such as greeting cards, books, paperware, puzzles, games, novelty items—all with a Jewish theme to party stores, temples, bookstores, supermarkets and chain stores." Publishes greeting cards, novelties, coloring books, children's books, giftwrap, tableware and puzzles. 60% of products are made for kids or have kids' themes.

Writing: Looks for greeting card writing which can be sent by children to adults and sent by adults to children (of all ages). Makes 10-20 freelance writing assignments/year. To contact, send cover letter. To query with specific ideas, write to request disclosure form first. Reports in 2 weeks. Materials returned with SASE; materials filed. For greeting cards, pays flat fee (this includes artwork). Pays on acceptance. Buys exclusive product rights.

Illustration: Needs freelance illustration for children's greeting cards, books, novelties, games. Makes 10-20 illustration assignments/year. "The only requirement is a Jewish theme." To contact, send cover letter and photocopies, color if possible. To query with specific ideas, write to request disclosure form first. Reports in 2 weeks. Returns materials with SASE; materials filed. For children's greeting cards, pays flat fee (this includes

FOR EXPLANATIONS OF THESE SYMBOLS, SEE THE INSIDE FRONT AND BACK COVERS OF THIS BOOK

"The artist managed to capture the Jewish motifs in a naive contemporary style," says Miriam Gutfeld, president of Shulsinger Sales. "The artist's style has established a new trend in Jewish greeting cards and has been copied unsuccessfully." Artist Claudia Fehr-Levin created this Bat Mitzvah card using acrylic ink. Her artwork can be found on calendars, notebook covers and other stationery products.

writing). For other artwork, pays by the project. Pays on acceptance. Buys exclusive product rights. Credit line sometimes given. Artist's guidelines not available.

Tips: Seasonal material should be submitted 6 months in advance. "An artist may submit an idea for any item that is related to our product line. Generally, there is an initial submission of a portfolio of the artist's work, which will be returned at the artist's expense. If the art is appropriate to our specialized subject matter, then further discussion will ensue regarding particular subject matter. We request a sampling of at least 10 pieces of work, in the form of tearsheets, or printed samples, or high quality color copies that can be reviewed and then kept on file, if accepted. If art is accepted and published, then original art will be returned to artist. Shulsinger Sales, Inc. maintains the right to re-publish a product for a mutually agreed upon time period. We pay an agreed upon fee per project."

 SMART ART, INC., P.O. Box 661, Chatham NJ 07928-0661. (973)635-1690. Fax: (973)635-2011. E-mail: smartart1@mindspring.com. Website: www.smartart.net. President: Barb Hauck-Mah. Estab. 1992. Greeting card company. Publishes photo-insert cards for card, gift and photo shops. About 10% of products are made for kids or have kids' themes.

Illustration: Needs freelance illustration for photo-insert cards. Makes 12-14 illustration assignments/year. Uses color artwork only. To contact, send color photocopies. To query with specific ideas, write to request confidentiality form. Reports in 2-3 months. Materials returned with SASE; materials not filed. For greeting cards, pays annual royalties for life of card or 5 years. Pays on publication. Credit line given. Artist's guidelines available for SASE.

Tips: Submit seasonal material 6-8 months in advance. "Smart Art specializes in a unique, premium quality line of photo-insert cards for the holidays, baby announcements, weddings and all-season occasions. Our cards feature watercolor or collage borders on textured, recycled paper. Designs should complement horizontal and vertical photos. Generally, our freelance designers are new to the greeting card/paper goods industry. Artists come from varied backgrounds, including an art teacher, a textile designer and several children's book illustrators. We are looking for 'border design' artwork rendered in pen & ink with watercolors or in cut/torn paper. We are interested in artists who can create interesting abstract textures as well as representational designs."

☑ **STANDARD PUBLISHING**, 8121 Hamilton Ave., Cincinnati OH 45231. (513)931-4050. Fax: (513)931-0950. Director: Diane Stortz. Children's Publishing: Ruth Frederick (church resources). Art Director: Colleen Davis. Estab. 1866. Publishes children's books and teacher helps for the religious market. 75% of products are made for kids or have kids' themes.

● Standard also has a listing in Book Publishers.

Writing: Considers puzzle books, activity books and games. Reports in 3 months. Payment method varies. Credit line given.

Illustration: Needs freelance illustration for puzzle, activity books, teacher helps. Makes 6-10 illustration assignments/year. To contact, send cover letter and photocopies. Reports back in 3 months if interested. Payment method varies. Credit line given.

Photography: Buys a limited amount of photos from freelancers. Wants mature, scenic and Christian themes.

Tips "Many of our projects are developed inhouse and assigned. Study our catalog and products; visit Christian bookstores."

☑ **TALICOR, INC.**, 4741 Murriet St., Chino CA 91710-5156. (909)517-1962. Fax: (909)517-1962. E-mail: webmaster@talicor.com. Website: www.talicor.com. President: Lew Herndon. Estab. 1971. Game and puzzle manufacturer. Publishes games and puzzles (adults' and children's). 70% of products are made for kids or have kids' themes.

Writing: Makes 1 writing assignment/month; 12/year.

Illustration: Needs freelance illustration for games and puzzles. Makes 12 illustration assignments/year. To contact, send promo piece. Reports in 6 months. Materials returned with SASE; materials filed. For artwork, pays by the hour, by the project or negotiable royalty. Pays on acceptance. Buys negotiable rights.

Photography: Buys stock and assigns work. Buys 6 stock images/year. Wants photos with wholesome family subjects. Makes 6 assignments/year. Uses 4×5 transparencies. To contact, send color promo piece. Reports only if interested. Materials returned with SASE; materials filed. Pays per photo, by the hour, by the day or by the project (negotiable rates). Pays on acceptance. Buys negotiable rights.

Tips: Submit seasonal material 6 months in advance.

☑ **WARNER PRESS**, P.O. Box 2499, Anderson IN 46018-9988. Fax: (765)640-8005. E-mail: jennieb@warnerpress.org. Website: www.warnerpress. Senior Editor: Jennie Bishop. Creative Director: John Silvey. Estab. 1880. Publishes church resources, coloring and activity books and children's supplies, all religious-oriented. 15% of products are made for kids.

Writing: To contact, request guidelines first (available for church resource products only). Contact: Jennie Bishop, senior editor. Reports in 4-6 weeks. Limited purchases of children's material right now. Materials may be kept on file for future use. Pays on acceptance. Buys all rights. Credit line sometimes given. Writer's guidelines for church resource products for SASE.

Illustration: "We purchase a very limited amount of freelance art at this time, but we are always looking for excellent coloring book artists."

Photography: Buys photography from freelancers for church bulletin covers. Contact: John Silvey, creative director.

Tips: Writers request guidelines for church resource products before submitting. No guidelines available for children's products at present. We purchase a very limited amount of children's material, but we may grow into more children's products and opportunities. Make sure to include SASE. Unsolicited material that does not follow guidelines will not be reviewed."

Play Publishers & Producers

Writing plays for children and family audiences is a special challenge. Whether creating an original work or adapting a classic, plays for children must hold the attention of audiences that often include children and adults. Using rhythm, repetition and dramatic action are effective ways of holding the attention of kids. Pick subjects children can relate to, and never talk down to them.

Theater companies often have limited budgets so plays with elaborate staging and costumes often can't be produced. Touring companies want simple sets that can be moved easily. Keep in mind that they may have as few as three actors, so roles may have to be doubled up.

Many of the companies listed here produce plays with roles for adults and children, so check the percentage of plays written for adult and children's roles. Most importantly, study the types of plays a theater wants and doesn't want. Many name plays they've recently published or produced, and some have additional guidelines or information available. For more listings of theaters open to submissions of children's and adult material and information on contests and organizations for playwrights, consult *Dramatists Sourcebook* (Theatre Communications Group, Inc.).

Information on play publishers listed in the previous edition but not included in this edition of *Children's Writer's & Illustrator's Market* may be found in the General Index.

☑ ♼ **A.D. PLAYERS**, 2710 W. Alabama, Houston TX 77098. (713)526-2721. Fax: (713)522-5475. E-mail: adplayer@hearn.org. Website: www.adplayers.org. Estab. 1967. Produces 4-5 children's plays/year in new Children's Theatre Series; 5 musicals/year. Produces children's plays for professional productions.
 • A.D. Players has received the Dove family approval stamp; an award from the Columbia International Film & Video Festival; and a Silver Angel Award.
Needs: 99-100% of plays/musicals written for adult roles; 0-1% for juvenile roles. "Cast must utilize no more than five actors. Need minimal, portable sets for proscenium or arena stage with no fly space and no wing space." Does not want to see large cast or set requirements or New Age themes. Recently produced plays: *Samson: The Hair Off His Head*, by William Shryoch (courage and obedience for preK-grade 6); *The Wizard of Oz*, by Danny Siebert (new adaptation for preK-grade 6).
How to Contact: Send script with SASE. No tapes or pictures. Will consider simultaneous submissions and previously performed work. Reports in 6-9 months.
Terms: Buys some residual rights. Pay negotiated. Submissions returned with SASE.
Tips: "Children's musicals tend to be large in casting requirements. For those theaters with smaller production capabilities, this can be a liability for a script. Try to keep it small and simple, especially if writing for theaters where adults are performing for children. We are interested in material that reflects family values, emphasizes the importance of responsibility in making choices, encourages faith in God and projects the joy and fun of telling a story."

☑ **AMERICAN STAGE**, P.O. Box 1560, St. Petersburg FL 33731. (727)823-1600. Artistic Director: Ken Mitchell. Managing Director: Lee Manwaring Lowry. Estab. 1977. Produces 3 children's plays/year. Produces children's plays for professional children's theater program, mainstage, school tour, performing arts halls.
Needs: Limited by budget and performance venue. Subject matter: classics and original work for children (ages K-12) and families. Recently produced plays: *A Christmas Carol*, by Doris Baisley (ages 5-up); *Puss-N-Boots*, by Bill Leavengood (ages 5-15). Does not want to see plays that look down on children. Approach must be that of the child or fictional beings or animals.
How to Contact: Query with synopsis, character breakdown and set description. Will consider simultaneous submissions and previously performed work.
Terms: Purchases "professional rights." Pays writers in royalties (6-8%); $25-35/performance. SASE for return of submission.
Tips: Sees a move in plays toward basic human values, relationships and multicultural communities.

ANCHORAGE PRESS, INC., P.O. Box 8067, New Orleans LA 70182-8067. (504)283-8868. Fax: (504)866-0502. Editor: Orlin Corey. Estab. 1935. Publishes 8-10 children's plays/year; 2-3 children's musicals/year.
Needs: "There is no genre, subject of preferred interest. We want plays of high literary/theatrical quality. Like music, such material—by nature of the stage—will appeal to any age capable of following a story. Obviously some appeal more to primary ages, some secondary." Does not want send-ups—cutesies—jargon-laden—pendantic/subject specific. "Plays—like ice cream—work only if they are superb. Teaching is not the purpose of theatre—entertainment is, and that may include serious subjects fascinatingly explored." Recently produced plays: *The Orphan Train*, by Aurand Harris (play about lives of 10 children who rode "orphan" trains of 1914 for ages 7-18); *Tokoloshe*, by Pieter Scholtz (Zulu tale of a water-sprite and a modern little Zulu girl seeking her father for ages 5-9).
How to Contact: Query for guidelines first. Will consider simultaneous submissions and previously performed work "essential to be proven." Reports 1-2 months.
Terms: Buys all stage rights. Pays royalty (varies extensively from 50% minimum to 80%). Submissions returned with SASE.
Tips: "Obtain guidelines, have proof of three distinct productions and get a catalog first. SASE essential."

N ARVADA CENTER FOR THE ARTS & HUMANITIES, 6901 Wadsworth Blvd., Arvada CO 80005. (303)431-3080. Fax: (303)431-3083. E-mail: kathy-k@arvadacenter.org. Website: www.arvadacenter.org. Artistic Director: Kathy Kuehn. Estab. 1976. Produces 3 children's plays/year; 3 musicals/year.
Needs: Produces professional adult productions for children; non-equity, summer theater. 95% of plays/musicals written for adult roles; 5% for juvenile roles. Productions must be 50-60 minutes in length, have participation, largest cast size 8, lower grade levels only. Musical needs: Up tempo, no ballads. Recently produced plays: *Strega Nona*, by Tomie De Paolo (adaptation of the book for preschool-6th grade); *Further Adventures of Little Red Riding Hood*, by David and Julie Payne (fairy tale for preschool-6th grade).
How to Contact: Plays/musicals: Query with synopsis, character breakdown and set description. Reports back only if interested.
Terms: Obtains a percentage of rights on mss and scores.

N BAKER'S PLAYS, P.O. Box 699222, Quincy MA 02269-9222. (617)745-0805. Fax: (617)745-9891. E-mail: info@bakersplays.com. Website: www.bakersplays.com. Associate Editor: Raymond Pape. Estab. 1845. Publishes 20 plays/year; 2 musicals/year.
Needs: Adaptations of both popular and lesser known folktales. Subject matter: full lengths for family audience and full lengths and one act plays for teens." Recently published plays: *Broadway Cafe*, by Cohen and Spencer (musical for young adults for ages 12-25); *Willabella Witch's Last Spell*, by Thomas Hischar (a witch wants to quit her job for ages 8-18).
How to Contact: Submit complete ms, score and tape of songs. Reports in 3-8 months.
Terms: Obtains worldwide rights. Pays writers in production royalties (amount varies) and book royalties.
Tips: "Know the audience you're writing for before you submit your play anywhere. 90% of the plays we reject are not written for our market. When writing for children, never be afraid to experiment with language, characters or story. They are fertile soil for fresh, new ideas."

✔ BILINGUAL FOUNDATION OF THE ARTS, 421 N. Avenue 19th, Los Angeles CA 90031. (323)225-4044. Fax: (323)225-1250. E-mail: bfateatro@aol.com. Artistic Director: Margarita Galban. Contact: Agustín Coppola, dramaturg. Estab. 1973. Produces 6 children's plays/year; 4 children's musicals/year.
Needs: Produces children's plays for professional productions. 60% of plays/musicals written for adult roles; 40% for juvenile roles. No larger than 8 member cast. Recently produced plays: *Second Chance*, by A. Cardona and A. Weinstein (play about hopes and fears in every teenager for teenagers); *Choices*, by Gannon Daniels (violence prevention, teens).
How to Contact: Plays: Query with synopsis, character breakdown and set description and submit complete ms. Musicals: Query with synopsis, character breakdown and set description and submit complete ms with score. Will consider simultaneous submissions and previously performed work. Reports in 6 months.
Terms: Pays royalty; per performance; buys material outright; "different with each play."
Tips: "The plays should reflect the Hispanic experience in the U.S."

N BIRMINGHAM CHILDREN'S THEATRE, P.O. Box 1362, Birmingham AL 35201. (205)458-8181. Managing Director: Bert Brosowsky. Estab. 1947. Produces 8-10 children's plays/year; some children's musicals/year.

TO RECEIVE REGULAR TIPS AND UPDATES about writing and Writer's Digest publications via e-mail, send an e-mail with "SUBSCRIBE NEWSLETTER" in the body of the message to newsletter-request@writersdigest.com

Needs: "BCT is an adult professional theater performing for youth and family audiences September-May." 99% of plays/musicals written for adult roles; 1% for juvenile roles. "Our 'Wee Folks' Series is limited to four cast members and should be written with preschool-grade 1 in mind. We prefer interactive plays for this age group. We commission plays for our 'Wee Folks' Series (preschool-grade 1), our Children's Series (K-6) and our Young Adult Series (6-12)." Recently produced plays: *The Little Red Hen*, by Patricia Muse (classic story retold in interactive format for children in preschool through grade 1; 4 actors) and *Rapunzel*, by Randy Marsh (classic story told with a twist for children in grades K-6; 6 actors). Does not want plays which have references to witches, spells, incantations, evil magic or devils. No adult language. Will consider musicals, interactive theater for Wee Folks Series. Prefer mainstage limited to 4-7 cast members.
How to Contact: Query first, query with synopsis, character breakdown and set description. Reports in 4 months.
Terms: Buys negotiable rights. Submissions returned with SASE.
Tips: "We would like our commissioned scripts to teach as well as entertain. Keep in mind the age groups (defined by each series) that our audience is composed of. Send submissions to the attention of Charlotte Dominick, executive director."

BOARSHEAD THEATER, 425 S. Grand Ave., Lansing MI 48933. (517)484-7800. Fax: (517)484-2564. Artistic Director: John Peakes. Director of P.R., Marketing and Outreach: Cathy Hansel. Estab. 1966. Produces 3 children's plays/year.
Needs: Produces children's plays for professional production. Majority of plays written for young adult roles. Prefers 5 characters or less for touring productions, 5 plus characters for mainstage productions; one unit set, simple costumes. Recently produced plays: *The Lion, the Witch & the Wardrobe*, by Joseph Robinette (fantasy for ages 6-12); *1,000 Cranes*, by Katharine Schultz Miller. *The Planet of the Perfectly Awful People*; and *Patchwork*. Does not want to see musicals.
How to Contact: Query with synopsis, character breakdown and set description. Send to Education Director. Include 10 pages of representative dialogue. Will consider previously performed work. Reports in 2 weeks on queries; 4 months "if we ask for submissions."
Terms: Submissions returned with SASE. If no SASE, send self-addressed stamped post card for reply.

☑ **CALIFORNIA THEATRE CENTER**, P.O. Box 2007, Sunnyvale CA 94087. (408)245-2979. Fax: (408)245-0235. E-mail: ctc@ctcinc.org. Website: www.ctcinc.org. Resident Director: Will Huddleston. Estab. 1975. Produces 15 children's plays and 1 musical for professional productions.
Needs: 75% of plays/musicals written for adult roles; 20% for juvenile roles. Prefers material suitable for professional tours and repertory performance; one-hour time limit, limited technical facilities. Recently produced *Thumbelina*, by Will Huddleston (fairy tale for ages K-4); *The Little Mermaid*, by Gayle Cornelison (fairy tale for ages K-5).
How to Contact: Query with synopsis, character breakdown and set description. Send to: Will Huddleston. Will consider previously performed work. Reports in 6 months.
Terms: Rights negotiable. Pays writers royalties; pays $35-50/performance. Submissions returned with SASE.
Tips: "We sell to schools, so the title and material must appeal to teachers who look for things familiar to them. We look for good themes, universality. Avoid the cute."

CHILDREN'S STORY SCRIPTS, Baymax Productions, PMB 130, 2219 W. Olive Ave., Burbank CA 91506-2648. (818)563-6105. Fax: (818)563-2968. E-mail: baymax@earthlink.net. Editor: Deedra Bebout. Estab. 1990. Produces 1-10 children's scripts/year.
Needs: "Except for small movements and occasionally standing up, children remain seated in Readers Theatre fashion." Publishes scripts sold primarily to schools or wherever there's a program to teach or entertain children. "All roles read by children except K-2 scripts, where kids have easy lines, leader helps read the narration. Prefer multiple cast members, no props or sets." Subject matter: scripts on all subjects that dovetail with classroom subjects. Targeted age range—K-8th grade, 5-13 years old. Recently published plays: *A Clever Fox*, by Mary Ellen Holmes (about using one's wits, grades 2-4); *Memories of the Pony Express*, by Sharon Gill Askelson (grades 5-8). No stories that preach a point, no stories about catastrophic disease or other terribly heavy topics, no theatrical scripts without narrative prose to move the story along, no monologues or 1-character stories.
How to Contact: Submit complete ms. Will consider simultaneous submissions and previously performed work (if rights are available). Reports in 2 weeks.
Terms: Purchases all rights; authors retain copyrights. "We add support material and copyright the whole package." Pays writers in royalties (10-15% on sliding scale, based on number of copies sold). SASE for reply and return of submission.
Tips: "We're only looking for stories related to classsroom studies—educational topics with a freshness to them. Our scripts mix prose narration with character dialogue—we do not publish traditional, all-dialogue plays." Writer's guidelines packet available for business-sized SASE with 2 first-class stamps. Guidelines explain what Children's Story Scripts are, give 4-page examples from 2 different scripts, give list of suggested topics for scripts.

CIRCA '21 DINNER THEATRE, P.O. Box 3784, Rock Island IL 61204-3784. (309)786-2667. Fax: (309)786-4119. Website: circa21.com. Producer: Dennis Hitchcock. Estab. 1977. Produces 3 children's musicals/year.
Needs: Produces children's plays for professional productions. 95% of musicals written for adult roles; 5% written for juvenile roles. "Prefer a cast of four to eight—no larger than ten. Plays are produced on mainstage sets." Recently produced plays: *Aladdin and Little Mermaid*, by Ted Morris and Bill Johnson (ages 5-12).
How to Contact: Send complete script with audiotape of music. Reports in 3 months.
Terms: Payment negotiable.

I.E. CLARK PUBLICATIONS, P.O. Box 246, Schulenburg TX 78956-0246. (409)743-3232. Fax: (409)743-4765. E-mail: ieclark@cvtv.net. General Manager: Donna Cozzaglio. Estab. 1956. Publishes 3 children's plays/year; 1 or 2 children's musicals/year.
Needs: Publishes plays for all ages. Published plays: *Little Women*, by Thomas Hischak (dramatization of the Alcott novel for family audiences); *Heidi*, by Ann Pugh, music by Betty Utter (revision of our popular musical dramatization of the Johanna Spyri novel). Does not want to see plays that have not been produced.
How to Contact: Submit complete ms and audio or video tape. Will consider simultaneous submissions and previously performed work. Reports in 2-4 months.
Terms: Pays writers in negotiable royalties. SASE for return of submission.
Tips: "We publish only high-quality literary works. Request a copy of our writer's guidelines before submitting. Please send only one manuscript at a time and be sure to include videos and audiotapes."

COLUMBIA ENTERTAINMENT COMPANY, % Betsy Phillips, 309 Parkade, Columbia MO 65202-1447. (573)874-5628. Artistic Director: Betsy Phillips. Estab. 1988. Produces 2-4 children's plays/year; 0-1 children's musicals/year.
Needs: "We produce children's theatre plays. Our theatre school students act all the roles. We cast adult and children roles with children from theatre school. Each season we have 5 plays done by adults (kid parts possible)—3 theatre school productions. We need large cast plays-20+, as plays are produced by theater school classes (ages 12-14). Any set changes are completed by students in the play." Musical needs: Musicals must have songs written in ranges children can sing. Recently produced: *Comedia Del Delight*, by Claudia Haas and Richard Cash (a spoof of 16th century Italian commedia, all ages).
How to Contact: Plays: Submit complete ms; use SASE to get form. Musicals: Submit complete ms and score; tape of music must be included, use SASE to get entry form. Will consider simultaneous submissions and previously performed work. Reports in 2-6 months.
Terms: Buys production (sans royalties) rights on mss. "We have production rights sans royalties for one production. Production rights remain with author." Pays $250 1st prize. Submissions returned with SASE.
Tips: "Please write a play/musical that appeals to all ages. We always need lots of parts, especially for girls."

CONTEMPORARY DRAMA SERVICE, Division of Meriwether Publishing Ltd., 885 Elkton Dr., Colorado Springs CO 80907-3557. (719)594-4422. Fax: (719)594-9916. E-mail: merpcds@aol.com. Website: www.meriwe therpublishing.com. Executive Editor: Arthur L. Zapel. Estab. 1979. Publishes 60 children's plays/year; 15 children's musicals/year.
Needs: Prefer shows with a large cast. 50% of plays/musicals written for adult roles; 50% for juvenile roles. Recently published plays: *The Best Christmas Present Ever*, by Rachel Olson (Sunday school pageant for ages 10-12); *Princess*, by Judy Wickland (fairy tale spoof/satire for middle school grades). "We publish church plays for elementary level for Christmas and Easter. Most of our secular plays are for teens or college level." Does not want to see "full-length, three-act plays unless they are adaptations of classic works or have unique comedy appeal."
How to Contact: Query with synopsis, character breakdown and set description; "query first if a musical." Will consider simultaneous submissions or previously performed work. Reports in 1 month.
Terms: Purchases first rights. Pays writers royalty (10%) or buys material outright for $200-1,000. SASE for return of submission.
Tips: "If the writer is submitting a musical play, an audiocassette of the music should be sent. We prefer plays with humorous action. We like comedies, spoofs, satires and parodies of known works. A writer should provide credentials of plays published and produced. Writers should not submit items for the elementary age level."

DRAMATIC PUBLISHING, INC., 311 Washington St., Woodstock IL 60098. (815)338-7170. Fax: (815)338-8981. E-mail: plays@dramaticpublishing.com. Website: www.dramaticpublishing.com. Acquisitions Editor: Linda Habjan. Estab. 1885. Publishes 10-15 children's plays/year; 4-6 children's musicals.
Needs: Recently published: *The Cay*, by Dr. Gayle Cornelison and Robert Taylor; *The Dream Thief*, by Robert Schenkkan (fantasy classic by Pulitzer prize winning author); and *Alexander and the Terrible, Horrible, No Good, Very Bad Day*, book lyrics by Judith Viorst and Shelly Markham (for family audiences).
How to Contact: Submit complete ms/score and cassette/video tape (if a musical); include SASE if materials are to be returned. Reports in 4-6 months. Pays writers in royalties.
Tips: "Scripts should be from ½ to 1½ hours long, and not didactic or condescending. Original plays dealing with hopes, joys and fears of today's children are preferred to adaptations of old classics."

N EARLY STAGES CHILDREN'S THEATRE @ STAGES REPERTORY THEATRE, 3201 Allen Parkway, Suite 101, Houston TX 77019. (713)527-0220. Fax: (713)527-8669. E-mail: chesleyk@stagestheatre.com. Artistic Director: Rob Bundy. Early Stages Director: Chesley Krohn. Estab. 1978. Produces 5 children's plays/year; 1-2 children's musicals/year.

Needs: In-house professional children's theatre. 100% of plays/musicals written for adult roles. Cast size must be 8 or less. Performances are in 2 theaters—Arena has 230 seats; Thrust has 180 seats. Musical needs: Shows that can be recorded for performance; no live musicians. Recently produced plays: *Little Red Riding Hood*, by Sidney Berger/Rob Landes (musical fairytale for ages 4-adult); and *Sundiata: The Lion King*, by Kim Hines (historical play about king of Mali Empire for ages 4-adult).

How to Contact: Plays/musicals: Query with synopsis, character breakdown and set description. Will consider simultaneous submissions and previously performed work. Reports back only if interested.

Terms: Mss optioned exclusively. Pays 3-8% royalties. Submissions returned with SASE.

Tips: "Select pieces that are intelligent, as well as entertaining, and that speak to a child's potential for understanding."

ELDRIDGE PUBLISHING CO. INC., P.O. Box 1595, Venice FL 34284-1595. (941)496-4679. Fax: (941)493-9680. E-mail: info@histage.com. Website: www.histage.com or www.95church.com. Editor: Nancy Vorhis. Estab. 1906. Publishes approximately 25 children's plays/year; 4-5 children's musicals/year.

Needs: Prefers simple staging; flexible cast size. "We publish for junior and high school, community theater and children's theater (adults performing for children), all genres, also religious plays." Recently published plays: *Oliver T*, by Craig Sodaro ("Oliver Twist" reset behind 1950s TV for ages 12-14); *teensomething*, book, music, lyrics by Michael Mish (a revue of teen life for ages 12-19). Prefers work which has been performed or at least had a staged reading.

How to Contact: Submit complete ms, score and tape of songs (if a musical). Will consider simultaneous submissions ("please let us know, however"). Reports in 2-3 months.

Terms: Purchases all dramatic rights. Pays writers royalties of 50%; 10% copy sales; buys material outright for religious market.

Tips: "Try to have your work performed, if at all possible, before submitting. We're always on the lookout for comedies which provide a lot of fun for our customers. But other more serious topics which concern teens, as well as intriguing mysteries, and children's theater programs are of interest to us as well. We know there are many new talented playwrights out there and we look forward to reading their fresh scripts."

ENCORE PERFORMANCE PUBLISHING, P.O. Box 692, Orem UT 84059. (801)225-0605. Fax: (807)765-0489. E-mail: encoreplay@aol.com. Website: www.Encoreplay.com. Contact: Mike Perry. Estab. 1978. Publishes 20-30 children's plays/year; 10-20 children's musicals/year.

Needs: Prefers close to equal male/female ratio if possible. Adaptations for K-12 and older. 60% of plays written for adult roles; 40% for juvenile roles. Recently published plays: *Boy Who Knew No Fear*, by G. Riley Mills/Mark Levenson (adaptation of fairy tale, ages 8-16); *Two Chains*, by Paul Burton (about drug abuse, ages 11-18).

How to Contact: Query first with synopsis, character breakdown, set description and production history. Will only consider previously performed work. Reports in 2 months.

Terms: Purchases all publication and production rights. Author retains copyright. Pays writers in royalties (50%). SASE for return of submission.

Tips: "Give us issue and substance, be controversial without offense. Use a laser printer! Don't send an old manuscript. Make yours look the most professional."

N THE ENSEMBLE THEATRE, 3535 Main, Houston TX 7002. (713)520-0055, ext. 317. Fax: (713)520-1269. Artistic Director: Michael Washington. Estab. 1976. Produces 6 children's plays/year; 1 children's musical/year.

Needs: Produces children's plays for professional productions (in-house and touring). 70% of plays/musicals written for adult roles; 30% for juvenile roles. Limited to cast of 6 or less, with limited staging, costuming and props. Musical needs: appropriate for limited or recorded accompaniment. Recently published *Tales of the Mouse*, by Anita Gustafson (you're not too small to be smart for ages 4-11); *Once on this Island*, by Lynn Ahrens (love and belief for ages 6-96).

How to Contact: Plays: Query with synopsis, character breakdown and set description; submit complete ms. Musicals: Query with synopsis, character breakdown and set description. Will consider simultaneous submissions and previously performed work. Reports only if interested.

Terms: Pays $20-75/performance.

Tips: "Entertain, educate and enlighten."

✓ THE FOOTHILL THEATRE COMPANY, P.O. Box 1812, Nevada City CA 95959-1812. (530)265-9320. Fax: (530)265-9325. E-mail: ftc@foothilltheatre.org. Website: www.foothilltheatre.org. Literary Manager: Gary Wright. Estab. 1977. Produces 0-2 children's plays/year; 0-1 children's musicals/year. Professional nonprofit theater.

Needs: 95% of plays/musicals written for adult roles; 5% for juvenile roles. "Small is better, but will consider anything." Produced *Peter Pan*, by J.M. Barrie (kids vs. grownups, for all ages); *The Lion, the Witch and the Wardrobe*, by Joseph Robinette (adapted from C.S. Lewis, for all ages). Does not want to see traditional fairy tales.

How to Contact: Query with synopsis, character breakdown and set description. Will consider simultaneous submissions and previously performed work. Reports in 6 months.

Terms: Buys negotiable rights. Payment method varies. Submissions returned with SASE.

Tips: "Trends in children's theater include cultural diversity, real life issues (drug use, AIDS, etc.), mythological themes with contemporary resonance. Don't talk down to or underestimate children. Don't be preachy or didactic—humor is an excellent teaching tool."

THE FREELANCE PRESS, P.O. Box 548, Dover MA 02030. (508)785-8250. Managing Editor: Narcissa Campion. Estab. 1979.

Needs: Casts are comprised of young people, ages 8-15, and number 25-30. "We publish original musicals on contemporary topics for children and adaptations of children's classics (e.g., Rip Van Winkle)." Published plays: *The Tortoise and the Hare* (based on story of same name, for ages 8-12); *Monopoly*, 3 (young people walk through board game, for ages 11-15).

• The Freelance Press does not accept plays for adult performers.

How to Contact: Submit complete ms and score with SASE. Will consider simultaneous submissions and previously performed work. Reports in 3 months.

Terms: Pays writers 10% royalties on book sales, plus performance royalties. SASE for return of submission.

HAYES SCHOOL PUBLISHING CO. INC., 321 Pennwood Ave., Wilkinsburg PA 15221. (412)371-2373. Fax: (412)371-6408. Estab. 1940.

Needs: Wants to see supplementary teaching aids for grades K-12. Interested in all subject areas, especially music, foreign language (French, Spanish, Latin), early childhood education.

How to Contact: Query first with table of contents, sample page of activities. Will consider simultaneous and electronic submissions. Reports in 4-6 weeks.

Terms: Purchases all rights. Work purchased outright. SASE for return of submissions.

HEUER PUBLISHING COMPANY, P.O. Box 248, Cedar Rapids IA 52406. (319)364-6311. Fax: (319)364-1771. E-mail: editor@hitplays.com. Website: www.hitplays.com. Associate Editor: Geri Albrecht. Estab. 1928. Publishes 10-15 plays/year for young audiences and community theaters; 5 musicals/year.

Needs: "We publish plays and musicals for schools and community theatres (amateur)." 100% for juvenile roles. Single sets preferred. Props should be easy to find and costumes, other than modern dress, should be simple and easy to improvise. Stage effects requiring complex lighting and/or mechanical features should be avoided. Musical needs: "We need musicals with large, predominantly female casts. We publish plays and musicals for middle, junior and senior high schools." Recently published plays: *Mushroom Blues*, by Ray Sheers (Marx Brothers style comedy in three acts for all ages); *Lost City of the Nunus*, by Martin Follose (group of young archaeologists find adventure deep in the jungle in this three act comedy for all ages).

How to Contact: Plays: Query with synopsis. Musicals: Query with synopsis. Will consider simultaneous submissions and previously performed work. Reports in 2 months.

Terms: Buys amateur rights. Pays royalty or purchases work outright. Submissions returned with SASE.

Tips: "We sell almost exclusively to junior and smaller senior high schools so the subject matter and language should be appropriate for schools and young audiences."

N **☑** **INTERNATIONAL READERS' THEATRE**, 73 Furby St., Winnipeg, Manitoba R3C 2A2 Canada. (204)775-2923. Fax: (204)775-2947. E-mail: irt@blizzard.mb.ca. Website: www.blizzard.mb.ca/catalog/IRT.html. Production Coordinator: David Fuller. Estab. 1996. Produces 5-10 children's plays/year.

Needs: "We publish plays of all genres and age ranges, from elementary school-level drama to professional, adult-oriented drama (comedies, drama, etc.)." Recently published plays: *I am a Survivor*, by Susan F.J. Daniel (Remembrance Day, war for young adults); *How the Jellyfish Lost His Bones*, by Roy C. Booth and Cynthia Booth (fairy tale for young children).

How to Contact: Plays/musicals: Query first. Will consider previously performed work. Reports in 6 months.

Terms: Obtains a license to publish and sell the play; writers retain rights. For scores "we direct inquiries about music in plays we publish to the composer." Pays 85% royalties (amateur performance rights). Submissions returned with SASE.

FOR EXPLANATIONS OF THESE SYMBOLS,
SEE THE INSIDE FRONT AND BACK COVERS OF THIS BOOK

Tips: "If submitting from the U.S.A., include an SAE with an International Reply Coupon, not a U.S. stamp! U.S. postage is not valid in Canada."

N MERRY-GO-ROUND YOUTH THEATRE, P.O. Box 506, Auburn NY 13021. (315)255-1305. Fax: (315)252-3815. E-mail: mgrplays@dreamscape.com. Website: www.merry-go-round.com. Artistic Director: Edward Sayles. Estab. 1958. Produces 10 children's plays/year; 3 children's musicals/year.
Needs: 100% of plays/musicals written for adult roles. Cast maximum, 4-5 and staging must be tourable. Recently produced plays: *The Muser's Holiday*, by David Eliet (holidays, fables, sharing for ages 6-7); *There Once Was a Longhouse, Where Now There is Your House*, (Native Americans of New York state).
How to Contact: Plays/musicals: query with synopsis, character breakdown and set description; submit complete ms and score. Will consider simultaneous submissions, electronic submissions via disk/modem and previously performed work. Reports in 2-3 weeks.
Tips: "Realize that our program is grade/curriculum specific. And understanding of the NYS Learning Standards may help a writer to focus on a point of curriculum that we would like to cover."

MIDWEST THEATRE NETWORK/ROCHESTER PLAYWRIGHT FESTIVAL, 5031 Tongen Ave. NW, Rochester MN 55901. (507)281-8887. Executive Director/Dramaturg: Joan Sween. Estab. 1992. Produces 1-8 plays biennially, some children's.
Needs: "The Rochester Playwright Festival is an event wherein four to eight different theatres, usually amateur, all simultaneously produce a new play. The plays are generated by a play writing competition administered by Midwest Theatre Network. The festival is biennial. The first festival was in 1996, the second will occur October, 1998, and the next will be January, 2001. The contest leading to the 2001 festival will run from January 1, 1999 to November 30, 1999. One of the participating theatres is usually specifically a children's theatre. Others may be community theatres with adjunct children's programs. Any of the other theatres, however, may elect to produce a children's play if one engages their enthusiasm. Our participating theatres are oriented toward theatre for children (product), as opposed to theatre by children (process). However, they remain motivated solely by the quality of the script. The age of the performer required is not an issue." No limitations such as cast, props, staging, etc., other than the resources of the various participating theatres, whose annual budgets vary from $500,000 to $20,000. Musical needs: "We have no specific musical needs or preferences—whatever engages. Generally, overly simplistic progressions and repetitive tempi are not competitive. We'll read anything, but there are certain types of plays that are never successful with our theatres: plays with bunny rabbits and other creatures using off-color language; plays full of adult double entendre, sly adult humor, and sexual orientation; uninspired rehashes of folk tales with no fresh direction or characters; plays with knives, poison, guns, torture, bigotry or humor based on disabilities and body shape; plays with no structure, no conflict, no point; plays of egregious length; plays that condescend to young people." Recently produced plays: *The Robin and the Raven*, by Scott Burroughs (adventure/Celtic mythological characters for ages 6-12).
How to Contact: Plays: Submit complete ms. Musicals: Submit complete ms and audio tape. Will consider simultaneous submissions. Send #10 SASE for guidelines and required entry form after January 1, 1999. The first submission from any author is free, succeeding submissions require a $10 (each) reading fee. Reports in 3-8 weeks.
Terms: All a winning author relinquishes is permission for one of our cooperating theatres to produce his/her play royalty-free at the festival, and permission for that theatre to make sufficient copies of the ms for actors, technicians, development people. The author receives expenses to attend festival and a cash prize.
Tips: "Best advice: (If I could do this in neon that would leap off the page and smack the playwright in the face, I would.) *Do not send your play in close to the contest deadline.* We receive 4% of our submissions in the first seven months of the contest and 96% during the last three months. The former receive thoughtful leisurely readings by our panel and are more likely to receive helpful feedback. The latter are read by panelists who are rushed and jaded and are less likely to receive any feedback at all. We are eager to receive children's scripts. We do not receive nearly as many as we'd like. We receive between 700 and 1,000 scripts each competition, but only 25-40 of them are children's scripts, and the majority of them are inept or offensively adult. Where are the good children's scripts?"

N NEBRASKA THEATRE CARAVAN, 6915 Cass St., Omaha Ne 68132. (402)553-4890, ext. 154. Fax: (402)553-6288. E-mail: caravan@radiks.net. Director: Marya Lucca-Thyberg. Estab. 1976. Produces 2 children's plays/year; 1-2 children's musicals/year.
Needs: Produces children's plays for professional productions with a company of 5-6 actors touring. 90% of plays/musicals written for adult roles; 10% for juvenile roles. Limited to 5-6 touring actors, stage must be flexible and 75 minute show for grades 7-12; 60 minutes for elementary. Musical need: 1 piano or keyboard accompaniment. Recently produced plays: *The Ice Wolf*, by Joanna Halpert Kraus (folktale for grades 2-8); *The Masque of the Red Death*, by Rachel Hauben-Combs (Edgar Allan Poe for grades 7-12).
How to Contact: Plays: query with synopsis, character breakdown and set description. Musicals: query first. Will consider simultaneous submissions and previously performed work. Reports in 3 months.
Terms: Pays $10-40/performance; pays commission—option 1—own outright, option 2—have right to produce at any later date—playwright has right to publish and produce. Submissions returned with SASE.
Tips: "Be sure to follow guidelines."

THE NEW CONSERVATORY THEATRE CENTER, 25 Van Ness Ave., San Francisco CA 94102-6033. (415)861-4914. Fax: (415)861-6988. Executive Director: Ed Decker. Estab. 1981. Produces 6 children's plays/year; 1 children's musical/year.

Needs: Limited budget and small casts only. Produces children's plays as part of "a professional theater arts training program for youths ages 4-19 during the school year and 2 summer sessions. The New Conservatory also produces educational plays for its touring company. We do not want to see any preachy or didactic material." Recently produced plays: *Charlie and The Chocolate Factory*, by Roald Dahl (good overcomes all, for ages 4-12); *Puss in Boots and Other Cat Tails*, by Stephanie Leverage (geography, for ages 4-12).

How to Contact: Query with synopsis, character breakdown and set description, or submit complete ms and score. Reports in 3 months.

Terms: Rights purchased negotiable. Pays writers in royalties. SASE for return of submission.

Tips: "Wants plays with name recognition; i.e., *The Lion, the Witch and the Wardrobe* as well as socially relevant issues. Plays should be under 50 minutes in length."

NEW PLAYS INCORPORATED, P.O. Box 5074, Charlottesville VA 22905-0074. (804)979-2777. Fax: (804)984-2230. E-mail: patwhitton@aol.com. Website: www.newplaysforchildren.com. Publisher: Patricia Whitton. Estab. 1964. Publishes 3-4 plays/year; 1 or 2 children's musicals/year.

Needs: Publishes "generally material for kindergarten through junior high." Recently published: *Ugly Duckling*, by Pamela Sterling (adaptation of Hans Christian Andersen for ages 4-10); *Masterpiece in Purple*, by Lisa Railsback (child artist for ages 7-12). Does not want to see "adaptations of titles I already have. No unproduced plays; no junior high improvisations. Read our catalog."

How to Contact: Submit complete ms and score. Will consider simultaneous submissions and previously performed work. Reports in 2 months (usually).

Terms: Purchases exclusive rights to sell acting scripts. Pays writers in royalties (50% of production royalties; 10% of script sales). SASE for return of submission.

Tips: "Write the play you really want to write (not what you think will be saleable) and find a director to put it on."

☑ **NEW YORK STATE THEATRE INSTITUTE**, 155 River St., Troy NY 12180. (518)274-3200. Fax: (518)274-3815. E-mail: nysti@capital.net. Website: www.nysti.org. Artistic Director: Patricia B. Snyder. Estab. 1976. Produces 5 children's plays/year; 1-2 children's musicals/year.

Needs: Produces family plays for professional theater. 90% of plays/musicals are written for adult roles; 10% for juvenile roles. Does not want to see plays for children only. Produced plays: *The Snow Queen*, by Adrian Mitchell and Richard Penslee (ages 10-100); *A Canterville Ghost*, adapted by John Vreeke from Oscar Wilde (all ages).

How to Contact: Query with synopsis, character breakdown and set description; submit tape of songs (if a musical). Will consider simultaneous submissions and previously performed work. Reports in 1 month for queries. SASE for return of submission.

Tips: Writers should be mindful of "audience *sophistication*. We do not wish to see material that is childish. Writers should submit work that is respectful of young people's intelligence and perception—work that is appropriate for families, but that is also challenging and provocative."

☑ **THE OPEN EYE THEATER**, P.O. Box 959, Margaretville NY 12455. Phone/fax: (914)586-1660. E-mail: openeye@catskill.net. Website: www.theopeneye.com. Producing Artistic Director: Amie Brockway. Estab. 1972 (theater). Produces 3 plays/year for a family audience. Most productions are with music but are not musicals.

Needs: "Casts of various sizes. Technical requirements are kept to a minimum for touring purposes." Produces professional productions combining professional artists and artists-in-training (actors of all ages). Recently produced plays: *The Nightingale*, by William E. Black and Amie Brockway (adaptation of Hans Christian Andersen story for ages 6-adult); and *A Liars Stew*, by Mark Rosenwinkel (Mark Twain stories for families).

How to Contact: "No videos or cassettes. Letter of inquiry only." Will consider previously performed work. Reports in 6 months.

Terms: Rights agreement negotiated with author. Pays writers one-time fee or royalty negotiated with publisher. SASE for return of submission.

Tips: "Send letter of inquiry only. We are interested in plays for a multigenerational audience (8-adult)."

PHOENIX THEATRE'S COOKIE COMPANY, 100E. McDowell, Phoenix AZ 85004. (602)258-1974. Fax: (602)253-3626. Artistic Director: Alan J. Prewitt. Estab. 1980. Produces 4 children's plays/year.

Needs: Produces theater with professional adult actors performing for family audiences. 95% of plays/musicals written for adult roles; 5% for juvenile roles. Requires small casts (4-7), small stage, mostly 1 set, flexible set or ingenious sets for a small space. "We're just starting to do plays with music—no musicals per se." Does not want to see larger casts, multiple sets, 2 hour epics. Recently produced *Mother Goose on the Loose*, by Alan J. Prewitt (Mother Goose gets a makeover, for ages 4-11); *Cinderella*, by Alan J. Prewitt (1950s version, for ages 4-12).

How to Contact: Plays/musicals: Query with synopsis, character breakdown and set description. Will consider simultaneous submissions. Reports back only if interested within 2 weeks.

Terms: Submissions returned with SASE.
Tips: "Only submit innovative, imaginative work that stimulates imagination and empowers the child. We specialize in producing original scripts based on classic children's literature."

PIONEER DRAMA SERVICE, P.O. Box 4267, Englewood CO 80155-4267. (303)779-4035. Fax: (303)779-4315. E-mail: piodrama@aol.com. Website: www.pioneerdrama.com. Submissions Editor: Beth Somers. Publisher: Steven Fendrich. Estab. 1960. Publishes more than 10 new plays and musicals/year.
Needs: "We are looking for plays up to 90 minutes long, large casts and simple sets." Publishes plays for ages preschool-12th grade. Recently published plays/musicals: *The Real Story of Little Red Riding Hood*, by Judy Wolfner, music and lyrics by David Reiser (a musical for young audiences); *Rapunzel*, by Karen Boetteher-Tate (preK-4th grade). Wants to see "script, scores, tapes, pics and reviews."
How to Contact: Query with synopsis, character breakdown, running time and set description. Submit complete ms and score (if a musical) with SASE. Will consider simultaneous submissions, CAD electronic submissions via disk or modem, previously performed work. Contact: Beth Somers, submissions editor. Reports in 3-4 months. Send for writer's guidelines.
Terms: Purchases all rights. Pays writers in royalties (10% on sales, 50% royalties on productions). Research Pioneer through catalog and website.
Tips: "Research the company. Include a cover letter and a SASE."

PLAYERS PRESS, INC., P.O. Box 1132, Studio City CA 91614-0132. (818)789-4980. Vice President: R. W. Gordon. Estab. 1965. Publishes 10-20 children's plays/year; 3-12 children's musicals/year.
Needs: Subject matter: "We publish for all age groups." Recently published: *African Folk Tales*, by Carol Korty (for ages 10-14).
How to Contact: Query with synopsis, character breakdown and set description; include #10 SASE with query. Considers previously performed work only. Reports on query in 2-4 weeks; submissions in 1-12 months.
Terms: Purchases stage, screen, TV rights. Payment varies; work purchased possibly outright upon written request. Submissions returned with SASE.
Tips: "Submit as requested—query first and send only previously produced material. Entertainment quality is on the upswing and needs to be directed at the world, no longer just the U.S. Please submit with two #10 SASEs plus ms-size SASE. Please do not call."

PLAYS, The Drama Magazine for Young People, 120 Boylston St., Boston MA 02116-4615. (617)423-3157. Fax: (617)423-2168. E-mail: writer@user1.channel1.com. Website: www.channel1.com/plays/. Managing Editor: Elizabeth Preston. Estab. 1941. Publishes 70-75 children's plays/year.
Needs: "Props and staging should not be overly elaborate or costly. There is little call among our subscribers for plays with only a few characters; ten or more (to allow all students in a class to participate, for instance) is preferred. Our plays are performed by children in school from lower elementary grades through junior-senior high." 100% of plays written for juvenile roles. Subject matter: Audience is lower grades through junior/senior high. Recently published plays: *Kid Avalanche*, by John Murray (unexpected inheritance—a prizefighter causes havoc in college dorm, junior/senior high); *Matchmaking for Mother*, by Helen Louise Miller (middle-grade play about brother and sister trying to marry off their hardworking mom); and senior high adaptation of *The Invisible Man*, by H.G. Wells. "Send nothing downbeat—no plays about drugs, sex or other 'heavy' topics."
How to Contact: Query first on adaptations of folk tales and classics; otherwise submit complete ms. Reports in 2-3 weeks.
Terms: Purchases all rights. Pay rates vary. Guidelines available; send SASE. Sample copy $4.
Tips: "Get your play underway quickly. Keep it wholesome and entertaining. No preachiness, heavy moral or educational message. Any 'lesson' should be imparted through the actions of the characters, not through unbelievable dialogue. Use realistic situations and settings without getting into downbeat, depressing topics. No sex, drugs, violence, alcohol."

RIVERSIDE CHILDREN'S THEATRE, 3280 Riverside Park Dr., Vero Beach FL 32963. (561)234-8052. Fax: (561)234-4407. Education Director: Linda Downey. Estab. 1980. Produces 4 children's plays/year; 2 children's musicals/year.
Needs: Produces amateur youth productions. 100% of plays/musicals written for juvenile roles. Musical needs: For children ages 6-18. Produced plays: *Schoolhouse Rock Live* (general audiences); *Romeo & Juliet* (general audiences).
How to Contact: Plays/musicals: Query with synopsis, character breakdown and set description. Will consider simultaneous submissions, electronic submissions via disk/modem and previously performed work. Reports back only if interested.
Terms: Pays royalty or $40-60 per performance. Submissions returned with SASE.
Tips: "Interested in youth theatre for children ages 6-18 to perform."

SEATTLE CHILDREN'S THEATRE, P.O. Box 9640, Seattle WA 98109. Fax: (206)443-0442. Website: www.sct.org. Literary Manager and Dramaturg: Deborah Frockt. Estab. 1975. Produces 5 full-length children's plays/year; 1 full-length children's musical/year. Produces children's plays for professional productions (September-June).

Needs: 95% of plays/musicals written for adult roles; 5% for juvenile roles. "We generally use adult actors even for juvenile roles." Prefers no turntable, no traps. Produced plays: *The King of Ireland's Son*, by Paula Wing (mythology and Hero Quest for ages 8 and older); *Pink and Say*, by Oyamo (adaptation from Patricia Polacco); and *Civil War Friendship* (for ages 8 and older). Does not want to see anything that condescends to young people—anything overly broad in style.

How to Contact: Accepts agented scripts or those accompanied by a professional letter of recommendation (director or dramaturg). Reports in 6-12 months.

Terms: Rights vary. Payment method varies. Submissions returned with SASE.

Tips: "Please *do not* send unsolicited manuscripts. We prefer sophisticated material (our weekend performances have an audience that is half adults)."

✓ **STAGE ONE: THE LOUISVILLE CHILDREN'S THEATRE**, 501 W. Main, Louisville KY 40202-2957. (502)589-5946. Fax: (502)588-5910. E-mail: stageone@kca.org. Website: www.stageone.org. Producing Director: Moses Goldberg. Estab. 1946. Produces 6-8 children's plays/year; 1-4 children's musicals/year.

Needs: Stage One is an Equity company producing children's plays for professional productions. 100% of plays/musicals written for adult roles. "Sometimes we do use students in selected productions." Produced plays: *Pinocchio*, by Moses Goldberg, music by Scott Kasbaum (ages 8-12); and *John Lennon & Me*, by Cherie Bennett (about cystic fibrosis; peer acceptance for ages 11-17). Does not want to see "camp or condescension."

How to Contact: Submit complete ms, score and tape of songs (if a musical); include the author's résumé if desired. Will consider simultaneous submissions, electronic submissions via disk or modem and previously performed work. Reports in 3-4 months.

Terms: Pays writers in royalties (5-6%) or $25-75/performance.

Tips: Looking for "stageworthy and respectful dramatizations of the classic tales of childhood, both ancient and modern; plays relevant to the lives of young people and their families; and plays directly related to the school curriculum."

N: THEATRE FOR YOUNG AMERICA, 4881 Johnson Dr., Mission KS 66205. (913)831-2131. Artistic Director: Gene Mackey. Estab. 1974. Produces 9 children's plays/year; 3-5 children's musicals/year.

Needs: "We use a small cast (4-7), open thrust stage." Theatre for Young America is a professional equity company. 90% of plays/musicals written for adult roles; 10% for juvenile roles. Produced plays: *The Wizard of Oz*, by Jim Eiler and Jeanne Bargy (for ages 6 and up); *A Partridge in a Pear Tree*, by Lowell Swortzell (deals with the 12 days of Christmas, for ages 6 and up); *Three Billy Goats Gruff*, by Gene Mackey and Molly Jessup (Norwegian folk tales, for ages 6 and up).

How to Contact: Query with synopsis, character breakdown and set description. Will consider simultaneous submissions and previously performed work. Reports in 2 months.

Terms: Purchases production rights, tour rights in local area. Pays writers in royalties or $10-50/performance.

Tips: Looking for "cross-cultural material that respects the intelligence, sensitivity and taste of the child audience."

THEATREWORKS/USA, 151 W. 26th, 7th Floor, New York NY 10001. (212)647-1100. Fax: (212)924-5377. Associate Artistic Director: Barbara Pasternack. Estab. 1960. Produces 3-4 children's plays and musicals/year.

Needs: Cast of 5 or 6 actors. Play should be 1 hour long, tourable. Professional children's theatre comprised of adult equity actors. 100% of shows are written for adult roles. Produced plays: *Curious George*, book and lyrics by Thomas Toce, music by Tim Brown (adaptation, for grades K-3); *Little Women*, by Allan Knee, incidental music by Kim Oler and Alison Hubbard (adaptation, for grades 4-8). No fractured, typical "kiddy theater" fairy tales or shows written strictly to teach or illustrate.

How to Contact: Query first with synopsis, character breakdown and sample songs. Will consider previously performed work. Reports in 6 months.

Terms: Pays writers royalties of 6%. SASE for return of submission.

Tips: "Plays should be not only entertaining, but 'about something.' They should touch the heart and the mind. They should not condescend to children."

N: THIS MONTH ON STAGE, P.O. Box 62, Hewlett NY 11557-0062. (800)536-0099. E-mail: tmosmail@aol.com. Publisher: David Lefkowitz. Estab. 1991. Publishes 1-2 children's plays/year.

Needs: Prefers material for older audiences, or universally relevant material. Does not want to see: Patronizing, moralistic, Sunday School, etc.

How to Contact: Submit complete ms. Will consider simultaneous submissions and electronic submissions via disk/modem. Reports in 4-6 months.

Terms: Buys one-time rights. Work purchased outright ($1-2); copies. Submissions returned with SASE (separate SASE for each ms please).

Tips: "Ask yourself: will adults enjoy it too?"

Young Writer's & Illustrator's Markets

The listings in this section are special because they publish work of young writers and artists (under age 18). Some of the magazines listed exclusively feature the work of young people. Others are adult magazines with special sections for the work of young writers. There are also a few book publishers listed that exclusively publish the work of young writers and artists. Many of the magazines and publishers listed here pay only in copies, meaning authors and illustrators receive one or more free copies of the magazine or book to which they contributed.

As with adult markets, markets for children expect writers to be familiar with their editorial needs before submitting. Many of the markets listed will send guidelines to writers stating exactly what they need and how to submit it. You can often get these by sending a request with a self-addressed, stamped envelope (SASE) to the magazine or publisher, or by checking a publication's website (a number of listings include web addresses). In addition to obtaining guidelines, read through a few copies of any magazines you'd like to submit to—this is the best way to determine if your work is right for them.

A number of kids' magazines are available on newsstands or in libraries. Others are distributed only through schools, churches or home subscriptions. If you can't find a magazine you'd like to see, most editors will send sample copies for a small fee.

Before you submit your material to editors, take a few minutes to read Before Your First Sale on page 8 for more information on proper submission procedures. You may also want to check out two other sections—Contests & Awards and Conferences & Workshops. Some listings in these sections are open to students (some exclusively)—look for the phrase **"open to students"** in bold. Additional opportunities for writers can be found in *Market Guide for Young Writers* (Writer's Digest Books) and *A Teen's Guide to Getting Published: the only writer's guide written by teens for teens*, by Danielle and Jessica Dunn (Prufrock Press). More information on these books are given in the Helpful Resources section in the back of this book. Also be sure to read the Insider Report with Susan Napoli Picchietti, editor of *Potluck Children's Literary Magazine*, on page 286.

Information on companies listed in the previous edition but not included in this edition of *Children's Writer's & Illustrator's Market* **may be found in the General Index**.

THE ACORN, 1530 Seventh St., Rock Island IL 61201. (309)788-3980. Newsletter. Estab. 1989. Editor: Betty Mowery. Audience consists of "kindergarten-12th grade students, parents, teachers and other adults. Purpose in publishing works for children: "to expose children's manuscripts to others and provide a format for those who might not have one. We want to showcase young authors who may not have their work published elsewhere and present wholesome writing material that will entertain and educate—audience grades K-12." Children must be K-12 (put grade on manuscripts). Guidelines available for SASE.

Magazines: 100% of magazine written by children. Uses 6 fiction pieces (500 words); 20 pieces of poetry (32 lines). No payment; purchase of a copy isn't necessary to be printed. Sample copy $3. Subscription $10 for 4 issues. Submit mss to Betty Mowery, editor. Send complete ms. Will accept typewritten, legibly handwritten and/or computer printout. Include SASE. Reports in 1 week. Will not respond without SASE.

Artwork: Publishes artwork by children. Looks for "all types; size 4×5. Use black ink in artwork." No payment. Submit artwork either with ms or separately to Betty Mowery. Include SASE. Reports in 1 week.

Tips: "My biggest problem is not having names on the manuscripts. If the manuscript gets separated from the cover letter, there is no way to know whom to respond to. Always put name, age or grade and address on manuscripts, and if you want your material returned enclose a SASE. Don't send material with killing of humans or animals, or lost love poems or stories."

AMELIA MAGAZINE, 329 "E" St., Bakersfield CA 93304-2031. (805)323-4064. Magazine. Published quarterly. Strives to offer the best of all genres. Purpose in publishing works for children: wants to offer first opportunities to budding writers. Also offers the annual Amelia Student Award for high school students. Submissions from young writers must be signed by parent, teacher or guardian verifying originality. Guidelines are not specifically for young writers; they cover the entire gamut of publication needs. For sample of past winner send $3 and SASE.

Magazines: 3% of magazine written by children. Uses primarily poetry, often generated by teachers in creative writing classes. Uses 1 story in any fiction genre (1,500 words); 4 pieces of poetry, usually haiku (3 lines). Would like to receive more general poetry from young writers. Pays in copies for haiku; $2-10 for general poetry. Regular $35 rate for fiction or nonfiction. Submit mss to Frederick A. Raborg, editor. Submit complete ms (teachers frequently submit student's work). Will accept typewritten ms. Include SASE. Reports in 3 weeks.

Artwork: Publishes artwork and photography by children. Looks for photos no smaller than 5×7; artwork in any method; also cartoons. Pays $5-20 on publication. Submit well-protected artwork with SASE. Submit artwork/photos to Frederick A. Raborg, Jr., editor. Include SASE. Reports in 3 weeks. Sample issue: $9.95.

Tips: "Be neat and thorough. Photos should have captions. Cartoon gaglines ought to be funny; try them out on someone before submitting. We want to encourage young writers because the seeds of literary creativity are sown quite young with strong desires to read and admiration for the authors of those early readings."

AMERICAN GIRL, 8400 Fairway Place, Middleton WI 53562. (608)836-4848. Fax: (608)831-7089. Website: www.americangirl. Contact: Magazine Department Assistant. Bimonthly magazine. Audience consists of girls ages 8-12 who are joyful about being girls. Purpose in publishing works by young people: "self-esteem boost and entertainment for readers. *American Girl* values girls opinions and ideas. By publishing their work in the magazine, girls can share their thoughts with other girls! Young writers should be 8-12 years old. We don't have writer's guidelines for children's submissions. Instruction for specific solicitations appears in the magazine."

Magazines: 5% of magazine written by young people. "A few pages of each issue feature articles that include children's answers to questions or requests that have appeared in a previous issue of *American Girl*." Pays in copies. Submit to address listed in magazine. Will accept legibly handwritten ms. Include SASE. Reports in 8-12 weeks.

Tips: "Please, no stories, poems, etc. about American Girls Collection Characters (Felicity, Samantha, Molly, Kirsten, Addy or Josefina). Inside *American Girl*, there are several departments that call for submissions. Read the magazine carefully and submit your ideas based on what we ask for."

✔ **BEYOND WORDS PUBLISHING, INC.**, 20827 NW Cornell Rd., Suite 500, Hillsboro OR 97124-9808. (503)531-8700. Fax: (503)531-8773. E-mail: marianne@beyondword.com. Website:www.beyondword.com. Book publisher. Managing Editor of Children's Department: Marianne Monson. Publishes 2-3 books by children/year. Looks for "books that inspire integrity in children ages 5-15 and encourages creativity and an appreciation of nature." Wants to "encourage children to write, create, dream and believe that it is possible to be published. The books must be unique, be of national interest and the child author must be personable and promotable." Writer's guidelines available with SASE.

Books: Holds yearly writing contests for activity/advice books written by and for children/teens. Also occasionally publishes nonfiction advice books for and by children such as joke books, or guides for kids about pertinent concerns. Submit mss to Marianne Monson, managing editor. Reports in 4 months.

Artwork/Photography: Publishes artwork by children. Submit artwork to Marianne Monson, managing editor.

Tips: "Write about issues that affect your life. Winners in the past have written chapters on great slumber parties, analyzing dreams, jokes and understanding peers with disabilities. Trust your own instincts. You know best!"

Ⓝ **CHILDREN WRITING FOR CHILDREN FOUNDATION (CWC)**, 7142 Dustin Rd., Galena OH 43021-7959. (800)759-7171. Executive Director: Susan Schmidt. Purpose of organization: A non-profit corporation established to educate the public at large about children's issues through literary works created by children and to celebrate and share the talents of children as authors. Books must be written and/or illustrated by children aged 6-18. "We look for kids to write about personal experiences that educate and reveal solutions to problems." Open submissions are accepted. In addition, submissions are accepted through two annual contests, usually announced through *Teacher's Magazine*.

Books: Publishing focus is on nonfiction writings about children's issues such as peer pressure, illness, and special challenges or opportunities. Stories with educational value are preferred. Writer's guidelines available with SASE. Pays royalties, but no advances. Will accept typewritten, legibly handwritten and computer-printed ms. Include SASE for ms return and/or comments. Reports in 3-6 months.

A SELF-ADDRESSED, STAMPED ENVELOPE (SASE) should always be included with submissions within your own country. When sending material to other countries, include a self-addressed envelope (SAE) and International Reply Coupons (IRCs).

Artwork/Photography: Publishes books with artwork and/or photography accompanying nonfiction stories written and illustrated by children.
Tips: Write about personal experiences in challenging situations, painting a word picture of the people involved, the story, how you resolved or responded to the situation and what you learned or gained from the experience.

N **CICADA**, Carus Publishing Company, P.O. Box 300, 315 Fifth St., Peru IL 61354. (815)224-6656. Fax: (815)224-6615. E-mail: cicada@caruspub.com. Website: www.cicadamag.com. Editor-in-chief: Marianne Carus. Editor: Deborah Vetter. Senior Editor: John D. Allen. Senior Art Director: Ron McCutchan.
• *Cicada* publishes work of writers and artists of high-school age. See the Insider Report with Editor Deborah Vetter in the Magazines section (as well as the *Cicada* listing in that section) for more information.

N **THE CLAREMONT REVIEW**, 4980 Wesley Rd., Victoria, British Columbia Canada V8Y 1Y9. (604)658-5221. Fax: (250)658-5387. E-mail: aurora@home.com. Magazine. Publishes 2 books/year by young adults. Publishes poetry and fiction with literary value by students aged 13-19 anywhere in North America. Purpose in publishing work by young people: to provide a literary venue.
Magazines: Uses 10-12 fiction stories (200-2,500 words); 30-40 poems. Pays in copies. Submit mss to editors. Submit complete ms. Will accept typewritten mss. SASE. Reports in 6 weeks (except during the summer).
Artwork: Publishes artwork by young adults. Looks for b&w copies of imaginative art. Pays in copies. Send picture for review. Negative may be requested. Submit art and photographs to editors. SASE. Reports in 6 weeks.
Tips: "Read us first—it saves disappointment. Know who we are and what we publish. We're closed July and August. SASE a must."

N **CLUBHOUSE**, P.O. Box 15, Berrien Springs MI 49103. (616)471-9009. Editor: Krista Hainey. Magazine. Estab. 1949. Published monthly. Occasionally publishes items by kids. "Audience consists of kids ages 9-13; philosophy: "kids are smart and capable and display Christian attributes. We like to focus on these positive elements." Purpose in publishing works by young people: "to give encouragement and demonstration of talent; to give children the opportunity to see their work appreciated and published." Children must be ages 9-14; must include parent's note verifying originality.
Magazines: Uses adventure, historical, everyday life experience (fiction/nonfiction-1,200 words); health-related short articles; poetry (4-24 lines of "mostly mood pieces and humor"). Pays in prizes for children, money for adult authors. Query. Will accept typewritten, legibly handwritten and computer printout mss. "Will not be returned without SASE." Reports in 6 weeks.
Artwork: Publishes artwork by children. Looks for all types of artwork—white paper, black pen. Pays in prizes for kids. Send b&w art to Christa Hainey, editor. "Won't be returned without SASE."
Tips: "All items submitted by kids are held in a file and used when possible. We normally suggest they do not ask for return of the item."

CREATIVE KIDS, P.O. Box 8813, Waco TX 76714-8813. (800)998-2208. Fax: (254)756-3339. E-mail: creative_kids@prufrock.com. Website: www.prufrock.com. Editor: Libby Lindsey. Magazine published 4 times/year. Estab. 1979. "All material is by children, for children." Purpose in publishing works by children: "to create a product that provides children with an authentic experience and to offer an opportunity for children to see their work in print. *Creative Kids* contains the best stories, poetry, opinion, artwork, games and photography by kids ages 8-14." Writers ages 8-14 must have statement by teacher or parent verifying originality. Writer's guidelines available on request with SASE.
Magazines: Uses "about 6" fiction and nonfiction stories (800-900 words); poetry, plays, ideas to share (200-750 words) per issue. Pays "free magazine." Submit mss to submissions editor. Will accept typewritten mss. Include SASE. Reports in 1 month.
Artwork/Photography: Publishes artwork and photos by children. Looks for "any kind of drawing, cartoon, or painting." Pays "free magazine." Send original or a photo of the work to submissions editor. Include SASE. Reports in 1 month.
Tips: "*Creative Kids* is a magazine by kids, for kids. The work represents children's ideas, questions, fears, concerns and pleasures. The material never contains racist, sexist or violent expression. The purpose is to provide children with an authentic experience. A person may submit one piece of work per envelope. Each piece must be labeled with the student's name, birth date, grade, school, home address and school address. Include a photograph, if possible. Recent school pictures are best. Material submitted to *Creative Kids* must not be under consideration by any other publication. Items should be carefully prepared, proofread and double checked (perhaps also by a parent or teacher). All activities requiring solutions must be accompanied by the correct answers. Young writers and artists should always write for guidelines and then follow them. It is very frustrating to receive submissions that are not complete."

✓ **CREATIVE WITH WORDS, Thematic anthologies**, Creative with Words Publications, P.O. Box 223226, Carmel CA 93922. Fax: (831)655-8627. E-mail: cwwpub@usa.net. Website: members.tripod.com/~CreativeWithWords. Editor: Brigitta Geltrich. Nature Editor: Bert Hower. Publishes 14 anthologies/year. Estab. 1975. "We publish the creative writing of children (4 anthologies written by children; 4 anthologies written by adults; 4-6 anthologies written by all ages)." Audience consists of children, schools, libraries, adults, reading programs.

Purpose in publishing works by children: to offer them an opportunity to get started in publishing. "Work must be of quality, original, unedited, and not published before; age must be given (up to 19 years old) and home address." SASE must be enclosed with all correspondence and mss. Writer's guidelines and theme list available on request with SASE, via e-mail or on website.

Books: Considers all categories except those dealing with sensationalism, death, violence, pornography and overly religious. Uses fairy tales, folklore items (up to 1,500 words) and poetry (not to exceed 20 lines, 46 characters across). Published *Nature Series: Seasons, Nature, School, Love* and *Relationships* (all children and adults). Pays 20% discount on each copy of publication in which fiction or poetry by children appears. Best of the month is published on website and author receives one free copy of issue. Submit mss to Brigitta Geltrich, editor. Query; child, teacher or parent can submit; teacher and/or parents must verify originality of writing. Will accept typewritten and/or legibly handwritten mss. SASE. "Will not go through agents." Reports in 2-4 weeks after deadline of any theme.

Artwork/Photography: Publishes b&w artwork, b&w photos and computer artwork by children (language art work). Pays 20% discount on every copy of publication in which work by children appears. Submit artwork to Brigitta Geltrich, editor, and request info on payment.

Tips: "Enjoy the English language, life and the world around you. Look at everything from a different perspective. Look at the greatness inside all of us. Be less descriptive and use words wisely. Let the reader experience a story through a viewpoint character, don't be overly dramatic. Match illustrations to the meaning of the story or poem."

FREE SPIRIT PUBLISHING INC., 400 First Ave. North, Suite 616, Minneapolis MN 55401-1730. (612)338-2068. Fax: (612)337-5050. E-mail: help4kids@freespirit.com. Website: www.freespirit.com. Publishes 15-20 books/year. "We specialize in SELF-HELP FOR KIDS® and SELF-HELP FOR TEENS®. We aim to help kids help themselves. We were the *first* publisher of self-help materials for children, and today we are the *only* publisher of SELF-HELP FOR KIDS® materials. Our main audience is children and teens, but we also publish for parents, teachers, therapists, youth workers and other involved in caring for kids. Our main interests include the development of self-esteem, self-awareness, creative thinking and problem-solving abilities, assertiveness and making a difference in the world. We do not publish fiction or poetry. We do accept submissions from young people ages 14 and older; however, please send a letter from a parent/guardian/leader verifying originality." Request catalog, author guidelines, and "student guidelines" before submitting work. Send SASE.

Books: Publishes self-help for kids, how-to, classroom activities. Pays advance and royalties. Submit mss to acquisitions editor. Send query and sample table of contents. Will accept typewritten mss. SASE required. Reports in 3-4 months.

Artwork/Photography: Submit samples to acquisitions editor.

Tips: "Free Spirit publishes very specific material, and it helps when writers request and study our catalog before submitting work to us, and refer to our author guidelines (our catalog and guidelines are available by mail or via our website.) We do not accept general self-help books, autobiographies or children's books that feature made-up stories. Our preference is books that help kids to gain self-esteem, succeed in school, stand up for themselves, resolve conflicts and make a difference in the world. We do not publish books that have animals as the main characters."

THE GOLDFINCH, Iowa History for Young People, 402 Iowa Ave., Iowa City IA 52240-1806. (319)335-3916. Fax: (319)335-3935. E-mail: mfrese@blue.weeg.uiowa.edu. Magazine published quarterly. Audience is 4th-8th graders. "Magazine supports creative work by children: research, art, writing. *The Goldfinch* puts the fun back into history. We publish young Iowans' work to show them that they and their creative efforts are an important part of Iowa history." Submitted work must go with the historical theme of each issue.

Magazines: 10-20% written by children. Uses at least 1 nonfiction essay, poem, story/issue (500 words). Pays complimentary copies. Submit mss with SASE to Millie K. Frese, editor. Submit complete ms. Will accept typewritten, legibly handwritten, computer disk (Apple) mss. Reports in 1 month.

Artwork/Photography: Publishes artwork/photographs by children. Art and photos must be b&w. Pays complimentary copies. Query first with SASE to Millie Frese.

Tips: "We make the subject of Iowa history come alive through short features, games/puzzles/activities, fiction and cool historical photographs. Good research is the key to success; the Goldfinch is a history magazine, so its vital historical details are accurate."

N KIDS' WORLD, The Magazine That's All Kids!, 1300 Kicker Rd., Tuscaloosa AL 35404. (205)553-2284. Magazine. Published 4 times a year. Audience consists of young children up to age 10. "I'm creating a fun magazine for kids to read and a good place for young writers to get a start." Purpose in publishing works by young people: "So that my magazine will be unique—edited by a kid, for kids, by kids (all kids!). Authors must be under 17—no horror or romance." Writer's guidelines available on request.

Magazines: 100% of magazine written by young people. Uses 4-10 short stories; 1-2 essays about favorite things, etc.; 4-10 poems and art. Pays one free copy per ms or artwork. Submit mss to Morgan Kopaska-Merkel, editor. Submit complete mss. Will accept typewritten and legibly handwritten mss. Include SASE. Reports in 2-6 months.

Artwork/Photography: Publishes artwork and photography by children. Looks for "children/babies and things of interest to them (food, toys, animals . . .)." Must be b&w in pen. Pays one free copy per artwork. Send the artwork, plus a note and SASE. Reports in 2-4 weeks.

Tips: "Have an adult check spelling, punctuation and grammar. I get a lot of submissions, so I can only publish the really good ones, within reason for a child's age."

✓ ❖ **KWIL KIDS PUBLISHING, The Little Publishing Company That Kwil Built**, Kwilville, P.O. Box 29556, Maple Ridge, British Columbia V2X 2V0 Canada. Phone/fax: (604)466-5712. E-mail: kwil@bc.symp atico.ca. Website: www.netmanor.com/kwilkids. Publishes books, greeting cards, newspaper column, newsletter and web page. Publishes 30-40 books/year by children (at cost, nonprofit). Publishes weekly column in local paper, two monthly newsletters; books—2 launches/year and greeting cards (fundraiser). "*Kwil Kids* come in all ages, shapes and sizes—from 4-64 and a whole lot more! Kwil does not pay for or profit from the creative work of children but provides opportunity/encouragement. We promote literacy, creativity and written 'connections' through written and artistic expression and to publish autobiographical, inspirational, fantastical, humorous stories of gentleness, compassion, truth and beauty. Our purpose is to foster a sense of pride and enthusiasm in young writers and artists, to celebrate the voice of youth and encourage growth through joy-filled practice and cheerleading, not criticism." Must include name, age, school, address and parent signature (if a minor). Will send newsletter upon request as a sample and an application to join "The Kwil Club."

Books: Publishes autobiographical, inspirational, creative stories (alliterative, rhyming refrains, juicy words) fiction; short rhyming and non-rhyming poems (creative, fun, original, expressive, poetry). Length: 1,000 words for fiction; 8-16 lines for poetry. No payment—self published and sold "at cost" only (1 free copy). Submit mss to Kwil publisher. Submit complete ms; send copy only—expect a reply but will not return ms. Will accept typewritten and legibly handwritten mss and e-mail. Include SASE. Publishes greeting cards with poems, short stories and original artwork. Pays 5¢ royalty on each card sold (rounded to the nearest dollar and paid once per year) as a fundraiser. Reports in 1 month.

Newsletter: 95% of newsletter written by young people. Uses 15 short stories, poems, jokes (20-100 words). No payment—free newsletters only. Submit complete ms. Will accept typewritten and legibly handwritten mss and e-mail. Reports in 1 month.

Artwork: Publishes artwork and photography by children with writing. Looks for black ink sketches to go with writing and photos to go with writing. Submit by postal mail only; white background for sketches. Submit artwork/photos to Kwil publisher. Include SASE. Reports in 1 month.

Tips: "We love stories that teach a lesson or encourage peace, love and a fresh, new understanding. Just be who you are and do what you do—then all of life's treasures will come to you. In other words: be creative, have fun, and remember that we all have important thoughts, feelings, and ideas to share. Trust that your thoughts, feelings and experiences are worthy of expression and that your 'craft' will evolve and 'improve' over time. It is our policy not to judge, compare or critique young writers and artists. Kwil very much wants to hear yours. Kwil's motto: 'Keep your pencil moving!' Kwil always writes back."

MERLYN'S PEN: Fiction, Essays, and Poems by America's Teens, P.O. Box 1058, East Greenwich RI 02818. (800)247-2027. Fax: (401)885-5222. Website: www.merlynspen.com. Magazine. Published annually. "By publishing student writing, *Merlyn's Pen* seeks to broaden and reward the young author's interest in writing, strengthen the self-confidence of beginning writers and promote among all students a positive attitude toward literature. We publish 75 manuscripts annually by students in grades 6-12. The entire magazine is dedicated to young adults' writing. Our audience is classrooms, libraries and students from grades 6-12." Writers must be in grades 6-12 and must send a completed *Merlyn's Pen* cover sheet with each submission. When a student is accepted, he/she, a parent and a teacher must sign a statement of originality. Writer's guidelines available on request.

Magazines: Uses 20 short stories (no word limit); plays; 8 nonfiction essays (no word limit); 25 pieces of poetry; letters to the editor; editorials; reviews of previously published works. Published authors receive 3 contributor's copies and payment of $20-200. Also, a discount is offered for additional copies of the issue. Submit up to 3 titles at one time. Will only accept typewritten mss. Reports in 10 weeks.

Artwork/Photography: Publishes artwork by children.

Tips: "All manuscripts and artwork must be accompanied by a completed copy of *Merlyn's Pen* official cover sheet for submissions. Call to request cover sheet, or download from our website."

NATIONAL GEOGRAPHIC WORLD, 1145 17th St. NW, Washington DC 20036-4688. (202)857-7000. Magazine published monthly. Picture magazine for ages 8 and older. Purpose in publishing work by young people: to encourage in young readers a curiosity about the world around them.
● *National Geographic World* does not accept unsolicited manuscripts.

Tips: Publishes art, letters, poems, games, riddles, jokes and craft ideas by children in mailbag section only. No payment given. Send by mail to: Submissions Committee. "Sorry, but *World* cannot acknowledge or return your contributions."

✓ **NEW MOON: The Magazine For Girls & Their Dreams**, New Moon Publishing, Inc., P.O. Box 3620, Duluth MN 55803-3620. (218)728-5507. Fax: (218)728-0314. E-mail: girl@newmoon.org. Website: www.newm oon.org. Magazine. Published bimonthly. *New Moon*'s primary audience is girls ages 8-14. "We publish a magazine that listens to girls." More than 70% of *New Moon* is written by girls. Purpose in publishing work by children/teens: "We want girls' voices to be heard. *New Moon* wants girls to see that their opinions, dreams, thoughts and ideas count." Writer's guidelines available for SASE or online.

Magazine: 75% of magazine written by young people. Uses 4 fiction mss (300-900 words); 12 nonfiction mss (300-900 words) per year. Submit to Deb Mylin or Bridget Grosser, managing editor. Submit query, complete mss for fiction and nonfiction. Will accept typewritten, legibly handwritten mss and disk (IBM compatible). "We do not return or acknowledge unsolicited material. Do not send originals—we will not return any materials." Reports in 6 months if interested.

Artwork/Photography: Publishes artwork and photography by children. Looks for cover and inside illustrations. Pay negotiated. Submit art and photographs to Bridget Grosser, managing editor. "We do not return unsolicited material."

Tips: "Read *New Moon* to completely understand our needs."

☑ POTLUCK CHILDREN'S LITERARY MAGAZINE, P.O. Box 546, Deerfield IL 60015-0546. Fax: (847)317-9492. E-mail: nappic@aol.com. Website: http://members.aol.com/nappic. Quarterly magazine. "We look for works with imagery and human truths. Occasionally we will work with young authors on editing their work. We are available to the writer for questions and comments. The purpose of *Potluck* is to encourage creative expression and to supply young writers with a forum in which they can be heard. We also provide informative articles to help them become better writers and to prepare them for the adult markets. For example, recent articles dealt with work presentation, tracking submissions and rights." Writer's guidelines available on request with a SASE.

Magazines: 99% of magazine written by young people. Uses fiction (300-400 words); nonfiction (300-400 words); poetry (30 lines); book reviews (150 words). Pays with copy of issue published. Submit mss to Susan Napoli Picchietti, editor. Submit complete ms; teacher may send group submissions, which have different guidelines and payment schedules. Will accept typewritten and e-mailed mss. Include SASE. Reports 6 weeks after deadline.

Artwork/Photography: Publishes artwork by children. Looks for all types of artwork—no textured works. Must be 8½×11 only. Pays in copies. Do not fold submissions. If you want your work returned, you must include proper postage and envelope. Submit artwork to Susan Napoli Picchietti, editor. Include SASE. Reports in 6 weeks.

Tips: "Relax—observe and acknowledge all that is around you. Life gives us a lot to draw on. Don't get carried away with style—let your words speak for themselves. If you want to be taken seriously as a writer, you must take yourself seriously. The rest will follow. Enjoy yourself and take pride in every piece, even the bad, they keep you humble."

SKIPPING STONES, Multicultural Children's Magazine, P.O. Box 3939, Eugene OR 97403. (541)342-4956. Website: www.nonviolence.org/skipping. Articles/Poems/Fiction Editor: Arun N. Toké. 5 issues a year. Estab. 1988. Circulation 3,000. "*Skipping Stones* is a multicultural, nonprofit, children's magazine to encourage cooperation, creativity and celebration of cultural and environmental richness. It offers itself as a creative forum for communication among children from different lands and backgrounds. We prefer work by children under 18 years old. International, minorities and under represented populations receive priority, multilingual submissions are encouraged."

● *Skipping Stones*' theme for the 2000 Youth Honor Awards is multicultural and nature awareness. Send SASE for guidelines and for more information on the awards.

Magazines: 50% written by children. Uses 5-10 fiction short stories and plays (500-750 words); 5-10 nonfiction articles, interviews, letters, history, descriptions of celebrations (500-750 words); 15-20 poems, jokes, riddles, proverbs (250 words or less) per issue. Pays in contributor's copies. Submit mss to Mr. Arun Toké, editor. Submit complete ms for fiction or nonfiction work; teacher may submit; parents can also submit their contributions. Submissions should include "cover letter with name, age, address, school, cultural background, inspiration piece, dreams for future." Will accept typewritten, legibly handwritten and computer/word processor mss. Include SASE. Responds in 4 months. Accepts simultaneous submissions.

Artwork/Photography: Publishes artwork and photography for children. Will review all varieties of ms/illustration packages. Wants comics, cartoons, b&w photos, paintings, drawings (preferably ink & pen or pencil), 8×10, color photos OK. Subjects include children, people, celebrations, nature, ecology, multicultural. Pays in contributor's copies.

Terms: "*Skipping Stones* is a labor of love. You'll receive complimentary contributor's (up to four) copies depending on the length of your contribution and illustrations." Reports back to artists in 4 months. Sample copy for $5 and 4 first-class stamps.

Tips: "Let the 'inner child' within you speak out—naturally, uninhibited." Wants "material that gives insight on cultural celebrations, lifestyle, custom and tradition, glimpse of daily life in other countries and cultures. Please, no mystery for the sake of mystery! Photos, songs, artwork are most welcome if they illustrate/highlight the points. Upcoming features: Turning points in life, cooperative games and sports, religions and cultures from around the world, modern technology and its impact, Native American cultures, street children, songs and recipes from around the world, resource conservation and sustainable lifestyles, indigenous architecture, building commu-

insider report

Feeding the souls of hungry young writers

"Interviews always end up being about me when I really want them to be about the magazine and what it has to offer young writers," says Susan Napoli Picchietti, editor and publisher of *Potluck Children's Literary Magazine*. But it's difficult to discount a person who devotes so much time and energy to encouraging young writers and helping them learn the craft and business of freelancing.

Susan Napoli Picchietti

"I had wanted to do a children's magazine since I was young," Picchietti says. "I had always written and it was a way for me to come to terms with whatever was happening in my life at the time." The idea for the magazine became a reality when Picchietti's husband encouraged her to cash in some savings bonds given to her throughout her childhood by her grandfather, who died when she was 13. "About $1,400 had accumulated and I put it into a separate account because I didn't want to just stick it into the regular account where it would probably go for groceries. That money was my grandfather, in essence, and it just seemed sacrilegious." Instead the money went into printing and finding subscribers for her magazine.

The bulk of *Potluck*'s 30 pages is taken up by poems and short stories by writers age 8 to 16. But what makes the magazine very different from others that publish the work of young writers are Picchietti's short pieces about being a professional writer and developing creativity. "I didn't want *Potluck* just to be a showplace. I wanted young people to learn how to write, how to be a writer, how to submit. I wanted them to be aware that what they were doing wasn't just sending off their work because their teachers told them they had to or Mom thought it was a good idea, but they were actually doing a job—they were being freelance writers. I wanted them to understand the rights of a writer, the responsibilities of a writer and how to present their work in a professional manner."

This mission to help young writers means Picchietti does much more than just publish a small magazine from her home in Deerfield, Illinois. It also means she spent most of 1997 calling individual Border's stores around Chicago and across the country to ask them to carry the magazine. And that she took out ads in the *Chicago Tribune* and *The New York Times* to find new subscribers. And that she's willing to help a teenage girl edit her collection of poems and publish them in a chapbook or advise an 18-year-old writer from Nigeria where to find adult markets for her work. "That's basically what I feel I'm here for," Picchietti says. "It's not just to publish work. It's to enable young writers, to have them move beyond this, which is an odd thing for a magazine to do in some respects."

Part of what helps Picchietti craft a magazine, not only for kids but by kids, is her experience as a mother of three children, ages 13, 11 and 8. Her background as a school librarian choosing books for children also contributes to her expertise. But for Picchietti, being able to appreciate young writers comes most from remembering what writing meant to her as a child and as a teenager. "I have everything I've ever written," she says. "I review some of my stuff that makes my hair go white, then I go back to the kids' work and it's not that bad. You really do have to look at it through eyes of a child the age of the writer."

Those same eyes help Picchietti craft personal rejection letters with comments and encouragement for young writers who have clearly tried. "I try to give them something and not just leave them rejected because that doesn't teach them anything. That just tells them, 'Oh, I'm not a good writer. I better not submit anywhere else.' You really don't want that because everyone has potential." And Picchietti believes she isn't the only one who is seeing potential in so many young writers. Parents and teachers are taking children and teens more seriously and encouraging them to express their feelings in creative ways. "As far as the schools go and a teacher working with her students to get them published—I can't think of a better connection you can make with your student. You can bet you will be remembered in that child's life."

To facilitate that student/teacher connection Picchietti accepts bulk submissions from schools. "They can send en masse and it doesn't cost anything beyond a self-addressed, stamped envelope. We do like them to buy a subscription but nothing is ever required. When these kids get published, you don't know how it changes their lives."

Susan Napoli Picchietti started *Potluck Children's Literary Magazine* as not just an outlet for young writers to be published, but also as a publication to help them become better writers. "I didn't want *Potluck* just to be a showplace," says Picchietti. "I wanted young people to learn how to write, how to be a writer, how to submit. I wanted them to be aware they weren't just sending off their work because their teachers told them they had to or Mom thought it was a good idea, but they were actually doing a job—they were being freelance writers." To learn more about the magazine, visit the *Potluck* website at http://members.aol.com/nappic.

Potluck

Children's Literary Magazine
THE magazine for the serious young writer

Summer 1999   Vol. 2, No. 3 $4.95

* Poetry * Short Stories *
* Two Book Reviews *
Creative Corner: *Free Verse Poetry*

When Picchietti's life is overwhelmed by all the unexpected tasks that go into publishing a magazine, she thinks of her grandfather. "He was a very simple man. He worked constantly," she remembers. She also remembers the little things he did for his family to show his love. "We had a cottage on a lake and he would get up before everybody and go to the bakery and get the first batch of donuts. He'd buy everybody's favorite. We'd wake up and there they would be. He just did it, and never asked a thing, because he loved us."

Picchietti does the same thing for each young writer she publishes in *Potluck*. "I'm the easiest person to submit to," she says. "I say 'SASE required,' but I've never been able to trash anything. I just can't do that." And even though postage costs have gone up and her husband wonders when she'll ever turn a profit on her venture, Picchietti believes her life is full of riches. "Every subscriber is payment," she says. "Every letter is payment. Every new Border's store that carries the magazine is payment for me, to my soul."

—*Megan Lane*

nity and networking, grandparents, Humor Unlimited, Raising Caring Children, creative problem-solving, rewards and punishments and fear and loss."

☑ **SKYLARK**, Purdue University Calumet, 2200 169th St., Hammond IN 46323-2094. (219)989-2273. Fax: (219)989-2165. Editor: Pamela Hunter. Young Writers' Editor: Shirley Jo Moritz. Annual magazine. Circ. 1,000. 20% of material written by juvenile authors. Presently accepting material by children. "*Skylark* wishes to provide a vehicle for creative writing of all kinds (with emphasis on an attractive synthesis of text and layout), especially by writers ages 5-18, who live in the Illinois/Indiana area and who have not ordinarily been provided with such an outlet. Children need a place to see their work published alongside that of adults." Proof of originality is required from parents or teachers for all authors. "We feel that creativity should be nurtured as soon as possible in an individual. By publishing young, promising authors and illustrators in the same magazine which also features work by adults, perhaps we will provide the impetus for a young person to keep at his/her craft." Writer's guidelines available upon request with a SASE.

Magazines: 20% of magazine written by young people. In previous issues, *Skylark* has published mysteries, fantasy, humor, good narrative fiction stories (400-800 words), personal essays, brief character sketches, nonfiction stories (400-650 words), poetry (no more than 20 lines). Does not want to see material that is obviously religious or sexual. Pays in contributor's copies. One copy per piece published (if two poems are published by one author, that author receives two (2) complimentary copies.) Submit ms to Shirley Jo Moritz, Young Writers' editor. Submit complete ms. Prefers typewritten ms. Must include SASE for response or return of material. Reports in 4 months. Byline given.

Artwork/Photography: Publishes artwork and photographs by children. Looks for "photos of animals, landscapes and sports, and for artwork to go along with text." Pays in contributor's copies. One copy per each piece of artwork published. Artwork and photos may be b&w or color. Use unlined paper. Do not use pencil and no copyrighted characters. Markers are advised for best reproduction. Include name and address on the back of each piece. Package properly to avoid damage. Submit artwork/photos to Pamela Hunter, editor-in-chief. Include SASE. Reports in 5 months.

Tips: "We're looking for literary work. Follow your feelings, be as original as you can and don't be afraid to be different. You are submitting to a publication that accepts work by adults and young people alike. Be responsible. Abide by our guidelines, especially the one concerning an SASE for return of your work or notification of acceptance."

▣ **SPRING TIDES**, 824 Stillwood Dr., Savannah GA 31419. (912)925-8800. Annual magazine. Audience consists of children 5-12 years old. Purpose in publishing works by young people: To promote and encourage writing. Requirements to be met before work is published: must be 5-12 years old. Writers guidelines available on request.

Magazines: 100% of magazine written by young people. Uses 5-6 fiction stories (1,200 words maximum); autobiographical experiences (1,200 words maximum); 15-20 poems (20 lines maximum) per issue. Writers are not paid. Submit complete ms or teacher may submit. Will accept typewritten mss. SASE. Reports in 2 months.

Artwork: Publishes artwork by children. "We have so far used only local children's artwork because of the complications of keeping and returning pieces."

☑ **STONE SOUP, The Magazine by Young Writers and Artists**, Children's Art Foundation, P.O. Box 83, Santa Cruz CA 95063. (831)426-5557. Fax: (831)426-1161. E-mail: editor@stonesoup.com. Website: www.st

onesoup.com. Articles/Fiction Editor, Art Director: Ms. Gerry Mandel. Magazine published 6 times/year. Circ. 20,000. "We publish fiction, poetry and artwork by children through age 13. Our preference is for work based on personal experiences and close observation of the world. Our audience is young people through age 13, as well as parents, teachers, librarians." Purpose in publishing works by young people: to encourage children to read and to express themselves through writing and art. Writer's guidelines available upon request with a SASE.

Magazines: Uses animal, contemporary, fantasy, history, problem-solving, science fiction, sports, spy/mystery/adventure fiction stories. Uses 5-10 fiction stories (100-2,500 words); 5-10 nonfiction stories (100-2,500 words); 2-4 poems per issue. Does not want to see classroom assignments and formula writing. Buys 65 mss/year. Byline given. Pays on publication. Buys all rights. Pays $25 each for stories and poems, $25 for book reviews. Contributors also receive 2 copies. Sample copy $4. Free writer's guidelines. "We don't publish straight nonfiction, but we do publish stories based on real events and experiences." Send complete ms to Ms. Gerry Mandel, editor. Will accept typewritten and legibly handwritten mss. Include SASE. Reports in 1 month.

Artwork/Photography: Publishes any type, size or color artwork/photos by children. Pays $15 for b&w or color illustrations. Contributors receive 2 copies. Sample copy $4. Free illustrator's guidelines. Send originals if possible. Send submissions to Ms. Gerry Mandel, editor. Include SASE. Reports in 1 month. Original artwork returned at job's completion. All artwork must be by children through age 13.

Tips: "Be sure to enclose a SASE. Only work by young people through age 13 is considered. Whether your work is about imaginary situations or real ones, use your own experiences and observations to give your work depth and a sense of reality. Read a few issues of our magazine to get an idea of what we like."

STRAIGHT, Standard Publishing, 8121 Hamilton Ave., Cincinnati OH 45231. (513)931-4050. Fax: (513)931-0950. Magazine published quarterly in weekly parts. Estab. 1951. Magazine includes fiction pieces and articles for Christian teens 13-19 years old to inform, encourage and uplift them. "*Straight* is a magazine for today's Christian teenagers. We use fiction and nonfiction to address modern-day problems from a Christian perspective." Purpose in publishing works by young people: to provide them with an opportunity to express themselves and communicate with their peers through poetry, fiction and nonfiction. Children must submit their birth dates and Social Security numbers. Writer's guidelines available on request, "included in regular guidelines."

● At presstime *Straight* was in the process of changing formats and changing names. Changes will be in effect in 2000. Contact them for more information.

Magazines: Uses fiction, personal experience pieces, poetry. Submit complete mss to Heather E. Wallace, editor. Will accept typewritten and computer printout mss. Reports in 1-2 months.

Artwork/Photography: Publishes artwork and photography by children. Send samples for review for consideration for assignment. Send samples for file to Heather Wallace, editor.

Tips: "Remember that we are a religious publication. Any submissions, including poetry should have a religious slant."

☑ ▼ **VIRGINIA WRITING**, Longwood College, 201 High St., Farmville VA 23909-1839. (804)395-2160. Fax: (804)392-1916. E-mail: tdean@longwood.lwc.com. Submit entries to: Billy C. Clark, editor. Magazine published twice yearly. "*Virginia Writing* publishes prose, poetry, fiction, nonfiction, art, photography, music and drama from Virginia high school students and teachers. The purpose of the journal is to give "promising writers, artists and photographers, the talented young people of Virginia, an opportunity to have their works published. Our audience is mainly Virginia high schools, Virginia public libraries, Department of Education offices, and private citizens. The magazine is also used as a supplementary text in many of Virginia's high school classrooms. The children must be attending a Virginia high school, preferably in no less than 9th grade (though some work has been accepted from 8th graders). Originality is strongly encouraged. The guidelines are in the front of our magazine or available with SASE." No profanity or racism accepted.

● *Virginia Writing* is the recipient of 14 national awards, including the 1997 Golden Shoestring Honor Award, eight Distinguished Achievement Awards for Excellence in Educational Journalism and the Golden Lamp Honor Award as one of the top four educational magazines in the U.S. and Canada.

Magazines: 85% of magazine written by children. Uses approximately 7 fiction and nonfiction short stories and essays, 56 poems per issue. Submit complete ms. Will accept typewritten mss. Reports in 1-4 months, "but must include SASE to receive a reply in the event manuscript is not accepted."

Artwork/Photography: Publishes artwork by children. Considers all types of artwork, including that done on computer. Color slides of artwork are acceptable. All original work is returned upon publication in a non-bendable, well protected package. Reports as soon as possible.

Tips: "All works should be submitted with a cover letter describing student's age, grade and high school currently attending. Submit as often as you like and in any quantity. We cannot accept a work if it features profanity or racism."

VISIT THE WRITER'S DIGEST WEBSITE at www.writersdigest.com for hot new markets, daily market updates, writers' guidelines and much more.

WHOLE NOTES, P.O. Box 1374, Las Cruces NM 88004-1374. (505)541-5744. Magazine published twice yearly. "We encourage interest in contemporary poetry by showcasing outstanding creative writing. We look for original, fresh perceptions in poems that demonstrate skill in using language effectively, with carefully chosen images and clear ideas. Our audience (general) loves poetry. We try to recognize excellence in creative writing by children as a way to encourage and promote imaginative thinking." Writer's guidelines available for SASE.
Magazines: Every fourth issue is 100% by children. Writers should be 21 years old or younger. Uses 30 poems/ issue (length open). Pays complimentary copy. Submit mss to Nancy Peters Hastings, editor. Submit complete ms. "No multiple submissions, please." Will accept typewritten and legibly handwritten mss. SASE. Reports in 2 months.
Artwork/Photography: Publishes artwork and photographs by children. Looks for b&w line drawings which can easily be reproduced; b&w photos. Pays complimentary copy. Send clear photocopies. Submit artwork to Nancy Peters Hastings, editor. SASE. Reports in 2 months.
Tips: Sample issue is $3. "We welcome translations. Send your best work. Don't send your only copy of your poem. Keep a photocopy."

✓ **WORD DANCE**, Playful Productions, Inc., P.O. Box 10804, Wilmington DE 19850-0804. (302)322-6699. Fax: (302)322-4531. E-mail: playful@worddance.com. Website: www.worddance.com. Director: Stuart Unger. Magazine. Published quarterly. "We're a magazine of creative writing and art that is for *and* by children in kindergarten through grade eight. We give children a voice."
Magazines: Uses adventure, fantasy, humorous, etc. (fiction); travel stories, poems and stories based on real life experiences (nonfiction). Publishes 250 total pieces of writing/year; maximum length: 3 pages. Submit mss to Stuart Ungar, articles editor. Sample copy $3. Free writer's guidelines and submissions form. SASE. Reports in 6-9 months.
Artwork: Illustrations accepted from young people in kindergarten through grade 8. Accepts illustrations of specific stories or poems and other general artwork. Must be high contrast. Query. Submit complete package with final art to art director. SASE. Reports in 6-8 months.
Tips: "Submit writing that falls into one of our specific on-going departments. General creative writing submissions are much more competitive."

✓ **THE WRITERS' SLATE**, (The Writing Conference, Inc.), P.O. Box 27288, Overland Park KS 66225-7288. (913)681-8894. Fax: (913)681-8894. E-mail: jbushman@writingconference.com. Website: www.writingco nference.com. Magazine. Publishes 3 issues/year. *The Writers' Slate* accepts original poetry and prose from students enrolled in kindergarten-12th grade. The audience is students, teachers and librarians. Purpose in publishing works by young people: to give students the opportunity to publish and to give students the opportunity *to read* quality literature written by other students. Writer's guidelines available on request.
Magazines: 90% of magazine written by young people. Uses 10-15 fiction, 1-2 nonfiction, 10-15 other mss per issue. Submit mss to Dr. F. Todd Goodson, editor, Kansas State University, 364 Bluemont Hall, Manhattan KS 66506-5300. Submit complete ms. Will accept typewritten mss. Reports in 1 month. Include SASE with ms if reply is desired.
Artwork: Publishes artwork by young people. Bold, b&w, student artwork may accompany a piece of writing. Submit to Dr. F. Todd Goodson, editor. Reports in 1 month.
Tips: "Always accompany submission with a letter indicating name, home address, school, grade level and teacher's name. If you want a reply, submit a SASE."

✓ **WRITES OF PASSAGE**, P.O. Box 1935, Livingston NJ 07039. E-mail: wopassage@aol.com. Website: www.writes.org. Contact: Wendy Mass. Journal. Publishes 2 issues/year by teenagers (spring/summer and fall/ winter). "Our philosophy: 'It may make your parents cringe, your teacher blush, but your best friend will understand.' " Purpose in publishing works by young people: to give teenagers across the country a chance to express themselves through creative writing. "We publish poems and short stories written by teens across the U.S. providing an outlet for their thoughts and feelings. It gives teens an opportunity to see that they are not alone with their fears and confusion and rewards them for creative writing. It sends a message that their thoughts are important." Writers must be 12-19 years old, work must be original and short biography and a SASE must be included.
Magazines: Uses short stories (up to 4 double-spaced pages) and poetry. Pays in 2 copies. Submit to Wendy Mass, publisher. Will accept typewritten and legibly handwritten mss. SASE. Reports in 2 months. Sample copies available for $6. Writer's guidelines for SASE.
Tips: "We began *Writes of Passage* to encourage teenage reading and writing as fun and desirable forms of expression and to establish an open dialogue between teenagers in every state. Our selection process does not censor topics and presents submissions according to the authors' intentions. It gives teens an opportunity to expand on what they have learned in reading and writing classes in school by opening up a world of writing in which they can be free. As a result, submissions often reveal a surprising candidness on the part of the authors, including topics such as love, fear, struggle and death and they expose the diverse backgrounds of contributors."

Resources
Agents & Art Reps

This brand new section features listings of literary agents and art reps who either specialize in or represent a good percentage of children's writers or illustrators. While there are a number of children's publishers who are open to nonagented material, using the services of an agent or rep can be beneficial to a writer or artist. Agents and reps can get your work seen by editors and art directors more quickly. They are familiar with the market and have insights into which editors and art directors would be most interested in your work. Also, they negotiate contracts and will likely be able to get you a better deal than you could get on your own.

Agents and reps make their income by taking a percentage of what writers and illustrators receive from publishers. The standard percentage for agents is 10-15 percent; art reps generally take 25-30 percent. We have not included any agencies in this section that charge reading fees.

WHAT TO SEND

When putting together a package for an agent or rep, follow the guidelines given in their listings. Most agents open to submissions prefer initially to receive a query letter describing your work. (For tips on queries, see Writing Effective Query Letters on page 20.) For novels and longer works, some agents ask for an outline and a number of sample chapters, but you should send these only if you're asked to do so. Never fax or e-mail a query letter or sample chapters to agents without their permission. Just as with publishers, agents receive a large volume of submissions. It may take them a long time to reply, so you may want to query several agents at one time. It's best, however, to have a complete manuscript considered by only one agent at a time. Always include a self-addressed, stamped envelope (SASE).

For initial contact with art reps, send a brief query leter and a self-promo piece. Again, follow the guidelines given in the listings. If you don't have a flier or brochure, send photocopies. (For

---

An Organization for Agents

In some listings of agents you'll see references to AAR (The Association of Authors' Representatives). This organization requires its members to meet an established list of professional standards and code of ethics.

The objectives of AAR include keeping agents informed about conditions in publishing and related fields; encouraging cooperation among literary organizations; and assisting agents in representing their author-clients' interests. Officially, members are prohibited from directly or indirectly charging reaging fees. They offer writers a list of member agents on their website or through the mail (for $7 plus 55¢ postage). They also offer a list of recommended questions an author should ask an agent. They can be contacted at AAR, 10 Astor Place, Third Floor, New York NY 10003. (212)252-3695. Website: www.aar-online.org. (Note: at presstime, AAR was preparing to move. Check their website for updated address.)

tips on creating promotional material see For Illustrators: Super Self-Promotion Strategies on page 67.) Always include a SASE.

For those who both write and illustrate, some agents listed will consider the work of author/illustrators. Read through the listings for details.

As you consider approaching agents and reps with your work, keep in mind that they are very choosy about who they take on to represent. Your work must be high quality and presented professionally to make an impression on them. For insights from an agent on what impresses him in a submission, read the Insider Report with Steven Malk, agent for Writers House, on page 297. For more listings of agents and more information and tips see *Guide to Literary Agents*; for additional listing of art reps see *Artist's & Graphic Designer's Market* (both Writer's Digest Books).

AGENTS

N: BOOKS & SUCH, 3093 Maiden Ln., Altadena CA 91001. (626)797-1716. Fax: (626)398-0246. E-mail: jkgbooks@aol.com. **Contact:** Janet Kobobel Grant. Estab. 1996. Associate member of CBA. Represents 20 clients. 10% of clients are new/unpublished writers. Specializes in "general and inspirational fiction, romance, specializes in the Christian booksellers market but is expanding into the ABA market as well as children's and young adult market."
  ● Before becoming an agent, Ms. Grant was an editor for Zondervan and managing editor for Focus on the Family.
Represents: 34% juvenile books. Considers: nonfiction, fiction, picture books, young adult.
How to Contact: Query with SASE. Accepts queries by e-mail. Considers simultaneous queries. Reports in 3 weeks on queries; 6 weeks on mss. Returns material only with SASE.
Needs: Actively seeking "material appropriate to the Christian market or that would crossover to the ABA market as well." Obtains new clients through recommendations and conferences.
Terms: Agent receives 15% commission on domestic and foreign sales. Offers written contract. 2 months notice must be given to terminate contract. Charges for postage, photocopying, fax and express mail.
Tips: "The heart of my motivation is to develop relationships with the authors I serve, to do what I can to shine the light of success on them, and to help be a caretaker of their gifts and time."

N: ANDREA BROWN LITERARY AGENCY, INC., P.O. Box 371027, Montara CA 94037-1027. (650)728-1783. President: Andrea Brown. Estab. 1981. Member of AAR, SCBWI and Authors Guild. 10% of clients are new/previously unpublished writers. Specializes in "all kinds of children's books—illustrators and authors."
  ● Prior to opening her agency, Brown served as an editorial assistant at Random House and Dell Publishing and as an editor with Alfred A. Knopf.
Member Agents: Andrea Brown, Laura Rennert.
Represents: 98% juvenile books. Considers: nonfiction (animals, anthropology/archaeology, art/architecture/design, biography/autobiography, current affairs, ethnic/cultural interests, history, how-to, nature/environment, photography, popular culture, science/technology, sociology, sports); fiction (historical, science fiction); picture books, young adult.
How to Contact: Query. Reports in 1-4 weeks on queries; 1-3 months on mss.
Needs: Mostly obtains new clients through recommendations, editors, clients and agents.
Terms: Agent receives 15% commission on domestic sales; 20% on foreign sales. Written contract.
Tips: Query first. "Taking on very few picture books. Must be unique—no rhyme, no anthropomorphism. Do not call, or fax queries or manuscripts." Agents at Andrea Brown Literary Agency attend Austin Writers League; SCBWI, Orange County Conferences; Mills College Childrens Literature Conference (Oakland CA); Asilomar (Pacific Grove CA); Maui Writers Conference, Southwest Writers Conference; San Diego State University Writer's Conference; Big Sur Children's Writing Workshop (Director). Recent sales include *Bus Driver From the Black Lagoon*, by Mike Thaler (Scholastic).

N: PEMA BROWNE LTD., HCR Box 104B, Pine Rd., Neversink NY 12765-9603. (914)985-2936. Website: www.geocities.com/~pemabrowneltd. **Contact:** Perry Browne or Pema Browne ("Pema rhymes with Emma"). Estab. 1966. Member of SCBWI. Represents 50 clients. Handles selected commercial fiction, nonfiction, romance, business, new age, reference, pop culture, juvenile and children's picture books.
  ● Prior to opening their agency, Perry Browne was a radio and TV performer; Pema Browne was a fine artist and art buyer.
Member Agents: Pema Browne (children's fiction and nonfiction, adult nonfiction); Perry Browne (adult fiction and nonfiction).
Represents: 35% juvenile books. Considers: nonfiction, fiction, picture books, young adult.

How to Contact: Query with SASE. No fax queries. No e-mail queries. Reports in 3 weeks on queries; within 6 weeks on mss. Prefers to be the only reader. "We do not review manuscripts that have been sent out to publishers."Returns materials only with SASE.

Needs: Actively seeking nonfiction, juvenile, middle grade, some young adult, picture books. Obtains new clients through "editors, authors, *LMP, Guide to Literary Agents* and as a result of longevity!"

Terms: Agent receives 15% commission on domestic sales, 20% on foreign sales.

Tips: "In nonfiction, one must have credentials to lend credence to a proposal. Make sure of margins, double-space and use clean, dark type." This agency sold 25 books in the last year.

[N] RUTH COHEN, INC. LITERARY AGENCY, P.O. Box 7626, Menlo Park CA 94025. (650)854-2054. **Contact:** Ruth Cohen or Sally Driscoll. Estab. 1982. Member of AAR, Authors Guild, Sisters in Crime, Romance Writers of America, SCBWI. Represents 45 clients. 15% of clients are new/previously unpublished writers. Specializes in "quality writing in contemporary fiction; women's fiction; mysteries; thrillers and juvenile fiction."

● Prior to opening her agency, Cohen served as directing editor at Scott Foresman & Company (now HarperCollins).

Represents: 35% juvenile. Considers: nonfiction, fiction, picture books, young adult.

How to Contact: *No unsolicited mss.* Send outline plus 2 sample chapters. "Please indicate your phone number or e-mail address." *Must include SASE.* Reports in 3 weeks on queries.

Needs: Obtains new clients through recommendations from others and through submissions.

Terms: Agent receives 15% commission on domestic sales; 20% on foreign sales, "if a foreign agent is involved." Offers written contract, binding for 1 year "continuing to next." Charges for foreign postage, phone calls, photocopying submissions and overnight delivery of mss when appropriate.

Tips: "As the publishing world merges and charges, there seem to be fewer opportunities for new writers to succeed in the work that they love. We urge you to develop the patience, persistence and perseverance that have made this agency so successful. Prepare a well-written and well-crafted manuscript, and our combined best efforts can help advance both our careers."

[N] DWYER & O'GRADY, INC., P.O. Box 239, Lempster NH 03605-0239. (603)863-9347. Fax: (603)863-9346. E-mail: dosouth@mindspring.com. **Contact:** Elizabeth O'Grady. Estab. 1990. Member of SCBWI. Represents 20 clients. 70% of clients are new/unpublished writers. Represents only writers and illustrators of children's books.

● Prior to opening their agency, Dwyer and O'Grady were booksellers and publishers.

Member Agents: Elizabeth O'Grady (children's books); Jeff Dwyer (children's books).

Represents: 100% juvenile books. Considers: nonfiction, fiction, picture books, young adult.

How to Contact: Send outline and 1 sample chapter with SASE. Does not accept queries by fax or e-mail. Considers simultaneous submissions. Reports in 2 months. Returns material only with SASE.

Needs: Obtains new clients through referrals or direct approach from agent to writer whose work they've read.

Terms: Agent receives 15% commission on domestic sales; 20% on foreign sales. Offers written contract. Thirty days notice must be given to terminate contract. Charges for "photocopying of longer manuscripts or mutually agreed upon marketing expenses."

Tips: Agents from Dwyer & O'Grady attend Book Expo; American Library Association; Society of Children's Book Writers & Illustrators conferences. They sold 13 titles in the last year. These include *A Gardener's Alphabet*, by Mary Azarian (Houghton Mifflin); *Many Many Moons*, by Mary Azarian (Little Brown); *Hinkley Fire*, by Ted Rose (Houghton Mifflin); *Talkin Bout Bess*, by Earl B. Lewis (Orchard Books). Other clients include Kim Ablon, Tom Bodett, Odds Bodkin, Donna Clair, Pat Lowery Collins, Leonard Jenkins, Robert H. Miller, Rebecca Rule, Steve Schuch, Virginia Stroud, Natasha Tarpley, Zong-Zhour Wang and Rashida Watson.

[N] ETHAN ELLENBERG LITERARY AGENCY, 548 Broadway, #5-E, New York NY 10012. (212)431-4554. Fax: (212)941-4652. E-mail: eellenberg@aol.com. **Contact:** Ethan Ellenberg. Estab. 1983. Represents 70 clients. 10% of clients are new/previously unpublished writers. Specializes in commercial fiction, especially thrillers and romance/women's fiction.

● Prior to opening his agency, Ellenberg was contracts manager of Berkley/Jove and associate contracts manager for Bantam.

Represents: "We do a lot of children's books." Considers: nonfiction, fiction, picture books, young adult.

How to Contact: Send outline plus 3 sample chapters. Accepts queries by e-mail; does not accept fax queries. Considers simultaneous queries and submissions. Reports in 10 days on queries; 3-4 weeks on mss. Returns materials only with SASE.

Terms: Agent receives 15% on domestic sales; 10% on foreign sales. Offers written contract, "flexible." Charges for "direct expenses only: photocopying, postage."

Tips: "We do consider new material from unsolicited authors. Write a good clear letter with a succinct description of your book. We prefer the first three chapters when we consider fiction. For all submissions you must include SASE for return or the material is discarded. It's always hard to break in, but talent will find a home. We continue to see natural storytellers and nonfiction writers with important books." This agency sold over 100 titles in the last year, including *Puppy and Me* series, by Julia Noonan (Scholastic).

N FLANNERY LITERARY, 1140 Wickfield Court, Naperville IL 60563-3300. (630)428-2682. Fax: (630)428-2683. **Contact:** Jennifer Flannery. Estab. 1992. Represents 33 clients. 90% of clients are new/previously unpublished writers. Specializes in children's and young adult, juvenile fiction and nonfiction.

• Prior to opening her agency, Ms. Flannery was an editorial assistant.

Represents: 95% juvenile books. Considers: nonfiction, fiction, picture books, young adult.

How to Contact: Query. Reports in 2-4 weeks on queries; 6-8 weeks on mss.

Needs: Obtains new clients through referrals and queries.

Terms: Agent receives 15% commission on domestic sales; 20% on foreign sales. Offers written contract, binding for life of book in print, with 30 day cancellation clause. 100% of business is derived from commissions on sales.

Tips: "Write an engrossing succinct query describing your work." Jennifer Flannery attends SCBWI conferences. Flannery Literary sold 20 titles in the last year.

N THE CHARLOTTE GUSAY LITERARY AGENCY, 10532 Blythe, Los Angeles CA 90064-3312. (310)559-0831. E-mail: gusay1@aol.com. **Contact:** Charlotte Gusay. Estab. 1988. Member of Authors Guild and PEN, signatory of WGA. Represents 30 clients. 50% of clients are new/previously unpublished writers. Specializes in fiction, nonfiction, children's (multicultural, nonsexist), children's illustrators, screenplays, books to film.

• Prior to opening her agency, Gusay was a vice president for an audiocassette producer and also a bookstore owner.

Represents: Considers: nonfiction, fiction.

How to Contact: SASE always required for response. "Queries only, *no* unsolicited manuscripts. Initial query should be 1- to 2-page synopsis with SASE." Reports in 4-6 weeks on queries; 6-10 weeks on mss.

Needs: Does not want to receive poetry, science fiction, horror. Usually obtains new clients through referrals and queries.

Terms: Agent receives 15% commission on domestic sales; 10% on dramatic sales; 25% on foreign sales. Offers written contract, binding for "usually 1 year." Charges for out-of-pocket expenses such as long distance phone calls, fax, express mail, postage, etc.

Tips: "Please be professional."

N KIRCHOFF/WOHLBERG, INC., AUTHORS' REPRESENTATION DIVISION, 866 United Nations Plaza, #525, New York NY 10017. (212)644-2020. Fax: (212)223-4387. Director of Operations: John R. Whitman. Estab. 1930s. Member of AAR. Represents 50 authors. 10% of clients are new/previously unpublished writers. Specializes in juvenile through young adult trade books and textbooks.

Member Agents: Liza Pulitzer-Voges (juvenile and young adult authors).

Represents: 80% juvenile books, 5% young adult. "We are interested in any original projects of quality that are appropriate to the juvenile and young adult trade book markets. But, we take on very few new clients as our roster is full."

How to Contact: "Send a query that includes an outline and a sample; SASE required." Reports in 1 month on queries; 2 months on mss. Please send queries to the attention of Liza Pulitzer-Voges.

Needs: "Usually obtains new clients through recommendations from authors, illustrators and editors."

Terms: Agent receives standard commission "depending upon whether it is an author only, illustrator only, or an author/illustrator book." Offers written contract, binding for not less than 1 year.

Tips: Kirchoff/Wohlberg has been in business for over 50 years and sold over 50 titles in the last year."

N BARBARA S. KOUTS, LITERARY AGENT, P.O. Box 560, Bellport NY 11713. (516)286-1278. **Contact:** Barbara Kouts. Estab. 1980. Member of AAR. Represent 50 clients. 10% of clients are new/previously unpublished writers. Specializes in adult fiction and nonfiction and children's books.

Represents: 60% juvenile books. Considers: nonfiction, fiction, picture books, young adult.

How to Contact: Query. Reports in 2-3 days on queries; 4-6 weeks on mss.

Needs: Obtains new clients through recommendations from others, solicitation, at conferences, etc.

Terms: Agent receives 10% commission on domestic sales; 20% on foreign sales. Charges for photocopying.

Tips: "Write, do not call. Be professional in your writing." Recent sales of this agency include *Dancing on the Edge*, by Han Nolan (Harcourt Brace); *Cendrillon*, by Robert San Souci (Simon & Schuster).

A SELF-ADDRESSED, STAMPED ENVELOPE (SASE) should always be included with submissions within your own country. When sending material to other countries, include a self-addressed envelope (SAE) and International Reply Coupons (IRCs).

N IRENE KRAAS AGENCY, 220 Copper Trail, Santa Fe NM 87505. (505)474-6212. Fax: (505)474-6216. Estab. 1990. Member of Authors Guild. Represents 30 clients. 75% of clients are new/unpublished writers. Specializes in fiction only, middle grade through adult.
Represents: 30% juvenile books. Considers: fiction (middle grade, young adult).
How to Contact: Send cover letter and first 30 pages. Must include return postage and/or SASE. Does not accept e-mail queries. Considers simultaneous submissions. Returns materials only with SASE.
Needs: Actively seeking "books that are well written with commercial potential." Obtains new clients through recommendations from others, conferences.
Terms: Agent receives 15% commission on domestic sales; 20% on foreign sales. Offers written contract, binding for 1 year "but can be terminated at any time for any reason with written notice." Charges for photocopying and postage.

N RAY LINCOLN LITERARY AGENCY, Elkins Park House, Suite 107-B, 7900 Old York Rd., Elkins Park PA 19027. (215)635-0827. **Contact:** Mrs. Ray Lincoln. Estab. 1974. Represents 30 clients. 35% of clients are new/previously unpublished writers. Specializes in biography, nature, the sciences, fiction in both adult and children's categories.
Member Agents: Jerome A. Lincoln.
Represents: 20% juvenile books. Considers nonfiction, fiction, young adult.
How to Contact: Query first, then on request send outline, 2 sample chapters and SASE. "I send for balance of manuscript if it is a likely project." Reports in 2 weeks on queries; 1 month on mss.
Needs: Obtains new clients usually from recommendations.
Terms: Agent receives 15% commission on domestic sales; 20% on foreign sales. Offers written contract, binding "but with notice, may be cancelled." Charges only for overseas telephone calls. "I request authors to do manuscript photocopying themselves. Postage, or shipping charge on manuscripts accepted for representation by agency."
Tips: "I always look for polished writing style, fresh points of view and professional attitudes." Recent sales of this agency include *Best Halloween Ever*, by Barbara Robinson (HarperCollins); *Daddy and Me*, by Jerry Spinelli (Knopf).

N GINA MACCOBY LITERARY AGENCY, P.O. Box 60, Chappaqua NY 10514. (914)238-5630. **Contact:** Gina Maccoby. Estab. 1986. Represents 35 clients. Represents illustrators of children's books.
Represents: 33% juvenile books. Considers: nonfiction, fiction, young adult.
How to Contact: Query with SASE. "Please, no unsolicited mss." Considers simultaneous queries and submisssions. Reports in 2 months. Returns materials only with SASE.
Needs: Usually obtains new clients through recommendations from own clients.
Terms: Agent receives 15% commission on domestic sales; 25% on foreign sales. Charges for photocopying. May recover certain costs such as airmail postage to Europe or Japan or legal fees.
Tips: This agency sold 18 titles last year including *The Art of Keeping Cool*, by Janet Taylor Lisle (DK Ink).

N THE NORMA-LEWIS AGENCY, 311 W. 43rd St., Suite 602, New York NY 10036. (212)664-0807. **Contact:** Norma Liebert. Estab. 1980. 50% of clients are new/previously unpublished writers. Specializes in juvenile books (pre-school to high school).
Represents: 60% juvenile books. Considers: nonfiction, fiction, picture books, young adult.
How to Contact: Prefers to be only reader. Reports in 6 weeks. Returns materials only with SASE.
Terms: Agent receives 15% commission on domestic sales; 20% on foreign sales.

N PESHA RUBINSTEIN LITERARY AGENCY, INC., 1392 Rugby Rd., Teaneck NJ 07666-2839. (201)862-1174. Fax: (201)862-1180. E-mail: peshalit@aol.com. **Contact:** Pesha Rubinstein. Estab. 1990. Member of AAR, RWA, MWA, SCBWI. Represents 35 clients. 25% of clients are new/previously unpublished writers. Specializes in commercial fiction and nonfiction and children's books.
   ● Prior to opening her agency, Rubenstein served as an editor at Zebra and Leisure Books.
Represents: 30% juvenile books. Considers: fiction.
How to Contact: Send query, first 10 pages and SASE. Reports in 2 weeks on queries; 6 weeks on requested mss.
Needs: Does not want to receive poetry or westerns.
Terms: Agent receives 15% commission on domestic sales; 20% on foreign sales. Offers written contract. Charges for photocopying and overseas postage. No weekend or collect calls accepted.
Tips: "Keep the query letter and synopsis short. Please send first ten pages of manuscript rather than selected chapters from the manuscript. I am a stickler for correct grammar, spelling and punctuation. The work speaks for itself better than any description can. Never send originals. A phone call after one month is acceptable. Always include a SASE covering return of the entire package with the submission."

N STERNIG & BYRNE LITERARY AGENCY, 3209 S. 55th St., Milwaukee WI 53219-4433. (414)328-8034. Fax: (414)328-8034. E-mail: jackbyrne@aol.com. **Contact:** Jack Byrne. Estab. 1950s. Member of SFWA and MWA. Represents 30 clients. 20% of clients are new/unpublished writers. Sold 12 titles in the last year. "We have a small, friendly, personal, hands-on teamwork approach to marketing."

Member Agents: Jack Byrne.

Represents: 40% juvenile books. Considers: nonfiction, fiction, young adult.

How to Contact: Query. Considers simultaneous queries; no simultaneous submissions. Reports in 3 weeks on queries; 3 months on mss. Returns materials only with SASE. "No SASE equals no return."

Needs: Actively seeking science fiction/fantasy. Does not want to receive romance, poetry, textbooks, highly specialized nonfiction.

Terms: Agent receives 15% commission on domestic sales; 20% on foreign sales. Offers written contract, open/ non binding. 60 days notice must be given to terminate contract.

Tips: "Don't send first drafts; have a professional presentation . . . including cover letter; know your field (read what's been done . . . good and bad)." Reads *Publishers Weekly*, etc. to find new clients. Looks for "whatever catches my eye."

S©OTT TREIMEL NEW YORK, 434 Lafayette St., New York NY 10003. (212)505-8353. Fax: (212)505-0664. E-mail: mescottyt@earthlink.net. **Contact:** Scott Treimel. Estab. 1995. Represents 20 clients. 30% of clients are new/unpublished writers. Specializes in children's book from concept board books through young adult novels: tightly focused segment of the trade and educational markets.

● Prior to becoming an agent, Treimel was a rights agent for Scholastic, Inc.; a book packager and rights agent for United Feature Syndicate; and the founding director of Warner Bros. Worldwide Publishing.

Represents: 100% juvenile books. Considers all juvenile fiction and nonfiction areas.

How to Contact: Query with SASE. For picture books, send entire ms. Does not accept queries by fax or e-mail. Prefers to be only reader. Prefers "30 day exclusive read on manuscripts/request." Reports in 2 weeks on queries; 1 month on mss. Returns materials only with SASE or discards.

Needs: Actively seeking picture book illustrators, picture book authors, first chapter books, middle-grade fiction and nonfiction, young adult fiction. Obtains new clients through recommendations and queries.

Terms: Agent receives 15% commission on domestic sales; 20% on foreign sales. Offers verbal or written contract, binding on a "contract-by-contract basis." Charges for photocopying, overnight/express postage, messengers and book orders.

Tips: Attends Society of Children's Book Writers & Illustrators (Los Angeles, August). Sold 20 titles in the last year.

WECKSLER-INCOMCO, 170 West End Ave., New York NY 10023. (212)787-2239. Fax: (212)496-7035. **Contact:** Sally Wecksler. Estab. 1971. Represents 25 clients. 50% of clients are new/previously unpublished writers. "However, I prefer writers who have had something in print." Specializes in nonfiction with illustrations (photos and art).

● Prior to becoming an agent, Wecksler was an editor at *Publishers Weekly*; publisher with the international department of R.R. Bowker; and international director at Baker & Taylor.

Member Agents: Joann Amparan (general, children's books), S. Wecksler (general, foreign rights/co-editions, fiction, illustrated books, children's books).

Represents: 25% juvenile books. Considers: nonfiction, fiction, picture books.

How to Contact: Query with outline plus 3 sample chapters. Include brief bio. Reports in 1 month on queries; 2 months on mss.

Needs: Actively seeking "illustrated books for adults or children with beautiful photos or artwork." Does not want to receive "science fiction or books with violence." Obtains new clients through recommendations from others and solicitations.

Terms: Agent receives 12-15% commission on domestic sales; 20% on foreign sales. Offers written contract, binding for 3 years.

Tips: "Make sure a SASE is enclosed. Send three chapters and outline, clearly typed or word processed manuscript, double-spaced, written with punctuation and grammar in approved style. *We do not like to receive presentations by fax.*"

WRITERS HOUSE, 21 W. 26th St., New York NY 10010. (212)685-2400. Fax: (212)685-1781. Estab. 1974. Member of AAR. Represents 280 clients. 50% of clients were new/unpublished writers. Specializes in all types of popular fiction and nonfiction. No scholarly, professional, poetry or screenplays.

Member Agents: Amy Berkower (major juvenile authors); Merrilee Heifetz (quality children's fiction); Susan

insider report

Going on instincts and playing author's advocate

Agent Steven Malk's conference appearances have been known to cause whispering among the writers in the crowd. He's a guy in his mid-twenties? What could he possibly know about children's books? What conference-goers don't know (until he tells them) is that Malk has been surrounded by children's books and authors his whole life. His mother owns The White Rabbit Children's Bookstore in La Jolla, California (www.whiterabbit-childbooks.com), and his grandmother opened one of the world's first children's bookstores in Johannesburg, South Africa, in the '50s. "How many people can say they're the third generation of something?" he says.

Steven Malk

Malk, an agent for New York-based Writers House, works out of San Diego. He reads all the manuscripts he receives himself, speaks at a number of SCBWI conferences, and has led several online chats for children's writers. Recent and upcoming work from his authors include *Video* (Greenwillow), the second novel from Karen Romano Young, author of the well-received *The Beetle and Me: A Love Story*; *I Hate to Go to Bed* (Harcourt), by author/illustrator Katie Davis; award-winning novelist Franny Billingsley's *The Folk Keeper* (Atheneum); Elise Primavera's *Auntie Claus*, Harcourt's lead fall title featured in New York Saks Fifth Avenue Christmas window displays; and *Stop Pretending: What Happened When My Big Sister Went Crazy* (HarperCollins), a YA poetry collection by Sonya Sones. (See First Books on page 45 for an interview with Sones.)

Here Malk talks about the advantages of having an agent, offers tips on choosing one, reveals what impresses him in a submission, and shares his advice to unpublished writers.

How did working at your mom's bookstore affect your career path?

I could not overstate how important it was. I started working there when I was sixteen, and I continued all through high school and college. I loved it and I developed really strong instincts. Matching up customers with books was great experience—it's similar to what I do now with publishers. I learned how to read people's tastes, as well as how to pitch books. It's a great store with a great selection, so I learned everything that was out there and developed a strong sense about what I like and don't like.

How did you end up becoming an agent? Why did agenting interest you?

After working at The White Rabbit for a while, I realized I wanted to be in publishing, but I wasn't sure if I wanted to be an editor or an agent. I interned for the Sandra Dijkstra Agency when I was still in college, and then worked there full time as soon as I graduated. It seemed like the best of all worlds. These days, agents do a lot of editorial work. I get to be involved in the business side of things, and I can be very creative. I'm involved in every single facet of an author's career.

How do you maintain relationships with editors and get a feel for their tastes and interests?

That's really important. I do have to get a feel for an editor's personality and what she likes, further than "she likes to do novels." It's something that's learned; it takes a little while; it's trial and error. I start to get a sense, the more I deal with an editor, of what she likes. If she buys something from me or if she turns something down, it's all educational. Usually I start to see a pattern and get an idea of her taste. There are certain editors I work with more than others. I have a really good idea, if I have a certain type of project, who I'm going to send it to—if I have a young picture book as opposed to an edgy novel or a longer picture book.

You probably don't have an "average" day, do you?

Every day is different. I can tell you this—I'm not sitting in the office all day reading manuscripts. A lot of writers think that. I'm most likely talking to a couple of editors. On any given day, I might be negotiating a contract. Or I'm sending a project out. I'm writing a pitch letter. I'm making my submission list of editors. I'm calling editors and pitching something. I'm following up on a project. Or I'm dealing with sub rights. There's so much involved.

Why should an author have an agent?

There are a lot of reasons. It's different for every person. I don't think it's going to work for every single author necessarily. If you're a control freak, you shouldn't have an agent. You relinquish a certain amount of control of your career. You have to do a lot of research when you're deciding if you want an agent. You should decide why you want an agent, and what you expect from an agent. You really have to find someone you like and trust. You should feel like you and your agent share a common vision.

An agent is going to be able to place your work, and not just place your work with a house, but place your work with the right editor and the right house. The response time is going to be quicker. I can say with a lot of confidence that the offer is going to be higher. And you're going to have an expert negotiating your contract for you. Placing manuscripts is what agents do for a living. It's our job to know what's going on and who's publishing what and how much money authors are getting.

The most important thing to keep in mind is that an agent is someone who's working for you and is in your corner; he's your advocate. Editors are ultimately working for their company, so as nice and friendly as they may be, it's not in their best interest to get you a great deal.

Your agent is only going to be making money if you're making money. With companies merging these days, editors are losing their jobs or changing companies. Even though an author/editor relationship might seem stable, you never know when it's going to end or change. Having an agent, someone you know and trust, someone who's working for you and is in your corner no matter what, is extremely valuable.

If a writer is unpublished, will it be just as difficult to find an agent as it is to find a publisher, generally?

It can be really hard to find an agent. You have to do your research. All agents are different.

I'm not the right agent for everyone. I have my own style—everyone has his own style—so you have to do your homework. Some agents are biased against first-time authors and don't really want to take them on. I love to work with first-time authors. I don't care if someone's published 60 books or none.

What makes you excited about a manuscript when you read it?

It's hard to define—it's my instincts. Some might look at a manuscript and think about what niche it would fall into, what market; try to define it. I don't care about that stuff—whether it's "marketable" or not doesn't matter to me. What matters is how much it speaks to me, and whether or not it has a voice, and voice itself is hard to define. I look for books that I can't stop thinking about. They can be funny, or really haunting or sad, or just very well written. But whatever they are, the books I take on tend to stay with me—days later, I'll still be thinking about them. That's when I know I want to be representing something.

Have you "discovered" authors at conferences?

At the 1998 SCBWI conference in L.A., I found two. One was Sonya Sones. Her book *Stop Pretending* (HarperCollins) came out in fall 1999. That's a perfect example. When I got that book, I read it in one sitting. I didn't even get up, I just called her and said, "I want to represent this—this is going to be a huge book." It's young adult poetry about a really difficult subject. It's not, on the fact of it, the most marketable story. I totally go on my instincts, and that was such an easy call—talk about voice. And it's so moving.

I also met Bruce Hale. Harcourt bought his three-book Chet Gecko series. It's also been optioned as a television series. The first book comes out spring 2000. Again, there's a really great voice. His and Sonya's could not be more different. Sonya's is a really serious, intense book and Bruce's is fun and humorous.

What's your final advice to a writer looking for an agent?

Be professional. It's amazing to me how many people don't send a SASE, or write their cover letters in pencil with things misspelled, or send me something, then three weeks later send a whole new draft saying, "I sent you the wrong story." I really like a good cover letter—it makes an impression on me. But your work's going to speak for itself no matter what.

    —Alice Pope

Cohen (juvenile and young adult fiction and nonfiction); Susan Ginsberg; Fran Lebowitz (juvenile and young adult); Robin Rue (YA fiction).
Represents: 35% juvenile books. Considers: nonfiction, fiction, picture books, young adult.
How to Contact: Query. Reports in 1 month on queries.
Needs: Obtains new clients through recommendations from others.
Terms: Agent receives 15% commission on domestic sales; 20% on foreign sales. Offers written contract, binding for 1 year.
Tips: "Do not send manuscripts. Write a compelling letter. If you do, we'll ask to see your work."

N WRITERS HOUSE, (West Coast Office), 3368 Governor Dr., #224F, San Diego CA 92122. (619)678-8767. Fax: (619)678-8530. **Contact:** Steven Malk.
    ● See Writers House listing above for more information.
Represents: Nonfiction, fiction, picture books, young adult.

ART REPS

N ARTISTS INTERNATIONAL, 320 Bee Brook Rd., Washington CT 06777-1911. (860)868-1011. Fax: (860)868-1272. E-mail: artsintl@javanet.com. **Contact:** Michael Brodie. Commercial illustration representative. Estab. 1970. Represents 20 illustrators. Specializes in children's books. Markets include: design firms; editorial/magazines; licensing.
Handles: Illustration.
Terms: Rep receives 30% commission. No geographic restrictions. Advertising costs are split: 70% paid by talent; 30% paid by representative. "We have our own full-color brochure, 24 pages, and featured in *Picture Book '97*."
How to Contact: For first contact, send slides, photocopies and SASE. Reports in 1 week.
Tips: Obtains new talent through recommendations from others, solicitation, conferences, *Literary Market Place*, etc. "SAE with example of your work; no résumés please."

N ASCIUTTO ART REPS., INC., 1712 E. Butler Circle, Chandler AZ 85225. (602)899-0600. Fax: (602)899-3636. **Contact:** Mary Anne Asciutto. Children's illustration representative. Estab. 1980. Member of SPAR, Society of Illustrators. Represents 20 illustrators. Specializes in children's illustration for books, magazines, posters, packaging, etc. Markets include: publishing/packaging/advertising.
Handles: Illustration only.
Terms: Rep receives 25% commission. No geographic restrictions. Advertising costs are split: 75% paid by talent; 25% paid by representative. For promotional purposes, talent should provide "prints (color) or originals within an 8½×11 size format."
How to Contact: Send a direct mail flier/brochure, tearsheets, photocopies and SASE. Reports in 2 weeks. After initial contact, send appropriate materials if requested. Portfolio should include original art on paper, tearsheets, photocopies or color prints of most recent work. If accepted, materials will remain for assembly.
Tips: In obtaining representation "be sure to connect with an agent who handles the kind of accounts you (the artist) *want*."

N CAROL BANCROFT & FRIENDS, 121 Dodgingtown Rd., P.O. Box 266, Bethel CT 06801. (203)748-4823. Fax: (203)748-4581. **Owner:** Carol Bancroft. Illustration representative for children's publishing. Estab. 1972. Member of SPAR, Society of Illustrators, Graphic Artists Guild. Represents 40 illustrators. Specializes in illustration for children's publishing—text and trade; any children's-related material. Clients include Scholastic, Houghton Mifflin, HarperCollins, Penguin, Viking. Client list available upon request.
Handles: Illustration for children of all ages. Seeking multicultural and fine artists.
Terms: Rep receives 25-30% commission. Advertising costs are split: 75% paid by talent; 25% paid by representative. For promotional purposes, talent must provide "laser copies (not slides), tearsheets, promo pieces, good color photocopies, etc.; 6 pieces or more is best; narrative scenes and children interacting." Advertises in *RSVP*, *Picture Book*.
How to Contact: "Call for information or send samples and SASE." Reports in 1 month.
Tips: "We're looking for artists who can draw animals and people well. They need to show characters in an engaging way with action in situational settings. Must be able to take a character through a story."

N SAL BARRACCA ASSOC. INC., 381 Park Ave. S., New York NY 10016. (212)889-2400. Fax: (212)889-2698. **Contact:** Sal Barracca. Commercial illustration representative. Estab. 1988. Represents 23 illustrators. "90% of our assignments are book jackets." Markets include: advertising agencies; publishing/books.
Handles: Illustration.
Terms: Rep receives 25% commission. Exclusive area representation is required. Advertising costs are split: 75% paid by talent; 25% paid by representative. For promotional purposes "portfolios must be 8×10 chromes that are matted. We can shoot original art to that format at a cost to the artist. We produce our own promotion and mail out once a year to over 16,000 art directors."
How to Contact: For first contact, send direct mail flier/brochure, tearsheets and SASE. Reports in 1 week; 1 day if interested. After initial contact, drop off or mail in appropriate materials for review. Portfolio should include tearsheets, slides.
Tips: "Make sure you have at least three years of working on your own so that you don't have any false expectations from an agent."

N SAM BRODY, ARTISTS & PHOTOGRAPHERS REPRESENTATIVE & CONSULTANT, 77 Winfield St., Apt. 4, E. Norwalk CT 06855-2138. Phone/fax: (203)854-0805 (for fax, add 999). **Contact:** Sam Brody. Commercial illustration and photography representative and broker. Estab. 1948. Member of SPAR. Represents 4 illustrators, 3 photographers, 2 designers. Markets include: advertising agencies; corporations/client direct; design firms; editorial/magazines; publishing/books; sales/promotion firms.
Handles: Illustration, photography, design, "great film directors."
Terms: Agent receives 30% commission. Exclusive area representation is required. For promotional purposes, talent must provide back-up advertising material, i.e., cards (reprints—*Workbook*, etc.) and self-promos.

How to Contact: For first contact, send bio, direct mail flier/brochure, tearsheets. Reports in 3 days or within 1 day if interested. After initial contact, call for appointment or drop off or mail in appropriate materials for review. Portfolio should include tearsheets, slides, photographs. Obtains new talent through recommendations from others, solicitation.

Tips: Considers "past performance for clients that I check with and whether I like the work performed."

PEMA BROWNE LTD., HCR Box 104B, Pine Rd., Neversink NY 12762. (914)985-2936 or (914)985-2062. Fax: (914)985-7635. **Contact:** Pema Browne or Perry Browne. Commercial illustration representative. Estab. 1966. Represents 10 illustrators. Specializes in general commercial. Markets include: all publishing areas; children's picture books; collector plates and dolls; advertising agencies. Clients include HarperCollins, Thomas Nelson, Bantam Doubleday Dell, Nelson/Word, Hyperion, Putnam. Client list available upon request.

Handles: Illustration. Looking for "professional and unique" talent.

Terms: Rep receives 30% commission. Exclusive area representation is required. For promotional purposes, talent must provide color mailers to distribute. Representative pays mailing costs on promotion mailings.

How to Contact: For first contact, send query letter, direct mail flier/brochure and SASE. If interested will ask to mail appropriate materials for review. Portfolios should include tearsheets and transparencies or good color photocopies, plus SASE. Obtains new talent through recommendations and interviews (portfolio review).

Tips: "We are doing more publishing—all types—less advertising." Looks for "continuity of illustration and dedication to work."

CORNELL & MCCARTHY, LLC, 2-D Cross Hwy., Westport CT 06880. (203)454-4210. Fax: (203)454-4258. E-mail: cmartreps@aol.com. **Contact:** Merial Cornell. Children's book illustration representative. Estab. 1989. Member of SCBWI and Graphic Artists Guild. Represents 30 illustrators. Specializes in children's books: trade, mass market, educational.

Handles: Illustration.

Terms: Agent receives 25% commission. Advertising costs are split: 75% paid by talent; 25% paid by representative. For promotional purposes, talent must provide 10-12 strong portfolio pieces relating to children's publishing.

How to Contact: For first contact, send query letter, direct mail flier/brochure, tearsheets, photocopies and SASE. Reports in 1 month. Obtains new talent through recommendations, solicitation, conferences.

Tips: "Work hard on your portfolio."

CREATIVE FREELANCERS MANAGEMENT, INC., 99 Park Ave., #210A, New York NY 10016. (800)398-9544. Fax: (203)532-2927. Website: www.freelancers.com. **Contact:** Marilyn Howard. Commercial illustration representative. Estab. 1988. Represents 30 illustrators. "Our staff members have art direction, art buying or illustration backgrounds." Specializes in children's books, advertising, architectural, conceptual. Markets include: advertising agencies; corporations/client direct; design firms; editorial/magazines; paper products/greeting cards; publishing/books; sales/promotion firms.

Handles: Illustration. Artists must have published work.

Terms: Rep receives 30% commission. Exclusive area representation is preferred. Advertising costs are split: 75% paid by talent; 25% paid by representative. For promotional purposes, talent must provide "printed pages to leave with clients. Co-op advertising with our firm could also provide this. Transparency portfolio preferred if we take you on but we are flexible." Advertises in *American Showcase*, *Workbook*.

How to Contact: For first contact, send tearsheets or "whatever best shows work." Reports back only if interested.

Tips: Looks for experience, professionalism and consistency of style. Obtains new talent through "word of mouth and website."

DWYER & O'GRADY, INC., P.O. Box 239, Lempster NH 03605. (603)863-9347. Fax: (603)863-9346. E-mail: donorth@srnet.com. **Contact:** Elizabeth O'Grady. Agents for children's picture book artists and writers. Estab. 1990. Member of Society of Illustrators, SCBWI, ABA. Represents 12 illustrators and 12 writers. Staff includes Elizabeth O'Grady, Jeffrey Dwyer. Specializes in children's picture books (middle grade and young adult). Markets include: publishing/books, audio/film.

Handles: Illustrators and writers of children's books. "Favor realistic and representational work for the older age picture book. Artist must have full command of the figure and facial expressions."

Terms: Receives 15% commission domestic, 20% foreign. Additional fees are negotiable. Exclusive representation is required (world rights). Advertising costs are paid by representative. For promotional purposes, talent must provide both color slides and prints of at least 20 sample illustrations depicting the figure with facial expression.

VISIT THE WRITER'S DIGEST WEBSITE at www.writersdigest.com for hot new markets, daily market updates, writers' guidelines and much more.

How to Contact: When making first contact, send query letter, slides, photographs and SASE. Reports in 6 weeks. After initial contact, call for appointment and drop off or mail appropriate materials for review. Portfolio should include slides, photographs.

⊠ HK PORTFOLIO, 666 Greenwich St., New York NY 10014. (212)675-5719. E-mail: harriet@hkportfolio.com. Website: www.hkportfolio.com. **Contact:** Harriet Kasak or Mela Bolinao. Commercial illustration representative. Estab. 1986. Member of SPAR, Society of Illustrators and Graphic Artists Guild. Represents 50 illustrators. Specializes in illustration for juvenile markets. "Sub-agent for Peters, Fraser & Dunlop (London)." Markets include: advertising agencies; editorial/magazines; publishing/books.
Handles: Illustration.
Terms: Rep receives 25% commission. No geographic restrictions. Advertising costs are split: 75% paid by talent; 25% paid by representative. Advertises in *American Showcase*, *Picturebook*.
How to Contact: No geographic restrictions. For first contact, send query letter, direct mail flier/brochure, tearsheets, slides, photographs, photostats and SASE. Reports in 1 week. After initial contact, drop off or mail in appropriate materials for review. Portfolio should include tearsheets, slides, photographs, photostats, photocopies.
Tips: Leans toward highly individual personal styles.

⊠ KIRCHOFF/WOHLBERG, ARTISTS' REPRESENTATION DIVISION, 866 United Nations Plaza, #525, New York NY 10017. (212)644-2020. Fax: (212)223-4387. **Director of Operations:** John R. Whitman. Estab. 1930s. Member of SPAR, Society of Illustrators, AIGA, Associaton of American Publishers, Bookbuilders of Boston, New York Bookbinders' Guild. Represents over 50 illustrators. Artist's Represenative: Elizabeth Ford. Specializes in juvenile and young adult trade books and textbooks. Markets include: publishing/books.
Handles: Illustration and photography (juvenile and young adult).
Terms: Rep receives 25% commission. Exclusive representation to book publishers is usually required. Advertising costs paid by representative ("for all Kirchoff/Wohlberg advertisements only"). "We will make transparencies from portfolio samples; keep some original work on file." Advertises in *American Showcase*, *Art Directors' Index*, *Society of Illustrators Annual*, children's book issues of *Publishers Weekly*.
How to Contact: Please send all correspondence to the attention of Elizabeth Ford. For first contact, send query letter, "any materials artists feel are appropriate." Reports in 4-6 weeks. "We will contact you for additional materials." Portfolios should include "whatever artists feel best represents their work. We like to see children's illustration in any style."

⊠ LINDGREN & SMITH, 250 W. 57th St., #521, New York NY 10107. (212)397-7330. E-mail: inquiry@lindgrensmith.com. Website: www.lindgrensmith.com. **Assistant:** Wini Barron. Commercial illustration representative. Estab. 1984. Member of SPAR. Markets include advertising agencies; corporations/client direct; design firms; editorial/magazines; paper products/greeting cards; publishing/books, children books.
Handles: Illustration.
Terms: Exclusive representation is required. Advertises in *American Showcase*, *The Workbook*, *The Black Book* and *Picturebook*.
How to Contact: For first contact, send direct mail flier/brochure, tearsheets, photocopies. "We will respond by mail or phone."
Tips: "Check to see if your work seems appropriate for the group. We only represent experienced artists who have been professionals for some time."

⊠ S.I. INTERNATIONAL, 43 E. 19th St., New York NY 10003. (212)254-4996. Fax: (212)995-0911. E-mail: hspiers@tiac.net. Website: www.si-i.com. Commercial illustration representative. Estab. 1983. Member of SPAR, Graphic Artists Guild. Represents 50 illustrators. Specializes in license characters, educational publishing and children's illustration, digital art and design, mass market paperbacks. Markets include design firms; publishing/books; sales/promotion firms; licensing firms; digital art and design firms.
Handles: Illustration. Looking for artists "who have the ability to do children's illustration and to do license characters either digitally or reflexively."
Terms: Rep receives 25-30% commission. Advertising costs are split: 70% paid by talent; 30% paid by representative. "Contact agency for details. Must have mailer." Advertises in *Picturebook*.
How to Contact: For first contact, send query letter, tearsheets. Reports in 3 weeks. After initial contact, write for appointment to show portfolio of tearsheets, slides.

Clubs & Organizations

Contacts made through organizations such as the ones listed in this section can be quite beneficial for children's writers and illustrators. Professional organizations provide numerous educational, business and legal services in the form of newsletters, workshops or seminars. Organizations can provide tips about how to be a more successful writer or artist, as well as what types of business records to keep, health and life insurance coverage to carry and competitions to consider.

An added benefit of belonging to an organization is the opportunity to network with those who have similar interests, creating a support system. As in any business, knowing the right people can often help your career, and important contacts can be made through your peers. Membership in a writer's or artist's organization also shows publishers you're serious about your craft. This provides no guarantee your work will be published, but it gives you an added dimension of credibility and professionalism.

Some of the organizations listed here welcome anyone with an interest, while others are only open to published writers and professional artists. Organizations such as the Society of Children's Book Writers and Illustrators (SCBWI) have varying levels of membership. SCBWI offers associate membership to those with no publishing credits, and full membership to those who have had work for children published. (See the Insider Report with SCBWI Executive Director Lin Oliver on page 307.) Many national organizations such as SCBWI also have regional chapters throughout the country. Write or call for more information regarding any group that sounds interesting, or check the websites of the many organizations that list them. Be sure to get information about local chapters, membership qualifications and services offered.

Information on organizations listed in the previous edition but not included in this edition of *Children's Writer's & Illustrator's Market* may be found in the General Index.

✓ **AMERICAN ALLIANCE FOR THEATRE & EDUCATION**, Theatre Department, Arizona State University, Box 872002, Tempe AZ 85287-2002. (480)965-6064. Fax: (480)965-5351. E-mail: aate.info@asu.edu. Website: www.aate.com. Administrative Director: Christy M. Taylor. Purpose of organization: to promote standards of excellence in theatre and drama education by providing the artist and educator with a network of resources and support, a base for advocacy, and access to programs and projects that focus on the importance of drama in the human experience. Membership cost: $90 annually for individual in US and Canada, $120 annually for organization, $55 annually for students, $65 annually for retired people; add $20 outside Canada and US. Annual conference. Newsletter published quarterly (on website only); must be member to subscribe. Contests held for unpublished play reading project and annual awards for best play. Awards plaque and stickers for published playbooks. Publishes list of unpublished plays deemed worthy of performance in newsletter and press release and staged readings at conference.

N **ARIZONA AUTHORS ASSOCIATION**, P.O. Box 87857, Phoenix AZ 85080-7857. Website: home.rmci .net/vijayaschartz/azauthors.htm. President: Vijaya Schartz. Purpose of organization: to offer professional, educational and social opportunities to writers and authors, and serve as a network. Members must be authors, writers working toward publication, agents, publishers, publicists, printers, etc. Membership cost: $45/year writers; $30/year students; $60/year other professionals in publishing industry. Holds regular workshops and meetings. Publishes bimonthly newsletter and Arizona Literary Magazine. Sponsors Annual Literary Contest in poetry, essays, short stories, novels, with cash prizes and awards bestowed at a public banquet in Phoenix. Winning entries are also published in the Arizona Literary Magazine. Send SASE for guidelines.

N **ASSITEJ/USA**, % Steve Bianchi, 724 Second Ave. S., Nashville TN 37210. (615)254-5719. Fax: (615)254-3255. E-mail: usassitej@aol.com. Website: www.assitej-usa.org. Editor, *TYA Today*: Katherine Krzys. Purpose of organization: to promote theater for children and young people by linking professional theaters and artists together; sponsoring national, international and regional conferences and providing publications and information. Also serves as US Center for International Association of Theatre for Children and Young People. Holds conference: One Theatre World 2000. Join producers, educators and theater artists from every part of America to celebrate the turn of the century by seeing what is best in our national fields, and challenging ourselves to do better. May 31-June 4, 2000. Different levels of membership include: organizations, individuals, students, retirees, libraries. *TYA Today* includes original articles, reviews and works of criticism and theory, all of interest to theater practitioners (included with membership). Sponsors workshops or conferences. Publishes journal that focuses on information on field in US and abroad.

[N] THE AUTHORS GUILD, 29th Floor, 330 W. 42nd St., New York NY 10036-6902. (212)563-5904. Fax: (212)564-8363. E-mail: staff@authorsguild.org. Website: www.authorsguild.org. Executive Director: Paul Aiken. Purpose of organization: to offer services and materials intended to help authors with the business and legal aspects of their work, including contract problems, copyright matters, freedom of expression and taxation. Guild has 7,000 members. Qualifications for membership: Must be book author published by an established American publisher within 7 years or any author who has had 3 works (fiction or nonfiction) published by a magazine or magazines of general circulation in the last 18 months. Associate membership also available. Annual dues: $90. Different levels of membership include: associate membership with all rights except voting available to an author who has a firm contract offer or is currently negotiating a royalty contract from an established American publisher. "The Guild offers free contract reviews to its members. The Guild conducts several symposia each year at which experts provide information, offer advice and answer questions on subjects of interest and concern to authors. Typical subjects have been the rights of privacy and publicity, libel, wills and estates, taxation, copyright, editors and editing, the art of interviewing, standards of criticism and book reviewing. Transcripts of these symposia are published and circulated to members. The *Authors Guild Bulletin*, a quarterly journal, contains articles on matters of interest to writers, reports of Guild activities, contract surveys, advice on problem clauses in contracts, transcripts of Guild and League symposia and information on a variety of professional topics. Subscription included in the cost of the annual dues."

LEWIS CARROLL SOCIETY OF NORTH AMERICA, 18 Fitzharding Place, Owingsmills MD 21117. (410)356-5110. E-mail: eluchin@erols.com. Website: www.lewiscarroll.org/carroll.html. Secretary: Ellie Luchinsky. "We are an organization of Carroll admirers of all ages and interests and a center for Carroll studies." Qualifications for membership: "An interest in Lewis Carroll and a simple love for Alice (or even the Snark)." Membership cost: $20/year. There is also a contributing membership of $50. Publishes a quarterly newsletter.

THE CHILDREN'S BOOK COUNCIL, INC., 568 Broadway, New York NY 10012. (212)966-1990. Website: www.cbcbooks.org. Purpose of organization: "A nonprofit trade association of children's and young adult publishers, CBC promotes the enjoyment of books for children and young adults and works with national and international organizations to that end. The CBC has sponsored National Children's Book Week since 1945." Qualifications for membership: US trade publishers and packagers of children's and young adult books and related literary materials are eligible for membership. Membership cost: "Individuals wishing to receive mailings from the CBC (our semi-annual newsletter *CBC Features*—and our materials brochures) may be placed on our mailing list for a one-time-only fee of $60. Publishers wishing to join should contact the CBC for dues information." Sponsors workshops and seminars. Publishes a newsletter with articles about children's books and publishing and listings of free or inexpensive materials available from member publishers. Sells reading encouragement graphics and informational materials suitable for libraries, teachers, booksellers, parents, and others working with children.

[✓] FLORIDA FREELANCE WRITERS ASSOCIATION, Cassell Network of Writers, P.O. Box A, North Stratford NH 03590. (603)922-8338. Fax: (603)922-8339. E-mail: danakcnw@ncia.net. Website: www.writers-editors.com. Executive Director: Dana K. Cassell. Purpose of organization: To act as a link between Florida writers and buyers of the written word; to help writers run more effective communications businesses. Qualifications for membership: "None—we provide a variety of services and information, some for beginners and some for established pros." Membership cost: $90/year. Publishes a newsletter focusing on market news, business news, how-to tips for the serious writer. Non-member subscription: $39—does not include Florida section—includes national edition only. Annual *Directory of Florida Markets* included in FFWA newsletter section. Publishes annual *Guide to CNW/Florida Writers*, which is distributed to editors around the country. Sponsors contest: annual deadline March 15. Guidelines available fall of each year. Categories: juvenile, adult nonfiction, adult fiction and poetry. Awards include cash for top prizes, certificate for others. Contest open to non-members.

**FOR EXPLANATIONS OF THESE SYMBOLS,
SEE THE INSIDE FRONT AND BACK COVERS OF THIS BOOK**

☑ **GRAPHIC ARTISTS GUILD**, 90 John St., Suite 403, New York NY 10038. (212)791-3400. Fax: (212)791-0333. E-mail: execdir@gag.org. Website: www.gag.org/. Executive Director: Paul Basistà, CAE. Purpose of organization: "to promote and protect the economic interests of member artists. It is committed to improving conditions for all creators of graphic arts and raising standards for the entire industry." Qualification for full membership: 50% of income derived from artwork. Associate members include those in allied fields, students and retirees. Initiation fee: $25. Full memberships $120, $165, $215, $270; student membership $55/year. Associate membership $115/year. Publishes *Graphic Artists Guild Handbook, Pricing and Ethical Guidelines* and quarterly *Guild News* (free to members, $12 to non-members). "The Guild is an egalitarian union that embraces all creators of graphics arts intended for presentation as originals or reproductions at all levels of skill and expertise. The long-range goals of the Guild are: to educate graphic artists and their clients about ethical and fair business practices; to educate graphic artists about emerging trends and technologies impacting the industry; to offer programs and services that anticipate and respond to the needs of our members, helping them prosper and enhancing their health and security, to advocate for the interests of our members in the legislative, judicial and regulatory arenas; to assure that our members are recognized financially and professionally for the value they provide; to be responsible stewards for our members by building an organization that works efficiently on their behalf."

THE INTERNATIONAL WOMEN'S WRITING GUILD, P.O. Box 810, Gracie Station, New York NY 10028. (212)737-7536. Executive Director and Founder: Hannelore Hahn. IWWG is "a network for the personal and professional empowerment of women through writing." Qualifications: open to any woman connected to the written word regardless of professional portfolio. Membership cost: $35 annually; $45 annually for foreign members. "IWWG sponsors several annual conferences a year in all areas of the US. The major conference is held in August of each year at Skidmore College in Saratoga Springs NY. It is a week-long conference attracting close to 500 women internationally." Also publishes a 32-page newsletter, *Network*, 6 times/year; offers health insurance at group rates, referrals to literary agents.

JEWISH PUBLICATION SOCIETY, 1930 Chestnut St., Philadelphia PA 19103-4599. (215)564-5925. Editor-in-Chief: Dr. Ellen Frankel. Children's Editor: Bruce Black. Purpose of organization: "To publish quality Jewish books and to promote Jewish culture and education. We are a non-denominational, nonprofit religious publisher. Our children's list specializes in fiction and nonfiction with substantial Jewish content for pre-school through young adult readers." Qualifications for membership: "One must purchase a membership of at least $50, which entitles the member to a 20% discount off every book purchase. Our membership is nondiscriminatory on the basis of religion, ethnic affiliation, race or any other criteria." "*The JPS Bookmark* reports on JPS Publications; activities of members, authors and trustees; JPS projects and goals; JPS history; children's books and activities." All members receive *The Bookmark* with their membership.

☑ **LEAGUE OF CANADIAN POETS**, 54 Wolseley St., 3rd Floor, Toronto, Ontario M5T 1A5 Canada. (416)504-1657. Fax: (416)504-0096. Executive Director: Edita Petrauskaite. President: Roger Nash. Inquiries to Program Manager: Sandra Drzewiecki. The L.C.P. is a national organization of published Canadian poets. Our constitutional objectives are to advance poetry in Canada and to promote the professional interests of the members. Qualifications for membership: full—publication of at least 1 book of poetry by a professional publisher; associate membership—an active interest in poetry, demonstrated by several magazine/periodical publication credits, student—an active interest in poetry, 12 sample poems required; supporting—any friend of poetry. Membership fees: full—$175/year, associate—$60, student—$30, supporting—$100. Holds an Annual General Meeting every spring; some events open to nonmembers. "We also organize reading programs in schools and public venues. We publish a newsletter which includes information on poetry/poetics in Canada and beyond. Also publish the books *Poetry Markets for Canadians*; *Who's Who in the League of Canadian Poets*; *Poets in the Classroom* (teaching guide) and its accompanying anthology of Canadian poetry *Vintage*; plus a series of cassettes. We sponsor a National Poetry Contest, open to Canadians living here and abroad." Rules: Unpublished poems of any style/subject, under 75 lines, typed, with name/address on separate sheet. $6 entry fee (includes GST) per poem. $1,000-1st prize, $750-2nd, $500-3rd; plus best 50 published in an anthology. Inquire with SASE. Contest open to Canadian nonmembers. Sponsors an annual chapbook ms contest. Organizes 2 annual awards: The Gerald Lampert Memorial Award for the best first book of poetry published in Canada in the preceding year and The Pat Lowther Memorial Award for the best book of poetry by a Canadian woman published in the preceding year. Deadline for poetry contest is November 1 each year, for awards December 31. Send SASE for more details. Sponsors youth poetry competition. Deadline: December 1 of each year. Send SASE for details.

☑ **THE NATIONAL LEAGUE OF AMERICAN PEN WOMEN**, 1300 17th St. N.W., Washington D.C. 20036-1973. (202)785-1997. Fax: (202)452-6868. E-mail: nlapw1@juno.com. Website: members.aol.com/penwomen/pen.htm. National President: Judith E. LaFourest. Purpose of organization: to promote professional work in art, letters, and music since 1897. Qualifications for membership: An applicant must show "proof of sale" in each chosen category—art, letters, and music. Membership cost: $40 ($10 processing fee and $30 National dues); Annual fees—$30 plus Branch/State dues. Different levels of membership include: Active, Associate, International Affiliate, Members-at-Large, Honorary Members (in one or more of the following classifications: Art, Letters, and Music). Holds workshops/conferences. Publishes magazine 6 times a year titled *The Pen Woman*.

Nonmember subscription $18 per year. Sponsors various contests in areas of Art, Letters, and Music. Awards made at Biennial Convention. Biannual scholarships awarded to non-Pen Women for mature women. Awards include cash prizes—up to $1,000. Specialized contests open to non-members.

N: NATIONAL WRITERS UNION, 113 University Place, 6th Floor, New York NY 10003. (212)254-0279. **Open to students.** Purpose of organization: Advocacy for freelance writers. Qualifications for membership: "Membership in the NWU is open to all qualified writers, and no one shall be barred or in any manner prejudiced within the Union on account of race, age, sex, sexual preference, disability, national origin, religion or ideology. You are eligible for membership if you have published a book, a play, three articles, five poems, one short story or an equivalent amount of newsletter, publicity, technical, commercial, government or institutional copy. You are also eligible for membership if you have written an equal amount of unpublished material and you are actively writing and attempting to publish your work." Membership cost: annual writing income under $5,000—$90/year; annual writing income $5,000-25,000—$145/year; annual writing income over $25,000—$195/year. Holds workshops throughout the country. Offers national union newsletter quarterly, *American Writer*, issues related to freelance writing and to union organization for members.

PEN AMERICAN CENTER, 568 Broadway, New York NY 10012. (212)334-1660. Fax: (212)334-2181. E-mail: jm@pen.org. Purpose of organization: "To foster understanding among men and women of letters in all countries. International PEN is the only worldwide organization of writers and the chief voice of the literary community. Members of PEN work for freedom of expression wherever it has been endangered." Qualifications for membership: "The standard qualification for a writer to join PEN is that he or she must have published, in the United States, two or more books of a literary character, or one book generally acclaimed to be of exceptional distinction. Editors who have demonstrated commitment to excellence in their profession (generally construed as five years' service in book editing), translators who have published at least two book-length literary translations, and playwrights whose works have been professionally produced, are eligible for membership." An application form is available upon request from PEN Headquarters in New York. Candidates for membership should be nominated by 2 current members of PEN. Inquiries about membership should be directed to the PEN Membership Committee. Friends of PEN is also open to writers who may not yet meet the general PEN membership requirements. PEN sponsors public events at PEN Headquarters in New York, and at the branch offices in Boston, Chicago, New Orleans, San Francisco and Portland, Oregon. They include tributes by contemporary writers to classic American writers, dialogues with visiting foreign writers, symposia that bring public attention to problems of censorship and that address current issues of writing in the United States, and readings that introduce beginning writers to the public. PEN's wide variety of literary programming reflects current literary interests and provides informal occasions for writers to meet each other and to welcome those with an interest in literature. Events are all open to the public and are usually free of charge. The Children's Book Authors' Committee sponsors biannual public events focusing on the art of writing for children and young adults and on the diversity of literature for juvenile readers. The PEN/Norma Klein Award was established in 1991 to honor an emerging children's book author. The bimonthly *PEN Newsletter* covers PEN activities, features interviews with international literary figures, transcripts of PEN literary symposia, reports on issues vital to the literary community. All PEN publications are available by mail order directly from PEN American Center. Individuals must enclose check or money order with their order. Subscription: $8 for 6 issues; sample issue $2. Pamphlets and brochures all free upon request. Sponsors several competitions per year. Monetary awards range from $700-7,500.

PUPPETEERS OF AMERICA, INC., #5 Cricklewood Path, Pasadena CA 91107. (818)797-5748. Membership Officer: Gayle Schluter. Purpose of organization: to promote the art of puppetry. Qualifications for membership: interest in the art form. Membership cost: single adult, $40; youth member, $25; retiree, $25 (65 years of age); family, $60; couple, $50. Membership includes a bimonthly newsletter. Sponsors workshops/conferences. Publishes newsletter. *The Puppetry Journal* provides news about puppeteers, puppet theaters, exhibitions, touring companies, technical tips, new products, new books, films, television, and events sponsored by the Chartered Guilds in each of the 8 P of A regions. Subscription: $35 (libraries only).

✓ SOCIETY OF CHILDREN'S BOOK WRITERS AND ILLUSTRATORS, 8271 Beverly Blvd., Los Angeles CA 90048. (323)782-1010. E-mail: info@scbwi.org (autoresponse). Website: www.scbwi.org. President: Stephen Mooser. Executive Director: Lin Oliver. Chairperson, Board of Directors: Sue Alexander. Purpose of organization: to assist writers and illustrators working or interested in the field. Qualifications for membership: an interest in children's literature and illustration. Membership cost: $50/year. Plus one time $10 initiation fee. Different levels of membership include: full membership—published authors/illustrators; associate membership—unpublished writers/illustrators. Holds 100 events (workshops/conferences) around the country each year. Open to nonmembers. Publishes a newsletter focusing on writing and illustrating children's books. Sponsors grants for writers and illustrators who are members.

✓ SOCIETY OF ILLUSTRATORS, 128 E. 63rd St., New York NY 10021-7303. (212)838-2560. Fax: (212)838-2561. Website: www.societyillustrators.org. Director: Terrence Brown. Purpose of organization: to promote interest in the art of illustration for working professional illustrators and those in associated fields. Membership cost: Initiation fee—$250. Annual dues for non-resident members (those living more than 125 air miles

insider report

Creating a unified voice for quality children's literature

Lin Oliver has been producing quality family movies, most of them based on children's books, for over 20 years. But she began her career as a writer of educational children's books, and out of her own personal need for a conference to train young writers, co-founded the Society of Children's Book Writers and Illustrators in 1971. "I could not have predicted the enormous generosity of the membership," says Oliver.

As the executive director, she personally produces the annual national conference, and together with the president Stephen Mooser, oversees the publication of the SCBWI bimonthly bulletin, supervises the national office and works with the regional advisors to plan and support regional activities. Here she discusses the past, present and future of SCBWI.

Lin Oliver

How has SCBWI changed over the years?
Everybody who is a writer, an illustrator, an agent or an editor of children's books has joined SCBWI. We started out with a handful of members, but with almost 12,000 members today, we have become the largest writer's organization in the country, with an active professional membership. At our national conference, for instance, we have nightly forums on book promotion, on building a career, on establishing a website, all for people who are already published. SCBWI has become a regional organization, in addition to being a national organization. We now have regional advisors in every state and several in many of the larger states. We have chapters in France, South America and Okinawa. So we have grown not only in size but in coverage. We delegate to regions the responsibility of organizing local critique groups and conferences; we sponsor 25 to 30 conferences a year throughout the country, in addition to the national conference. We could not have predicted this grass roots movement which makes it easier for our membership to participate. My greatest joy in having begun SCBWI is to see the network of friends that has evolved over the years. Our goal has always been to build a community. I think we have done that.

What specifically does SCBWI offer new writers?
One thing we have tried to do is improve the quality of our members' submissions to publishing houses. When people join SCBWI, they get *The SCBWI Publications Guide to Writing and Illustrating for Children*, including market surveys of book, magazine and education publishers; an explanation of contracts; a listing of agents; and a guide to magazine formatting. We don't think we can teach talent, of course, but we can teach professionalism.

What would you do differently if you were starting SCBWI today?

We began as an organization just of writers. But when you work in the children's book field, illustrators are half the equation. So now I would set out to include artists, along with people who create for children in other media. We are known as book writers, but in fact many of our members work in television, in film, in live theater, on the Internet, and in all kinds of electronic publishing. The organization is for everybody who creates literary material for children.

What are SCBWI's goals for the future?

We have both philosophical and operational goals. Philosophically, we want the organization to become the unified voice for quality children's literature in literacy, free speech and library advocacy. We are trying to create white papers in such areas as the relationship between books and other entertainments for children. We would like to be able to present these views in the political and educational arenas for politicians, teachers, librarians and parents. That's the first goal.

Operationally, we would like to create programs with archival significance. For instance, we are talking about establishing a museum to house exhibits, both stationary and traveling, devoted to the creation of children's books. The museum would archive material from our members. It would include a gallery of new artists' works and historical retrospectives of children's books over the ages.

Both those goals fall into the category of statesmanship that we couldn't afford to do when we were struggling to grow and establish ourselves. But now that we are who we are, an organization that comprises virtually everybody who writes, illustrates, agents, edits or cares about children's books, I think we have to assume an activist role in issues that concern children, and in documenting and celebrating children's books in our culture.

How do you choose speakers for each SCBWI national conference?

They have to be what we consider writers or illustrators of quality children's books. They have to be willing to prepare, because when they come to the conference they're doing something different than they do in their "sub-careers" as speakers to schools. If you are talking to a school or a library, it's one thing. If you are talking to a group of your peers, you have to think about your work in a different way. So it's important to me that people who come on the faculty are willing to think hard about their work and come with something other than their usual canned presentation. It helps if someone is a good speaker. Usually I will check around. But I'm not looking for entertainers—I'm looking for people who can share. And that's the final criteria. They have to be willing to give of themselves. The editors who come have to be willing to look at manuscripts; the authors and the illustrators have to be willing to give individual consultations.

You've listened to hundreds of writers and illustrators speak at the SCBWI conferences. What makes some of them stand out?

One thing I've observed, if I can generalize about the writers and illustrators who have been with us over the years, is that they are individualistic. I imagine most creative people are, but the children's field tends to attract people who are not your run-of-the-mill normal adults. They are often oddballs. So you see this parade of wonderful eccentrics come through, and you can hear it when they speak. They reach kids who feel the same way. All children feel powerless in some way, of course. They feel they don't quite fit in, that there is something different about them. That's because they are new in the world and have nothing to compare themselves to. So when you hear the grownup version of these children, which is what the best of our writers and artists are—people who are in touch with their childhood and can express that to their audience—you hear an unmistakable quality of voice.

How do you think writers and illustrators grow?
I think they grow by holding to a vision, by not being corrupted by material concerns or concerns in the marketplace. It's like an onion. You peel off layer after layer as you continue to dig inside yourself. You reach different levels of awareness, and you bring that to your work without consideration of what you've done before or how people will judge you.

How can members best take advantage of SCBWI?
The most important thing they can do is to participate. If they attend the conferences, contribute to the newsletters, participate in the critique groups, if they make friends and continue to stay in touch with their friends, there is no way they can't benefit. It's like everything else in life. The more you put in, the more you get back.
—*Anna Olswanger*

from SI's headquarters) are $277. Dues for Resident Artist Members are $460 per year; Resident Associate Members $535. Different levels of membership: *Artist Members* "shall include those who make illustration their profession" and through which they earn at least 60% of their income. *Associate Members* are "those who earn their living in the arts or who have made a substantial contribution to the art of illustration." This includes art directors, art buyers, creative supervisors, instructors, publishers and like categories. "All candidates for membership are admitted by the proposal of one active member and sponsorship of four additional members. The candidate must complete and sign the application form which requires a brief biography, a listing of schools attended, other training and a résumé of his or her professional career." Candidates for *Artist* membership, in addition to the above requirements, must submit examples of their work. Sponsors "The Annual of American Illustration." Awards include gold and silver medals. Open to nonmembers. Deadline: October 1. Sponsors "The Original Art: The Best of Children's Book Illustration." Deadline: mid-September. Call for details.

SOCIETY OF MIDLAND AUTHORS, % SMA, P.O. 10419, Chicago IL 60610-0419. E-mail: rclwriter @aol.com. Website: www.midlandauthors.com. Purpose of organization: create closer association among writers of the Middle West; stimulate creative literary effort; maintain collection of members' works; encourage interest in reading and literature by cooperating with other educational and cultural agencies. Qualifications for membership: author or co-author of a book demonstrating literary style and published by a recognized publisher and be identified through residence with Illinois, Indiana, Iowa, Kansas, Michigan, Minnesota, Missouri, Nebraska, North Dakota, Ohio, South Dakota or Wisconsin. Membership cost: $25/year dues. Different levels of membership include: regular—published book authors; associate, nonvoting—not published as above but having some connection with literature, such as librarians, teachers, publishers and editors. Program meetings at Cliff Dwellers, 200 S. Michigan Ave., Borg-Warner Bldg. Chicago, held 5 times a year, featuring authors, publishers, editors or the like individually or on panels. Usually second Tuesday of October, November, February, March and April. Also holds annual awards dinner at Cliff Dwellers, 200 S. Michigan Ave., Chicago, in May. Publishes a newsletter focusing on news of members and general items of interest to writers. Non-member subscription: $5. Sponsors contests. "Annual awards in six categories, given at annual dinner in May. Monetary awards for books published which premiered professionally in previous calendar year. Send SASE to contact person for details." Categories include adult fiction, adult nonfiction, juvenile fiction, juvenile nonfiction, poetry, biography. No picture books. Contest open to non-members. Deadline for contest: January 30.

VOLUNTEER LAWYERS FOR THE ARTS, 1 E. 53rd St., 6th Floor, New York NY 10022-4201. (212)319-2787 (administration), ext. 10 (the Art Law Line). Fax: (212)752-6575. E-mail: vlany@bway.net. Executive Director: Amy Schwartzman. Purpose of organization: Volunteer Lawyers for the Arts is dedicated to providing free arts-related legal assistance to low-income artists and not-for-profit arts organizations in all creative fields. Over 800 attorneys in the New York area donate their time through VLA to artists and arts organizations unable to afford legal counsel. There is no membership required for our services. Everyone is welcome to use VLA's Art Law Line, a legal hotline for any artist or arts organization needing quick answers to arts-related questions. VLA also provides clinics, seminars and publications designed to educate artists on legal issues which affect their careers. Membership is through donations and is not required to use our services. Members receive discounts on publications and seminars as well as other benefits. Some of the many publications we carry are *All You Need to Know About the Music Business*; *Business and Legal Forms for Fine Artists, Photographers & Authors & Self-Publishers*; *Contracts for the Film & TV Industry*, plus many more. Please call Steven Malmberg, publications coordinator at ext. 10 to order. VLA's Seminars include "Not-for-Profit Incorporation and Tax Exemption Seminar" and "Copyright Basics for all Seminars."

☑ **WESTERN WRITERS OF AMERICA, INC.**, 1012 Fair St., Franklin TN 37064-2718. (615)791-1444. Fax: (615)791-1444. E-mail: candywwa@aol.com or tncrutch@aol.com. Website: www.imt.net/~gedison/wwahome.html or www.imt.net/~gedison/wwa.html. Secretary/Treasurer: James A. Crutchfield. **Open to students.** Purpose of organization: to further all types of literature that pertains to the American West. Membership requirements: must be a *published* author of Western material. Membership cost: $75/year ($90 foreign). Different levels of membership include: Active and Associate—the two vary upon number of books published. Holds annual conference. The 2000 conference will be held in Kerrville, TX. Publishes bimonthly magazine focusing on market trends, book reviews, news of members, etc. Non-members may subscribe for $30 ($40 foreign). Sponsors contests. Spur awards given annually for a variety of types of writing. Awards include plaque, certificate, publicity. Contest open to nonmembers.

WRITERS CONNECTION, P.O. Box 24770, San Jose CA 95154-4770. (408)445-3600. Fax: (408)445-3609. Sponsors annual Selling to Hollywood scriptwriting conference in the Los Angeles area each August.

⚑ **WRITERS' FEDERATION OF NEW BRUNSWICK**, Box 37, Station A, 404 Queen St., Fredericton, New Brunswick E3B 4Y2 Canada. (506)459-7228. E-mail: aa821@fan.nb.ca. Website: www.sjfn.nb.ca/communi ty_hall/W/Writers_FEDERATION_NB/index.htm. Project Coordinator: Anna Mae Snider. Purpose of organization: "to promote the work of New Brunswick writers and to help them at all stages of their development." Qualifications for membership: interest in writing. Membership cost: $30, basic annual membership; $20, student/unemployed; $40, family membership; $50, institutional membership; $100, sustaining member; $250, patron; and $1,000, lifetime member. Holds workshops/conferences. Publishes a newsletter with articles concerning the craft of writing, member news, contests, markets, workshops and conference listings. Sponsors annual literary competition (for New Brunswick residents). Categories: fiction, nonfiction, poetry, children's literature—3 prizes per category of $150, $75, $50; Alfred Bailey Prize of $400 for poetry ms; The Richards Prize of $400 for short novel, collection of short stories or section of long novel; The Sheree Fitch Prize for writing by young people (14-18 years of age). Contest open to nonmembers (residents of New Brunswich only).

☑ ⚑ **WRITERS GUILD OF ALBERTA**, 11759 Groat Rd., 3rd Floor, Percy Page Centre, Edmonton, Alberta T5M 3K6 Canada. (780)422-8174. Fax: (780)422-2663. E-mail: wga@oanet.com. Website: www.writers guild.ab.ca. Executive Director: Mr. Miki Andrejevic. Purpose of organization: to provide meeting ground and collective voice for the writers in Alberta. Membership cost: $60/year; $20 for seniors/students. Holds workshops/conferences. Publishes a newsletter focusing on markets, competitions, contemporary issues related to the literary arts (writing, publishing, censorship, royalties etc.). Nonmembers may subscribe to newsletter. Subscription cost: $60/year. Sponsors annual literary awards program in 7 categories (novel, nonfiction, short fiction, children's literature, poetry, drama, best first book). Awards include $500, leather-bound book, promotion and publicity. Open to nonmembers.

VISIT THE WRITER'S DIGEST WEBSITE at www.writersdigest.com for hot new markets, daily market updates, writers' guidelines and much more.

Conferences & Workshops

Writers and illustrators eager to expand their knowledge of the children's publishing industry should consider attending one of the many conferences and workshops held each year. Whether you're a novice or seasoned professional, conferences and workshops are great places to pick up information on a variety of topics and network with experts in the publishing industry, as well as your peers.

Listings in this section provide details about what conference and workshop courses are offered, where and when they are held, and the costs. Some of the national writing and art organizations also offer regional workshops throughout the year. Write or call for information.

Writers can find listings of more than 500 conferences (searchable by type, location and date) at The Writer's Digest/Shaw Guides Directory to Writers' Conferences, Seminars and Workshops—www.writersdigest.com/conferences/index/htm.

Members of the Society of Children's Book Writers and Illustrators can find information on conferences in national and local SCBWI newsletters. Nonmembers may attend SCBWI events as well. SCBWI conferences are listed in the beginning of this section under a separate subheading. For information on SCBWI's annual national conferences, contact them at (323)782-1010 or check their website for a complete calendar of national and regional events (www.scbwi.org).

Information on conferences listed in the previous edition but not this edition of *Children's Writer's & Illustrator's Market* may be found in the General Index.

SCBWI Conferences

The Society of Children's Book Writers and Illustrators (SCBWI) is an international organization with about 12,000 members. SCBWI offers an array of regional events that can be attended by both members and nonmembers. Listings of regional events follow. For more information, contact the conference coordinators listed or visit SCBWI's website, www.scbwi.org for a complete calendar of events. SCBWI members will also find event information listed in the bimonthly SCBWI *Bulletin*, free with membership. In addition to the regional events, SCBWI offers two national conferences—one in August in Los Angeles, the other in February in New York City. For information about conferences or membership in SCBWI, check www.scbwi.org or contact the SCBWI offices: 8271 Beverly Blvd., Los Angeles CA 90048, (323)782-1010.

N̄ SCBWI—ARIZONA; RETREAT, P.O. Box 11834, Prescott AZ 86304. (520)443-5481. Fax: (520)717-2426. E-mail: karylbob@juno.com. Regional Advisor: Karyl Dahlbom. Writer workshops geared toward intermediate, advanced and professional levels. Illustrator workshops geared toward intermediate level. **Open to students.** Offers hands-on critique sessions of mss in progress (art as well as text). Annual workshop. Workshop held the end of September or early October. Registration limited to 35. The facility is a camp—very basic. Cost of workshop: $200; includes 2 nights lodging and 4 meals. Deposits are accepted to reserve a space beginning in March.

N̄ SCBWI—ARIZONA; WRITERS DAY, 735 W. Pine St., Tucson AZ 85704. (520)544-2650. E-mail: desertmorn@aol.com. Regional Advisor: Dawn Dixon. Writer and illustrator workshops geared toward all levels. **Open to students.** Four editors are invited to speak to book and illustration needs. Usually includes 2-3 book publishers, a magazine editor, a special interest publisher. Q&A sessions included. Annual workshop. Usually has 75-85 participants. No limit on registration. Cost of workshop: $80-90. Information available on SCBWI website; registration begins in January.

✔ SCBWI—CAROLINAS ANNUAL FALL CONFERENCE, 104 Barnhill Place, Chapel Hill NC 27514-9224. (919)967-2452. Fax: (919)929-6643. E-mail: earl-frandavis@prodigy.net. Website: www.SCBWI.org. Contact: Frances A. Davis. **Open to students.** Writer and illustrator conference geared toward beginner, intermediate, advanced and professional levels. Sessions include: Marketing Your Children's Manuscript; Writing for the Middle Grade Child; The Ins and Outs of Illustration; Exploration of the Changing Face of Nonfiction; Finding the Magic Words We Love, Developing Skills; Writing for Young Adults; Picture Books—Editorial Thoughts. Annual conference held September or October, 2000. Cost of conference is $60 for SCBWI members; $65 for NCWN members; $70 for non-members before October 1st. Critiques for writing. Portfolios will be displayed, not critiqued. Write for more information.

SCBWI—FLORIDA REGION, 2158 Portland Ave., Wellington FL 33414. (561)798-4824. E-mail: barcafer@ aol.com. Florida Regional Advisor: Barbara Casey. Writer and illustrator workshops geared toward beginner, intermediate, advanced and professional levels. **Open to students.** Subjects to be announced. Annual workshop. Workshop held second Saturday of September in the meeting rooms of the Palm Springs Public Library, 217 Cypress Lane, Palm Springs FL. Registration limited to 100/class. Cost of workshop: $50 for members, $55 for non-members. Special rates are offered through the West Palm Beach Airport Hilton Hotel for those attending the conference who wish to spend the night. Write for more information.

☑ **SCBWI—HOUSTON**, 17522 Brushy River Court, Houston TX 77095. (281)304-9502. Fax: (281)256-3442. E-mail: marydwade@aol.com. Regional Advisor: Mary Wade. Writer and illustrator workshops geared toward all levels. **Open to students.** Annual conference. Conference covers picture books, text and illustration, middle grade novels and nonfiction. Conference and workshops held February, 2000. Cost of workshop: $75; includes lunch; critiques $20 extra. Contact Mary Wade for more information.

N: SCBWI—INDIANA; CONFERENCE AT INDIANA STATE UNIVERSITY, 934 Fayette St., Indianapolis IN 46202. (317)262-9823. E-mail: s_murray@iquest.net. Regional Advisor: Sara Murray-Plumer. Writer workshops geared to all levels. **Open to students.** Workshop held July 28-30, 2000. Cost and conference program TBA; check SCBWI website for information.

◀ **N: SCBWI—INDIANA; RECEPTION FOR JANE YOLEN**, 934 Fayette St., Indianapolis IN 46202. (317)262-9823. E-mail: s_murray@iquest.net. Regional Advisor: Sara Murray-Plumer. Writer workshops geared toward all levels. **Open to students.** Workshop held April 30, 2000. Presentation by Jane Yolen with time for Q&A. Cost and location TBA; check SCBWI website for information.

☑ **SCBWI—IOWA CONFERENCE**, 4408 Topaz Ave. NW, Cedar Rapids IA 52405. (319)390-5780. Iowa SCBWI Regional Advisor: Dori Butler. Writer workshops geared toward all levels. "Usually speakers include one to two acquiring book editors who discuss the needs of their publishing house and manuscripts that caught their attention. Also, we usually have several published Iowa authors discussing specific genres and/or topics like promotion, marketing, school visits, etc." Annual conference. Iowa has 1 or 2 conferences a year, usually in May and October. Cost of conference: usually about $60; less for SCSWI members. Individual critique costs $30 extra. Work must be submitted in advance.

✓ **N: SCBWI—MICHIGAN ANNUAL WORKING WRITER'S RETREAT**, 446 Kensington Rd., East Lansing MI 48823. E-mail: celenzaa@pilot.msu.edu. Retreat Chairs: Anna Celenza and Kara Marsee. Writer and illustrator workshops geared toward intermediate and advanced levels. Program focus: the craft of writing. Features peer facilitated critique groups, creativity, motivation and professional issues. Retreat held October 6-8, 2000 in Gull Lake (near Battle Creek and Kalamazoo). Registration limited. Cost of retreat: TBA but approximately $200 to members; includes meals, lodging, linens and tuition. Write or e-mail for additional information.

N: SCBWI—MICHIGAN EDITOR AND ART DIRECTOR DAY, 1152 Stellma Ln., Rochester Hills MI 48309. Fax: (248)651-6489. E-mail: bsz@flash.net. Event Chairs: Brenda Yee and Debbie Stewart. Writer and illustrator workshops geared toward beginner One day event in Detroit featuring two editors and two art directors from major publishing houses. Topics include what editors and art directors look for; ms/portfolio critiques and a juried show for illustrators. Registration fee TBA but approximately $75, including lunch. Additional $35 charge for ms/portfolio critiques. Write or e-mail for additional information.

N: SCBWI—MIDSOUTH CONFERENCE, 2802 Acklen Ave., Nashville TN 37212. (615)297-5818. E-mail: scbwi.midsouth@juno.com. Regional Advisor: Tracy Barrett. Writer workshops geared toward all levels. Illustrator workshops geared toward beginner and intermediate levels. **Open to students.** Previous workshop topics have included Editor's Market Report, Writing the Biographical Novel, Screenwriting, Successful Self-Promotion, Introduction to Magazine Illustration. There are also opportunities for ms and portfolio critiques and critique groups can be formed at the conference. Workshop held April 15, 2000. Cost of workshop: $60 SCBWI members; $65 nonmembers; ms critiques extra. Manuscripts for critique must be typed, double-spaced, and submitted in advance with payment. Portfolios are brought to the conference, but reservations for critique time and payment must be made in advance.

SCBWI—NEW YORK; CONFERENCE FOR CHILDREN'S BOOK ILLUSTRATORS & AUTHOR/ ILLUSTRATORS, 32 Hillside Ave., Morisey NY 10952. (914)356-7273. Conference Chair: Frieda Gates. Illustrator conference. Held May 2000. Registration limited to 125; 80 portfolios will be accepted for review. Cost of conference: with portfolio—$85, members, $95 others; without portfolio—$55 members, $65 others; $50 additional for 30-minute portfolio evaluation; $25 additional for 15-minute book dummy evaluation. "In addition to an exciting program of speakers, this conference provides a unique opportunity for illustrators and author/illustrators to have their portfolios reviewed by scores of art buyers and agents from the publishing and allied industries. Our reputation for exhibiting high-quality work of both new and established children's book illustrators, plus the ease of examining such an abundance of portfolios, has resulted in a large number of productive contacts between buyers and illustrators."

SCBWI—NORTH CENTRAL CALIFORNIA; MARCH IN MODESTO, 8931 Montezuma Rd., James-town CA 95327. (209)984-5556. Fax: (209)984-0636. E-mail: trigar@mlode.com. SCBWI North Central CA Regional Advisor: Tricia Gardella. Writer and illustrator workshops geared toward all levels. **Open to students.** Offers talks on different genres, illustration evaluations and afternoon question breakout sessions. Annual confer-ence. Conference held March 2000. Cost of conference: $50; $55 for nonmembers. Write for more information.

N: SCBWI—OREGON, P.O. Box 336, Noti OR 97461. E-mail: robink@rio.com. Regional Advisor: Robin Koontz. Writer and illustrator workshops and presentations geared toward all levels. "We invite editors, agents, authors, illustrators and others in the business of writing and illustrating for children. They present lectures, workshops and critiques." Annual retreat and conference. Two events per year: Working Writers and Illustrators Retreat: Retreat held in September (3-5 days). Cost of retreat: $200-350 (depending on length); includes double occupancy and all meals; Spring Conference: Held in Tualatin, Oregon (1-day event); includes continental break-fast and lunch. Registration limited to 100 for the conference and 50 for the retreat.

N: SCBWI—SAN DIEGO CHAPTER, WORKSHOP AND CONFERENCE, Society of Children's Book Writers and Illustrators/San Diego Chapter, 16048 Lofty Trail Dr., San Diego CA 92127. Chapter voice mail: (619)230-9342. E-mail: arlene821@aol.com. Conference Chairman: Arlene Bartle. Writer and illustrator workshops geared toward all levels. Topics vary but emphasize writing and illustrating for children. Annual workshop; conference held every other year. Cost of workshop: $35-50. Cost of conference: $65-100. Write or e-mail for more information. "The San Diego chapter holds meetings the second Saturday of each month from September-May at University of San Diego's Harmon Hall, usually 2-4 p.m. Chapter newsletter subscription cost $16/year and includes market updates."

SCBWI—SOUTHERN BREEZE (ALABAMA/GEORGIA/MISSISSIPPI REGION), P.O. Box 26282, Birmingham AL 35260. Fax: (205)979-0274. E-mail: joanbroer@aol.com. Website: hometown.aol.com/southb rez/. Regional Advisor: Joan Broerman. "The fall conference, Writing and Illustrating for Kids, offers more than 20 workshops on craft, from entry level to professional track, picture books to young adult. Annual conference held October 23, 2000. Cost of workshop: $50-60 for SCBWI members; $60-80 for nonmembers; ms critiques and portfolio review available for additional cost. Write for more information (include SASE). "Our spring conference, Springmingle!, is in different parts of the three-state region. Springmingle 2000! will be held in Atlanta, Georgia, March 17-19, 2000." This conference is geared towards intermediate to professional level. Preregistration important for both conferences.

✔ SCBWI—UTAH/IDAHO; SPRING INTO ACTION, 1194 E. 11000 S., Sandy UT 84094. (801)523-6311. E-mail: kimorchid@aol.com. Website: members.aol.com/kimorchid/utahscbw.htm. Utah/Idaho SCBWI Re-gional Advisor: Kim Williams-Justesen. Writer workshops geared toward all levels. Illustrator workshops geared toward beginners and intermediate. **Open to students.** Topics for children's writing and illustration "A Day in the Life of an Illustrator;" "Getting Your Feet Wet;" "Understanding Your Audience;" Local editor's panel; plot and character; effective dialogue. Annual conference. Conference held April 22, 2000. Cost of conference: $45 SCBWI members; $55 nonmembers; includes workshops, registration packet. Write or e-mail for more information.

SCBWI—WASHINGTON STATE, 4037 56th Ave. SW, Seattle WA 98116. (206)932-3157. Regional Advi-sor: D. Bergman. Writer workshops geared toward all levels. **Open to students.** All aspects of writing and illustrating children's books are covered from picture books to YA novels, from contracts to promotion. An editor, art director and published authors and illustrators serve as conference faculty. Annual conference and workshop. Conference held April 22, 2000. Registration limited to about 200. Cost of conference: $55-75; includes registra-tion, morning snack and lunch. The conference is a one-day event held at Seattle Pacific University. Hour to hour and ½ sessions run back-to-back so attendees have 2 or 3 choices. "In this way we can meet the needs of both those at the entry-level and those more advanced."

⬇ SCBWI—WISCONSIN ANNUAL FALL RETREAT, Rt. 1, Box 137, Gays Mills WI 54631. (608)735-4707. Fax: (608)735-4700. E-mail: pfitsch@mwt.net. Co-Regional Advisor: Patricia Pfitsch. Writer workshops geared toward working writers. Some years we offer group critique sessions with faculty and participant participation—each full time participant receives critique from well-known editors, writers and or agents as well as other participants. Other years we offer the opportunity for individual critique. Also talks by faculty on various aspects of writing and selling your work. "We try to have major New York editors, agents and well-known writers on the faculty. The entire retreat is geared *only* to children's book writing; addresses writing skills and marketing of work." Annual workshop. Retreat held October 13-15, 2000, from Friday evening to Sunday afternoon. Registration limited to approximately 60. Cost of workshop: about $250; includes room, board and program. Critique may be extra. "We strive to offer an informal weekend with an award-winning children's writer, an agent or illustrator and an editor from a trade house in New York in attendance." There's usually a waiting list by mid-July. Send SASE for flier.

Other Conferences

Many conferences and workshops included here focus on children's writing or illustrating and related business issues. Others appeal to a broader base of writers or artists, but still provide information that can be useful in creating material for children. Illustrators may be interested in painting and drawing workshops, for example, while writers can learn about techniques and meet editors and agents at general writing conferences. For more information visit the websites listed or contact conference coordinator.

☑ **AMERICAN CHRISTIAN WRITERS CONFERENCE**, P.O. Box 110390, Nashville TN 37222-0390. 1(800)21-WRITE or (615)834-0450. Fax: (615)834-7736. E-mail: regaforder@aol.com. Website: www.ecpa.org/acw. Director: Reg Forder. Writer and illustrator workshops geared toward beginner, intermediate and advanced levels. Classes offered include: fiction, nonfiction, poetry, photography, music, etc. Workshops held in two dozen US cities. Call or write for a complete schedule of conferences. 75 minutes. Maximum class size: 30 (approximate). Cost of conference: $89, 1-day session; $149, 2-day session (discount given if paid 30 days in advance) includes tuition only.

ARKANSAS WRITERS' CONFERENCE, 6817 Gingerbread Lane, Little Rock AR 72204. (501)565-8889. Fax: (501)565-7220. Counselor: Peggy Vining. Writer workshops geared toward beginner, intermediate and advanced levels. **Open to students.** Annual conference. Conference always held the first full weekend in June. "2000 will be our 56th annual conference." Cost of conference: $5/day; includes registration and workshops. Contest fees, lodging and food are not included. Write for more information. Offers 34 different awards for various types of writing, poetry and essay.

☑ **AUSTIN WRITERS' LEAGUE CONFERENCE WORKSHOP SERIES**, 1501 W. Fifth St., Suite E-2, Austin TX 78703. (512)499-8914. Fax: (512)499-0441. E-mail: writersleague.org. Executive Director: Jim Bob McMillan. Writer and illustrator workshops and conferences geared toward all levels for children and adults. Annual conferences. Classes are held during the week and workshops are held on Saturdays during March, April, May, September, October and November. Annual Teddy Children's Book Award of $1,000 presented each spring to book published in previous year. Write for more information. The Austin Writers' League has available audiotapes of past workshop programs.

AUTUMN AUTHORS' AFFAIR XV, 1507 Burnham Ave., Calumet City IL 60409. (708)862-9797. President: Nancy McCann. Writer workshops geared toward beginner, intermediate, advanced levels. **Open to students.** Emphasizes writing for children and young adults. Sessions include children/teen/young adult writing, mysteries, romantic suspense, romance, nonfiction, etc. Annual workshop. Workshops held in October. Cost of workshop: $75 for 1 day, $120 for weekend, includes meals Friday night, Saturday morning and Saturday afternoon; dessert buffet Saturday night and breakfast/brunch Sunday morning. Write for more information.

☑ **BE THE WRITER YOU WANT TO BE—MANUSCRIPT CLINIC**, Villa 30, 23350 Sereno Court, Cupertino CA 95014-6507. (415)691-0300. Fax: (650)903-5920. Contact: Louise Purwin Zobel. Writer workshops geared toward beginner, intermediate and advanced levels. **Open to students.** Annual workshop. "Participants may turn in manuscripts at any stage of development to receive help with structure and style, as well as marketing advice. Manuscripts receive some written criticism and an oral critique from the instructor, as well as class discussion." Annual workshop. Usually held in the spring. Registration limited to 20-25. Cost of workshop: $45-65/day, depending on the campus; includes an extensive handout. SASE for more information.

√ **BUTLER UNIVERSITY CHILDREN'S LITERATURE CONFERENCE**, 4600 Sunset Drive, Indianapolis IN 46208. (317)940-9861. Fax: (317)940-9644. E-mail: sdaniell@butler.edu. Contact: Shirley Daniell. Writer and illustrator conference geared toward intermediate level. Open to college students. Annual conference, held January 29, 2000. Includes sessions such as The Joy of Writing Nonfiction, Creating the Children's Picture Book and Nuts and Bolts for Beginning Writers. Registration limited to 300. Cost of conference: $80; includes meals, registration, 3 plenary addresses, 2 workshops, book signing, reception and conference bookstore. Write for more information. "The conference is geared toward three groups: teachers, librarians and writers/illustrators."

N CAPE COD WRITERS CONFERENCE, Cape Cod Writers' Center, P.O. Box 186, W. Barnstable MA 02655. (508)362-2718. E-mail: ccwc@capecod.net. Website: www.capecod.net/writers. President: Don Ellis. Executive Director: Arlene Pollack. Writer conference and workshops geared toward beginner, intermediate and professional levels. **Open to students.** "We hold one children's writing course and a week long young writer's workshop at our annual conference each summer (2 sessions per day with youngsters ages 12-16)." Annual conference. Conference held third week in August. Cost of conference includes $60 to register; $85 per course (we offer 9); manuscript evaluation, $60; personal conference, $30. Write for more information.

N CAT WRITERS ASSOCIATION ANNUAL WRITERS CONFERENCE, P.O. Box 1904, Sherman TX 75091-1904. (903)868-1022. Fax: (903)893-1731. E-mail: amy@shojai.com. Website: www.catwriters.org. President: Amy D. Shojai. Writer workshops geared toward beginner, intermediate, advanced and professional levels. Illustrator workshops geared toward intermediate, advanced and professional levels. **Open to students.** Annual workshop. Workshop held in November. Cost of workshop: approximately $90; includes 9-10 seminars, 2 receptions, 1 banquet, 1 breakfast, press pass to other events, interviews with editors and book signing/art sale event. Conference information becomes available in June/July prior to event and is posted on the website (including registration material). Seminars held/co-sponsored with the Dog Writers Association ("We often receive queries from publishers seeking illustrators or writers for particular book/article projects—these are passed on to CWA members").

✓ CELEBRATION OF CHILDREN'S LITERATURE, Montgomery College, 51 Mannakee St., Office of Continuing Education, Room 220, Rockville MD 20850. (301)251-7914. Fax: (301)251-7937. E-mail: ssonner@mc.cc.md.us. Senior Program Director: Sandra Sonner. Writer and illustrator workshops geared toward all levels. **Open to students.** Past topics included The Publisher's Perspective, Successful Picture Book Design, The Oral Tradition in Children's Literature, The Best and Worst Children's Books, Websites for Children, The Pleasures of Nonfiction and The Book as Art. Annual workshop. Will be held April 22, 2000. Registration limited to 200. Writing/art facilities, continuing education classrooms and large auditorium. Cost of workshop: approximately $65; includes workshops, box lunch and coffee. Write for more information.

CHILDREN'S LITERATURE CONFERENCE, 250 Hofstra University, U.C.C.E., Hempstead NY 11549. (516)463-5016. Fax: (516)463-4833. E-mail: dcekah@hofstra.edu. Website: ContinuingLearners@www.hofstra.edw. Writers/Illustrators Contact: Kenneth Henwood, director. Writer and illustrator workshops geared toward all levels. Emphasizes: fiction, nonfiction, poetry, submission procedures, picture books. Workshops will be held April 15, 2000. Length of each session: 1 hour. Registration limited to 35/class. Cost of workshop: approximately $75; includes 2 workshops, reception, lunch, 2 general sessions, and panel discussion with guest speakers and/or critiquing. Write for more information. Co-sponsored by Society of Children's Book Writers & Illustrators.

✓CHILDREN'S WRITER'S CONFERENCE, St. Charles County Community College, P.O. Box 76975, 103 CEAC, St. Peters MO 63376-0975. (314)213-8000 ext. 4108. E-mail: suebe@inlink.com. SCBWI MO Regional Advisor: Sue Bradford Edwards. Writer and illustrator conference geared toward all levels. **Open to students.** Speakers include editors, writers and other professionals, mainly from the Midwest. Topics vary from year to year, but each conference offers sessions for both writers and illustrators as well as for newcomers and published writers. Previous topics included: "What Happens When Your Manuscript is Accepted" by Dawn Weinstock, editor; "Writing—Hobby or Vocation?" by Chris Kelleher; "Mother Time Gives Advice: Perspectives from a 25 Year Veteran" by Judith Mathews, editor; "Don't Be a Starving Writer" by Vicki Berger Erwin, author; and "Words & Pictures: History in the Making," by author-illustrator Cheryl Harness. Annual conference held in early November. Registration limited to 50-70. Cost of conference: $50-70; includes one day workshop (8:00 a.m. to 5:00 p.m.) plus lunch. Write for more information.

CLEVELAND HEIGHTS/UNIVERSITY HEIGHTS WRITER'S MINI-CONFERENCE, 34200 Ridge Rd., #110, Willoughby OH 44094-2954. (440)943-3047. E-mail: fa837@po.cwru.edu. Coordinator: Lea Leever Oldham. Writer workshops geared toward all levels. **Open to students.** Conference will cover children's writing, young adult fiction, nonfiction, poetry, marketing, query letters, tax and bookkeeping, copyright protection and other topics of interest to the beginning or advanced writer. Annual conference. Conference held October 23,

**FOR EXPLANATIONS OF THESE SYMBOLS,
SEE THE INSIDE FRONT AND BACK COVERS OF THIS BOOK**

2000 at Taylor Academy in Cleveland Heights, OH. Cost of conference: $39; includes half-day sessions by published authors and refreshments.

THE COLLEGE OF NEW JERSEY WRITERS' CONFERENCE, English Dept., The College of New Jersey, P.O. Box 7718, Ewing NJ 08628-0718. (609)771-3254. E-mail: write@tcnj.edu. Director: Jean Hollander. Writer workshops geared toward all levels. Offers workshop in children's literature. Workshops held in April of every year. Length of each session: 2 hours. Registration limited to 50. Cost of workshop: $50 (reduced rates for students); includes conference, workshop and ms critique. Write for more information.

PETER DAVIDSON'S HOW TO WRITE A CHILDREN'S PICTURE BOOK SEMINAR, 982 S. Emerald Hills Dr., P.O. Box 497, Arnolds Park IA 51331-0497. Fax: (712)362-8363. Seminar Presenter: Peter Davidson. "This seminar is for anyone interested in writing and/or illustrating children's picture books. Beginners and experienced writers alike are welcome. **Open to students.** If participants have a manuscript in progress, or have an idea, they are welcome to bring it along to discuss with the seminar presenter." *How to Write a Children's Picture Book* is a one-day seminar devoted to principles and techniques of writing and illustrating children's picture books. Topics include Definition of a Picture Book, Picture Book Sizes, Developing an Idea, Plotting the Book, Writing the Book, Illustrating the Book, Typing the Manuscript, Copyrighting Your Work, Marketing Your Manuscript and Contract Terms. Seminars are presented year-round at community colleges. Even-numbered years, presents seminars in Minnesota, Iowa, Nebraska, Kansas, Colorado and Wyoming. Odd-numbered years, presents seminars in Illinois, Minnesota, Iowa, South Dakota, Missouri, Arkansas and Tennessee (write for a schedule). One day, 9 a.m.-4 p.m. Cost of workshop: varies from $40-59, depending on location; includes approximately 35 pages of handouts. Write for more information.

DOWNEAST MAINE WRITER'S WORKSHOPS, P.O. Box 446, Stockton Springs ME 04981. (207)567-4317. Fax: (207)567-3023. E-mail: redbaron@ime.net. Website: www.maineweb.com/writers/. Director: Janet J. Barron. Writing workshops geared towards beginning writers. **Open to students.** We hold 1 or 2 workshops during the summer each year. Workshop usually held the first or second Friday-Sunday in August. Workshops topics include Writing for the Children's Market, Creative Writing (basics of Fiction & Nonfiction), How to Get Your Writing Published and a Sampler (a half day gourmet taste of Fiction, Nonfiction, Writing for the Children's Market, Poetry, Scriptwriting, and How to Get Published). Tuition: $295 includes lunch and a 3-day workshop (we accept Visa and MC). There are additional charges of $19.95 for 300 page textbook and $4 for shipping and handling. Reasonable local accommodations additional. Expert, individual, personal, practical instruction on the fundamentals of writing for publication. We also offer a writer's clinic for writing feedback if participants seek this type of guidance. No requirements prior to registration. For more information, contact DEMWW.

DUKE CREATIVE WRITER'S WORKSHOP, Box 90702, Room 203, The Bishop's House, Durham NC 27708. (919)684-2827. Fax: (919)681-8235. E-mail: kprice@mail.duke.edu. Website: www.learnmore.duke.edu. Director: Kim Price. Writer workshops geared toward intermediate to advanced levels. The Creative Writer's Workshop allows each participant to explore creative writing in-depth with the instructor of their choice. Each instructor focuses on a particular style or area of creative writing; for example, Short Fiction, Personal Narrative, Playwriting, Poetry and others. Annual workshop. Every summer there is one 2-week session in July. Registration limited to 40. All participants have access to University facilities including computer clusters, libraries and classrooms. Costs for 1999 were $1,195 for this 2-week residential session. This cost includes room, board, activity and course expenses, special events and meals, and 1 camper T-shirt. Interested participants are requested to send a sample of their writing and a letter of introduction prior to registration. Write or call for more information.

DUKE YOUNG WRITER'S CAMP, P.O. Box 90702, Room 203, The Bishop's House, Durham NC 27708. (919)684-2827. Fax: (919)681-8235. E-mail: kprice@mail.duke.edu. Website: www.learnmore.duke.edu. Director: Kim Price. Contact: Duke Youth Programs (919)684-6259. Writer workshops geared toward beginner and intermediate levels. **Open to students** (ages 6-11). Summer Camp. The Young Writer's Camp offers courses that help participants to increase their skills in Creative Writing, Expository Writing and Journalism. The courses are divided into lower and upper age groups. Specific examples of courses offered this summer for the older age group are: Writing the Short Story, Essays Made Fun and Film Review. Some examples of the lower age group classes are: Humor Writing, Children's Literature and Journal Writing. Annual workshop. Every summer there are 3 2-week sessions in June and July. Registration limited to 140. All participants have access to University facilities including computer clusters, libraries and classrooms. Costs for 1999 were $1,195 for residential campers and $695 for day campers. The cost for residential campers includes room, board, activity and course expenses, and 1 camp T-shirt. The cost for day campers includes all course expenses, and 1 camp T-shirt. Write or call for more information.

FEMINIST WOMEN'S WRITING WORKSHOPS, P.O. Box 6583, Ithaca NY 14850. Co-director: Kit Wainer. Writer's workshop geared toward beginner, intermediate, advanced and professional levels. **Open to students**. Annual workshop. Workshop held July, 2000. Registration limited to 45 women. Writing facilities available: 4-6 one day workshops; 4-5 four day work groups. Cost: $550; includes tuition, private room, 3 meals for 8 days. 3-10 page writing sample required for new participants. Write for more information. "We don't have 'writing for children' workshops every year. A brochure available in late February will specify."

✓ FISHTRAP, INC., P.O. Box 38, Enterprise OR 97828-0038. (541)426-3623. Fax: (541)426-3324. E-mail: rich@fishtrap. Website: www.fishtrap.org. Director: Rich Wandschneider. Writer workshops geared toward beginner, intermediate, advanced and professional levels. **Open to students.** Not specifically writing for children, although we have offered occasional workshops such as children's poetry—teaching and writing; illustrating "The Children's Storybook"; book making for children; and teaching methods for elementary writing teachers. A series of eight writing workshops (enrollment 12/workshop) and a writers' gathering is held each July; a winter gathering concerning writing and issues of public policy (e.g. "Violence," "Fire") held in February. Dates for the winter gathering are February 25-27, 2000; and for the summer gathering July 9-16, 2000. During the school year Fishtrap brings writers into local schools and offers occasional workshops for teachers and writers of children's and young adult books. Also brings in "Writers in Residency" (10 weeks). Cost of workshops: $175-220 for 1-4 days; includes workshop only. Food and lodging can be arranged. College credit is available. Please contact for more information.

FLORIDA CHRISTIAN WRITERS CONFERENCE, 2600 Park Ave., Titusville FL 32780. (407)269-6702, ext. 202. Fax: (407)383-1741. E-mail: writer@digital.net. Website: www.Kipertek.com/writer. Conference Director: Billie Wilson. Writer workshops geared toward all levels. **Open to students.** "We offer 48 one-hour workshops and 7 five-hour classes. Approximately 24 of these are for the children's genre: Seeing Through the Eyes of an Artist; Characters . . . Inside and Out; Seeing Through the Eyes of a Child; Picture Book Toolbox; and CD-ROM & Interactive Books for Children. Annual workshop held January 27-31, 2000. We have 30 publishers and publications represented by editors teaching workshops and reading manuscripts from the conferees. The conference is limited to 200 people. Usually workshops are limited to 25-30. Advanced or professional workshops are by invitation only via submitted application." Cost of workshop: $400; includes food, lodging, tuition and manuscript critiques and editor review of your manuscript. Write for more information.

GREAT LAKES WRITER'S WORKSHOP, Alverno College, 3400 S. 43rd St., P.O. Box 343922, Milwaukee WI 53234-3922. (414)382-6176. Fax: (414)382-6332. Assistant Director: Cindy Jackson. Writing workshops geared toward beginner and intermediate levels; subjects include writing techniques/focuses such as character development, scene development, etc.; techniques for getting over writer's block; marketing strategies; and publishing strategies. Annual workshop. Workshop held on a weekend in June. Average length of each session: 2 hours. Write for more information.

GREEN RIVERS WRITERS NOVELS-IN-PROGRESS WORKSHOP, 11906 Locust Rd., Middletown KY 40243-1413. (502)245-4902. President: Mary O'Dell. Writer workshops geared toward intermediate and advanced levels. Workshops emphasize novel writing. Format is 6 novelist instructors working with small groups (5-7 people); one of these novelists may be young adult novelist. Workshop held March 12-19, 2000. Registration limited to 49. Participants will need to bring own computers, typewriters, etc. Private rooms are available for sleeping, working. No art facilities. Cost of workshop: $375; includes organization membership, buffet banquet with agents and editors, registration, manuscript reading fee (60 pages approximately with outline/synopsis). Writers must supply 40-60 pages of manuscript with outline, synopsis or treatment. Write for more information. Conference held on Shelby Campus at University of Louisville; private rooms with bath between each 2 rooms. Linens furnished. $22 per night.

THE HEIGHTS WRITER'S CONFERENCE, Sponsored by Writer's World Press, 35 N. Chillicothe Rd. #D, Aurora OH 44202-8741. (330)562-6667. Fax: (330)562-1216. E-mail: writersworld@juno.com. Conference Director: Lavern Hall. Writer workshops geared toward beginner and intermediate. **Open to students.** Program includes 1-hour seminars and 2½-hour workshops. "Our workshop topics vary yearly. We *always* have children's literature." Annual workshop held first Saturday in May. Registration is open for seminars. The 2 teaching workshops are limited to 25 and pre-registration is a must. Cost of conference: $85; includes continental breakfast, registration packet, lunch, seminars and/or workshops, general session and networking reception at the end of the day. SASE for brochure.

HIGHLAND SUMMER CONFERENCE, Box 7014 Radford University, Radford VA 24142-7014. (540)831-5366. Fax: (540)831-5004. E-mail: jasbury@runet.edu. Website: www.runet.edu/~arsc. Director: Grace Toney Edwards. Assistant to the Director: Jo Ann Asbury. **Open to students.** Writer workshops geared toward beginner, intermediate and advanced levels. Emphasizes Appalachian literature, culture and heritage. Annual workshop. Workshop held (last 2 weeks in June annually). Registration limited to 20. Writing facilities available: computer center. Cost of workshop: Regular tuition (housing/meals extra). Must be registered student or special status student. E-mail, fax or call for more information. Past visiting authors include: Wilma Dykeman, Sue Ellen Bridgers, George Ella Lyon, Lou Kassem.

HOFSTRA UNIVERSITY SUMMER WRITERS' CONFERENCE, 250 Hofstra University, UCCE, Hempstead NY 11549. (516)463-5016. Fax: (516)463-4833. E-mail: dcekah@hofstra.edu. Director, Liberal Arts Studies: Kenneth Henwood. Writer workshops geared toward all levels. Classes offered include fiction, nonfiction, poetry, children's literature, stage/screenwriting and other genres. Children's writing faculty has included Pam Conrad, Johanna Hurwitz, Tor Seidler and Jane Zalben, with Maurice Sendak once appearing as guest speaker. Annual workshop. Workshops held for 2 weeks July 10-21, 2000. Each workshop meets for 2½ hours daily for a total of 25 hours. Students can register for 2 workshops, schedule an individual conference with the writer/ instructor and submit a short ms (less than 10 pages) for critique. Enrollees may register as certificate students or credit students. Cost of workshop: certificate students enrollment fee is approximately $375 plus $26 registra-tion fee; 2-credit student enrollment fee is approximately $1,000/workshop undergraduate and graduate (2 credits); $2,000 undergraduate and graduate (4-credits). On-campus accommodations for the sessions are available for approximately $350/person for the 2-week conference. Students may attend any of the ancillary activities, a private conference, special programs and social events.

N HOUSTON WRITER'S CONFERENCE 2000, P.O. Box 742683, Houston TX 77274-2683. (281)342-5924. E-mail: houwriters@aol.com. Website: www.houstonwriters.com. Chair: Ted Simmons. Writer's confer-ence geared toward beginner, intermediate and advanced levels. **Open to students**. Annual conference. Confer-ence held March 16-19, 2000. No limit on registration. Cost: $255; 240 prior to February 1, 2000; includes access to all workshops; cocktails Thursday evening; Friday and Saturday lunch; Saturday evening banquet, breakfast Sunday; appointments with agents and editors.

HUDSON WRITERS MINI CONFERENCE, 34200 Ridge Rd., #110, Willoughby OH 44094-2954. (440)943-3047. E-mail: lealoldham@aol.com. Coordinator: Lea Leever Oldham. Writer workshops geared toward all levels. **Open to students.** Covers children's writing, young adult, fiction, nonfiction, poetry, marketing, query letters, fax and bookkeeping, copyright protection and other topics of interest. Annual conference. Conference held at Hudson High School in Hudson, OH, May 2000. Cost of conference: $39; includes half-day sessions and refreshments.

INSPIRATIONAL WRITERS ALIVE!, Rt. 4, Box 81-H, Rusk TX 75785. Director: Maxine E, Holder. Guest speakers for 1999: Norma Jean Lutz and Cecil Murphey. Annual conference held 1st Saturday in August. **Open to students** and adults. Registration usually 60-75 conferees.Writing/art facilities available: First Baptist Church, Christian Life Center, Houston TX. Cost of conference: member $65; nonmember $80; seniors $60; at the door: members $85; nonmembers $100. Write for more information. "Annual IWA Contest presented. Manuscripts critiqued along with one-on-one 15 minute sessions with speaker(s). (Extra ms. if there is room.)" For more information send for brochure: Attn: Martha Roger, 6038 Greenmont, Houston TX 77092, (713)686-7209 or Maxine Holder, (903)795-3986 or Pat Vance, (713)477-4968.

N INTERNATIONAL READERS THEATRE WORKSHOP, P.O. Box 17193, San Diego CA 92177. (619)276-1948. Fax: (619)576-7369. Website: www.readers-theatre.com. Director: Dr. Bill Adams. Writer work-shops geared toward all levels. **Open to Students.** Program includes scriptmaking, direction, performance, story-telling, theater seminar and more. Annual workshop. Workshop held 2 weeks in July. Registration limited to 70. Full conference facilities, Wellington Hall, King's College, London. Cost of workshop: $1,395; includes room, large English breakfast, refreshments, workshop fees. Write for more information.

INTERNATIONAL WOMEN'S WRITING GUILD "REMEMBER THE MAGIC" ANNUAL SUM-MER CONFERENCE, P.O. Box 810, Gracie Station, New York NY 10028. (212)737-7536. Executive Director: Hannelore Hahn. Writer and illustrator workshops geared toward all levels. Offers 65 different workshops— some are for children's book writers and illustrators. Also sponsors 13 other events throughout the US. Annual workshops. Workshops held 2nd or 3rd week in August. Length of each session: 1 hour-15 minutes; sessions take place for an entire week. Registration limited to 500. Cost of workshop: $350 (plus $350 room and board). Write for more information. "This workshop always takes place at Skidmore College in Saratoga Springs NY."

I'VE ALWAYS WANTED TO WRITE BUT—BEGINNERS' CLASS, Villa 30, 23350 Sereno Ct., Cuper-tino CA 95014. (415)691-0300. Contact: Louise Purwin Zobel. Writer workshops geared toward beginner and intermediate levels. "This seminar/workshop starts at the beginning, although the intermediate writer will benefit, too. There is discussion of children's magazine and book literature today, how to write it and how to market it. Also, there is discussion of other types of writing and the basics of writing for publication." Annual workshops. "Usually held several times a year; fall, winter and spring." Sessions last 1-2 days. Cost of workshop: $45-65/ day, depending on the campus; includes extensive handout. Write with SASE for more information.

LIGONIER VALLEY WRITERS CONFERENCE, P.O. Box B, Ligonier PA 15658-1602. (724)537-3341. Fax: (724)537-0482. Conference Director: Tina Thoburn. Contact: Sally Shirey. Writer programs geared toward all levels. Annual conference features fiction, nonfiction, poetry and other genres. Conference held July 7-9, 2000. Write or call for more information.

LORAIN COUNTY COMMUNITY COLLEGE WRITER'S MINI-CONFERENCE, 34200 Ridge Rd., #110, Willoughby OH 44094-2954. (440)943-3047. E-mail: lealoldham@aol.com. Coordinator: Lea Leever Oldham. Writer workshops geared toward all levels. **Open to students.** Offers sessions on children's writing, poetry, self-publishing, fiction, nonfiction, articles and other topics of interest to the beginning to advanced writer. Conference held March 25, May 6, October 21, 2000. Cost of conference: $39. A full day conference is held September 9, 2000. Cost $59.

MANHATTANVILLE WRITERS' WEEK, Manhattanville College, 2900 Purchase St., Purchase NY 10577-2103. (914)694-3425. Fax: (914)694-3488. E-mail: rdowd@mville.edu. Dean, School of Graduate & Professional Studies: Ruth Dowd. Writer workshops geared toward beginner, intermediate and advanced levels. **Open to students.** Writers' week offers a special workshop for writers interested in children's/young adult writing. We have featured such workshop leaders as: Patricia Gauch, Patricia Horner, Elizabeth Winthrop and Lore Segal. Annual workshop held last week in June. Length of each session: one week. Cost of workshop: $560 (non-credit); includes a full week of writing activities, 5-day workshop on children's literature, lectures, readings, sessions with editors and agents, etc. Workshop may be taken for 2 graduate credits. Write for more information.

MAPLE WOODS COMMUNITY COLLEGE WRITERS' CONFERENCE, 2601 NE Barry Rd., Kansas City MO 64156. (816)437-3011. Fax: (816)468-0479. E-mail: schumacp@maplewoods.cc.mo.us. Director Community Education: Paula Schumacher. Contact: Sherry Skinner. Writer workshops geared toward beginner, intermediate levels. Various writing topics and genres covered. Covers where do you get your ideas for children books; how to write childrens books and get published; panels comprised of childrens books authors, librarians and book sellers. Conference held September 2000. Registration limited to 350. Cost of workshop: $79; includes continental breakfast, refreshments and two networking sessions.

☑ 🍁 **MARITIME WRITERS' WORKSHOP**, Department Extension & Summer Session, P.O. Box 4400, University of New Brunswick, Fredericton, New Brunswick E3B 5A3 Canada. Phone/fax: (506)474-1144. E-mail: k4jc@unb.ca. Website: www.unb.ca/web/coned/writers/marritrs.html. Coordinator: Rhona Sawlor. Week-long workshop on writing for children, general approach, dealing with submitted material, geared to all levels and held in July. Annual workshop. 3 hours/day. Group workshop plus individual conferences, public readings, etc. Registration limited to 10/class. Cost of workshop: $350 tuition; meals and accommodations extra. Room and board on campus is approximately $280 for meals and a single room for the week. 10-20 ms pages due before conference (deadline announced). Scholarships available.

🔃 **MENDOCINO COAST WRITERS CONFERENCE**, College of the Redwoods, 1211 Del Mar Dr., Ft. Bragg CA 95437. (707)961-6248. E-mail: mcwc@jps.net. Website: www.mcwcwritewhale.com. Registrar: Jan Boyd. Writer and illustrator workshops geared toward beginner, intermediate and advanced levels. **Open to Students.** Those conducting sessions include Kathy Dawson, senior editor Penguin Putnam (specializes in children's and young adult fiction); Ian Schoenherr, children's book illustrator Penguin Putnam; and Dennis Lee, children's poet and editor. Annual conference in its 11th year. This year's conference will take place June 1-3, 2000. Registration limited to 99. Conference is held on the campus of College of Redwoods. Cost of conference (early registration): $200-245; $200 includes Friday and Saturday lecture sessions, 2 social events; 2 lunches; 2 breakfasts; 1 dinner; editor/agent panels. $245 includes all of the above plus Thursday intensive workshops (choice of one) in poetry, fiction, nonfiction, screen and playwriting. After April 2000 price increases to $250/295. Not for registration but for the intensives we would like to have a writing sample. Artists/illustrators may bring samples of their work, if they wish, for one-on-one conference with Kathy Dawson, $20/20 minutes. "What we offer for children's writers varies from year to year. This year children's writing is one of our focuses. Having Ian Schoenherr is a special event and will not necessarily be repeated."

🔃 **MIDLAND WRITERS CONFERENCE**, Grace A. Dow Memorial Library, 1710 W. St. Andrews, Midland MI 48640-2968. (517)835-7151. Fax: (517)835-9791. E-mail: kred@vlc.lib.mi.us. Conference Chair: Katherine Redwine. **Open to students.** Writer and illustrator workshops geared toward all levels. "Each year, we offer a topic of interest to writers of children's literature. Last year, Jan Wuhl spoke on writing and illustrating picture books for children." Classes offered include: how to write poetry, writing for youth, your literary agent/what to expect. Annual workshop. Workshops held usually second Saturday in June. Length of each session: concurrently, 4 1-hour sessions repeated in the afternoon. Maximum class size: 50. "We are a public library." Cost of workshop: $60; $50 seniors and students; includes choice of workshops and the keynote speech given by a prominent author (last year Peggy Noonan). Write for more information.

MISSISSIPPI VALLEY WRITERS CONFERENCE, 3403 45th St., Moline IL 61265. E-mail: kimseuss@aol. com. Conference Director: David R. Collins. Writer workshops geared toward all levels. Conference open to students. Classes offered include Juvenile Writing—1 of 9 workshops offered. Annual workshop. Workshops held June 5-10, 2000; usually it is the second week in June each year. Length of each session: Monday-Friday, 1 hour each day. Registration limited to 20 participants/workshop. Writing facilities available: college library. Cost of workshop: $25 registration; $50 to participate in 1 workshop, $90 in 2, $40 for each additional; $25 to audit a workshop. Write for more information.

☑ **MONTROSE CHRISTIAN WRITER'S CONFERENCE**, 5 Locust St., Montrose PA 18801-1112. (570)278-1001. Fax: (570)278-3061. E-mail: mbc@montrosebible.org. Website: www.montrosebible.org. Executive Director: Jim Fahringer. **Open to students.** Writer workshops geared toward beginner, intermediate and advanced levels. Annual workshop. Workshop held in July. Cost of workshop: $100; includes tuition. Write for more information.

MOUNT HERMON CHRISTIAN WRITERS CONFERENCE, Mount Hermon Christian Conference Center, P.O. Box 413, Mount Hermon CA 95041-0413. (831)335-4466. Fax: (831)335-9218. E-mail: davidtalbott@mhcamps.org. Website: www.mountherman.org. Director of Specialized Programs: David R. Talbott. Writer workshops geared toward all levels. Open to students over 16 years. Emphasizes religious writing for children via books, articles; Sunday school curriculum; marketing. Classes offered include: Suitable Style for Children; Everything You Need to Know to Write and Market Your Children's Book; Take-Home Papers for Children. Workshops held annually over Palm Sunday weekend: April 14-18, 2000. Length of each session: 5-day residential conferences held annually. Registration limited 45/class, but most are 10-15. Conference center with hotel-style accommodations. Cost of workshop: $500-700 variable; includes tuition, resource notebook, refreshment breaks, full room and board for 13 meals and 4 nights. Write for more information.

THE NATIONAL WRITERS ASSOCIATION CONFERENCE, 3140 S. Peoria #295, Aurora CO 80014. (303)841-0246. Executive Director: Sandy Whelchel. Writer workshops geared toward all levels. Classes offered include marketing, agenting, "What's Hot in the Market." Annual workshop. "In 2000 the workshop will be held in Denver, Colorado, June 9-11. Write for more information.

☑ **NORTH CAROLINA WRITERS' NETWORK FALL CONFERENCE**, P.O. Box 954, Carrboro NC 27510-0954. (919)967-9540. Fax: (919)929-0535. E-mail: mail@nc@ncwriters.org. Website: www.ncwriters.org. Program and Services Director: Bobbie Collins-Perry. Writer workshops geared toward beginner, intermediate, advanced and professional levels. **Open to students.** "We offer workshops and critique sessions in a variety of genres: fiction, poetry, children's. Past young adult and children's writing classes included: 'Everybody's Got a Story to Tell—or Write!' with Eleanora Tate; 'Writing Young Adult Fiction' with Sarah Dessen and 'Writing for Children' with Carole Boston Weatherford." Annual conference. Conference held November 10-12, 2000 in Fayetteville, NC. Cost of workshop: approximately $175/NCWN members, $190/nonmembers; includes workshops, panel discussions, round table discussions, social activities and 3 meals. "Cost does not include fee for critique sessions or accommodations."

[N] OAKLAND UNIVERISTY WRITER'S CONFERENCE, 231 Varner Hall, Oakland University, Rochester MI 48309-4401. (248)370-3125. Fax: (248)370-4280. E-mail: gjboddy@oakland.edu. Program Director: Gloria J. Boddy. Writer and illustrator conference geared toward beginner, intermediate, advanced and professional levels. **Open to students.** Offers sessions in Children's Poetry, Marketing a Children's Book Manuscript, Writing Nonfiction for Teens. Annual conference. Conference held October, 2000. Limited to 10 per workshop. Cost of conference: $78; includes attendance at a choice of 40 presentations; $38; includes hands on workshops, chance to read work and receive feedback. Write for more information.

[N] OF DARK AND STORMY NIGHTS, P.O. Box 1944, Muncie IN 47308-1944. (765)288-7402. E-mail: spurgeonmwa@juno.com. Director: W.W. Spurgeon. Writer workshops geared toward beginner, intermediate, advanced and professional. **Open to students.** Topics include mystery and true crime writing for all ages. Annual workshop. Workshop held June 10, 2000. Registration limited to 175. "This is a concentrated one-day program with panels and speakers." Cost of workshop: $150; includes all sessions, continental breakfast and full luncheon. Mss critiques available for an extra charge. Write for more information.

☑ **OHIO KENTUCKY INDIANA CHILDREN'S LITERATURE CONFERENCE**, % Greater Cincinnati Library Consortium (GCLC), 3333 Vine St., Suite 605, Cincinnati OH 45220-2214. (513)751-4422. Fax: (513)751-0463. E-mail: gclc@one.net. Website: www.libraries.uc.edu/gclc. Staff Development Coordinator: Judy Malone. Writer and illustrator conference geared toward all levels. **Open to students.** Annual conference. Emphasizes multicultural literature for children and young adults. November conference keynote speakers were Valiska Gregory, author and Christopher Canyon, illustrator. Workshops by children's literature specialists/authors/illustrators: Tara Calahan King, Charlotte Decker, Darwin Henderson, Alice Pope, Margaret Reige, Rick Sowash, Carolmarie Stock, Nina Strauss, Connie Woodridge. Next conference November 4, 2000. Contact GCLC for more information. Registration limited to 250. Cost of conference: $35; includes registration/attendance at all workshop sessions, continental breakfast, lunch, author/illustrator signings. Write for more information.

N THE OLDER'S CHILDREN'S WRITING WORKSHOP, 84 New St., Albany VT 05820-0163. (802)755-6774. E-mail: julvt@together.net. Contact: Jules Older. Writer workshop geared toward beginner, intermediate, advanced and professional levels; illustrator workshops geared toward beginner and intermediate levels. **Open to students.** "Our overarching aim is getting published. We discuss contracts, agents, illustrators, submissions format and style. We show what editors are really interested in and what turns them off. A professional critique is included." Annual workshop. Workshop held in the fall. Registration limited to 12. Writing/art facilities available: conference room. Cost of workshop: $200; includes critique, seminar, lunch, beverage breaks and handouts. Write, phone or e-mail for more information.

✓ OUTDOOR WRITERS ASSOCIATION OF AMERICA ANNUAL CONFERENCE, RD 1, Box 177, Spring Mills PA 16875-9633. (814)364-9557. Fax: (814)364-9558. E-mail: eking4owaa@compuserve.com. Meeting Planner: Eileen King. Writer workshops geared toward all levels. Annual workshop. Workshop held in June. Cost of workshop: $130; includes attendance at all workshops and most meals. Attendees must have prior approval from Executive Director before attendance is permitted. Write for more information.

OZARK CREATIVE WRITERS, INC. CONFERENCE, 6817 Gingerbread Lane, Little Rock AR 72204. (501)565-8889. Fax: (510)565-7220. E-mail: pvining@aristotle.net. Director: Peggy Vining. **Open to students.** Writer's workshops geared to all levels. "All forms of the creative process dealing with the literary arts. We sometimes include songwriting. We invite excellent speakers who are selling authors. We also promote writing by providing competitions in all genres." Always the second full weekend in October at Inn of the Ozarks in Eureka Springs AR (a resort town). Morning sessions are given to main attraction author . . . 6 1-hour satellite speakers during each of the 2 afternoons. Two banquets. "Approximately 200 attend the conference yearly . . . many others enter the creative writing competition." Cost of registration/contest entry fee approximately $40-50. Includes entrance to all sessions, contest entry fees. "This does not include meals or lodging. We block off 70 rooms prior to August 15 for OCW guests." Send #10 SASE for brochure by May 1st. "Reserve early."

N PERSPECTIVES IN CHILDREN'S LITERATURE CONFERENCE, School of Education, 226 Furcolo Hall, University of Massachusetts, Amherst MA 01003-3035. (413)545-4325 or (413)545-1116. Fax: (413)545-2879. E-mail: rudman@educ.umass.edu. Director of Conference: Dr. Masha K. Rudman. Writer and illustrator workshops geared to all levels. Emphasis varies from year to year. The Perspectives in Children's Literature Conference celebrates 30 years of fantastic stories, fabulous art, an exploration of culture and unlimited learning. Conference 2000 will feature James Ransome and Pat Mora as keynote speakers, in addition to Norma Simon, Nancy Hope Wilson, Barry Moser and other workshop presenters. Presenters talk about what inspires them, how they bring their stories to life and what their visions are for the future. Next conference is scheduled for Saturday, April 8, 2000 at the University of Massachusetts. For more information contact the School of Education, by phone call, fax or e-mail."

PHOTOGRAPHY: A DIVERSE FOCUS, 895 W. Oak St., Zionsville IN 46077-1220. Phone/fax: (317)873-0738. Director: Charlene Faris. Writer and illustrator workshops geared to beginners. "Conferences focus primarily on children's photography; also literature and illustration. Annual conferences are held very often throughout year." Registration is not limited, but "sessions are generally small." Cost of conference: $165 (2 days), $85 (1 day). "Inquiries with a SASE only will receive information on seminars."

✓ GARY PROVOST'S WRITERS RETREAT WORKSHOP, % Write It/Sell It, 2507 S. Boston Place, Tulsa OK 74114. (800)642-2494 (for brochure). Fax: (918)583-1471. E-mail: wrwwisi@aol.com. Website: www.c hannel1.com/wisi. Director: Gail Provost Stockwell. Contact: Lance Stockwell, assistant director. Writer workshops geared toward beginner, intermediate and advanced levels. Workshops are appropriate for writers of full length novels for children/YA. Also, for writers of all novels or narrative nonfiction. Annual workshop. Workshops held May 26-June 4, 2000. Registration limited to small groups: beginners and advanced. Writing facilities available: private rooms with desks. Cost of workshop: $1,620; includes tuition, food and lodging for nine nights, daily classes, writing space, time and assignments, consultation and instruction. Requirements: short synopsis required to determine appropriateness of novel for our nuts and bolts approach to getting the work in shape for publication. Write for more information. For complete details, call 800 number.

N PUBLISH AND PROSPER IN 2000, 1501 Broadway, Suite 302, New York NY 10036. (212)997-0947. Fax: (212)768-7414. E-mail: asjany@ibn.net. Website: asja.org. Executive Director: Alexandra Owens. Writer's workshop geared toward beginner, intermediate, advanced and professional levels. **Open to students.** Topics include: Writing for Children and Young Adults. Annual workshop. Workshop held May, 2000. Registration limited to 600. Write for more information.

ROBERT QUACKENBUSH'S CHILDREN'S BOOK WRITING AND ILLUSTRATING WORK-SHOP, 460 E. 79th St., New York NY 10021-1443. Phone/fax: (212)861-2761. E-mail: rqstudios@aol.com. (E-mail inquirers please include mailing address). Website: www.rquackenbush.com. Contact: Robert Quackenbush. Writer and illustrator workshops geared to all levels. **Open to students.** Five-day extensive workshop on writing and illustrating books for children, emphasizes picture books from start to finish. Also covered is writing fiction and nonfiction for middle grades and young adults, if that is the attendees' interest. Current trends in illustration are also covered. Workshops held fall, winter and summer. Courses offered fall and winter include 10 weeks each—1½ hour/week; July workshop is a full 5-day (9 a.m.-4 p.m) extensive course. Next workshop July 10-14, 2000. Registration limited to 10/class. Writing and/or art facilities available; work on the premises; art supply store nearby. Cost of workshop: $650 for instruction. Cost of workshop includes instruction in preparation of a ms and/or book dummy ready to submit to publishers. Class limited to 10 members. Attendees are responsible for arranging their own hotel and meals, although suggestions are given on request for places to stay and eat. "This unique workshop, held annually since 1982, provides the opportunity to work with Robert Quackenbush, a prolific author and illustrator of children's books with more than 170 fiction and nonfiction books for young readers to his credit, including mysteries, biographies and song-books. The workshop attracts both professional and beginning writers and artists of different ages from all over the world."

☑ **QUARTZ MOUNTAIN**, (formerly Oklahoma Fall Arts Institutes), P.O. Box 18154, Oklahoma City OK 73154. (405)842-0890. Fax: (405)848-4538. Website: www.okartinst.org. Website: www.okartinst.org. Assistant Program Director: Christina Newendorp. Writer and illustrator workshops geared toward intermediate, advanced and professional levels. Writing topics include children's writing, fiction, nonfiction, poetry, and the art of teaching writing. Other arts workshops include finding illustrators, getting published, working with agents. Registration is limited to 20 participants per workshop; 5 workshops each weekend. Cost of workshop: $450; includes tuition, double-occupancy room and board. Write for more information. "Catalogs are available. Each workshop is taught by a professional artist of national reputation."

READER'S DIGEST WRITER'S WORKSHOP, 7632 Deerfield Dr., Prescott AZ 86305. (520)541-9625. Fax: (520)541-0433. National Coordinator: Ray Newton. Writer workshops geared toward all levels. Classes offered include major emphasis on nonfiction magazine articles for major popular publications. Annual workshops in various locations in US. Time of year varies, depending on location. Registration limited to 250. Cost of workshop: $150 registration fee; includes three meals. Does not include travel or lodging. "Participants will have opportunity for one-on-one sessions with major editors, writers representing national magazines, including the *Reader's Digest*." Write or call for more information.

ST. DAVIDS CHRISTIAN WRITERS CONFERENCE, % Audrey Stallsmith, Registrar, 87 Pines Rd. E, Hadley PA 16130. (412)253-2738. Registrar: Audrey Stallsmith. Writer workshops geared toward all levels. **Open to students.** Annual conference. Conference held in June. Writing/art facilities available: college computer lab. Cost of conference: $425; includes tuition with room and board (double room, $25 extra for single room). Write for more information.

☑ **SAN DIEGO STATE UNIVERSITY WRITERS' CONFERENCE**, The College of Extended Studies, San Diego CA 92182-1920. (619)594-2517. Fax: (619)594-8566. E-mail: ppierce@mail.sdsu.edu. Website: www. ces.sdsu.edu. Conference Facilitator: Paula Pierce. Writer workshops geared toward beginner, intermediate and advanced levels. Emphasizes nonfiction, fiction, screenwriting, advanced novel writing; includes sessions specific to writing and illustrating for children. Workshops offered by children's editors, agents and writers. Workshops held third weekend in January each year. Registration limited. Cost of workshop: approximately $225. Write for more information or see our home page at the above website.

☒ **THE WILLIAM SAROYAN WRITER'S CONFERENCE**, P.O. Box 5331, Fresno CA 93755. Phone/fax: (559)224-2516. E-mail: law@pacbell.net. President: Linda West. Writer and illustrator workshops geared toward advanced level. **Open to Students.** Annual conference. Confrence held April 7-9, 2000 at Piccadilly Inn-airport. Registration limited to 250. Cost of conference: $225. Friday noon to Sunday noon workshops (39 to choose from) most meals, critique groups, one-on-ones with agents, editors. Write for more information. "We try to cover a wide variety of writing. Children's books would be one topic of many."

SEATTLE CHRISTIAN WRITERS CONFERENCE, sponsored by Writers Information Network, P.O. Box 11337, Bainbridge Island WA 98110. (206)842-9103. Fax: (206)842-0536. Director: Elaine Wright Colvin. Writer workshops geared toward all levels. Conference open to students. Past conferences have featured subjects such as 'Making It to the Top as a Children's Book Author,' featuring Debbie Trafton O'Neal. Quarterly workshop (4 times/year). Workshop dates to be announced. Cost of workshop: $25. Write for more information and to be added to mailing list.

SELF PUBLISHING YOUR OWN BOOK, 34200 Ridge Rd., #110, Willoughby OH 44094-2954. (440)943-3047. E-mail: fa837@po.cwru.edu. Coordinator: Lea Leever Oldham. **Open to students.** Covers options for

---

VISIT THE WRITER'S DIGEST WEBSITE at www.writersdigest.com for hot new markets, daily market updates, writers' guidelines and much more.

publishing, ISBN, copyright, fair use, pricing, bar codes, size and binding and other topics of interest to the potential self publisher. Quarterly workshop. Workshop will be offered at several locations in Cleveland Heights, Kirtland, Euclid and Chardon, Ohio, on February 9, 1999; April 14, 1999; July 12, 1999; and October 7, 1999. Cost of workshop varies.

☑ **SOUTHWEST WRITERS WORKSHOP**, 8200 Mountain Rd., NE, Suite 106, Albuquerque NM 87110-7835. (505)265-9485. Fax: (505)265-9483. E-mail: swriters@aol.com. Website: www.US1.net/sww. Contact: Lori Johnson. **Open to students.** Writer workshops geared toward all genres at all levels of writing. Various aspects of writing covered including children's. Examples from conferences: Preconference workshops on the juvenile/young adult/novel taught by Penny Durant; on picture books by April Halprin Wayland; on Writing a Juvenile Novel in 6 weeks by Shirley Raye Redmond; on writing for children's magazines by D. Vetter (of Cricket). Annual conference. Conference held August 19-22, 2000 at the Alburquerque Hyatt Hotel. Length of each session: Thursday-Sunday. Cost of workshop: $250 for members and $305 for nonmembers by July 15; after this date $305 for members and $375 for nonmembers; includes all sessions, most meals and one ten-minute session with an editor or agent. Also offers critique groups (for $60/year, offers 2 monthly meetings, monthly newsletter, annual writing contest and occasional workshops). Write for more information.

SPLIT ROCK ARTS PROGRAM, University of Minnesota, 335 Nolte Center, 315 Pillsbury Dr., SE, Minneapolis MN 55455-0139. (612)624-6800. Fax: (612)624-5891. E-mail: srap@ucumn.edu. Contact: Vivien Oja, program associate. Writer and illustrator workshops geared toward intermediate, advanced and professional levels. Workshops offered in writing and illustrating books for children and young people. Workshops begin in July for 5 weeks. Two college credits available. Registration limited to 16 per class. Workshops held on the University of Minnesota-Duluth campus. Cost of workshop: $440; includes tuition and fees. Amounts vary depending on course fee, determined by supply needs, etc. "Moderately priced on-campus housing available." Complete catalogs available in March. Call or write anytime to be put on mailing list. Some courses fill very early.

☑ **STATE OF MAINE WRITERS' CONFERENCE**, 18 Hill Rd., Belmont MA 02478. (207)934-9806 (summer). (413)596-6734 (winter). Fax: (413)796-2121. Chairs: June Knowles and Mary Pitts. Writers' workshops geared toward beginner, intermediate, advanced levels. **Open to students.** Emphasizes poetry, prose, mysteries, editors, publishers, etc. Annual conference held August 15-18, 2000. Cost of workshop: $100; includes all sessions and supper, snacks, poetry booklet. Send SASE for more information.

STEAMBOAT SPRINGS WRITERS CONFERENCE, P.O. Box 774284, Steamboat Springs CO 80477. (970)879-8079. E-mail: freiberger@compuserve.com. Conference Director: Harriet Freiberger. Writers' workshops geared toward intermediate levels. **Open to students.** Some years offers topics specific to children's writing some years. Annual conference since 1982. Workshops held July 22, 2000. Registration limited to 25-30. Cost of workshop: $45; includes 4 seminars and luncheon. Write or e-mail for more information.

⟨N⟩ SUNSHINE COAST FESTIVAL OF THE WRITTEN ARTS, P.O. Box 2299, Sechelt, British Columbia V0N-3A0 Canada. (604)885-9631, 1-800-565-9631. Fax: (604)885-3967. E-mail: written_arts@sunshine.net. Website: www.sunshine.net/rockwood. Festival Producer: Gail Bull. Writer and illustrator workshops geared toward professional level. **Open to Students.** Annual literary festival held August 10-13, 2000. Writers-in-residence workshops. Pavilion seating, 500 per event. Festival pass $150; individual events $12. Writer's workshops are 3 days. Fee schedule available upon request.

⟨N⟩ SURREY WRITER'S CONFERENCE, Guilford Continuing Education, 10707 146th St., Surrey, British Columbia U3R IT5 Canada. (604)589-2221. Fax: (604)588-9286. E-mail: lkmason@6c.sympatico.cw. Website: www.vcn.6c.ca/swc/. Coordinator: Lisa Mason. Writer and illustrator workshops geared toward beginners, intermediate and advanced levels. **Open to students**. Topics include marketing, children's agents and editors. Annual Conference. Conference held October 20-22, 2000 and October 19-21, 2001. Cost of conference: $290; includes all events for 3 days and most meals. Write for more information.

TO WRITE, WRITERS' GUILD OF ACADIANA, P.O. Box 51532, Lafayette LA 70505-1532. Contact: Marilyn Continé (318)981-5153 or Ro Foley (318)234-8694. Fax: (318)367-6860. E-mail: mmcontine@aol.com. Writer conference geared toward beginner and intermediate levels. "We invite children's writers and agents, among other genres. The conference is not geared only to children's writings." Annual conference. Conference held March 23-24, 2000. Registration limited to 150. Cost of workshop: $115 member/$140 nonmember; includes 2 days of about 20 various sessions, some geared to children's writers; Friday night dinner, Saturday continental breakfast and luncheon; Friday and Saturday autograph teas; a chance to have your ms looked at by agents. Also includes a year membership to Writer's Guild of Acadiana. Write for more information or call.

⟨N⟩ TUSCAN CASTLE ART'S RETREAT, GREAT TRAVELS, INC., 5506 Connecticut Ave., NW, Suite 23, Washington DC 20015. (800)411-3728. Fax: (209)966-6972. E-mail: gtravels@erols.com. Website: www.great-travels.com. Writer and illustrator retreat geared toward all levels. **Open to Students.** Retreat held each

October. Registration limited to 18 writers, 12 artists. Cost of retreat: $1,659 double occupancy; $350-550 for single occupancy; includes transfers, accommodations in the castle, 6 gourmet dinners served with mineral water or wine, welcome reception, Florence walking tour. Send writing sample for writers. "You will reside in the heart of Tuscany, birthplace of Dante, Boccaccio, Leonardo da Vinci and Michelangelo. Your home and studio is the medieval fortress, Castello di Montegufoni built in the 11th century, later refined by the Renaissance. Montegufoni stands on a peaceful country road, the same Via Volterrana once followed by Charlemagne to Rome. In World War II the *Birth of Venus* and the *Primavera*, paintings by Botticelli, were hidden in the cellars of Montegufoni. Our retreat brings artists and writers to this special place once again."

☑ ☒ **VANCOUVER INTERNATIONAL WRITERS FESTIVAL**, 1398 Cartwright St., Vancouver, British Columbia V6H 3R8 Canada. (604)681-6330. Fax: (604)681-8400. E-mail: viwf@writersfest.bc.ca. Website: www.writersfest.bc.ca. Artistic Director: Alma Lee. Annual literary festival. The Vancouver International Writers Festival strives to encourage an appreciation of literature and to promote literacy by providing a forum where writers and readers can interact. This is accomplished by the production of special events and an annual Festival which feature writers from a variety of countries whose work is compelling and diverse. The Festival attracts over 11,000 people and presents approximately 40 events in four venues during five days on Granville Island, located in the heart of Vancouver. The first 3 days of the festival are programmed for elementary and secondary school students. Held third week in October (5-day festival). All writers who participate are invited by the A.D. The events are open to anyone who wishes to purchase tickets. Cost of events ranges from $10-25.

VASSAR COLLEGE CHILDREN'S BOOK INSTITUTE OF PUBLISHING AND WRITING, (formerly Institute of Publishing and Writing: Children's Books in the Marketplace), Vassar College, 124 Raymond Ave., Poughkeepsie NY 12604-0300. (914)437-5903. Fax: (914)437-7209. E-mail: mabruno@vassar.edu. Website: www.vassar.edu. Associate Director of College Relations: Maryann Bruno. Writer workshops geared toward all levels. **Open to students.** Offers six days of intensive instruction and advice from working professionals. Conference covers writing fiction and nonfiction, the picture book, editing, production process, how to get your work published. Directed by Jean Marzollo, author of the popular I Spy series. Annual conference. Conference held mid June. Registration limited to 25-30. Writing/art facilities available: computer center. Cost of conference: $900, includes tuition, room and full board, use of Vassar's athletic facilities. Write for more information.

☒ **THE VICTORIA SCHOOL OF WRITING**, P.O. Box 8152, Victoria, British Columbia V8W 3R8 Canada. (250)598-5300. Fax: (250)598-0066. E-mail: writeawy@islandnet.com. Website: www.islandnet.com/writeawy. Registrar: Margaret Dyment. Writer conference geared toward intermediate level. In the 2000 conference there may be 1 workshop on writing for children and young adults. Annual conference. Workshop held July 20-23. Registration limited to 100. Conference includes close mentoring from established writers. Cost of conference: $475 (Canada); includes tuition and some meals. To attend, submit 3-10 pages of writing samples. Write for more information.

☒ **VIRGINIA FESTIVAL OF THE BOOK**, 145 Ednam Dr., Charlottesville VA 22903. (804)924-3296. Fax: (804)296-4714. Website: www.vabook.org. Program Director: Suzanne Liola. **Open to students.** Readings, panel discussions, presentations and workshops by author and book-related professional for children and adults. Most programs are free and open to the public. Workshop held March 22-26, 2000 in Charlottesville. See website for more information.

WESLEYAN WRITERS CONFERENCE, Wesleyan University, Middletown CT 06459. (860)685-3604. Fax: (860)685-2441. E-mail: agreene@wesleyan.edu. Website: www.wesleyan.edu/writing/conferen.html. Director: Anne Greene. Writer workshops geared toward all levels. "This conference is useful for writers interested in how to structure a story, poem or nonfiction piece. Although we don't always offer classes in writing for children, the advice about structuring a piece is useful for writers of any sort, no matter who their audience is." Classes in the novel, short story, fiction techniques, poetry, journalism and literary nonfiction. Guest speakers and panels offer discussion of fiction, poetry, reviewing, editing and publishing. Individual ms consultations available. Conference held annually the last week in June. Length of each session: 6 days. "Usually, there are 100 participants at the Conference." Classrooms, meals, lodging and word processing facilities available on campus. Cost of workshop: tuition—$450, room—$105, meals (required of all participants)—$185. "Anyone may register; people who want financial aid must submit their work and be selected by scholarship judges." Call for a brochure or look on the web at address above.

WESTERN RESERVE WRITERS AND FREELANCE CONFERENCE, Lakel and Community College, 7700 Clocktower Dr., Kirtland OH 44094. (440)943-3047. E-mail: lealoldham@aol.com. Coordinator: Lea Leever Oldham. Writer workshops geared toward all levels. **Open to students.** Emphasizes fiction, nonfiction, articles, children's writing, poetry, marketing, tax for freelancers, copyright issues and other topics of interest to the beginning or advanced writer. All-day conference, September 2000. Cost of workshop: $59 includes lunch and all-day sessions by a published author and other experts. Held at Lakeland Community College, Kirtland, OH.

WESTERN RESERVE WRITERS MINI CONFERENCE, 34200 Ridge Rd. #110, Willoughby OH 44094-2954. E-mail: fa837@po.cwru.edu. Coordinator: Lea Leever Oldham. Writer workshops geared toward beginner, intermediate and advanced levels. **Open to students.** Topics include children's writing, fiction, nonfiction, poetry, articles, marketing and other topics or intereest to the beginning or advanced writer. Annual conference March 27, 1999. Held at Lakeland Community College, Kirtland OH. Cost of conference: $39. Write for more information.

N WHIDBEY ISLAND WRITERS' CONFERENCE, 5456 Pleasant View Ln., Freeland WA 98249. (360)331-2739. E-mail: writers@whidbey.com. Website: www.Whidbey.com/writers. Director: Celeste Mergens. Writer and illustrator workshops geared toward beginner, intermediate and advanced levels. **Open to students.** Topics include "Writing for Children," "Writing in a Bunny Eat Bunny World," "The Art of Revision." Annual conference. Workshop held March 3-5, 2000. Registration limited to 275. Cost of conference: $258; includes all workshops and events, 2 receptions, activities and daily luncheons. "For writing consultations participants pay $35 for 20 minutes to submit the first five pages of a chapter book, youth novel or entire picture book idea with a written one-page synopsis." Write, e-mail or check website for more information. "This is a uniquely personable weekend that is designed to be highly interactive. Friday's venue has an entire workshop series dedicated to children's writing."

WILLAMETTE WRITERS ANNUAL WRITERS CONFERENCE, 9045 SW Barbur Blvd., Suite 5A, Portland OR 97219. (503)452-1592. Fax: (503)452-0372. E-mail: wilwrite@teleport.com. Office Manager: Bill Johnson. Writer workshops geared toward all levels. Emphasizes all areas of writing, including children's and young adult. Opportunities to meet one-on-one with leading literary agents and editors. Workshops held in August. Cost of conference: $246; includes membership.

N WRITE ON THE SOUND WRITERS CONFERENCE, 700 Main St., Edmonds WA 98020-3032. (206)771-0228. Fax: (206)771-0253. E-mail: wots@ei.edmonds.wa.us. Website: www.ci.edmonds.wa.us. Cultural Resources Coordinator: Frances Chapin. Writer workshops geared toward beginner, intermediate, advanced and professional levels with some sessions on writing for children." Annual conference held the first weekend in October with 2 full days of a variety of lectures and workshops." Registration limited to 200. Cost of workshop: approximately $50/day, or $85 for the weekend, includes 4 workshops daily plus one ticket to keynote lecture. "Brochures are mailed in August. Attendees must preregister. Write, e-mail or call for brochure."

WRITERS' FORUM, 1570 E. Colorado Blvd., Pasadena CA 91106-2003. (626)585-7608. Coordinator of Forum: Meredith Brucker. Writer workshops geared toward all levels. Workshops held March 4, 2000. Length of sessions: 1 hour and 15 minutes including Q & A time. Cost of day: $100; includes lunch. Write for more information to Extended Learning, Pasadena City College, 1570 E. Colorado Blvd., Pasadena CA 91106-2003.

N WRITER'S ROUNDTABLE CONFERENCE, P.O. Box 461572, Garland TX 75046-1572. (800)473-2538 ext. 5. Fax: (972)414-2839. E-mail: directors@wrc-online.com. Website: www.wrc-online.com. Contact: Registrar. Writer workshops geared toward intermediate, advanced and professional levels. **Open to students.** "In 2000 we will feature among our speakers Diane Hess (Senior Editor/Scholastic), who will address a variety of writing and marketing topics specific to children's publishing." Annual workshop. Workshop held March 31-April 2, 2000. Registration limited to 300. WRC 2000 will be held at the Renaissance Dallas North Hotel (main ballroom and three breakouts). Cost of workshop: $195 (early registration); $325 (at door). Cost includes: full weekend of workshops, Friday evening snack buffet, breakfast and lunch Saturday, full set of conference tapes. Saturday-only registration also available. Professional track registrants only—required to submit clips/credits upon registration. "WRC is a multi-genre conference heavily geared toward the marketing of work and advancement of writing careers rather than how-to-write. Over half of paying attendees are full-time, professional writers."

WRITING CHILDREN'S FICTION, (formerly Children's Writers' Intensive Workshop), Rice University, Houston TX 77005. (713)527-4803. Fax: (713)285-5213. E-mail: scs@rice.edu. Website: www.scs.rice.edu. Contact: School of Continuing Studies. Children's writing courses and workshops geared toward all levels. Topics include issues in children's publishing, censorship, multiculturalism, dealing with sensitive subjects, submissions/formatting, the journal as resource, the markets—finding your niche, working with an editor, the agent/author connection, the role of research, contract negotiation. Annual week-long workshop held every July. Weekly evening courses held year-round. Contact Rice Continuing Studies for current information on course offerings.

TO RECEIVE REGULAR TIPS AND UPDATES about writing and Writer's Digest publications via e-mail, send an e-mail with "SUBSCRIBE NEWSLETTER" in the body of the message to newsletter-request@writersdigest.com

N WRITING TODAY, Birmingham-Southern College, Box 549003, Birmingham AL 35254. (205)226-4921. Fax: (205)226-3072. E-mail: dcwilson@bsc.com. Director of Special Events: Martha Andrews. Writer's workshop geared toward all levels. **Open to students**. "The Writing Today Conference brings together writers, editors, publishers, playwrights, poets and other literary professionals from around the country for two days of workshops and lectures on the literary arts, as well as practical information necessary to the craft of writing. Programs explore poetry, playwriting, children's books, novels, short stories, etc." Major speakers for the 1999 conference included Connie Mae Fowler, Richard North Patterson and David Sedaris and Grand Master Pat Conroy. Annual Conference. Conference held April 7-8, 2000. Registration limited to 500. Cost of Conference: $120; includes all workshop sessions, continental breakfast and lunch both days and a Friday and Saturday reception. Individual mss critiques available for an additional fee. Write for more information.

N NORMAN ZOLLINGER'S TAOS SCHOOL OF WRITING, P.O. Box 20496, Albuquerque NM 87154-0496. (505)294-4601. Fax: (505)294-7049. E-mail: spletzer@swcp.com. Website: www.us1.net/zollinger. Administrator: Suzanne Spletzer. Writer's school geared toward all levels. **Open to Students.** Covers all writing and publishing topics such as plotting, dialogue, characterization, why you need an agent, how to work with an editor, etc. Annual school. Workshop held mid July. Registration limited to 60. Cost of school: $1,200; includes tuition, meals and room (double occupancy). Submit ms of up to 20 pages with synopsis (if novel) of up to 3 pages. Held at Thunderbird Lodge in beautiful Taos Ski Valley at 9,000 feet. Student readings. Guest speakers such as W. Michael Gear, Kathleen Gear, Tony Hillerman, Stephen Donaldson.

Contests & Awards

Publication is not the only way to get your work recognized. Contests can also be viable vehicles to gain recognition in the industry. Placing in a contest or winning an award validates the time spent writing and illustrating. Even for those who don't place, many competitions offer the chance to obtain valuable feedback from judges and other established writers or artists.

When considering contests, be sure to study guidelines and requirements. Regard entry deadlines as gospel and note whether manuscripts and artwork should be previously published or unpublished. Also, be aware that awards vary. While one contest may award a significant amount of money or publication, another may award a certificate or medal instead.

Note that some contests require nominations. For published authors and illustrators, competitions provide an excellent way to promote your work. Your publisher may not be aware of local competitions such as state-sponsored awards—if your book is eligible, have the appropriate person at your publishing company nominate or enter your work for consideration.

To select potential contests for your work, read through the listings that interest you, then send for more information about the types of written or illustrated material considered and other important details, such as who retains the rights to prize-winning material. A number of contests offer such information through websites given in their listings. If you are interested in knowing who has received certain awards in the past, check your local library or bookstores or consult *Children's Books: Awards & Prizes*, compiled and edited by the Children's Book Council (www.c bcbooks.org). Many bookstores have special sections for books that are Caldecott and Newbery Medal winners. Visit these websites for more information on award-winning children's books: The Caldecott—www.ala.org/alsc/caldecott.html; The Newbery—www.ala.org/alsc/newbery.h tml; The Coretta Scott King Award—www.ala.org/srrt/csking; The Boston Globe-Horn Book Award—www.hbook.com/bghb.html; The Golden Kite Award—www.scbwi.org/goldkite.htm.

Information on contests listed in the previous edition but not included in this edition of *Children's Writer's & Illustrator's Market* may be found in the General Index.

AIM Magazine Short Story Contest, P.O. Box 1174, Maywood IL 60153-8174. (773)874-6184. Contest Directors: Ruth Apilado, Mark Boone. Annual contest. **Open to students.** Estab. 1983. Purpose of contest: "We solicit stories with social significance. Youngsters can be made aware of social problems through the written word and hopefully they will try solving them." Unpublished submissions only. Deadline for entries: August 15. SASE for contest rules and entry forms. SASE for return of work. No entry fee. Awards $100. Judging by editors. Contest open to everyone. Winning entry published in fall issue of *AIM*. Subscription rate $12/year. Single copy $4.50.

ALCUIN CITATION AWARD, The Alcuin Society, P.O. Box 3216, Vancouver, British Columbia V6B 3X8 Canada. (604)888-9049. Fax: (604)888-9049. E-mail: deeddycibm.net. Website: www.slais.ubc.ca/users/ Alcuin. Secretary: Doreen E. Eddy. Annual award. Estab. 1983. **Open to students.** Purpose of contest: Alcuin Citations are awarded annually for excellence in Canadian book design. Previously published submissions only, "in the year prior to the Awards Invitation to enter; i.e., 1999 awards went to books published in 1998." Submissions made by the author, publishers and designers. Deadline for entries: March 15. SASE. Entry fee is $10. Awards certificate. Judging by professionals and those experienced in the field of book design. Requirements for entrants: Winners are selected from books designed and published in Canada. Awards are presented annually at the Annual General Meeting of the Alcuin Society held in late May or early June each year.

AMERICA & ME ESSAY CONTEST, Farm Bureau Insurance, Box 30400, 7373 W. Saginaw, Lansing MI 48909-7900. (517)323-7000. Fax: (517)323-6615. Website: farmbureauinsurance-mi.co. Contest Coordinator: Lisa Fedewa. Annual contest. **Open to students.** Estab. 1968. Purpose of the contest: to give Michigan 8th graders the opportunity to express their thoughts/feelings on America and their roles in America. Unpublished submissions only. Deadline for entries: mid-November. SASE for contest rules and entry forms. "We have a school mailing list. Any school located in Michigan is eligible to participate." Entries not returned. No entry fee. Awards savings bonds and plaques for state top ten ($500-1,000), certificates and plaques for top 3 winners from each school. Each school may submit up to 10 essays for judging. Judging by home office employee volunteers. Requirements for entrants: "Participants must work through their schools or our agents' sponsoring schools. No individual submissions will be accepted. Top ten essays and excerpts from other essays are published in booklet form following the contest. State capitol/schools receive copies."

☑ **AMERICAN ASSOCIATION OF UNIVERSITY WOMEN, NORTH CAROLINA DIVISION, AWARD IN JUVENILE LITERATURE**, North Carolina Literary and Historical Association, 4610 CMS Center, Raleigh NC 27699-4610. (919)733-9375. Fax: (919)733-8807. Award Coordinator: Dr. Jerry C. Cashion. Annual award. Purpose of award: to reward the creative activity involved in writing juvenile literature and to stimulate in North Carolina an interest in worthwhile literature written on the juvenile level. Book must be published during the year ending June 30 of the year of publication. Submissions made by author, author's agent or publisher. Deadline for entries: July 15. SASE for contest rules. Awards a cup to the winner and winner's name inscribed on a plaque displayed within the North Carolina Division of Archives and History. Judging by Board of Award selected by sponsoring organization. Requirements for entrants: Author must have maintained either legal residence or actual physical residence, or a combination of both, in the State of North Carolina for three years immediately preceding the close of the contest period.

AMHA LITERARY CONTEST, American Morgan Horse Association Youth, P.O. Box 960, Shelburne VT 05482. (802)985-4944. Website: www.morganhorse.com. Contest Director: Susan Bell. Annual contest. Open to students. Purpose of contest: "to award youth creativity." The contest includes categories for both poetry and essays. The 1999 theme was "Morgans Helping Youth." Entrants should write to receive the 1999 entry form and theme. Unpublished submissions only. Submissions made by author. Deadline for entries: October 1. SASE for contest rules and entry forms. No entry fee. Awards $50 cash and ribbons to up to 5th place. "Winning entry will be published in *AMHA News and Morgan Sales Network*, a monthly publication."

AMHA MORGAN ART CONTEST, American Morgan Horse Association, Box 960, Shelburne VT 05482. (802)985-4944. Fax: (802)985-8897. E-mail: amha@together.net. Website: www.morganhorse.com. Membership Recognition Coordinator: Susan Bell. Annual contest. The art contest consists of two categories: Morgan art (pencil sketches, oils, water colors, paintbrush), Morgan specialty pieces (sculptures, carvings). Unpublished submissions only. Deadline for entries: October 1. Contest rules and entry forms available for SASE. Entries not returned. Entry fee is $5. Awards $50 1st Prize in 2 divisions (for adults) and AMHA gift certificates to top 6 places (for children). Judging by *The Morgan Horse* magazine staff. "All work submitted becomes property of The American Morgan Horse Association. Selected works may be used for promotional purposes by the AMHA." Requirements for entrants: "We consider all work submitted." Works displayed at the annual convention and the AMHA headquarters; published in *AMAHA News* and *Morgan Sales Network* and in color in the *Morgan Horse Magazine* (TMHA). The contest divisions consist of Junior (to age 17), Senior (18 and over) and Professional (commercial artists). Each art piece must have its own application form and its own entry fee. Matting is optional.

☑ ❀ **ATLANTIC WRITING COMPETITION**, Writer's Federation of Nova Scotia, 1113 Marginal Rd., Halifax, Nova Scotia B3H 4P7 Canada. (902)423-8116. Fax: (902)422-0881. E-mail: writers1@fox.nstn.ca. Website: www.chebucto.ns.ca/Culture/WFNS/. Open to students. Annual contest. Estab. 1970s. Purpose is to encourage new and emerging writers and encourages all writers in Atlantic Canada to explore their talents by sending in new, untried work to any of five categories: novel, short story, poetry, writing for children or magazine article. Unpublished submissions only. Submissions made by author. Deadline for entries: July 31, 2000. SASE for contest rules and entry forms. Entry fee is $15 (Canadian). Judging by a writer, bookseller and publisher. Only open to residents of Atlantic Canada who are unpublished in category they enter. Judges return comments to all entrants.

🅽 **BAKER'S PLAYS HIGH SCHOOL PLAYWRITING CONTEST**, Baker's Plays, P.O. Box 6992222, Quincy MA 02269-9222. Fax: (617)745-9891. E-mail: info@bakersplays.com. Website: www.bakersplays.com. Contest Director: Raymond Pape. Annual contest. Estab. 1990. Purpose of the contest: to acknowledge playwrights at the high school level and to insure the future of American theater. Unpublished submissions only. Postmark deadline: January 30, 2000. Notification: May. SASE for contest rules and entry forms. No entry fee. Awards $500 to the 1st Place playwright and Baker's Plays will publish the play; $250 to the 2nd Place playwright with an honorable mention; and $100 to the 3rd Place playwright with an honorable mention in the series. Judged anonymously. Open to any high school student. Plays must be accompanied by the signature of a sponsoring high school drama or English teacher, and it is recommended that the play receive a production or a public reading prior to the submission. "Please include a SASE." Teachers must not submit student's work. The first place playwright will have their play published in an acting edition the September following the contest. The work will be described in the Baker's Plays Catalogue, which is distributed to 50,000 prospective producing organizations.

THE IRMA S. AND JAMES H. BLACK BOOK AWARD, Bank Street College of Education, 610 W. 112th St., New York NY 10025-1898. (212)875-4450. Fax: (212)875-4558. E-mail: lindag@bnkst.edu. Website: www.bnkst.edu/html/library/isb.html. Contact: Linda Greengrass. Annual award. Estab. 1972. Purpose of award: "The award is given each spring for a book for young children, published in the previous year, for excellence of both text and illustrations." Entries must have been published during the previous calendar year (between January '00 and December '00 for 2000 award). Deadline for entries: January 1. "Publishers submit books to us by sending them here to me at the Bank Street library. Authors may ask their publishers to submit their books. Out of these, three to five books are chosen by a committee of older children and children's literature professionals. These books are then presented to children in selected second, third and fourth grade classes here and at a few other cooperating schools on the East Coast. These children are the final judges who pick the actual award. A scroll (one each for the author and illustrator, if they're different) with the recipient's name and a gold seal designed by Maurice Sendak are awarded in May."

WALDO M. AND GRACE C. BONDERMAN/IUPUI NATIONAL YOUTH THEATRE PLAYWRITING COMPETITION AND DEVELOPMENT WORKSHOP AND SYMPOSIUM, Indiana University-Purdue University at Indianapolis, 425 University Blvd. #309, Indianapolis IN 46202-5140. (317)274-2095. Fax: (317)278-1025. E-mail: dwebb@iupui.edu. Website: www.iupui.edu/~comstudy/playsym/symwork.html. Director: Dorothy Webb. **Open to students.** Entries should be submitted to Priscilla Jackson, Literary Manager. Contest every two years; next competition will be 2000. Estab. 1983. Purpose of the contest: "to encourage writers to create artistic scripts for young audiences. It provides a forum through which each playwright receives constructive criticism of his/her work and, where selected, writers participate in script development with the help of professional dramaturgs, directors and actors." Unpublished submissions only. Submissions made by author. Deadline for entries: September 1, 2000. SASE for contest rules and entry forms. No entry fee. "Awards will be presented to the top ten finalists. Four cash awards of $1,000 each will be received by the top four playwrights whose scripts will be given developmental work culminating in polished readings showcased at the symposium held on the IUPUI campus. This symposium is always held opposite years of the competition. Major publishers of scripts for young audiences, directors, producers, critics and teachers attend this symposium and provide useful reactions to the plays. If a winner is unable to be involved in preparation of the reading and to attend the showcase of his/her work, the prize will not be awarded. Remaining finalists will receive certificates." Judging by professional directors, dramaturgs, publishers, university professors. Write for guidelines and entry form.

 **BOOK OF THE YEAR FOR CHILDREN**, Canadian Library Association, 200 Elgin St., Suite 602, Ottawa, Ontario K2P 1L5 Canada. (613)232-9625. Fax: (613)563-9895. Contact: Chairperson, Canadian Association of Children's Librarians. Annual award. Estab. 1947. "The main purpose of the award is to encourage writing and publishing in Canada of good books for children up to and including age 14. If, in any year, no book is deemed to be of award calibre, the award shall not be made that year. To merit consideration, the book must have been published in Canada and its author must be a Canadian citizen or a permanent resident of Canada." Previously published submissions only; must be published between January 1 and December 1 of the previous year. Deadline for entries: January 1. SASE for award rules. Entries not returned. No entry fee. Awards a medal. Judging by committee of members of the Canadian Association of Children's Librarians. Requirements for entrants: Contest open only to Canadian authors or residents of Canada. Winning books are on display at CLA headquarters.

 THE BOSTON GLOBE-HORN BOOK AWARDS, The Boston Globe & The Horn Book, Inc., The Horn Book, 56 Roland St., Suite 200, Boston MA 02129. (617)628-0225. Fax: (617)628-0882. E-mail: info@hbook.com. Website: www.hbook.com/bghb.html. Award Directors: Stephanie Loer and Roger Sutton. Writing Contact: Stephanie Loer, children's book editor for *The Boston Globe*, 298 North St., Medfield MA 02052. Annual award. Estab. 1967. Purpose of award: "to reward literary excellence in children's and young adult books. Awards are for picture books, nonfiction and fiction. Up to two honor books may be chosen for each category." Books must be published between June 1, 1998 and May 31, 1999. Deadline for entries: May 15. "Publishers usually submit books. Award winners receive $500 and silver engraved bowl, honor book winners receive a silver plate." Judging by 3 judges involved in children's book field who are chosen by Roger Sutton, editor-in-chief for The Horn Book, Inc. (*The Horn Book Magazine* and *The Horn Book Guide*) and Stephanie Loer, children's book editor for *The Boston Globe*. "*The Horn Book Magazine* publishes speeches given at awards ceremonies. The

**FOR EXPLANATIONS OF THESE SYMBOLS,
SEE THE INSIDE FRONT AND BACK COVERS OF THIS BOOK**

book must have been published in the U.S. The awards are given at the fall conference of the New England Library Association."

BUCKEYE CHILDREN'S BOOK AWARD, State Library of Ohio, 65 S. Front St., Columbus OH 43215-4163. (614)644-7061. Fax: (614)728-2788. E-mail: rmetcalf@winslo.state.oh.us. Website: www.wpl.lib.oh.us/buckeyebook/. Chairperson: Nancy Smith. Correspondence should be sent to Ruth A. Metcalf at the above address. **Open to students.** Award offered every two years. Estab. 1981. Purpose of the award: "The Buckeye Children's Book Award Program was designed to encourage children to read literature critically, to promote teacher and librarian involvement in children's literature programs, and to commend authors of such literature, as well as to promote the use of libraries. Awards are presented in the following three categories: grades K-2, grades 3-5 and grades 6-8." Previously published submissions only. Deadline for entries: February 1. "The nominees are submitted by this date during the even year and the votes are submitted by this date during the odd year. This award is nominated and voted upon by children in Ohio. It is based upon criteria established in our bylaws. The winning authors are awarded a special plaque honoring them at a banquet given by one of the sponsoring organizations. The BCBA Board oversees the tallying of the votes and announces the winners in March of the voting year in a special news release and in a number of national journals. The book must have been written by an author, a citizen of the United States and originally copyrighted in the U.S. within the last three years preceding the nomination year. The award-winning books are displayed in a historical display housed at the Columbus Metropolitan Library in Columbus, Ohio."

☑ **BYLINE MAGAZINE CONTESTS**, P.O. Box 130596, Edmond OK 73013-0001. Website: www.bylinemag.com. Contest Director: Marcia Preston. Purpose of contest: *ByLine* runs 4 contests a month on many topics to encourage and motivate writers. Past topics include first chapter of a novel, children's fiction, children's poem, nonfiction for children, personal essay, general short stories, valentine or love poem, etc. Send SASE for contest flier with topic list. Unpublished submissions only. Submissions made by the author. "We do not publish the contests' winning entries, just the names of the winners." SASE for contest rules. Entry fee is $3-4. Awards cash prizes for first, second and third place. Amounts vary. Judging by qualified writers or editors. List of winners will appear in magazine.

☑ **BYLINE MAGAZINE STUDENT PAGE**, P.O. Box 130596, Edmond OK 73013. (405)348-5591. Website: www.bylinemag.com. Contest Director: Marcia Preston, publisher. Estab. 1981. "We offer writing contests for students in grades 1-12 on a monthly basis, September through May, with cash prizes and publication of top entries." Previously unpublished submissions only. "This is not a market for illustration." Deadline for entries varies. "Entry fee usually $1." Awards cash and publication. Judging by qualified editors and writers. "We publish top entries in student contests. Winners' list published in magazine dated 2 months past deadline." Send SASE for details.

RANDOLPH CALDECOTT MEDAL, Association for Library Service to Children, Division of the American Library Association, 50 E. Huron, Chicago IL 60611. (312)280-2163. Website: www.ala.org/alsc/caldecott.html. Executive Director ALSC: Susan Roman. Annual award. Estab. 1938. Purpose of the award: to honor the artist of the most distinguished picture book for children published in the US (Illustrator must be US citizen or resident.) Must be published year preceding award. Deadline for entries: December. SASE for award rules. Entries not returned. No entry fee. "Medal given at ALA Annual Conference during the Newbery/Caldecott Banquet."

☑ **CALIFORNIA YOUNG PLAYWRIGHTS CONTEST**, Playwrights Project, 450 B St., Suite 1020, San Diego CA 92101. (619)239-8222. E-mail: youth@playwright.com. Director: Deborah Salzer. **Open to Californians under age 19.** Annual contest. Estab. 1985. "Our organization, and the contest, is designed to nurture promising young writers. We hope to develop playwrights and audiences for live theater. We also teach playwriting." Submissions required to be unpublished and not produced professionally. Submissions made by the author. Deadline for entries: April 1. SASE for contest rules and entry form. No entry fee. Award is professional productions of 3-5 short plays each year, participation of the writers in the entire production process, with a royalty award of $100 per play. Judging by professionals in the theater community, a committee of 5-7; changes somewhat each year. Works performed in San Diego at the Cassius Carter Centre Stage of the Old Globe Theatre. Writers submitting scripts of 10 or more pages receive a detailed script evaluation letter.

CALLIOPE FICTION CONTEST, Writers' Specialized Interest Group (SIG) of American Mensa, Ltd., P.O. Box 466, Moraga CA 94556-0466. E-mail: cynthia@theriver.com. Fiction Editor: Sandy Raschke. Submit entries to Sandy Raschke, fiction editor. **Open to students.** Annual contest. Estab. 1991. Purpose of contest: To promote good writing and opportunities for getting published. To give our member/subscribers and others an entertaining and fun exercise in writing. Unpublished submissions only (all genres, no violence, profanity or extreme horror). Submissions made by author. Deadline for entries: changes annually but usually around September 15. Entry fee is $2 for non-subscribers; subscribers get first entry fee. Awards small amount of cash (up to $25 for 1st Place, to $5 for 3rd), certificates, full or mini-subscriptions to *Calliope* and various premiums and books, depending on donations. All winners are published in subsequent issues of *Calliope*. Judging by fiction editor, with concurrence of other editors, if needed. Requirements for entrants: one-time rights. Open to all writers. No special considerations—other than following the guidelines. Contest theme, due dates and sometimes entry fees change annually. Always send SASE for complete rules; available after April 1 each year.

N **CANADA COUNCIL GOVERNOR GENERAL'S LITERARY AWARDS**, 350 Albert St., P.O. Box 1047, Ottawa, Ontario K1P 5V8 Canada. (613)566-4376. Officer, Writing and Publishing Section Officer: Josiane Polidori. Annual award. Estab. 1937. Purpose of award: given to the best English-language and the best French-language work in each of the seven categories of Fiction, Literary Nonfiction, Poetry, Drama, Children's Literature (text), Children's Literature (illustration) and Translation. Books must be first-edition trade books that have been written, translated or illustrted by Canadian citizens or permanent residents of Canada. In the case of Translation, the original work written in English or French, must also be a canadian-authored title. Titles must be published between September 1, 1999 and September 30, 2000. Books must be submitted by publishers. Books published between September 1, 1999 and April 30, 2000 must reach the Canada Council no later than May 15, 2000. For books and bound proofs published between May 1, 2000 and September 30, 2000, the deadline is August 15, 2000. Awards $10,000 (Canadian).

RAYMOND CARVER SHORT STORY CONTEST, English Dept. Humboldt State University, Arcata CA 95521-8299. (707)826-5946, ext. 1. Fax: (707)826-5939. E-mail: kce1@humboldt.edu. Submit entries to Student Coordinator. **Open to students**, US citizens and writers living in the US. Annual contest. Estab. 1982. Unpublished submissions only. Submissions made by author. Deadline for entries: December 1. SASE for contest rules and entry forms. Entry fee is $10. Awards $1,000 1st place and publication in TOYON; $500 2nd place and honorable mention in TOYON; 3rd place honorable mention. Judges change every year. Must be US citizen or writers living in US.

N **CHILDREN WRITING FOR CHILDREN NATIONAL CONTEST**, 7142 Dustin Rd., Galena OH 43021-7959. (800)759-7171. Executive Director: Susan Schmidt. CWC is a nonprofit corporation established to educate the public at large about children's issues through literary works created by children and to celebrate and share the talents of children as authors. Books must be written by children ages 6-18. Two annual contests (fall and spring) are announced in September and January. Manuscript guidelines are available only with SASE. Awards include publication and/or scholarships. For more information contact CWC or watch for announcement in *Teacher's Magazine*.

CHILDREN'S WRITERS FICTION CONTEST, Goodin Williams Goodwin Literary Associates, P.O. Box 8863, Springfield MO 65801-8863. (417)863-7670 or (417)866-0744. Fax: (417)864-4745. Coordinator: V.R. Williams. Annual contest. Estab. 1994. Purpose of contest: to promote writing for children, by giving children's writers an opportunity to submit work in competition. Unpublished submissions only. Submissions made by the author. Deadline for entries: July 31. SASE for contest rules and entry forms. Entry fee is $5. Awards cash prize, certificate and publication in newsletter; certificates for Honorable Mention. Judging by Goodin, Williams and Goodwin. First rights to winning material acquired or purchased. Requirements for entrants: Work must be suitable for children and no longer than 1,000 words. "Send SASE for list of winners."

THE CHRISTOPHER AWARD, The Christophers, 12 E. 48th St., New York NY 10017. (212)759-4050. E-mail: tci@idt.net. Website: www.christophers.org. Christopher Awards Coordinators: Peggy Flanagan and Virginia Armstrong. Annual award. Estab. 1969 (for young people; books for adults honored since 1949). "The award is given to works, published in the calendar year for which the award is given, that 'have achieved artistic excellence, affirming the highest values of the human spirit.' They must also enjoy a reasonable degree of popular acceptance." Previously published submissions only; must be published between January 1 and December 31. "Books should be submitted all year. Two copies should be sent to Peggy Flanagan, 12 E. 48th St., New York NY 10017 and two copies to Virginia Armstrong, 22 Forest Ave., Old Tappan NJ 07675." Entries not returned. No entry fee. Awards a bronze medallion. Books are judged by both reading specialists and young people. Requirements for entrants: "only published works are eligible and must be submitted during the calendar year in which they are first published."

CHRISTOPHER COLUMBUS SCREENPLAY DISCOVERY AWARDS, Christopher Columbus Society of the Creative Arts, #600, 433 N. Camden Dr., Beverly Hills CA 90210. (310)288-1988. Fax: (310)288-0257. E-mail: awards@hollywoodawards.com. Website: screenwriters.com. Award Director: Mr. Carlos Abreu. Annual and monthly awards. Estab. 1990. Purpose of award: to discover new screenplay writers. Unpublished submissions only. Submissions are made by the author or author's agent. Deadline for entries: August 1st and monthly (last day of month). Entry fee is $55. Awards: (1) Feedback—development process with industry experts. (2) Financial rewards—option moneys up to $10,000. (3) Access to key decision makers. Judging by entertainment industry experts, producers and executives.

THE COMMONWEALTH CLUB'S BOOK AWARDS CONTEST, The Commonwealth Club of California, 595 Market St., San Francisco CA 94105. (415)597-6700. Fax: (415)597-6929. E-mail: cwc@sirius.com. Website: www.commonwealthclub.org. Attn: James Wilson. Chief Executive Officer: Gloria Duffy. Annual contest. Estab. 1932. Purpose of contest: the encouragement and production of literature in California. Juvenile category included. Previously published submission; must be published from January 1 to December 31, previous to contest year. Deadline for entries: January 31. SASE for contest rules and entry forms. No entry fee. Awards gold and silver medals. Judging by the Book Awards Jury. The contest is only open to California writers/ illustrators (must have been resident of California when ms was accepted for publication). "The award winners will be honored at the Annual Book Awards Program." Winning entries are displayed at awards program and advertised in newsletter.

CRICKET LEAGUE, *Cricket Magazine*, P.O. Box 300, 315 Fifth St., Peru IL 61354. (815)224-6633. Website: www.cricketmag.com. Address entries to: Cricket League. Monthly. Estab. 1973. "The purpose of Cricket League contests is to encourage creativity and give young people an opportunity to express themselves in writing, drawing, painting or photography. There is a contest each month. Possible categories include story, poetry, art or photography. Each contest relates to a *specific theme* described on each *Cricket* issue's Cricket League page. Signature verifying originality, age and address of entrant required. Entries which do not relate to the current month's theme cannot be considered." Unpublished submissions only. Deadline for entries: the 25th of each month. Cricket League rules, contest theme, and submission deadline information can be found in the current issue of *Cricket*. "We prefer that children who enter the contests subscribe to the magazine, or that they read *Cricket* in their school or library." No entry fee. Awards certificate suitable for framing and children's books or art/writing supplies. Judging by *Cricket* editors. Obtains right to print prizewinning entries in magazine. Refer to contest rules in current *Cricket* issue. Winning entries are published on the Cricket League pages in the *Cricket* magazine 3 months subsequent to the issue in which the contest was announced. Current theme, rules, and prizewinning entries also posted on the website.

⊞ CUNNINGHAM PRIZE FOR PLAYWRITING, The Theatre School, Depaul University, 2135 N. Kenmore Ave., Chicago IL 60614-4111. Submit entries to: Cunningham Prize Selection Committee. Annual award. Estab. 1990. Purpose of award: to recognize and encourage the writing of dramatic works which affirm the centrality of religion, broadly defined and the human quest for meaning, truth and community. It is the intent of the endowment to consider submissions of new dramatic writing in all genres, including works for children and young people. Submissions made by the author. Playwrights who have won the award within the last five years are not eligible. Candidates must be writers whose residence is in the Chicago area, defined as within 100 miles of the loop. Deadline for entries: December 1. SASE for return of materials. Awards $5,000. Judging by The Selection Committee, composed of distinguished citizens including members of DePaul University, representatives of the Cunnningham Prize Advisory Committee, critics, and others from the theatre professions and is chaired by the dean of the Theatre School.

MARGUERITE DE ANGELI PRIZE, Bantam Doubleday Dell Books for Young Readers, 1540 Broadway, New York NY 10036. Estab. 1992. Fax: (212)782-9452 (note re: Marguerite De Angeli Prize). Annual award. Purpose of the award: to encourage the writing of fiction for children aged 7-10, either contemporary or historical; to encourage unpublished writers in the field of middle grade fiction. Unpublished submissions only. No simultaneous submissions. Length: between 40-144 pages. Submissions made by author or author's agent. Entries should be postmarked between April 1st and June 30th. SASE for award rules. No entry fee. Awards a $1,500 cash prize plus a hardcover and paperback book contract with a $3,500 advance against a royalty to be negotiated. Judging by Bantam Doubleday Dell Books for Young Readers editorial staff. Open to US and Canadian writers who have not previously published a novel for middle-grade readers (ages 7-10). Works published in an upcoming Bantam Doubleday Dell Books for Young Readers list.

DELACORTE PRESS PRIZE FOR A FIRST YOUNG ADULT NOVEL, Delacorte Press, Books for Young Readers Department, 1540 Broadway, New York NY 10036. (212)354-6500. Fax: (212)782-9452. Annual award. Estab. 1982. Purpose of award: to encourage the writing of contemporary young adult fiction. Previously unpublished submissions only. Mss sent to Delacorte Press may not be submitted to other publishers while under consideration for the prize. "Entries must be submitted between October 1 and New Year's Day. The real deadline is a December 31 postmark. Early entries are appreciated." SASE for award rules. No entry fee. Awards a $1,500 cash prize and a $6,000 advance against royalties on a hardcover and paperback book contract. Works published in an upcoming Bantam Doubleday Dell Books for Young Readers list. Judged by the editors of the Books for Young Readers Department of Bantam Doubleday Dell. Requirements for entrants: The writer must be American or Canadian and must *not* have previously published a young adult novel but may have published anything else. Foreign-language mss and translations and mss submitted to a previous Delacorte Press are not eligible. Send SASE for new guidelines.

MARGARET A. EDWARDS AWARDS, American Library Association, 50 East Huron St., Chicago IL 60611-2795. (312)944-6780 or (800)545-2433. Fax: (312)664-7459. E-mail: yalsa@ala.org. Website: www.ala.org/yalsa. Annual award administered by the Young Adult Library Services Association (YALSA) of the American Library Association (ALA) and sponsored by *School Library Journal* magazine. Purpose of award: "ALA's Young Adult Library Services Association (YALSA), on behalf of librarians who work with young adults in all types of libraries, will give recognition to those authors whose book or books have provided young adults with a window through which they can view their world and which will help them to grow and to understand themselves and their role in relationships, society and the world." Previously published submissions only. Submissions are nominated by young adult librarians and teenagers. Must be published five years before date of award. SASE for award rules and entry forms. No entry fee. Judging by members of the Young Adult Library Services Association. Deadline for entry: June 1. "The award will be given annually to an author whose book or books, over a period of time, have been accepted by young adults as an authentic voice that continues to illuminate their experiences and emotions, giving insight into their lives. The book or books should enable them to understand themselves, the world in which they live, and their relationship with others and with society. The book or books must be in print at the time of the nomination."

☑ ⬇ **ARTHUR ELLIS AWARD**, Crime Writers of Canada, 3007 Kingston Rd., Box 113, Scarborough, Ontario M1M 1P1 Canada. (416)461-9826. Fax: (416)461-4489. E-mail: ap113@torfree.net.on.ca. Submit entries to: Secretary/Treasurer. Annual contest. Estab. 1984. Purpose of contest: to honor the best juvenile writing with a theme of crime, detective, espionage, mystery, suspense and thriller, fictional or factual accounts of criminal doings. Includes novels with a criminous theme. Previously published submissions only. Submissions made by author or by author's agent or publisher. Must be published during year previous to award. Deadline for entries: January 31. SASE for contest rules and entry forms. Awards a statuette of a hanged man—with jumping jack limbs. Judging by 2 nonmembers and one member per category. Can be any publication, regardless of language, by a writer, regardless of nationality, resident in Canada or a Canadian writer resident abroad.

FLORIDA STATE WRITING COMPETITION, Florida Freelance Writers Assocociation, P.O. Box A, North Stratford NH 03590. (603)922-8338. Fax: (603)922-8339. E-mail: danakcnw@ncia.net. Website: www.writers-editors.com. Executive Director: Dana K. Cassell. Annual contest. Estab. 1984. Categories include children's literature (length appropriate to age category). Entry fee is $5 (members), $10 (nonmembers). Awards $75 1st Prize, $50 2nd Prize, $25 3rd Prize, certificates for honorable mentions. Judging by teachers, editors and published authors. Judging criteria: interest and readability within age group, writing style and mechanics, originality, salability. Deadline: March 15. For copy of official entry form, send #10 SASE or go to www.writers-editors.com. List of 1999 winners on website.

FOR A GOOD TIME THEATRE COMPANY'S ANNUAL SCRIPT CONTEST, For A Good Time Theatre Company, P.O. Box 5421, Saginaw MI 48603-0421. (517)753-7891. Fax: (517)753-5890. E-mail: theatre co@aol.com. Contest Director: Lee-Perry Belleau, artistic director. Annual contest. Estab. 1997. Purpose of contest: To award top-notch playwrights in theater for young audiences with a production by a critically acclaimed regional theater company. Unpublished submissions only. Submissions made by author or by author's agent. Deadline for entries: May 1 (postmark). SASE for contest rules and entry forms. Entry fee is $10. Awards production of the winning script; cash award of $1,000 and a videotape of the produced script. Judging by For A Good Time Theatre's staff dramaturg (prescreening). Screening is then done by the producer. Final judging is done by the artistic director. Acquires regional production rights for the year of the contest. Plays must be 50 minutes long; must be a musical (composed music is not necessary, just song lyrics); written for multiple characters played by three actors, with roles for men and women. Other criteria, such as subject matter, varies from year to year. Send SASE for details.

☑ **DON FREEMAN MEMORIAL GRANT-IN-AID**, Society of Children's Book Writers and Illustrators, 8271 Beverly Blvd., Los Angeles CA 90048. E-mail: scbwi@juno.com. Website: www.scbwi.org. Estab. 1974. Purpose of award: to "enable picture book artists to further their understanding, training and work in the picture book genre." Applications and prepared materials will be accepted between January 15 and February 15. Grant awarded and announced on June 15. SASE for award rules and entry forms. SASE for return of entries. No entry fee. Annually awards one grant of $1,000 and one runner-up grant of $500. "The grant-in-aid is available to both full and associate members of the SCBWI who, as artists, seriously intend to make picture books their chief contribution to the field of children's literature."

⬇ **AMELIA FRANCES HOWARD GIBBON AWARD FOR ILLUSTRATION**, Canadian Library Association, Suite 602, 200 Elgin St., Ottawa, Ontario K2P 1L5 Canada. (613)232-9625. Contact: Chairperson, Canadian Association of Children's Librarians. Annual award. Estab. 1971. Purpose of the award: "to honor excellence in the illustration of children's book(s) in Canada. To merit consideration the book must have been published in Canada and its illustrator must be a Canadian citizen or a permanent resident of Canada." Previously published submissions only; must be published between January 1 and December 31 of the previous year. Deadline for entries: January 1. SASE for award rules. Entries not returned. No entry fee. Awards a medal. Judging by

---

MARKET CONDITIONS are constantly changing! If you're still using this book and it is 2001 or later, buy the newest edition of *Children's Writer's & Illustrator's Market* at your favorite bookstore or order directly from Writer's Digest Books.

selection committee of members of Canadian Association of Children's Librarians. Requirements for entrants: illustrator must be Canadian or Canadian resident. Winning books are on display at CLA Headquarters.

☑ **GOLD MEDALLION BOOK AWARDS**, Evangelical Christian Publishers Association, 1969 East Broadway Rd., Suite Two, Tempe AZ 85282. (480)966-3998. Fax: (480)966-1944. E-mail: jmeegan@ecpa.org. Website: www.ecpa.org. President: Doug Ross. Annual award. Estab. 1978. Categories include Preschool Children's Books, Elementary Children's Books, Youth Books. "All entries must be evangelical in nature and cannot be contrary to ECPA's Statement of Faith (stated in official rules)." Deadlines for entries: December 1. SASE for award rules and entry form. "The work must be submitted by the publisher." Entry fee is $300 for nonmembers. Awards a Gold Medallion plaque.

☑ **GOLDEN ARCHER AWARD**, Wisconsin Educational Media Association, 1300 Industrial Dr., Fennimore WI 53809. Website: www.wema.org/goldkite.htm. Award Director: Annette R. Smith. **Open to students.** Annual award. Estab. 1974. Purpose of award: to encourage young readers to become better acquainted with quality literature written expressly for them, to broaden students' awareness of reading and literature as life-long pleasure and to honor favorite books and their authors. Previously published submissions only. Submissions nominated by Wisconsin students. No entry fee. Three awards are given—one in each of 3 categories, Primary, Intermediate and Middle/Junior High.

☑ **GOLDEN KITE AWARDS**, Society of Children's Book Writers and Illustrators, 8271 Beverly Blvd., Los Angeles CA 90048. (323)782-1010. E-mail: scbwi@juno.com. Website: www.scbwi.org/goldkite.htm. Coordinator: Sue Alexander. Annual award. Estab. 1973. "The works chosen will be those that the judges feel exhibit excellence in writing, and in the case of the picture-illustrated books—in illustration, and genuinely appeal to the interests and concerns of children. For the fiction and nonfiction awards, original works and single-author collections of stories or poems of which at least half are new and never before published in book form are eligible—anthologies and translations are not. For the picture-illustration awards, the art or photographs must be original works (the texts—which may be fiction or nonfiction—may be original, public domain or previously published). Deadline for entries: December 15. SASE for award rules. Self-addressed mailing label for return of entries. No entry fee. Awards statuettes and plaques. The panel of judges will consist of two children's book authors, a children's book artist or photographer (who may or may not be an author), a children's book editor and a librarian." Requirements for entrants: "must be a member of SCBWI." Winning books will be displayed at national conference in August. Books to be entered, as well as further inquiries, should be submitted to: The Society of Children's Book Writers and Illustrators, above address.

Ⓝ **AURAND HARRIS MEMORIAL PLAYWRITING AWARD**, The New England Theatre Conference, c/o Department of Theatre, Northeastern University, 360 Huntington Ave., Boston MA 02115. Annual award. Estab. 1997. Unpublished submissions only. Submissions by author. Deadline for entries: April 15. Handling fee is $20; no fee to current members of New England Theatre Conference. Awards 2 cash prizes: 1st Prize of $1,000 and 2nd Prize of $500. Judging by a panel of judges named by the NETC Executive Board. Playwrights may submit only 1 play/year. Contest open only to New England residents and any NETC member. Playwrights living outside of New England may participate by joining NETC. No scripts will be returned. Winners notified by mail.

☑ **HIGHLIGHTS FOR CHILDREN FICTION CONTEST**, 803 Church St., Honesdale PA 18431-2030. (717)253-1080. Fax: (570)251-7847. E-mail: highlights@ezaccess.net. Mss should be addressed to Fiction Contest. Editor: Kent L. Brown Jr. Annual contest. Estab. 1980. Purpose of the contest: to stimulate interest in writing for children and reward and recognize excellence. Unpublished submissions only. Deadline for entries: February 28; entries accepted after January 1 only. SASE for contest rules and return of entries. No entry fee. Awards 3 prizes of $1,000 each in cash and a pewter bowl (or, at the winner's election, attendance at the Highlights Foundation Writers Workshop at Chautauqua). Judging by *Highlights* editors. Winning pieces are purchased for the cash prize of $1,000 and published in *Highlights*; other entries are considered for purchase. Requirements for entrants: open to any writer. Winners announced in June. Length up to 900 words. Stories for beginning readers should not exceed 500 words. Stories should be consistent with *Highlights* editorial requirements. No violence, crime or derogatory humor. Send SASE for guidelines and contract theme."

☑ ❖ **INFORMATION BOOK AWARD**, Children's Literature Roundtables of Canada, Dept. of Language Education, University of British Columbia, 2125 Main Mall, Vancouver, British Columbia V6T 1Z4 Canada. (604)822-5788. Fax: (604)922-1666. E-mail: aprilg@direct.ca. Website: www.library.ubc.ca/edlib/rdtable.html. Award Directors: April Gill and Dr. Ron Jobe. Annual contest. Estab. 1987. Purpose of contest: The Information Book Award recognizes excellence in the writing of information books for young people from 5 to 15 years. It is awarded to the book that arouses interest, stimulates curiosity, captures the imagination, and fosters concern for the world around us. The award's aim is to recognize excellence in Canadian publishing of nonfiction for children. Previously published submissions only. Submissions nominated by a person or group of people. Work must have been published the calendar year previous to the award being given. Deadline for entries: June. SASE for contest rules. Certificates are awarded to the author and illustrator and they share a cash prize of $500

(Canadian). Judging by members of the children's literature roundtables of Canada. In consultation with children's bookstores across Canada, a national committee based in Vancouver sends out a selective list of over 20 titles representing the best of the information books from the preceding year. The Roundtables consider this preliminary list and send back their recommendations, resulting in 5-7 finalists. The Roundtables make time at their Fall meetings to discuss the finalists and vote on their choices, which are collated into one vote per Roundtable (the winner is announced in November for Canada's Book Week). The award is granted at the Serendipity Children's Literature Conference held in February in Vancouver, British Columbia.

☑ **INSPIRATIONAL WRITERS ALIVE! OPEN WRITERS COMPETITION**, Texas Christian Writer's Forum, 6038 Greenmont, Houston TX 77092-2332. Fax: (713)686-7209. E-mail: mrogers353@aol.com or patav @aol.com. Contact: Contest Director. Annual contest. Estab. 1990. Purpose of contest: to help aspiring writers in the inspirational/religion markets and to encourage writers in their efforts to write for possible future publication. Our critique sheets give valuable information to our participants. Unpublished submissions only. Submissions made by author. Deadline: May 15. SASE for contest rules. Entry fee is $10 (devotional, short story or article); $10 (3 poems). Awards certificate of merit for 1st, 2nd and 3rd Place; plus a small monetary award of $25 1st, $15 2nd, $10 3rd. Requirements for entrants: Cannot enter published material. "We want to aid especially new and aspiring writers." Contest has 5 categories—to include short story (adult), short story (for children and teens) article, daily devotions, and poetry and book proposal. Request complete guidelines from M. Rogers. Entry forms and info available after December 1, 1999. "*Must* include a cover sheet with every category."

N IOWA TEEN AWARD, Iowa Educational Media Association, 306 E. H Ave., Grundy Center IA 50638. (319)824-6788. Contest Directors: Joel Shoemaker (shoemaker@iowacity.k12.ia.us). Nancy Geiken (ngeiken@vi nton-shellsburg.k12.ia.us). Annual award. Estab. 1983. Previously published submissions only. Purpose of award: to allow students to read high quality literature and to have the opportunity to select their favorite from this list. Must have been published "in last 3-4 years." Deadline for entries: April 1999 for 2000-2001 competition. SASE for award rules/entry forms. No entry fee. "Media specialists, teachers and students nominate possible entries." Awards an inscribed brass apple. Judging by Iowa students in grades 6-9. Requirements: Work must be of recent publication, so copies can be ordered for media center collections. Reviews of submitted books must be available for the nominating committee. Works displayed "at participating classrooms, media centers, public libraries and local bookstores in Iowa."

N JOSEPH HENRY JACKSON AND JAMES D. PHELAN LITERARY AWARDS, The San Francisco Foundation, 446 Valencia St., San Francisco CA 94103. (415)626-2787. Fax: (415)626-1636. E-mail: intrsect@w enet.net. Submit entries to Awards Coordinator. **Open to Students.** Annual award. Estab. 1937. Purpose of award: to encourage young writers for an unpublished manuscript-in-progress. Submissions must be unpublished. Submissions made by author. Deadline for entry: January 31. SASE for contest rules and entry forms. Judging by established peers. All applicants must be 20-35 years of age. Applicants for the Henry Jackson Award must be residents of northern California or Nevada for 3 consecutive years immediately prior to the January 31, deadline. Applicants for the James D. Phelan awards must have been born on California but need not be current residents.

N THE EZRA JACK KEATS NEW WRITER AWARD, Ezra Jack Keats Foundation/Administered by the New York Public Library Early Childhood Resource and Information Center, 66 Leroy St., New York NY 10014. (212)929-0815. Fax: (212)242-8242. E-mail: jjonas@nypl.org. Program Coordinator: JoAnn Jonas. **Open to students.** Annual award. Purpose of the award: "The award will be given to a promising new writer of picture books for children. Selection criteria include books for children (ages nine and under) that reflect the tradition of Ezra Jack Keats. These books portray: the universal qualities of childhood, strong and supportive family and adult relationships, the multicultural nature of our world." Submissions made by the author, by the author's agent or nominated by a person or group of people. Must be published in the preceding year. Deadline for entries: December 15, 1999. SASE for contest rules and entry forms. No entry fee. Awards $1,000 coupled with Ezra Jack Keats Silver Medal. Judging by a panel of experts. "The author should have published no more than six books. Entries are judged on the outstanding features of the text, complemented by illustrations. Candidates need not be both author and illustrator. Entries should carry a 1999 copyright (for the 2000 award)." Winning book and author to be presented at reception at The New York Public Library.

N KERLAN AWARD, University of Minnesota, 109 Walter Library, 117 Pleasant St. SE, Minneapolis MN 55455. (612)624-4576. Website: www.lib.umn.edu/special/kerlan. Curator: Karen Nelson Hoyle. Annual award. Estab. 1975. "Given in recognition of singular attainments in the creation of children's literature and in appreciation for generous donation of unique resources to the Kerlan Collection." Previously published submissions only. Deadline for entries: November 1. Anyone can send nominations for the award, directed to the Kerlan Collection. No materials are submitted other than the person's name. Requirements for entrants: open to all who are nominated. "For serious consideration, entrant must be a published author and/or illustrator of children's books (including young adult fiction) and have donated original materials to the Kerlan Collection."

⬛ CORETTA SCOTT KING AWARD, Coretta Scott King Task Force, Social Responsibility Round Table, American Library Association, 50 E. Huron St., Chicago IL 60611. Website: www.ala.org/srrt/csking. "The Coretta Scott King Award is an annual award for a book (1 for text and 1 for illustration) that conveys the spirit of brotherhood espoused by M.L. King, Jr.—and also speaks to the Black experience—for young people. There is an award jury that judges the books—reviewing over the year—and making a decision in January. A copy of an entry must be sent to each juror. Acquire jury list from SRRT office in Chicago."

ANNE SPENCER LINDBERGH PRIZE IN CHILDREN'S LITERATURE, The Charles A. and Anne Morrow Lindbergh Foundation, 2150 Third Ave., Suite 310, Anoka MN 55303. (612)576-1596. Fax: (612)576-1664. E-mail: lindbergh@isd.net. Website: www.isd.net/lindbergh. Contest Director: Kelley A. Wolf. Competition open to adults. Contest is offered every 2 years. Estab. 1996. Purpose of contest: To recognize the children's fantasy novel judged to be the best published in the English language during the 2-year period. Prize program honors Anne Spencer Lindbergh, author of a number of acclaimed juvenile fantasies, who died in late 1993 at the age of 53. Previously published submissions only. Submissions made by author, author's agent or publishers. Must be published between January 1 of odd numbered years and December 31 of even numbered years. Deadline for entries: November 1 of even numbered years. Entry fee is $25. Awards $5,000 to author of winning book. Judging by panel drawn from writers, editors, librarians and teachers prominent in the field of children's literature. Requirements for entrants: Open to all authors of children's fantasy novels published during the 2-year period. Entries must include 4 copies of books submitted. Winner announced in January.

✅ LOUISE LOUIS/EMILY F. BOURNE STUDENT POETRY AWARD, Poetry Society of America, 15 Gramercy Park, New York NY 10003-1705. (212)254-9628. Fax: (212)673-2352. E-mail: timothyd@poetrysociety.org. Website: www.poetrysociety.com. Contact: Award Director. **Open to students.** Annual award. Purpose of the award: award is for the best unpublished poem by a high or preparatory school student (grades 9-12) from the US and its territories. Unpublished submissions only. Deadline for entries: Oct. 1 to Dec. 21. SASE for award rules and entry forms. Entries not returned. "High schools can send an unlimited number of submissions with one entry per individual student for a flat fee of $10." Award: $250. Judging by a professional poet. Requirements for entrants: Award open to all high school and preparatory students from the US and its territories. School attended, as well as name and address, should be noted. PSA submission guidelines must be followed. These are printed in our fall calendar and are readily available if those interested send us a SASE. Line limit: none. "The award-winning poem will be included in a sheaf of poems that will be part of the program at the award ceremony and sent to all PSA members."

✅ MAGAZINE MERIT AWARDS, Society of Children's Book Writers and Illustrators, 8271 Beverly Blvd., Los Angeles CA 90048. Fax: (323)782-1010. Website: www.scbwi.org/magmerit.htm. Award Coordinator: Dorothy Leon. Annual award. Estab. 1988. Purpose of the award: "to recognize outstanding original magazine work for young people published during that year and having been written or illustrated by members of SCBWI." Previously published submissions only. Entries must be submitted between January 31 and December 15 of the year of publication. For brochure (rules) write Award Coordinator. No entry fee. Must be a SCBWI member. Awards plaques and honor certificates for each of the 3 categories (fiction, nonfiction, illustration). Judging by a magazine editor and two "full" SCBWI members. "All magazine work for young people by an SCBWI member—writer, artist or photographer—is eligible during the year of original publication. In the case of co-authored work, both authors must be SCBWI members. Members must submit their own work." Requirements for entrants: 4 copies each of the published work and proof of publication (may be contents page) showing the name of the magazine and the date of issue. The SCBWI is a professional organization of writers and illustrators and others interested in children's literature. Membership is open to the general public at large.

✅ MAJESTIC BOOKS WRITING CONTEST, Majestic Books, P.O. Box 19097, Johnston RI 02919-0097. E-mail: majesticbk@aol.com. Contest Director: Cindy MacDonald. **Open to Rhode Island students only.** Annual contest. Estab. 1992. Purpose of contest: to encourage students to write to the best of their ability and to be proud of their work. Unpublished submissions only. Submissions made by the author or teacher. Deadline for entries: December 31. No entry fee; however, we do ask for a large SASE (9×12) for our reply and certificate. Winners are published in an anthology. All entrants receive a certificate acknowledging their efforts. Judging by a panel of published writers and an English teacher. One-time publishing rights to submitted material required or purchased. "Our contest is open to all students, age 6-17 in Rhode Island. *Anthology* comes off the press in December and a presentation ceremony is held for all winning students. Students must include their age, grade, school and statement of authenticity signed by the writer and a parent or teacher. Entries must be neat and will not be returned. In order to encourage all children, every entrant receives a personalized award acknowledging their efforts."

⬛ MILKWEED PRIZE FOR CHILDREN'S LITERATURE, Milkweed Editions, 430 First Ave. N., Suite 400, Minneapolis MN 55401-1473. (612)332-3192. Fax: (612)332-6248. E-mail: greg_larson@milkweed.org. Website: www.milkweed.org. Award Director: Emilie Buchwald, publisher/editor. Annual award. Estab. 1993. Purpose of the award: to find an outstanding novel for readers ages 8-13 and encourage writers to turn their attention to readers in this age group. Unpublished submissions only "in book form." Must send SASE for award guidelines. The prize is awarded to the best work for children ages 8-13 that Milkweed agrees to publish in a calendar year by a writer not published by Milkweed before. The Prize consists of a $5,000 advance against royalties agreed to at the time of acceptance. Submissions must follow our usual children's guidelines. Must send SASE with submission form.

N NATIONAL CHILDREN'S THEATRE FESTIVAL, Actor's Playhouse at the Miracle Theatre, 280 Miracle Mile, Coral Gables FL 33134. (305)444-9293. Fax: (305)444-4181. Director: Earl Maulding. **Open to Students**. Annual contest. Estab. 1994. Purpose of contest: to encourage new, top quality musicals for young audiences. Submissions must be unpublished. Submissions are made by author or author's agent. Deadline for entries: August 1, 2000. SASE for contest rules and entry forms. Entry fee is $10. Awards: first prize of $1,000 plus production; second prize of $100, plus reading. Judging by local panel of theatre professionals. Final judges are of national reputation. Past judges include Joseph Robinette and Moses Goldberg. Rights to winning material acquired.

NATIONAL PARENTING PUBLICATIONS AWARD (NAPPA), National Parenting Publications Awards, 443 E. Irving Dr., Suite D, Burbank CA 91504. (818)864-0400, ext. 250. E-mail: laparent@family.com. Website: www.laparent.com. Contact person: NAPPA Coordinator. Annual contest. Estab. 1991. Purpose of award: To recognize high-quality media and toys that enrich the educational and entertainment experiences of children. Submissions made by author, by author's agent, nominated by a person or group, or may be submitted by anyone. Deadline for entries: July 31. Call for contest rules and entry forms. Entry fee is $89. Gold winners receive editorial mention in each of the participating parenting publications throughout the US. Judged by distinguished reviewers, educators, editors and authors. The most important criteria is that each product must enrich both the educational and entertainment experiences of children, helping today's kid prepare for tomorrow. Call for categories and entry form.

NATIONAL WRITERS ASSOCIATION SHORT STORY CONTEST, 3140 S. Peoria, Suite 295, Aurora CO 80014. (303)841-0246. Executive Director: Sandy Whelchel. Annual contest. Estab. 1971. Purpose of contest: "To encourage writers in this creative form and to recognize those who excel in fiction writing." Submissions made by the author. Deadline for entries: July 1. SASE for contest rules and entry forms. Entry fee is $15. Awards 3 cash prizes, choice of books and certificates for Honorable Mentions. Judging by "two people read each entry; third person picks top three winners." Judging sheet copies available for SASE. Top three winners are published in an anthology published by National Writers Association, if winners agree to this.

N.C. WRITERS' NETWORK INTERNATIONAL LITERARY PRIZES, N.C. Writers' Network, 3501 Hwy. 54 W, Studio C, Chapel Hill NC 27516. (919)967-9540. Fax: (919)929-0535. E-mail: mail@ncwriters.org. Website: www.ncwriters.org. Program Coordinator: Frances Dowell. **Open to students.** Annual contest. *Thomas Wolfe Fiction Prize* (TWFP), est. 1994, awards $1,000 prize for best piece of fiction (short story or novel excerpt not to exceed 12 pp.), winning entry will be considered for publication in Carolina quarterly; *Paul Green Playwrights Prize* (PGPP), est. 1995, awards $500 prize for best play, any length, no musicals, winning entry will be considered for production by a consortium of North Carolina theaters. *Randall Jarrell Poetry Prize* (RJPP), est. 1990, awards $1,000 prize, publication and reading/reception for best poem, winning poem published in Parnassus: Poetry in Review. Unpublished submissions only. Submissions made by the author. Deadline for entries: TWFP—Aug. 31; PGPP—Sept. 30; RJPP—Nov. 1. SASE for award rules and entry forms. Entry fee is $7-TWFP; $7-RJPP; $10-PGPP ($7.50 for NCWN members). Judging by published writers or editors. Previous judges have included: Anne Tyler, Barbara Kingsolver, Donald Hall, Lucille Clifton, Romulus Linney.

NEW ENGLAND BOOK AWARDS, New England Booksellers Association, 847 Massachusetts Ave., Cambridge MA 02139. (617)576-3070. Fax: (617)576-3091. E-mail: neba@neba.org. Award Director: Nan Sorensen. Annual award. Estab. 1990. Purpose of award: "to promote New England authors who have produced a body of work that stands as a significant contribution to New England's culture and is deserving of wider recognition." Previously published submissions only. Submissions made by New England booksellers; publishers. "Award given to authors 'body of work' not a specific book." Entries must be still in print and available. Deadline for entries: October 31. SASE for contest rules and entry forms. No entry fee. Judging by NEBA membership. Requirements for entrants: Author/illustrator must live in New England. Submit written nominations only; actual books should not be sent. Member bookstores receive materials to display winners' books.

N JOHN NEWBERY MEDAL, Association for Library Service to Children, Division of the American Library Association, 50 E. Huron, Chicago IL 60611. Website: www.ala.org/alsc/newbery.html. (312)280-2163.

Executive Director, ALSC: Susan Roman. Annual award. Estab. 1922. Purpose of award: to recognize the most distinguished contribution to American children's literature published in the US. Previously published submissions only; must be published prior to year award is given. Deadline for entries: December. SASE for award rules. Entries not returned. No entry fee. Medal awarded at Caldecott/Newbery banquet during annual conference. Judging by Newbery Committee.

N: THE NOMA AWARD FOR PUBLISHING IN AFRICA, Kodansha Ltd., P.O. Box 128, Witney, Oxon OX8 5XU England. 44-1993-775235. Fax: 44-1993-709265. E-mail: maryljay@aol.com. Secretary of the Managing Committee: Mary Jay. **Open to students.** Annual award. Estab. 1979. Purpose of award: to encourage publications of works by African writers and scholars in Africa, instead of abroad, as is still too often the case at present. Books in the following categories are eligible: scholarly or academic, books for children, literature and creative writing, including fiction, drama and poetry. Previously published submissions only. 2000 award given for book published in 1999. Deadline for entries: end of February 2000. Submissions must be made through publishers. Conditions of entry and submission forms are available from the secretariat. Entries not returned. No entry fee. Awards $10,000. Judging by the Managing Committee (jury): African scholars and book experts and representatives of the international book community. Chairman: Walter Bgoya. Requirements for entrants: Author must be African, and book must be published in Africa. "Winning titles are displayed at appropriate international book events."

N: NORTH AMERICAN INTERNATIONAL AUTO SHOW SHORT STORY HIGH SCHOOL POSTER CONTEST, Detroit Auto Dealers Association,. 1800 W. Big Beaver Rd., Troy MI 48084-3531. (248)643-0250. Fax: (248)637-0734. E-mail: aprice@dada.org. Website: naias.com. Director of Communications: Sharon Kelsey. **Open to students.** Annual contest. Submissions made by the author and illustrator. Deadline to be determined for 2000. Contact DADA for contest rules and entry forms. No entry fee. Five winners of the short story contest will each receive $500. Entries will be judged by an independent panel comprised of knowledgeable persons engaged in the literary field in some capacity. Entrants must be Michigan residents, including high school students enrolled in grades 9-12. Junior high school students in 9th grade are also eligible. Awards in the High School Poster Contest are as follows: Best Theme, Best Use of Color, Best Use of Graphics & Most Creative. A winner will be chosen in each category from grades 9, 10, 11 and 12. Each winner in each grade from each category will win $250. The winner of the Chairmans Award will receive $1,000. Entries will be judged by an independent panel of recognized representatives of the art community. Entrants must be Michigan high school students enrolled in grades 9-12. Junior high students in 9th grade are also eligible. Winners will be announced during the North American International Auto Show in January and may be published in the *Auto Show Program* at the sole discretion of the D.A.D.A.

N: THE SCOTT O'DELL AWARD FOR HISTORICAL FICTION, 1700 E. 56th St., Suite 3907, Chicago IL 60637-1936. Award Director: Mrs. Zena Sutherland. Annual award. Estab. 1981. Purpose of the award: "To promote the writing of historical fiction of good quality for children and young adults." Previously published submissions only; must be published between January 1 and December 31 previous to deadline. Deadline for entries: December 31. "Publishers send books, although occasionally a writer sends a note or a book." SASE for award rules. No entry fee. There is only 1 book chosen each year. Award: $5,000. Judging by a committee of 3. Requirements for entrants: "Must be published by a U.S. publisher in the preceding year; must be written by an American citizen; must be set in North or South America; must be historical fiction."

✓ OHIOANA BOOK AWARDS, Ohioana Library Association, 65 S. Front St., Suite 1105, Columbus OH 43215. (614)466-3831. Fax: (614)728-6974. E-mail: ohioana@winslo.state.oh.us. Website: www.oplin.lib.oh.us/ OHIOANA/. Director: Linda R. Hengst. Annual award. "The Ohioana Book Awards are given to books of outstanding literary quality. Purpose of contest: to provide recognition and encouragement to Ohio writers and to promote the work of Ohio writers. Up to six are given each year. Awards may be given in the following categories: fiction, nonfiction, children's literature, poetry and books about Ohio or an Ohioan. Books must be received by the Ohioana Library during the calendar year prior to the year the award is given and must have a copyright date within the last two calendar years." Deadline for entries: December 31. SASE for award rules and entry forms. No entry fee. Winners receive citation and glass sculpture. "Any book that has been written or edited by a person born in Ohio or who has lived in Ohio for at least five years" is eligible. The Ohioana Library Association also awards the "Ohioana Book Award in the category of juvenile books." Send SASE for more information.

✓ OKLAHOMA BOOK AWARDS, Oklahoma Center for the Book, 200 NE 18th, Oklahoma City OK 73105. (405)521-2502. Fax: (405)525-7804. E-mail: gcarlile@oltn.odl.state.ok.us. Website: www.odl.state.ok.us/ ocb. Annual award. **Open to students.** Estab. 1989. Purpose of award: "to honor Oklahoma writers and books about our state." Previously published submissions only. Submissions made by the author, author's agent, or entered by a person or group of people, including the publisher. Must be published during the calendar year preceding the award. Awards are presented to best books in fiction, nonfiction, children's, design and illustration, poetry and books about Oklahoma or books written by an author who was born, is living or has lived in Oklahoma. Deadline for entries: early January. SASE for award rules and entry forms. No entry fee. Awards a medal—no cash prize. Judging by a panel of 5 people for each category—a librarian, a working writer in the genre, booksellers, editors, etc. Requirements for entrants: author must be an Oklahoma native, resident, former resident or have written a book with Oklahoma theme. Winner will be announced at banquet at the Cowboy Hall of Fame in Oklahoma City. The Aarell Gibson Lifetime Achievement Award is also presented each year to an Oklahoma author for a body of work.

N: ORBIS PICTUS AWARD FOR OUTSTANDING NONFICTION FOR CHILDREN, The National Council of Teachers of English, 1111 W. Kenyon Rd., Urbana IL 61801-1096. (217)328-3870, ext. 3603. Co-Chairs, NCTE Committee on the Orbis Pictus Award for Outstanding Nonfiction for Children: Karen P. Smith, Queens College, New York and Richard Kemper, Millersville University, Pennsylvania. Annual award. Estab. 1989. Purpose of award: to honor outstanding nonfiction works for children. Previously published submissions only. Submissions made by author, author's agent, by a person or group of people. Must be published January 1-December 31 of contest year. Deadline for entries: November 30. Call for award information. No entry fee. Awards a plaque given at the NCTE Elementary Section Luncheon at the NCTE Annual Convention in November. Judging by a committee.

☑ HELEN KEATING OTT AWARD FOR OUTSTANDING CONTRIBUTION TO CHILDREN'S LITERATURE, Church and Synagogue Library Association, P.O. Box 19357, Portland OR 97280-0357. (503)244-6919. Fax: (503)977-3734. E-mail: csla@worldaccessnet.com. Website: www.worldaccessnet.com/~csla. Chair of Committee: Evelyn Pockrass. Annual award. Estab. 1980. "This award is given to a person or organization that has made a significant contribution to promoting high moral and ethical values through children's literature." Deadline for entries: April 1. "Recipient is honored in July during the conference." Awards certificate of recognition and a conference package consisting of all meals day of awards banquet, two nights' housing and a complementary 1 year membership. "A nomination for an award may be made by anyone. It should include the name, address and telephone number of the nominee plus the church or synagogue relationship where appropriate. Nominations of an organization should include the name of a contact person. A detailed description of the reasons for the nomination should be given, accompanied by documentary evidence of accomplishment. The person(s) making the nomination should give his/her name, address and telephone number and a brief explanation of his/her knowledge of the nominee's accomplishments. Elements of creativity and innovation will be given high priority by the judges."

☑ ❀ OWL MAGAZINE CONTESTS, Writing Contest, Photo Contest, Poetry Contest, *OWL Magazine*, 179 John St., Suite 500, Toronto, Ontario M5T 3G5 Canada. (416)340-2700. Fax: (416)340-9769. E-mail: owl@owlkids.com. Website: www.owl.on.ca. Contact: Children's Page editor. Annual contests. Purpose of contests: "to encourage children to contribute and participate in the magazine. Unpublished submissions only. Deadlines change yearly. Prizes/awards "change every year. Often we give books as prizes." Winning entries published in the magazine. Judging by art and editorial staff. Entries become the property of Bayard Press. "The contests and awards are open to children up to 14 years of age. Check the Hoot section of *OWL* for information and updates on contests."

PATERSON PRIZE FOR BOOKS FOR YOUNG PEOPLE, Poetry Center at Passaic County Community College, One College Blvd., Paterson NJ 07505-1179. (973)684-6555. Fax: (973)684-5843. E-mail: mgillan@pccc.cc.nj.us. Website: www.pccc.cc.nj.us/poetry. Award Director: Maria Mazziotti Gillan. **Open to students.** Estab. 1996. Poetry Center's mission is "to recognize excellence in books for young people." Previously published submissions only. Submissions made by author, author's agent or publisher. Must be published between January 1, 1998-December 31, 1999. Deadline for entries: March 15, 2000. SASE for contest rules and entry forms. Awards $500 for the author in either of 3 categories: PreK-Grade 3; Grades 4-6, Grades 7-12. Judging by a professional writer selected by the Poetry Center. Contest is open to any writer/illustrator. Write for guidelines.

PENNSYLVANIA YOUNG READER'S CHOICE AWARDS, Pennsylvania School Librarians Association, 148 S. Bethelehem Pike, Ambler PA 19002-5822. (215)643-5048. Fax: (215)628-8441. E-mail: bellavance@erols.com. Coordinator: Jean B. Bellavance. Annual award. Estab. 1991. Submissions nominated by a person or group. Must be published within 5 years of the award—for 1999-2000 books published 1995 to present. Deadline for entries: September 15, 1999. SASE for contest rules and entry forms. No entry fee. Framed certificate to winning authors. Judging by children of Pennsylvania (they vote). Requirements for entrants: currently living in North America. Reader's Choice Award is to promote reading of quality books by young people in the Commonwealth of Pennsylvania, to promote teacher and librarian involvement in children's literature, and to honor authors whose work has been recognized by the children of Pennsylvania. Three awards are given, one for each of the following grade levels: K-3, 3-6, 6-8.

☑ PLEASE TOUCH MUSEUM® BOOK AWARD, Please Touch Museum, 210 N. 21st St., Philadelphia PA 19103-1001. (215)963-0667. Fax: (215)963-0667. E-mail: sey@libertynet.org. Website: www.pleasetouchmuseum.org. **Open to students.** Annual award. Estab. 1985. Purpose of the award: "to recognize and encourage the publication of books for young children by American authors that are of the highest quality and will aid them in enjoying the process of learning through books. Awarded to two picture books that are particularly imaginative and effective in exploring a concept or concepts, one for children age three and younger, and one for children ages four-seven." Previously published submissions only. "To be eligible for consideration a book must: (1) Explore and clarify an idea for young children. This could include the concept of numbers, colors, shapes, sizes, senses, feelings, etc. There is no limitation as to format. (2) Be distinguished in both text and illustration. (3) Be published within the last year by an American publisher. (4) Be by an American author and/or illustrator." Deadline for entries: (submissions may be made throughout the year). SASE for award rules and entry forms. No entry fee. Judging by selected jury of children's literature experts, librarians and early childhood educators. Education store purchases books for selling at Book Award Celebration Day and throughout the year. Receptions and autographing sessions held in bookstores, Please Touch Museum, and throughout the city.

EDGAR ALLAN POE AWARD, Mystery Writers of America, Inc., 6th Floor, 17 E. 47th St., New York NY 10017. (212)888-8171. Fax: (212)888-8107. Website: www.mysterywriters.org. Administrative Director: Mary Beth Becker. Annual award. Estab. 1945. Purpose of the award: to honor authors of distinguished works in the mystery field. Previously published submissions only. Submissions made by the author, author's agent; "normally by the publisher." Work must be published/produced the year of the contest. Deadline for entries: November 30 "except for works only available in the month of December." SASE for award rules and entry forms. No entry fee. Awards ceramic bust of "Edgar" for winner; scrolls for all nominees. Judging by professional members of Mystery Writers of America (writers). Nominee press release sent after first Wednesday in February. Winner announced at the Edgar Banquet, held in late April.

☑ ✿ THE PRISM AWARDS, The Kids Netword, 90 Venice Crescent, Thornhill, Ontario L4J 7T1 Canada. (877)908-9900 or (905)882-9755. Fax: (403)932-9901. Award Manager: Lucy La Grassa. Annual award. Estab. 1989. Purpose of the award: Children have an opportunity to submit mss for review. Winners are chosen based on originality of ideas and self-expression. Unpublished submissions only. Deadline for entries: January 2000. SASE for award rules and entry forms. Entry fee is $2. Award consists of $500 cash and editorial training and possible publication. Judging by more than 20 independent judges. Requirements for entrants: a Native Indian, Canadian or landed immigrant in Canada, ages 7-14; story must be written solely by the submitter. No less than 4 pages, no more than 16 pages. Copyright only to winning ms acquired by The Kids Netword upon winning.

☑ ✿ PRIX ALVINE-BELISLE, Association pour l'avancement des sciences et des techniques de la documentation (ASTED) Inc., 3414 Avenue Du Parc, Bureau 202, Montreal, Québec H2X 2H5 Canada. (514)281-5012. Fax: (514)281-8219. E-mail: info@asted.org. Award President: Micheline Patton. Award open to children's book editors. Annual award. Estab. 1974. Purpose of contest: To recognize the best children's book published in French in Canada. Previously published submissions only. Submissions made by publishing house. Must be published the year before award. Deadline for entries: June 1. Awards $500. Judging by librarians jury.

QUILL AND SCROLL INTERNATIONAL WRITING/PHOTO CONTEST, *Quill and Scroll*, School of Journalism, University of Iowa, Iowa City IA 52242-1528. (319)335-5795. Fax: (319)335-5210. E-mail: quill-scroll@uiowa.edu. Website: www.niowa.edu/~quill-sc. Contest Director: Richard Johns. **Open to students.** Annual contest. Previously published submissions only. Submissions made by the author or school newspaper adviser. Must be published February 6, 1999 to February 4, 2000. Deadline for entries: February 5. SASE for contest rules and entry forms. Entry fee is $2/entry. Awards engraved plaque to junior high level sweepstakes winners. Judging by various judges. *Quill and Scroll* acquires the right to publish submitted material in the magazine if it is chosen as a winning entry. Requirements for entrants: must be students in grades 9-12 for high school division.

THE ERIN PATRICK RABORG POETRY AWARD, *AMELIA Magazine*, 329 E St., Bakersfield CA 93304-2031. (805)823-4064. Fax: (805)323-5326. E-mail: amelia@lightspeed.net. Submit entries to: Frederick A. Raborg, Jr., editor. **Open to students.** Estab. 1992. Purpose of contest: To draw attention to childhood lifestyles and consequences. Also, to explore the humor as well as the pathos of childhood. Unpublished submissions only. Submissions made by author. Deadline for entries: December 1 annually. SASE for contest rules. Entry fee is $3 each entry. Award consists of $50 and publication in *AMELIA*. Judging is done in-house. Rights to winning material acquired: first North American serial only. "Be consistent within the form chosen."

☑ ANNA DAVIDSON ROSENBERG AWARD FOR POEMS ON THE JEWISH EXPERIENCE, Judah L. Magnes Museum, 2911 Russell St., Berkeley CA 94705. Poetry Award Director: Paula Friedman. Annual award. Estab. 1986-87. Purpose of the award: to encourage poetry in English on the Jewish experience (writer does not need to be Jewish). Previously unpublished submissions only. Deadline for entries: August 31. SASE for award rules and entry forms by July 31. Entry forms must be included with submissions. SASE for mandatory list of winners. Awards $100-1st Prize, $50-2nd Prize, $25-3rd Prize; honorable mention certificates; $25 Youth Commendation (poets under 19); $25 Emerging Poet Award. Judging by committee of 3 well-published poets with editing/teaching experience. There will be a reading of top award winners in December at Magnes Museum. Write for entry form and guidelines *first*; entries must follow guidelines and be accompanied by entry form. *Please do not phone.* Note: "We are not a contest for works for children—though our Youth Commendation is for authors under 19 (to date, winners have been as young as 9 years old)."

N: CARL SANDBURG LITERARY ARTS AWARDS, Friends of the Chicago Public Library, Harold Washington Library Center, 400 S. State St., Chicago IL 60605. (312)747-4907. Fax: (312)747-4077. Annual award. Categories: fiction, nonfiction, poetry, children's literature. Purpose of contest: to recognize Chicago area and Chicago connected authors. Published submissions only; must be published between June 1 and May 31 (the following year). Deadline for entries: August 15. SASE for award rules. Entries not returned. $25 entry fee. Awards medal and $1,000 prize. Judging by authors, reviewers, book buyers, librarians from Chicago literary community. Requirements for entrants: native born Chicagoan or presently residing in the 6 county metropolitan area. Two copies must be submitted by August 15. All entries become the property of the Friends.

SASKATCHEWAN BOOK AWARDS: CHILDREN'S LITERATURE, Saskatchewan Book Awards, Box 1921, Regina, Saskatchewan S4P 3E1 Canada. (306)569-1585. Fax: (306)569-4187. E-mail: sk.bookawards @dlewest.com. Award Director: Joyce Wells. **Open to students.** Annual award. Estab. 1995. Purpose of contest: to celebrate Saskatchewan books and authors and to promote their work. Previously published submissions only. Submissions made by author, author's agent or publisher by September 30. SASE for contest rules and entry forms. Entry fee is $15 (Canadian). Awards $1,000 (Canadian). Judging by two children's literature authors outside of Saskatchewan. Requirements for entrants: Must be Saskatchewan resident; book must have ISBN number; book must have been published within the last year. Award winning book will appear on TV talk shows and be pictured on book marks distributed to libraries, schools and bookstores in Saskatchewan.

SEEDHOUSE MAGAZINE'S SUMMER WRITING CONTEST, Seedhouse Magazine, P.O. Box 883009, Steamboat Springs CO 80488-3009. Fax: (970)879-6978. E-mail: seedhouse98atyahoo.com. Website: seedhouse mag.org. **Open to students.** Annual contest. Purpose of contest: "*Seedhouse Magazine* sponsors this annual contest to give published and nonpublished writers a chance to share their work. We are not looking for specific genre or form, but rather for fresh perspectives on whatever 'unlimbers' your keyboard. The contest is open to all genres of fiction and all types of poetry. We welcome entries from published and nonpublished writers. The winning story and poem will appear in the September/October issue of *Seedhouse Magazine*. Prizes will be awarded in both categories. 1st Place $50 and 1 year subscription to *Seedhouse* to winner in each category. 2nd Place $30, 3rd Place $20." Submissions made by author. Deadline for entries: July. Requirements for entrants: "Please put your name, address and telephone number on a separate piece of paper and include a two-three-sentence biography. Your name must not appear anywhere on your entry. Short story: 5,000 words or less. Poetry: two page maximum, up to three poems may be submitted as one entry."

SEVENTEEN FICTION CONTEST, 850 Third Ave., 9th Floor, New York NY 10022. Annual contest. Estab. 1945. Fax: (212)407-9899. E-mail: seventeenm@aol.com. Unpublished submissions only. Deadline for entries: April 30. SASE for contest rules and entry forms; contest rules also published in November issue of *Seventeen*. Entries not returned. No entry fee. Awards cash prize and possible publication in *Seventeen*. Judging by "inhouse panel of editors, external readers." If 1st Prize, acquires first North American rights for piece to be published. Requirements for entrants: "Our annual fiction contest is open to anyone between the ages of 13 and 21 who submit on or before April 30 (check November issue of *Seventeen* for details). Submit only original fiction that has not been published in any form other than in school publications. Stories should be between 1,500 and 3,000 words in length (6-12 pages). All manuscripts must be typed double-spaced on a single side of paper. Submit as many original stories as you like, but each story must include your full name, address, birth date and signature in the top right-hand corner of the first page. Your signature on submission will constitute your acceptance of the contest rules."

SHUBERT FENDRICH MEMORIAL PLAYWRIGHTING CONTEST, Pioneer Drama Service, Inc., P.O. Box 4267, Englewood CO 80155-4267. Fax: (303)779-4315. E-mail: piodrama@aol.com. Website: www.pioneer drama.com. Director: Beth Somers. Annual contest. **Open to students.** Estab. 1990. Purpose of the contest: "to encourage the development of quality theatrical material for educational and family theater." Previously unpublished submissions only. Deadline for entries: March 1. SASE for contest rules and guidelines. No entry fee. Cover letter must accompany all submissions. Awards $1,000 royalty advance and publication. Upon receipt of signed contracts, plays will be published and made available in our next catalog. Judging by editors. All rights acquired with acceptance of contract for publication. Restrictions for entrants: Any writers currently published by Pioneer Drama Service are not eligible.

SKIPPING STONES YOUTH HONOR AWARDS, *Skipping Stones*, P.O. Box 3939, Eugene OR 97403-0939. (541)342-4956. E-mail: skipping@efn.org. Website: www.nonviolence.org/skipping. Annual award. Purpose of contest: "to recognize youth, 7 to 17, for their contributions to multicultural awareness, nature and ecology, social issues, peace and nonviolence. Also to promote creativity, self-esteem and writing skills and to recognize important work being done by youth organizations." Submissions made by the author. The theme is "Multicultural and Nature Awareness." Deadline for entries: June 20. SASE for contest rules. Entries must include certificate of originality by a parent and/or teacher and background information on the author written by the author. Entry fee is $3. Judging by *Skipping Stones'* staff. "Up to ten awards are given in three categories: (1) Compositions—(essays, poems, short stories, songs, travelogues, etc.) should be typed (double-spaced) or neatly handwritten. Fiction or nonfiction should be limited to 750 words; poems to 30 lines. Non-English writings are also welcome. (2) Artwork—(drawings, cartoons, paintings or photo essays with captions) should have the artist's name, age and address on the back of each page. Send the originals with SASE. Black & white photos are especially welcome. Limit: 8 pieces. (3) Youth Organizations—Tell us how your club or group works to: (a) preserve the nature and ecology in your area, (b) enhance the quality of life for low-income, minority or disabled or (c) improve racial or cultural harmony in your school or community. Use the same format as for compositions." The winners are published in the September-October issue of *Skipping Stones*.

☑ KAY SNOW WRITERS' CONTEST, Williamette Writers, 9045 SW Barbur Blvd. #5A, Portland OR 97219-4027. (503)452-1592. Fax: (503)452-0372. E-mail: wilwrite@teleport.com. Website: www.teleport.com/~wilwrite/. Contest Director: Liam Cullen. Annual contest. **Open to students.** Purpose of contest: "to encourage beginning and established writers to continue the craft." Unpublished, original submissions only. Submissions made by the author or author's agent. Deadline for entries: May 15. SASE for contest rules and entry forms. Entry fee is $10, Williamette Writers' members; $15, nonmembers; free for student writers 6-18. Awards cash prize of $200 per category (fiction, nonfiction, juvenile, poetry, script writing), $50 for students in three divisions: 1-5, 6-8, 9-12. "Judges are anonymous."

☒ SOCIETY OF MIDLAND AUTHORS AWARDS, Society of Midland Authors, P.O. Box 10419, Chicago IL 60610-0419. E-mail: rclwriter@aol.com. Website: www.midlandauthors.com. **Open to students.** Annual award. Estab. 1915. Purpose of award: "to stimulate creative literary effort, one of the goals of the Society. There are six categories, including children's fiction, children's nonfiction, adult fiction and nonfiction, biography and poetry." Previously published submissions only. Submissions made by the author or publisher. Must be published during calendar year previous to deadline. Deadline for entries: January 30. SASE for award rules and entry forms. No entry fee. "Rules, forms and other information can now be downloaded from our website." Awards plaque given at annual dinner, cash (minimum $300). Judging by panel (reviewers, university faculty, writers, librarians) of 3 per category. "Award is for book published in the awards year." Author to be currently residing in the Midlands, i.e., Illinois, Indiana, Iowa, Kansas, Michigan, Minnesota, Missouri, Nebraska, North Dakota, South Dakota, Ohio or Wisconsin.

SPUR AWARDS, Western Writers of America, 60 Sandpiper Court, Conway AR 72032. (501)450-0086. Award Director: W.C. Jameson. Annual award. Estab. 1953. Previously published submissions only. Submissions made by author, author's agent or publisher. Must be published the year previous to the award. SASE for contest rules and entry forms. Awards plaque. Judging by panel of 3 published writers. Awards given in June 2000 at Kerrville TX.

☑ THE STANLEY DRAMA AWARD, Stanley-Tomolat Foundation, Wagner College, One Campus Rd., Staten Island NY 10301. (718)390-3325. Fax: (718)390-3323. E-mail: lterry@wagner.edu. Award Director: Liz Terry. **Open to students.** Annual award. Estab. 1957. Purpose of contest: to support new works and playwrights. Unpublished submissions only. Submissions made by author. Deadline for entries: October 1. SASE for contest rules and entry forms. Entry fee is $20. Awards $2,000. Judging by committee. Award is to a full-length play or musical, previously unpublished and/or produced. One-act plays must be a full evening of theater; accepts series of one-acts related to one theme. "We will consider only one submission per playwright."

GEORGE G. STONE CENTER FOR CHILDREN'S BOOKS RECOGNITION OF MERIT AWARD, George G. Stone Center for Children's Books, Claremont Graduate University, 131 E. 10th St., Claremont CA 91711-6188. (909)607-3670. Fax: (909)621-8390. Award Director: Doty Hale. Annual award. Estab. 1965. Purpose of the award: to recognize an author or illustrator of a children's book or a body of work exhibiting the "power to please and expand the awareness of children and teachers as they have shared the book in their classrooms." Previously published submissions only. SASE for award rules and entry forms. Entries not returned. No entry fee. Awards a scroll. Judging by a committee of teachers, professors of children's literature and librarians. Requirements for entrants: "Nominations are made by students, teachers, professors and librarians. Award made at annual Claremont Reading Conference in spring (March)."

☑ JOAN G. SUGARMAN CHILDREN'S BOOK AWARD, Washington Independent Writers Legal and Educational Fund, Inc., #220, 733 15th St. NW, Washington DC 20005. (202)347-4973. Fax: (202)628-0298. E-mail: washwriter@aol.com. Website: www.washwriter.org. Director: Isolde Chapin. Open to residents of D.C., Maryland, Virginia. Award offered every 2 years. Next awards presented in 2000 for publications done in 1997-

1998. Estab. 1987. Purpose of award: to recognize excellence in children's literature, ages 1-15. Previously published submissions only. Submissions made by the author or author's agent or by publishers. Must be published in the 2 years preceeding award year. Deadline for entries: January 31, 2000. SASE for award rules and entry forms. No entry fee. Awards $1,000. Judging by selected experts in children's books. Requirements for entrants: publication of material; residence in DC, Maryland or Virginia. No picture-only books. Works displayed at reception for award winners and become part of the Sugarman Collection at The George Washington University.

N **SUGARMAN FAMILY AWARD FOR JEWISH CHILDREN'S LITERATURE**, District of Columbia Jewish Community Center, 1529 16th St. NW, Washington DC 20036. (202)518-9400. Fax: (202)518-9420. Award director: Rabbi Panava Miller. **Open to students.** Biannual award. Estab. 1994. Purpose of contest: to enrich all children's appreciation of Jewish culture and to inspire writers and illustrators for children. Newly published submissions only. Submissions are made by the author, made by the author's agent. Must be published January-December of year previous to award year. SASE for entry deadlines, award rules and entry forms. Entry fee is $25. Award at least $750. Judging by a panel of 3 judges—a librarian, a children's bookstore owner and a reviewer of books. Requirements for entrants: must live in the United States. Work displayed at the D.C. Jewish Community Center Library after March.

SWW ANNUAL CONTEST, Southwest Writers Workshop, 1338 B Wyoming NE, Albuquerque NM 87112. (505)265-9485. Fax: (505)265-9483. E-mail: swriters@aol.com. Website: www.us1.net/sww. Submit entries to: Contest Chair. Annual contest. Estab. 1982. Purpose of contest: to encourage writers of all genres. Previously unpublished submissions only. Submissions made by author. Deadline for entries: May 1, 1999. SASE for contest rules and entry forms. Entry fee. Award consists of cash prizes in each of over 15 categories. Judging by national editors and agents. Official entry form is required.

✓ **SYDNEY TAYLOR MANUSCRIPT COMPETITION**, Association of Jewish Libraries, 1327 Wyntercreek Lane, Dunwoody GA 30338-3816. Fax: (770)394-2060. E-mail: m-psand@mindspring.com. Website: www.jewishlibraries.org. Coordinator: Paula Sandfelder. **Open to students.** Annual contest. Estab. 1985. Purpose of the contest: "This competition is for unpublished writers of fiction. Material should be for readers ages 8-11, with universal appeal that will serve to deepen the understanding of Judaism for all children, revealing positive aspects of Jewish life." Unpublished submissions only. Deadline for entries: January 15. SASE for contest rules and entry forms must be enclosed. No entry fee. Awards $1,000. Award will be given at the Association of Jewish Libraries annual convention. Judging by qualified judges from within the Association of Jewish Libraries. Requirements for entrants: must be an unpublished fiction writer; also, books must range from 64-200 pages in length. "AJL assumes no responsibility for publication, but hopes this cash incentive will serve to encourage new writers of children's stories with Jewish themes for all children."

TREASURE STATE AWARD, Missoula Public Library, Missoula County Schools, Montana Library Assoc., 301 E. Main, Missoula MT 59802. (406)721-2005. Fax: (406)728-5900. E-mail: bammon@missoula.lib.mt. Website: www.missoula.lib.mt. Award Directors: Bette Ammon and Carole Monlux. Annual award. Estab. 1990. Purpose of the award: Children in grades K-3 read or listen to a ballot of 5 picture books and vote on their favorite. Previously published submissions only. Submissions made by author, nominated by a person or group of people—children, librarians, teachers. Must be published in previous 5 years to voting year. Deadline for entries: March 20. SASE for contest rules and entry forms. No entry fee. Awards a plaque or sculpture. Judging by popular vote by Montana children grades K-3.

VEGETARIAN ESSAY CONTEST, The Vegetarian Resource Group, P.O. Box 1463, Baltimore MD 21203. (410)366-VEGE. Fax: (410)366-8804. E-mail: vrg@vrg.org. Website: www.vrg.org. Address to Vegetarian Essay Contest. Annual contest. Estab. 1985. Purpose of contest: to promote vegetarianism in young people. Unpublished submissions only. Deadline for entries: May 1 of each year. SASE for contest rules and entry forms. No entry fee. Awards $50 savings bond. Judging by awards committee. Acquires right for The Vegetarian Resource Group to reprint essays. Requirements for entrants: age 18 and under. Winning works may be published in *Vegetarian Journal*, instructional materials for students. "Submit 2-3 page essay on any aspect of vegetarianism, which is the abstinence of meat, fish and fowl. Entrants can base paper on interviewing, research or personal opinion. Need not be vegetarian to enter."

✓ **VFW VOICE OF DEMOCRACY**, Veterans of Foreign Wars of the U.S., 406 W. 34th St., Kansas City MO 64111. (816)968-1117. Fax: (816)968-1149. Website: www.vfw.org. **Open to students.** Annual contest. Estab. 1960. Purpose of contest: to give high school students the opportunity to voice their opinions about their responsibility to our country and to convey those opinions via the broadcast media to all of America. Deadline for entries: November 1st. No entry fee. Winners receive awards ranging from $1,000-20,000. Requirements for entrants: "Ninth-twelfth grade students in public, parochial, private and home schools are eligible to compete. Former first place state winners are not eligible to compete again. Contact your participating high school teacher, counselor or your local VFW Post to enter."

THE STELLA WADE CHILDREN'S STORY AWARD, *Amelia* Magazine, 329 E St., Bakersfield CA 93304. (805)323-4064. Editor: Frederick A. Raborg, Jr. Annual award. Estab. 1988. Purpose of award: "With decrease in the number of religious and secular magazines for young people, the juvenile story and poetry must be preserved and enhanced." Unpublished submissions only. Deadline for entries: August 15. SASE for award rules. Entry fee is $7.50 per adult entry; there is no fee for entries submitted by young people under the age of 17, but such entry must be signed by parent, guardian or teacher to verify originality. Awards $125 plus publication. Judging by editorial staff. Previous winners include Maxine Kumin and Sharon E. Martin. "We use First North American serial rights only for the winning manuscript." Contest is open to all interested. If illustrator wishes to enter, only an illustration without a story, the entry fee remains the same. Illustrations will also be considered for cover publication. Restrictions of mediums for illustrators: Submitted photos should be no smaller than 5×7; illustrations (drawn) may be in any medium. "Winning entry will be published in the most appropriate issue of either *Amelia*, *Cicada* or *SPSM&H*—subject matter would determine such. Submit clean, accurate copy." Sample issue: $9.95.

WASHINGTON CHILDREN'S CHOICE PICTURE BOOK AWARD, Washington Library Media Association, P.O. Box 99121, Seattle WA 98199-0121. E-mail: galantek@edmonds.wednet.edu. Award Director: Kristin Galante. Submit entries to: Kristin Galante, chairman. Annual award. Estab. 1982. Previously published submissions only. Submissions nominated by a person or group. Must be published within 3 years prior to year of award. Deadline for entries: February 1. SASE for contest rules and entry forms. Awards pewter plate, recognition. Judging by WCCPBA committee.

WASHINGTON POST/CHILDREN'S BOOK GUILD AWARD FOR NONFICTION, % Marcy Ramsey. President of the Children's Book Guild of Washington, D.C., 140 Bright Meadow Lane, Chestertown MD 21620. Fax: (410)778-4070. E-mail: deepland@dmv.com. Website: www.childrensbookguild.org. **Open to students.** Annual award. Estab. 1977. Purpose of award: "to encourage nonfiction writing for children of literary quality. Purpose of contest: "to call attention to an outstanding nonfiction author of several works, judged on the author's total output, to encourage authors to write nonfiction." Awarded for the body of work of a leading American nonfiction author." Awards $1,000 and an engraved crystal paperweight. Judging by a jury of Children's Book Guild librarians and authors and a *Washington Post* book critic. "One doesn't enter. One is selected. Authors and publishers mistakenly send us books. Our jury annually selects one author for the award."

☑ **WE ARE WRITERS, TOO!**, Creative With Words Publications, P.O. Box 223226, Carmel CA 93922. Fax: (831)655-8627. E-mail: cwwpub@usa.net. Website: members.tripod.com/~CreativeWithWords. Contest Director: Brigitta Geltrich. Quarterly contest. Estab. 1975. Purpose of award: to further creative writing in children. Unpublished submissions only. Can submit year round on any topic. Deadlines for entries: June 1 and December 1. SASE for contest rules and entry forms. SASE for return of entries "if not on accepted entry." No entry fee. Awards publication in an anthology, on website and a free copy for "Best of the Month." Judging by selected guest editors and educators. Contest open to children only (up to and including 19 years old). Writer should request contest rules. SASE with all correspondence. Age of child and home address must be stated and manuscript must be verified of its authenticity. Each story or poem must have a title. Creative with Words Publications publishes the top 100-120 manuscripts submitted to the contest and also publishes anthologies on various themes throughout the year to which young writers may submit. Request theme list, include SASE, or visit our website. "Website offers special contests to young writers with prizes."

WESTERN WRITERS OF AMERICA AWARD, Western Writers of America, Inc., 60 Sandpiper, Conway AR 72032. (501)450-0086. E-mail: carlj@mail.uca.edu. Website: www.imt.net/~gedison/wwahome.html. Award Director: W.C. Jameson. **Open to students.** Submit entries to: W.C. Jameson. Annual award. Purpose of award: to recognize the best western writing. Western material is defined by the WWA, Inc. as that which is set in the territory west of the Mississippi River or on the early frontier. Previously published submissions only. Submissions made by author. Must be published in the previous year. Deadline for entries: December 31. SASE for contest rules and entry forms. Entry fee is $10. Awards include the Spur Awards, the Medicine Pipe Bearer Award for Best First Novel and the Storyteller Award for the Best Children's Picture Book of the West.

JACKIE WHITE MEMORIAL NATIONAL CHILDREN'S PLAY WRITING CONTEST, Columbia Entertainment Company, 309 Parkade Blvd., Columbia MO 65202-1447. (573)874-5628. Contest Director: Betsy Phillips. Annual contest. Estab. 1988. Purpose of contest: to find good plays for 30-45 theater school students, grades 6-9, to perform in CEC's theater school and to encourage writing production of large cast scripts suitable for production in theater schools. Previously unpublished submissions only. Submissions made by author. Deadline for entries: June 1. SASE for contest rules and entry forms. Entry fee is $10. Awards $250, production of play, travel expenses to come see production. Judging by board members of CEC and at least one theater school parent. Play is performed during the following season, i.e. 1997 winner to be presented during CEC's 1997-98 season. We reserve the right to award 1st place and prize monies without a production.

Ⓝ LAURA INGALLS WILDER AWARD, Association for Library Service to Children, Division of the American Library Association, 50 E. Huron, Chicago IL 60611. (312)280-2163. Website: www.ala.org/alsc.

Executive Director, ALSC: Susan Roman. Award offered every 3 years. Purpose of the award: to recognize an author or illustrator whose books, published in the US, have over a period of years made a substantial and lasting contribution to children's literature. Awards a medal presented at banquet during annual conference. Judging by Wilder Committee.

N PAUL A. WITTY SHORT STORY AWARD, International Reading Association, P.O. Box 8139, 800 Barksdale Rd., Newark DE 19714-8139. (302)731-1600. The entry must be an original short story appearing in a young children's periodical for the first time during 1999. The short story should serve as a literary standard that encourages young readers to read periodicals. Deadline for entries: The entry must have been published for the first time in the eligibility year; the short story must be submitted during the calendar year of publication. Anyone wishing to nominate a short story should send it to the designated Paul A. Witty Short Award Subcommittee Chair by December 1. Send SASE for guidelines. Award is $1,000 and recognition at the annual IRA Convention.

✓ WOMEN IN THE ARTS ANNUAL CONTESTS, Women In The Arts, P.O. Box 2907, Decatur IL 62524-2907. (217)872-0811. Submit entries to Vice President. **Open to students.** Annual contest. Estab. 1995. Purpose of contest: to encourage beginning writers, as well as published professionals by offering a contest for well-written material in fiction, essay and poetry. Submissions made by author. Deadline for entries: November 15 annually. SASE for contest rules and entry forms. Entry fee is $2/item. Prize consists of $30 1st Place; $25 2nd Place; $15 3rd Place. Send SASE for complete rules.

✓ ALICE LOUISE WOOD OHIOANA AWARD FOR CHILDREN'S LITERATURE, Ohioana Library Association, 65 S. Front St., Suite 1105, Columbus OH 43215. (614)466-3831. Fax: (614)728-6974. E-mail: ohioana@winslo.state.oh.us. Website: www.oplin.lib.oh.us/OHIOANA/. Director: Linda R. Hengst. Annual award. Estab. 1991. Purpose of award: "to recognize an Ohio author whose body of work has made, and continues to make a significant contribution to literature for children or young adults." SASE for award rules and entry forms. Award: $1,000. Requirements for entrants: "must have been born in Ohio, or lived in Ohio for a minimum of five years; established a distinguished publishing record of books for children and young people; body of work has made, and continues to make, a significant contribution to the literature for young people; through whose work as a writer, teacher, administrator, or through community service, interest in children's literature has been encouraged and children have become involved with reading."

✓ WORK-IN-PROGRESS GRANTS, Society of Children's Book Writers and Illustrators, 8271 Beverly Blvd., Los Angeles CA 90048. Fax: (323)782-1892. E-mail: scbwiqjuno.com. Website: www.scbwi.org. Annual award. "The SCBWI Work-in-Progress Grants have been established to assist children's book writers in the completion of a specific project." Five categories: (1) General Work-in-Progress Grant. (2) Grant for a Contemporary Novel for Young People. (3) Nonfiction Research Grant. (4) Grant for a work whose author has never had a book published. (5) Grant for a picture book writer. Requests for applications may be made beginning October 1. Completed applications accepted February 1-May 1 of each year. SASE for applications for grants. In any year, an applicant may apply for any of the grants except the one awarded for a work whose author has never had a book published. (The recipient of this grant will be chosen from entries in all categories.) Five grants of $1,000 will be awarded annually. Runner-up grants of $500 (one in each category) will also be awarded. "The grants are available to both full and associate members of the SCBWI. They are not available for projects on which there are already contracts." Previous recipients not eligible to apply.

✓ ♦ WRITER'S BLOCK LITERARY CONTEST, *Writer's Block* Magazine, #32, 9944-33 Ave., Edmonton, Alberta T6N 1E8 Canada. (403)464-6623. Fax: (780)464-5524. Contest Director: Shaun Donnelly. Submit entries to: Shaun Donnelly, editor. **Open to students.** Biannual contest. Estab. 1994. Purpose of contest: to discover outstanding fiction/poetry by new writers for inclusion in *Writer's Block* magazine. Unpublished submissions only. Submissions made by author. Deadline for entries: March 30 and September 30. SASE for contest rules and entry forms. Entry fee is $5. Prize consists of publication, $100-150 cash, hardcover books in author's genre. Judging by independent judges (usually writers).

WRITER'S EXCHANGE POETRY CONTEST, 100 Upper Glen Dr., Blythewood SC 29016. E-mail: eboon e@aol.com. Website: members.aol.com/WriterNet or members.aol.com/WEBBASE1. Contest Director: Gene Boone. Quarterly contest. **Open to students.** Estab. 1985. Purpose of the contest: to promote friendly competition among poets of all ages and backgrounds, giving these poets a chance to be published and win an award. Submissions are made by the author. Continuous deadline; entries are placed in the contest closest to date received. SASE for contest rules and entry forms. Entry fee is $2 first poem, $1 each additional poem. Awards 50% of contest proceeds, usually $35-100 varying slightly in each quarterly contest due to changes in response. Judging by Gene Boone or a guest judge such as a widely published poet or another small press editor. "From the entries received, we reserve the right to publish the winning poems in an issue of *Writer's Exchange*, a literary newsletter. The contest is open to any poet. Poems on any subject/theme, any style, to 30 lines, may be entered. Poems should be typed, single-spaced, with the poet's name in the upper left corner."

WRITERS' INTL. FORUM CONTESTS, (formerly Writer's International Forum for Young Authors Contests), Bristol Services Int'l., P.O. Box 516, Tracyton WA 98393-0516. Website: www.bristolservicesintl.com. Contest Director: Sandra E. Haven. Estab. 1997. Purpose of contest: to inspire excellence in the traditional short story format and for tightly focused essays. "In fiction we like identifiable characters, strong storylines, and crisp, fresh endings. Open to all ages." Unpublished submissions only. Deadlines, fees, and cash award prizes vary per contest. SASE or see website for dates of each upcoming contest, contest rules and entry forms. Judging by *Writer's Int'l Forum* staff. "We reserve the right to publish cash award winners." For young writers, please state age of author and birth date in cover letter. Contest winners announced at website. Word count maximum: 2,500. Please request guidelines for contest you want to enter or visit website to request guidelines.

✅ **WRITING CONFERENCE WRITING CONTESTS**, The Writing Conference, Inc., P.O. Box 27288, Overland Park KS 66225-7288. Phone/fax: (913)681-8894. E-mail: jbushman@writingconference.com. Website: www.writingconference.com. Contest Director: John H. Bushman. **Open to students.** Annual contest. Estab. 1988. Purpose of contest: to further writing by students with awards for narration, exposition and poetry at the elementary, middle school and high school levels. Unpublished submissions only. Submissions made by the author or teacher. Deadline for entries: January 8. SASE for contest rules and entry form or consult website. No entry fee. Awards plaque and publication of winning entry in *The Writers' Slate*, March issue. Judging by a panel of teachers. Requirements for entrants: must be enrolled in school—K-12th grade.

YEARBOOK EXCELLENCE CONTEST, *Quill and Scroll*, School of Journalism, University of Iowa, Iowa City IA 52242-1528. (319)335-5795. Fax: (319)335-5210. E-mail: quill-scroll@uiowa.edu. Website: www.uiowa. edu/~quill-sc. Executive Director: Richard Johns. **Open to students.** Annual contest. Estab. 1987. Purpose of contest: to recognize and reward student journalists for their work in yearbooks and to provide student winners an opportunity to apply for a scholarship to be used freshman year in college for students planning to major in journalism. Previously published submissions only. Submissions made by the author or school yearbook adviser. Must be published between November 1, 1998 and November 1, 1999. Deadline for entries: November 1. SASE for contest rules and entry form. Entry fee is $2 per entry. Awards National Gold Key; sweepstakes winners receive plaque; seniors eligible for scholarships. Judging by various judges. Winning entries may be published in *Quill and Scroll* magazine.

YOUNG ADULT CANADIAN BOOK AWARD, The Canadian Library Association, Suite 602, 200 Elgin St., Ottawa, Ontario K2P 1L5 Canada. (613)232-9625. Fax: (613)563-9895. Contact: Committee Chair. Annual award. Estab. 1981. Purpose of award: "to recognize the author of an outstanding English-language Canadian book which appeals to young adults between the ages of 13 and 18 that was published the preceding calendar year. Information is available for anyone requesting. We approach publishers, also send news releases to various journals, i.e., *Quill & Quire*." Entries are not returned. No entry fee. Awards a leather-bound book. Requirement for entrants: must be a work of fiction (novel or short stories), the title must be a Canadian publication in either hardcover or paperback, and the author must be a Canadian citizen or landed immigrant. Award given at the Canadian Library Association Conference.

YOUNG READER'S CHOICE AWARD, Pacific Northwest Library Association, Box 352930, University of Washington, Graduate School of Library and Information Science, Seattle WA 98195-2930. (206)543-1897. Award Director: named annually. Annual award for published authors. Estab. 1940. Purpose of award: "to promote reading as an enjoyable activity and to provide children an opportunity to endorse a book they consider an excellent story." No unsolicited mss or published novels are accepted. Deadline for entries: February 1. SASE for award rules and entry forms. No entry fee. Awards a silver medal, struck in Idaho silver. "Children vote for their favorite (books) from a list of titles nominated by librarians, teachers, students and other interested persons."

"WE WANT TO PUBLISH YOUR WORK."

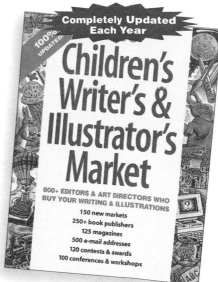

Completely Updated Each Year

Children's Writer's & Illustrator's Market

800+ EDITORS & ART DIRECTORS WHO BUY YOUR WRITING & ILLUSTRATIONS

- 150 new markets
- 250+ book publishers
- 125 magazines
- 500 e-mail addresses
- 120 contests & awards
- 100 conferences & workshops

You would give anything to hear an editor speak those six magic words. So you work hard for weeks, months, even years to make that happen. You create a brilliant piece of work and a knock-out presentation, but there's still one vital step to ensure publication. You still need to submit your work to the right buyers. With rapid changes in the publishing industry it's not always easy to know who those buyers are. That's why each year thousands of writers and illustrators turn to the most current edition of this indispensable market guide.

Keep ahead of the changes by ordering *2001 Children's Writer's & Illustrator's Market* today! You'll save the frustration of getting your work returned in the mail stamped MOVED: ADDRESS UNKNOWN. And of NOT submitting your work to new listings because you don't know they exist. All you have to do to order the upcoming 2001 edition is complete the attached order card and return it with your payment. Order now and you'll get the 2001 edition at the 2000 price—just $21.99— no matter how much the regular price may increase!

2001 Children's Writer's & Illustrator's Market will be published and ready for shipment in January 2001.

More books to help you get published

Get Your Children's Stories Published
with Help from These Writer's Digest Books!

2000 Guide to Literary Agents
Agents can open doors for you in the publishing industry. You can team up with an agent using this invaluable directory (now in its 9th year). Over 500 listings of literary and script agents, plus inside information on the industry will help you choose the right agent to represent you.
#10627/$21.99/335p/pb

You Can Write Children's Books
Writer and editor Tracey Dils gives you the essential writing and submission guidelines you need to get your work in print. She reveals the hot trends in children's publishing, how to maintain a structured format, ways to target the right age group, how to produce a professional package, and more.
#10547/$12.99/128p/pb

Writing and Illustrating Children's Books for Publication
Create a good, publishable manuscript in eight weeks using this self-taught writing course. Easy-to-follow lessons and exercises cover everything from getting ideas to writing, polishing and publishing.
#10448/$24.95/128p/200 illus./hc

How To Write and Sell Children's Picture Books
If you yearn to put smiles on little faces, you need this charming guide. You'll discover how to put your picture book on paper and get it published—whether you're retelling a wonderful old tale, or spinning a splendid new yarn.
#10410/$17.99/192p/hc

New in paperback!

Children's Writer's Word Book
This fast-reference guide will help to ensure your writing speaks to your young audience. Complete with word lists, thesaurus of synonyms, and tips on word usage and sentence length.
#10649/$16.99/352p/pb

The Children's Writer's Reference
Get the inside information you need to write and illustrate stories kids will love and publishers will buy. You'll get 8 easy-to-reference chapters on Children and Books, Ideas, Age Groups, Format, Characters, Setting, Plot, Writing and Thinking Visually.
#10604/$16.99/272p/pb

NEW!

Books are available at your local bookstore, or directly from the publisher using the order card on the reverse.

Helpful Books & Publications

The editor of *Children's Writer's & Illustrator's Market* suggests the following books and periodicals to keep you informed on writing and illustrating techniques, trends in the field, business issues, industry news and changes, and additional markets.

BOOKS

N AN AUTHOR'S GUIDE TO CHILDREN'S BOOK PROMOTION, by Susan Salzman Raab with Johanna Bierwirth, 19 Price Lane, Rose Valley PA 19065. (610)565-8188. E-mail: info@raabassociates.com. Website: www.raabassociates.com/books.htm.

CHILDREN'S WRITER GUIDE, (annual), The Institute of Children's Literature, 95 Long Ridge Rd., West Redding CT 55104. (800)443-6078.

CHILDREN'S WRITER'S REFERENCE, by Berthe Amoss and Eric Suben, Writer's Digest Books, 1507 Dana Ave., Cincinnati OH 45207. (800)289-0963. Website: www.writersdigest.com.

CHILDREN'S WRITER'S WORD BOOK, by Alijandra Mogilner, Writer's Digest Books, 1507 Dana Ave., Cincinnati OH 45207. (800)289-0963. Website: www.writersdigest.com.

GETTING STARTED AS A FREELANCE ILLUSTRATOR OR DESIGNER, by Michael Fleischman, North Light Books, 1507 Dana Ave., Cincinnati OH 45207. (800)289-0963. Website: www.writersdigest.com.

GUIDE TO LITERARY AGENTS, (annual) edited by Donya Dickerson, Writer's Digest Books, 1507 Dana Ave., Cincinnati OH 45207. (800)289-0963. Website: www.writersdigest.com.

HOW TO GET YOUR TEACHING IDEAS PUBLISHED, by Jean Stangl, Walker and Company, 435 Hudson St., New York NY 10014. (212)727-8300.

N HOW TO PROMOTE YOUR CHILDREN'S BOOK: A SURVIVAL GUIDE, by Evelyn Gallardo, Primate Production, P.O. Box 3038, Manhattan Beach CA 90266, Website: www.evegallardo.com/promote.html.

HOW TO SELL YOUR PHOTOGRAPHS & ILLUSTRATIONS, by Elliot & Barbara Gordon, North Light Books, 1507 Dana Ave., Cincinnati OH 45207. (800)289-0963.

HOW TO WRITE A CHILDREN'S BOOK & GET IT PUBLISHED, by Barbara Seuling, Charles Scribner's Sons, 1230 Avenue of the Americas, New York NY 10020. (212)702-2000.

HOW TO WRITE AND ILLUSTRATE CHILDREN'S BOOKS AND GET THEM PUBLISHED, edited by Treld Pelkey Bicknell and Felicity Trottman, Writer's Digest Books, 1507 Dana Ave., Cincinnati OH 45207. (800)289-0963. Website: www.writersdigest.com.

HOW TO WRITE AND SELL CHILDREN'S PICTURE BOOKS, by Jean E. Karl, Writer's Digest Books, 1507 Dana Ave., Cincinnati OH 45207. (800)289-0963. Website: www.writersdigest.com.

HOW TO WRITE ATTENTION-GRABBING QUERY & COVER LETTERS, by John Wood, Writer's Digest Books, 1507 Dana Ave., Cincinnati OH 45207. (800)289-0963. Website: www.writersdigest.com.

HOW TO WRITE, ILLUSTRATE, AND DESIGN CHILDREN'S BOOKS, by Frieda Gates, Lloyd-Simone Publishing Company, distributed by Library Research Associates, Inc., Dunderberg Rd. RD 6, Box 41, Monroe NY 10950. (914)783-1144.

LEGAL GUIDE FOR THE VISUAL ARTIST, by Tad Crawford, North Light Books, 1507 Dana Ave., Cincinnati OH 45207. (800)289-0963.

MARKET GUIDE FOR YOUNG WRITERS, Fifth Edition, by Kathy Henderson, Writer's Digest Books, 1507 Dana Ave., Cincinnati OH 45207. (800)289-0963. Website: www.writersdigest.com.

A TEEN'S GUIDE TO GETTING PUBLISHED, by Danielle Dunn & Jessica Dunn, Prufrock Press, P.O. Box 8813, Waco TX 76714-8813. (800)998-2208.

TEN STEPS TO PUBLISHING CHILDREN'S BOOKS, by Berthe Amoss & Eric Suben, Writer's Digest Books, 1507 Dana Ave., Cincinnati OH 45207. (800)289-0963. Website: www.writersdigest.com.

THE ULTIMATE PORTFOLIO, by Martha Metzdorf, North Light Books, 1507 Dana Ave., Cincinnati OH 45207. (800)289-0963.

THE WRITER'S DIGEST GUIDE TO MANUSCRIPT FORMATS, by Dian Dincin Buchman & Seli Groves, Writer's Digest Books, 1507 Dana Ave., Cincinnati OH 45207. (800)289-0963. Website: www.writersdigest.com.

THE WRITER'S ESSENTIAL DESK REFERENCE, Second Edition, Writer's Digest Books, 1507 Dana Ave., Cincinnati OH 45207. (800)289-0963. Website: www.writersdigest.com.

WRITING AND ILLUSTRATING CHILDREN'S BOOKS FOR PUBLICATION: TWO PERSPEC-TIVES, by Berthe Amoss and Eric Suben, Writer's Digest Books, 1507 Dana Ave., Cincinnati OH 45207. (800)289-0963. Website: www.writersdigest.com.

WRITING & PUBLISHING BOOKS FOR CHILDREN IN THE 1990s: THE INSIDE STORY FROM THE EDITOR'S DESK, by Olga Litowinsky, Walker & Co., 435 Hudson St., New York NY 10014. (212)727-8300.

WRITING BOOKS FOR YOUNG PEOPLE, Second Edition, by James Cross Giblin, The Writer, Inc., 120 Boylston St., Boston MA 02116-4615. (617)423-3157.

WRITING FOR CHILDREN & TEENAGERS, Third Edition, by Lee Wyndham and Arnold Madison, Writer's Digest Books, 1507 Dana Ave., Cincinnati OH 45207. (800)289-0963. Website: www.writersdigest.com.

WRITING FOR YOUNG ADULTS, by Sherry Garland, Writer's Digest Books, 1507 Dana Ave., Cincinnati OH 45207. (800)289-0963. Website: www.writersdigest.com.

WRITING TOGETHER, by Dawn Denham Haines, Susan Newcomer and Jacqueline Raphael, The Berkley Publishing Group, Penguin Putnam, Inc., 375 Hudson St., New York NY 10014. (212)366-2000.

WRITING WITH PICTURES: HOW TO WRITE AND ILLUSTRATE CHILDREN'S BOOKS, by Uri Shulevitz, Watson-Guptill Publications, 1515 Broadway, New York NY 10036. (212)764-7300.

YOU CAN YOU CAN WRITE CHILDREN'S BOOKS, by Tracey E. Dils, Writer's Digest Books, 1507 Dana Ave., Cincinnati OH 45207. (800)289-0963. Website: www.writersdigest.com.

PUBLICATIONS

☑ **BOOK LINKS**, editor Judith O'Malley, American Library Association, 50 E. Huron St., Chicago IL 60611. (800)545-2433. Website: www.ala.org/BookLinks. *Magazine published 6 times a year (September-July) for the purpose of connecting books, libraries and classrooms. Features articles on specific topics followed by bibliographies recommending books for further information. Subscription: $19.95/year.*

CHILDREN'S BOOK INSIDER, editor Laura Backes, 901 Columbia Rd., Ft. Collins CO 80525-1838. (970)495-0056 or (800)807-1916. E-mail: mail@write4kids.com. Website: www.write4kids.com. *Monthly newsletter covering markets, techniques and trends in children's publishing. Subscription: $29.95/year. Official update source for* Children's Writer's & Illustrator's Market, *featuring quarterly lists of changes and updates to listings in CWIM.*

☑ **CHILDREN'S WRITER**, editor Susan Tierney, The Institute of Children's Literature, 95 Long Ridge Rd., West Redding CT 55104. (800)443-6078. Website: www.childrenswriter.com. *Monthly newsletter of writing and publishing trends in the children's field. Subscription: $24/year; special introductory rate: $15.*

THE FIVE OWLS, editor Susan Stan, Hamline University Crossroads Center, MS-C1924, 1536 Hewitt Ave., St. Paul MN 55104. (612)644-7377. Fax: (612)641-2956. *Bimonthly newsletter for readers personally and professionally involved in children's literature. Subscription: $35/year.*

THE HORN BOOK MAGAZINE, editor-in-chief Robert Sutton, The Horn Book Inc., 56 Roland St., Suite 200, Boston MA 02129. (800)325-1170. E-mail: info@hbook.com. Website: www.hbook.com. *Bimonthly guide to the children's book world including views on the industry and reviews of the latest books. Subscription: $42/ year; special introductory rate: $24.95.*

THE LION AND THE UNICORN: A CRITICAL JOURNAL OF CHILDREN'S LITERATURE, editors Jack Zipes and Louisa Smith, The Johns Hopkins University Press—Journals Publishing Division, 2175 N. Charles St., Baltimore MD 21218-4319. (410)516-6987. *Magazine published 3 times a year serving as a forum for discussion of children's literature featuring interviews with authors, editors and experts in the field. Subscription: $26/year.*

ONCE UPON A TIME . . . , editor Audrey Baird, 553 Winston Court, St. Paul MN 55118. (651)457-6223. Fax: (651)457-9565. Website: http://members.aol.com/OUATMAG/. *Quarterly support magazine for children's writers and illustrators and those interested in children's literature. Subscription: $24.25/year.*

PUBLISHERS WEEKLY, editor-in-chief Nora Rawlinson, Bowker Magazine Group, Cahners Publishing Co., 249 W. 17th St., New York NY 10011. (800)278-2991. *Weekly trade publication covering all aspects of the publishing industry; includes coverage of the children's field (books, audio and video) and spring and fall issues devoted solely to children's books. Subscription: $139/year. Available on newsstands for $4/issue. (Special issues are higher in price.)*

RIVERBANK REVIEW of books for young readers, editor Martha Davis Beck, University of St. Thomas, 2115 Summit Ave., CHC-131, St. Paul MN 55105. (612)962-5373. Fax: (612)962-5169. *Quarterly publication exploring the world of children's literature including book reviews, articles and essays. Subscription: $20/year.*

☑ **SOCIETY OF CHILDREN'S BOOK WRITERS AND ILLUSTRATORS BULLETIN**, editors Stephen Mooser and Lin Oliver, SCBWI, 8271 Beverly Blvd., Los Angeles CA 90048. (323)782-1010. Website: www.scbwi.org. *Bimonthly newsletter of SCBWI covering news of interest to members. Subscription with $50/ year membership.*

Useful Online Resources

The editor of *Children's Writer's & Illustrator's Market* suggests the following websites to keep you informed on writing and illustrating techniques, trends in the field, business issues, industry news and changes, and additional markets.

AMAZON.COM: www.amazon.com
Calling itself "A bookstore too big for the physical world," Amazon.com has more than 3 million books available on their website at discounted prices, plus a personal notification service of new releases, reader reviews, bestseller and suggested book information. Be sure to check out Amazon.com Kids.

N ASSOCIATION FOR LIBRARY SERVICE TO CHILDREN: www.ala.org/alsc/awards.html
This site provides links to information about Newbery, Caldecott and Coretta Scott King Awards as well as a host of other awards for notable children's books.

N AUTHORS AND ILLUSTRATORS FOR CHILDREN WEBRING: www.webring.org/cgi-bin/webring?ring = aicwebring;list
Here you'll find a list of link of sites of interest to children's writers and illustrators or created by them.

N THE AUTHORS GUILD ONLINE: www.authorsguild.org/
The website of The Authors Guild offers articles and columns dealing with contract issues, copyright, electronic rights and other legal issues of concern to writers.

BARNES & NOBLE ONLINE: www.barnesandnoble.com
The world's largest bookstore chain's website contains 600,000 in-stock titles at discount prices as well as personalized recommendations, online events with authors and book forum access for members.

BOOKWIRE: www.bookwire.com
A gateway to finding information about publishers, booksellers, libraries, authors, reviews and awards. Also offers frequently asked publishing questions and answers, a calendar of events, a mailing list and other helpful resources.

CANADIAN CHILDREN'S BOOK CENTRE: www3.sympatico.ca/ccbc/
The site for the CCBC includes profiles of illustrators and authors, information on recent books, a calendar of upcoming events, information on CCBC publications, and tips from Canadian children's authors.

THE CHILDREN'S BOOK COUNCIL: www.cbcbooks.org/
This site includes a complete list of CBC members with addresses, names and descriptions of what each publishes, and links to publishers' websites. Also offers previews of upcoming titles from members; articles from CBC Features, *the Council's newsletter; and their catalog.*

CHILDREN'S LITERATURE WEB GUIDE: www.ucalgary.ca/~dkbrown/index.html
This site includes stories, poetry, resource lists, lists of conferences, links to book reviews, lists of awards (international), and information on books from classic to contemporary.

N CHILDREN'S PUBLISHERS' SUBMISSION GUIDELINES: www.signaleader.com/chldwrit.html
This site features links to at least 140 websites of children's publishers and includes information on which publishers offer submission guidelines online.

N CHILDREN'S WRITER'S AND ILLUSTRATOR'S RESOURCE LIST: http://people.ne.mediaone.net/peter_davis/cwrl.html
Maintained by Peter Davis, this site includes lists of books on writing and illustrating, books on the business of illustration, organizations and periodicals and Internet resources.

CHILDREN'S WRITERS RESOURCE CENTER: www.write4kids.com
This site includes highlights from the newsletter Children's Book Insider; *definitions of publishing terms; answers to frequently asked questions; information on trends; information on small presses; a research center for Web information; and a catalog of material available from CBI.*

THE DRAWING BOARD: http://members.aol.com/thedrawing
This site for illustrators features articles, interviews, links and resources for illustrators from all fields.

EDITOR & PUBLISHER: www.mediainfo.com
The Internet source for Editor & Publisher, *this site provides up-to-date industry news, with other opportunities such as a research area and bookstore, a calendar of events and classifieds.*

INKSPOT: www.inkspot.com
An elaborate site that provides information about workshops, how-to information, copyright, quotations, writing tips, resources, contests, market information (including children's writers marketplace), publishers, booksellers, associations, mailing lists, newsletters, conferences and more.

N KEYSTROKES: www.writelinks.com/keystrokes/
This online monthly newsletter for writers features articles on an array of topics, including topics related to writing for children. The site offers a years' worth of the newsletter.

ONCE UPON A TIME: members.aol.com/OUATMAG
This companion site to Once Upon A Time *magazine offers excerpts from recent articles, notes for prospective contributors, and information about OUAT's 11 regular columnists.*

PUBLISHERS' CATALOGUES HOME PAGE: www.lights.com/publisher/index.html
A mammoth link collection of publishers around the world arranged geographically. This site is one of the most comprehensive directories of publishers on the Internet.

THE PURPLE CRAYON: www.users.interport.net/~hdu/
Editor Harold Underdown's site includes articles on trends, business, and cover letters and queries as well as interviews with editors and answers to frequently asked questions. He also includes links to a number of other sites helpful to writers.

N SLANTVILLE: www.slantville.com/
An online artists community, this site includes a yellow pages for artists, frequently asked questions and a library offering information on a number of issues of interest to illustrators. This is a great site to visit to view artists' portfolios.

SOCIETY OF CHILDREN'S BOOK WRITERS AND ILLUSTRATORS: www.scbwi.org
This site includes information on awards and grants available to SCBWI members, a calendar of events listed by date and region, a list of publications available to members, and a site map for easy navigation. Balan welcomes suggestions for the site from visitors.

UNITED STATES POSTAL SERVICE: www.usps.gov/welcome.htm
Offers domestic and International postage rate calculator, stamp ordering, zip code look up, express mail tracking and more.

N VERLA KAY'S WEBSITE: www.mlode.com/~verlakay/
Author Verla Kay's website features writer's tips, articles, a schedules of online workshops (with transcripts of past workshops), a good news board and helpful links.

WRITERSDIGEST.COM: www.writersdigest.com
Brought to you by Writer's Digest *magazine and* Writer's Market, *this site features a hot list, markets of the day, and a searchable database of more than 1,150 writer's guidelines.*

WRITES OF PASSAGE: www.writes.org
Run by Writes of Passage *(a literary magazine for teens), this site includes features from the magazine; links to a list of teen resources on the Web, including high school and college newspapers and online dictionaries; and a database of high school websites.*

Glossary

AAR. Association of Authors' Representatives.

ABA. American Booksellers Association.

ABC. Association of Booksellers for Children.

Advance. A sum of money a publisher pays a writer or illustrator prior to the publication of a book. It is usually paid in installments, such as one half on signing the contract; one half on delivery of a complete and satisfactory manuscript. The advance is paid against the royalty money that will be earned by the book.

ALA. American Library Association.

All rights. The rights contracted to a publisher permitting the use of material anywhere and in any form, including movie and book club sales, without additional payment to the creator. (See The Business of Writing & Illustrating.)

Anthology. A collection of selected writings by various authors or gatherings of works by one author.

Anthropomorphization. The act of attributing human form and personality to things not human (such as animals).

ASAP. As soon as possible.

Assignment. An editor or art director asks a writer, illustrator or photographer to produce a specific piece for an agreed-upon fee.

B&W. Black and white.

Backlist. A publisher's list of books not published during the current season but still in print.

Biennially. Occurring once every 2 years.

Bimonthly. Occurring once every 2 months.

Biweekly. Occurring once every 2 weeks.

Book packager. A company that draws all elements of a book together, from the initial concept to writing and marketing strategies, then sells the book package to a book publisher and/or movie producer. Also known as book producer or book developer.

Book proposal. Package submitted to a publisher for consideration usually consisting of a synopsis, outline and sample chapters. (See Before Your First Sale.)

Business-size envelope. Also known as a #10 envelope. The standard size used in sending business correspondence.

Camera-ready. Refers to art that is completely prepared for copy camera platemaking.

Caption. A description of the subject matter of an illustration or photograph; photo captions include persons' names where appropriate. Also called cutline.

CD-ROM. Compact disc read-only memory. Non-erasable electronic medium used for digitalized image and document storage capable of holding enormous amounts of information. A computer user must have a CD-ROM drive to access a CD-ROM.

Clean-copy. A manuscript free of errors and needing no editing; it is ready for typesetting.

Clips. Samples, usually from newspapers or magazines, of a writer's published work.

Concept books. Books that deal with ideas, concepts and large-scale problems, promoting an understanding of what's happening in a child's world. Most prevalent are alphabet and counting books, but also includes books dealing with specific concerns facing young people (such as divorce, birth of a sibling, friendship or moving).

Contract. A written agreement stating the rights to be purchased by an editor, art director or producer and the amount of payment the writer, illustrator or photographer will receive for that sale. (See The Business of Writing & Illustrating.)

Contributor's copies. The magazine issues sent to an author, illustrator or photographer in which her work appears.

Co-op publisher. A publisher that shares production costs with an author, but, unlike subsidy publishers, handles all marketing and distribution. An author receives a high percentage of royalties until her initial investment is recouped, then standard royalties.

Copy. The actual written material of a manuscript.

Copyediting. Editing a manuscript for grammar usage, spelling, punctuation and general style.

Copyright. A means to legally protect an author's/illustrator's/photographer's work. This can be shown by writing ©, the creator's name, and year of work's creation. (See The Business of Writing & Illustrating.)

Cover letter. A brief letter, accompanying a complete manuscript, especially useful if responding to an editor's request for a manuscript. May also accompany a book proposal. (See Before Your First Sale.)

Cutline. See caption.

Disk. A round, flat magnetic plate on which computer data may be stored.

Division. An unincorporated branch of a company.

Dummy. Handmade mock-up of a book.

Electronic submission. A submission of material by modem or on computer disk.

E-mail. Electronic mail. Messages sent from one computer to another via a modem or computer network.

Final draft. The last version of a polished manuscript ready for submission to an editor.

First North American serial rights. The right to publish material in a periodical for the first time, in the United States or Canada. (See The Business of Writing & Illustrating.)

Flat fee. A one-time payment.

Galleys. The first typeset version of a manuscript that has not yet been divided into pages.

Genre. A formulaic type of fiction, such as horror, mystery, romance, science fiction or western.

Glossy. A photograph with a shiny surface as opposed to one with a non-shiny matte finish.

Gouache. Opaque watercolor with an appreciable film thickness and an actual paint layer.

Halftone. Reproduction of a continuous tone illustration with the image formed by dots produced by a camera lens screen.

Hard copy. The printed copy of a computer's output.

Hardware. All the mechanically-integrated components of a computer that are not software—circuit boards, transistors and the machines that are the actual computer.

Hi-Lo. High interest, low reading level.

Home page. The first page of a World Wide Web document.

Imprint. Name applied to a publisher's specific line of books.

Interactive. A type of computer interface that takes user input, such as answers to computer-generated questions, and acts upon them.

Internet. A worldwide network of computers that offers access to a wide variety of electronic resources.

IRA. International Reading Association.

IRC. International Reply Coupon. Sold at the post office to enclose with text or artwork sent to a foreign buyer to cover postage costs when replying or returning work.

Keyline. Identification, through signs and symbols, of the positions of illustrations and copy for the printer.

Layout. Arrangement of illustrations, photographs, text and headlines for printed material.

Line drawing. Illustration done with pencil or ink using no wash or other shading.

Mass market books. Paperback books directed toward an extremely large audience sold in supermarkets, drugstores, airports, newsstands and bookstores.

Mechanicals. Paste-up or preparation of work for printing.

Middle reader. The general classification of books written for readers approximately ages 9-11.

Modem. A small electrical box that plugs into the serial card of a computer, used to transmit data from one computer to another, usually via telephone lines.

Ms (mss). Manuscript(s).

NCTE. National Council of Teachers of English.

One-time rights. Permission to publish a story in periodical or book form one time only. (See The Business of Writing & Illustrating.)

Outline. A summary of a book's contents in 5-15 double-spaced pages; often in the form of chapter headings with a descriptive sentence or two under each heading to show the scope of the book.

Package sale. The sale of a manuscript and illustrations/photos as a "package" paid for with one check.

Payment on acceptance. The writer, artist or photographer is paid for her work at the time the editor or art director decides to buy it.

Payment on publication. The writer, artist or photographer is paid for her work when it is published.

Photostat. Black and white copies produced by an inexpensive photographic process using paper negatives; only line values are held with accuracy. Also called stat.

Picture book. A type of book aimed at preschoolers to 8-year-olds that tells a story using a combination of text and artwork.

Print. An impression pulled from an original plate, stone, block, screen or negative; also a positive made from a photographic negative.

Proofreading. Reading a typescript to correct typographical errors.

Query. A letter to an editor designed to capture interest in an article or book you have written or propose to write. (See Before Your First Sale.)

Reading fee. Money charged by some agents and publishers to read a submitted manuscript.

Reprint rights. Permission to print an already published work whose first rights have been sold to another magazine or book publisher. (See The Business of Writing & Illustrating.)

Response time. The average length of time it takes an editor or art director to accept or reject a query or submission and inform the creator of the decision.

Rights. The bundle of permissions offered to an editor or art director in exchange for printing a manuscript, artwork or photographs. (See The Business of Writing & Illustrating.)

Rough draft. A manuscript that has not been checked for errors in grammar, punctuation, spelling or content.

Roughs. Preliminary sketches or drawings.

Royalty. An agreed percentage paid by a publisher to a writer, illustrator or photographer for each copy of her work sold.

SAE. Self-addressed envelope.

SASE. Self-addressed, stamped envelope.

SCBWI. The Society of Children's Book Writers and Illustrators. (See listing in Clubs & Organizations section.)

Second serial rights. Permission for the reprinting of a work in another periodical after its first publication in book or magazine form. (See The Business of Writing & Illustrating.)

Semiannual. Occurring once every 6 months.

Semimonthly. Occurring twice a month.

Semiweekly. Occurring twice a week.

Serial rights. The rights given by an author to a publisher to print a piece in one or more periodicals. (See The Business of Writing & Illustrating.)

Simultaneous submissions. Queries or proposals sent to several publishers at the same time. (See Before Your First Sale.)

Slant. The approach to a story or piece of artwork that will appeal to readers of a particular publication.

Slush pile. Editors' term for their collections of unsolicited manuscripts.

Software. Programs and related documentation for use with a computer.

Solicited manuscript. Material that an editor has asked for or agreed to consider before being sent by a writer.

SPAR. Society of Photographers and Artists Representatives.

Speculation (spec). Creating a piece with no assurance from an editor or art director that it will be purchased or any reimbursements for material or labor paid.

Stat. See photostat.

Subsidiary rights. All rights other than book publishing rights included in a book contract, such as paperback, book club and movie rights. (See The Business of Writing & Illustrating.)

Subsidy publisher. A book publisher that charges the author for the cost of typesetting, printing and promoting a book. Also called a vanity publisher.

Synopsis. A brief summary of a story or novel. Usually a page to a page and a half, single-spaced, if part of a book proposal.

Tabloid. Publication printed on an ordinary newspaper page turned sideways and folded in half.

Tearsheet. Page from a magazine or newspaper containing your printed art, story, article, poem or photo.

Thumbnail. A rough layout in miniature.

Trade books. Books sold strictly in bookstores, aimed at a smaller audience than mass market books, and printed in smaller quantities by publishers.

Transparencies. Positive color slides; not color prints.

Unsolicited manuscript. Material sent without an editor's or art director's request.

Vanity publisher. See subsidy publisher.

Word processor. A computer that produces typewritten copy via automated text-editing, storage and transmission capabilities.

World Wide Web. An Internet resource that utilizes hypertext to access information. It also supports formatted text, illustrations and sounds, depending on the user's computer capabilities.

Work-for-hire. An arrangement between a writer, illustrator or photographer and a company under which the company retains complete control of the work's copyright. (See The Business of Writing & Illustrating.)

Young adult. The general classification of books written for readers approximately ages 12-18.

Young reader. The general classification of books written for readers approximately ages 5-8.

Age-Level Index

This index lists book and magazine publishers by the age-groups for which they publish. Use it to locate appropriate markets for your work, then carefully read the listings and follow the guidelines of each publisher. Use this index in conjunction with the Subject Index to further narrow your list of markets. **Picture Books** and **Picture-Oriented Material** are for preschoolers to 8-year-olds; **Young Readers** are for 5- to 8-year-olds; **Middle Readers** are for 9- to 11-year-olds; and **Young Adults** are for ages 12 and up.

BOOK PUBLISHERS

MAGAZINES

Picture-Oriented Material

Young Readers

Middle Readers

Young Adult/Teen

Subject Index

This index lists book and magazine publishers by the fiction and nonfiction subject area in which they publish. Use it to locate appropriate markets for your work, then carefully read the listings and follow the guidelines of each publisher. Use this index in conjunction with the Age-Level Index to further narrow your lists of markets.

BOOK PUBLISHERS: FICTION

Fantasy

Folktales

BOOK PUBLISHERS: NONFICTION

SUBJECT INDEX

MAGAZINES: FICTION

MAGAZINES: NONFICTION

SUBJECT INDEX

Poetry Index

This index lists markets that are open to poetry submissions and is divided into book publishers and magazines. It's important to carefully read the listings and follow the guidelines of each publisher to which you submit.

Photography Index

This index lists markets that buy photos from freelancers, and is divided into book publishers, magazines and greeting cards. It's important to carefully read the listings and follow the guidelines of each publisher to which you submit

General Index

Companies that appeared in the 1999 edition of *Children's Writer's & Illustrator's Market* but do not appear in this edition are identified with a two-letter code explaining why the market was omitted: (**NR**)—No (or late) Response to Listing Request; (**OB**)—Out of Business; (**RR**)—Removed by Market's Request.